The Art
and Practice
of Court
Administration

PUBLIC ADMINISTRATION AND PUBLIC POLICY

A Comprehensive Publication Program

Executive Editor

JACK RABIN
Professor of Public Administration and Public Policy
School of Public Affairs
The Capital College
The Pennsylvania State University—Harrisburg
Middletown, Pennsylvania

Assistant to the Executive Editor
T. Aaron Wachhaus, Jr.

Available Electronically

The Art and Practice of Court Administration

Alexander B. Aikman

Redding, California, U.S.A.

CRC Press
Taylor & Francis Group
Boca Raton London New York

CRC Press is an imprint of the
Taylor & Francis Group, an informa business

Auerbach Publications
Taylor & Francis Group
6000 Broken Sound Parkway NW, Suite 300
Boca Raton, FL 33487-2742

© 2007 by Taylor & Francis Group, LLC
Auerbach is an imprint of Taylor & Francis Group, an Informa business

No claim to original U.S. Government works
Printed in the United States of America on acid-free paper
10 9 8 7 6 5 4 3 2 1

International Standard Book Number-10: 0-8493-7221-6 (Hardcover)
International Standard Book Number-13: 978-0-8493-7221-6 (Hardcover)

Library of Congress Cataloging-in-Publication Data

Aikman, Alexander B.
    The art and practice of court administration / Alexander B. Aikman.
        p. cm. -- (Public administration and public policy ; 128)
    Includes bibliographical references and index.
    ISBN-13: 978-0-8493-7221-6 (alk. paper)
    ISBN-10: 0-8493-7221-6 (alk. paper)
    1. Court administration--United States.   I. Title.

    KF8732.A945 2007
    347.73'13--dc22

                                                                        2006034586

Visit the Taylor & Francis Web site at
http://www.taylorandfrancis.com

and the Auerbach Web site at
http://www.auerbach-publications.com

To my wife, Ruth Grace Aikman,
my partner, my inspiration, my love.

Contents

Acknowledgments

This book is the product of over 30 years in court administration. Thus, it owes a great deal to the literally thousands of mentors I have had over those years, some of whom knew they were helping me learn about the field and many who did not. I learned from every consulting and research assignment I have had, both while with the National Center for State Courts and as an independent consultant. Judges, administrators, court line staff and managers, officials and staffs of other government agencies, and attorneys across the nation all were my teachers. They have enriched my understanding of how courts work and, sometimes, how they do not work. My former colleagues at the National Center for State Courts, in particular, were superb faculty in a 20-year seminar in sound court administration.

Among these thousands of mentors, several stand out for special acknowledgment. Larry L. Sipes saw something in a young attorney who had never worked in a court that led him to invite me into a lifelong commitment to court administration. He then carefully and wisely nurtured and guided my enthusiasm while allowing me sufficient rein to make mistakes, from which I learned much.

Edward B. McConnell gave me my first and second management positions, another valued learning experience. More importantly, in countless ways he modeled excellence in management. Often as a court administrator faced with a difficult situation, I would ask myself what Ed would have done and try to do likewise.

Within three months of my joining the staff of the National Center for State Courts, Hank Rogers, the executive officer of one of the two courts in which I was undertaking my first assignment, invited me to join administrators from throughout California for a series of workshops on court administration being presented by the Institute for Court Management. That opportunity, together with the exceptional support Hank provided during and following that assignment, cemented my commitment to court administration.

Ernie Friesen was the lead faculty member for that entire series of ICM workshops and particularly for the workshop on caseflow management. I learned things in those workshops that I still draw on today. Over the intervening years, Ernie has been exceptionally generous in sharing his extraordinary depth and breadth of understanding of management generally and of court administration in particular. He also encouraged me specifically to undertake the writing of this book.

The judges of the El Dorado County, California, Superior Court allowed me the opportunity to apply my consulting experience to a living, vibrant court environment. I deeply appreciate the support and guidance they provided and the many "real world" lessons learned during my years of service to that court. Equally important to whatever successes we achieved during those years were the hard-working, dedicated staff and managers of the court. They worked diligently and faithfully to implement the many initiatives that the judges and I undertook. Without their skill and support, we could not have achieved half of all we were able to achieve in a relatively few years.

I also have benefited from skilled support in the production of this book. Mary Ann Pruitt applied her graphic skills to design the figures representing Maslow's Hierarchy of Needs and my Hierarchy of Court Administration. I could not have produced them on my own. Andrea Logue and Erika Rickard were invaluable research assistants. They patiently and skillfully checked the hundreds of citations and quotations in this book to assure their accuracy. I am solely responsible for any errors that may have passed into the final version; their help materially improved the quality of the research effort that has gone into this book. Jeanelle Couch-Metzger also provided timely and important assistance with the references.

Four friends and colleagues, Ed McConnell, Ernie Friesen, John Hudzik, and Marcus Reinkensmeyer reviewed the manuscript. I deeply appreciate the time they gave to the effort and their thoughts and counsel. The opinions expressed in the book are mine alone; they do not necessarily reflect the views of these reviewers.

My wife Ruth patiently and wisely applied her considerable English and writing skills to drafts of the book. I value her assistance and benefited throughout production of the book from her suggestions, support, and encouragement.

To all those on whose shoulders I have stood to produce this book, I offer my heartfelt appreciation. As always, any errors of judgment or of facts, or omissions, are my responsibility alone.

Alexander B. Aikman

About the Author

Alexander B. Aikman has been in court administration for over 33 years. He has been a court executive officer for an eight-judge court in Northern California, a consultant to trial courts, appellate courts, and state administrative offices of the courts as a senior staff member, and vice president of the National Center for State Courts. He also has served as a researcher in a half-dozen national-scope studies of court administration issues. He has authored eight books and eight journal articles on various aspects of court administration. He joined the staff of the National Center after litigating business, civil rights, and criminal cases for five years as an associate with a major San Francisco law firm. Aikman holds a BA from Wesleyan University, Middletown, Connecticut and JD and LLM degrees from The University of Chicago Law School, where he was a member of the Order of the Coif and executive editor of the *Law Review*.

Chapter 1

Introduction

1.1   Why This Book?

Everyone knows about courts and judges. It's just that they "know" different things, depending on their experiences and the experiences of acquaintances, their news sources, and their philosophical and political preferences. What people know about courts is determined almost entirely by what judges do in individual cases and what people claim they have done, either good or bad, depending on whether one likes the result. People's knowledge is based almost entirely on a few well-publicized cases and their own experiences, normally involving traffic tickets, divorce, and maybe jury duty. People see and hear about only the proverbial tip of the iceberg of what courts do and how they operate. Even judges do not "see" a lot of what happens to filed civil cases because a large proportion (maybe two-thirds) are resolved with little or no judicial involvement. They are filed and then are abandoned by the filing party, settled by the parties and then dismissed before a response is filed, or the other side files an answer, the parties work on the case outside of court, and then settle it without getting a judge involved. Most traffic tickets are paid without violators ever coming to court. Other than cases in which they are personally involved, the cases that get publicity—and thus form the basis of what people "know"—are a tiny fraction of what courts do.

People's perceptions about courts also ignore a critical component of what it means to be a "court": the institutional support processes of a government agency that also is a separate branch of government. Courts have employees, budgets, complex computerized information systems, jurors, and facilities to be managed. They interact with scores of government, nonprofit, community, and volunteer entities in countless ways that are largely invisible to everyone who "knows" courts and judges. The story of the management of this government branch is hardly ever told and hardly ever of public concern,[1] except to those within the judicial branch. Indeed, most citizens may believe it is terribly boring and irrelevant to their lives. The discipline of court administration is virtually invisible even among political and social scientists. Yet, court administration can profoundly influence whether and how courts work well, whether judges can fill their adjudication role effectively, whether citizens' experiences with their courts are positive or negative, and even whether other government agencies and private entities can effectively fulfill their missions.

This book is about the administration of courts, both currently and how the courts and their administration might change and grow through the bulk of the 21st century. It is a tale of creating and providing the infrastructure that enables judges to provide the justice that courts are charged by law to provide. It is not the tale normally associated with courts, but it is important and deserves examination.

Modern court administration is not yet 60 years old. The first person hired to assist a chief justice to bring professional management to a state's courts was appointed in 1947.[2] The first trial court administrator, that is, someone hired by and responsible only to the judges, was not hired until 1950.[3] Until the advent of modern court administration, the judicial branch presented the façade of a functioning institution, but in truth, judges, to whom the public mistakenly ascribes "control" had—and in important respects still have—no management control over critical aspects of their institution. In most courts, the clerk of court is independently elected or appointed by the local government's legislative or executive branch. Because these clerks see themselves as "equal" to elected judges and also independent, they may or may not manage court operations and records as the judges believe to be necessary. Court security has been and largely remains the province of the local Sheriff or police chief, an elected or appointed law en-forcement officer independent of the judiciary. For 200 years court reporters were almost all independent contractors; many remain so today, as do the increasingly critical language interpreters. Attorneys, the ultimate independent contractors in a court context, are administratively independent of courts. Even public defender offices, whose funds may be funneled through the judicial branch and whose chief public defender may be appointed by the judges, have ethical obligations to their clients that judges can neither breach nor manage. It is only since the mid-1950s that courts, the "third branch," actually have started to create a coherent institu-tion, in contrast to an unconnected conglomerate of independent, locally funded and managed entities.[4] Extraordinary strides in court administration and in courts themselves have been made since 1947. The judiciary has gone a long way toward establishing itself as a viable, truly independent, responsible, and accountable, branch of government.[5] Part of that growth and maturation is attributable to the growth and maturation of court administration.

Hundreds of practice books and research reports on specific tasks and func-tions of courts have been published since the early 1970s, but only a few books and articles have examined the field of court administration.[6] Since the 1970s, when the last broad examination of court administration was published, few aspects of court administration have been untouched by change: the use of technology, funding, the organization and number of trial courts; the role of state-level administration and policy making versus local administration and policy making; the largely universal use of court administrators in addition to or instead of clerks of court; the number and types of employees; the introduction of more "business" management; and the increasing emphasis on public access and accountability. Steven Hays and Cole Blease Graham, two political scientists who edited a 1993 book that addressed court administration and management issues, said in their preface to the book that, "since the early 1970s, every single court in the United States has been positively influenced by innovation springing out of the court management movement."[7] It is time to look anew at the field of court administration.

As we look ahead to the balance of the 21st century, there is need to look at what the term *court administration* means and should mean. There also is need for a fresh eye on the complex environment in which court administration is practiced. The context within which court administration operates is addressed in part I of this book.

There is a need to examine what court administrators do and the qualities and traits they need in addition to the skills, knowledge, and abilities currently identified for them. This is particularly necessary in the near term because a large percentage of the current administrators in some states are projected to retire in the next five years.[8] Judges, who normally hire the court administrator, believe they know what they need in an administrator, but their description often is narrow and short-sighted. They might believe they need someone with a strong budget background, often gained in the executive or legislative branch, because their budgets have been constricted in recent years and they attribute the lack of new funds to a deficiency in the former administrator. They may want someone with a strong technology background because they know they need to install new computers or a new computerized case management information system. They may desire someone with a strong human resources background because some of their staff (or some of the judges) believe the previous administrator did not do a good job with human resource issues and now there are morale problems. In other words, judges often look at the immediate past or the immediate future to identify what they need over the next five, seven, or more years. The critical issue of year one will pass while scores of issues no one anticipated when the administrator was hired arise during the balance of the administrator's tenure. The skills the judges deemed to be critical may be germane to some of these issues, but they are as likely to be irrelevant. Many administrators rise to the challenge and are effective in addressing these other issues, too. When they are not, however, the judges are likely to blame the administrator rather than their own narrow selection criteria. Their perspective is more like that through a telescope than through binoculars or even the unaided eye. Because of this tunnel vision, judges who hire based on today's issue run a substantial risk of being disappointed with their administrator as time goes by.

Administrators need a large set of skills and abilities to be effective. The National Association for Court Management (NACM), an international association of court managers plus a smattering of judges interested in judicial administration, has defined the "knowledge, skills, and abilities" needed by court managers.[9] As NACM itself recognizes, court managers also need qualities, traits, and skills that are not part of the core competencies.[10] Most judges do not reference NACM's core competencies when they seek a new administrator. Judges may not even recognize the qualities and traits that go beyond the core competencies. Even if some judges do recognize them, they seldom articulate them in advance and maybe not even during the final selection discussion; they may vote for or against a candidate without sharing with their colleagues all the factors they took into account. There are no guarantees of success no matter how broad or narrow the selection criteria when a new administrator is hired, but courts can do better. At the same time, administrators need to understand the unique environment in which they must operate and its limitations and idiosyncrasies. Those who have worked in courts for years have that understanding, but those new to courts when they become administrators have a sharp learning curve. Court administration would benefit from fresh eyes and ideas, but bringing in "outsiders" who can be successful is a challenge.

In the early days of court administration, the tasks assigned to the new administrator were only those not performed by the clerk of court. Administrators were brought in to relieve judges of the burden of budget administration plus the details of personnel administration and maybe some of the interbranch coordination requirements. In a few instances, they were hired to address perceived deficiencies in the clerk of court operation. The position has changed and grown along with the growth and increasing complexity of courts themselves. Yet, some are suggesting that court administration and court administrators have grown "stale" as the field has matured, that there is a lack of new ideas and a loss of the old "energy."[11] This assessment may be too harsh, yet there does seem to have been a pause in recent years for everyone to catch their collective breath and think about what courts have to do next while still implementing a number of changes that occurred toward the end of the last century.

Before the field moves on, there is merit in examining court administration through a new conceptual framework. That framework should provide, in particular, fresh thinking about decision making when budgets are frozen or cut as well as when resources are added. The framework should indicate priorities when it is difficult to respond to all the internal and external demands on one's resources and when a court is trying to introduce new programs and perspectives. I call that framework the "hierarchy of court administration," borrowing broadly from the hierarchy of needs created by Abraham Maslow after he had studied human psychological health.[12] Courts need a fresh perspective so that they will not continue to think in linear terms about change and management when they must operate in a disjointed, rapidly changing, short-attention-span, and increasingly demanding world. And it is a world that, to many people, appears to be increasingly hostile to the courts. The court administrator's position and responsibilities plus the new framework are presented in part II of this book.

Courts are highly complex institutions, which are difficult to manage on a number of levels and for a number of reasons.[13] We will explore those levels and reasons throughout this book. It often is said within the field of judicial administration that court reform is not for the short-winded. Court administration also is not for those who have difficulty with complexity, who crave certainty, who have limited tolerance for change and ambiguity, who have limited mediation skills, and who prefer structured organizations and one boss.

This book offers some guidance in the second part about how to address some specific issues faced by administrators, but this is not a "how to" book. As indicated above, there are hundreds of such books devoted to specific topics and functions in courts. There also are thousands of books on business, nonprofit, and government management that contain good, specific suggestions applicable to courts. This book will emphasize how to *approach* issues and problems. It will examine policy not practices, functions not tasks, goals not operations, and approaches not solutions.

The focus here is on state trial courts, because that is where the bulk of my experience for over 30 years has been centered. I share some personal experiences and observations. My experiences are not definitive, but they are illustrative. The book should prove most helpful to court administrators and senior court managers and those interested in those positions. It also offers information and perspectives that should benefit judges with administrative roles in their courts or who are considering moving into such roles. In particular, the discussion in chapter 7 about what court administrators do and the qualities and traits they should possess might assist judges as they consider applicants for top management positions.

1.2 Judicial Administration and Court Administration

Judicial administration and court administration are different. There is considerable overlap, but there also are important components of each that are unique. Just as political science and public administration are two separate disciplines that examine the overall organization and operation of government in general, so when one looks at the judicial branch, there are two areas of interest, judicial administration and court administration. In very broad terms, political science and judicial administration are similar; in academic circles, court administration increasingly is being viewed as a subset of public administration.

The difference between judicial administration and court administration is not one of judges versus administrators or managers. Rather, the difference is that judicial administration embraces jurisdictional, procedural, and administrative law issues beyond the purview of those who practice court administration. Judicial administration issues are the responsibility of policy makers (normally, judges through rule making and the legislature). The policy choices affect what judges do and how they do it in adjudicating cases. These same choices are "givens" for court administration; they provide the context within which administrators manage and staffs operate. Court administration has many components untouched by decisions about judicial administration, as well.

What are the elements that are unique to each subject and which elements are shared? Since at least the early 20th century, the American Bar Association (ABA) has shown a special interest in judicial administration (Roscoe Pound's famous speech to the ABA in 1906 was referred for consideration to the ABA's Committee on Judicial Administration and Remedial Procedures).[14] When the ABA's Section on Judicial Administration was established in 1938, it was assigned six areas for attention:

- Integration of the judiciary through establishment and active functioning of judicial councils, judicial conferences, administrative judges, and administrative offices of the courts
- Delegation of rule making to courts of highest jurisdiction and consistent improvement of pleading, trial practice, and appellate procedures
- Improvement of the jury system
- Adoption of pretrial conferences and pretrial discovery procedures
- Simplification of the laws of evidence
- Improvement of administrative tribunals and practice before them.

In 1937, the ABA had committed to improving the methods of judicial selection.[15] It is these seven topics that have come to define "judicial administration."[16] This definition not only applies to the ABA, but it has been discussed in many articles and books.[17] The ABA itself did not include a discussion of court administration, per se, in its periodic updates on judicial administration, until 1981.[18]

Five topics regularly addressed within judicial administration do not directly involve court administration: integrating court systems; giving the courts of highest jurisdiction rule-making authority (instead of placing it with the legislature); judicial selection procedures; changes in the rules of evidence; and administrative tribunals. Decisions made in these judicial administration areas may impact court administration significantly, but they are not part of court administration. However, court administration is directly involved in two items that are part of the ABA's judicial administration agenda: jury management and the use of pretrial conferences and special rules of discovery. These are the specific areas of overlap between judicial administration and court administration.[19] At times, trial court administrators or state court administrators may be asked to study the management impact of changes and advise policy makers on specific changes in judicial administration, or even to help the branch lobby for desired changes. These assignments are made because of the individuals' expertise in court administration, not because judicial administration and court administration are the same thing.

Judicial administration is very important, just as political science plays an important role in informing legislative and executive branch decision making in areas within those branches' purview. Judicial administration has received substantial attention since the late 1930s, and it will continue to receive attention in the 21st century because the goals set by the ABA and others are not yet fully realized in all states. Also, views about how courts should operate and be organized change over time and previous positions may need to be reviewed. This book, however, addresses court administration.

Court administration is the totality of support and infrastructure tasks and functions that enable judicial officers to fulfill the court's adjudicative functions and the court as an institution to fulfill the obligations of a branch of government. Court administration is what court administrators, clerks of court, and numerous supporting personnel (case processing staff, courtroom staff, court reporters, interpreters, jury clerks, computer and other technical staff, human resources staff, accounting staff, and facilities support staff) do to enable the delivery of justice by judicial officers.

Although they are distinct endeavors, judicial administration and court administration are symbiotic. The rise of court administration might never have occurred or, at minimum, it would not have been so substantial, were it not for the improvements in judicial administration. In particular, changes in how courts are organized and moving policy making within the branch to the court of highest jurisdiction (or a comparable policy-making body), created a need for more professional administration while also establishing the environment within which court administration could demonstrate its competence. The growing move in the latter half of the 20th century to funding trial courts from the state's budget also contributed to both the need for and value of professional management. In like fashion, the advancements rendered through court administration gave policy makers comfort that changes they would make in judicial administration would be well implemented.

For decades, if not longer, legislators and many in the executive branch at both state and federal levels saw the judicial branch as unmanaged and the source of many fiscal and budgeting nightmares. They also often viewed judges and their managers as incapable of effective management. These views have not been displaced entirely, but to a large degree they have disappeared or been scaled way back because of increasingly professional management within the branch, both at the state level and in trial courts.

The distinctions between judicial administration and court administration are significant, but they also can be seen as opposite sides of the same coin. They both have been essential in the development and maturation of the third branch of government during the last half of the 20th century and will continue to act symbiotically in the 21st century. Three sage observers of courts emphasized the importance of both judicial and court administration when they noted: "A court's effectiveness in contributing to social justice depends on both its judicial and its administrative structure."[20]

If we were to use the image of Lady Justice to represent the courts, her sword, scales, and partial blindfold would be the work of judicial officers and, in key respects, of judicial administration; court administration would be Lady Justice's skeleton and the people and mechanisms that keep her gown clean and orderly and her implements in working order. A similar metaphor was suggested in the final report of a leadership forum held late in 2004. The forum brought together 30 leaders prominent in judicial administration and court administration in the 1970s and 1980s to review the accomplishments of their era plus suggest a leadership agenda for the 21st century. That report said, in part: "the great challenge of a free society has been to maintain both a social order and preserve individual liberty; a competent judicial system is the key to maintaining that balance; and competent court administration provides the framework for maintaining a competent judicial system and keeping that essential balance healthy."[21]

Federal judge John Parker, an important figure in judicial reform efforts in the 1930s and 1940s, said:[22]

> If democracy is to live, democracy must be made efficient, for the survival of the fit is as much a law of political economy as it is of the life of the jungle. If we would preserve free government in America, we must make free government, good government. Nowhere does government touch the life of the people more intimately than in the administration of justice; and nowhere is it more important that the government process be shot through with efficiency and common sense.

Peter Drucker, management expert, talking generically about management, said: "Without institution there is no management. But without management, there is no institution."[23]

Court administration is important because courts are important and court administration enables courts to work effectively, with efficiency, and, it is to be hoped, common sense. When courts work well, our democratic system of government is preserved and enhanced. Court administration does not embrace all the aspects of courts and justice that receive the legitimate attention and concern of scholars, lawyers, and citizens, but it increasingly impacts how well courts are able to deliver justice. This point was made by two political scientists who looked at court administration in the early 1990s: "It is probably safe to say that since the early 1970s, every single court in the United States has been positively influenced by innovation springing out of the court management movement."[24] Court administration is an aspect of public administration that uniquely advances democracy and thus is worthy of careful attention.

1.3 Court Administration and Maslow's Hierarchy of Needs

Abraham Maslow, a founder of humanistic psychology in the mid-20th century—roughly 1940 to 1960—first articulated his hierarchy of needs in 1954.[25] Disturbed by psychological theories that were based on pathologies (Freud) and animal experiments (Skinner), Maslow sought to understand what led to mental health by studying what animals and humans do when they are healthy. Maslow identified various needs of humans, starting with basic physiological needs such as air, water, and food. Then, when those needs were satisfied, he posited that people seek to satisfy safety needs (physical and emotional safety), then love and belonging (love, affiliation), then esteem (self-esteem and the recognition and esteem of others), and, finally, self-actualization. Maslow posited that people seek to satisfy the needs at each level before they turn to attaining their needs at the next level. That is, if people are hungry, they will seek to satisfy that need before concerning themselves with security needs or the need to be loved and to love. If they have moved up the hierarchy but then come to lack food or shelter, they will focus on the lower level needs until they again are satisfied. They must feel physically and emotionally secure before they turn their attention to finding and providing love. Maslow called this ascending catalog his "hierarchy of needs." This idea can be displayed graphically as a triangle (Figure 1.1).

Physiological needs were at the base, then the security needs, and on up the triangle until one reached self-actualization. The term self-actualization refers to individuals operating at their highest, most fulfilled level: "Musicians must make music, artists must paint, poets must write, if they are to be ultimately at peace with themselves. What humans *can* be, they *must* be. They must be true to their own nature. This need we may call self-actualization."[26] The specific elements within each level of need are set forth in Table 1.1.

Maslow's theory has received substantial acceptance and been used as a guide in education, management, human resource management, sales, and numerous other contexts.[27] It contains an intuitive "truthfulness" to which many people relate. The theory has its critics,[28] including claims that there is an insufficiently researched basis for all five levels, but especially for self-actualization. Some

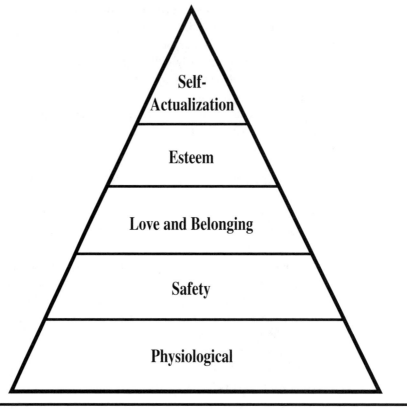

Figure 1.1 Maslow Hierarchy of Needs.

Table 1.1 **Specific elements within each level of Maslow's hierarchy**

⇒ Physiological

Oxygen, water, protein, salt, sugar, calcium, other minerals & vitamins, maintain pH balance, temperature, activity, rest, sleep, waste disposal, avoidance of pain, sex

⇒ Safety/security

Safe circumstances, stability, protection, avoiding fears and anxieties

⇒ Belonging and love

Friends, sweetheart, children, affectionate relationships, organizational affiliations

⇒ Esteem

Respect of others: status, fame, glory, recognition, attention, reputation, achievement; self-esteem: confidence, appreciation, dignity, dominance, mastery, independence, freedom

⇒ Self-actualization

Growth, motivation, desire to fulfill one's potential

psychologists have restructured the needs Maslow cites into different groupings with different names.[29]

What is striking to a layperson is the broad acceptance of Maslow's basic thesis, that there are certain needs that humans share and that they can be arrayed along a continuum, from the most basic, survival-level needs to various higher or "more desirable" states. When humans reach these higher states or conditions, they are more "actualized," that is, closer to their full potential, than if they must constantly struggle with basic physical and economic needs.

If the court as an institution is substituted for humans in Maslow's hierarchy, the parallel between human needs and court administration's needs is striking. Courts have certain basic needs and functions that must be performed if they are to operate effectively and fulfill their mission. These tasks and functions are akin to Maslow's physiological needs for humans. When the mission critical needs are satisfied, courts can move into new programs, improved operations, and more community outreach. If budgets are later cut, courts revert back to the mission critical tasks until they can again start enhancing their funds.

Thinking of the mission critical tasks and functions as akin to humans' basic physiological needs would be an important change in the debate over the resources that courts need every time the business cycle—and hence government revenue—turns down. When courts face frozen or reduced budgets, the debate about how much of a cut a court can or should take often turns on which tasks and functions of a court are deemed to be "mandated," meaning constitutionally or statutorily required to be performed. Each time this debate is engaged, courts scramble to review the current statutes and any new court rules and judicial decisions rendered since the last budget crunch that define a task or need as legally required. For courts that are locally funded, a state statute is a mandate. In the periodic but perennial budget debates about what courts "must" do, this gives the locally funded courts an advantage. For courts that are state funded, the legislature can change its mind and de facto repeal a previous mandate by not funding the courts to perform that function or task during a fiscal year. So in state-funded systems, courts, legislatures, and governors may end up debating whether a statute is or should be regarded as critical to court functioning and thus "mandated."

There is a major flaw in this debate about mandates: statutes and judicial decisions do not address all the tasks and functions of a court. Nor do they attempt to define the most critical or necessary tasks and functions. Statutes address specific issues one at a time, even if they are part of a "codification" that brings all individual laws on a subject together into one title or section. No legislature, and certainly no court when asked to adjudicate as to whether something is constitutionally required, thinks in terms of all the functions and tasks courts must perform to meet their assigned constitutional role. There also are many tasks that courts must perform to be viable institutions, that are not mentioned in any statute. This absence does not reflect a legislative choice that the task should not be performed during tight budgetary times or that everything in statutes should have a higher priority. Indeed, many legislators as well as most in the courts may assume the function is needed and not see a need to articulate that need in a statute.[30] The assumption that a court has certain basic needs that must be met for it to function is related to the concept of "inherent powers": this is a concept that has been used by courts to mandate the funding of certain individual items or even large portions of a budget. As such, it carries some negative connotations for the two other branches of government. Using the term *mission critical tasks and functions* avoids the legal and political implications attached to inherent powers. It also might negate arguments occasionally made by judges that a new desk chair or a raise for the judge's secretary is "inherently" critical to the court providing justice and therefore can be mandated using a court's inherent powers. A "hierarchy of need" analogy enables courts to define which functions are akin to the physiological needs of humans, without which the judicial institution could not survive and perform its constitutional duties. These tasks will include "institutional" needs such as accounting for and depositing cash, paying employees, and storing and preserving case records, in addition to case-based requirements such as issuing warrants, holding hearings, and advising prisons of certain information about sentenced defendants. These are the "mission critical" needs of a court; they exist whether or not a legislature or a court case recognizes or addresses them and they are as essential to a court as are the physiological needs of humans. Chapter 9 defines the tasks and functions that should be regarded as "physiological" for courts.

There is one further point regarding statutory mandates and mission critical needs. A few courts believe that mandates must be followed no matter what, including periods when there are reduced budgets. Other courts will lower the priority given to some statutory mandates or will stop complying with some statutes altogether. Law enforcement and prosecutors make similar judgments. Law enforcement will choose not to patrol in some areas as often or not to arrest for certain behavior. Prosecutors will choose not to file and pursue charges on certain crimes while resources are limited. Likewise, each court makes its own decisions. The result is a patchwork of activities that courts perform across a state during tight budget periods. Agreeing on the tasks and functions that are mission critical may not end this divergence, but it may limit it.

Courts have significant security needs, as do humans. Both human beings and courts need to know they are physically secure, which, in turn, for courts leads to psychological security for judges, staff, and all those who visit the courthouse. Security breaches of all kinds receive wide and normally very negative press coverage. They all affect how the public feels about courts and how judges and staff feel about coming to work each day. Court administration's need for safety and security is as great as the need of individuals in Maslow's hierarchy; it also is a need that should be addressed immediately after a court has addressed its mission critical (physiological) needs.

The parallel between human needs to love and belong and something similar for a court is not as clear as it is for the first two levels of need.[31] It is not much of a stretch, however, to see a parallel between humans' need to connect with others on an emotional level and the need for courts to engage positively with scores of external agencies and organizations. In the hierarchy of court administration, the third level is the need to have positive and effective external relationships.

At the fourth level in Maslow's hierarchy, human beings seek two types of esteem: first, self-esteem and then the esteem of and confirmation from others. The comparable level for courts would be improving service and internal processes by introducing new programs, new technologies, more refined procedures, and broader and more effective ways to provide public access. In doing these things, courts demonstrate both within the judiciary and to the public that courts are viable, vibrant enterprises worthy of public support (esteem). These enhancements not only bring courts closer to achieving their mission and goals, but also show outside observers that the court is focusing on improving and enhancing staff productivity and is moving beyond the merely necessary to doing better. This is the proactive management level of need for courts.

It has been said that Clarence Darrow and even Thomas Jefferson or Samuel Adams could walk into a courtroom today and feel reasonably comfortable with both the appearance and the procedures used, except, probably, for the computers that now dot courtrooms. This is not intended as a compliment, although in some ways it reflects the conservative nature of courts and the development of law that is not necessarily bad. Even so, from a management perspective, if this statement could be applied validly to the administration of courts in 50 or 100 years, it would be a death knell.

In today's world, being a proactive court in administrative terms is essential to continued viability. As resources become available—and that means seeking the resources, not waiting for the legislature to bestow them—courts have to look to being proactive to remain relevant and worthy of esteem. Courts moving into this level of the hierarchy can start initiating and innovating and thereby improving productivity and service. Courts able to operate at this level are open to new ideas and recognize their merits, and as a result adopt new procedures and approaches on a regular basis.

The highest level for a court is to be a leadership organization, which is akin to the self-actualization level for humans. Just as Maslow says self-actualized individuals have "become everything that one is capable of becoming,"[32] so leadership courts are model institutions, recognized as such both within the third branch and in their communities. They are "early adopters" of new technologies, new procedures, and new ways to organize staff and workflow. They care for their staff

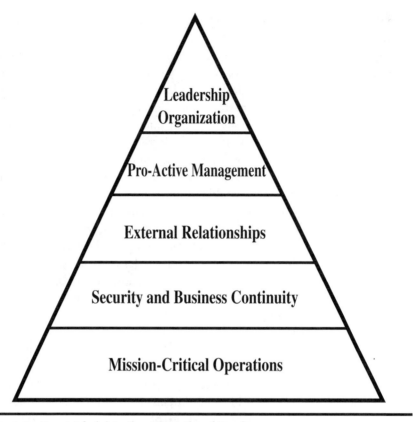

Figure 1.2 Court Administration Hierarchy of Needs.

financially and by nurturing and encouraging staff's professional development. They scan the environment and use strategic planning to guide budget development, expenditures, and management decisions. They reach out to the community in new ways, they find new ways to obtain community feedback on how they are working and what more needs to be done, and they find new ways to open up their administrative processes to public scrutiny. They look at their mission and judge a new idea by whether or not that idea advances achieving their mission.

The hierarchy of court administration is shown graphically in Figure 1.2. The details behind these labels are discussed in part II of this book.

1.4 Structure of This Book

To understand court administration, it helps to understand the context in which it is practiced. That is the purpose of part I, "The Context of Court Administration." The word *context* here refers to a short overview of the history of the field and how courts are organized across the country and in the federal system. To conduct a dialogue about courts, there needs to be a common vocabulary. There is no common vocabulary across states for trial courts' names, for the scope of their jurisdiction, or for the title of the judge with primary administrative responsibility. Nor is there agreement on the names of the court of last resort, the state-level office responsible for administration of the branch, or of the person who heads that office. Chapter 3 offers an overview of the variations and establishes the vocabulary of this book. Chapter 4 explores the "environmental" conditions in which court administration is practiced: courts as the third branch, courts' role in society, and court funding. Chapter 5 discusses the special impact on courts of the elected clerk of court, the prosecutor, and the sheriff. The final chapter of part I, chapter 6, explores judges' administrative roles and how judges' judicial and administrative roles fit and do not fit with management.

Part II, "The Art of Practicing Court Administration," starts with an examination of the administrator's roles, both those shared with any senior manager in government and in many respects the private sector, and in the specific context of courts. This chapter also examines the qualities and skills needed by a court administrator, particularly those that are not covered in NACM's Core Competencies. Also discussed is the need for administrators to display leadership and the hiring process for administrators. The balance of part II reviews the many aspects of court administration within the framework provided by the hierarchy of court administration. Courts' mission critical functions embrace almost all of the elements of a court's operations, both purely administrative and case-related. These same mission critical functions are found at the proactive management level as well. At the mission critical level, they must be done at the minimally accepted level to meet courts' mission and goals. At the proactive management level, a court can move beyond the minimum to provide enhancements, to improve productivity, and to apply new or improved technologies to accomplish the same functions. The difference is that the mission critical functions create the floor below which a court should not fall in order to meet its mission. At the proactive management level, the court addresses these same functions, but with improved operations and enhanced productivity. If necessary, these enhancements can be suspended or abandoned in order to preserve the mission critical level of functioning. At the proactive management level, as well, courts are starting to introduce new programs, which they cannot do at the mission critical level.

Each level in the hierarchy of court administration is discussed in a chapter in part II. Taken together, these chapters, but especially the chapter on leadership organizations, define the blueprint for administration of courts in the 21st century.

Notes

1. When I have been on airplanes or attending social events and mention that I am (was) a court administrator or a management consultant to courts, I usually face quizzical silence. People generally do not know where to go next when "court administration" is the topic of conversation.

2. Edward McConnell, the lead law clerk and administrative assistant for Chief Justice Arthur Vanderbilt of New Jersey, had a master's degree in business administration in addition to his law degree when named as the state court administrator.

3. Edward C. Gallas was named the court executive officer of the Los Angeles, California, Superior Court.

4. See Tobin, Robert W., *Creating the Judicial Branch: The Unfinished Reform.* Williamsburg, VA: National Center for State Courts, 1999.

5. Ibid.

6. For example, Saari, David, "New Ideas for Trial Court Administration—Applying Social Science to Law," *Judicature*, vol. 51, p. 82 (1967); Gallas, Edward, "The Profession of Court Management," *Judicature*, vol. 51, p. 334 (1968); Friesen, Ernest C. Jr., Edward C. Gallas, and Nesta Gallas, *Managing the Courts.* Indianapolis, IN: Bobbs-Merrill, 1971; Hays, Steven W., and Cole Blease Graham, Jr., eds., *Handbook of Court Administration and Management.* New York: Marcel Dekker, 1993.

7. Hays, Steven W., and Cole Blease Graham, Jr., eds., *Handbook of Court Administration*, p. iii.

8. For example, a membership survey of the National Association for Court Management as of April 3, 2006, indicates that 661 of the 1,325 (50%) responding members are aged 50 or older. One hundred and seventy-three (13%) are over 60. Most government retirement programs provide pension benefits based on the number of years of service, not age, so someone who has worked for government for 30 years could retire with a substantial pension even if that person were still in his or her 50s.

9. National Association for Court Management, *Core Competency Curriculum Guidelines: What Court Leaders Need to Know and Be Able To Do.* Williamsburg, VA: National Association for Court Management, 2005.

10. Ibid., p. 4.

11. For example, Gallas, Geoff, and Gordy Griller, "The Court Management Profession: Questions and Issues," *Court Manager*, vol. 19, no. 2, 2004, pp. 5–12.

12. See, for example, Maslow, Abraham H., *Motivation and Personality*, 2nd ed. New York: Harper & Row, 1970.

13. See Friesen, Ernest C. Jr., Edward C. Gallas, and Nesta Gallas, *Managing the Courts*, chap. 4, esp. p. 119.

14. See Gossett, William T., Bernard G. Segal, and Chesterfield Smith, "Foreword," to Levin, A. Leo, and Russell R. Wheeler, eds., *The Pound Conference: Perspectives on Justice in the Future.* St. Paul, MN: West Publishing, 1979, p. 7.

15. Section of Judicial Administration, *The Improvement of the Administration of Justice*, 5th ed. Chicago: American Bar Association, 1971, p. 2.

16. Vanderbilt, Arthur T., ed., *Minimum Standards of Judicial Administration.* New York: The Law Center of New York University, 1949; Section of Judicial Administration, *The Improvement of the Administration of Justice*, 5th ed. Chicago: American Bar Association, 1971; Klein, Fannie J., ed., *The Improvement of the Administration of Justice*, 6th ed. Chicago: ABA Press, 1981; American Bar Association, Judicial Administration Division, *Standards Relating to Court Organization.* Chicago: ABA Press, 1990; American Bar Association Judicial Administration Division, *Standards Relating to Trial Courts.* Chicago: ABA Press, 1992.

17. For example, Hays, Steven W., and Cole Blease Graham, Jr., eds., *Handbook of Court Administration* (as the title suggests, this book also covers some issues of court administration); Epstein, Lee, *Contemplating Courts.* Washington, D.C.: CQ Press, 1995; Carp, Robert A., and Ronald Stidham, *Judicial Process in America.* Washington, D.C.: CQ Press, 2001.

18. Klein, Fannie J., ed., *Improvement of the Administration of Justice, 1981*, chap. 3.

19. Administrative tribunals need the skills and results of court administration and the topics reviewed in this book generally are germane, but administrative law and administrative tribunals are part of the executive branch and thus not directly part of court administration.

20. Friesen, Ernest C. Jr., Edward C. Gallas, and Nesta Gallas, *Managing the Courts*, p. 237.

21. *Final Report, Judicial System Leadership Forum*, Dec. 16–17, 2004. Washington, D.C.: Bureau of Justice Assistance and American University, 2005, p. 5, retrieved Sept. 12, 2005 from http://www.american.edu/justice/resources.

22. Parker, John J., "Improving the Administration of Justice," *American Bar Association Journal*, vol. 27, 1941, at p. 71, quoted in Section of Judicial Administration, *Improvement of the Administration of Justice, 1971*, p. 5.

23. Drucker, Peter F., *Management: Tasks, Responsibilities, Practices*. New York: Harper & Row, 1973, p. 6.

24. Hays, Steven W., and Cole Blease Graham, Jr., eds., *Handbook of Court Administration*, p. iii.

25. *Motivation and Personality*. New York: Harper & Row, 1980.

26. Ibid., p. 22.

27. An Internet search for "Maslow's Hierarchy of Needs" turns up over 19,000 results, many of which are articles and academic papers relating Maslow's hierarchy to the fields cited plus others.

28. For example, Heylighen, Francis, "A Cognitive Systematic Reconstruction of Maslow's Theory of Self-Actualization," *Behavioral Science*, vol. 37, pp. 39–58, 1992; Wahba, M., and L. Bridwell, "Maslow Reconsidered: A Review of Research on the Need Hierarchy Theory," *Organizational Behavior and Human Performance*, vol. 15, pp. 212–240.

29. Huitt, W., "Maslow's Hierarchy of Needs," *Educational Psychology Interactive*, Valdosta, GA: Valdosta Univ., retrieved Sept. 12, 2005 from http://chiron.valdosta.edu/whuitt/col/regsys/maslow.html.

30. Assuring the payment of bills incurred by courts would be just one example. See chapter 8 for more detail.

31. In truth, many in courts, especially judges who must run for election or reelection, would like to feel that citizens "love" them and the courts. Public opinion surveys over the years suggest this wish is not realized as much as desired (see, e.g., chapter 4). There is some evidence, however, that efforts to improve the administration of court systems will be recognized by citizens. Rottman, David B., *Trust and Confidence in the California Courts*. Williamsburg, VA: National Center for State Courts, 2005, p. 3. Legislatures and governors also recognize and reward administrative improvements, normally with increased funding but also with laws that facilitate or institutionalize a documented, positive change.

32. Maslow, Abraham H., *Motivation and Personality*, p. 22.

THE CONTEXT
FOR COURT
ADMINISTRATION

I

Chapter 2

An Historical Context

Modern court administration is not yet two generations old, and a few of its original pioneers are still alive. Even so, there are at least three reasons why there is value in examining the historical context of the field at this juncture.

First, some people have a sense that there is ennui or loss of forward movement in the field.[1] A brief reminder of how far the field has come may make those still involved feel better about where courts are today and what might yet be accomplished. Second, as noted in the previous chapter, substantial turnover in trial courts' top managers is likely in the next five to ten years. Those who follow the retirees should know and understand the history so they will have a context for both their profession and new proposals.[2] Third, both a society and a profession should know and appreciate its heroes. This chapter will not provide extended biographies, but it will at least acknowledge some brilliant and visionary pioneers. There also is a need to note and acknowledge the important contributions made by a number of organizations. A thumbnail sketch of each organization's contribution to court administration's advancement is offered in this chapter.

2.1 The Pioneers

Every field of endeavor needs "heroes," but new fields that already may be in "pause" mode may need them more. The thumbnail sketches that follow, of ten pioneers who helped to establish and shape modern court administration, are offered to remind readers of our heroes. Identification of the ten individuals in this section is not meant to diminish or demean the important contributions, both nationally and in their states, of countless other pioneers who helped to shape both judicial administration and court administration in the 20th century. These other men and women each brought their own special visions, insights, political acumen, and talents to reform efforts, particularly from the 1960s through the

1980s. Were this a full history of judicial administration and court administration, the list of people to be profiled would have to extend well beyond ten. The ten cited here deserve special recognition for their multiple efforts and the influence they had and continue to have.

These ten individuals accomplished a lot. That alone, however, is not why they are cited here. They all shared passions: a passion for justice; a derivative passion for courts because courts are the primary vehicle through which our society provides individual justice; a passion for public service, even when, at times, headlines, commentators, and some polls suggest public service and public servants are somehow tainted or unworthy of respect. They had a passion for integrity, both personal and professional, and a passion for hard work, because the ends were so significant. They are models for today's and tomorrow's court leaders because of who they were as much as for what they did. Had they only done significant things, they would be remembered but not honored. If the profession today is suffering, perhaps it is passion that has faded. If we can find and develop those with both passion and skill, the profession, and courts, will leap forward again.

Discussions of modern judicial administration efforts always start with *Dean Roscoe Pound*'s 1906 address to the American Bar Association (ABA) titled, "The Causes of Popular Dissatisfaction with the Administration of Justice." Some have suggested from the perspective of 70 years that this was "the most influential paper ever written by an American legal scholar."[3] Many, perhaps most of those in attendance that August day did not recognize the address as great, however. When a member of the audience moved that the speech be copied and distributed to all 4,000 members of the ABA, the motion was roundly defeated, with some members bitter and upset at Pound's "unwarranted" attack on America's courts and legal system. A motion to refer the speech to a standing committee barely passed.[4] Yet, over time, the concerns expressed and the call to action in this speech became the foundation for much of the ABA's judicial administration reform efforts later in the 20th century. If one compares the points made by Pound in this speech with the six items identified in the 1938 charter of the ABA's Section on Judicial Administration, the parallels are clear. And this list has guided the ABA since that time in its agenda to address issues of judicial and court administration. Distressingly, some of the causes of dissatisfaction cited by Pound remain today. The speech is important, nonetheless, as a rallying point for judicial administration reform.

Arthur Vanderbilt deserves note both for his inspired guidance of the ABA's early efforts at judicial administration reform and for his unique, seminal step for court administration as a Chief Justice. As noted in chapter 1, Chief Justice Vanderbilt reached out and appointed the first person named to be a state court administrator because of his professional managerial skills.[5] His understanding that the courts of New Jersey would benefit from the assistance of a professional manager earns him a very special place in the "court administration Hall of Fame," even if he had not made important contributions to judicial administration, as well. Chief Justice Vanderbilt was a wordsmith. It is he who first said that, "judicial reform is no sport for the short-winded or for lawyers who are afraid of temporary defeat. Rather must we recall the sound advice given by General Jan Smuts to the students at Oxford: 'When enlisted in a good cause, never surrender, for you can never tell what morning reinforcements in flashing armour will come marching over the hilltop.'"[6]

Justice Tom Clark, who served on the United States Supreme Court from 1949 until 1967, was deeply involved in many of the early initiatives for the advancement of both judicial administration and court administration through the ABA's Section on Judicial Administration, which he chaired in 1956, and on his own. He was involved in the 1958 creation of the National Conference of State Trial Judges (NCSTJ), an association of state trial judges of general jurisdiction. In 1961, he chaired the ABA's Joint Committee for the Effective Administration of Justice. Through the auspices of the NCSTJ, he was instrumental in the creation of the National College of State Trial Judges, which held its first training session in 1964; now the National Judicial College, it is located in Reno, Nevada. Following his retirement from the U.S. Supreme Court, Justice Clark served as the first director of the Federal Judicial Center, the research arm of the federal judiciary, and Chair of the Board of Directors of the American Judicature Society. He also was an ally of Chief Justice Warren Burger in the establishment of the Institute for Court Management (ICM) and the National Center for State Courts (NCSC), founded in 1970 and 1971, respectively.

Justice Paul C. Reardon of Massachusetts is not a household name in court administration other than, perhaps, the fact that the NCSC gives the Paul C. Reardon Award annually to a judge who has made outstanding contributions to the improvement of justice and to the NCSC. Justice Reardon did both. Like several other dedicated facilitators of improvement in judicial and court administration during the 1960s and 1970s, Justice Reardon often worked quietly behind the scenes, but always for improved judicial and court administration and always effectively. Nationally, he may be best known as the chair of the ABA's Advisory Committee on Fair Trial and Free Press. Following release of the committee's report in 1966, it became known—and still often is referred to—as the Reardon Report. It was the first attempt to codify a balance between these two important constitutional rights. Its recommendations became part of the statutes and ethical rules of all 50 states. Its precepts remain the foundation for bench-bar-press relations, helping to guide courts' handling of today's notorious cases. Justice Reardon was an original organizer of the National Conference of State Trial Judges while he was serving as Chief Justice of the Superior Court of Massachusetts; he served as its second chair. He also helped organize the first National Conference on the Judiciary, which ended with passage of a resolution to create a national center for state courts. He then became one of six drafters of the Center's charter and served as its first President. Thereafter, he played a significant role in helping the Center raise the funds needed to build its headquarters building in Williamsburg, Virginia. He had a burning commitment both to justice and to the courts fulfilling their assigned constitutional role. It was this passion that underlay his commitment to reform during his years on the trial and appellate benches and following his retirement.

Chief Justice of the United States Warren Burger deserves a special place in the annals of judicial and court administration reform. The Federal Judicial Center (FJC) was created at the end of 1967 and began operating in January 1968. Chief Justice Burger assumed office in June 1969 and was soon receiving reports originating in the FJC. Chief Justice Burger knew five things: (1) the FJC reports were very informative and helpful; (2) state courts did not have access to these reports; (3) state courts would benefit as much as federal courts from such reports; (4) because each state's courts were independent of each other and there were so many state courts, it was difficult for them to share and coordinate across state lines information about successful programs and procedures; and (5) state courts heard substantially more cases than the federal courts (see section 3.4, chapter 3) and were in closer touch with average citizens than federal courts. Chief Justice Burger was an activist for administrative reform. He convinced Richard Nixon, then U.S. President, to cosponsor a National Conference on the Judiciary (effectively, the *states'* judiciaries), which was held in March 1971. Burger took an active role in the planning process, gave a keynote address, and assured that the resolution to establish a national center for state courts would be adopted at the end of the conference. During his remaining years, both as U.S. Chief Justice and, following his retirement in 1986, as a private citizen, Chief Justice Burger lent his personal attention and his prestige to the development and support of the National Center for State Courts. In recognition of his special place in the Center's history, he was named honorary chairman of the Board.

Chief Justice Burger's vision was not limited to a research, consulting, and coordination organization for state courts. Recognizing the value of professional management for both federal and state courts, he helped establish the Institute for Court Management (ICM) in 1970. ICM was and remains the premier training organization for court managers. The original concept of Chief Justice Burger was that ICM would train people from other areas of government, especially retired military officers, and from the private sector, in the intricacies of courts. They then would become the nucleus of the new profession of court administrator. ICM also was to provide ongoing training. In time, the model ICM candidate changed to someone already working in courts who needed to learn management skills, but Burger's core vision of a need to train professional managers for courts has remained the touchstone for ICM to this day.

Burger convinced Congress to create the position of Circuit Court Executive for the federal courts. Again, he did so to bring a cadre of professional managers into the federal system to assist judges in the federal circuits to administer their courts more professionally and effectively.[7]

Howell Heflin, Chief Justice of Alabama and then U.S. Senator, deserves recognition for his accomplishments in both careers. First as President of the Alabama State Bar and then as Chief Justice, Heflin fought for and oversaw substantial improvements in the organization and administration of the courts in his state. Improving the courts of Alabama was significant, but perhaps not much more so than the efforts of chief justices in several other states during the 1970s and 1980s. Heflin is included in this list of pioneers for his untiring efforts in support of the federal quasi-government institution, the State Justice Institute (SJI). SJI was the logical and necessary conclusion of a series of federal programs that provided grants to states for various federal initiatives, some of which went to state courts.

The infusion of federal funds to state courts was a key ingredient in the substantial progress in judicial and court administration reform in the 1970s and 1980s.[8] The availability of federal funds initially was a consequence of the "war on crime" started by President Richard Nixon in the late 1960s. The Law Enforcement Assistance Administration (LEAA) was created by Congress within the Department of Justice to funnel federal funds to states to fight crime (as well as to fund a number of nationally oriented projects directly from Washington). Almost all of the funds sent to state governments for local distribution (80 percent of the total congressional appropriation) ended up with law enforcement and prosecutors, with small amounts going to corrections and even less to defense services. The authorizing legislation included courts as potential grantees, but their funding was not much higher than the funds given for defense services. Courts were not attuned to seeking federal funding from either Washington or in the state capitals and did not operate effectively within the political environments of state-level funding. Eventually, through hard work by the Conference of Chief Justices (CCJ), the Conference of State Court Administrators (COSCA), and the two LEAA senior managers assigned to oversee court funding, LEAA became a very important funding source for many states' reform efforts.[9]

There were two difficulties with LEAA as a funding source for reform, however. First, the funds were set aside for criminal law efforts (the "war on crime") while many of the state courts' needs involved civil justice concerns. The funding agencies at times were very generous in their interpretation of their mandate when courts argued that improvements in civil justice would make it easier for courts to address criminal case processing, but this argument could take state courts only so far over the long term. Second, almost all of those making the decisions about what would be funded, whether in Washington or in state capitals, had law enforcement or prosecutorial backgrounds and little or no understanding of courts. So projects deemed to be of critical importance to courts were not seen as critical by those making funding decisions. The state courts' leadership, through the CCJ and COSCA, decided that the best solution was to have a federal agency devoted solely to state courts' shared needs. It took many years of lobbying, but this decision eventually led to establishment of SJI. Senator Heflin was critical to convincing Congress first, that federal money should be earmarked for state courts and second, that the need was important enough to the whole country to justify a quasi-governmental funding agency. During Heflin's years in the U.S. Senate, SJI never received enormous funding from Congress, but in the context of state courts' needs, the funding was significant and substantial and, most critically, continuing. (As courts' budgets normally are barely sufficient or slightly deficient, the marginal utility of the federal funds to support research and training was enormous.) After Senator Heflin retired, the funding totals started to slip and support in Congress began to fade, to the point that in fiscal 2006, SJI was barely able to continue as a viable source of project, conference, and training funding. The importance of federal funding in meeting the needs of state courts in those years has been recognized by some.[10] Even so, the virtual lack of federal funding is not included as much as it should be when possible "ennui" or "stagnation" in the field is discussed. The number and value of new ideas within judicial and court administration are not truly known today because federal funding is not nearly as available as it was in the 1970s through the early 1990s. Few states are able and willing to support research and implementation projects that have national impact, so new ideas are not getting tested or the exposure they need to have a national impact. Howell Heflin's efforts on behalf of federal funding to assist state courts were critical to advancing the reform agenda.

Except for Dean Pound, all those cited to this point were judges. Three administrators and one researcher deserve special recognition: Edward B. McConnell, Edward C. Gallas, Ernie Friesen, and William Pabst.

Ed McConnell became the administrative and legal assistant to New Jersey Chief Justice Vanderbilt in 1950. He was named the New Jersey state court administrator in 1953 because of his skills as a manager.[11] He pioneered a role that has grown in both importance and visibility in the years since, especially in the states where all or most of trial courts' funding comes from state government. McConnell performed at a high level throughout his 20 years of service in New Jersey; in many respects his tenure was a model for state court administrators across the country. Had McConnell left court administration at the end of his tenure in New Jersey, his service there, alone, might warrant his inclusion on this list. But McConnell cemented his stature when he moved from New Jersey to become Executive Director of the National Center for State Courts in 1973 (the position was renamed "president" in the 1980s). The first executive director of the NCSC was an appellate judge from California, Winslow Christian, who took a leave of absence to help the fledgling organization. He worked diligently during his two-year tenure and instituted some important organizational steps, but when McConnell joined the Center its future was uncertain. Over the course of his 17 years with the Center, McConnell:

- Steered the organization through some perilous fiscal times to relative fiscal health;
- Oversaw the fund-raising, design, and construction of the national headquarters building in Williamsburg, Virginia;
- Reorganized the governing structure of the Center to establish a critical bond between the Center and CCJ and COSCA, through which these two organizations now provide the Chair and Vice Chair of the Board, respectively, and provide a critical mass of Board members;
- Expanded and contracted the Center's regional offices to fit available resources and the needs of client courts;
- Expanded the secretariat function of the Center to the point where its staff now serves as staff for most of the key volunteer organizations in the field;
- Assured that the Center's research efforts and consulting undertakings met the needs of trial courts and state-level administrative offices and were of high quality;
- Initiated the Center's move to provide assistance to courts around the globe, which is now the largest single area of expenditures for the Center.

McConnell saved the National Center when it was weak and strengthened it into the premier organization in the field. His management skills, political acumen, and understanding of people remain models to which all court managers should aspire.

Ed Gallas was the first professional manager appointed by a trial court to be responsible for the functions and tasks that were not the direct responsibility of the clerk of court. He became the court executive officer of the Los Angeles Superior Court in 1950. Gallas was every bit as much of a pioneer as was McConnell. He worked in the largest general jurisdiction court in the country in one of the most populated counties in the nation. He had to negotiate and carve out his place in a court where the clerk of court, up to that point, had been the manager of court operations and other county officials provided all other support. Ed Gallas also was a coauthor of the first book devoted to court administration, *Managing the Courts*. That book, although now out of print, remains an enlightening and informative read for current and aspiring court managers.[12] Had Gallas not been as wise, astute, and competent as he was, professional court management in trial courts might have taken much longer to develop.

Ernie Friesen is a giant in the field on several levels. He was the Director of the Administrative Office of the United States Courts. He was the first executive director of ICM. He was a coauthor with Ed Gallas and Gallas's sociologist wife, Nesta, of *Managing the Courts*. Mostly through ICM, but also often as an independent trainer, Friesen has taught aspiring court managers for four decades. He has conducted research on several aspects of court administration, but is best known for and still sought out for his expertise in caseflow management. His distillation of the purposes of courts and how they relate to the need to reduce delay is a classic that still should guide anyone interested in caseflow management. He is an astute student of management and, most importantly, of management in the context of courts, who has helped court managers across the country to understand their role and their responsibilities better.

William Pabst at first blush seems out of place on this list.[13] He was never a judge and never a court administrator. He managed only a few people in what eventually became the Center for Jury Studies. Bill Pabst is on this list because of his vision, his commitment to effective public administration, and because he used these two qualities to demonstrate the value of analysis, evaluation, and data to guide management in a critical area of court administration.

Bill Pabst was an engineer who was called to jury duty in Washington, DC, where he and many others sat and waited for days to be called to a courtroom and, perhaps, placed on a trial jury. The experience was frustrating. Unlike many citizens who merely walk away from jury service (or the lack of jury service) angry, Pabst reexamined his experience and decided to use his analytic skills to see if he could find ways to improve the jury experience. He sought and obtained a small "acorn" grant from LEAA to test his theory. With his colleague and fellow engineer Tom Munsterman, who today is recognized internationally as *the* expert on jury trials and jury management in the United States, he applied his scientific skills to determine if there was a better way to call and use jurors. He determined that if the court in the District were to apply his formulas to guide their summoning and use of jurors, it could save $300,000 a year. Following this initial effort, Pabst, with Munsterman, formed the Center for Jury Studies.[14] They demonstrated that sound management decisions could be guided by wisely used statistics, even in the face of resistance by judicial officers. They showed courts in concrete terms how to improve jury service for all citizens. And they documented over and over again that doing so also saved money. They not only made pioneering contributions to jury management, but to court administration generally through their data-driven, rational approach to management of a complex, difficult function. The latter lesson still has not been fully learned and understood by many court managers, but it was a critically important lesson, nonetheless. Pabst's efforts to collect and analyze data and then to use those data to guide decision making was a model that deserves to be held up to and applied by all court managers.

2.2 Critical Nurturing and Facilitating Organizations

Just as individuals were important to the development of court administration in the last third of the 20th century, so were institutions.

The *American Bar Association* (ABA) already has been referenced several times. Those references reflect the central role this national voluntary association of attorneys has played in advancements in judicial administration. Without the advances in judicial administration, the advances in court administration in the last half of the 1900s would not have been possible. Significant amounts of the ABA's attention and efforts have been focused on organization, procedure, and judicial selection issues, but its efforts have not stopped there. In its 1976 *Trial Court Standards*, a prestigious group of attorneys from across the nation for the first time affirmed that courts, rather than attorneys, should be responsible for the pace of litigation. In the early 1980s, the Judicial Administration Section's case processing time standards for civil and criminal cases—and their subsequent adoption by the full ABA in 1984—were a critical element in advancing efforts throughout the country to promote courts' responsibility for the pace of litigation and to improve case processing techniques. The ABA's actions in both 1976 and 1984 provided strong moral suasion for both judges and attorneys who were uncertain that courts should take responsibility for caseflow management. The ABA reaffirmed its positions in this area in 1992 when it updated its *Standards Relating to Trial Courts*. The ABA currently is deeply involved with one of the six agenda items set for the Section of Judicial Administration in 1938: improvement of the jury system. Both caseflow management and jury management are critical responsibilities of court administration. The ABA has been a staunch supporter in these areas for many years.

The *American Judicature Society* (AJS), located in Chicago for decades but now associated with Drake University in Des Moines, Iowa, was founded in 1913 by Herbert Harley, a newspaper editor in Michigan. Its original purpose was to improve the administration of justice by conducting research and issuing proposals for reform. Until late in the 20th century, it focused its effort on issues centered on judges, particularly improvement of the judicial selection process. Through its magazine, *Judicature*, it also has disseminated reports on research, opinion pieces, and reports on state developments touching both judicial and court administration. *Judicature* articles have contributed significantly to both judicial and court administration over the years. Since the early 1990s, AJS has expanded its formal emphases to include discipline and removal of judges, ethics for both judicial and support staff, jury management, and judicial independence.

AJS joined with the North American Judges Association in 1970 to establish the American Academy of Judicial Education for judges of special and limited jurisdiction courts. That same year, AJS supported the formation of ICM. As mentioned above in the discussion of Chief Justice Burger, ICM was established to train court managers. As such, it was an effective complement to the American Academy of Judicial Education.

The *Institute for Court Management* remained an independent organization devoted to training court managers until the late 1980s, when it merged with the National Center for State Courts. Its purposes have not changed; it merely has a new institutional association.

In 1976, Chief Justice Burger called the *National Center for State Courts* "the most important single development for the state courts in the administration of justice in this century."[15] He and a number of others have repeated that sentiment many times since. The NCSC was established in 1971 to accomplish five goals:[16]

1. To help state courts set and observe satisfactory standards of judicial administration;
2. To support and coordinate, but not supplant, the efforts of all organizations active in the field of court improvement;[17]
3. To act as a clearinghouse for information concerning state courts;
4. To initiate and support research into problems of courts and to help states consider and implement recommended solutions;
5. To work with the Federal Judicial Center to coordinate research into problems common to both federal and state courts.

Today, it is the nation's premier research, consulting, and clearinghouse organization in support of state courts. Its research and consulting efforts, in particular regarding caseflow management; data collection, analysis, and presentation; the use of technology, including case management software; performance standards; judgeship needs; and problem-solving courts, have been critical to advancing these areas of interest.

Its institutional support, referred to by the Center as its secretariat function, has helped essential organizations grow, develop, and articulate positions, and represent the field, particularly before the two other branches of government at both the state and federal levels. Its federal liaison function quietly but effectively has represented state courts in Congress and to administrative agencies so that state court concerns and needs are not overlooked or trampled.

In terms of need and responsiveness, its information clearinghouse function has been its most highly rated service since the very first client survey undertaken by the Center in the 1970s. The ability of courts across the country to share information about what works, how to design and implement specific programs, and what to look for or avoid has contributed substantially to advancements in court administration over the past 35 years. The Center also is undertaking considerable work throughout the world to inform developing nations how American courts are administered and to help them establish administrative infrastructures of their own.

As indicated above, William Pabst and G. Thomas Munsterman formed the *Center for Jury Studies* (CJS) in the early 1970s. It produced its first manual on jury management in 1974; the manual was updated in 1996. Pabst and Munsterman focused on one thing and did it very well. Munsterman continues to do so today. As a result, virtually every court in the country has been exposed to techniques for improving jury service for citizens and improving juror administration by courts. Hundreds of courts have benefited from direct assistance by the CJS. The savings courts have achieved over the years from using the techniques developed, disseminated, and taught by the CJS must be well into the millions.

Rand's Institute for Civil Justice (ICJ) was funded initially (1980) by insurance carriers and corporations as a counterweight to perceptions that existing research and research organizations did not fully reflect all perspectives on important civil justice issues. Its research has provided valuable insights that otherwise might not have been gained through existing research avenues because the other researchers were asking different questions. Its willingness and ability to ask questions that might not be central to a court or to a university-based researcher and to access different data sources advances the development of judicial administration policy, at least insofar as public policy is shaped by research. Over the years, ICJ's research has touched on many issues involved in the civil justice system, but most especially, tort liability, mass torts and how best to resolve them, the use of alternative dispute resolution mechanisms, discovery practices, and delay reduction.

The *National Judicial College* (NJC) has been providing judges from throughout the nation with critically important substantive and management knowledge and skills since it opened its doors. As noted above, the NJC is the successor to the National College of State Trial Judges, which was founded in 1964. Most of the NJC's courses cover substantive law developments, but the NJC's support for court administration over the years has been significant. The NJC was an "early adopter" of the NCSC's research findings regarding caseflow management; it cosponsored and helped administer a series of workshops across the country for judges, administrators, and attorneys on the subject. It continues to offer courses on the subject today. In the 1990s, it pioneered a course for judges on court administration with faculty teams of judges and administrators. It has offered multiple courses every year on other topics of court administration, particularly on chief judge-administrator management teams and jury management. The NJC has been an essential partner of administrators in advancing concepts of court administration among judges.

Former employees of the National Center formed the *Justice Management Institute* (JMI) in 1993. In the years since, JMI has made important research and training contributions in caseflow management, sentencing alternatives in criminal cases, drug court implementation and evaluation, and records management. It also has conducted important evaluations of new programs or initiatives in several states affecting either judicial or court administration.

The importance of federal funding of research, training, and consulting work for state courts was cited above. The key federal agencies—although certainly not the only ones—have been the *Law Enforcement Assistance Administration* (LEAA), followed by the *Bureau of Justice Assistance* (BJA), the *Bureau of Justice Statistics* (BJS), and the *State Justice Institute* (SJI). LEAA no longer exists, but BJA and BJS continue to support court initiatives, as does SJI to the extent that its limited appropriation allows.

The main difficulty with federal funding of projects for state courts over the years, and today, is that funding for research and even training must fit within the priority categories of each agency. As suggested in the discussion of LEAA, federal funding is designed to achieve specific goals of the Congress or the executive branch. Those goals may match the needs of state courts, but often they do not. At one point in the mid-1990s, one of these agencies was focused solely on "the war on drugs," which was the political hot button of the day. I had what I thought was a good idea for a project in the civil justice area that paralleled and extended a project this agency had funded about five years earlier. When I talked to the agency about my idea, the person to whom I spoke agreed that the idea may be worthy of study, but unless I could find a way to tie it to the war on drugs, there was no way a proposal would even be considered. I could not figure out any relationship between my idea and the war on drugs, so I did not submit a proposal. My experience is repeated year in and year out in countless local courts, state administrative offices of the courts, and the NCSC.

The war on drugs was important then and still is today, but it does not represent the universe of issues with which courts must deal or, necessarily, courts' priorities.[18] Often, federal priorities simply do not reflect the institutional priorities of courts. Research and needed new programs of particular concern to courts are not funded when they cannot be tied to the current federal priority. Without federal dollars, often state and local dollars are insufficient to undertake the work. Even if the state or local courts can find the funds for a new initiative, the results often are not disseminated as they are when ICM and the NJC can build training programs or when a research organization can publish evaluation reports and conduct workshops around the country to spread the word about a new approach or program. Valuable lessons are never learned or are not shared as they should be to advance the field.

The need for dissemination and sharing is partially filled by three membership organizations: The *Conference of Chief Justices*, the *Conference of State Court Administrators*, and the *National Association for Court Management* (NACM). The membership of the first two organizations is apparent from their titles. These organizations have played an increasingly critical role in sharing information about effective new initiatives in individual states and in representing state court interests in Washington, DC. At times, they also can be effective in a state's capital by sharing positive experiences from around the country to give legislators and governors assurance that a new initiative in their state will be effective. By adopting resolutions supporting various programs and positions of importance to state courts, CCJ and COSCA have increased their influence in both state capitals and in Washington, DC.

NACM is a voluntary organization whose membership in 2006 stood at 2,500. It is the largest organization of court managers in the world (plus a few judges particularly interested in court administration). Indeed, it had almost 70 members from other counties in 2005. If NACM did nothing beyond its annual and mid-year conferences, it would be important, because these educational opportunities to gain new knowledge, to share perspectives, and to learn how others deal with similar problems is incomparable in helping the field to advance and mature. Beyond its conferences, NACM has been represented on the oversight or advisory committees for most of the major research initiatives undertaken by the NCSC, and policy makers in Washington, DC solicit its institutional views. More critically for the field, it has developed and broadly disseminated a code of ethics for court personnel and its ten "core competencies" (knowledge, skills, and abilities that court leaders should know or possess in key areas of court administration). It also produces a series of miniguides on various topics of court administration, which are brief outlines (30–35 pages) that identify key information about or decisions germane to each topic and offer suggestions for handling the topics covered based on members' experiences. Its *Court Manager* quarterly magazine is the leading periodical in the field. NACM also is collaborating with Michigan State University on a noncredit certificate program to advance members' professional development. All these steps help to advance both the professionalism and the knowledge of court managers across the country.

Society, institutions, and professions constantly change, sometimes purposively and sometimes in spite of themselves. Those most likely to adjust positively also are those most likely to know, honor, and learn from the past. The individuals cited in this chapter have gone, or in time no longer will be with us. The institutions remain, however, and continue to inform and to assist court and judicial administration to advance. The value each has added to the advancement of court administration provides lessons for those still here and those yet to come.

NOTES

1. See, for example, Gallas, Geoff, and Gordy Griller, "The Court Management Profession: Questions and Issues," *Court Manager*, vol. 19, no. 2, 2004, pp. 5–12.
2. See also, Tobin, Robert W., *Creating the Judicial Branch: The Unfinished Reform.* Williamsburg, VA: National Center for State Courts, 1999, p. 257.
3. Gossett, William T., Bernard G. Segal, and Chesterfield Smith, "Foreword," to Levin, A.

Leo and Russell R. Wheeler, eds., *The Pound Conference: Perspectives on Justice in the Future*. St. Paul, MN: West Publishing, 1979, p. 7.

4. Ibid.

5. In his Introduction to the ABA's 1949 *Minimum Standards of Judicial Administration*, New Jersey Chief Justice Vanderbilt notes the assistance provided by New Jersey's state court administrator, who was Ed McConnell's predecessor. It is not appropriate, therefore, to say that McConnell was the first state court administrator. He was, however, the first named to the post to be a professional manager and to assist the chief justice to implement statewide budgetary and organizational reform.

6. Vanderbilt, Arthur, "Foreword," *Reports of the Section of Judicial Administration*. Chicago: American Bar Association, 1938, p. xix.

7. Chief Justice Burger also was very concerned about prison conditions and the need for correctional reform. Among other ways in which he evidenced this concern, he was instrumental in the creation of the National Institute of Corrections, a training organization for correctional officers that paralleled ICM in some respects.

8. See Tobin, Robert W., *Creating the Branch*, p. 155.

9. LEAA was the source of almost one-third of the funds needed to build the headquarters building for the NCSC, in addition to supporting the National Conference on the Judiciary and several very important early projects of the NCSC, plus supporting state reform efforts.

10. See Tobin, Robert W., *Creating the Branch*, pp. 140, 218; *Final Report*, Judicial System Leadership Forum, Dec. 16–17, 2004. Washington, D.C.: Bureau of Justice Assistance and American University, 2005, p. 3.

11. McConnell was a faculty member at Rutgers University's School of Business Administration from 1947 until 1952. See Zaffarano, Mark A., "A Profile of Ed McConnell," *The Court Manager*, Summer 1990, pp. 21–23.

12. Copies of the book still can be found through the World Wide Web.

13. I acknowledge my debt to Bob Tobin, *Creating the Branch*, for reminding me of the significance of Bill Pabst's contribution.

14. The Center for Jury Studies originally was part of the engineering firm for which Pabst worked. Later, it was spun off as an independent entity. In the late 1980s, the Center for Jury Studies merged with the National Center for State Courts.

15. Cited in, *Annual Report*, National Center for State Courts, 1975, p. 2.

16. Charter, National Center for State Courts, adopted June 1971.

17. The words, "but not supplant," in this goal were very important to gain the support of existing organizations, which were concerned that the size and support accorded to the Center from the beginning would jeopardize their institutional health. All of the organizations that predate the NCSC remain in existence today, although in a few cases their size or their program focus has shifted somewhat as a result of the Center's programs and efforts over the years.

18. Had Bill Pabst sought his "acorn" grant during the renewed war on drugs, the Center for Jury Studies might not have been funded even for the initial exploratory work.

Chapter 3

Context Associated with Court Organization, Vocabulary, and Filings

Court structures within states and across states and the federal government might be better termed court dis*organization* than court *organization*. Courts in each state and the federal courts have their own organizational structure, but there is only the barest commonality. "All [states] . . . make a distinction between trial courts and appellate courts, and all of them arrange their courts in some form of a hierarchical system."[1] The names assigned to different courts also vary markedly. Even the word *court* means different things in different contexts. To understand the complexities of court administration, it helps to understand the foundational complexities of organization and vocabulary. These are explored in this chapter.

Beyond current structure and vocabulary, there has been substantial interest since the mid-1970s among legislators, governors, some judges and court administrators, and some public administration academics in reducing the number and broadening the jurisdiction of trial courts. The reasons for this interest and the arguments that have slowed or forestalled more consolidations at the trial court level are explored in the second portion of this chapter.

Finally, this chapter offers a brief look at the number of cases filed in state and federal courts and the implications of those numbers.

3.1 Current Organizational Constructs for Handling Caseload Across the States

At its most pristine, court structure would provide for two courts per state: a single trial court geographically distributed across a state in branches that would hear all cases of first instance plus one appellate court in which all appeals, both mandatory and discretionary, would be filed. Only South Dakota, the District of Columbia, and the territories of American Samoa, Guam, and the Virgin Islands have been able to operate with this pristine structure. Various factors interact when trial court organization issues are decided in state legislatures: the historical development of law and courts, state and local politics, the value of judges specializing, and legitimate issues about career ladders for judges. State constitutions normally create one trial court of general jurisdiction, with a further provision for "such other courts as the legislature may from time to time create," or words to that effect. As a consequence, the dominant model is for one trial court of general jurisdiction and one or more of limited jurisdiction, although a few states have only one trial court that has jurisdiction over all cases of first instance. California is the largest and most recent state in this latter class. At the appellate level, often the number of appeals and the workload associated with these appeals lead to creation of an intermediate court (often referred to as the "court of appeals") to which all appeals of right are taken. Appeals from decisions of the intermediate appellate court then are granted or denied at the discretion of the court of last resort (normally but not universally, the "supreme court"). In almost all states, the court of last resort is mandated to accept capital punishment cases (if a state has capital punishment) and one or two other categories of cases.

The federal judiciary has a single general jurisdiction trial court but two specialized trial courts, the Court of Federal Claims for money claims against the federal government and the Court of International Trade. Plus, the federal system has two levels of appellate courts, the 11 branches of the Circuit Court of Appeals and the Supreme Court. Bankruptcy courts, which have their own staff and judges and their own courtrooms, are nonetheless considered to be a component of the federal district courts.[2]

When there are two levels of trial courts, one level typically handles high-volume, smaller-value cases such as traffic, small claims, criminal infractions and misdemeanors, sometimes smaller civil cases (up to some monetary cap), and landlord–tenant disputes. This level of court is referred to as the court of "limited jurisdiction" because the cases it can hear are limited to those specifically assigned to it by the legislature. Some states have created additional specialty courts of limited jurisdiction, such as housing courts, juvenile courts, tax courts, water courts, and probate courts. On top of the state-created courts, a number of states have allowed cities and towns to establish their own ordinance, traffic, and misdemeanor courts. These are limited jurisdiction courts, as well, but their jurisdiction is limited geographically as well as by subject matter.

Normally, the second trial court is a court of "general jurisdiction" that hears all trial-level disputes not specifically assigned to the court(s) of limited jurisdiction. In a few states, the cases that can be heard in the general jurisdiction and state-created limited jurisdiction court overlap, but normally the cases heard in each court are distinct to that court. More often than not, when there are multiple limited jurisdiction courts, there is a state-created court that has jurisdiction in each county or portion of a county, one or more city or town courts, and, perhaps, a specialty court. New York's trial court structure is the most complex, with ten trial-level courts. There has been a modest trend nationally since the mid-1970s toward consolidating several limited jurisdiction trial courts into a single, state-created court of limited jurisdiction.

Often, for the cases originating in the limited jurisdiction courts, appeals go to the general jurisdiction court rather than to the appellate court. Any further appeal then would go to the appellate court as if the case had originated in the court of general jurisdiction. In many instances, the appealed limited-jurisdiction case is allowed to start all over in the general jurisdiction court, including the right to retry the case as if it had not been determined in the first court (a trial de novo or "new trial"). Less often, these appealed cases are decided on the record made in the limited jurisdiction court, with the general jurisdiction court accepting the facts as found in the first court, just as happens in an appellate court with an appeal from the general jurisdiction court.

On the administrative side of the judiciary, every state and territory has an office responsible to the policy-making body for the state's judicial branch, which normally is the court of last resort. This office usually is called the "administrative office of the courts," although there are several variations that convey the same thought. The person responsible for the administrative office normally is the "state court administrator," although, again, there are some variations in the title across the country. Most state court administrators are not judges, but in several eastern states, there is a strong tradition of judges filling the position of state court administrator. Administrators who are not judges bring a variety of backgrounds and experiences to the position. Most have come from within the judicial branch, sometimes from a trial court but more often from the administrative office of the courts itself or from the state supreme court's staff. In recent years, a number of administrators have been named after serving as staff for a legislative committee—often either a budget or judiciary committee—or as senior staff to the governor. These latter appointments often reflect a perceived need for more effective advocacy by the judiciary with the two other branches of state government. A strong majority of state court administrators in the early years (1960s into the 1980s) and possibly a plurality today were and are attorneys. In most states today, however, nonattorneys fill the position, selected, as was McConnell in 1950 (see chapter 2), for their management skills, policy understanding, and, normally, political skills rather than their knowledge of the law. A parallel set of skills and backgrounds exists for trial court administrators, except that being a lawyer has not been and is not critical in most trial courts. Promotions from amongst long-term employees have been much more common in trial courts.

3.2 A Common Vocabulary

Whatever the structure of each state's court system, each court is assigned a name that identifies its role and jurisdictional level. As varied as the structures are state to state, the nomenclature is even more varied. The courts of limited jurisdiction in the various states each have their own names. For example, in some states, the sole or most prominent court of limited jurisdiction might be called a "district court." In other states and in the federal system, however, the "district court" is the court of general jurisdiction. In some states, "municipal courts" are the courts established by cities and towns; in California before the merger of its two trial courts, the "municipal courts" were the state-created limited jurisdiction courts, there being no city or town courts in California. As indicated, the court of last resort in most states is called the "supreme court," but in New York, the "supreme court" is one of two trial courts of general jurisdiction. The only way to know for sure what a limited jurisdiction and the general jurisdiction court is called in a particular state is to look it up. The proverbial Martian—and our many friends from other countries who visit to learn how American courts operate—have to learn anew what each court is called when moving from state A to state B to state C or the federal system. This learning process is required at the appellate level as well as at the trial level, although there is less variety in nomenclature at that level. And not only will the names probably be different in states A and B, but the cases that will be heard in the limited jurisdiction court and in the general jurisdiction court in state A likely will be different in the corresponding courts of state B. There is no way to know the structure or its nomenclature other than knowing state to state.[3]

This "Tower of Babel" and the "Babel of structure" both are the result of each state and the federal courts being free to establish its courts and court system as it sees fit. That is what happens in a republic, but it makes it hard to have common understandings or a common vocabulary across states. From a national perspective, "usually," "often," "sometimes," and "some" become both common and necessary qualifiers.

To compound matters further, the term *court* has different meanings. Mostly, the word means an institution established by law that has one or more judges, its own staff, and a defined group of cases that it hears. The group of cases it hears defines its jurisdiction. A court's jurisdiction can be statewide, countywide, citywide, or regional. In Texas, each judge is elected to a specific courtroom and has a judicial district or county court number assigned to that courtroom. Judges share courthouses and some administrative staff, but each judge is a "court."

Today, courts across the nation have established "problem-solving courts," such as drug courts, mental health courts, family courts, domestic violence courts, and homeless courts (for more about these courts, see section 12.8, chapter 12). In days past, these "courts" might have been called calendars or divisions, depending on the number of judges and cases involved. Today, these courts are likely to be one judge handling only one type of case all the time or a special calendar handled by one judge once or twice a week (homeless courts tend to be held for one day only once a year or quarterly).

The concept has been extended in some states to embrace "business courts," as well. Business courts are one, two, or more judges on a court assigned to hear only civil cases involving predefined business disputes. As with the problem-solving courts, these courts might as easily be called special calendars, but they are not. The business community lobbied for business courts in several states. Delaware's business court was the first of its kind, but it really is the state's Chancery Court, a court in the traditional sense that is assigned equity and many business-based disputes. Because of Delaware's strong position as a state in which to incorporate, the Chancery Court simply grew into being a business court. Other states have established their business courts, in part, to compete with Delaware to be the sites for corporate headquarters and to compete with private judges offering dispute resolution for pay.

In California, the legislature established "complex litigation" at the request of the judicial branch after years of lobbying by the business lawyers of the state. In New York, the judicial branch established them administratively. These courts offer procedural rules that facilitate resolution of defined business disputes plus specially assigned judges who either had a business law background before coming to the bench or had gained substantial experience with business cases after getting on the bench.

There are three major arguments in support of business courts. First, that certain business disputes, especially involving corporate governance, corporate finance, and substantial contract disputes between large companies, require expertise that the many judges who have come to the bench from an exclusively criminal law, family law, or personal injury law background do not have. Second, because of the makeup of the bench, business litigants had to spend considerable time (and attorney fees) educating judges about the law and normal business practices associated with their cases. The risk of an adverse decision was seen to be high for both sides because the judges might not understand business practice or the nuances of business law, so might rule improperly and thus generate an appeal. And, finally, the processing time before a decision is made might be excessive compared to the litigants' need to get the matter resolved and move on, which a former business lawyer probably would understand better than a former prosecutor.

These concerns are legitimate and would support special business calendars, which is what has been created; but we call them "business courts." And we put the label of court on the special procedures set up for addressing and overcoming drug abuse, domestic violence, anger, and criminal records and lifestyles that make it hard for people to do better. If we were to extend the concept, we could have "tort courts," "contract courts," and "major felony courts," and, like Texas, each judge might end up as his or her own court.

The multiple uses of the term *court* can be confusing to someone not working daily in and with courts. This concern probably comes too late in the game, however. These special calendars have been called courts since at least the late 1980s. The term has a certain caché and also is widely used and accepted. New "courts" are being created with some regularity. Thus, this book will use the appellation, although with a reminder that not all "courts" are, indeed, courts.

To simplify the discussion in the balance of this book, I will adopt the following nomenclature:

- "Court" will be an institution with assigned judges, staff, and facilities, and its own budget, that hears cases defined by statute, unless it is used in the context of "problem-solving courts" or is attached to other special calendars that broadly are being called courts.
- "Court of limited jurisdiction" will refer normally to the court handling the high-volume, lesser-value cases referenced above, but can embrace specialty courts, as well.
- "Court of general jurisdiction" will mean the court assigned all other cases, normally higher-value civil cases, family-related cases, probate, juvenile, and felony criminal cases.
- "Intermediate appellate court" will mean the first-level appellate court in which all appeals of right are filed
- "Court of last resort" will mean the highest court in the state to which an appeal can be taken; normally, these courts have discretion to accept or not accept cases for further review, except as noted above.[4]
- "Administrative office of the courts" (AOC) will refer to the state-level office that serves as the staff arm of the policy-making body for the third branch, which normally is the state supreme court.
- "State court administrator" will refer to the person who heads the AOC.

A few other terms are important throughout the book, although they are not part of the structural issues discussed in this chapter:

- "Chief judge" will mean the judge with primary administrative responsibilities for an entire trial court; other terms used in courts but not in this book include presiding judge and administrative or chief administrative judge; large urban courts may also have "supervising judges," that is, the judges with administrative responsibility for a division (civil, criminal, family, etc.); this latter term will be retained in this book

■ "Court administrator" will mean the chief manager of staff and support operations that are not otherwise assigned to a separate clerk of court and who is appointed by and responsible as an at-will employee to the judges; other terms used in courts but not in this book include court executive, court executive officer, trial court administrator, trial court executive, and district administrator

■ "Clerk of court" or "clerk" is the person elected by citizens or appointed by the local-government executive or legislative body who has responsibility for the creation, maintenance, protection, and dissemination of the case records of a trial court (except for the record created by court reporters, which ordinarily is part of the court administrator's responsibilities).[5]

■ "Court leaders" and "court leadership" is the chief judge and, ideally, both the court administrator and the clerk of court; much of the court administration literature uses the term to reference only the team of the chief judge and the administrator; at times and on certain issues, the court leaders can be a judge other than the chief judge and a staff member other than the administrator or clerk; the concept of "leader" is somewhat fluid; it will be discussed more fully in chapter 7.

3.3 Alternatives to Current Trial Court Structure

The movement in state courts toward fewer courts of limited jurisdiction (and, to a lesser extent, to a single trial court) gained momentum in the last third of the 20th century. It probably will continue as a topic of discussion well into the 21st century because of perceptions that it will save money and, secondarily, reduce citizen confusion about the appropriate court for their cases. There are management benefits, as well, that will be mentioned in section 3.3.3. Court organization is one of the "overlap" topics mentioned in chapter 1. It has been part of the agenda for judicial administration reform since Dean Pound's speech in 1906. Court structure affects how court administration is conducted. Therefore, court administration expertise and experience can inform the debate about organization. The arguments for and against more consolidation that address efficiency, access, caseflow management, and budget impacts are court administration issues.

Whether or not to consolidate courts is not conceptually or politically clear-cut.[6] This section will examine how and why states might reorganize their trial courts. Sound arguments can be marshaled by each side; they are collected and offered here to inform the debate, not to try to determine it. The first option discussed is consolidating two or more courts of limited jurisdiction into a single court of limited jurisdiction. Consolidating specialty courts into existing courts of limited or general jurisdiction will be addressed second. The third subsection will discuss unifying all trial courts into a single court of first instance. The funding arrangements for trial courts are addressed in chapter 4. Moving funding responsibility from localities to the state may well be part of the consolidation debate for any of the three options, but conceptually, funding and consolidation need not be tied together.

3.3.1 Consolidating Different Limited Jurisdiction Courts into a Single Limited Jurisdiction Court

When one talks about consolidating two or more courts of limited jurisdiction, it almost always involves counties and cities. Occasionally, it can mean consolidating two courts funded by a county.[7] In these instances, the legislature must make the decision. Judges and citizens in the rural communities make the same arguments against consolidation to the legislature as cities do when they face consolidation. Thus, the pros and cons of consolidation apply to almost any merger of courts.

Interestingly, the conceptual labels applied to the arguments for and against merger are the same on both sides: efficiency (i.e., saving money); effectiveness (i.e., making better use of staff and judges or achieving better results); access to courts; and quality of justice. The facts in support of the concepts, and their interpretation and weight, are different, however. Then there are other arguments unique to retaining the status quo. Each argument for and against consolidation is set forth in Table 3.1.

Two factors are unique to city or town courts: (1) city and town courts are seen (and desired) as positive contributors to the city's or town's revenue stream; and (2) city and town judges are appointed by the city manager, mayor, or city council, often for relatively short terms. These factors intertwine; they are troubling elements of the anticonsolidation argument that "local justice" and "understanding of the community" needs to be retained.

Cities and towns normally favor having their own courts because they think they can enhance their revenue stream. That attitude derives in part from the view that local police can be induced to aggressively enforce local traffic or parking laws and all or most of the resulting revenue stays in the community's coffers. In addition, because the city leaders appoint "their" judges, they normally believe they can exercise administrative or moral suasion to induce them to impose significant fines on the guilty or to find a very high percentage of all those coming before them to be guilty. Abstract concepts such as "due process," "fair hearings," and arguments about understanding the local community are not as important to the city or town leaders as the revenue. Regrettably, some city officials have not relied solely on moral suasion to assure the desired revenue stream. Some city

Table 3.1   Arguments For and Against Consolidating Two or More Courts of Limited Jurisdiction

Issue	Arguments for and against	Counterarguments
Efficiency	Consolidation will lead to elimination of overlapping and duplicative positions and reduce the need for senior and some middle managers; we can bring significant economies of scale to the new court; new staff positions can be deferred because of the increased productivity achieved through the larger operation.	If staff in each court is fully occupied now, the work will not decrease, so combining their caseloads will not save staff positions; the only likely savings are a few middle and senior manager positions that won't produce savings sufficient to cover the increased costs; middle managers' span of control cannot be expanded too much without losing the benefit of supervision, so even those savings may be illusory.
	Each separate court has an administrator, accounting staff, and maybe other duplicative support positions that can be reduced in number to save money	In fact, each court administrator after consolidation is given some job in the new court, so there are no savings; if savings develop, it is only over time when positions are vacated through voluntary departure or retirement.
		The larger, new court will need a bigger bureaucracy for its infrastructure, which will produce new costs for staff that do not process cases, thus offsetting any savings from fewer senior or middle managers.
	Judges in smaller courts work part-time or do not have enough cases to warrant their full-time position, so merger will assure their time will be used better (they can be on the bench longer handling more cases).	Part-time judges work part-time because the workload does not justify more; if courts are consolidated, cases will have to be moved out of town to another facility, which imposes a burden on local citizens and reduces access; further, all courts do not have part-time judges, so a judge with a full calendar and responsibilities still will have those in a new court, saving nothing.
	Courthouses can be consolidated and the abandoned courthouses either sold or used by other units of government, thus bringing in revenue or avoiding new facility costs, and eliminating building maintenance costs for a courthouse.	A merger will itself involve costs that might be significant, including moving, possibly new furniture and furnishings, new stationery, business cards, and all court forms, training for staff on cases they do not now handle, and maybe new computer hardware and software.

Continued

Table 3.1 Continued

Issue	Arguments for and against	Counterarguments
	The new court can undertake enhanced fine and fee collection efforts, thus improving revenue and better enable the court to enforce its judgments.	Enhanced fine and fee collection efforts could be undertaken without consolidation if it were a priority.
	If citizens do not get to court on time or at all because of travel problems, processing costs will increase because more warrants will be issued and served for failure to appear or failure to pay.	Virtually everyone owns or has access to cars today and almost all communities have public transportation that goes to or near a courthouse, so citizens will adjust and do fine; if there is a community in which a significant number of people lack the means to own cars and public transportation is insufficient, video conferencing, "kiosks" for information and payments, and even occasional on-site appearances by a judge all can solve the access issue at much lower on-going costs than on-site staff; a few very inefficient courts should not preclude courts saving substantial funds through consolidation.
Effectiveness	If there are part-time judges, a larger court can support full-time judges who are attorneys and who will become more expert and thus more effective in handling cases; a larger court will attract better lawyers to be judges and better lawyers will be better judges.	Local judges know local defendants and can both adjudicate their cases more effectively and impose sentences appropriate for each person; local judges know our citizens and how they expect and want cases to be handled.
	Courts with more judges have greater flexibility in scheduling and matching judges to calendars and thus can improve judicial productivity.	Judicial productivity is a function of personal commitment and the number and type of cases to be heard, not how many judges sit in a courthouse.
	Many of these courts are one judge courts; bringing two judges from two one-judge courts into one building is more than twice as effective in calendar management.	
	The new court will be better able to support staff training; cities and towns may not have resources—or be willing to commit them—to training court staff, seeing that cost as an unnecessary diminution of income.	Improving staff training is not dependent on either a larger court or consolidation; if a court's leadership wishes to provide it, they can find the funds within the budget.

Issue	Arguments for and against	Counterarguments
	A larger court will attract staff in critical infrastructure operations, e.g., accounting and technology, who are more expert and thus will keep up with the work better and make fewer mistakes. Courts that are large enough to have their own support staff are better off, as city and town staff seldom make court support a high priority.	City and county IT staff are fully qualified now and they support the courts' operations, as do the city's and county's auditor or treasurer staff; these government units can attract better people than a court can to one or two positions because they offer variety and advancement opportunities.
	There is no substantive, or crime-reduction or prevention, or traffic safety advantage to having two courts doing the same thing.	Local law enforcement officers can get in and out of court faster in a smaller court and the local judges will accommodate their schedules better than judges who are not part of the community; both of these benefits put more officers on the street, which is how and where crime is stopped.
	If both courts can have jury trials, they are competing for the same citizens and citizens may be called more often than they need to be; once jurors appear, larger courts can use them more efficiently and effectively.	There are not enough jury trials in courts of limited jurisdiction to create much conflict for jurors or to warrant these material changes just to reduce a theoretical conflict.
	If both courts need interpreters, they will not be competing with each other for a limited supply and interpreters' time will be used better when they are in court.	A community has or does not have enough people willing and able to be interpreters; the supply, which is the real issue, is not affected by how many courts there are.
Access to justice	Citizens are confused by multiple courts with similar jurisdiction and often go to the wrong courthouse, call the wrong court, or send money to the wrong court, thus, at minimum, wasting time and maybe missing deadlines.	Our courthouse is close to our citizens; they know where to go and are served by their neighbors; [If two courthouses are within a short distance of each other, as often is the case in urban areas,] only a few people get confused; the number is not sufficient to disrupt everything and incur the costs of consolidation.
	A larger court can provide assistance to the self-represented litigant that neither smaller court can provide at present.	Our procedures are not that complicated; almost everyone represents him- or herself, except for more serious misdemeanors, and they do so well.

Continued

Table 3.1 Continued

Issue	Arguments for and against	Counterarguments
	The new court can use computers and video hook-ups to provide access in remote areas that will be almost the same as now; the new court still can schedule cases to be heard in ____, if necessary.	Travel time and distance will increase for our citizens if our courthouse is closed; some of our citizens will not be able to travel to the new courthouse because they lack a car or the public bus system is inadequate to meet the need.
Quality of Justice	Full-time judges will be better able to keep up with the law than part-time judges, which will enhance the justice they can dispense.	Our judges know our litigants and citizens and provide the justice desired in this community. Mandatory continuing education can solve the quality issues without consolidating.
	Judges of the new court will be more independent and thus freer to rule on the facts presented rather than be concerned about the impact on the city's revenue.	Maybe that's a problem somewhere, but not here; our judges are not pressured to produce revenue at the expense of justice; we will not discuss personnel issues, but when judges have not been reappointed, it has not been because we desired more revenue.
	If staff are moving from a part-time to a full-time status, full-time staff can be trained and monitored more effectively to reduce processing errors, including mistakes made in reports sent to other government agencies.	We monitor and correct errors by staff now.
	Certain local attorneys will lose their undue influence over the judges.	Neither our judges nor our attorneys are corrupt and we resent any implication that they are.
	Because our judges know our citizens, they know whose word can be trusted and whose cannot.	Judges who "know" who is telling the truth and who is not risk not hearing or recognizing truth; there is no neutrality in the dispensation of justice if witnesses are prejudged.
	Our judges can and do accommodate local citizens' needs, particularly in scheduling or continuing hearings.	True needs for continuances or other "accommodations" are readily accepted by all judges; judges who accommodate local citizens over those they do not know are not providing even-handed justice.
Out-of-touch bureaucracy	We don't want a bureaucrat [in the county seat/in the state capital] making rules that won't work in this community or that ignore our needs and special circumstances.	There is no appearance of justice when each small court has its own rules and procedures; citizens have a right to expect that they will be treated the same in every court in the state.

Issue	Arguments for and against	Counterarguments
		The rule-making process normally is flexible enough to accommodate important local variation that requires accommodation.
Political considerations	Judges will have to run for election (or reelection) in a bigger area and that will discourage our attorneys from seeking the position because the cost of election will increase or the larger town/city in the new court's area will have a majority of voters, so our attorneys will be unable to get elected.	No attorneys running for a judgeship can be or should be assured of winning.
		Judges rule on the facts and law in the case before them, not on where someone lives.
		Judges running for reelection are almost always reelected, whether they run in their local community or in a larger area.
		If the cost of running increases for a judge, it also increases for an attorney considering running against that judge, which might actually reduce challenges rather than increase them.
		We cannot give up the benefits of consolidation to accommodate the desires of a few attorneys in some small communities.
	We have a good relationship between the judges and our city/county council and we don't want to lose that.	The dynamics of the budget process will change, which may or may not benefit the court's budget; sometimes changing relationships is just a cost that must be borne by some for the greater good, as there are as many or more courts with poor relationships with their local council as there are with good relationships.
	The income split will not be favorable to us.	This is a political/fiscal matter that can be addressed independent of the merits or demerits of consolidation.
	The city/town would lose patronage positions.	This political interest seldom is acknowledged, but may be a sub rosa reason in some communities; it cannot be allowed to drive a statewide decision designed to improve the delivery of justice.

Continued

Table 3.1 Continued

Issue	Arguments for and against	Counterarguments
Civic Pride	The court/courthouse has been here since ___; it helps to define our community and a new court would not provide that.	Consolidation does not necessarily require that local historical landmarks be abandoned; when it does, the building can be retained and used for other purposes by local government or even the private sector and remain a source of local pride.
	The people in the county seat are always putting us down.	This perception, even if true, reflects political perspectives and maybe some personal animosity, but neither factor has a legitimate place in a courtroom, so should not be controlling or even accorded much weight.
	Our court gives us enhanced status as a community.	A community's status is not driven by the presence or absence of a courthouse or a court; communities will have to find their status somewhere else."

and town judges across the country have been fired or not reappointed because the appointing city or town officials were displeased with revenue received. The judges' demeanor and decision making, even their oversight of staff, all might be seen as good, but if they find too many defendants not guilty or impose fines that are deemed to be too small, they are not "good" judges and lose their jobs.

In one jurisdiction in a state that is strongly committed to the value of city courts, I had a chance during a consulting assignment to talk to defense attorneys practicing in both the city courts and the county court. Several said it was hard to practice in some of the city courts because basic rights and procedures were not accorded to self-represented defendants by the city judges. Too often, the attorneys felt uneasy watching the disposition of city court cases. They did not feel that way when practicing in the county-supported court. Even county judges who had previously practiced in these same city courts expressed similar thoughts without knowing what others had told me. City and town courts tend to have to fight harder for their independence than do state-created courts, even if counties financially support the latter.

City managers and elected city officials also tend to see their courts as merely another city agency, subject to the same administrative orders and constraints as the social services or roads department. Most of the time, this perception does not impact judicial independence, but it can if city officials feel court employees are not aggressive enough or, perhaps, successful enough in collecting fines and fees. I have consulted with city courts in which the city was asserting the right to select a person to be the administrator over the objections of the judges or to take over certain staff functions the city manager or treasurer thought were not operating properly. Since the city manager or the city council appoints the judge(s), they tend to believe they also have the right and authority to control what happens administratively in the court. The judges tend to view the court the same way county judges do, as an independent branch of city government that is different from the other city agencies. When I have consulted in city courts, I normally have had to include a section early in my report on independence of the judiciary. That is not an issue when I consult in county-supported courts. The tension is almost inherent in the structure, and, once it arises, tends to be constant. It simply seems to be harder for city and town officials to see their court as an independent judicial entity.

In county-supported courts, judges usually are elected or the governor appoints them, so the county-based court can operate more as an independent entity even if the county provides fiscal and administrative support. People concerned with good judicial administration should note these concerns about possible financial pressures on city and town courts. If the city and town courts are to continue, their independence needs more protection. If they are merged with the county courts, the issue normally disappears.

A conclusion for or against consolidation normally turns on either the financial arrangements or the philosophical value to the decision makers of "local justice." In the short term, local political forces, the inertia associated with changing governmental institutions, and cities' and towns' perceived budgetary needs usually are determinative. Because of the belief in cities and towns about their need for revenue, some states have simply "bought out" the cities or counties through partial or complete state funding as part of the consolidation scheme. If some state-level fiscal relief is not part of the discussion, consolidation becomes a much harder sell.

3.3.2 Consolidating Specialty Courts into Limited or General Jurisdiction Courts

Specialty courts pose special issues regarding an independent existence or consolidation. Clearly, the states that have created them believed at one point and may still believe that the type of case or the litigants deserve an independent, stand-alone court with dedicated judges and staff. Less often, the judges of the state have not wanted to handle these cases and have successfully argued that other judges should be doing it in their own court. Especially when the specialty court is a juvenile, family, probate, tax, or water court, strong arguments are available that these case types deserve specialized treatment.

The arguments for and against retaining these separate courts have to start with the decision that they require specialization. There is no need for specialty courts if specialization does not add value. (Judges are the last great generalist professionals and, for the most part, cling steadfastly to remaining so.)

When judges rotate calendar assignments, they sit on one type of calendar for, normally, a year (but occasionally six months or as little as a month), and they then either "re-up" for another year or move to handling different cases. Regularly rotating assignments—that is, *not* becoming a specialist—offers several advantages:

(1) all judges can expect to handle the "interesting" or intellectually stimulating cases from time to time in their careers; (2) all judges can expect to share the burden of handling the less intellectually stimulating or desired case types (e.g., family law, traffic, and small claims); (3) variety rejuvenates judges who have been on the bench for a while; (4) reassigning judges on a schedule allows the chief judge to move a judge who is not handling an assignment well without directly confronting his or her performance, which helps collegiality; (5) judges who hear the same cases all the time tend to look at them more minutely and with more technicality, which can be a problem; (6) judges who do not rotate tend to develop some boredom even if they generally like the subject area; and (7) judges who do not rotate tend to become predictable, which may lead to concern within the Bar, to judge shopping, or to situations where attorney-represented litigants have a tactical advantage over the self-represented litigant.

The benefits of specialization are relatively clear. First, the law and procedures in almost all areas, even traffic and small claims, are becoming more complex. Almost all other professionals, including practicing attorneys, now specialize because it is so hard to keep up with developments in all aspects of the profession. If judges truly were merely neutral referees who exercise judgment based on the law and facts both sides present to them, their generalist bent would not be a big issue. This Platonic view of judging is far too simplistic in today's world, however. Advocates may overlook an important case or statute and advocates may misinterpret or misrepresent the facts or holdings of decided cases. So, a judge with in-depth knowledge of the law in a particular area has a clear advantage over one without such knowledge. For some case types, such as juvenile and family law, a judge's temperament also is germane. Some judges are energized by dealing with and assisting children or have the appropriate temperament to deal with and resolve family squabbles all day. As a general proposition, these judges are rare. A separate court assures that the judges and staff know in advance what they are getting into and choose to do so. In a number of general jurisdiction courts, finding a judge willing to take a family law calendar or a juvenile calendar is hard work. How much easier it would be if all the judges *wanted* to handle these cases! And, as suggested above, judges with a general caseload prefer specialized courts because they remove the burden of these cases from the general caseload.

On the other hand, some judges may see specialized courts as providing growth or advancement opportunities.[8]

Probate is becoming increasingly complex and it is a niche practice for most attorneys. A probate calendar or court also normally includes conservatorship cases involving people unable to manage their affairs, an increasingly important area with the maturing of the "baby boomer" segment of the population. Water courts have been created in some Western states because each case has many parties, difficult issues, and possibly hundreds of thousands of documents. Plus, many of these cases last for years. These cases can overwhelm the normal calendars of a court. If a special court handles only water cases, the existing court can continue to handle the "regular" caseload. In addition, the water court can obtain software designed for these cases and adopt case management procedures that fit specific case needs. Further, the original court may get a de facto increase in space if the water judge(s) and the records are moved to a new facility.

Thus, specialized courts may serve important policy and operational needs. The issue, therefore, is not specialization per se, but whether the need for specialization is so substantial that it cannot be realized within the existing structure of other courts.

There are three management-related factors, possibly four, that weigh against independent specialized courts. The first is a general concern with specialization.[9]

> In general, the higher the degree of specialization used by an organization, the less flexible it becomes; that is, the less able it is to adjust to changes in objectives, environment, resources, or technology.... The way in which work is divided or partitioned will be a major influence in determining in which dimensions an organization will be inflexible.

The second factor is the incremental cost of creating and sustaining a separate institution and maintaining one or more suitable courthouses. Infrastructure costs, including management, are unnecessarily duplicated.

Third, one of the primary advantages of larger courts is economies of scale, which provides significant flexibility in the assignment of cases among judges and judges to various court needs. If one judge gets some free time, he or she can step in and pick up a different kind of case or a calendar for a temporarily overwhelmed judge. When some judgeships are pulled out and put into a separate court, this flexibility in the original court is diminished.[10] Flexibility in the assignment of staff also is diminished. Another factor is the obverse of this problem. Specialized courts are created to meet a current and projected future need; if the number of cases goes up or down significantly from time to time (e.g., in juvenile courts), specialized courts do not have the same flexibility to change the number of judges assigned as the workload ebbs and flows.

The final, possible, factor is the size of the bar from which judges can be drawn.

If there are only a few attorneys in the area practicing law in the specialized field, it may be hard to find enough qualified attorneys to meet the need. Training judges on existing courts might be preferable. Some might argue that "an attorney is an attorney and a judge is a judge," and more than one judge has gotten to the bench because of that attitude.[11] Good courts—and citizen support for these courts—require something more than "any attorney is fine," however.

For juvenile courts, the basic legal and factual issues presented by the cases are not necessarily complex. The main challenge in case management is short, statutorily set deadlines for case events, which can be difficult at times, but usually are not an overwhelming burden. The clientele, however, often require and generally are seen as needing special treatment. The court operates as much as a social service agency as it does as a preserver of public order and imposer of sanctions. The original intent of juvenile courts, to develop special procedures and sanctions that would enable offenders to become law-abiding and productive adults without the stigma of a criminal record, readily could justify using judges specially trained to deal with children.

Four factors weigh against a separate juvenile court beyond whatever fiscal savings might be achieved from abandoning a separate court. First, separate juvenile courts remain an exception across the country. One cannot assume that the states without separate juvenile courts care less about their children, so one has to assume there are ways to meet the goal of juvenile courts without having a separate court. And there are. Every general jurisdiction court handling juvenile cases has a distinct juvenile division or separate calendars reserved only for juvenile cases. Statutes normally dictate the privacy accorded juvenile records and hearings, but even if these laws did not exist, sound case management would warrant separate calendars. Judges are specially assigned. Court leaders normally regard training for these judges as important, and, usually, as essential. The expertise of judges new to these cases may be limited at the beginning, but grows materially over a year's time. Judges assigned to juvenile calendars or divisions may not remain on those calendars as long as judges in separate juvenile courts, but an adequate level of specialization and expertise is a recognized management need, so tenure on these assignments tends to be longer than for civil or criminal calendars. Because the length of service on juvenile calendars is discretionary, long tenure is not assured, but tenure on these cases is getting longer across the country.[12] Good management can address the need without having to create or maintain a separate court.

Second, society is not as protective of offending juveniles as it once was, especially as the juveniles move closer to adulthood. The number of juveniles referred to adult courts for prosecution has increased significantly in the last ten or so years.[13] This trend is both a reflection of less tolerance for what unabashedly can be terrible crimes and the change in attitude about the need to protect and nurture children versus punishment and the deterrence of others. Separate juvenile courts tend to reflect the "old" attitude of protecting, nurturing, and teaching better ways and thus may be out of step with how citizens now want older juveniles' criminal acts and acts that are particularly heinous to be treated.

Third, the number of juveniles most likely to be seen in a juvenile court tends to fluctuate up and down over time. (Compare the size of the "boomer" generation with the X generation and again with the Y generation, which in size is in between the two.). As suggested above, a separate court has much less flexibility in adjusting its resources up and down, so sometimes its judges and staff will be very overworked and at other times they will be expanding work to fill the available time. A juvenile calendar or juvenile division in a general jurisdiction court can adjust more quickly and appropriately.

Finally, there is a growing national trend toward problem-solving courts that use criminal or family-law based cases as an opportunity to deal with an entire family and the issues that have resulted in criminal charges or civil law suits being filed. The trigger might be a juvenile case, or a criminal or family case involving one or both parents, but whatever the triggering event, the family thereafter is dealt with as a unit. Their cases and their issues are addressed in a coordinated fashion by various public and private social agencies to try to reverse socially destructive behaviors. A separate juvenile court makes these court-based problem-solving techniques for the entire family much harder to create and manage.

The argument for separate juvenile courts, therefore, turns on how one balances three considerations: (1) the "generic" arguments in Table 3.1 regarding consolidated or separate courts; (2) the traditional therapeutic approach to handling juveniles versus the newer "punishment" orientation; and (3) the new therapeutic approaches being developed by courts for handling dysfunctional families versus the more traditional case-by-isolated-case approach. As both the law and courts' management of juveniles from dysfunctional families changes, the case for separate juvenile courts becomes harder to sustain.

Separate, independent family courts present policy issues similar to those involving independent juvenile courts, but with additional elements. As suggested above, a substantial majority of the judges on general jurisdiction courts have no law practice experience with family law cases.[14] A like or greater number do not *want* to have any experience with family law cases as judges. Judges often see assignment to a family law calendar as punishment or as a "rite of passage" for new judges because they have the least leverage as to where they will be assigned. These cases are very important, however, not only to the parties but also to society at large. They deserve better treatment. A family court assures the interest and expertise of the judicial officers while also relieving judges on the original court of having to deal with these cases. A family court's jurisdiction can be defined so it can take a "problem-solving" approach to all of a family's problems and challenges, even helping the parents with education needs or learning disabilities in addition to the more obvious drug, anger, parenting skills, and job training challenges. Of less importance but a factor nonetheless, a family court courthouse can be designed to accommodate children and the special needs created by dealing with families with problems. A brand new courthouse for an existing court *could* include these design features, but many courthouses operate at or above capacity, so cannot readily be adapted now to meet these special needs.

The counterarguments are similar to those against having separate juvenile courts. A growing number of courts are creating problem-solving "family courts" in the sense of special calendars and dedicated judges, without setting up separate institutions. Only a few states have separate family courts. If most states can deal with these issues within the structure of a general jurisdiction court, perhaps all can.

Separate probate and tax courts present issues very similar to those discussed for family and juvenile courts. Legislatures may believe tax disputes need to be resolved quickly by judges who are well versed in the complexities of tax law. It also is a fact of life that tax law, like family law, is not a common practice area for attorneys or for attorneys who have become judges. These are legitimate interests, but ones that do not necessarily require a separate court. If a tax court is really a misnamed administrative tribunal, it should be in the executive branch rather than the judicial branch. If the tax court is in the judicial branch, it is not clear that properly trained judges on the court of general jurisdiction could not handle these cases in a proper and expeditious manner.[15]

As suggested above, there are some sound management reasons for creating separate water courts. Even here, however, a new, temporary judgeship (or judgeships) with dedicated staff might be a better approach than creating a new institution with an indefinite life span, all the trappings and infrastructure associated with independent courts, and a built-in constituency that will lobby to retain the separate entity.

Special housing courts exist in only a few states. The experience of almost all states with housing court type cases in either a court of limited jurisdiction or the general jurisdiction court suggests that the management imperatives for a separate housing court are weak. Inertia and local political considerations seem to be important factors in the continuation of these courts. Management advantages are not apparent.

3.3.3 Consolidating Limited and General Jurisdiction Courts

The arguments for and against creating one trial court out of an existing general jurisdiction court and one or more limited jurisdiction courts extend beyond those in Table 3.1, although most of those apply here, too. These other factors are reviewed in Table 3.2. Balancing all these factors, almost all states have chosen not to create a single trial court.[16] The route to a single trial court in California may be instructive, nonetheless.

Table 3.2   Arguments For and Against Unifying Two or More Courts into a Single Court of General Jurisdiction

Issue	Arguments for and against	Counterarguments
Judicial quality and usage	The judges on the limited jurisdiction court do not need to have practiced law as long as the judges on the general jurisdiction court and are not qualified to handle general jurisdiction cases, especially general civil cases and major felonies	In fact, judges in both courts, whether appointed initially or elected, usually have practiced law longer than needed for the general jurisdiction court or have been on the limited jurisdiction court for many years and can handle a wide variety of cases
	Judges on the general jurisdiction court will refuse to handle limited jurisdiction cases and many limited jurisdiction judges have no interest in handling general jurisdiction cases, especially family and probate cases	If necessary, sitting judges can be "grandparented" into hearing only cases that would have been within the jurisdiction of the court on which they are sitting at the time of unification; their replacements then would understand that the court hears all cases of first instance.
		Many of the general jurisdiction court judges used to serve on the limited jurisdiction court; they might wish to move beyond limited jurisdiction cases, but they know how to handle them so their ego should not defeat an otherwise good idea.
		In point of fact, after unification, the judges get comfortable with each other and with the set-up; in short order virtually all "grand parented" judges agree to hear cases they originally refused to hear.
		A chief judge will not assign a judge of either court to a calendar for which he or she is unqualified; we give tremendous discretion to judges, yet this argument improperly assumes the chief judge will not use discretion wisely in assigning judges to calendars.
		Training is needed for judges of both courts, as general jurisdiction judges also need to learn the law associated with limited jurisdiction cases; this is a management challenge, not a reason for the status quo.

Continued

Table 3.2 Continued

Issue	Arguments for and against	Counterarguments
	General jurisdiction courts need high-quality lawyers willing to accept a judicial appointment; the best civil lawyers in the community will not desire judgeships if they think they risk being put on a traffic or small claims or even a family law calendar	Good attorneys interested in public service will not be deterred by a unified jurisdiction; they recognize that judges with strong civil law backgrounds are not common and that chief judges want to use judges to their best advantage, both to please the judges and to enable the court to give the best service. A good civil lawyer is not at risk of hearing traffic or small claims cases unless it is the tradition of the court that all judges must take a turn on those calendars; if that is the tradition, it would not necessarily be a deterrent to a good attorney.
	Unification provides more flexibility in assigning judges to take best advantage of their skills and to match caseload better with available resources.	Most judges are kept busy today without unification; they also are on the court that best fits their interests and skills, so unification is not needed.
	The judiciary needs a career ladder just as any business or even a law firm does; having two trial courts allows testing of a judge's skills in the court of limited jurisdiction and promotion of the best, so litigants in general-jurisdiction-court cases, where the stakes normally are higher, get tested and mature judges, while the best judges at the limited jurisdiction level are rewarded.	If general jurisdiction court judges came only from the limited jurisdiction courts, this argument would have more weight, but that is not the case; many general jurisdiction court judges go onto that court without ever having served on the court of limited jurisdiction.
	Judges would not get lazy or bored in the limited jursidiction court because of the "carrot" of appointment to the general jurisdiction court.	The case management skills and temperament for handling cases at each court level are different; a judge who is good at the limited jurisdiction court level is not necessarily a good candidate for the general jurisdiction court
	Unification provides new challenges for judges of both courts, which instills energy and new enthusiasm for the job; the variety of calendars available when a court hears all cases of first instance preclude judges from getting bored or jaded.	Even if true, this is a short-term benefit that will wear off and five or ten years from now will not be a factor; few courts stick with rotating all judges every year or two, so the theoretical advantage of new cases and calendars is not really germane

Issue	Arguments for and against	Counterarguments
	In large urban counties, combining two or more courts into a single court could produce *dis*econo-mies of scale, where size starts to introduce inefficiencies and bureaucratic controls in the name of uniformity of the entire organiza-tion that are counterproductive to doing justice and that add rather than subtract costs.	Rules shared by all branches of a single court are not counterproduc-tive, but actually ease the practice of law for attorneys who have cases in several branches. A single court does not require that administration be located in a single site; the Los Angeles Superior Court has 11 administrative districts to try to avoid some of these diseconomies of scale; policies are set for the entire court, with implementation left to the administrative districts
Staff Utilization	A unified court offers new career options for staff and creates new opportunities for advancement and learning new skills; it expands the variety of work opportunities avail-able to employees, making court employment more attractive to both current and prospective employees.	Most courts are understaffed, so combined courts will not free up staff time for training and learning how to handle new case types; a unified court still will be organized with a lot of case processing staff and a few supervisors, so the career ladder is not changed materially.
	The larger staff will provide econo-mies of scale that will improve staff productivity which, in turn, will de-fer the need to add staff positions.	The larger staff will require more bureaucratic controls and more "infrastructure" staff such as human resources and technology support, which will undermine increases in productivity
	Staff can be allocated to branch locations and to work areas in a way that better reflects workload, improving productivity and provid-ing for more timely completion of work	If branch locations don't have room for additional staff, facility con-straints will preclude this type of staff movement, as will large distances between branches, as staff will resist new long commutes to accommodate management's desire to balance work and staff
	Staff training needs will increase materially, which will diminish the time staff can devote to processing cases or produce frustration at the difficulty associated with complet-ing their jobs.	Staff training is enriching and ap-preciated and is resisted only if staff members feel it is taking time away from completing time-critical tasks. With more staff, work can be ad-justed to free time for training. A lot of staff training today is done by peers; staff new to an assignment will not need to learn it all without help.

Continued

Table 3.2 Continued

Issue	Arguments for and against	Counterarguments
Improved technology	A unified court creates an occasion to upgrade hardware, standardize software so case information can be shared in all branches by all judges and staff, and to introduce new technology that advances access or improves communication with other justice agencies.	Courts can create a way to share data about cases that move across jurisdictional lines without going to unification; today's software advances allow communication across hardware and software platforms without everyone having the same hardware and software.
		The cost of new hardware and software can be substantial, both in dollar terms and in terms of disrupted operations and stress on staff; these costs could materially undermine any dollar savings associated with unification.
Public Access	With unified courts and judges, case types that could not be heard in limited jurisdiction court locations now will be heard by general jurisdiction judges, allowing domestic violence matters, juvenile hearings, larger civil cases, and other matters to be heard in courthouses that are spread around the county more than the general jurisdiction courthouse(s) used to be; this provides more convenient and more timely access, especially to those at risk of physical harm.	Moving all these cases to outlying courthouses presents three problems: (1) training judges to handle all these new case types, which can remove judges from the bench; (2) keeping calendar size manageable; and (3) finding time during the court day to hear these new case types.
		Limited jurisdiction courthouses may not be designed to accommodate special proceedings like juvenile hearings and may not have courtrooms available to allow moving judges to these outlying sites to expand the cases heard there; nothing about unification carries any promise of new courthouses.
Court Management	Rules, policies, and procedures can be standardized county-wide or region-wide, which makes it easier for litigants and attorneys who have cases in different locations and also reduces the impression that how cases are treated by judges varies by location. If a location has a special need for a variation in the rules or a different rule, the other judges will recognize that and write in the exception or different rule for that location.	Even within a county, there may be legitimate reasons for rules to be different in a particular location; standardization does not advance justice in these cases. A court may develop standardized rules, but the real problem is standardized interpretation and enforcement of those rules. Many courts have great rules and almost no uniformity because judges choose to apply them differently; a larger court has a harder time identifying and addressing various interpretations and enforcement approaches

Issue	Arguments for and against	Counterarguments
	A wider range of calendars and more locations allows a chief judge to match judicial temperament and skills to calendar needs more precisely; this is good for both the individual judges and the system.	This argument assumes too much. A chief judge may not be that wise or the range of calendars and locations still may not be sufficient to match each judge to a calendar for which he or she is best suited and that he or she desires
	The court administrator can reorganize staff and workflow to better match needs and staff assignments and also to enrich individual jobs.	See the counterargument directly above; even if the court administrator can do this, it merely rearranges deck chairs; it does not save any money, which should be the primary goal of unification
	The judges and management of the single court can formulate one policy and speak to the community, to justice agencies, and to legislators with one voice rather than compete against each other while representing separate courts.	If you have a dozen judges in a room, you will get a dozen opinions about how to approach a problem or issue; it is unrealistic to expect the independent professionals who sit on the bench to be willing to adhere to a common policy or decision in each instance. For some judges, "independence" from administrative control is a refined art.
	A larger court means more committees, larger committees, and slower approval processes for new court policies and procedures; valuable time can be lost in responding to a new issue or problem.	Most courts of size have an executive committee or another procedure set up to deal with issues and problems that require prompt action; some rules, procedures, or policies may take longer to adopt than in the smaller separate courts, but imminent issues still will be addressed.
	A larger court can obtain some economies of scale in purchasing and in the cost of some fringe benefits, which saves money.	Many cities and counties belong to joint powers entities that provide the benefits of purchasing economies of scale and courts, whether one or more, can take advantage of these without unification
	A single court can stop competing with other courts in the county for freelance court reporters and for interpreters and also can use these contractors more efficiently when they are brought in, thus decreasing the cost per case for these services.	The interpreter problem is one of supply, not competition among courts; a unified court cannot increase the supply any more than two or more courts can.
		Court reporters are struggling against technological obsolescence, so there is a supply issue here, too, starting with the court reporting schools' reduced enrollments. Courts are contributing to this problem by pushing audio and video recording of proceedings; having one court or many will not improve the supply issue.

California is the most recent state (1998) to create a single trial court. The political and administrative factors that spurred this decision may be informative for both those who desire a single trial court and those who oppose it. Two factors appealed to the legislators who supported the change for years and placed the final constitutional amendment on the ballot:[17] a belief, supported by data provided by the judicial branch, that substantial budget savings would follow consolidation across the state[18] and a further belief that many judges statewide were underutilized and consolidation would defer the need for new judgeships.[19] Because of these beliefs, the legislature over a period of about ten years had pushed for greater "cooperation" between the two independent courts (superior, which was the general jurisdiction court, and municipal, which was the limited jurisdiction court). Through a 1991 statute and the use of budgetary pressure starting in fiscal year 1996, the legislature mandated "coordination" of the courts' staffs and their judicial calendars to "achieve maximum utilization of judicial and other court resources and statewide cost reductions in court operations....[20] The policy-making body for the judicial branch, the Judicial Council, was charged with making annual reports to the legislature about progress in implementing these statutes. Full state funding of trial courts had preceded the consolidation vote by two years, which materially increased the legislature's ability to apply pressure on the entire judicial branch. Because of its reporting duty, the Judicial Council, in turn, required substantive progress from trial courts. In the two fiscal years prior to the June 1998 vote to amend the constitution to allow unification on a county-by-county basis, the Council did not accept "paper" cooperation but required meaningful changes before it would approve budget increases for reluctant courts.

Several elements came together to lead to a single trial court in California:

■ The data about cost savings were not effectively challenged, either in the legislature or by those in the judicial branch who might have been able to do so.

■ Legislative antagonism toward the judicial branch kept the issue on legislators' radar; the antagonism was fueled by several factors: anger over several years about a state supreme court opinion that indicated in a statement not necessary to its decision that legislators probably did not need more staff; adverse media stories about some judges in a major metropolitan area taking off two afternoons a week to play golf; the anecdotal inability of legislators to find judges in their chambers late in the afternoon; and anecdotes from constituents about "bad" or "lazy" judges.

■ A respected legislative "champion" of the idea who did his homework, worked with the Judicial Council on refinements to the proposal, kept pushing for the change, and was willing and able to take the heat from judges and to give straight talk back to them without being antagonistic.

- Years of cooperation in almost all counties and, in a number of courts, true consolidation of staffs and management, softened the opposition of judges and court administrators.
- The Judicial Council cooperated to the extent that it sought "workable" legislation rather than steadfastly opposing the change.
- State funding preceded consolidation by two years, which gave the state legislature leverage it never would have had if funding had remained largely a county responsibility.

To its credit, California undertook a comprehensive evaluation of its structural change. Bear in mind that the two arguments that carried the most weight with the legislature over a number of years were: (1) substantial cost savings; and (2) reduced need for new judges. The latter may have been realized, but the former was not. It is interesting that "financial savings" is not on the list of the overall benefits identified by trial court personnel and judges as a benefit of consolidation. Rather, public access, better relations with other justice agencies, and improvements in internal communications and flexibility were most cited by trial court representatives. Progress in these areas is important because both the justice system and citizens benefit. They do not produce the dollar savings legislators often seem to require, however. Simply improving citizens' and other agencies' interactions with the courts and providing better internal use of resources may not be seen as sufficient benefits if legislatures make fiscal savings their highest priority. Because the conditions affecting courts and the demands on them are constantly changing, cost increases may be contained by unification, but a decrease in the branch's budget is doubtful. The overall benefits cited by trial court participants in the evaluation are: [21]

- Greater cooperation and teamwork exists between the judiciary, other branches of government, and the community.
- More uniformity and efficiency in case processing, and timelier disposition of cases.
- Enhanced opportunities for innovation, self-evaluation, and reengineering of court operations.
- More coherence brought to the governance of the courts and greater understanding by other branches of government and the public.
- Courts become a unified entity and speak with one voice in dealings with the public, county agencies, and justice system partners.
- Public has greater access to the courts and an increased focus on accountability and service.

Even though these overall benefits touch only lightly on the two most important considerations for the legislature, the unification did not fail to provide those benefits. The evaluation examined the four areas that prior to unification were expected to be impacted by unification: (1) utilization of judicial resources; (2) organization and efficiency of court staff; (3) efficiency of court operations; and (4) quality of services provided. The "headline" conclusions in each area are set forth below, along with a few of the subconclusions that support the general statement.[22]

- The use of judicial resources improved.
  - There was greater flexibility in assigning judges to cases.
  - Courts could organize judicial assignments more flexibly, most often on the basis of case type rather than geography.
  - Judges heard a wider variety of cases, which they saw as a positive.
- Improved administrative efficiencies begun while courts were coordinating continued with unification, which offered enhanced opportunities for staff efficiencies.
  - Duplication of effort was reduced through creating a countywide coordinator for divisions (civil, criminal, family, etc.).
  - The need for staff training increased substantially.
- Court managers, most staff, and judges believe that unification potentially will be more efficient.
  - Courtrooms are more fully utilized.
  - Backlogs of cases were reduced.
  - Rules, policies, and procedures were standardized countywide.
  - Technology was improved to accommodate unification needs.
- Court users have been provided improved quality of service.
  - More cost-effective use of judicial officers and staff facilitated program expansion (e.g., problem-solving courts and services to juveniles).
  - Improved access results from reorganization of operations and facilities, new hours of operation, alternative filing processes, and new or alternative payment options.
  - Courts can speak with one voice when dealing with the public and other organizations.
  - Justice system partners reported either improved working relations or no change in relations.

Robert Tobin cites another consideration surrounding unification that may be important for the judicial branch. He argues that unification gives "organizational form to the concept that the state judicial branch is more than a group of semi-independent judges loosely held together by a common appellate process. It is an integrated organism."[23] There seems to be little doubt that today California's trial courts are seen by government at all levels and by a growing number of citizens as a unified state entity with policy and significant operational decisions made at the state level for all trial courts. Because state funding came first, however, it is uncertain how much of this derives from state financing and how much from unification. Doubtless, both were important, but their relative contribution to the establishment of an integrated third branch is less clear.

Before leaving this topic, one other phenomenon associated with single trial courts should be noted: the continuing phenomenon of two or more levels of judges even in unified trial courts. Idaho, Illinois, the District of Columbia, Wisconsin, Puerto Rico, and the federal courts all have a single general jurisdiction trial court. They also have two levels of judges, one for general jurisdiction cases, and one for limited jurisdiction cases, although they do not necessarily refer to the distinction in this way. The "regular" judges appoint the "limited jurisdiction" judges. In Illinois, the "associate" judges by law cannot preside over felony cases absent special Supreme Court permission. In the District of Columbia, all judges used to rotate among all the calendars monthly. Now, lesser jurisdiction judicial officers exclusively hear some case types. Puerto Rico has one court, but two divisions that look very much like a general jurisdiction division and a limited jurisdiction division. In the federal district courts, appointed magistrates used to handle preliminary matters in criminal cases, perhaps handle misdemeanors, and assist judges with discovery motions in civil cases. Now, these judicial officers are "magistrate judges." They are not "Article III" judges—those established by the Constitution and who serve as district court judges—but their judicial powers and jurisdiction have expanded and the district court judges have gained some relief from handling some types of cases.

California has converted to a single court too recently for a movement to start to reintroduce limited jurisdiction judges. Before unification, California's municipal courts used appointed full-time "traffic referees" to hear traffic cases and many regularly used volunteer attorneys to hear small claims, family, and juvenile cases as pro tem judges. And in fact, pro tem judges remain part of the makeup of the unified courts.[24] In the superior court, there were and are judicially appointed "commissioners" who had a limited jurisdiction that litigants could waive, so they were de facto "regular" judges; commissioners most often are assigned to family law, juvenile, and probate cases. Today, California is trying to move away from limited jurisdiction judicial officers, with a legislative proposal pending that will mandate that over time commissioner positions be converted to full judicial positions. This legislation is being proposed because of the belief that too many commissioners, unaccountable to the public, were appointed in years past and that they are hearing too many sensitive cases.

There are reasons for desiring secondary or supplemental judicial resources that go beyond judges' desire not to hear certain kinds of cases. Some matters, especially discovery disputes in civil and family cases, fights between former spouses about who can have the children during what hours and for which holiday, or how much notice is required to change a visitation plan, and highly technical evidence such as complex accounting issues in a divorce or contract case, may require substantial amounts of a judge's time. In the larger picture, a judge's time could be spent more productively on the many other cases seeking judicial attention. This rationale does not apply to traffic or small claims calendars, however.

Professor Maurice Rosenberg had a less complimentary view of why judges seek subordinate judicial officers. He said that many judges like the idea of using auxiliary court personnel in a limited judicial capacity because "they look on most aspects of pre-trial processing of cases as too hum-drum for their talents and conceive of trial work as their destiny."[25]

Whether one views the existence of subordinate, limited jurisdiction judicial officers as justified or as bowing to judicial egos, it is found widely, almost always with the sanction of law. Therefore, it should be neither dismissed nor ignored. The tendency of many judges to try to hand off "lesser" cases or emotionally draining cases to subordinate judicial officers suggests that two levels of court, either de facto or by law, may be inevitable, even if not desirable for all case types. It simply appears that too many judges in both general and limited jurisdiction courts do not want to handle certain cases or have a legitimate need to spend their time otherwise. Therefore, they continually will seek ways to avoid the undesired duties or case types, including doing all they can to establish subordinate judicial positions.[26] There are sound policy arguments one can make as to why our best judges—or, at least, judges—should sit on and decide these high-volume or difficult and stressful cases. Experience to date suggests, however, that the human tendency to want to slough off cases that bore or bother will find a way to prevail regardless of—and almost with indifference to—the policy arguments.

3.4 Caseloads in State and Federal Courts

The number of cases to be managed in state courts is another factor that is part of the context of court administration. For many reasons, a lot of cases that used to be solely state court matters are becoming subject to federal law and thus moving to federal courts. For example, class actions involving a certain level of dollar claim for tort damages or the number or residence of parties in these cases, and certain crimes against persons are now to be filed in federal courts.[27] The federal judiciary does not necessarily support these changes, at least not without additional judicial resources, but Congress sees them as desirable and state court representatives have not convinced Congress that the status quo is sufficient. Further, the popular media seems to focus more on federal cases than on state cases, except for criminal cases, and in 2005 and 2006 focused substantial attention on federal judges, particularly nominees for the U.S. Supreme Court. This emphasis mistakenly has led the general public to believe that federal courts play a larger role in the nation's judicial business than they do. This is not meant in any way to denigrate the work of the federal courts, but to suggest that the impression among many citizens that federal courts are more important than state courts is not supported by the evidence. More cases of all kinds—except, of course, for those exclusively within federal jurisdiction—are filed and resolved in state courts, by a wide margin, than in federal courts.

The NCSC publishes an annual report on state court caseloads. The most recent figures available cover cases filed and disposed in 2003. In that year, just over 100 million cases of all kinds were filed in state trial courts.[28] Limited jurisdiction courts, which handle almost all of the high-volume cases, received slightly fewer than 67 million of these cases. Between October 1, 2002 and September 30, 2003, just over 328,500 cases were filed in the federal district courts.[29] Traffic cases represent almost 55 percent of all state cases (roughly 54,700,000 cases in 2003).[30] Because traffic cases distort the comparison with federal courts, removing them from the state total makes the comparison more apt. Still, state courts received almost 45,400,000 cases in 2003, about 138.5 nontraffic cases filed in state courts for every one case filed in a federal court.

On a per judge basis, 483 cases per federal district court judge were filed during the federal fiscal year of 2003.[31] The overall national average of cases filed per judge in unified and general jurisdiction state courts—the courts with caseloads roughly similar to those of federal district courts—in 2003 was 1,626.[32] Federal district courts do not handle domestic relations or juvenile cases (except for de minimis exceptions), either. Even if one were to eliminate all traffic, domestic, and juvenile cases from state courts' caseload, leaving only civil and criminal caseloads, state general jurisdiction and unified jurisdiction judges carry about three times as many cases per judge as federal district court judges do.

This comparison is not offered to suggest that federal judges work less hard than state judges—or any other potentially negative comparison—or that the work of federal courts somehow is less important than some suggest, but merely to make two points. First, state courts are where the "action" is from a judicial and court administration perspective, despite the significance of federal courts in the legal firmament. The point is stronger when one considers that family law and juvenile matters are such important case types from a societal viewpoint. Second, state courts' caseload is substantial no matter how one examines it, which confirms the wisdom of Chief Justice Burger's desire to enhance the management skills and research and consulting assistance available to state courts through the NCSC and ICM.[33] The size and variety of the caseload and the management challenges these create also makes the business of court administration in state courts very important.

The numbers for state courts suggest another point. Between federal and state courts, federal courts normally are seen as more prestigious, particularly by judges and attorneys. Within state courts, general jurisdiction courts are seen as having more prestige than limited jurisdiction courts, again mostly among judges and lawyers (and many legislators). This perspective regarding state courts is explainable in large part because most states require more years of practice for an attorney who becomes a judge on a court of general jurisdiction than for an attorney who becomes a judge on a court of limited jurisdiction. Plus, so many limited jurisdiction judges preside in city and town courts and may or may not be attorneys and, regardless, often are part-time judicial officers. Also, attorneys seldom practice in courts of limited jurisdiction except as prosecutors and public defenders in misdemeanor cases.[34] This combination of factors could well lead to an unfounded sense of superior quality on the benches of general jurisdiction courts.

Traditionally, most judges and attorneys felt strongly that their needs and concerns were and should be the primary if not the exclusive focus of administrators. This remains the view of many judges and attorneys today. There is a growing outward perspective developing, however, that sees the primary focus of court administration in coming years as access, accountability, and community outreach, all of which make citizens and litigants key beneficiaries of court administration.[35] From this perspective, the triangle of prestige should be turned upside down, at least for court administration. Far more people interact with state courts of limited jurisdiction than with state general jurisdiction or federal courts, by a minimum of three or four to one. So it is through courts of limited jurisdiction that the third branch most impacts the public, and from which the public's views about courts mostly are fashioned. Arthur Vanderbilt, while President of the American Bar Association, pointed out in 1938 that it is in courts that, "men and women feel the keen cutting edge of the law and therefore judge the law by what they see and hear in courts…"[36] If courts of limited jurisdiction are not operating well, citizens will judge all courts poorly. Stumpf and Culver also point out that courts of limited jurisdiction often define the legal rules for a community: "In their day-in, day-out processing of thousands of seemingly trivial cases, the lowest of our [state] courts significantly shape the contours of legal rules for the community. That so few of these decisions are ever appealed seems to enhance their role further in shaping policy at the state and local level."[37]

From an administrative perspective, if courts of limited jurisdiction are not well managed, access, the enforcement of courts' orders, public understanding of courts, and public support of courts all suffer. The high volume in these courts creates unique challenges in public service and interactions, the use of technology to extend and facilitate access, calendar management, and cash management. From the perspective of attorneys and judges, a prestige hierarchy of federal, state general jurisdiction, and state limited jurisdiction courts may make sense. From a court administration perspective, a similar view would be unwise.

Notes

1. Green, Milton D., "The Business of the Trial Courts," in Jones, Harry W., ed., *The American Assembly, The Courts, the Public, and the Law Explosion.* Englewood Cliffs, NJ: Prentice-Hall, 1965, p. 8.
2. There also is a "court" that operates in secret to review requests for search warrants and electronic intercepts in national security cases. The judges are judges of existing courts who are specially assigned.

3. One book includes a multipage table showing the names—just court names—of the general jurisdiction courts in all 50 states and a full-page table showing the names and size of the courts of last resort. See Stumpf, Harry P., and John H. Culver, *The Politics of State Courts*. White Plains, NY: Longman Publishing Group, 1992, chap. 2.

4. Texas and Oklahoma have a civil court of last resort and a criminal court of last resort. For administrative purposes, one of these courts is designated as the administrative and rule-making body for the judicial branch.

5. Appellate courts have clerks of court, as well. Appellate clerks are appointed by the judges and serve only that court. In federal trial courts, the clerk is appointed by the judges.

6. See, for example, Rottman, David B., and William E. Hewitt, *Trial Court Structure and Performance: A Contemporary Reappraisal*. Williamsburg, VA: National Center for State Courts, 1996; Flango, Victor E., "Court Unification and Quality of State Courts," *Justice System Journal*, vol. 16, no. 3, 1994, pp. 33–55.

7. For many decades, California's counties supported both "municipal" courts that served larger population centers and "justice " courts that served their rural areas. (Judges in justice courts normally were not attorneys—although they could be—and served a small geographic area on a part-time basis.) Starting in the late 1950s and continuing into the 1980s, justice courts were phased out. The first move usually was to convert one or more justice courts to a municipal court serving a larger geographic area and with a full-time attorney judge and then, finally, merging the several municipal courts into a single, countywide municipal court.

8. See Tobin, Robert W., *Creating the Judicial Branch: The Unfinished Reform*. Williamsburg, VA: National Center for State Courts, 1999, p. 228.

9. Litterer, J. A., *The Analysis of Organizations,* 1965, p. 185, cited in Friesen, Ernest C., Jr., Edward C. Gallas, and Nesta Gallas, *Managing the Courts*. Indianapolis, IN: Bobbs-Merrill, 1971, p. 178.

10. Most states address this issue, at least partially, by having some provision for cross-assigning judges between courts. Clearly this helps if assignments are for a week or more so both the helping judge and the recipient court can make appropriate plans, but it offers limited relief when a court needs help for a day or two, particularly if the problem appears without warning.

11. See, for example, Vanderbilt, Arthur T., "Foreword," *Reports of the Section of Judicial Administration*. Chicago: American Bar Association, 1938, reprinted in Section of Judicial Administration, *Improvement of the Administration of Justice*, 5th ed. Chicago: American Bar Association, 1971, p. xxiii.

12. Some states now require by rule or otherwise that assignments to juvenile and family calendars be for a minimum of two or three years in recognition of the special needs associated with these cases.

13. In 1972, 1.3 percent of juveniles taken into police custody were referred to adult courts. That percentage jumped from 3.3 percent in 1995 to 6.2 percent in 1996 and has remained over 6 percent every year since. Pastore, Ann L., and Kathleen Maguire, eds., *Sourcebook of Criminal Justice Statistics, 2003*. Washington, D.C.: U.S. Dept. of Justice, Bureau of Justice Statistics, 2005, Table 4.26.

14. For whatever reason, family law practitioners very seldom are either appointed or elected to courts of general jurisdiction.

15. Particularly when I was a young attorney but even in later years, when I would meet tax attorneys I was struck by how many said they did not like tax law in law school and never thought they would practice tax law, but now found it fun and very interesting. These are anecdotes, but some sitting judges might have the same experience if properly trained.

16. Single trial courts exist in California, the District of Columbia, Idaho (but with a "magistrates division" that functions as a limited jurisdiction court), Illinois (but with "associate judges" who cannot preside over felonies), Iowa, Minnesota, Puerto Rico (but with two "divisions"), and South Dakota. Kansas, North Dakota, and Wisconsin have one trial court of general jurisdiction created by the state but also have multiple courts of limited jurisdiction established by municipalities. Schauffler, Richard Y., et al., *State Courts Caseload Statistics, 2004*, Williamsburg, VA: National Center for State Courts, 2005, chap. 1: State Court Structure Charts.

17. The constitutional amendment left the final decision of whether to consolidate to a majority vote of the judges of each court in each county, with both courts agreeing. One of the last of the 58 counties to vote for a single trial court, Los Angeles, did so at the end of 1999 after two previous negative votes by superior court judges. A substantial majority of counties voted to consolidate within three months of the June 1998 approval by voters of the constitutional amendment. These votes were made easier by the previous years of increasing consolidation of staffs and coordination of judicial calendars induced by statutory "encouragements."

18. There was some inventive math that supported these claims of material fiscal savings. The numbers were accepted by the legislature, however, and were used over several years to support the benefits of a single trial court. In point of fact, for a variety of reasons not germane here, the total judicial branch budget has increased substantially since 1998, although the increase is largely associated with issues involved in state funding rather than consolidation.

19. In 2005, the Judicial Council of California, using a weighted caseload methodology, determined that 150 new judgeships should be sought statewide, which it will seek to spread over three fiscal years. The study showed that 360 judgeships were needed. Judicial Council of California, *Cornerstones of Democracy: California Courts Enter a New Era of Judicial Branch Independence*. San Francisco: Judicial Council of California, 2005, p. 25, retrieved from http://www.courtinfo.ca.gov/reference/2_annual.htm.

20. *Trial Court Realignment and Efficiency Act of 1991*, Chap. 90, Statutes of 1991, 1991–1992, California State Legislature, Regular Session (June 30, 1991), 406–409, § 6.

21. Lahey, Mary Anne, Bruce A. Christenson, and Robert J. Rossi, *Analysis of Trial Court Unification in California: Final Report*. Palo Alto, CA: American Institutes for Research, 2000, p. vii.

22. Ibid. at pp. iv–vii.

23. Tobin, Robert W., *Creating the Judicial Branch*, p. 139.

24. In December 2005, the California Judicial Council passed new rules regarding the selection, training, and evaluation of pro tem judges. Freedman, Robert B., "'Promise and Potential for Pro Tems," *California Courts Review*, Spring 2006, pp. 21–23. It remains to be seen whether this is the first step toward a new class of quasi-judge.

25. Rosenberg, Maurice, "Court Congestion Status, Causes, and Proposed Remedies," in Jones, Harry W., ed., *American Assembly*, p. 42.

26. Tobin, Robert W. *Creating the Judicial Branch*, p. 138.

27. For example, Donn, Jeff, "Feds Assuming Expanded Role against Common Crime," Redding (CA) *Record Searchlight*, Dec. 28, 2003, p. A-12.

28. Schauffler, Richard Y., et al., *Examining the Work of State Courts, 2004: A National Perspective from the Court Statistics Project*. Williamsburg, VA: National Center for State Courts, 2005, p. 14.

29. *Judicial Caseload Profile Report*, 2002, retrieved Oct. 20, 2005, from http://www/iscpirts/gpvcgo-bin/cmsd/2002.

30. Schauffler, Richard Y., et al., *Work of State Courts*, p. 18.

31. *Judicial Caseload Profile*.

32. "Overview," Schauffler, Richard Y., et al., *Work of State Courts*, p. 12.
33. See chapter 2.
34. On my first day of work for a major business law firm in San Francisco, fresh out of law school, I was given two cases, one of which needed an answer to a civil complaint in municipal court. Just in case the format for municipal court differed from the format for superior court or the U.S. District Court, where most of the firm's work was done, I asked several partners if they had any municipal court answers I could use as a guide. In a litigation department of a dozen attorneys, no one had or knew of a pleading—complaint or answer—from a municipal court case.
35. See, Tobin, Robert W., *Creating the Judicial Branch,* pp. 195–198, 202; Commission on Trial Court Performance Standards, *Trial Court Performance Standards.* Williamsburg, VA: National Center for State Courts and Bureau of Justice Assistance, 1990.
36. Vanderbilt, Arthur T., "Foreword," p. xxxii.
37. Stumpf, Harry P., and John H. Culver, *Politics of State Courts*, p. 3.

Chapter 4

The Environmental Context: Social and Political Factors

Court administration occurs in an environment. Part of that environment is external, fashioned by social and political forces that often are beyond a court's control. This environmental context is the subject of this chapter.

4.1 Courts in Our Government Structure: Separation of Powers, Checks and Balances, and Court Administration

In late July 2005, HarrisInteractive conducted a telephone survey of a representative sample of Americans on behalf of the American Bar Association (ABA). The survey sought to assess the public's understanding of and support for certain fundamental concepts of American government.[1] Eighty-two percent of respondents said they feel the concept of separation of powers is important, but less than half (45%) could correctly identify what the concept means.[2] Eighty-six percent believe the concept of checks and balances is important, but over one-third could not correctly identify the principle. Only slightly more respondents (48%) could correctly identify the responsibilities of the judiciary than those who could not (44%). Almost half of the respondents (45%) could not name the three branches of government. Only one in five (21%) correctly answered all four of the civics questions.[3]

The reasons why people support the separation of powers and checks and balances are unclear. They may reflect support for an independent judiciary, as suggested by the incoming president of the ABA. Instead, they might suggest that courts should not "legislate"—a frequent charge of social conservatives—or should not interfere with legislative decisions, a suggestion of some senators in statements surrounding the confirmation hearings of Chief Justice Roberts and Justice Alito.[4]

At both the federal and state levels, government is divided into three separate, mostly independent, but also interdependent branches: executive, legislative, and judicial. The concept of separation of powers supports the independence of each branch of government within its assigned sphere. The concept of checks and balances covers the mutual dependencies of all three branches as well as the legal power of one branch to overrule, change or modify, and enforce the decisions or actions of the other coordinate branches.

Our government structure affects court administration in several ways. The ABA survey results hint at a subtle influence. If the public's support for the separation of powers reflects support for courts' independence, this response is a positive for courts and court administration.[5] Courts need to seek ways to harness and build on that support. If the support for separation of powers instead suggests the public believes courts have been too "activist" and should "stay out of" legislative matters, as suggested often during the 2004 presidential campaign and the confirmation hearings for Chief Justice Roberts and Justice Alito, it may reflect irritation with courts that might negatively impact court administration.[6]

The public's views about courts generally are not well informed.[7] If the public does not understand courts' role, both in the government structure and in support of democracy, this lack of understanding can lead to a negative view of courts that turns into resistance to courts' agendas to improve court administration at the local or state level. In a world of 24/7 news outlets and Internet blogs, a decision by any court at any level that generates a lot of strong negative reactions can hurt.[8] Courts' efforts to obtain budget increases, to introduce new programs, to protect their institutional prerogatives against legislative erosion, or even to obtain new courthouses or increases in the salaries of judges or staff might be opposed simply because of one or two recent cases, possibly in another state. Because government structure and its import are not well understood, because news outlets' discussions of court cases often are not as informing as they should be about what was decided by a court and why—and what was not decided or involved—all courts are affected by outrage about a case anywhere. A case in, say, California that results in a lot of negative publicity could affect the ability of a local court in Arkansas or Maine to increase staff's salaries or to obtain new security equipment for a courthouse. Citizens who believe that courts declare war (4% in the ABA survey) or raise taxes (3%) may not understand the subtleties of the differences between state and federal judiciaries and the fact that the judiciary of California has nothing to do with the judiciary of Maine or Arkansas. When a court's leadership seeks to reach out to the public with information or for support, the challenges posed by a citizenry unfamiliar with basic civics needs to be taken into account.[9]

Many judges and lawyers believe these distinctions among different states' judiciaries and relevant local issues are obvious and clear. Thus, they may not appreciate the impact of 24/7 television and the Internet on their local issues. Even if they understand the impact, judges face two limitations in trying to counter these negative forces. The first are the canons of ethics that govern judges and place strict limits on acceptable political activity. Even though these ethical restraints normally make an exception for political activity to support or improve the administration of justice, judges by and large cannot participate in the rough-and-tumble of politics to the same degree as all other government officials and as ordinary citizens can. Only in the rarest of instances would judges wish to join a debate about the propriety or wisdom of a case in another state or in the federal system. The second limitation is that even in states where all judges come to the bench through election, only a few judges have experience as legislators or were involved on the political side of the executive branch before coming to the bench. Consequently, they do not have finely honed political skills or instincts. This limits how a trial court or the state-level judicial branch responds to adverse publicity from other states and a lack of understanding about the role of courts in government. Certainly, each state has both trial and appellate judges who have excellent political skills and instincts as well as experience. These judges use them to benefit the branch as much as they can. Even so, the number of such judges is relatively small, they are not full-time politicians, and they are largely removed from politics by their job. The task of countering the impact of the news media and the Internet may simply be too large for judges to undertake. Court administrators can help, but their capacity to help is limited, too. At the trial level, political and marketing skills are seldom part of court administrators' job descriptions. Political skill is more often explicitly part of the job expectation for state court administrators. On court-related issues, however, administrators do not get the same attention from the media as a judge or a high-profile attorney would and an administrator's words normally are not given the same weight by the media as those of a judge. Administrators can help to design and manage a campaign to counter a general lack of understanding about courts' roles, but normally they cannot be the people in front of the camera or given attribution for blogs on the Internet.

Courts have a lot of good stories to tell about the job that they are doing in trying to improve the delivery of justice and in their stewardship of government resources. Telling them will be harder, however, if basic civic lessons have not been learned by significant portions of the community. Some approaches to counter these problems are addressed in chapter 11. For now, it is sufficient to note that if significant portions of the citizenry have trouble understanding the role assigned to courts in our government structure, courts can be adversely affected. Having said that, however, neither judges nor court administrators should assume, as many judges have said over the years, that if only people understood courts and how they work, courts would receive greater public support. This belief runs counter to opinion polls taken over several decades that indicate that people with experience of courts are less favorable in their views than those who are without such experience.[10] As Peter Drucker has noted in a broader context: "The temptation is great...to respond to lack of results by redoubling efforts....The temptation, above all, is to blame the outside world for its stupidity or its reactionary resistance, and to consider lack of results a proof of one's own righteousness and a reason in itself for keeping on with the good work."[11] Civics lessons alone are not sufficient to overcome citizens' generally negative feelings about courts.

4.1.1 Separation of Powers

Separation of powers is one of our country's most important contributions to political theory and, in the 20th century, to the advances in judicial and court administration. It is a brilliant response to the training and perceptions of our founding fathers that as power is accumulated, it can be used cruelly against citizens by nefarious people and over time even tends to distort the values of people of good will. Democracies also are subject to the "tyranny of the majority." So our founding fathers invented a way to assure that government is not usurped and individuals do not gain undue power: divide power up and keep any one branch of government (and officials in those branches) from being able to accumulate or claim too much power. Also, insert the judiciary as a protection against the majority's tyranny of a minority.

The separation of powers concept has been critical for those who have been responsible since the mid-1950s and 1960s for the growth and strengthening of the third branch.[12] It has driven their vision of what courts can be and has been used effectively to argue for greater state-level control of the judiciary, consolidation and rationalization of court structure, and state funding of trial courts. It probably will continue to be a highly important spur for and ally of the judiciary in the 21st century. It works best for courts at the federal and state levels, however; it is challenged from time to time for county-funded courts and often is on the defensive in city and town courts (see chapter 3).

The concept of judicial independence envisioned by the nation's founding fathers addressed decisional independence. Judges should be free to decide individual cases based on the proven facts and the applicable law as written by the legislative branch or determined by the common law in the absence of legislative action. The judiciary's decisions should be made without regard to what a majority might desire and without fear of reprisal by the political arms of government. "The strict, mechanical justice favored by some legislators is a caricature of justice; real justice must ultimately deal with the application of law to a specific situation and to specific organizations and individuals. Judges have to consider the dignity and worth of an individual in a way that is not possible in the legislative process."[13] Decisional independence is the cornerstone of America's judiciary; it should be guarded jealously by all judges and lawyers, but also by all those in court administration. Court administrators should join judges in defending it against outside attacks, while also being vigilant that no internal administrative decision undermines that independence. This is not a startling idea. I know of no administrator who knowingly would threaten or challenge a judge's decisional independence. At the same time, occasionally judges claim that management decisions threaten their decisional independence.[14] While the perception of the threat often is overblown and might more accurately reflect disagreement with the decision, every administrator must be careful to review any decision so challenged and assure it is changed or abandoned if a judge is correct.

Separation of powers and court administration intersect in three ways: (1) public perceptions about whether courts are doing their job properly; (2) courts' use of "inherent powers" to obtain resources not provided by the two other branches; and (3) local governments' efforts to control courts through threats to budgets and manipulation of support services.

There is an element of separation of powers that is becoming "muddy" in today's world and is not working to the advantage of courts. As indicated, courts are to apply the facts proven by the parties to the law as enunciated by the legislature. When there is no law, American courts reach back to the English common law tradition and "make" law. They extend or apply the common law only in the absence of legislative direction for the facts involved in the case. There is a third area, however, where courts, particularly appellate courts, have to act, which from time to time becomes a source of friction with the other branches of government. If a statute exists but its meaning is unclear or there appears to be a gap in its coverage, the lack of clarity or the gaps often end up being tested in court. Judges are asked to provide the needed interpretation or to fill in the gap. People go to the courts for aid because courts are set up to reach closure. That is, their job is to resolve cases, not leave them dangling forever or until a difficult political accommodation can be reached by the body politic.[15] Given courts' institutional imperative to decide and given a problem or question about a statute, judges act. In some cases they act by saying the law's wording and the legislative history are not clear enough to fill the gap or provide the requested interpretation. In those cases, the issue goes back to the legislative arena. Most of the time, the law's language and the legislative history allow courts to rule and fill a gap or provide an interpretation. In these instances, the decision normally is accepted and everyone moves on. Sometimes the legislature decides the judge(s) did not get it right and will amend the statute to clarify or complete its intention. Sometimes a court's decision is needed because the legislature did not have or take the time to review a bill's language closely before voting for it.[16] Or, compromise language needed to assure enough affirmative votes turned out upon implementation to be too ambiguous. Again, the reason the legislation is contested is not as critical as people's need or desire for clarity. Judicial review is part of the normal ebb and flow of each branch's duties and part of the normal checks and balances anticipated by the founding fathers. Judges, legislators, and most of the public understand this is how government works and should work.

Courts get in trouble, however, when a statute addresses a politically sensitive issue. Too often, the only way the legislature (often in consultation with the executive) can get a bill passed is to compromise on "fuzzy" language or not to address a particularly difficult point. The two other branches know that the judicial branch will get involved because of the ambiguity and often count on that fact.[17] When the lawsuit(s) is filed and the court(s) makes a decision, the political debate rages again. Those who agree with the court's ruling are pleased, but those who disagree attack the courts for all sorts of malfeasance, ignorance, and shameless legislating. These attacks protect the attackers politically, but weaken the judicial branch in the eyes of many citizens who do not understand the dynamics that led to the court's intervention or, more fundamentally, do not understand the role of each branch of government. Separation of powers is operating as planned, but the courts, in effect, have been "set up" by the other branches because those branches would not exercise the political will to resolve the issue(s) in their houses. Ethical constraints on judges largely preclude them from responding to the charges in kind or, in most instances, at all. Most urban and state bar associations have set up committees specifically designed to respond on the judiciary's behalf in these circumstances, but they are not always accorded equal status or response opportunities by the media. Courts have a hard time playing in the political "blame game." Doing poorly weakens courts politically may hurt when they seek to improve court administration.

George Will, a respected conservative political columnist with the *Washington Post*, wrote a column about "activist" judges as the political debate was heating up in late Summer 2005 about "judicial restraint" and "strictly applying, not creating, the law":[18]

> There are…impeccably conservative reasons for regarding judicial review as a valuable restraint on majorities, and hence for having high regard for some judicial activism….
>
> Lincoln's greatness was inseparable from his belief that there are some things that majorities should not be permitted to do—things that violate natural rights, the protection of which is the Constitution's principal purpose….
>
> In their book, "Desperately Seeking Certainty: The Misguided Quest for Constitutional Foundations," Daniel Farber and Suzanna Sherry of the Berkeley and Vanderbilt law schools, respectively, note that judicial review amounts to blocking a contemporary majority in

the name of a past majority—the one that produced the Constitution through democratic ratification conventions....

There are, inescapably, policymaking dimensions of, or consequences from, what these unelected [federal judicial] officials do.

Will's column was written in the context of a debate about filling U.S. Supreme Court vacancies. It applies equally to the states' judiciaries except for the caveat that some states still elect their appellate judges.

Will's column supports the normal checks-and-balances process and even the occasional rejection of majoritarian legislative decisions as a proper and expected part of both independence and checks and balances. Even if Will speaks for most Americans, however, those for whom he does not speak can make it hard for courts in the arena of public opinion.

Why is this germane for court administration? Because initiatives on the court administration side can be undermined or halted by citizen mistrust of or anger at judicial decision making. If courts are constantly drawn into and then quartered over intensely difficult political issues, their status can be weakened. Politicians and then citizens start talking about "Republican" and "Democratic" judges, about "liberal" and "conservative" judges, and believe that courts do not resolve cases based on an application of the facts to the law but on the same political grounds and processes used by the other branches of government.[19] Professor Cass Sunstein of The University of Chicago Law School is heading a study of federal appellate judges' behavior based on their political party affiliation and that of their appointing presidents.[20] He and his team of researchers have reviewed thousands of federal appellate decisions. The results are intriguing on several levels, but two are germane here. First, Republican judges tend to rule more conservatively when all the judges on the panel are Republican and the Democrats tend to rule more liberally when the panel consists of three Democrats. Republicans and Democrats tend to differ in areas such as abortion, capital punishment, environmental regulation, and sex discrimination, among others. When the panel is mixed, however, the minority judge moves in the direction of the majority judges, regardless of whether the sole judge is a Republican or Democrat. At this level, then, the growing belief of many that judging is just an exercise in politics in a different forum has some surface validity, but not of the character or extent argued by some. And the belief is largely untrue when panels are mixed.

It also cannot be assumed that this result has always existed. Presidents of both parties (and governors) in recent years have been looking for more "reliable" appointees, that is, ones whose votes can be "counted on" on certain issues. So, when like-minded judges sit together, the tendency to rule consistent with "expectations" may not be so remarkable. More remarkable, perhaps, is the movement in the opposite direction when one sits with those having different tendencies. The second result may be more critical in terms of the impact being discussed here. It also should be noted that the tendency to rule "conservatively" or "liberally" is not present for all case types. In criminal cases and property rights cases, for example, that is, cases found often in state courts at both the trial and appellate level, there is great commonality in results. All judges are seen to rule in accordance with the facts and established law. At least based on the findings of Sunstein's study to date, except when three judges of the same party are on a panel together, the blanket application of political labels to judges by critics is unfounded.

As at least a partial counterweight to Sunstein's findings, two new faculty members of The University of Chicago Law School commented in 2005 for the alumni magazine about their recent federal court of appeals' clerkships. Jacob Gersen came away from his clerkship impressed by "how careful most judges are in their reasoning and decision. The judges we sat with were almost universally prepared, diligent, engaged, and cared a great deal about getting the law right." Todd Henderson noted that "... the law isn't all about politics, and that justice is not always about power. It's easy to fall into the trap of becoming cynical about law and justice in our society. [United States Judge Dennis Jacobs of the Court of Appeals for the Second Circuit] taught me that integrity and fairness can coexist with strong convictions."[21]

Because of growing beliefs that judges are just legislators in robes, we now see demonstrations outside the Supreme Court building in Washington, DC and in state capitals in an effort to influence decisions. We see letter-writing campaigns to judges and the release of polls about how citizens think appellate courts should decide cases, implying that judges should follow the majority view regardless of how the facts and law sort out. When a court finally decides, those whose views did not prevail see it as a political decision only and are open to punishing that court and, sometimes, all courts, for the "wrong" decision. Rather than being seen as separate and independent, courts are seen as extensions of the political process in the two other branches. In such an atmosphere, attempts by courts' leaders to gain additional fiscal resources, to introduce new programs, to reach out to the community through education programs, or to gain citizens' input into how the court is operating all become more difficult and might be fruitless. Local court administrators probably have no control over these forces, but it is prudent to be aware of them as new local initiatives are put together or more resources are sought for existing staff or programs.

The concept of separation of powers affects courts in one other way. It is the foundation of the concept of "inherent powers." The defining book on the subject states the following about inherent powers:[22]

> The rhetoric... of inherent powers has a tendency to be fulsome and talismanic, so that the mere statement of the concept becomes a sub-stitute for any analysis of whether its use is appropriate or justified....

Further, the application of inherent powers also has been dealt with as though it encompassed one idea.... Basically, inherent powers operate to support judicial independence through four separate applications, not always related....

These are:

Separation of powers...;

Court governance (...*e.g.*, rulemaking, supervision of the bar and judiciary, contempt, attorneys fees, etc.);

Implementation of the adjudicative function, *i.e.*, the common law tradition...; and

Logistical support (ensuring that the court has the necessary personnel, including salaries, equipment, space and other operational essentials).

Inherent powers and court administration intersect primarily in the fourth application, although specific cases affecting court administration may fall into one of the other categories, as well. Often, state courts that are funded locally have called upon their "inherent powers" to mandate the appropriation of additional resources by county government. State-funded courts, including courts of last resort, have used the concept much less often, in a few instances trying to force the state legislature to appropriate additional funds. Anecdotally, court leaders report that when they have obtained a favorable judicial decision, their victory turns out to be largely Pyrrhic, in that they might have won the battle for more funds now, but they probably lost the long-term war. The long-term loss is tied to a souring of relations with the two other branches to the point that it took several years—sometimes longer—to rebuild trust, communication, and positive relations. Even in a government of separate powers, there is a comity and inter-dependence that requires good working relationships among the three branches, whether at the local level or state level. The checks and balances built into our system can be used to punish as well as to support and facilitate. Lawsuits that result in the legislative branch (local or state) having to appropriate funds it does not wish to appropriate—possibly at the expense of programs legislators or the executive desires—do little or nothing to advance comity.

4.1.2 Checks and Balances

The two other branches check courts through the budget process, legislation, and whether, how, and when the executive enforces judicial orders.[23] In a democracy, the legislative and executive branches determine the laws under which we are governed and through which we maintain social and economic order, how we enforce the laws, and how many resources will be allotted to governing. With its originally limited role of adjudicating issues case by case, the judiciary originally was thought of as the "least dangerous branch."[24] In light of the intense debates in recent years about the role of courts in matters thought by many to be "political," it is unclear whether courts still are seen as "least dangerous," but that appellation was apt probably into the 20th century. Some would argue it remains apt today despite contrary rhetoric.

The founding fathers did not address legislatures specifically trying to influence decisions (or protesting decisions made) by threatening or cutting budgets, but they denied Congress the right to lower judges' salaries during their tenure, implying that they understood how budgets could be used as a weapon against courts. A number of legislators, however, have threatened or used the budget process from time to time to express their distaste for courts' decisions.[25]

While the importance of decisional independence is largely unchallenged, the parallel issue of the independence of a court's administration seldom is debated. Yet, if the judiciary is to establish and sustain its independence as a fully functioning branch of government, the independence of its administration also is essential.[26]

There are significant "checks" on trial courts that operate at the administrative level that probably were never thought of by constitutional draftsmen and almost never rise to public attention. The pressures exerted by local government on the administration of courts are effective because of two strong traditions in trial courts: local funding and elected judges. A third factor is local government's inclination to see the court as no different from any other department when it comes to administrative support and budgets.

Locally funded courts remain in less than half the states today, but in that minority of states and in states where state funding is not complete, local funding almost always is accompanied by the county or city providing core administrative services to the court. The local infrastructure (e.g., accounting, purchasing, and facilities maintenance) already exists and is serving all other local departments and agencies, so it is natural and cost-effective for the court to be served as well. If the services are of high quality and provided in a timely manner, both the court and local taxpayers are well served. If they are not, the court's management often has to compromise regarding the level or quality of services that support the judicial function. Court administrators are caught in a bind that has four components: poor or untimely service is too common in local government; local government officials often accept poor service as simply part of being in government; courts are supposed to put up with it like everyone else; and, because it is a "fact of life," not complain. Judges and court administrators understand they cannot change a county's policies or personnel just for the court, but they also believe that being a co-equal branch of government entitles a court to greater consideration than a department within the executive branch. The one area where friction most often surfaces seems to be the budget, where courts often argue they are special and either cannot be cut like the other departments or require increases not provided to other departments. When it comes to the level or quality of service, however, courts seldom are aggressive.

However much the court administrator may jump up and down or seek to persuade other department heads that a court has a special or a time-critical need that requires a higher priority, a special status for or need in the court seldom is acknowledged. There are three reasons why. First, "if we give you special attention, every other department will seek it," with the clear implication that they could not provide the service requested to everyone or do not believe it is appropriate for anyone. Second, they are doing the best they can with the funds and staff available and you just have to accept that. Or, third, the court administrator is trying to "jump the line" by claiming "separate branch" and "special status" and the local officials do not accept that rationale and do not appreciate the court "always" trying to be special.

Three thoughts are suggested by this third explanation. First, it must be noted that the attitude that courts are identical to every other department is far from universal. Many local officials recognize that the court is not like any other department and try to accommodate its needs within the constraints of the first and second reasons. It is just that, more than one might expect, local officials reject the idea that a court's status as a separate branch entitles it to special consideration when allocating or performing support services.[27] Second, many department heads and personnel do not understand how courts operate, the statutory and public safety requirements for prompt action by a court, and the hundreds or thousands of people who enter a courthouse daily compared to the dozens or scores at most other departments. This lack of understanding leads to the third thought: the lack of appreciation of a special status for the court within the local government structure should be recognized by the court's leaders as one of the challenges of the job. Careful, reasoned presentations over time, starting at the top and moving down as low as necessary in the government hierarchy, often are required. In many respects, people in other departments of local government are just like those surveyed for the ABA, they do not understand separation of powers and coequal branches of government.[28] So the court administrator must carry his or her education campaign to colleagues in local government as well as to the general citizenry. Trying to reason with other department heads and personnel will not produce immediate results for today's emergency, but it may produce improved results longer term.

Although frustrating when a court needs services, local officials often are correct that the general lack of resources is simply a fact that must be accepted. There are many demands made on local government and it seldom has sufficient resources to respond to them all. The courts still are part of government and should be subject to the ebbs and flows of income just as other units of government are.[29]

Less appropriate is an effort to punish a court by local political or bureaucratic representatives who are unhappy with the chief judge or court administrator over some real or imagined problem. Common irritants are the court continually requesting better service; trying to insist on service not provided to other departments or agencies; and not accepting any cuts in budget or insisting on a much smaller cut than the locality's chief administrator desires. On rare occasions, local elected officials strongly disagree with a local judge's decision affecting government and seek ways to make their dissatisfaction clearly known. Few threats carry as much weight with government officials, including judges, as the threat or reality of a cut in one's budget (or the absence of an increase when costs increase).

Beyond budgetary threats, when local government officials believe, correctly or not, that the court is not being a "team player," retaliation might occur through degradation in the level or timeliness of services. This affects a trial court in two ways: (1) much of a court's work is time-critical, with statutory deadlines for case events and some time constraints on handling funds and on notifications to other government agencies; and (2) depending on a court's size, scores, hundreds, or even thousands of citizens pass through a courthouse daily who can be adversely affected by a nonresponsive support department. There are many stories of trials being postponed or recessed because a heating or air conditioning unit was broken and repair was delayed, or because a computer glitch precluded the court's staff getting enough jurors to the courthouse. If a court's vendors—including appointed counsel paid by the court—are not paid on a timely basis, the court's management is blamed, not the county or city auditor or controller. If a court's computers go down and repair service is slow, police agencies or jails may not receive important notices on time, possibly jeopardizing public safety, and calendars might not be ready for the opening of court the next day. In the ordinary course, judges look to their administrator to assure that these glitches do not occur. When glitches do arise, judges expect that the problem will be corrected as quickly as possible. If the city or county is stonewalling the court because of perceived affronts, the administrator appears to the judges and maybe the public to be ineffective and his or her status is undermined. Sometimes just the threat of antagonism toward the administrator is sufficient to catch the judges' attention and get them to override an administrator's decision, thereby weakening the administrator.

Local officials are not always villains in these scenarios.[30] The desire that everyone, including the court, be treated equally has a surface rationality from an administrative perspective. It is much easier to manage and saves the county administrator, city manager, or department head difficult explanations to other departments if the court gets no special treatment. Difficulties arise because courts are not like every other part of local government any more than the local elected council or board can be treated like the roads department when budget or support decisions are made. Changing one's perspective in this regard is hard, however. Also, judges may be no more sensitive to the institutional imperatives of the county or city than they are to the institutional imperatives of the court (see section 6.3, Chapter 6). Thus, for judges, the most important concern is the thing they believe will facilitate the performance of their professional duties. The second most important concern is that the staff immediately around them who help them daily, are happy. Because of judges' perspectives, courts may make demands on judges' behalf that pose legitimate problems for local government as an institution.

One court many years ago claimed that unless it got the full amount in its budget request, it would have to shut down in May (the fiscal year ended June 30). To keep that from happening, it said it would sue the county for all the funds it said it needed. The budget request included funds for expanding programs and upgrading technology that already were cutting edge in the state. Over the previous three fiscal years, the court received more dollars each year than it had the year before. This particular court had programs most courts in the state did not have. Its budget, both on a per judge basis and a per case basis, was in the top 20 percent in the state. Further, a manager who said he could accept the adjustments suggested by an outside consulting team because the quality of his unit's work would not suffer, was told to keep quiet, that the court wanted to insist on all or nothing. For this court to claim that it could not provide justice without its full requested budget, and that it would have to close if it could not upgrade its special programs, was an abuse of the concepts of separate but equal and independence. Regrettably, this court is not entirely unique in making these types of claims. When such claims are made, county administrators have a right to be both skeptical and annoyed. The administrative desire for uniformity and the fiscal pressures on a county or city are very low on judges' priority list. Local officials quite reasonably can see this as unfair and unacceptable.[31]

The court administrator, as the representative of the judges in dealing with local officials, carries the judges' desires, whether or not the administrator would take a similar position left to his or her own devices. Some local officials are unable to separate the role of advocate on the court's behalf from the personality and person of the administrator, however. That is when the administrator may get in trouble.

Before these situations arise, the chief judge and administrator must be in sync, both with respect to what the court needs and how best to approach the county (or city) to meet those needs.[32] If both individuals are in agreement, the leadership team will support one another and give a consistent message to local officials. If the administrator at any point senses that he or she is getting out ahead of the chief judge or is pressing for something to which the chief judge is not fully committed, the administrator must quickly reassess his or her position and seek firm directions from the chief judge. If the administrator is not sensitive to the political winds both within the court and between the judges and local officials, he or she may be left dangling in the proverbial wind if a confrontation occurs with local officials.

If it looks as though there might be a big fight, especially over the budget, it also is important to inform and obtain the support of all judicial officers. One would want this support in almost all instances, regardless, but in a disagreement over the budget, it is likely that some local officials will "back door" the leadership team to complain directly to individual judges, seeking judicial allies who then will weaken the leadership team's position. Most judges back their leadership team in these circumstances and indicate clearly when contacted that the chief judge and administrator speak for and represent the court, so the county or city should cease and desist. When the bench does this, in most instances the local officials back off and seek an accommodation. On occasion, however, the chief judge or the administrator will press the court's position more strongly than some judicial opinion leaders think is prudent and these other judges will tacitly or explicitly support the local officials' position. When that happens, it is the administrator whose position is at risk. The chief judge cannot be removed as a judge and normally has a limited term as chief that fellow judges would not seek to truncate. The judges may feel they cannot affect the leaders of the other branches so it may appear that the easiest way to resolve the problem is to fire the court administrator.[33] In virtually all trial courts, the judges, not the county administrator, city manager, or the local legislative body hire and fire the court administrator. By acceding to the pressure from local officials, however, judges also cede their authority over their administrative structure. The field of court administration is strewn with the figurative bodies of court administrators whose judges have not provided the needed support, resulting in the administrator being sacrificed to eliminate friction with officials in the other branches.[34]

In such circumstances, the local officials de facto exercise control over a court's administrative support without any legal right to do so. Because judges' decisional independence is supported by and intertwined with a court's administrative independence,[35] the overall independence of the judiciary is affected. Judges do not always recognize the connection between their decisional independence and administrative independence in this context, however, so may not see the dispute as involving the independence of the judiciary. Once in a while, administrative independence on a particular issue is not deemed critical enough to fight "city hall," so to speak. There arises a de facto "check" on court independence that was not anticipated in the formal constitutional structure.[36]

The "crocodile in the bathtub"[37] for local judges is periodically having to face the electorate. Judges are subject to election in 39 states, some throughout their careers and some for reelection or retention after an initial appointment by the governor.[38] Judges worry about fights with the county or city coming back to haunt them in one of two ways: (1) other elected officials will "punish" the judges for not doing as they wish by finding an attorney to run against them, thereby dramatically increasing the time commitment and cost of the next election even if the sitting judge wins;[39] or (2) local officials will publicly attack the court for its poor administration and the electorate will blame the judges and turn them out. Since it is very hard to garner any electorate's interest in arcane administrative issues, general attacks about bad management and irresponsibility are much easier to make than to defend. I have never heard of a judgeship being lost because of an administrator's poor performance, but no judge wants to be the first to whom that happens. The judges' self-interest in securing their jobs trumps any institutional integrity arguments, either resulting in the administrator's evisceration or removal. This occurs even if privately the judges believe the administrator is right. The result not only weakens the independence of the institution, but also is one of the arguments that supports state funding and state administration of trial courts; local officials lose their leverage when they no longer control the purse strings and the infrastructure support.[40] Our government structure at the state level does not insulate courts from checks and balances and from crocodiles in the bathtub, but at least with a state judicial branch and state funding, the separation of powers and the independence of courts are not undermined sub rosa at the local level.

4.2 Courts in Society

Courts' place in society is complex and ambiguous. Courts are to help maintain social order. They also are to protect individuals from the abuse of power by government. They are to protect citizens' safety and sense of well-being. They also are to assure that individuals who are guilty of crimes are identified and punished and those who are not are released. The system is set up to err on the side of releasing the guilty in order to protect the innocent from government abuse. When someone perceived to be guilty by the public is released, however, the public often demands that the system err on the side of convicting the innocent. Courts face a dilemma at this point. Policy makers made a conscious choice centuries ago to lean toward release in order to prevent what was perceived to be a greater evil. It seems that citizens today might make a different choice, but that debate has not been engaged. It is unknown whether, after a full debate, they would choose the appearance of security over limiting abuses by government. Courts must play by the rules that exist, however, not the rules that some in the community might prefer. When the public, or a segment of the public, is outraged over the release of someone thought to be guilty, there are few options for courts. Courts could try to improve civics instruction, but that is of no use in the immediacy of public debate about a specific case. Further, judges have ethical restraints that make it difficult to respond in full.[41] Judges also feel political constraints related to not pointing fingers at others in the system who might use their political muscle against a judge or the court later. Finding the proper balance point is hard in a world that many citizens see as hostile and dangerous. Abuses by government are not seen to be as threatening or as prevalent as the dangers of crime or terrorism. When there is a gap between what citizens view to be the correct result and the result determined in court, the court, not the perception, is faulted.[42]

Judges also are to show wisdom when sanctioning criminals, when dealing with delicate and emotional family matters, and when resolving issues involving children, the mentally ill, and the disabled. Tobin puts the point this way: "The range of social problems demanding the attention of the courts includes alcohol and drug control, juvenile delinquency, the recidivism and rehabilitation of crimes, and the protection of dependent children, the senile, the elderly, the psychotic, and the heirs to property. Each category contains persons subject to harm if treated with distaste, dishonesty, disinterest, or incompetency."[43] Yet legislatures often seek to limit or eliminate judges' discretion, which restricts judge's opportunities to be wise in individual cases. The legislature imposes mandatory sentencing requirements to assure "proper" sentencing, changes the burden of proof on some matters to limit judges' and juries' decision making, and mandates conditions of probation for a number of case types, just to be sure judges do not "mess up."[44] The emotions within families that brought them to court for a divorce often come to be directed toward a judge, and there is frequent second-guessing about how judges deal with those in society least able to care for themselves.[45] Courts are seen by citizens of all political views as safety valves or last resorts for legislation that is flawed or opposed, yet also are to "apply, not make" law. "Justice delayed is justice denied," but attorneys and a few judges are quick to argue that forcing quick dispositions denies justice, too, so there is pressure both to resolve cases more quickly and more slowly. Seldom does the public feel that judges, as in the fairy tale Goldilocks, get it "just right."

Everyone can make mistakes, yet the public has a very low tolerance for mistakes made by government officials, especially if public safety or children are involved. When a mistake occurs in a court case, it often is headline material, with no grace for "everyone makes mistakes." The public understands and appreciates that courts provide finality. If the final decision involves a matter around which there are intense feelings, however, the side that does not like the result will cite the case as another reason why judges cannot be trusted or call the judge's decision "improper legislating" or "judges imposing their personal views." *Activist* and *extremist* are currently popular terms applied to judges whose decisions displease.

The advent of "problem-solving courts" is changing the traditional court model. In courts traditionally, everything is defined by "the case." Each case is adjudicated without reference to other cases that might be pending with this individual, or new cases that arise while the first case is still active, or a party's history of cases. (There are some legal and operational exceptions to this statement, but they are limited and not germane here.) Problem-solving courts focus on the individual and the circumstances that brought that person (or his or her family) into court. Interestingly, the general approach taken in problem-solving courts is not new; what has changed is its application to a broader range of issues and cases. Kerwin, Henderson, and Baar identified the general approach two years before the first "problem-solving court" was created; they called it the "diagnostic approach." The diagnostic approach, they said, "is largely devoted to determining the cause of a problem and devising the proper treatment to eliminate it, or mitigate its most damaging effects. More important... is the representation of society in these proceedings." The authors go on to say that, "perhaps the most distinctive feature of diagnostic adjudication is the role of non-judicial personnel in defining issues and securing outcomes...."[46] The "nonjudicial personnel" they reference are the government and private social service agencies that actually deliver the services needed. Problem-solving courts focus on the individual and the conditions, circumstances, or addictions that brought this person and this case into court. They seek to address these underlying factors through coordinating relevant government and private agencies and services so that in the future this person will not violate more laws or will correct dysfunctional family and personal relationships. The facts and law remain relevant because the defendant or family has to accept the court's authority over the underlying case[47] and they have to agree to participate. Then, however, the focus shifts from the facts in this case and from sanctions and "adjudication," to helping the person or family get control of the things that have made his or her life dysfunctional. The judge serves as the amalgamator and coordinator of the services.

Most people agree that without judicial involvement and oversight, the problem-solving approach would not be effective. The moral authority of the judge and the power of a court to issue orders mandating compliance are essential to gain an individual's acquiescence and conformance to conditions. They also are essential to getting cooperation from the various agencies involved. Drug addicts are placed in rehabilitation programs, but with intense supervision by the judge and immediate and graduating sanctions when the person defaults. As progress is made by the individual, the frequency and intensity of the court's supervision eases until the person demonstrates through his or her actions that a drug-free life is attained. Drug court regimens usually take 12 to 18 months. The person also may be given educational help, job assistance, housing assistance, and anger management skills, depending on his or her needs. Families that have several cases in court have all their cases consolidated before one judge, who then applies the same techniques and restorative treatments to the family as a drug court would to a drug addict. The model for this approach was based on the best drug rehabilitation programs that a judge in Miami, Florida, could find in 1989. The model now also is applied in thousands of courtrooms across the nation to helping the mentally ill, the homeless, those with alcohol addictions, and those who engage in domestic violence.

The model not only changes the way courts address cases, but also has led to new models for cooperation among government and private social service agencies and new ways of thinking among these agencies about how to address problem clients. The Conference of Chief Justices and the Conference of State Court Administrators twice have endorsed problem-solving courts since 2000 and also called for trial courts to explore extension of the model to new case types.[48] Problem-solving courts have proven to be highly effective in addressing the social, physiological, and psychological issues individuals confront.[49] They have inserted courts into social management more extensively and intensively than ever before. They may yet prove to be the foundation for changing courts' role in society and the meaning of the term *resolution of disputes*, although to date that is not the case.

Virtually every judge tries to be fair to all litigants and the legal process seeks to assure that they are, but perceptions of the process vary considerably among court users based on race, ethnicity, gender, and economic status. By and large, white, well-educated, and higher-income citizens view the courts favorably, often quite favorably. When public opinion polls divide answers along racial and income lines, however, courts often do not fare well with people of color and the poor.[50] Gender-bias commissions in a number of state also have found that women do not feel equally treated. A number of state court systems have recognized this issue; many have set up racial and gender bias commissions to document the issues statewide and to formulate ways to address the identified problems. Even so, the latest survey in California, which has had commissions addressing both racial and gender bias and has tried hard to address the perception gaps, shows that by a substantial margin African-Americans view the courts' processes more negatively than others.[51] Court leaders across the nation recognize that there is need to address two important issues highlighted by these surveys: (1) actual bias and undesirable actions; and (2) perceptions of bias that are not consistent with reality. They are trying to remedy both. In the meantime, it makes the courts' assigned role of social stabilizer difficult to achieve and presents challenges to those responsible for court administration. The 1999 national opinion survey poses a direct challenge to court administrators when it reports that 76 percent of whites/non-Hispanic and 72 percent of Hispanics agree or strongly agree with the statement that "court personnel are helpful and courteous," compared to only 66 percent of African Americans.[52]

Many associated with courts, led by judges, say that courts have trouble gaining people's support because half the people who come to court go away mad. While this may soothe some consciences, many opinion surveys, including surveys of self-represented litigants as they leave the courtroom, document that winning is not the most important factor in how people view courts. Courteous treatment, a chance to make a full presentation of their position, and a sense that judges listen are important and possibly more important than prevailing.[53] All three of these can be addressed as management issues. If addressed successfully, general citizens' views about courts would improve even if half the people who come to court continue to lose.

Courts are assigned multiple roles in society, some of which are conflicting. It is not surprising, therefore, that many citizens express concerns about courts in public opinion polls. Fulfilling most of the assigned and perceived roles successfully is made harder by the many sources of information about courts that present inaccurate or incomplete information. The difficulties cannot all be ascribed to others, however. Addressing the perceptions among minorities and women of less just treatment by courts, is a internal matter. Nonetheless, the political attacks on courts referenced in this chapter, particularly on the national stage, demean courts' status and the respect citizens accord both the institution and the process used. Some observers are concerned that if the attacks on courts continue and gain strength, courts' stature and democracy itself will be in jeopardy.[54]

Court administrators can support the judges, attorneys, and informed citizens willing to step forward in support of courts when there are political attacks. More directly, administrators can directly address issues of courtesy, assistance provided to court users, the quality of information provided to court users and citizens, and the ease of access to information, all of which will help with perception challenges. The experience in California of a fairly significant turnaround in favorable opinions about its courts provides encouragement.

4.3 Funding and Its Influence on Court Administration

Cities and towns fund their courts. State-created trial courts, whether limited or general jurisdiction, are funded locally by each county, fully funded by the state, or are funded by a mixture of local and state funding.[55] The second half of the 20th century saw a clear trend toward fully state-funded trial courts, to the point where today, more than half of the states have state-funded trial courts of general jurisdiction, while 15 also mostly fund their courts of limited jurisdiction.

Some of the implications of locally funded courts have been discussed already, both in chapter 3 and above in this chapter. They will not be repeated here. Rather, this section will review how the source of funding affects the focus of trial court leaders and how the leadership interacts with other units of government.

4.3.1 Locally Funded Courts

There are four consequences for trial courts that receive all or most of their operating budget locally. First, their orientation is to the locality. That may seem obvious, but it has several implications. The court tends to view itself as a local institution rather than part of a state system.[56] Statewide rules promulgated by the court of last resort (or other policy-making body) are not seen as quite so compelling. Even if acknowledged as controlling, local interpretation is likely to be more common and varied. Local rules of practice and procedure are seen as appropriate and maybe as necessary. This makes the practice of law by attorneys more difficult if they have a practice encompassing more than one county, as most attorneys today do. Rules and procedures that vary county to county can translate to higher costs for litigants. Forms tend to be developed locally even if there are some state-mandated forms, so multicounty attorneys need a separate set of forms for each county. Even state-developed forms might be modified to "fit" local practice and procedures. And each innovation has to be replicated or "invented" anew county to county, as the state's authority to impose a new program is limited because the state lacks the "hammer" of funding. The obverse is that each court can choose not to adopt a successful new program, leading to unequal treatment of litigants across a state.

Judges and administrators alike tend to see themselves as local officials rather than state officials, so their loyalties tend to be to the policy and political orientation of their county (or city) rather than to statewide concerns and needs of the judicial branch. Each county government develops its own relationships with state legislators, as does each county's trial court(s). As a result, the legislature may hear from the state judicial leadership about an issue of concern plus trial courts from across the state, which may or may not have the same perspective as the state judicial leadership. The issue may be procedural or one of substantive law, but as local courts, trial courts do not feel a strong need to follow the lead of the state policy-making body and may actively oppose the state leadership's position.[57] The legislature is unsure what "the courts" want because it is hearing many voices. This is a particular problem when one or two counties dominate in terms of population and political power in the legislature. If the largest courts oppose a state-level initiative, it may be defeated or materially changed. Thus, statutory changes that would benefit many if not all courts are stymied by the political strength of a few counties or by the cacophony of opposing views.

The second consequence is that court leaders spend considerable time building positive relationships with local officials, particularly those with budget authority. They also have to seek positive relationships with the heads of the departments that provide administrative services to the court(s) so that the service from local departments remains adequate. A substantial portion of court leaders' time *should* be devoted to external relationships. In a locally funded court, there are the elected legislative officials, the appointed city manager or county administrator and his or her budget staff, elected officials running departments such as the sheriff and the prosecutor, and appointed department heads. The time devoted to building positive relationships with all these officials is substantial. The time devoted to these external relations is lost for internal management purposes or internal time is pushed into overtime hours for the court's leaders. In a state with mixed local and state funding, trial court leaders must seek to establish and maintain positive relationships at both the state and local level, which is even more time consuming for a trial court's leaders.

The third consequence is that the court competes with local departments and agencies for funds, which is why positive relations with those with budget authority are so critical. A court's budgetary needs are assessed against local concerns and priorities (e.g., fish and game, tourism, roads, crime, or mandated state costs for welfare or other state priorities). A court in county A may be competing against mental health priorities while a court in the neighboring county may have to compete against funding to support new commercial development to increase revenue. Most court administrators at one time or another have heard some variation of the following question: "How do I tell our citizens that your additional law clerk (or file clerk, or computer software) is more important than children's meals, or putting more cops on the meth lab problem, or helping single mothers get off welfare?" When the county's coffers are relatively flush, questions such as these are negligible. All boats are raised by the rising tide. When revenue is tight or falling, how well or poorly a court does in terms of budget may turn on the strength of its relations with the local budget authorities, both elected and appointed.

Which brings us to the fourth consequence: the level of funding for the courts depends on the relative economic health of each county. In relatively rich counties, courts with good relations with local officials may have current-generation computer support and staff-to-judge ratios that are relatively high, and be able to initiate multiple new programs. Other courts may have trouble replacing outmoded computers, have staff-to-judge ratios that are half to two-thirds what the richer counties have, may restrict public-counter hours because of limited staffing, and have trouble instituting even one new program. "Rich" and "poor" is not necessarily determined by urban-rural-suburban locations or population differences; some courts in "poorer" or smaller counties still can do well in the budget wars if they have strong positive relations with their local legislators and appointed budget staff and there is a strong tradition of support for courts. But these funding disparities, however they have developed over the years, and which exist in every state with local funding, mean the quantity and quality of justice varies depending on where one lives. Similar funding disparities among locally funded schools have led the supreme courts of several states to mandate state funding of elementary and high school education. The issues are similar. Funding disparities among courts provide strong arguments for state funding of the judiciary, because state funding is seen as a way for state officials to begin to address and reduce the disparities. The problems associated with disparate funding and its consequences often are an important part of the movement to state funding.

4.3.2 State Funding

When states assume responsibility for trial court funding, three consequences follow: (1) total costs increase; (2) the focus shifts from local government to the state's judicial leadership and, indirectly, to the two other branches of state government; and (3) trial courts now must compete with each other for resources rather than with local departments and agencies.

Costs increase with state funding for three reasons. These three reasons are in addition to any added cost associated with making staff salaries more equal across the state. First, the funding disparity that is necessarily a result of county funding is corrected, at least to a degree. The well-funded courts are not cut, but courts that had been less well funded are brought up to more appropriate staffing levels and, usually, to better technology. There also often is a move to standardize computer hardware and software across the state to improve accountability and service and to enable decisions at the state level to be made with comparable data; the cost of these upgrades can be considerable. These added costs are not fully offset by any economies of scale that may result from statewide purchasing arrangements and greater uniformity.

Second, prior to state funding, counties either undervalue some of their services to courts within their budget structure or do not reflect some costs anywhere in the budget. When the state assumes funding for the courts, counties are quick to account for full costs for all services in order to enhance their reimbursement dollars. Merely totaling the counties' costs for courts immediately prior to the vote will not reveal these hidden costs. It probably is not even possible to ferret them all out in advance. Yet another wrinkle is that in some states that have made the switch, counties have adjusted their internal allocation of overhead costs in advance of the transfer date to push a higher percentage of those costs onto the court's budget, and, therefore, onto the state. Again, these costs, if allowed to stand by the state, cannot be determined in advance.

Finally, with state funding, the state administrative office of the courts must build an infrastructure to obtain funds and to manage them.[58] This results in a significant increase in staff at the administrative office even in a relatively small state. Trial courts may not need as many budget and accounting staff as in locally funded systems, but the reductions at the trial court level normally do not offset the increases at the state level because some local administration of and accounting for funds remains. Trial courts' staff is not eliminated and in smaller courts may not even be reduced. Local courts still need to develop budgets, only now to be submitted to and monitored for the state rather than the locality and the state may demand more than counties in fiscal reporting and monitoring.

State funding results in fiscal relief to localities. It may result in some beneficial economies of scale in some purchasing for trial courts. It may enhance uniformity in the allocation of funds among courts. It may lead to enhanced uniformity in procedure across a state. And it may produce other nonmonetary benefits (see chapter 3, section 3.3,3). It is not likely, however, to result in the total cost of funding courts going down.

The shift in administrative focus from the locality to the state affects local administrators in several ways. The leadership team must withdraw from local budgeting relationships built up over time and create new relationships with the state judicial leadership. They will be creating these relationships with people they know, since even in locally funded systems there are numerous state conferences, training programs, and written communications between the state leadership and local courts, but the relationships will have a different character, nonetheless. They also will have to change how they communicate. No longer is "separate but equal branch of government" a relevant argument, since the justification for new funding must be made first within the branch. No longer are local political interests and personalities germane. No longer is the argument, "the judge really wants it," as potentially powerful. Nor is the argument that "state law requires X" as compelling, because the request for funds goes to the body that created the state law and it can decide to suspend its implementation by not funding it this year. The justifications offered to document a need must be adjusted for a new audience.

The third consequence of state funding is that each trial court now is competing for budget dollars against every other trial court, not against the county's road department and welfare department. Now, a court must demonstrate that its need not only has objective merit, but also is greater than or at least equal to the needs of other courts in the state. The justification of a need shifts from interbranch considerations based, at least in part, on the special needs of a separate branch of government, to intrabranch justifications made to a tougher audience, followed by a second review by the legislature and, often, a third review by the executive. The judicial branch audience (the state administrative office's budget staff and probably the policy-making body for the branch) is tougher than local budget officials because it understands courts and probably can judge both absolute and relative need better than local officials.[59] It is harder at the local level to determine if the sheriff's new clerk is more needed than the court's, so the court can use its moral suasion plus separate branch status at times to secure its new clerk. It is less difficult for state officials to assess if court A's need for a clerk, first, is objectively justified, and second, greater than court B's. The positive side of intrabranch review is that the new audience also understands the nature of the need and the impact of the need not being filled. To that extent, the intrabranch review, at least in terms of justifying each court's individual need rather than its comparative need, is easier. Whether one is funded by the state legislature or locally, there never are enough funds for everyone to get whatever they want; choices must be made. State review of funding requests is as sophisticated as or more sophisticated than the local court leadership team, so quick tap-dancing about what a court needs is less likely to be successful. Decisions are more likely to be based on objective criteria than on personal and local political relationships. In some courts, that will be a positive development; in others, it will create difficulties.

New criteria of need for new funds must be developed for statewide application. A trial judge might know a local council or board member well and thus is able to get a new chair or a raise for staff with little difficulty. After state funding, that judge has to show other judges and court administrative staff not only that the court has this need, but also that these incremental costs benefit the entire branch and will be supportable in the state legislature. Even if the case is made successfully within the judicial branch, the total branch budget then will undergo another full review in the legislature and, probably, executive scrutiny. From a local perspective, the budget process becomes harder to manage than with local funding.

Courts that believe or can document that they have been historically under-funded by their localities usually benefit from state funding, even with the added levels of scrutiny. Well funded courts, that is, those funded above average or well above average, probably will not be hurt by state funding, in the sense of obtaining fewer operating funds, but the rate of increase in their budgets and their ability to introduce new programs or expand existing ones may diminish.

Notes

1. "Civics Education," released by the American Bar Association, retrieved on Nov. 18, 2005, from http://www.abanet.org.
2. This response may stand in contrast to the response in a 1983 survey conducted by the Hearst Corporation in which it seemed people understood the concept of separation of powers but did not believe it applied in the real world. See remarks of Frank A. Bennack, Jr., in National Center for State Courts, *How the Public Views the State Courts: A 1999 National Survey.* Williamsburg, VA: National Center for State Courts, p. 3.
3. In an August 2006 survey, 59% of respondents could not name the three branches. See Zogby Int'l, "More American know Snow White's dwarfs than U.S. Supreme Court Justices; Homer Simpson better known than Homer's Odessey; Harry Potter better known than Tony Blair," retrieved Aug. 19, 2006, from http://www.zogby.com/features.dbm.'ID+237. A 2006 survey for the McCormick Tribune Freedom Museum also revealed a woeful lack of knowledge about the First Amendment. See Johnson, Anna, "Study: Few Americans Know 1st Amend-ment," an Associated Press article retrieved on Mar. 1, 2006 from http://enews.earthlink.net/channel/news. As a general proposition, it seems that most Americans' understanding of basic government is not strong.
4. See, for example, Hofland, Gina, "Senator Complains to Nominee About Court," an Associ-ated Press news story retrieved Aug. 8, 2005, from http://start.earthlink.net/channel/news, in which Senator and Chair of the Judiciary Committee Arlen Specter, R-PA, is quoted as saying that, "he would question the nominee [John Roberts] on his thoughts about the court's attitude toward Congress and on two cases in which the court limited Congress' lawmaking ability."

5. The 15-year intrafamily struggle in Florida over whether a court's order that Terri Schiavo's life support could be removed led to an attempt by Florida Governor Jeb Bush, the Florida legislature, and the U.S. Congress to block the Florida judiciary's decisions in favor of removing the support. Those supporting the other branches' actions were intense in their support for maintaining the life support. In two polls, one (by ABC News) prior to Mrs. Schiavo's death and one (by the Harris Poll) following her death, however, a majority of those polled—two-thirds in the ABC poll regarding the efforts of the U.S. Congress—disapproved of the handling of the case by Governor Bush, President George W. Bush, the Congress, and the Florida legislature. Langer, Gary, "Poll: No Role for Government in Schiavo Case," retrieved Nov. 20, 2005 from http://abcnews.go.com/ Politics and The Harris Poll, "The Terri Schiavo Case: Paradoxically Most U.S. Adults Approve of How Both Her Husband and Her Parents Behaved," retrieved Nov. 20, 2005, from http://www.harrisinteractive. com/harris_poll/index. Mrs. Schiavo died April 1, 2005; the HarrisInteractive poll for the ABA was conducted about four months later.

6. "To the average person, the term *judicial independence* smacks of elitism and arrogance...the idea of independent judges...has a pejorative connotation in a democratic society fearful of untrammeled official power" (emphasis in original). Tobin, Robert W., *Creating the Judicial Branch: The Unfinished Reform*. Williamsburg, VA: National Center for State Courts, 1999, p. 14.

7. In a 1999 national survey of public opinion, 81 percent agreed that judges' decisions are influenced by politics and 78 percent agreed that judges' decisions are influenced by having to raise campaign funds. National Center for State Courts, *A 1999 National Survey*, pp. 41–42. "And this is just as likely to be a concern in states with partisan elections as in states without." Ibid., p. 3. Both African Americans' and Hispanics' level of agreement was even greater. In a 1992 public opinion survey in California, 58 percent of respondents felt that politics influenced court decisions. See Tobin, Robert W., *Creating the Judicial Branch*, p. 33. While there doubtless are occasional instances where these beliefs are true, they are not nearly as common as the strength of these answers suggests.

8. In the 1999 national survey of public opinion, 86 percent of respondents said they "regularly" or "sometimes" get their news about courts from TV, while 83 percent regularly or sometimes get their court information from print media. Interestingly, 41 percent get their court information from the TV "reality" court shows such as *People's Court* and *Judge Judy*. National Center for State Courts, *A 1999 National Survey*, pp. 19–20.

9. On the other hand, a recent survey of public opinion about California's courts shows an improved view of courts compared to the last statewide survey in 1992. Rottman, David B., "What Californians Think about Their Courts: Highlights from a New Survey of the Public and Attorneys," *California Courts Review*, Fall 2005, p. 7. This result suggests that substantial changes, accompanied by substantial publicity and outreach to the community, reap benefits.

10. See, for example, Yankelovich, Skelly & White, Inc., "Highlights of a National Survey of the General Public, Judges, Lawyers, and Community Leaders," in Fetter, Theodore J., ed., *State Courts: A Blueprint for the Future*. Williamsburg, VA: National Center for State Courts, 1978, p. 6; National Center for State Courts, *A 1999 National Survey*, pp. 7, 18. Rottman, David B., "What Californians Think," p. 8.

11. See Drucker, Peter F., *Management: Tasks, Responsibilities, Practices*. New York: Harper & Row, 1973, p. 145.

12. See Tobin, Robert W., *Creating the Judicial Branch*.

13. Ibid., p. 228.

14. Friesen, Ernest C., Jr., Edward C. Gallas, and Nesta Gallas, *Managing the Courts*. Indianapolis, IN: Bobbs-Merrill, 1971, p. 3.

15. The timeframe within which courts conclude cases varies across the nation (see the discussions of caseflow management in chapters 9 and 12) at both the trial and appellate levels, but even the slowest courts eventually conclude their cases. Because the two coordinate branches normally seek majority support before passing new laws and because there is no timeframe within which a consensus should be obtained, some difficult political decisions can be deferred for decades by the two other branches. That would not be acceptable for courts, which draws some people to go to court rather than back to the legislature.

16. California Assemblyman Jerome Horton was quoted in a Los Angles *Times* article as saying: "If we spend 30 minutes on an issue (in committee), everyone's attention deficit sets in. We're spending five, 10, 15 minutes on issues that will affect hundreds of thousands of people. Sometimes I think the only time a policy gets challenged effectively is when it gets to the floor. That can result in poor legislation. We're turning out broken products." Vogel, Nancy, "Lawmakers Say Nonvote as Significant as Yes, No," reprinted in Redding (CA) *Record Searchlight*, Aug. 29, 2005, p. B-3. This phenomenon is not limited to California.

17. This is not a new phenomenon. See Pound, Roscoe, "The Causes of Popular Dissatisfaction with the Administration of Justice," speech delivered Aug. 29, 1906, reprinted in Levin, A. Leo, and Russell R. Wheeler, eds., *The Pound Conference: Perspectives on Justice in the Future.* St. Paul, MN: West Publishing, 1979, p. 345.

18. Will, George F., "The Value of 'Activism'," *Washington Post,* Sept. 1, 2005, p. A-29.

19. See note 7.

20. "All Too Human," *The University of Chicago Law School Record,* Spring 2004, pp.3–5 and "The Chicago Judges Project," a transcript of a video interview, retrieved July 16, 2005, from http://research.uchicago.edu/highlights/documents/judges_transcript.htm.

21. "The Law School Welcomes Three New Faculty Members," *The University of Chicago Law School Record,* Fall 2005, pp. 26–27.

22. Stumpf, Felix. F., *Inherent Powers of the Courts: Sword and Shield of the Judiciary.* Reno, NV: The National Judicial College, 1994, pp. 1–2.

23. For example, the U.S. Supreme Court's decision in *Brown* v. *Board of Education,* 377 U.S. 74 (1954), would have been only an interesting philosophical dissertation if Presidents Kennedy and Johnson had not committed to assuring the enforcement of its pronouncements and President Johnson had not convinced the Congress to acquiesce.

24. See Hamilton, Alexander, *The Federalist Papers* (1788; Library of Congress), no. 78, http://thomas.loc.gov/home/histdox/fed_78.html. See also, Bickel, Alexander, *The Least Dangerous Branch: The Supreme Court at the Bar of Politics.* New Haven, CT: Yale University Press, 2nd ed., 1986. The judicial article in the Constitution, Article III, is a fraction of the length of the articles defining the legislative and executive branches' responsibilities and powers, because the scope of the judiciary's role was relatively narrow.

25. Congress is not immune from these thoughts. A member of the House of Representatives said in 2005 around the time of the debates about the Terri Schiavo case (note 5) that, "When their budget starts to dry up, we'll get their attention. If we're going to preserve our Constitution, we must get them in line." Quoted in a speech titled "Judicial Independence Under Attack," by Judge (ret.) Thomas W. Ross to the Mecklenburg County (NC) Bar Association's Law Day Luncheon, May 5, 2005, retrieved Nov. 20, 2005, from http://www.meckbar.org/newsevents/news_detail.

26. See Tobin, Robert W., *Creating the Judicial Branch,* p. 146.

27. This might not be such a sore point for courts if the legislative branch or even the county administrator or the city manager were treated similarly. They are not.

28. At times it seems county administrators understand the concepts, they just do not accept that courts should be treated as equal to the county legislative branch or the top executive(s)

of the county. In one county with which I am familiar, the county executive adamantly opposed any special treatment of or consideration for the court in the provision of county services, even though the court was state funded and would pay for any "extra" service, which a county department could not do.

29. There are budget devices that can reduce the impact of the ups and downs of revenue. These are beyond the scope of this discussion.

30. There have been rare instances of personal animus between local officials and a court administrator that has spilled over to operations and policy decisions, but these, fortunately, are very rare.

31. I recall one county executive telling me that she understood that the court was independent and could not be treated like every other part of government, but she needed some way to get the court to recognize it had responsibilities to the rest of county government, too. She could not accede to the fiscal demands being made by the court but did not want to be arbitrary in her response.

32. This is one of those circumstances where the clerk is not necessarily part of the leadership team. If the chief judge and administrator have the clerk's support, that can be very important politically. As the clerk is a local official, however, he or she may not be willing to use his or her political capital to support the court if the clerk sees too much personal risk in doing so. The clerk will fight for his or her budget and seek the chief judge's (and maybe the administrator's) support in that fight, but will not necessarily contribute in a dispute between the court and local officials that does not include the clerk's office.

33. In a few courts of which I am aware, local officials have been very explicit with the chief judge or the bench: "We won't work with your court administrator any more, so fire him or her or the court will continue to suffer degraded service or have continuing difficulties with its budget requests." These demands are blatant rejections of the idea that a court's independence is related to its administrative operations as much as to judges' decisional independence. But they have worked.

34. Tobin, Robert W., *Creating the Judicial Branch*, p. 162.

35. See Friesen, Ernest C., Jr., Edward C. Gallas, and Nesta Gallas, *Managing the Courts*, p 133.

36. Similar checks on courts' power also *could* exist in state-funded systems, depending on how many support functions are performed within the judiciary as part of its being a separate branch of state government and how many are provided by the executive branch. Rather than withholding or degrading administrative support, however, the state legislature and governor more often would seek to apply pressure through the budget or through legislation.

37. Otto Kaus, a retiring justice from the California Supreme Court, was asked in 1985 if he ever took into account public opinion or the specter of an upcoming election when reaching a decision. He replied that he knew he was not supposed to, that he hoped he had not, but the idea of having to face an electorate at some point that might not approve of the court's conclusion and did not understand its reasoning was like having a crocodile in the bathtub. You might try to ignore it, but it's hard to be sure you really have. See Schotland, Roy A., "The Crocodile in the Bathtub...and Other Arguments to Extend Terms for Trial Judges," *California Courts Review*, Fall 2005, p. 11.

38. See Tobin, Robert W., *Creating the Judicial Branch*, p. 13.

39. An Associated Press article entitled "Report: Judicial Election Spending Soars," states that candidates in state supreme court races across the nation spent $24.4 million for television advertising in 18 contests in 2004. In 2000, the total was $10.6 million. See a June 27, 2005, press release by Justice at Stake Campaign, the organization that compiled the data, at http://www.justiceatstake.org/files/JASnewsrelease062705.pdf.

No comparable figures are available for trial judges, but it is safe to assume that the out-of-pocket costs for candidates for trial benches across the nation are increasing comparably. This is critical because many, if not most, state judges over the past 25 years have come to the bench from a salaried public sector position and have limited financial reserves to support a campaign. Raising funds for a campaign poses problems for all judges.

40. They still could try to induce an attorney to run against a judge, however. Even without this, their leverage does not disappear completely unless the county or city is eliminated as a supplier of support for the court.

41. I believe courts have a greater capacity to respond than many judges believe—and a few judges have talked to reporters about the specifics of a case—but my views clearly are minority views.

42. It often is hard to know whether the perception is accurate. The perception that a guilty person was set free may in fact be accurate, but not for the reasons assumed by many citizens or reported by the media. There may have been police misconduct that the courts have made clear would be held against "the state" in a prosecution because the courts have no other way to attempt to influence undesirable or improper acts. Perhaps when a reporter recounts a witness's testimony, the facts seem clear, but when one hears the witness on the stand, the witness is not believable and thus the trier of fact discounts or disregards those reported "facts." It also may be a consequence of the general citizenry not being provided with all the facts or not recognizing the legal impact of some facts that it deems of no or little significance. A debate about a specific case is not the time or best opportunity for a court to offer a basic lesson in legal theory or the historical development of a legal principle. Finally, the public may be outraged because of a "moral certainty" of guilt that does not rise to the law's requirement of "guilt beyond a reasonable doubt." I represented a client on whose behalf I showed that it was scientifically impossible for the key witness to have observed what he said he observed. Therefore, my client was found not guilty. Even so, the judge was "morally certain" that my client must have done something, so lectured him not to try to do it again because next time he would be found guilty. If that was a judge's response, it should not be surprising that citizens also might find the process hard to accept at times. When a criminal verdict is "not guilty" and a civil judgment is "responsibility," lawyers and judges feel the system is working properly. The public does not necessarily agree; it may believe the criminal justice system is broken.

43. See, Tobin, Robert W., *Creating the Judicial Branch*, p. 237.

44. "In criminal law, the legislature looks at a social problem but the judge looks at an individual. The day that this distinction is blurred will be the end of judicial justice." Ibid., pp. 230–231.

45. In the 1999 public opinion survey, the highest percentage of "poor" answers regarding how courts handle cases was for family and juvenile delinquency cases. See National Center for State Courts, *A 1999 National Survey* p. 14. The same was true in California's 2005 survey. Rottman, David B., "What Californians Think," p. 8.

46. Kerwin, Cornelius, Thomas Henderson, and Carl Baar, "Adjudicatory Processes and the Organization of Trial Courts," *Judicature*, vol. 70, no. 2, 1986, p. 99.

47. In the traditional approach, facts control. The absence of facts or a lack of clarity about whether something is or is not true can be determinative. In a problem-solving court, the threshold for the validity of the facts is not reviewed as critically. (This is an important objection of some defense attorneys to the new approach.)

48. Aug. 3, 2000 and July 29, 2004. See Conference of Chief Justices, Conference of State Court Administrators, Resolution 22, "In Support of Problem-Solving Court Principles and Methods," adopted July 29, 2004, retrieved from http://ccj.ncsc.dni.us/CourtAdminResolutions/ProblemSolvingCourtPrinciplesAndMethods.pdf.

49. For example, Berman, Greg, and John Feinblatt, *Good Courts: The Case for Problem-Solving Justice*. New York: The New Press, 2005.

50. See, for example, the surveys cited in note 10, above, and the specific questions and responses cited in note 7, above. Comparable surveys in individual states are similar.

51. See Rottman, David B., "What Californians Think," p. 8.

52. National Center for State Courts, *A 1999 National Survey*, p. 26.

53. See, for example, Maryland Administrative Office of the Courts, *An Executive Program Assessment for State Court Projects to Assist Self-Represented Litigants: Final Report*. Annapolis, MD: Maryland Administrative Office of the Courts, 2005, pp. 4, 27–28.

54. See Ross, Thomas W.. "Judicial Independence."

55. Appellate courts are fully funded by state government.

56. See also, Stumpf, Harry P., and John H. Culver, *The Politics of State Courts*. White Plains, NY: Longman Publishing Group, 1992, pp. 7–8.

57. Tobin, Robert W., *Creating the Judicial Branch*, p. 181.

58. The state administrative office of the courts also may need to add staff to develop and monitor uniform practices and to expand training for trial court personnel. These are administrative consequences of state funding but they might be deemed to be severable from funding.

59. Bob Tobin expresses a counterview that is shared by many in trial courts, however: "It is a truism of court administration that many employees of state administrative offices have a very cursory knowledge of trial courts." Tobin, Robert W., *Creating the Judicial Branch*, p. 169.

Chapter 5

The Environmental Context: Clerks of Court, Prosecutors, and Sheriffs

There are three elected officials in the executive branch of local government who are critical in the operation of the court: clerk of court, prosecutor, and sheriff. (Elected local legislators, other elected department heads, probation departments that are in the executive branch, and some senior appointed officials also are very important, but this chapter is limited to these three elected officials, because their role is central to a court's overall effectiveness.) These officials deserve special attention because they have a direct impact on the proper functioning of the court yet are beyond the court's direct control and from time to time make decisions that work against the court's best interests. Probation officers also directly impact a court's operation, but normally the interests of probation and the court are parallel; negative impacts on a court from the probation function usually are tied to funding (and therefore staffing) limitations on probation rather than policy or operational differences.

5.1   Clerk of Court

In courts of limited jurisdiction, the clerk and administrator positions are combined. Because courts of limited jurisdiction are created or authorized by the legislature, there is no constitutional requirement for a separate clerk of court position. Without a constitutional imperative, legislatures merely provide for the functions; courts decide to assign all functions to one person. The issue of a separate, independent clerk applies only in courts of general jurisdiction.[1] Part of the reform effort of the second half of the 20th century in some states involved wresting control of the clerk's function in courts of general jurisdiction and placing it with the court administrator. As the clerk of court is a constitutional officer in most states, this was a long and difficult process; it succeeded in only a few states. The majority of states still have elected or appointed clerks of courts for their courts of general jurisdiction. These clerks normally are outside of the judicial branch and independent of the judges' control.

Historically, it made sense to have a local clerk of court who could retain and protect the court's records while the judge rode circuit on horseback, normally alone but sometimes with a court reporter, across a fairly large region. Because of the weather and the hazards of travel, it was prudent for the judge not to carry the case files with him as he rode. As communities grew the number of court cases increased, as did the number and size of case files, so weather and hazards aside, it became impractical for the judge to carry case files. Even in urban areas, judges in the early years might sit in several courthouses around the city, so, even there, carrying the files was not efficient.

The function filled by a clerk of court is essential. A court needs someone to be responsible for receiving, creating, storing, preserving, and providing access to case documents and files. Whatever the title of the responsible person, a court cannot operate without these functions being filled. The clerk's responsibilities extend beyond receiving documents and storing them; the clerk also is responsible for providing staff to record what happens in the courtroom (normally called taking "minutes" or creating "docket entries") and for sending notices of upcoming court dates and of case outcomes, either to other government agencies or to the parties. Without the clerical function, the concept of public court records would be meaningless.

There also was a public policy basis for a separate office: It was thought that if judges did not have to worry about the administrative side of court operations, they could work more effectively as adjudicators. "The underlying assumption was that judges could preserve their independence in matters of adjudication without control of the administrative aspects of court operations."[2]

The tasks are technical in nature; there are many details associated with each of the tasks just identified. In the Jacksonian era, during which most public officials became elected public officials, particularly at the local level, clerks of court were put on the list of those who should be elected. Since in those days the job of clerk of court often was less than a full-time job, other tasks were assigned, as well. In many communities, the clerk of court also is the clerk of the legislative branch (the board or council) and possibly the recorder of deeds. By combining several functions that originally required only a limited amount of time and normally involved similar tasks, localities created a full-time, responsible job of importance in the community.[3]

Clerks and court administrators are natural allies, in the sense that both serve the court and help judges achieve their mission. Both also serve the Bar and citizens using the court or seeking information about cases or how the court works.

They divide all the work involved in supporting a court, so each makes the other's job more manageable and easier. Administrators normally assist judges with the task of managing their cases so the clerk's case-based information is essential, as are management reports generated by the clerk and by the administrator using the clerk's data. When administrators are assigned responsibility for collecting fines or fines that are delinquent, the case records are essential, as is closing the loop back from the administrator to the clerk when payment is received. The two positions are, or should be, symbiotic.

By a factor of three or four to one, the clerk of court is responsible for more operations employees than the administrator. The budgets of the two offices are closer to comparable, however, since the administrator's budget includes court reporters' salaries and per diem charges, the cost of verbatim transcripts for indigents, fees paid to various professionals appointed by the court, security, and, depending on the state, adult or juvenile probation. Overall, a clerk's budget may be 80 to 90 percent personnel costs; salaried personnel in the budget managed by the court administrator may consume less than half of the total unless probation is a court responsibility, in which case personnel costs represent a much higher percentage of the total budget.

Despite the symbiotic nature of the two positions, there are natural tensions between them, as well. Clerks served courts for about 175 years before the first trial court administrator was appointed. They assumed responsibility for many of the items mentioned above as the administrator's responsibility by default as much as by design, but they had the responsibility, nonetheless. So in the early days of modern court administration (the 1950s through the 1970s), there were real power struggles in many communities. Many clerks felt threatened by the possibility that administrators eventually could take over their responsibilities, as some eventually did. Also, some clerks just did not want to surrender any control that had once been exclusively theirs. Although no clerk of court and only a very few administrators remain active from the days of those early struggles, some of the animus and distrust remains.[4]

There are a number of factors contributing to the tensions. In some instances, although fewer today than in the early days, court administrators have broader education and have more management experience when they are appointed than elected clerks of court have when they assume office. This has led some administrators to convey a lack of respect for clerks, which automatically generates tension. By the nature of the position, court administrators work closer with the judges than clerks are. This suits some clerks just fine, but others may resent it. Administrators tend to be the ones charged by judges with implementing new programs and thus become the messenger to a clerk that he or she must make some change in procedure or in data entry (and, often, in the supporting case management software). Often, the clerk is told, "This will happen and you will make the change(s)," rather than the clerk being asked for input in advance.

Some public-spirited individuals with relevant management experience, education, and some knowledge of courts run for and are elected to be clerks of court. Some long-term clerks upon retirement "pass on" the position to their chief deputies, thus assuring that the newly elected clerk knows the office's operations intimately and also understands the court. In most of these cases, although not universally, the relationships among the clerks, administrators, and judges are positive and supportive. There also have been many occasions, however, when a political party has desired to reward a hard-working official or volunteer with a reasonably safe sinecure and so runs that person for clerk of court. Management experience and knowledge of the office's and court's operations are not critical elements in the selection process. These individuals may be expected to employ party members in critical positions, to support party policy positions and other elected party officials, and to assist in achieving party goals locally and, sometimes, statewide. The individuals who come to the office in this fashion are good campaigners and usually have good people skills, but are not necessarily good managers.

Fortunately for courts and these individuals, some clerks grow in the job and become very competent and successful clerks of court. Unfortunately, there are numerous examples of poor performance. Sometimes, the only thing that saves the office and the court is the appointment of a chief deputy with the requisite knowledge and skills, although even then, the elected clerk retains final authority. When an administrator sees someone elected to clerk of court who fits this latter description, all his or her antennae go up and sensitivity is heightened. The administrator may find fault even with someone doing a credible job because of this heightened sensitivity. Clerks, both those trying to do their best and those less motivated, often sense this sensitivity in administrators and also may sense a lack of respect. When this happens, the stage is set for problems.

Administrators see the effects of a poorly managed clerk's office. They understand the impact of the nonoccurrence of or delay in a change the court desires.[5] When there are issues or problems, all they can do is negotiate, cajole, and plead for a change; they have no administrative authority over the clerk. Nor do the judges. When there are no problems, there is no frustration or irritation on the court's side. When there are problems, frustration follows quickly.

The circumstances that made a local, independent clerk of court necessary and desirable in the 17th and 18th centuries have long since disappeared. The position in many states is in the constitution, which makes changing the status quo very difficult regardless of the merits or demerits of doing so. The clerks of court normally are elected with the backing of the dominant political party in the locality, so even without a constitutional battle, the political battle in support of a change is hard for courts to win.[6] The code of ethics for judges makes it hard for them to fight politically, and attorney support (if provided) may not be sufficient. Putting the political issues aside, the substantive argument for the continuing independence of the clerk of court can be summarized simply:

Court records are public records that are critical for the proper and fair administration of justice and as a source of local history in many localities. To assure their integrity, someone other than judges (or someone responsible to judges for their job, i.e., the administrator) needs to be in charge. Otherwise, some judges might try to alter records or keep them from public scrutiny in return for bribes or political favors, or for personal friends, or surreptitiously to hide or to correct their mistakes. An independent clerk assures this will not happen.

This argument correctly identifies the importance of court records. It correctly states the risk: History tells us that a few judges have been corrupted by bribes or the need to appease political leaders who helped elect them. Most of these instances of bribes and political favors involve distorting the decision-making process, however, not changing the record after a decision has been made. The argument also overlooks several other points.

- No organization is or can be assured of being corruption free; corruption and law violations have occurred in the highest federal agencies, law enforcement agencies large and small, and in local government offices. The problems almost always can be traced to individuals gone bad and to bad monitoring of behavior, not to the organizational structure or who hired (or elected) the person in charge. Further, I suspect there are more instances in courts of embezzlement and improper sharing of information than of efforts to corrupt records.
- The federal trial courts and state appellate courts all appoint their clerks of court. No one suggests that the integrity of these courts records is or could be at risk. The argument is offered only where there are clerks of state trial courts selected by and responsible to someone outside the judiciary and these clerks are trying to keep or justify their independent status.
- I do not know of any tabulation, but based on my over-30 years in court administration, it seems that there are more instances of staff who, on their own, for friends, or as a consequence of bribes, have falsified records or improperly used records than of judges who have done so or who were responsible for staff doing so. Corrupted staff members have been employed in independent clerk of court offices and in offices managed by administrator-clerks. Independent clerks have not assured the absence of bad behavior. The incidence of bad behavior in courts of limited jurisdiction, which have clerk-administrators, might be higher than in courts of general jurisdiction, but if so, it is because of the nature of the cases assigned to the two courts, not to how the clerk is selected.
- If the only issue between clerks of court and judges were the integrity of the record, judges would have virtually no interest in assuming control of clerks' operations.

Before proceeding further with the difficulties associated with independent clerks, it is important to note that many clerks of courts across the country serve their courts admirably and with little or no friction regarding their activities or support of the court. The clerks recognize that the reason for their office's existence is to serve the court's needs as well as the public's and they do everything they can to respond positively. If an issue arises about treatment of the public, technology that is currently used or is needed, or personnel assigned to specific tasks, the clerk meets with the judge(s) affected and tries to respond to the need. If a judge or the chief judge and administrator want a new management report using the clerk's data, the clerk tries to produce it. If the clerk introduces new technology, the court is informed in advance, its needs and input are sought, and efforts are made to accommodate the court. If the court changes the way it organizes or manages its cases or wishes to introduce a new problem-solving court, the clerk is advised in advance and representatives of that office are involved in the planning and in monitoring implementation; the clerk's problems and issues are addressed during the planning phase. Communication is open and respectful of everyone's roles.

In these courts, the relationship between the clerk and the administrator is cordial, professional, and supportive. Each keeps the other informed and part of the planning process for new programs or changes in existing programs. Some disagreements and differences in institutional perspectives are inevitable, but when these surface, there is a respectful dialogue and an effort to accommodate the other's perspective and needs. The judges or administrator do not necessarily get everything they seek, but there is mutual respect, open communication, and a continuing effort to be supportive and responsive.

Fortunately for judges, administrators, and all of a court's stakeholders, courts that have these positive relationships with their clerks predominate. In these courts, the communication demands on the court's leadership is compounded because there is need for constant communication with an outside office, but that is an acceptable price given the constitutional requirement for a separate clerk of court.

Unfortunately, a significant minority of courts do not have these positive relationships with their clerks. Within this number, there are too many where the clerk and the court seem to be at war rather than part of the same management team. Many of the issues today revolve around computerized information systems or new forms, but sometimes involve personnel issues, as well.[7] In these latter courts, the clerks of court elevate being "equal" to the judges because they also are elected—or "independent" because they are appointed by one of the other branches—to a test of wills. It almost appears that to establish their equality or independence, they feel compelled to oppose many of the court's ideas, almost regardless of their merits. These clerks appear to believe there is a reason for their office's existence that is independent of service to the court and that they can faithfully fulfill their office without regard to the court and its needs or interests. Regrettably, the following are not isolated examples of how an independent clerk can harm a court (and taxpayers) far more than the theoretical possibility of a judge (or a judge's employee) seeking to alter records.

- The clerk refuses to capture in his or her automated information system data that judges need to manage their cases or refuses to modify the software to allow capture of the information desired. Either the court does without or creates procedures (and maybe information systems) that will provide the needed information.
- The clerk refuses to produce management reports the court needs to improve case management or operational decisions.
- Courts have set up parallel computerized information systems with their own data entry staff because they do not trust the clerk's data entry staff or because of deficiencies in the clerk's system. The public in these cases pays for the same information twice, but courts believe the additional expense is essential in order to do their assigned tasks.
- The clerk refuses to reassign a courtroom clerk who is not performing at the required level by either making too many mistakes, failing to capture needed information, or being too slow in updating records.
- The clerk tries to scuttle new forms created by the court by declining to have staff file them (thus requiring parallel files in the judges' offices) or record the data on the forms in the case management information system (ditto).
- The clerk does not address a significant problem of "unable to locate" files or a significant problem of documents not being put into case files in time for court hearings. (In response, I know several courts that require that one copy of a document be filed with the clerk—as required by law—and one copy with the judge. Alternatively, lawyers routinely bring an extra copy of a document to court to hand to the judge because there is an expectation that documents will not be in the file by the time a hearing is held.)
- Judges and administrators shy away from talking to the clerk of court because the level of distrust is so high or the quality of the discourse is so low that every meeting becomes a chore.
- Judges do not trust the data about cases sent by the clerk to the state, so are uncertain of the correct filing, disposition, pending, and other counts, both absolutely and in relation to those reported by other courts in the state. Thus, courts cannot effectively argue for needed resources, the data at the state level cannot be trusted to support a need for new judgeships, and the state administrative office has little or no leverage to require a clerk to improve the quality of data. (A few state AOCs audit the clerks'

statistical reports, but they have no authority to require the clerk to take corrective action if the data are shown by the audit to be inaccurate.)

■ The clerk's courtroom staff (or document-processing staff who have friends among court employees) become the ad hoc conduit to the judges about what is happening in the clerk's office and about what is planned because the clerk does not talk to the court's leadership.

■ Because of difficulties working with the clerk, the court creates work-arounds either for courtroom clerks or for its staff to get needed information and to get reactions to ideas that affect the clerk's office; decisions that should be made and implemented jointly are made unilaterally by the court and put into court rules or administrative orders to force the clerk to respond.

■ The court and the clerk submit separate budgets; the clerk may ask for resources the court believes are not needed or should be put toward different needs. Sometimes in a locally funded system, the clerk is given budget increases but the court is not. At a minimum, this produces frustration in the court. In bad situations, it becomes another source of contention.

■ A clerk will not make a software programming change because of budget limitations, but the court may have funds for such a change it cannot apply because the clerk has a separate budget and the information system is the clerk's, not the court's.[8]

■ If an elected clerk's staff works on political campaigns, at a minimum this can create some appearance of justice issues for the court. In a few cases, clerks have supported opponents of sitting judges, which can make the postelection atmosphere tense, at best, whether the judge wins or loses.

If the above rifts developed between the judges and an administrator-clerk, the administrator-clerk would be fired. When an independent clerk does them, a court's efforts to improve are thwarted, stakeholders and citizens are ill-served, and taxpayers end up paying more than they would in those few instances when an appointed administrator-clerk buckles to an unreasonable request of a judge or judges.

As suggested in section 6.2.2, chapter 6, judges are not always great managers and sometimes they put their personal interests above institutional interests. Therefore, one cannot assume that each time an elected (or independently appointed) clerk opposes something proposed by a judge or the entire court that he or she is simply being an obstructionist. The clerk may be correct in not acceding to the court's desire, either for substantive reasons or because of real budget restrictions. And in some of these cases, administrator-clerks would try to implement a judge's or the court's desire solely or mainly because he or she works for the judges. Thus, an independent clerk may on occasion serve as a desirable gatekeeper and "check" on a judge or a court. These circumstances are not sufficient to support the need for a separate clerk of court, however. The problems cited above are not excessive demands of judges or attempts to advance a personal agenda. They are normal operational needs to further the judge's role of providing justice and resolving cases. Further, even though administrators are hired and fired by the court, they still can act as a brake on excesses of judges in most instances. Without doubt, administrators have been fired for not doing what judges want; administrators know this and this knowledge can affect behavior. In some of these cases, an outside observer would conclude that the judges were wrong on the merits. The question in this context, however, is whether these instances relate to the completeness and integrity of the records—the clerk's responsibility—or other matters that would not involve a clerical function in any event. In virtually every instance, it is the latter, not the former.[9]

As the judicial branch in various states continues to seek to establish institutional cohesion and independence, the issue of the independently elected clerk of court will have to be addressed. No court can claim institutional integrity when most of those responsible for its working tools (case and financial information and hard-copy files) and who are the public "face" of the court, are outside the court's control and, too often, even its influence.[10]

5.2 The Prosecutor

The prosecutor's title varies around the country, so the generic "prosecutor" will be used here. Many outside officials influence what happens in courts, but other than the clerk, none has the impact of the prosecutor and his or her policies.

If courts were as they are depicted by the media, criminal cases would represent about 85 to 90 percent of all the cases filed. In fact, they represent about 21 percent of all filings in state courts, or 45 percent if traffic filings are removed. But of the roughly 20.6 million criminal cases filed nationally in 2003 (the most recent year for which data are available), about 17.6 million were misdemeanors filed in courts of limited and unified jurisdiction. Felonies, which get the most media attention, represented the balance of the criminal cases (about 7% of nontraffic filings). They were filed in general and unified jurisdiction courts.[11] Prosecutors filed and prosecuted most of these 20.6 million cases.[12]

"There is often a strange love-hate relationship between elected prosecutors and judges. Prosecutors can provide a buffer against weak cases and take the heat from law enforcement agencies, or they can open the floodgates to inundate the courts with weak cases, placing the onus on the courts to dismiss cases and to run the risk of being called soft on crime by the police public relations apparatus."[13] The latter prosecutors are the ones who have the greatest negative impact on courts.

The way in which prosecutors organize and allocate their staffs, their charging policies, and their decisions about accepting pleas or going to trial all significantly impact courts' workload, the time it takes to dispose of criminal cases, sentencing decisions, and judges' capacity to preside over the number of trials needed. There also is a trend toward more postdisposition proceedings than there were in the 1970s and 1980s. These postconviction proceedings also are affected by prosecutors' policies. They can file postconviction charges as new crimes or charge defendants with violations of probation. The processing of each type of filing is different, with violations of probation normally being easier to resolve (there is a lower threshold of proof) and resolution is faster than with new criminal charges. Again, a prosecutor's policy choice impacts the court's workload. The impact of their policies is not limited to criminal cases, either. Because criminal cases have priority under both constitutional and statutory provisions, when criminal cases require a substantial portion of a court's time and resources, the majority of other cases may be deferred, which often means more costs for parties in the deferred cases and may mean a de facto denial of justice because of a lack of a timely decision.

Obviously, the volume of misdemeanor cases is huge. Almost all of these cases are resolved by pleas of guilty or dismissal by the prosecutor, but the total time demand of these cases can be significant even though the time a judge devotes to any one case is relatively small. Also, misdemeanors include drunk driving cases, which are more time consuming from a judicial standpoint than most misdemeanors. Felonies, although much lower in number, demand substantial amounts of judge time for each case, among the heaviest demands of all case types.[14] There are more appearances per felony case prior to resolution and the overall time to disposition often is six months or more, depending on the court and how it manages its caseload.[15] Both of these facts also result in more staff time per case being spent on felonies. Trials are longer than for misdemeanors (three to five days in most courts compared to two days or less for most misdemeanors) and a higher percentage of felony charges are tried because the stakes are higher than with misdemeanors, both for society (as represented by the prosecutor) and for the defendants.

A prosecutor's policies can impact the court in several ways. Most prosecutors assign new assistants to handle misdemeanor cases. There are sound reasons for doing so, including the fact that the risk of serious consequences from mistakes is low and it is a good training opportunity before the assistants are assigned to felony cases. If the new assistants also screen the charges filed by the police and sheriff, however, they often do not have the perspective of more seasoned prosecutors so charges may exceed what the evidence will support. When that happens, rejections of the charges filed by law enforcement are relatively low, court filing numbers are high, and a number of cases may end up being pled to much lighter charges or dismissed altogether.[16] For newer assistants, handling misdemeanors, including how they charge these cases, provides opportunities to demonstrate that they deserve promotion. Their limited experience and their desire for advancement may lead to decisions about plea offers and when to go to trial that do not serve the entire system. Similarly, if screening of felony charges is not strict, a larger number of felony charges are filed in court but the end results again might be pleas to reduced charges or higher-than-average not guilty verdicts in cases that go to trial.

Some highly effective prosecutor offices put their most seasoned attorneys at the intake point. They are rigorous regarding the amount and quality of evidence required to file charges, so when charges are filed, the office either gets a plea to the original charge in a high percentage of cases or wins most of the cases that go to trial. Because the office insists that all or the most critical evidence be in hand when charges are filed, the cases also are resolved in a more timely way. New attorneys still can train on misdemeanor cases, but asking them to decide on the charges to be filed and the pleas to be taken, as well, may not be a wise use of resources. Most prosecutors recognize this, so at a minimum will have some system for prior approval of plea deals made by newer assistants. In some offices, however, this becomes a "choke point" that can delay resolution of cases unless managed well. Some prosecutors do not even trust senior attorneys to make "appropriate" plea deals in felony cases, so all pleas require prior approval of a managing attorney. This, too, normally results in delays in court.

When prosecutors are not rigorous about the charges they file or the plea bargains offered, court resources have to be devoted to disposing of weak cases and allocating precious time for criminal trials that may end up with pleas to reduced charges on the day of trial. Some court administrators track the data on criminal filings by charge and then by results; these courts can see patterns and identify points within the process that might benefit from reexamination by the prosecutor. Judges very seldom share these data with the prosecutor, however. When they are shared, it almost always is privately in an effort to suggest to the prosecutor that a reconsideration of charging or plea bargaining policies may be appropriate, but almost never are the data made public.[17]

When a court talks to a prosecutor about these policies, it is not "second guessing" the prosecutor in individual cases nor trying to substitute its policy preferences for the prosecutor's. Judges see almost all of the police reports and often see a lot of other evidence as a result of ruling on motions or presiding over settlement (plea) calendars. Judges are present when cases are tried and when juries return verdicts. They see patterns that may not be apparent to the elected prosecutor and often are not apparent to the individual assistants. Many judges are former assistant prosecutors and some were *the* prosecutor prior to going on the bench. They understand the operation of the office, but more critically understand what is happening in their courtrooms and whether the prosecutor's policies are effective in deterring crime and resolving the mountain of cases with which both that office and the court must deal. The court is worried about the use of its resources, but also about the resources of the defense bar, probation department, and jail facilities. It also can see the impact of policies on victims. If the prosecutor's policies are not effective in meeting that office's mission, judges' perspective of those policies may be better than the perspective of the prosecutor himself or herself.

In most communities, the police chief is the most powerful local political figure, followed closely by the sheriff and the prosecutor. All are "white knights" in the public's eyes because they are seen to be keeping us safe. It is almost always political suicide for a court to use its data and observations to take on a prosecutor in a public blame battle, both because he or she is seen as a "white knight" and because there are ethical constraints on judges that preclude equal footing in the battle. Also, a judge running for reelection does not want the prosecutor as an enemy. Among judges who have lost reelection bids, the loss often can be traced to their opponent(s) charging, rightly or wrongly, that they were "soft on crime."[18]

Trials as a percent of all dispositions in felony cases have been decreasing in both total number and percent of all dispositions in recent years.[19] Today, they range from a low of 2 percent to around 10 percent in most courts,[20] although in a few courts trial rates exceed 10 percent. The percentages vary because of policies in the prosecutor's office. Realistically, the court has little or no ability to modify those policies. In a few communities, mutual respect between the organizations (or a respected judge who used to be an assistant prosecutor or the prosecutor) will enable open dialogue, but prosecutors are rightfully jealous of their discretion and it would be improper for judges to seek to dictate a prosecutor's policies.

Even so, courts cannot be indifferent to prosecutors' policies, either. If a court disposes of 1,000 felonies in a year, the number of trials a court has to manage could range from 20 to 100, depending on how the prosecutor approaches his or her workload. Some prosecutors think if they are "tough" on plea offers, they will force defendants to plead to the original charges in a higher percent of cases and they can advise the public they do not "bargain away their interests." This works only if the prosecutor gets convictions in at least 70 percent of the trials, as good prosecutors will.[21] If the prosecutor insists on a lot of trials and then gets guilty verdicts on somewhere around half or even fewer of the cases, the "I'm tough because I don't plea bargain" policy is counterproductive. Defendants will feel they have nothing to lose by rolling the dice and insisting on a trial.[22] A court must respond by assuring a realistic threat of trial, which means assuring the availability of judges. The court, therefore, has to allocate resources for as few as 30 to 100 felony trial days per year (with a 2% trial rate) up to 500 trial days (in the 10% trial rate courts), based on prosecutorial decision making. Studies suggest a typical judge can average around 80 to 85 trial days a year, with the balance of the judge's time spent on pretrial and posttrial matters. A court, therefore, could assign as few as one judge to handle felony cases or might need five or six judges for the same number of felony filings, depending on the prosecutor. The resource impact of prosecutorial discretion is clear.[23]

Judges also understand that prosecutors do not necessarily feel any obligation to assist the court to deal with the criminal caseload or, for that matter, other cases impacted by a heavy criminal workload. I interviewed the prosecutor in one county where the trial rate was in the teens because the prosecutor had a "no plea bargain" policy. That is, close to trial he insisted on pleas to the original charge(s) or a trial. He told me that public safety is the paramount responsibility of government, so if the court has to devote all its judges to handling criminal cases, then that is what it should do. He was indifferent to the impact of his policies on all the civil, family, and probate litigants who also need judges' availability. He was very comfortable with his view of his role and with his policies. Therefore, I did not ask the follow-up question about how prosecutors in other communities managed to assure their citizens' safety with different charging and plea bargain policies and a willingness to work with their courts to ensure that the court's resources are available to all citizens who need them. That prosecutor's indifference to whatever problems his policies caused the court is not typical, but he is not alone, either. When a prosecutor with these or similar views serves a community, the court often struggles to meet all of its obligations.

Regular communication between the prosecutor and the court is very important. When there is regular communication, several good things happen. Both sides can be alerted in advance to planned changes in procedures or policies. The prosecutor can advise the court of an imminent spike in arrests directed at a certain type of crime or geographic area so the court will be prepared for higher than normal filings, arraignments, and case dispositions. If judges see systemic problems with plea offers or in the performance of an assistant, these can be discussed in private to the advantage of both organizations. Data about each operation can be shared and discussed as part of the normal communication, so there are no surprises; anomalies in the data can be studied and discussed based on the numbers and other available information rather than in an atmosphere of blame and finger pointing. Trust can be established over time so when there is a significant disagreement or concern, it can be discussed and resolved professionally for the benefit of the system and of citizens rather than to protect the ego of one side or the other.

Communication does not assure agreement, of course. Communication does not assure that the nature of the problem/issue will be seen the same way. Communication does not assure a meeting of the minds on a solution. Communication does not assure that either side will address a perceived problem as the other desires. Without communication, however, there is assurance that issues will not be identified, solutions will not be addressed or negotiated, and the status quo will continue.

5.3 The Sheriff

In almost every smaller court (15 judges and less) and in most large courts, security is provided by the county sheriff, almost all of whom are elected.

Security in many courts used to be close to an oxymoron. The deputy sheriffs used to be, and still are in many courts, deputies at or near the end of their careers who no longer can operate effectively on the street or who no longer desire to spend hours in a squad car. It was and sometimes still is a somewhat sick joke that the bailiffs are gray-haired, overweight, and slow.[24] There are too many stories of bailiffs falling asleep during court sessions. (Court sessions can be dull, but a bailiff's behavior should not emphasize that point.) As active law enforcement personnel, presumably they maintain currency in use of their firearms, but I have heard joking comments from judges that if an incident broke out in their courtroom they would duck behind their bench (which usually is bulletproof) to avoid being shot by their bailiff. In most courthouses, a bailiff is assigned to each courtroom. When budgets are tight, bailiffs may be withdrawn from courtrooms handling general civil cases, where there almost never is a security risk, in favor of more coverage in the high-risk family and criminal courtrooms, in some juvenile courtrooms, and for perimeter security.

Perimeter security is the security cordon set up at courthouse entrances (or outside courtrooms in some buildings when the court and other government agencies share a building) and around the outside of the courthouse. In most courthouses, sheriff's personnel also are responsible for perimeter security, although some courts have hired private security firms for this function because of the high cost of sheriff's deputies or concern about the quality of the deputies' performance.[25] A large number of courthouses in smaller communities still have no perimeter security, unless there is a specific case or particular individuals expected to pose security risks. This makes these courthouses and the people in them particularly vulnerable to random violence, including fights in hallways related to family law cases, because courtroom security alone often is not sufficient.

There are three issues for court administrators that involve the sheriff. The first is cost. In return for the protection provided, the county charges the court the cost of the sheriff's personnel. In a locally funded court, this is a paper exercise of moving funds from the court's budget to the sheriff's. In a state-funded court, dollars move from the state to the county. The components of those charges can be difficult for the court administrator to determine. The salary and benefit costs of the bailiffs and other assigned personnel are obvious. Management's costs attributable to court security are obvious. What about the bulletproof vests that some (or all) deputies wear? What about their guns and bullets? What about certification training and special training related to courthouse security? If sheriff's personnel transport prisoners to a courthouse, is the court paying actual time spent in transportation, or an average time, or an arbitrary number of hours that represents some outside limit calculated by the sheriff?[26]

Because bailiffs tend to be more senior deputies, their hourly cost, including benefits, is high compared to an "average" deputy. In an effort to assist with the court's budget situation and also to enable more active-duty deputy sheriffs to be on patrol, some sheriffs have created a special, lower-cost job classification of court security officer and assigned these individuals to courthouse security. These individuals may be retired law enforcement officers or younger individuals hoping to become regular deputies, but in any event they cost less than a "regular" deputy sheriff. The mutual advantages from such an arrangement reflect positive relations between the sheriff, the county, and the court.

Law enforcement is a 24/7 obligation, which creates a need for five people to fill one authorized full-time position, because of vacation, sick leave, training time, and 24-hour coverage. What load factor, if any, is applied to court security personnel, since courts other than high-volume big-city arraignment courts are not 24-hour operations? Even if not a 24-hour operation, courthouses normally are open more than eight hours per day. Is the court charged for just eight hours a day, for an eight-hour shift plus overtime, for extra deputies, or how? If a bailiff is sick, who is called in to cover that position and at what cost? (In the court for which I was the administrator, on occasion it might be a patrol officer for which my court was asked to pay overtime because the officer's current shift was not 8:00 to 5:00.)

Properly designed and executed security is expensive. Some courts will skimp on these costs because funds are not available or because of a perceived lack of threats. If there have been no serious security breaches or incidents in years, it is easy for a court's leadership to believe that the community and its courthouse are safe, so money can be saved by eschewing high security costs. Those perceptions are misplaced, as attested to by many stories every year from around the country of unexpected violence, injuries, and sometimes death in and around courthouses. Even so, the budget games played by a county and its sheriff to impose costs on the court rather than on the sheriff require constant vigilance and represent the downside of a court trying to be responsible about security needs. The court does not have a lot of leverage when it finds a problem, but it is incumbent on the administrator to monitor costs and to seek adjustments whenever appropriate.

The second interface between the court and the sheriff is the design and execution of the court's security plan. Every court should have a security plan (see section 10.2, chapter 10). Beyond reviewing plans developed by other courts and the court security miniguide developed and published by the National Association for Court Management in 2005,[27] each judge and court administrator ultimately relies on the sheriff and other local emergency personnel such as fire and health officials. They are the experts whose job it is both to advise the court on specifics of the plan and to execute the plan properly. But because they are the experts, it may be difficult for the court administrator and the representative judge(s) to get an equal place at the table when the plan is being developed or reviewed. Some sheriffs think very highly of their training and expertise and very little of the court's knowledge and expertise, so are dismissive of the court's ideas or stated requirements. Some sheriffs do not want to assume the new personnel obligations that a full plan might require. Some sheriffs downgrade the risks or believe their offices and officers are close enough to the courthouse to be able to respond to any emergency in a timely way.

Tragic incidents in two major cities in early 2005 should provide a court with support for remaining strong when faced with these types of reactions. The first was the killing of a federal judge's husband and mother in their Chicago home by someone seeking to kill the judge. For reasons unknown, he chose not to wait for the judge to come home after killing the first two people. To that point, home security was provided to federal judges only if there were specific, credible threats. There was an Internet message against this judge posted by a group involved in an entirely different case, but nothing suggesting this individual was a threat to this judge. So no special precautions were taken to help secure the judge's home. I was not privy to any of the discussions that went into the choices about home security prior to this incident, but I would be amazed if they were based on anything other than trying to balance budget considerations against perceptions of risk. In Atlanta, a lone deputy escorted a prisoner who had been caught the day before trying to smuggle a knife into the courtroom in which his state trial was being held. The prisoner allegedly overpowered the deputy, reportedly took her gun, shot her, then went to the courtroom and shot and killed the trial judge and his court reporter. The judge had asked for extra security because of the previous day's incident; the extra security was to be the officer in charge of courtroom bailiffs. He was to be a second bailiff in the courtroom, except he had not arrived in the courtroom by the time the defendant did. Apparently, no one in the sheriff's office recognized the risks associated with the transportation function. If they *were* recognized, the odds are high that the use of a single deputy to escort a defendant to a courtroom was driven by budget considerations, not security needs. The risks always seem to be acceptable until there is an incident. Then everyone is concerned and funds are found. [28]

These stories are offered not to disparage the security personnel involved in these two incidents, but to reinforce the will of court representatives to insist on measures they believe are necessary and then to audit implementation of the plan from time to time. The plan is the *court's* plan. A comprehensive plan may require significant funds, but if the funds are available, the sheriff should not be granted a veto based on "expertise" or to make his or her life easier. If all needed funds are not available, the sheriff and other experts can and should offer advice on priorities, but the priorities established should be the court's, not the experts'. [29]

The third area where the sheriff and court interact is the one most likely to involve a commonality of interest: the appearance of deputy sheriffs in court as witnesses. Law enforcement officers, at least those who regularly are assigned to patrol duties, rotate shifts from time to time. An officer who makes an arrest may have to appear in court as a witness while he or she is assigned to the swing shift (normally 4:00 p.m. to midnight) or the graveyard shift (normally 10:00 p.m. or midnight to 6:00 or 8:00 a.m.). Appearing in court between 8:00 a.m. and 5:00 p.m., therefore, means overtime hours for that officer. Most union contracts for law enforcement officers require that a certain minimum number of hours be paid (usually three or four) to that officer even if his or her actual time in court is less. If the officer's time exceeds the minimum, he or she receives pay for the actual hours in court, whether testifying or on standby. The costs associated with these appearances can add materially to a sheriff's budget. Every law enforcement leader desires to reduce these costs whenever possible. Thus, the court and sheriff have a shared interest in the court managing its calendars more efficiently. A well run calendar reduces the time officers must be in the courthouse and thus helps the sheriff to control costs. Sheriffs—and all leaders of law enforcement agencies—usually are happy to work with courts to improve the management of deputy sheriffs' time spent in the courthouse.[30]

The three elected local officials discussed in this chapter have multiple and profound effects on courts. Courts can and do negotiate regarding operations and new programs and procedures, but the process always involves negotiation and persuasion, not commands. In many courts, the negotiations are success-ful—although not always smooth—but there also are many instances where the negotiations are not successful and courts' desires to improve or to introduce new programs are stymied. An administrator must continually nurture and build his or her relationships with many outside agencies and organizations, but few are as important as a court's relationships with the clerk of court, the prosecutor, and the sheriff.

Notes

1. In states like Illinois, where the courts of limited jurisdiction were absorbed into the court of general jurisdiction, the executive branch clerk of court became the clerk for all functions and case types. By the time California consolidated its trial courts, the clerical function already had been removed from the executive branch and assigned to the general jurisdiction court's administrator.

2. Tobin, Robert W., *Creating the Judicial Branch: The Unfinished Reform*. Williamsburg, VA: National Center for State Courts, 1999, p. 146.

3. In Florida, the clerk of court is the clerk of the county legislative branch and also the county treasurer, so this person is serving all three branches of government in critical but largely technical jobs. This makes the clerk of court one of the most powerful local politicians in most Florida counties.

4. In 1985, the clerks' membership organization (the National Association of Court Admin-istrators) and the court administrators' association (the National Association of Trial Court Administrators) merged into a single organization, the National Association for Court Management. A conscious effort was made by the negotiating parties on both sides to melt

the divide that had existed and to welcome all senior executives in both offices into equal membership. The efforts of NACM's leadership over the years have helped further this goal, but without yet achieving full success. At the 2005 annual conference, there was a workshop titled, "Relationships: Elected Clerks, Appointed Clerks, Court Managers and Judges," for which the description talked about lessening the discord among the identified parties.

5. See Tobin, Robert W. *Creating the Judicial Branch*, p. 70.

6. Because of these political limitations and difficulties, several of the states where the courts have assumed responsibility for the clerk's office have done so through litigation rather than the ballot box.

7. See, Tobin, Robert W., *Creating the Judicial Branch*, p. 184.

8. "The situation [of trying to bring independently elected officials into harmonious relations with the court] is particularly stressful when independently directed employees point to lack of appropriations by a board as the reasons [sic] for failure to support judicial objectives." Friesen, Ernest C., Jr., Edward C. Gallas, and Nesta Gallas, *Managing the Courts*. Indianapolis, IN: Bobbs-Merrill, 1971, p. 17

9. "Locally funded courts are more often compromised by overinvolvement in local administrative practices than by unbridled autonomy." Tobin, Robert W., *Creating the Judicial Branch*, p. 69.

10. Ibid., p. 73; Friesen, Ernest C. Jr., Edward C. Gallas, and Nesta Gallas, *Managing the Courts*, pp. 73, 133.

11. National Center for State Courts, *Examining the Work of State Courts, 2004*. Williamsburg, VA: National Center for State Courts, 2005, p. 14. The percent of all filings represented by criminal cases and the distribution between felonies and misdemeanors varies state to state; these numbers represent the totals for all states combined.

12. Some prosecutors are not involved in the filing of minor misdemeanor complaints; the local law enforcement officers file charges directly with the court. A prosecutor becomes involved in these cases only if a defendant demands a trial.

13. Tobin, Robert W. *Creating the Judicial Branch*, p. 37.

14. For example, Lombard, Patricia, and Carol Krafka, *2003–2004 District Court Case-Weighting Study: Final Report to the Subcommittee on Judicial Statistics of the Committee on Judicial Resources of the Judicial Conference of the United States*. Washington, D.C.: Federal Judicial Center, 2005, pp. 60–62.

15. Cohen, Thomas H., and Brian A. Reaves, *Felony Defendants in Large Urban Counties, 2002*. Washington, D.C.: Dept. of Justice, 2006, p. 23, Table 22.

16. In one court for which I have data, more than half (52%) of the nontrial dispositions of misdemeanors are dismissals. The prosecutor obtained guilty pleas or guilty verdicts in only one-quarter (25%) of the trial dispositions. Yet when attorneys in that office were asked whether they could do anything different in deciding what charges to file or what pleas to offer (all pleas in the preliminary court need prior approval from one supervisor), they said no. The data suggest a significant waste of public resources, but the prosecutor does not share that perception.

17. I put some data into a report for a court that ultimately was shared with the prosecutor. It showed a high dismissal rate for certain case types. I suggested the court might want to share the data with the prosecutor so the prosecutor could investigate why this was happening. Within a couple of days of receiving the report, the prosecutor called the chief judge to request a meeting on this point.

18. In one election of which I am aware, the challenging attorney charged that the incumbent was "soft on crime," or words to that effect. In fact, the judge was handling a civil calendar and was generally viewed as "average" when he had been on criminal calendars in years past.

The media did not point out the facts, citizens got the wrong message, and the incumbent judge lost his reelection bid. This may be an extreme example, but it is not an isolated one.

19. See National Center for State Courts, *Caseload Highlights: Examining the Work of State Courts*, vol. 12, no. 1, Oct. 2005, p. 5.

20. Ibid.

21. Of felony defendants who went to trial in 2002, nationally, 85 percent were convicted. In jury trials, defendants charged with a felony offense were convicted of a felony 71 percent of the time. See, Cohen, Thomas H., and Brian A. Reaves, *Felony Defendants, 2002*, p. 26.

22. When I was an administrator, I personally reviewed all of the juror exit questionnaires. When three or more jurors added comments that the case never should have been tried or that the prosecuting attorney seemed unprepared, I sent the comments to the prosecutor for his information. He always expressed appreciation, but I never got any other feedback indicating anything had been changed.

23. These data are independent of the prosecutor's "conviction" rate that might be announced in a press release or annual report. There, a prosecutor normally would calculate "convictions" by the number of defendants who plead or are found guilty of some charge, often without reference to the original charge(s).

24. I have been in courts where bailiffs are younger and in outstanding shape and, as a consequence, I assume they are appropriately intimidating to anyone thinking about causing trouble. These bailiffs have stood out, however, because they are not the norm.

25. In some states, statutes require that the sheriff provide court security. Courts that use private security firms for some of their security either do not have such statutes or have interpreted the statutes to apply only to courtroom security.

26. In California, within months of the legislature approving state funding of the trial courts, the Sheriffs' Association obtained a law mandating use of the sheriff for court security in each county. Without the threat of competition, the counties and sheriffs took a very hard bargaining position regarding appropriate staffing levels and appropriate costs to be paid by the state. The negotiations between the judicial branch, counties, and sheriffs took four years to reach agreement on these issues.

27. Available through the National Center for State Courts on behalf of NACM: http://www.ncsconline.org.

28. A television show that reviewed the topic of court security indicated that in the next budget after this incident, 40 deputy sheriff positions were added for courthouse security. *American Justice*, Episode no. 247, first broadcast Apr. 27, 2005 by A&E Network. Produced by Judy Cole.

29. In one court with which I am familiar, individual deputies decided that sitting at the magnetometer when foot traffic was light was boring, so they left and went into a nearby courtroom as "extra" security. The judge whose courtroom was protected by the magnetometer screening, and into whose courtroom the deputies went, decided he liked the extra security in his courtroom. Therefore, he would not support the administrator complaining to the lieutenant in charge. When it was mentioned to the lieutenant nonetheless, he said he would look into it, but nothing changed. Both the judge and the lieutenant overlooked the point that eight court staff members were left without protection when the magnetometer was unattended, and that a restroom in which a weapon could be hidden for later retrieval was behind the unstaffed magnetometer. An individual deputy sheriff's boredom trumped a carefully worked out security plan.

30. On the other hand, deputy sheriffs and local police officers tend to oppose these efforts. Many come to rely on and build into their family budgets the extra funds associated with overtime

work. If a court improves its calendar management to the point of reducing officers' time in court, their income is adversely affected. I am aware of some police chiefs who have backed off of agreed-upon changes because of threats from their officers' union. I saw a news report in December 2005 after the Federal Emergency Management Administration terminated reimbursements for police overtime to New Orleans following Hurricane Katrina. A New Orleans police officer was estimating that his take-home pay would be reduced by 50 percent were his overtime income to terminate.

Chapter 6

The Environmental Context: Working with Trial Court Judges

It is essential for a court administrator to understand the roles judges assume on a court, their perspectives, and how they relate to institutional and management interests. Judges can make the administrator's job intellectually challenging, rewarding, and fun, but they also can make it uncertain, frustrating, and highly stressful; over time, an administrator will experience all of these responses. For a successful career, there should be more positive challenges, rewards, and fun than frustration, uncertainty, and stress.

6.1 Election, Tenure, and Removal of Judges

Eighty-seven percent of state judges are elected, both initially and at the end of each term of office.[1] This is one of the continuing influences of the populist Jacksonian Revolution in national and state politics in the early 1800s.[2] In many states in which judges are elected, the governor appoints people to judgeships that are vacated during a term of office. So if a trial judge is elevated to an appellate court, for example, or a trial judge retires or dies in the middle of a term of office, the governor will appoint a successor. This usually results in a high percentage (75% up to over 90%) of judges coming to the bench initially through gubernatorial appointment rather than election. The person so appointed may have to stand for election at the end of the term he or she is filling or at the next general election, but once someone is on the bench and runs as the incumbent, reelection occurs in a very high percent of cases. The number of challenges to the reelection of sitting judges appears to be increasing nationally, and the cost of elections for judicial offices clearly is increasing,[3] but the high reelection rate seems to be holding.[4] Since attorneys must abandon their practices (if in private practice when appointed) or leave their employment (if a government or corporate attorney), this level of job security is seen as a positive. Indeed, if attracting quality attorneys to be judges is one of the goals of the selection/appointment process, being able to provide a high level of job security to good attorneys would be one important way to advance that goal.

Part of the judicial administration revolution since the mid-1950s has minimized the bad effects of long-term tenure even more: there is widespread use of "judicial discipline" or 'judicial conduct" commissions with the power to remove from office or sanction judges who behave badly, lapse ethically, or are unable to perform their office, often because of disability or age. The wide range of possible responses to problem judges available to these commissions provides two advantages over either defeat at the polls or impeachment, both of which are draconian, time-consuming, expensive, and uncertain in their outcome. The first advantage is that problems that have not yet reached truly worrisome levels can be addressed, and if something is impinging on performance that is short of poor health or a permanent disability, problems can be halted or corrected before the situation becomes very serious. Second, when there are ethical lapses, habits that harm the perception of the judiciary, and other minor or limited problems, sanctions can be made proportional to the issue or problem; it is not "all or nothing." The use of proportional and graduated sanctions enhances both the accountability of the judicial branch and the appearance of justice, a key goal of the justice system.

6.2 Judges as Professionals and Managers

Judges are judges, not administrators. While seemingly obvious, this statement says a lot about the environment in which court administration is conducted. Compared to the general population, judges are high achievers with above-average intelligence and drive. Judges are highly skilled, highly trained, and usually hard working professionals who generally have a strong sense of independence and of self. Most judges also are committed to the law, to seeking justice, and to doing a good job.

Few judges are natural managers or, perhaps more accurately, they are not on the bench to be managers. Law schools do not teach management. Continuing education for lawyers rarely covers management. Judicial branch-sponsored training programs for judges that address management usually are offered only to chief judges and assistant chief judges. Judges mostly learn management by osmosis, from listening to their administrators, or by using their common sense and seeing if the result is positive, all of which can be hit-and-miss processes. Management is not a natural skill or a natural way of thinking about problems for lawyers. Plus, judges become judges to do judging, to resolve disputes and determine criminal cases, not to be managers. They normally are very busy as judges; most trial judges' caseloads are very demanding. Taking on management responsibilities takes time away from handling their calendars. Even if a judge is interested in management issues or is drawn to administration, his or her first priority is the cases that need attention, which is the reason they went on the bench. In larger courts, a chief judge normally is relieved of calendar responsibilities, so he or she can devote full attention to administration. This means his or her colleagues must handle the cases this judge otherwise would get, but in a large court it is accepted and recognized as necessary because of the demands of the position. Therefore, someone with an interest in administration at least gets time to focus on administration. In smaller courts and in divisions within larger courts, however, there normally is no relief for administrative time; the chief judge (and a supervising judge in a division) gets a full caseload. Thus, administration is an add-on. It must be fit in and around being in court, reviewing files while in chambers, meeting with counsel to discuss cases, legal research, and all the other responsibilities of a sitting judge. Even for one interested in and skilled at administration, this is a heavy burden. For one with only limited or no interest in administration, taking a management position becomes a burden. That is why in a number of courts the chief judge position is assigned by seniority, rotated every year, and often is filled by judges who would rather not have the "honor."[5] This colors both how judges respond to management issues and how administrators approach those issues with judges. Yet, many judges can be very helpful to administrators. Because judges normally are very bright, because their training and their years of legal practice have made them very good analysts, because of the personality preferences of some, and because their position requires that they consider and resolve policy questions, they often can learn quickly how to think like a manager and thus become wise counselors.

In 1971, Edward McConnell aptly described the administrative environment in a court system. It has not changed materially in the years since.[6]

> A judicial system from an administrative point of view is not un-like a university, in that it is staffed primarily by high-level professionals with a great sense and tradition of independence. Such an institution ... does not respond well to strong centralized administrative authority. ... historically judges have been little concerned with the overall performance and the administrative problems of the system of which they are a part. ... in most jurisdictions, some judges are literally working day and night in an all-out effort to make the court system work well, while other judges go along at a leisurely pace and show little concern for the problems of the courts.

Unlike a university, however, the court as an institution has no control over who becomes a judge, other than for subordinate judicial officers appointed by the judges. People outside the court select the judges. The administrative interest, administrative skills, concern with or interest in being part of a team, are of no interest to those who decide whether someone should or should not be a judge. Universities have rigorous standards for hiring even teaching assistants, but even more so for fully tenured professors. Those standards are applied first by their peers and then by the university's administration. Hospitals can screen doctors; they are not compelled to affiliate any doctor who wishes to be affiliated with them. Scientific research institutes can choose the scientists who will work under their auspices. Accounting and law firms require five to ten years of performance before admitting someone to a partnership. A governor is elected, but he or she gets to select those who serve as staff and the cabinet officials. The legislature and courts are unique in their lack of any capacity to select who will serve in their bodies.[7]

Virtually all institutions can, over time, seek and bring in as colleagues people with the requisite skill and knowledge, but who also share their values and aspirations, who are compatible personally, and who can work effectively as team players if that is a valued trait. Professionals with administrative skill can be brought in if that is needed and desired. Courts have none of these options with their judges. And skill in administrative matters is not even on the agenda for those making the choices prior to a judge joining a bench. Yet, court administration cannot be avoided once an individual reaches the bench. The court's leaders will bring policy decisions, and sometimes operational concerns, to the bench for resolution. People with complaints, those who want to avoid the consequences of a decision, or to seek a change, contact judges about administrative decisions. Institutions, including courts, usually structure and define both problems and solutions through committees, to which judges are expected to contribute and possibly chair. In time, a need to assume an administrative leadership role in the court may arise. Lawyers do not become judges to become involved in administration, but once they are on the bench, they cannot avoid it.

Most benches contain four types of judges, viewed from the perspective of their interest in and support of management.

1. Very interested in administrative matters with high skills in and understanding of management. On a smaller bench—under 15—there might be one or two such judges; on a larger bench, maybe 10 percent.
2. Limited interest in administrative matters but willing to help with them and to support leadership initiatives—up to about 25 percent.
3. Largely indifferent to administrative matters, preferring to concentrate on their judicial assignments, and to leave "administration" to the leadership, including the administrator; will cooperate with leadership initiatives and assist from time to time, so long as assisting with administration does not take too much time or energy away from judging—perhaps half of the bench.

4. Largely self-centered, "I'll do my own thing, so you can do whatever you want so long as it does not impact me," and often initially antagonistic to change that is seen as affecting them personally or those with whom they work most closely—about 10 to 15 percent.[8]

The consequence of these different personalities and perspectives is not good for court administration. "No [management] success results or should be expected unless the court is of a single mind in support of a managerial team. A unity of purpose is a prerequisite. In a judicial setting, this is a rarity."[9]

One caveat regarding the four categories, but particularly the first: A judge's interest in management and desire to be involved—or a judge's indifference—does not necessarily mean support for the administrator. As indicated, most judges are happy to leave administration to the administrator so they can concentrate on being a judge; that is why they became judges and that is why they hire administrators. Even so, when they are energized about a specific issue, most often personnel decisions involving individual employees or something that affects them personally, some judges assert authority as "the boss" and seek to control decisions. They simply have a hard time leaving management to the managers when they feel the manager is wrong, is not acting quickly enough, might make the wrong decision, or they feel personally affected. One judge told me that when he was the senior partner in his law firm, he was the final arbiter in personnel matters. Now that he was a judge, he viewed his role as unchanged and that everyone in the courthouse was his personal responsibility, so he was compelled to intervene when he felt a particular result was appropriate.[10]

Beyond undermining the authority of the administrator—staff quickly learn that they can dictate, stop, or reverse an administrator's decision by appealing to such a judge for a particular result—the judge puts him- or herself at risk legally. When making judicial decisions, a judge has absolute legal immunity. When making administrative decisions a judge lacks immunity and is as much at risk of being sued (and losing) as any staff manager. Some judges do not recognize the distinction or, if they do, rationalize their involvement as somehow being tied to their judicial decision making, thus preserving their authority and their immunity.[11]

Judges do not necessarily limit their concern and involvement to big issues or policy matters. They can, at times, be concerned about seemingly small, possibly inconsequential matters. Bob Tobin has observed: "Lawyers by training and inclination tend to be microcosmic in their thinking."[12] As a result, "Even though the ultimate test of credibility for the chief judge and administrator is the budget and the resources made available to judges, budgetary successes may not atone for consistent neglect of day-to-day judicial concerns, particularly parking."[13] Although concern about the allocation of parking spaces might seem like an exaggeration to make a point, many administrators have been upbraided because a judge believes he or she deserves or requires a better (read, "closer to the door of the courthouse") parking spot. Why does this happen? Friesen, Gallas, and Gallas provide an important clue: "Court organizations, whether large or small, must recognize the professionalism existing within its bounds. Machinery must be provided by which the ego needs of the professionals are recognized and met."[14] Unfortunately for administrators, there are only so many parking spaces close to doors in any given parking area, so the risk is high that someone will be disappointed. Many administrators dread the day that parking spot allocations are announced.

The tendency of some judges to try to intervene in daily administrative decision making, especially personnel matters, seems to vary by court. In some courts there is a strong tradition of judges not being involved in daily administrative matters. In most courts, it is understood but largely untested. In other courts—fortunately, a dwindling number—the tradition seems to be that inserting one's self into daily administration is okay if a judge wants to do so. The tradition is not driven by the skill of judges as managers, but by the vision of the judge mentioned above: judges remain "the boss" in all matters, including daily administration, and the administrator has scope to act on his or her own only until the boss wants a different result.[15] At that point, the administrator is akin to an administrative assistant who is to implement the boss's decision regardless of his or her personal views.[16] The concept that judging and managing are discrete, and that judges should judge and set administrative policy but not manage, has not caught hold in these courts. The better approach for courts is to allow the administrator to manage within his or her area of responsibility, enable a judge to counsel and mentor if the judge(s) feels a mistake is about to be or has been made, and then to monitor for changes in behavior. An administrator should listen to a judge's counsel. A judge(s) may properly see a possible legal or morale issue that the administrator has overlooked. The solution proposed by a judge may be better for the individual involved or for the court. So when a judge is giving the administrator the benefit of his or her perspectives, there is no problem. Problems normally arise after the counseling is completed. If the judge then seeks to remove the administrator's opportunity to exercise his or her discretion by "ordering" a particular result, the judge steps over the line between policy making and managing. A judge also steps over the line at the other end of the timing spectrum, when he or she acts first in response to a staff complaint or concern by "solving" the issue, telling staff what the solution is, and then telling the administrator what he or she has done.[17] When the judge believes he or she has the same authority to order a management decision as he or she has to rule on a legal matter in the courtroom, the judge is inserting him- or herself into administration counterproductively.

The administrator should have the wisdom to listen carefully and give due weight to a judge's advice, but should not be compelled to decide as an individual judge desires. If the administrator makes a terrible judgment that puts the court at some legal risk even after being counseled, or makes several poor judgments of the same kind, the court has a right to dismiss the administrator. If that is not the case, the administrator should have the right to exercise discretion and judgment within his or her sphere of authority without judicial interference; and, if a mistake is made, to learn and grow from the experience. Making mistakes and learning from them are part of the maturation of good managers and good leaders in the private sector. Court administrators deserve the same opportunities.

The best route to take when a judge seems to be stepping over the line from counselor to manager is for the administrator to have one or more heartfelt discussions with the judge about why the judge's actions are counterproductive and why the administrator should retain authority to make the final decision. Often, these discussions will be sufficient if the administrator has the respect of the bench and has previously demonstrated sound decision making. If the administrator cannot convince the judge to defer, or if there is continual backsliding from the judicial side as new situations arise, the administrator has to assess the viability of remaining in the position. The court cannot have two or more administrators. If judges feel it is appropriate for them to intervene when they wish, they do not want an administrator, they want an administrative assistant. The administrator then will have to assess whether to remain and function in the narrower role or to seek another opportunity.

This point is not made to suggest that this level of disagreement or conflict arises often. It does not. Rather, it is to suggest that this type of conflict can arise with any judge or group of judges over a wide variety of issues. One cannot necessarily predict the issue or question over which a major divergence of views might occur. A judge's normal predisposition regarding involvement with administrative issues does not assure support for or opposition to an administrator's position or recommendation. Support or opposition often is issue specific, so an administrator must be well prepared and informed in all instances to be effective.

A judge's training and professional perspective still lead judges to approach and analyze issues differently from the way an administrator would do. Sometimes professional perspectives color their conclusions in ways that are not helpful from an administrative perspective. Normally, an administrator can counter a judge's natural perspective and gain the judge's support, but sometimes professional (and personal) considerations prevail and the administrator has to adjust or abandon a plan. In most cases, if an administrator marshals his or her facts, presents them clearly, and lays out the practical and policy issues that support a recommendation or a decision, judges will understand the analysis and support the administrator. Nonetheless, there are inherent challenges for an administrator working daily with judges that shift the practice of court administration from technique to artful accommodation and adjustment.

As with every group, the degree to which judges' positive qualities are found on a bench can vary. Judges who do not work hard pose the greatest challenge for a court's leaders, particularly the chief judge. It is the chief judge who must find an assignment for such a judge that does not unduly hurt the court and litigants.

It is the chief judge who, occasionally, must field complaints about such a judge from the Bar and citizens. The other difficult personality is the passive-aggressive judge who sits in meetings and does not raise concerns or objections but then goes back to his or her courtroom and does whatever he or she chooses, seemingly indifferent to the corporate decision. The ethos of judicial interaction normally means that these judges are not confronted directly or even counseled or mentored much. They are independently elected, answerable to no one but the citizens at the ballot box, and equal to all their colleagues. Even if subject to reappointment rather than election at the end of a term of office, traits that negatively affect court administration may not be apparent to the appointing authority. If the judge is regarded as a good courtroom judge, even if he or she is not collegial and cooperative, the absence of these qualities may not be given much weight compared to the judge's judicial demeanor and skills. Colleagues and staff may talk about such judges behind their backs, the chief judge may agonize about what can be done, but "heart to heart" discussions are rare.[18]

Judges also are reluctant to act on a proposed change if even one judge is opposed. Perhaps, the willingness to allow one or two dissenters to postpone or kill a proposal is akin to "senatorial courtesy" in the U.S. Senate, where one senator can block discussion about confirming a presidential appointee for whatever reason he or she has, regardless of the merits. Perhaps, it is a consequence of dealing with disputes all day on the bench; when they step off the bench, they do not want to deal with more conflict, particularly with peers, regarding administrative matters. There also are the dynamics of small groups, discussed in section 12.2 of chapter 12. Whatever the reason, the willingness of a majority of judges to cede a de facto veto to dissenters rather than simply outvoting them often delays and sometimes terminates proposals for change. This kid glove treatment of coequal colleagues makes business and social gatherings more pleasant, but does little to build an institution.[19] The characteristics and qualities that lawyers bring to the bench have led many administrators and some chief judges to characterize managing in a court as like "herding cats." Whether or not this is a fair characterization in all courts, it is clear that judges' diverse personalities and perspectives make court administration a constant challenge.

6.3 The Different Perspectives of Judges and Administrators

When law students discuss an appellate court's decision, they start with the facts in that case and then stretch that set of facts with fewer, or additional, or changed facts in order to test the reasoning used in the opinion as well as the principles they are trying to learn. The goals of the classroom exercise are to create as many exceptional or similar scenarios as possible so the finished lawyer will think about all possibilities and learn to consider all foreseeable circumstances in order to protect a client's interests. This is great for an attorney representing a client. It also is a useful approach for most personnel rules and some operations policies. It is the worst perspective for other management rules and operations procedures. Sometimes, a rule, policy, or procedure written to cover every possible situation will hurt the "typical" case; managing to accommodate the unlikely but possible exception can hinder daily operations.[20] It also can become so complicated that staff dismisses it as unworkable or not understandable. An administrator can adjust to the extraordinary case when it arises because it may arise only once every several years. Staff is told to "consult with your supervisor" and the matter is addressed at that point, but in the meantime normal operations run smoothly. If every operation must be completed as if it were one of the exceptional instances, entirely unnecessary steps might be applied to every case and staff time and costs would increase. To an administrator, this is inefficient and often ineffective. To a judge, a rule or policy that covers all contingencies is natural and commonplace. A judge does not consider the impact on "typical" operations unless the administrator points out the need to do so.

The role of precedent also is different for a judge than for an administrator. The law is grounded in precedents, and trial judges, in particular, follow precedent. That is not necessarily true for administrative issues, however. For an administrator, a "rule" or operating practice is established so it will apply to everyone (or almost everyone); uniformity of operations and applications are a virtue. For a lawyer, a rule or procedure is just another "principle" that can tested and modified by the individual circumstances of individual situations. So if a uniform policy or rule disadvantages or hurts employee A and is thought to handicap the judge, the judge will look for ways to "interpret" the rule by focusing on facts that support "distinguishing" the rule or practice from its uniform application. If the application of a uniform practice produces a "bad" result in the judge's eye, a judge might favor changing the practice by distinguishing the facts of this case from the others—just as they did in law school and when they practiced law—to get a "good" result. The manager might foresee that the change could produce a number of bad results for others, but that perspective is not natural for a judge. The judge's thought process is, "fine, we'll deal with those other cases later, when they arise, just as we do with each case that comes into court." The administrator says, "We need to create and apply consistent policy positions so we don't need to address each individual case each time a new situation arises" and, sometimes, "so we don't violate our contract with the employees' union." They may end up at the same conclusion regarding a policy or procedure, but for the administrator, the policy then is set; for the judge, the policy or procedure is merely the starting point when a new situation arises.[21] The two perspectives are almost automatic for both judges and administrators; they also can lead to tension when specific situations arise. In administrative matters, the judges' perspective can be problematic.

Judges are contemplative and patient, often by disposition and always by the nature of their job. If they do not have all the facts or law for a decision in a case, they usually do further legal research on their own or continue the case and require the parties to fill the gaps. Once all the needed information is in hand, judges often take the issue "under submission," so they can think further about everything before deciding. Administrators seldom have these luxuries. Administrators often must make a decision with incomplete information and without time to contemplate. They might prefer a judicial approach, but understand that a contemplative approach is not possible or desirable in many of the matters brought to them daily for attention.[22] If an administrator takes an issue requiring fast action to judges, the judges' seeming lack of urgency may baffle the administrator. The different nature of decision making for the two positions can lead to frustrations on both sides, but more often for an administrator if he or she believes a quick response is needed and judges wish to defer.

Judges have an endearing belief in the self-executing nature of their orders in cases. In court, judges issue many orders of various kinds, some purely procedural or relate to scheduling, and others substantive and critical to proper case resolution. Most of the time, they seem to believe that all of these orders, whatever their nature, will be carried out according to their exact terms and in a timely manner. "[A]nyone long involved in court administration has encountered ... [judges'] assumptions about the miraculous power of the law to affect orderly change."[23] Cases come back to court almost every day because orders were ignored or, according to at least one party, were not executed properly, but this seems to have little or no impact on the perception that parties will follow an order simply because it exists. Perhaps the belief persists because so many orders *are* followed. When orders are executed, judges seldom see or know of parties' efforts to assure their proper execution. They appear to believe that the order was so clear and comprehensive that all the parties did was to follow the order and everything was fine. It often is not that easy. On the administrative side, they often seem to have a similar perspective. Once they have made a policy decision, it is seen as akin to an order in a case; it should be self-executing or there should be little difficulty implementing it. Because of this perspective, judges not only underestimate the complexity and level of detail involved in successfully implementing some decisions, but also may depreciate the skill sets of the person responsible for implementing their decisions, the administrator. This may be yet another factor as to why some judges do not see administrators as peers (see section 7.1.1, chapter 7). They simply do not understand the gap between making a policy decision and getting it implemented and thus see no great achievement when the result is as they said they wanted it to be.[24] Administrators' skill at closing the gap is overlooked. Many judges may feel insulted by this suggestion. Many judges not only recognize their administrators' contribution to the successful implementation of policy but also publicly acknowledge it on a regular basis. An administrator working in a court populated by a number of such judges is blessed. Regrettably, many administrators are not so blessed.

The way in which judges define themselves affects their role in and response to administrative matters and sometimes trumps good management. Judges see themselves first as skilled professionals doing a very difficult job (which they are), then as important members of the local body politic and the community (even in state-funded systems), then possibly as subject-matter experts, then as managers responsible for the well-being and happiness of those who work most directly with them (but normally only for those individuals), and, eventually, as part of an institution called "the court." For administrators, "the court" is first or second in their hierarchy of defining job characteristics.[25] Both judges and administrators must recognize that these perspectives lead to different responses to the same stimulus.

There are two factors that those in court administration, including chief judges, forget at their peril: (1) judges look at the same facts and circumstances seen by an administrator and see them first through the prism of how a decision or change will affect their professional work and status and occasionally how a decision will be viewed by attorneys or the broader community (looking ahead to the next election); and (2) considerations seen as institutional imperatives to a manager carry little or no weight with a judicial officer if they conflict with their professional imperatives.[26] As a footnote caveat for administrators, even chief judges and other judges with administrative responsibility, although more likely to understand and respond to an institutional perspective because making management decisions comes with the position, do not abandon the tug of professional need and integrity because they have administrative responsibilities. Even the best judicial managers and those easiest to work with are, and should be, judges first and managers second. This professional identity is not unique to judges; all professionals in organizational settings share it to greater or lesser degrees.[27] It is not to be feared, only to be recognized and understood by administrators as a condition of employment.

Peter Drucker gave managers the following advice in the mid-1970s about how to deal with professionals: [28]

> While the career professional needs a manager to be effective, the manager is not his boss. The manager is his "guide," his "tool," and his "marketing arm." The manager is the channel through which the career professional and especially the true specialist, can direct his knowledge, his work, and his capacities toward joint results, and through which, in turn, he finds out the needs, the capacities, and the opportunities of the enterprise of which he is a member.

Drucker's advice is offered in the context of a corporation, where a professional understands that he is an employee, albeit a professional employee. The part of Drucker's statement about a manager helping a professional to direct his knowledge, work, and capacities toward "corporate" goals—read "justice" in a court's context—is valid for court administrators and a central focus of what an administrator should be doing. The part about the professional finding out about and, presumably, supporting the entity's needs, capacities, and opportunities is more problematic in a court setting.

A judge is the boss in the sense that on most courts, all judges vote on the hiring and firing of administrators. The judge is the final policy maker on many issues, and yet also part of the court's workforce, albeit at the top of that workforce hierarchy. This distinguishes judges from members of a city council or a county's board or council and from the many appointed members of local commissions and boards overseeing various government activities. It also distinguishes them from private sector professionals, including doctors and scientists in research institutions. Plus, the people elect the judge in most trial courts, so the judge is subordinate to no one on or with the court, including the chief judge. Even if appointed, whether for a term or for life, each judge still is equal to every other judge in terms of judicial authority. Indeed, the position of "chief judge" is thought by many judges outside major urban courts to be largely titular. It entitles the incumbent to chair judges' meetings, to assign judges to various calendars, sometimes to assign cases to judges, to represent the court to outsiders, and to work with the administrator on management issues if so inclined.

Power within the court and being the "chief judge" are not the same thing. Power among judges comes from strong reasoning skills, people skills, and empathy for other judges' needs and values. Normally, it also involves an interest in and paying attention to administrative matters. These same qualities often are those identified for leaders in the literature on leadership. On a bench, any judge can be a leader, whether or not he or she has the title of "chief judge." This fact plus the dual role of boss and employee complicates an administrator's job and complicates lines of authority. In the early 1970s, Friesen, Gallas, and Gallas made the following suggestion about maintaining collegiality on a court: "An organization of equals finds its strength in a social system that values the status, rights, and independence of its individual members."[29] A chief judge who does that will succeed in keeping all the judges content and probably more willing to try new things. A judge or an administrator who overlooks this advice will not have a happy tenure.

6.4 The Independence of Trial Judges

Many court administrators and some judges contend that a judge is equal to every other judge in decisional independence and whatever is needed to assure that independence, yet subordinate to the needs of the institution insofar as administrative matters are involved. Except for chronic inability to dispose of one's cases, however, I am not aware of any judge being disciplined for ignoring or rejecting a management decision by the entire bench, the chief judge, or the administrator.[30] There are many courts in which most trial judges are happy to avoid administrative involvement and operational decisions and remain focused on what happens in their courtrooms. There are individual judges in virtually every court who feel that way and also judges who are team players when it comes to both setting administrative policies and practices and adhering to them. There also are many courts in which a significant number of judges, often a majority, do not make a distinction between decisional independence and independence from administrative constraint, or at least administrative constraint with which they disagree.[31]

Many courts may have three, four, or more versions of the same form because that many judges believe their version of the form is preferable. I have talked to lawyers who were embarrassed in front of their clients because they had learned in the courtroom that a judge was using a different form or required different steps in the disposition of a case than all the other judges in the court handling these cases. I worked with a number of judges in a large urban court on a pilot effort to reduce case processing delay. A committee of judges and attorneys worked for three months, supplemented by a staff committee advising about the operational implications of the proposed changes, meeting every two weeks, to hammer out a new set of rules for the pilot effort. All the judges in the pilot effort approved the new rules. In less than a year, almost every judge in the pilot had modified the rules, some a little and some a lot. Since no judge felt a need to return to the "official" rules, the administrative solution was to distribute a notebook with all the sets of rules to all attorneys handling cases assigned to the pilot so the attorneys would have some notice of how to approach their cases in each courtroom. The only thing that made this situation somewhat tolerable administratively was that each judge's staff worked only for one judge, so the judges' staffs had to learn only one set of rules and were not affected by all the other sets. The staff members who worked at the intake counter were not affected, either, because they merely had to accept for filing the documents the attorneys submitted, without checking whether the documents did or did not conform to all the various rules. In this same court, it took a judges committee and the administrative staff almost two years to develop a single guilty plea form because each judge handling criminal cases had his or her own ideas about how each item should be worded; compromise was very hard to achieve.

These are not extreme examples. I have designed new forms for an entire state where we collected dozens of variations of the same form from different courts and judges. I have worked with staff committees seeking to develop staff procedure manuals, both statewide and in a single court, where members of the drafting committee were amazed that their colleagues did something they thought was improper or unnecessary—or, sometimes, that was unique and great—yet each clerk thought that what she was doing was necessary because that is what her judge or judges required.

Judges' perception of a need for individuality regarding anything happening in or associated with the courtroom affects administration in other ways. It is harder to assign back-up staff when a member of the chamber's staff is ill or on vacation, harder to rotate courtroom staff periodically, very hard to establish procedures about which the public can be advised through brochures or a court's website, and it reinforces the judges' perception of "my" clerk, "my" bailiff, and "my" court reporter.

The point for court administration in these examples is that uniformity is a virtue for a manager most of the time and often it is seen by judges as unnecessary, an impediment, or a nuisance to be ignored if possible. In other words, the facts are the same, but different conclusions are reached based on different values and priorities. And this difference of perspective is not limited to rules and forms. It extends to personnel decisions, what should or should not be in computer programs, and in virtually every court, how cases should be managed in terms of target times to disposition, the granting or denying of continuances, and what will be deemed "good cause" for a continuance.

The judges hire the court administrator and then also have to work with and, to a limited extent, under the operations decisions of the administrator and chief judge. The situation inherently involves some role confusion for both judges and court administrators. In the early days of court administration, many judges did not see any problem, believing that they were the boss, the policy maker, and the manager when and as it suited them. The administrator, at best, was an administrative assistant. Over time, the number and percentage of judges who have that perspective has diminished as there has been judicial turnover, administrators have demonstrated their skills and value, and as court administration has become more established. Vestiges of these early attitudes remain, however. Peter Drucker, talking about the new corporate world in a world economy, observed that, "in a society of organizations there are no masters. The manager is not a master. He is a superior, but he is a fellow employee. For the first time in history, there is a society which lacks masters."[32] Chapter 5 of this book, in particular, has indicated how much a court operates in "a society of organizations." In courts, unfortunately for administrators, some judges do not and probably never will agree with Drucker.

Court administration literature for years has referred to the judges collectively as the "board of directors," who set policy but leave implementation to the leadership team and staff.[33] Courts in which the collective judiciary functions as a board of directors that remains isolated from implementation of policy are rare. This lack of detachment is not always negative.

Judges need to be involved in implementation decisions because they also are employees. Just as a file clerk might be affected by a policy decision and therefore his or her input can be valuable in deciding on final implementation details, so too with a judge. They also have unique skills and knowledge that is essential in a law-based institution. Further, both by training and their natural intelligence, judges' insights can be very helpful in problem solving. Perhaps, most importantly, the judge and what happens in the courtroom are the focal point for court administration; they are why we have courts. An administrator who believes any decision of significance involving procedure that affects what happens in the courtroom, even if it is procedure that only involves staff processing, can be made without some judicial input and advice does not understand the nature of courts. The "board of directors" may set a policy to develop a uniform procedure that will be reflected in a new form. A good administrator understands that unless judges play a major role in designing that form, the choice of language may not conform to current law and the uniform form may not be used. All of the judges may decide to open a center to assist self-represented litigants; designing such a center without judicial input would risk implementing decisions that do not conform to existing law and also risk judges not promoting use of the center because they see legal or policy weaknesses in its implementation. If staff designed new case management software without obtaining judicial input into what judges need when they are trying to manage cases, the system would fail.

Differences in perspective between judges and administrators can be a positive for a court. Sometimes they can result in a more complete understanding of a problem or of a solution. For example, a number of years ago both judges and administrators were asked to identify the major obstacles to implementing change in their court. Table 6.1 shows the top answers from both judges and administrators. Neither the judges' answers nor the administrators' are wrong. Both sets of answers show insight into both the institutional and personal interests

Table 6.1   Judges' and Administrators' Responses to the Question: What Are the Major Obstacles to Implementing Change In Your Court?

Judges	Court administrators
• Vested interest of judges in status quo	• Change mandated without providing funds
• Judges' priorities: i.e., judging more important than sound administration	• Court organizational structure not conducive to change
• Loss of budget authority	• Lack of unified judicial commitment to proposed change
• Reluctance of judges to yield to central authority	• Conflict with existing rules, statutes
• Protection of territory/turf; impact on existing power base	• Poor communication and coordination with those involved in proposed change
• Blurred administrator/judicial roles	• Judicial independence; vested interests

*Based on material prepared and presented by Dale Lefever, court consultant and trainer

involved. But note that there is only one item on each list that might be considered the same: reluctance of judges to yield to central authority on the judges' list and judicial independence, vested interests on the administrator's list. They both mention funding but from a different perspective: loss of budget authority for judges and lack of sufficient funding for administrators. In most instances, having different perspectives in a group strengthens both problem identification and the development of solutions. Likewise in courts, having both judicial and administrative perspectives at the table can be very synergistic; it also may result in significant communication gaps based on unarticulated assumptions or conflicts in professional perspectives. The other point to be recognized when selecting judges for committees is that some judges are not good team players. Judging at the trial level is an individual exercise. Judges also normally have great confidence in their conclusions. Someone who thinks alone and then feels very confident that his or her conclusion is the correct conclusion does not always work well on a team seeking both to understand the true nature of a problem and then to devise the best solution.

6.5 The Chief Judge–Administrator Team

From an administrative perspective, the relationship between the chief judge and the court administrator is the pivotal relationship on a court. Most of the literature of court administration for decades has talked about the chief judge and the court administrator as a team of more-or-less equals with different skill sets but each needed by the other for the team to be effective.[34] Most observers recommend that both parties assess their strengths and weaknesses and allocate responsibilities accordingly.[35] This approach requires that the chief judge see the administrator as a professional with strong administrative skills. The chief judge will always be the chief judge—the chair of the board, if you will—but he or she must recognize that the administrator possesses skills and perspectives that the chief judge lacks and that benefit both the chief judge and the court. The team needs continual communication and full and frank discussions about administrative matters and how they should be approached and/or resolved.[36] They both should operate on the principle of "no surprises." If the team operates in this fashion, it will be strong and effective.

In addition to mutual respect and full communication, the most effective teams are found where both the chief judge and administrator have things they wish to accomplish, both want their court to be among the best, and the chief judge has leadership skills. These courts usually also need several judges who are supportive of the chief judge's vision and two or three key managers who share the administrator's desire for positive change. If the chief judge comes to office without significant goals for new programs or improvements but is supportive of ideas of the administrator and staff, the court can advance, just not as far or as fast as in the first instance. When the chief judge is indifferent or resistent to seeking improvements, the court still can avoid backtracking if the administrator is respected and looks for opportunities for improvement. The court will not advance, and may retreat, if the team consists of a chief judge who is indifferent or ineffective and an administrator who is only playing a passive role in his or her job, because either he or she lacks the requisite skills or has, in effect, retired in place.

Certain assignments cannot be traded from the chief judge to the administrator. The chief judge must remain the main contact with the judges in chairing meetings, assigning both judicial and committee responsibilities, and in persuading judges about new ideas or programs.[37] In some courts and states, committee chairs are judges even if the issue is operational and staff members are the ones mainly impacted. The imprimatur of a committee recommendation when a judge is the chair of the committee is thought to be needed to gain other judges' acquiescence, even for recommendations that do not directly impact judges. When a recommendation impacts judges directly, a judicial chair may be essential. However skilled and experienced an administrator may be, most judges do not see the administrator as a peer, so do not assess an idea the same way as if it comes to them from a judge.[38] There simply are times when a "robe" must talk to a "robe" to sell a proposal.

In like fashion, from an institutional standpoint, the administrator must be seen to have the judges' confidence, particularly the confidence of the chief judge, and therefore should be the one to carry news to the staff.[39] Normally, the task of communicating with and interacting with the Bar, local and state government, other justice agencies, and community organizations is shared, as it would weaken the administrator if the chief judge were perceived to be the only one who could speak for the court with authority.

There is another respect in which "a robe," whether the chief's or another judge's, is critical for most successful initiatives. No significant change in a trial court or at the state level has been achieved without a judge as the leader. Consequently, all of the research stresses that programs in courts succeed when there is a judicial leader. Also, the core competencies developed by the National Association for Court Management stress the need for judicial leaders. Judges, administrators, or a staff person may initiate a substantial change. If a judge is unwilling to step forward and lead development and implementation of that change and to sell those who need to be sold (judges, staff, stakeholders), the idea will have little chance of success, no matter how conceptually sound it may be. The more general subject of leadership in a court will be discussed in chapter 7, section 7.3. In this context, however, it is important to note that the chief judge or another judge needs to be willing to be the champion of any significant change or new program. An administrator certainly can and often must provide support and assistance, but he or she should be the ally, not the leader. Judicial leadership is needed because any significant new initiative almost inevitably will impact judges' and their staffs' work. A new program also may impact stakeholders in significant ways. Judges, staff, and stakeholders need to know that judges support the new program; if they do not see a judge out front, they may question the court's commitment and take a wait and see attitude rather than provide active support. If a judge is not seen as the champion, no amount of assurance from the administrator or senior management will convince stakeholders that the judges are committed to success.

Of course, having a judge as the leader of a new initiative will not assure success, especially if other judges openly or even covertly oppose the initiative. Other stakeholders also have different priorities and values they bring to a new proposal that will not change just because a judge is leading the way for the court.[40] The absence of a judicial champion probably assures failure, however, in the long term if not the short term. One of the responsibilities of the leadership team is to assure that the proper judge leads significant new efforts.

Many court administrators in the 1970s and early 1980s were thought to be "old timers" if their tenure exceeded three years. There are no official statistics kept on length of tenure for administrators, but today the average or typical tenure is well above three years and probably is approaching six or seven years. Many administrators today hold their positions for ten years or more. This is a clear and positive sign of the profession's maturation. During an average tenure of seven years, the administrator might work with four to seven chief judges, the typical tenure for a chief judge now being two years, though it remains one year in many courts.[41] The administrator must adjust both the areas in which he or she will take the lead as part of the chief judge–administrator team and to the work styles and management preferences of each new personality. Some chief judges will be excellent managers and effective leaders. Some chief judges will be indifferent to the duties of the position, however. The latter serve as chief judge through seniority, or because no one else would take it. They may serve because their names are on the ballot at the next election and they want the chief judge title next to their name on the ballot. Alternatively, individuals may have pet projects to be implemented, but may otherwise be indifferent to the full range of duties that must be assumed. Some of these chief judges are content to hand more of the administrative load to the administrator. Some are not; they like the title and ostensible power, even though they are indifferent to the demands of the job and are unwilling or unable to delegate. The administrator must be flexible enough in outlook and skilled enough with people to adjust his or her style to the style of each chief judge.

Most administrators in most courts have been exceptionally adept at these adaptations, so chief judge transitions have worked well. Even so, after an administrator has been with a court for a period of time, a new chief judge may believe that a change is needed. The chief judge may feel he or she will have trouble working with the administrator or that the administrator is not the person to move the court in the direction desired by the new chief judge. Or, some judges and staff do not like the job done by the administrator and the new chief judge thinks a new team player will be better accepted. And, as suggested above, some administrators burn out, lose enthusiasm, and do little more than wait for retirement. So the administrator is asked or told to leave.[42] I also have known administrators who looked ahead to upcoming chief judges (when courts have succession ladders) or who have worked with a new chief judge for a few months and decided the adjustment task is too great; they have found another job or simply quit and then looked for something new.

The burden of adjustment is on the administrator, not the judge(s). However skilled or unskilled as a manager and leader the chief judge may be, he or she is still a judge and will remain on the court, in most instances until retirement. The administrator remains an employee, normally an at-will employee. The judge does not have to adjust, the administrator does.

Most administrators are hired by "the court," meaning at least a majority (it is hoped, all or a strong majority) of the judges. In some courts the chief judge alone is the hiring authority, but normally in these situations the chief judge seeks the endorsement of key judges, if not all of them. Firing authority usually follows hiring authority, although as implied above, if a chief judge or a strong minority of judges wants the administrator gone, the administrator almost always goes, whatever the formal hiring and firing modality. I know of a state court administrator who was hired by the entire supreme court of his state. When a new chief justice assumed office, he asked for the resignation of the state court administrator. The state court administrator said the entire court had hired him and he required a vote of all the justices before he would resign. He promised that if a majority of the justices desired his resignation, he would submit it immediately. His retention was put to the entire court; the new chief justice was the only vote for his departure. Nonetheless, the state court administrator submitted his resignation. He knew that in the end he could not be effective if he did not have the confidence and support of the chief justice, with whom he would have to work closely throughout the chief's term. I do not know of any comparable stories from trial courts,[43] but the point is the same: Without the confidence and support of the chief judge, an administrator cannot be effective. Sometimes that is not sufficient, but it always is necessary.

6.6 The Administrator and the Bench

Although the administrator's relationship with the chief judge is pivotal, it is not the only relationship in the court that an administrator must nurture. All judges on the bench are both the administrator's boss and his or her colleague. As suggested above, a court's leaders may be a judge or judges who do not currently have a management title. An administrator cannot be indifferent to the true leaders of the bench or to anyone who can initiate consideration of dismissal. Further, the court administrator owes each judge contact and communication about matters of personal interest to that judge (staff assignments to the judge's courtroom, procedures affecting the adjudication of cases assigned to that judge) as well as about matters affecting the entire court in which judges might be interested (e.g., facility plans, vacation policies, changes in personnel rules that might impact the judge's immediate support staff, or software changes affecting the case type the judge is hearing). Such communication is good management. It also is good internal politics.

If the administrator's tenure reaches double digits in length, several judges will become chief judge over those years; future chief judges cannot always be identified several years in advance. Having allies throughout the court cannot hurt an administrator. Many judges will serve on committees and chair committees. Staff members who might not like an administrator's decisions will talk to judges they know. A minority of judges can make an administrator's life very miserable even if the administrator has the support of a majority. I know one administrator of a large urban court who understood that over time his decisions might upset several different judges at any one time. Thus, only partially in jest he said that some judges at any given point would disagree with him and think he should be fired, so his job was to be sure that a majority of judges were not mad at him at the same time. An administrator in a small court can keep in touch with and inform his or her judges fairly easily. An administrator in a large court (over 15 judges) must build regular contact with all judges into his or her routine. An administrator who is not seen or heard from by trial judges except during court meetings will be seen as isolated, possibly as aloof, and will have little or no reservoir of good will when inevitably tough decisions must be made.

The administrator or a member of senior management should staff all judges' committees. Even if a judge puts a lot of time into the substantive aspects of a committee's work, staff work for the committee is needed to prepare agendas and minutes of meetings, undertake research and contact stakeholders between meetings, and assist in the drafting of rules, new procedures, or reports. Staff also may need to be contacted to see what effect a possible change would have on operations. If the administrator or a senior manager attends meetings, he or she also can introduce management considerations into the discussion and will be alert to changes coming along so others who need to prepare will not be caught unaware. Management's presence in these meetings serves important institutional purposes and is recognized as valuable by almost all judges.

6.7   The Relationship between Participation on Statewide Committees and Court Administration

There is another layer of committees relevant to trial court administration: statewide committees studying substantive or procedural topics. Whether a court is locally or state funded, membership on these committees by either judges or senior managers can be very helpful to a court. At a minimum, it gives visibility to those who serve, which is good for them and may assist the court to be seen within the judiciary as well managed and progressive. The benefits are largely psychic for the individuals, but should not be discounted. Indeed, there are few benefits a court can offer a judge and senior staff, so suggesting participation on a statewide committee is one way for court leaders to reward hard working and competent people. Participation on these committees also gives a court advance notice of changes that may occur. Such advance notice may be helpful for budget purposes and for identifying future judicial or staff training needs. In a state-funded system, budget decisions are not made because a court's representatives are on statewide committees, but such participation cannot hurt. If the court's representatives convey the aura of being with a well-run court, a budget request that is on the line between funding approval and rejection may get approval because of the perception that the funds will be spent responsibly by this well-managed court.

6.8   The "Elbow" Staff of Judges

All organizations are "political" in the following sense: people seek power within the organization, try to hurt or step over people they do not like, stroke egos for personal advantage, and desire advancement so act accordingly. Courts are no different. The internal politics that pose the greatest challenge for court administrators are not these, however, but those that involve the "elbow staff" of the judge: the courtroom clerk, the bailiff, and the court reporter. These are the staff closest to the seat of power. These are the staff who make a judge's on-bench time smooth and efficient or difficult. These are the people who sit and chat with the judge during breaks, serve as the judge's gatekeeper, and see the judge in his or her private moments as well as the public times.

Courtroom clerks are clerk of court or court employees who normally are at the top of the staff career ladder, short of becoming a manager. They are (or should be) among the court's best staff; they are expected to perform at a high level and usually do. They should be easy to manage but often are not because they recognize their special status and some (mis)behave accordingly. When courtroom clerks do not like a decision made by the administrator, the judge may hear about it before the administrator gets a chance to advise the judges. When courtroom clerks want something that they do not get from the administrator, the judge will hear about it. The relationship between judge and clerk is close; that closeness helps both parties perform their tasks effectively, but it also can pose difficulties for the clerk of court, the administrator, or both.

Court reporters have high verbal skills, normally are bright, are dexterous, and do work that very few people can do well. They are in relatively short supply in almost every community and their function is essential to the proper functioning of a court of record.[44] They work for the court while taking the record in the courtroom but are independent contractors when producing transcripts. The court itself is the largest consumer of transcripts for criminal cases because it is the court that normally pays for the transcripts ordered by indigents, and indigents often are 75 to 90 percent of criminal defendants. Court reporters are the only court employees allowed to have a private business based on their court work. They also are among the most independent-minded employees conceivable.

Virtually all court reporters were independent contractors until well into the second half of the 20th century. Then, in larger courts, they transitioned into being full-time employees. In smaller courts many became part-time employees (or regular contractors) for the purpose of taking the record in criminal cases, but remained independent contractors hired by the parties, as desired, in civil cases. In this partial employment status, they also usually continued to have a private business of deposition reporting, hired directly by civil litigants to report pretrial deposition testimony. The transition to full-time court employees for both criminal and civil cases—normally without the right to do deposition work—is another change in court administration that occurred in the second half of the 20th century. (In a minority of federal courts, estimated at about 20 percent, reporters still can maintain a private business for reporting depositions in civil cases.) Reporters had not been within the purview of the clerk of court's operation, so they became employees of "the court," and, hence, the responsibility of the court administrator. Because of their transcript business, almost every urban court and a few suburban and rural courts have more employee reporters who earn more per year than judges do.[45] Perhaps it is this history and context that leads many court reporters to approach their employment as if they still were independent contractors, especially vis-à-vis court management.

Judges work closely with their clerks and reporters daily, so they normally support and protect them. Accordingly, an administrator who makes a decision that is unpopular with these personnel not only has to deal with these personnel but also with a judge or judges. In most courts—thankfully, not all—some or all judges routinely stand against administrative decisions opposed by their "elbow" staff.[46]

Bailiffs in most courts are sheriff department employees, but they spend all their working time with "their" judge and in some respects see the judge more than the sheriff. Judges on occasion will support a bailiff regarding a management decision by a sheriff, but they seldom seek to intervene for bailiffs the way they do for clerks and reporters. When bailiffs are employees of the court, part of the "marshal's office," they enjoy the same special status in judges' eyes as clerks and reporters.

Assigning and reassigning clerks and reporters is harder than with any other personnel.[47] Discipline of elbow staff is harder in most courts, and occasionally, a judge will try to block or lessen a sanction. Performance reviews of elbow staff, if provided by a judge, almost uniformly are glowing; only if a judge is dissatisfied with the overall performance of a clerk is anything negative or needing improvement likely to appear in an evaluation. Most judges assert they want nothing to do with personnel matters, yet at the same time seek and often provide benefits for their elbow staff that are unavailable to other staff. Judges may grant "flex" hours around lunch or at the end of the day, or vacation days or time off not cleared with supervisors or other managers of the court. They also may seek pay increases for these staff not available to other staff. Benefits such as "flex" time and days off are justified in these judges' minds by the hard work and occasional extra hours put in by these staff, even if overtime is paid for those extra hours. Sometimes a judge and clerk have an "understanding" that the clerk will not claim overtime pay in return for flex hours, oblivious or indifferent to the labor law requirements regarding overtime pay. Beyond the legal issues, judges often are oblivious to the impact of these privileges on other staff who also are working hard and may be putting in even more overtime hours. But these other staff members are not working at a time and in a location where a judge can see them. The possibility that others who also may deserve this kind of accommodation will learn what the judge's clerk is doing and feel resentment does not seem to be recognized.

Most administrators long to break the tight working bond that exists between judges and their elbow staff. If they could, administrators could assure appropriate treatment of all staff, address some of the unhealthy attitude issues found in some of these staff, and be able to pursue ways to improve productivity without degrading the essential support provided to judges. Some administrators have succeeded in obtaining management control over these staff through persistence, patience, and the strong support of key judges who want to see the court become a coherent institution. In most courts, it is "Death Valley" for an administrator to openly challenge the special status of these staff.

Notes

1. Hall, Kermit L., "Judicial Independence and the Majoritarian Difficulty," in Hall, Kermit L., and Kevin T. McGuire, eds., *Institutions of American Democracy: The Judicial Branch.* New York: Oxford University Press, 2005, p. 60. See also, Tobin, Robert W., *Creating the*

Judicial Branch: The Unfinished Reform. Williamsburg, VA: National Center for State Courts, 1999, p. 30.

2. See Vanderbilt, Arthur T., "Foreword," *Reports of the Section of Judicial Administration.* Chicago: American Bar Association, 1938, reprinted in Section of Judicial Administration, *Improvement of the Administration of Justice,* 5th ed. Chicago: American Bar Association, 1971, p. xxiii.

3. An Associated Press article entitled "Report: Judicial Election Spending Soars," retrieved June 27, 2005, from http://start.earthlink.net/channel/news, states that candidates in state supreme court races across the nation spent $24.4 million for television advertising in 18 contests in 2004. In 2000, the total was $10.6 million. No comparable figures are available for trial judges, but it is safe to assume that the out-of-pocket costs for candidates for trial benches across the nation are increasing comparably. This is critical because many, if not most, state judges since the early 1980s, have come to the bench from a salaried public sector position and have limited financial reserves to support a campaign. Raising funds for a campaign poses problems for all judges.

4. In 2004, judges in Arizona, Iowa, and Kansas were targeted for defeat because of specific decisions. Schotland, Roy A., "The Crocodile in the Bathtub … and Other Arguments to Extend Terms for Trial Judges," *California Courts Review,* Fall 2005, p. 10.

5. "To place a judge who lacks the aptitude and appetite for administration in an executive position in the judicial establishment guarantees its mediocrity and is a disservice not only to the bench, the bar and public alike, but also to the individual judge." McConnell, Edward B., "Court Administration," Section of Judicial Administration, *Improvement of the Administration of Justice,* 5th ed. Chicago: American Bar Association, 1971, p. 18.

6. Ibid., p. 17. The university analogy also is used in Friesen, Ernest C., Jr., Edward C. Gallas, and Nesta Gallas, *Managing the Courts.* Indianapolis, IN: Bobbs-Merrill, 1971, pp. 107–108.

7. Some legislators with large campaign funds can give funds to candidates in other districts to garner "chits" that can be called on during a legislative session, but normally these legislators can only influence the election in the other district(s), not control it. Likewise, in small, normally rural communities, a highly regarded retiring judge can work with the Bar to anoint his or her successor if the position is determined through election (or to convince the governor to consider seriously only one person for appointment). Even in these communities, however, the retiring judge mostly influences rather than controls. And in a one-judge court, interest in and skill at administration and one's collegiality are not significant factors.

8. This individual or individuals often delay change until they are sure they can live with it or it will not affect them. They sometimes cause the leadership team to devise workarounds in order to implement a change without directly confronting the nay-sayers.

9. Friesen, Ernest C., Jr., Edward C. Gallas, and Nesta Gallas, *Managing the Courts,* p. 119.

10. He was one of several judges on the court, but he was the undisputed leader of the bench, so he did not have to consider what to do if another judge happened to disagree with him.

11. In one court, probation officers have to get a judge's approval to reschedule missed appointments with probationers; the judge approves the rescheduling, the date, and the time. This court has a legal opinion saying this approval authority falls within a judge's decision making because it implements the judge's sentencing decision, but if so, it skirts as close to the judicial–administrative line as possible. It is even arguably "judicial" only because it involves probation. Were a judge to exercise similar authority over actions of his or her administrator, it clearly would be administrative.

12. Tobin, Robert W., *Creating the Judicial Branch,* p. 108.

13. Ibid., p. 182.

14. Friesen, Ernest C., Jr., Edward C. Gallas, and Nesta Gallas, *Managing the Courts,* p. 108.

15. Judges also may claim final authority because they are elected and ultimately responsible to the electorate for everything that happens in a court. Were this to be a valid argument, they also should review all clerical entries, because a clerical error also negatively impacts a court's image.

16. See Tobin, Robert W., *Creating the Judicial Branch,* p. 112.

17. "Chief justices, chief judges, and all other judges feel few qualms about bypassing their court managers to deal directly with staff." Ibid., p. 115.

18. The Detroit Recorders Court, prior to its merger with the county's general jurisdiction court, is the only court I know that tried to formalize an approach to one type of problem judge. There, if a judge consistently was having trouble managing cases and achieving timely dispositions, the judge could be referred to a special committee of senior judges that would counsel the judge, provide a mentor, or remove the judge from a particular calendar. This would be regarded as unthinkable in virtually every other court in the country.

19. One caveat is in order regarding this statement. If delay and further consideration were to lead to a courtwide consensus in favor of a change, the accommodation of a colleague would make sense. My sense is that this positive result happens materially less often than simply killing change or materially weakening it.

20. The easiest example of this is case management rules designed to cover the "exceptional" case. The mindset of judges and attorneys is that the rule, even if it uses language such as "not to exceed" or "up to" a certain date or amount of time becomes the starting point rather than the end point. Thus, cases that can be resolved in less time tend to be delayed because the mindset is that the time in the rule is a minimum not a maximum.

21. It is the administrator's responsibility to recognize the difference in perspectives and to seek a dialogue with the judge(s) regarding the best approach for everyone.

22. See Drucker, Peter F. *Management: Tasks, Responsibilities, Practices.* New York: Harper & Row, 1973, p. 17. See also, former Lucky Stores executive Don Ritchey, quoted in Bennis, Warren, *Becoming a Leader,* p. 87: "You just haven't got the time or the resources, even if it was [sic] possible to actually get that last finite piece of information that lets you deal with certainty. You have to get 80 or 85 percent of it and then take your best shot and go on to something else."

23. Tobin, Robert W., *Creating the Judicial Branch,* p. 110.

24. When a court replaces a highly skilled administrator with one who is less skilled, the relative absence of skill in the new administrator may be apparent and regretted, but even this lesson does not always translate to assuring that future administrators are both skilled and seen as peers.

25. I owe this insight into the two professions' different perspectives to Dale Lefever, a hospital administrator who also has consulted with and trained judges for over 25 years. He suggests that when a stranger asks a judge what he does, he first will say he's a judge, then maybe mention the case type he or she is handling at the moment, and then third or fourth mention that he or she is a judge on XYZ Court. When a court administrator is asked what he or she does by this same stranger, the administrator most likely will say, "I work for the XYZ Court" or "I am the court administrator in XYZ Court." See also, Lefever, R. Dale, "Judge-Court Manager Relationships: The Integration of Two Cultures," *The Court Manager,* Summer 1990, pp. 8–9. In placing their professional status first, judges also provide astute administrators with insight into the relative importance to judges of administrative issues and responses. Bob Tobin makes a related point about court administration and judges when he observes that, "Practically all the literature of judge-administrator relations is written by court administrators or scholars. Judges rarely concern themselves with the subject," Tobin, Robert W., *Creating the Judicial Branch,* p. 112, note 5.

26. I know of one court in which a judge about to start a trial needed a courtroom clerk on an emergency basis because his clerk had become ill and stayed home. An experienced clerk was needed because of the special demands associated with a trial. After considering several options, the courtroom clerks' supervisor felt that moving another judge's clerk to the first courtroom and giving the second judge his regular backup clerk would work best. When the supervisor advised the second judge's clerk of her decision, the clerk refused, saying her judge would back her up. When the court administrator talked to the judge to explain the temporary and emergency nature of the need, the judge threatened the administrator with a contempt of court citation if his clerk were moved, seeing no difference between an administrative, institutional matter and legally contemptuous behavior in a courtroom. Rather than precipitate a confrontation, the supervisor was asked to find another way to cover the first courtroom (which she did). The second judge exhibited classic "silo" thinking: concern only for his courtroom and his needs, with no weight given to any of the institution's needs or concerns.

27. The analogy that seems to resonate most readily with both judges and court administrators is doctors, hospitals, and hospital administrators.

28. Drucker, Peter F., *Management*, p. 395.

29. Friesen, Ernest C., Jr., Edward C. Gallas, and Nesta Gallas, *Managing the Courts,* p. 115.

30. Judges have been disciplined for sexual and other harassment, an administrative issue, and misdeeds associated with their adjudicative role, but not, to my knowledge, for failing to cooperate with colleagues, for missing multiple days of work, for excessive vacation time, or failing to conform to administrative practices adopted for and by a majority of judges. The one exception of which I am aware is a California judge who claimed a medical disability to explain his hundreds of days' absence while he attended a Caribbean medical school. He was removed from the bench. In Arizona, some justices of the peace have been censured for poor attendance or chronic lateness.

31. Friesen, Ernest C., Jr., Edward C. Gallas, and Nesta Gallas, *Managing the Courts,* p. 3.

32. Drucker, Peter F., *Management*, p. 241.

33. For example, Friesen, Ernest C., Jr., Edward C. Gallas, and Nesta Gallas, *Managing the Courts,* p. 125. Robert Tobin argues the "board of directors" analogy is "very weak." See Tobin, Robert W., *Creating the Judicial Branch*, p. 109. One of the reasons is that judges are elected or appointed to fill a public office; they do not own stock and do not "own" courts the way a board member or senior manager of a corporation might.

34. For example, Clarke, John A., "The Role of the Executive Component of the Court, *The Court Manager*, Summer 1990, pp. 4–6. "Team management is not a psychological mechanism for making individuals [who are court managers] feel important; it is a functional necessity. Neither judges nor court managers have the total expertise necessary to lead and manage an effective court," Lefever, R. Dale, "Judge-Manager Relationships," p. 9.

35. Peter Drucker says the following about top management: "Top management work is work for a team rather than one man. It is quite unlikely that any one man will ...unite the divergent temperaments which the job requires. Moreover,... there is more work to be done than any one man can do," Drucker, Peter F. *Management*, p. 618. Although this might be thought to apply to top management in corporations, Drucker meant it to apply to the top management of any complex organization.

36. One now-retired administrator met with his chief judge each morning. He felt an obligation to have one or two things every day about which to advise the chief judge or about which to seek his opinion.

37. This is not to say that the chief judge always must be or should be the only one to communicate with and seek to persuade his or her colleagues. Sometimes another judge is the

most effective person to talk to a particular judge. It is to emphasize, however, that certain messages and efforts to persuade must be carried judge to judge even if the idea originates with the administrator and the administrator will be the one to implement it.

38. See Tobin, Robert W., *Creating the Judicial Branch*, p. 112. And herein lies the dilemma for administrators. To be effective, an administrator must be regarded as a peer even though the administrator's skills are not law based. See Friesen, Ernest C., Jr., Edward C. Gallas, and Nesta Gallas, *Managing the Courts,* p. 125. Yet, for reasons suggested in this chapter and in chapter 7, even if individual judges accept a strong administrator as a peer, the bench as a whole normally does not.

39. Occasionally, the message is so important to the court that both the chief judge and the administrator should present the matter together. In these instances, they both can contribute, but the administrator has to be seen by staff as having a key role in the decision and its implementation.

40. See Martin, John A., and Nancy C. Maron, "Courts, Delay, and Interorganizational Networks: Managing an Essential Tension," *The Justice System Journal*, vol. 14, no. 3 and vol. 15, no. 1, p. 278.

41. In states where the trial courts' chief judge is appointed by the state's chief justice, terms of office tend to be longer, at least three years and sometimes as high as five years. This additional time on the job for the chief judge helps both the chief judge and the administrator.

42. Cf. Richard B. Hoffman, "The Revolt of the Judges," *The Court Manager*, vol. 19, no.2, 2004, pp. 14–16.

43. There is a somewhat analogous story from an urban court in a small Western state in which the state chief justice asserted a role regarding the trial court administrator. A state statute provided that the trial court administrator was hired and fired by the chief judge of the trial court. The chief justice told the trial court chief judge to fire the administrator. The administrator submitted his resignation to the trial court chief judge and to the court, but they refused to accept it. The state's chief justice removed the chief judge, following which the trial court finally accepted the administrator's resignation. A subsequent lawsuit was settled, so the legal question regarding the chief justice's authority was not resolved.

44. Courts of general jurisdiction are courts of record, that is, a verbatim record is made of what happens in the courtrooms and appeals are based on the resulting written transcript. Courts of limited jurisdiction sometimes also are courts of record, but more commonly are not. Appeals from courts that are not courts of record normally are "de novo," that is, the parties present evidence all over again on appeal.

45. Court reporters in this position to whom I have spoken see no problem with this, arguing that they must work evenings and weekends, thus losing family time, to earn such large sums. (They are indifferent to or ignore the fact that many judges work evenings and some weekends, too.) The economics of court reporting is partially addressed in chapter 13, below.

46. In the half-dozen or so instances I have studied across the country, court reporters frequently overcharge for their transcripts, on occasion by as much as 25 percent. My studies are consistent with those undertaken on their own by administrative offices of the courts. Yet only a handful of states audit transcripts and the bills submitted for them. Judges rarely press for reform in billing even when faced with documentation of abuse.

47. See note 6.

THE ART OF
PRACTICING COURT
ADMINISTRATION

II

Chapter 7

On Being a Court Administrator

Courts are complex institutions for all the reasons cited to this point. Managing in this complex environment makes being a court administrator a complex and compelling job. The challenges are significant, but they are in the context of a public service that is critical to the continued strength and integrity of our political and social structures. There is substantial psychic satisfaction to be derived from serving courts when they work as they should, as well as from helping them to move closer to the desired ideal when they fall short.

This chapter will examine the position of court administrator from two perspectives: (1) the nature of the position and the tasks to be accomplished; and (2) the qualities and skills one should possess to perform effectively. Related to this latter perspective, the idea of court administrators as leaders and the need for leadership in courts also will be examined. The final section discusses how to approach hiring a court administrator.

Two political scientists, Steven W. Hays and Cole Blease Graham, Jr., argue that court administration is "simply a specialized form of public administration" and that court leaders should more aggressively apply and adapt public administration approaches.[1] There is much merit in both parts of this view. Saari, Planet, and Reinkensmeyer point out that the first trial court administrator, Edward Gallas, identified a parallel between the city manager concept and the court administrator approach. Both, they say, "are premised on the ideas of efficiency, effectiveness, honesty, and clean government."[2] Court administrators spend very little time learning of public administration principles, theories, or practice. There is little doubt that public administration could inform court administration. There also is a community of interest of which court administrators could take advantage.

Public administration is not the only perspective or set of experiences from which court administrators would benefit, however. If court administrators are to be strong and effective managers and if courts are to develop leaders for this century, courts also should look to the corporate and nonprofit sectors for guidance in two areas: to understand concepts of management and how it shapes and guides institutions in a changing world; and to be able to find best practices that can be applied in a court setting. In the early 1970s, business operated more as a hierarchy with most corporate leaders able to direct what would be done and who would do it and with limited need to negotiate for desired changes. Courts often try to operate in a hierarchical fashion, but cannot, for all the reasons reviewed to this point.[3] Today, the world economy has gained a stronger hold on corporate planning and operations, which has created a need for corporations to negotiate with and influence outside suppliers and to manage offices around the world. These changes have led corporate leaders and business literature to focus to a much greater degree on brokering what is needed and influencing others to enable their companies to succeed. Nonprofit organizations that rely heavily on volunteers, such as the Red Cross and both the Boy and Girl Scouts, also have to rely daily on those they cannot control but must influence to see the same vision and seek the same ends as headquarters. Thus, the private and nonprofit sectors are more parallel to courts today than they were when the modern court administration movement started.

The two perspectives, public administration and private sector, are not incompatible so much as they reflect different emphases. The emphasis in this work is on lessons to be learned from the private sector.

7.1 Nature of the Position

As is true of many elements of court operations and organization, there is no single model for a court administrator. States and individual trial courts have fashioned the position as best suits their needs and predilections.[4] Court administrators' duties range from fairly limited to very extensive with a substantial degree of both responsibility and independence. The latter, normally but not exclusively, are found in larger urban courts. Therefore, the specific duties discussed in this section will be too extensive for some and too narrow for others, at least in terms of scope and breadth of actual authority. They cover the range of duties for most administrators, however.

Tobin posits three professional levels among trial court administrators: administrative assistants, middle-management types, and executives. "Because of these gradations," he says, "there is no guaranteed upward mobility in the profession, because distinctly different skills are required at each level."[5] He argues for six categories of trial court administrators:[6]

1. "Intruders" have limited responsibility, a marginal role, and little or no political power.
2. "Technicians" have expertise in technology and may or may not have management skills.[7]

3. "High-level administrative assistants" are given routine responsibility with little or no role in caseflow management and a low profile in interbranch relations.

4. "Strong manager" has broad, clear authority from the chief judge, a large part in interbranch relations, public relations, and caseflow management.

5. "Entrepreneur" tends to "wheel and deal" to find resources, to reduce costs, and to achieve objectives.

6. "Fixture's" longevity brings a special security and respect.

These categories are not exclusive. For example, a technician with management skills also could be a strong manager. An entrepreneur could be a fixture or a high-level administrative assistant. In practice, most court administrators probably function as administrative assistants, strong managers, and entrepreneurs at various times during their tenure, even if one of the roles predominates. If they perform each of these roles well, they can become fixtures. If the expectations or desires of a chief judge or the bench change over time about the role predominantly to be filled, and there is concern that the incumbent might not be able to shift gears sufficiently, the administrator will not become (or remain) a fixture.

This chapter will treat the court administrator position as it were a strong manager position. There are two reasons for doing so: The first is influenced by an observation Friesen, Gallas, and Gallas made in the early 1970s: "The overall consideration in determining the value of court management to justice is the extent to which it contributes to maintaining the judiciary as an independent branch of the government as well as an independent unit of management."[8] Unless a court administrator is a strong manager, he or she cannot add the value indicated. Many judges do not necessarily subscribe to Friesen, Gallas, and Gallas's statement. Other judges believe the attainment of an independent branch depends on their management and political skills and strength rather than on the skills of an independently empowered administrator. Those who hold this view are not in touch with the complexity of court administration, the reality that administration is beyond the capacity of part-time manager-judges, and that court management should be a team undertaking. They do not see the weaknesses of a model that has judges as the primary instrument in court administration. Changing the minds of these judges remains one of the challenges of court administration in the 21st century.

The second reason for focusing on strong managers has just been suggested. Court administration that is effective requires a strong chief judge-administrator team that has two equals who recognize and respect each other's strengths and undertake to cover for each other's weaknesses. If the court administrator is not strong, the team will not be strong. If the team is not strong, the court will not gain the full benefits that professional management can bring. With the growing demands on and expectations of the public and the two other branches of government, courts need strong and effective professional management. This is as true for a court of three or four judges as it is for a court with one hundred judges. The community does not distinguish by size. The court with three or four judges is as much a major and critical institution in its community as the court with one hundred judges is in a major city, perhaps even more so. In the increasingly complex judicial environment, full-time judges who are part-time managers will not be able to respond sufficiently to the demands. The field of court administration is not advanced by a discussion of how to use an administrative assistant effectively.

7.1.1 Administrators as Professionals

Three observers, an academic and two court administrators, attribute the range of available models for court administrators, plus the perception among many judges that the position can be created or eliminated as they wish, as key to the acceptance and extension of the position across almost all courts.[9] That insight may well be valid. But it may be these very variances in what a court administrator does, and the shifting assignments as the chief judge changes, that contribute to some judges still being uncertain about the value and status of administrators. In this context, therefore, we should return briefly to the references in chapter 6 to administrators not being seen by judges as peers and sometimes not being seen as professionals, and how this contributes to difficulties implementing the "executive team" of the chief judge and the administrator.

Friesen, Gallas, and Gallas provide a four-part test for a professional.[10]

1. Mastery of an organized and growing body of specialized knowledge, including an understanding of both theory and practice, usually evidenced by completion of a distinctive educational program.
2. Distinctive skills representing special aptitude plus training and experience.
3. A professional attitude marked by determination to keep abreast of new developments in theory, research, and practice in the field of specialization.
4. Recognition of special public responsibility, usually marked by appropriate professional ethical codes.

A professional also has been defined as one who sets his or her own work schedule and tasks and determines his or her work hours. A few senior managers in most courts qualify as professionals insofar as they define the tasks they undertake daily, but otherwise, judges are the only ones who have some latitude in all three of these additional tests.

Peter Drucker, described by former General Electric CEO Jack Welch as, "the greatest management thinker of the ... [twentieth] century,"[11] almost single-handedly created the recognition today that management is a discrete undertaking with complex but defined tasks and responsibilities and that managers are professionals.[12] Judges are not necessarily students of Drucker, and they do not necessarily accept either part of Drucker's proposition.

Let us examine the "managers are professional" proposition first. Some of the early court administration leaders had strong management backgrounds in either the public or private sector and sometimes MBA, law, or other advanced degrees when they were appointed as court administrator. The preconditions for judges seeing these individuals as professionals with skills and knowledge judges lacked (or did not have time to use) were present. The preconditions were not always sufficient for them to be treated as professionals, but the potential existed. At the same time, however, and often over the years since, a number of those appointed as court administrators may have worked in the court for many years and advanced up the management ranks, finally to become the court administrator. They seldom had the specialized education[13] or obvious special knowledge of a professional. The field did not have a nationally developed code of ethics until the 1990s. The person promoted to court administrator might have learned a lot about management over the years and may have taken some management courses, but the indicia of "professional" involving specialized knowledge and advanced degrees were lacking. Even after the Institute for Court Management (ICM) was operational and giving sound management training to court employees,[14] ICM's certificates of workshop completion and its "court executive development program"[15] never rose, and still do not rise, to the level of a degree to which judges could relate as a "professional" degree.[16] Particularly in contrast to the very formal education, licensing, and practice requirements that judges experienced prior to coming to the bench, it was hard for judges to see incumbent administrators as professionals.

There also are important perception issues independent of degrees. First, if an administrator had worked his or her way up the ladder within a court eventually to become the administrator, he or she was known first as one of the staff or as a lower-level supervisor or manager of a section. Presumably, the person was one of the best performers or he or she would not have been appointed as the administrator, but he or she remains "one of the staff" in judges' eyes. The administrator may be liked and even admired as a person, but no professional status would be granted to "one of the staff" by the judges. Also, if administrators were seen as professionals, a few judges might feel that depreciates their own professional status because these administrators lack the normal indicia.

Second, as the position spread from large urban environments to smaller and more rural courts, clerks of court were more important politically and many also were responsive to judges' needs and desires. There was no need to upset the clerk or make the clerk an enemy by introducing a strong-management model for the court administrator. Plus, there were many questions in smaller courts in the early days as to whether there was enough work of consequence independent of what the clerk did to warrant a full-time court administrator. The administrative assistant model of court administrator was an easier fit in many of these courts. The model recognized a need to handle administrative details that judges did not want to handle or did not have time to handle, but also did not upset the political and social balances of the community. Once such a model is in place, it is hard to upgrade absent a scandal, a major dispute between the clerk and the court, or a mistake or oversight resulting from a judge's management decision. Once this model has been adopted, it also is hard for judges to see their administrator as a professional.

Third, as suggested in chapter 6, judges often come to view their orders and opinions as clear, comprehensive, and self-executing. If an order or an opinion is not clear and comprehensive, and parties in the case cannot agree, they will return to court and ask for clarification. If the parties do not come back to court, however, the judge has no idea why, but normally and sometimes inappropriately assumes it is because the opinion or order is being followed explicitly. If the parties are having trouble implementing it but do not come back for further guidance, the judge is unaware of the difficulties. There also may be a tendency for a judge to see the fashioning of an opinion and the resulting order as the complex part and the execution of the order as the simple part. "You haven't made a decision until you've found a way to implement it."[17] If a judge's opinion disposes of the case, execution of the judge's decision may not be simple at all, but if the judge is not involved at that stage, he or she is unaware of the planning and the skill involved in making it work. The judge says, in effect, "Here's your answer, now get it done as I say." There simply is a lack of exposure to the implementation side and a lack of recognition of the number of important steps that must be taken and managed before the order is effected.[18]

The judge may likewise think it is no big deal for a manager to implement a policy decision related to the court's human resources program; or put together the staff, physical facilities, workflow, forms, and sometimes new software needed to make a new problem-solving court work; or even develop and implement a strategic plan that the judge does not think is needed in the first place.[19] Just as some laypersons believe, incorrectly, that judging is a simple task that any attorney can do, so some judges seem to believe that successful management in a court setting is relatively simple and unworthy of being deemed professional.

The fourth perspective starts from the opposite end of the opinion spectrum. Its basis is a fear—or at least a concern—that the administrator, in fact, is a professional who can be effective. As an effective professional, the administrator may be seen as a threat to a judge's professional status or independence. This attitude was prevalent as the profession was starting and judges were uncertain just how administrators would operate and also interact with the clerk. It remains a concern for some judges today, as well. Those who see administrative decisions as something to be ignored, interpreted away, or modified to suit individual preferences do not want an effective manager making it harder to act as one wishes. To accord this person the status of a professional is also to grant status to his or her decisions, thus making it harder to ignore or reject them. To deny professional standing to an administrator is to lessen the value and import of the administrator's decisions or recommendations, thus preserving the individuality these judges crave.[20] A nonprofessional manager—or one accorded limited responsibility—can handle administrative details that a judge does not want to or should not handle (recruiting, hiring, payroll, purchasing, accounts payable, creating forms) without threatening the judge's status.

Different judges see administrators through different prisms, but the four perspectives identified above are the most prevalent. Some undervalue the administrator and some see his or her value and fight it. The result for the administrator is the same: difficulty establishing and sustaining recognition among all the judges that he or she is a professional worthy of professional status and courtesy.

7.1.2   Court Administration as a Profession

Drucker's proposition that management is a profession is a related but different issue. If a significant number of court administrators since the mid-1950s had obtained degrees in business, public administration, or economics, their knowledge and skills over time may have led many, if not most, judges to see management differently because these administrators would have had expertise that judges do not have. Within NACM's membership today, four in ten have masters', doctoral, or law degrees. Lawyers who become administrators prove for judges that management is not a special knowledge and skill because those lawyers were trained the same way the judges were and they are doing the job, so Drucker must be wrong that management involves defined and special skills and qualities. If judges have good management skills and instincts without having studied management or having spent much time thinking about it, some judges reason, then, management is not special and certainly not a unique discipline.

Since many judges do not want to think about administration and devote time to administrative matters almost under duress, they are not going to take the time to evaluate the unique skills and qualities that make management a profession and administrators professionals. And they will not see the work performed by administrators as professionally equal to their own work. This has nothing to do with whether judges like or do not like the administrator. In almost all courts, administrators and judges get along well on a personal level. In fact, most administrators are appreciated by most judges; it just is an appreciation more akin to that for a good automobile mechanic than to that for a good trial lawyer or a fellow judge. The perceptions of a lack of professional status flow from a general lack of concern about management, a lack of attention, a lack of knowledge about what being a manager means, and the historical context involved in creating the position.

Overcoming these attitudes is not easy. An administrator can contribute by being an example, approaching and performing his or her duties professionally and without concern that he or she may not be fully appreciated. The administrator can seek as many management training opportunities as possible, even a formal degree if he or she can afford it and fit in the course work. Ultimately, however, attitudes will change when judges who care about the institution and want it to advance take time to learn more about management itself[21] and, more specifically, what the administrator does and then take responsibility to help educate their fellow judges. Along with education, these judges also should be emissaries on the administrator's behalf by acknowledging and praising good work by the administrator, both in public settings and with colleagues.

7.2 Court Administrators' Skills and Qualities

In most respects, court administrators' duties and responsibilities are like those of other senior public administrators and senior executives in the private sector. There are internally focused and externally focused responsibilities. In terms of time commitments, the internally focused responsibilities dominate for a court's leadership team.

7.2.1 External Relationships

External relationships are all about communication, which involves exchanging information, facilitating planning, building understanding and trust, and serving as a vehicle for education of the community. The list of those with whom a court should have regular or at least periodic exchanges is long for several reasons: court's role in government; its limited capacity to control its assets, employees, key operatives, and working environment; the development of problem-solving courts; and the range of individuals and institutions who both impact and are impacted by courts (see also, chapter 11).

CEOs and presidents in the private and nonprofit sectors spend considerable time in external relations. They staff their offices to enable them both to coordinate these external contacts and also to cover or at least monitor internal operations while they are engaged externally. These staff positions are assigned to the CEO and president in addition to executives responsible for various substantive and support functions. The external communication needs of a court are every bit as demanding as those of corporate and nonprofit leaders, but chief judges and court administrators seldom are able to devote comparable amounts of time for two reasons. As indicated in chapter 6, administration is an "add on" for most chief judges, so they must handle a full or almost equal caseload on top of their administrative responsibilities. In smaller courts, a chief judge may not even have a secretary; his or her courtroom clerk may have to do double duty or there is a small pool of secretaries for all judges. The only backup that most chief judges have for both internal and external duties are the administrator and the administrator's support staff. Even the largest trial courts, in which the chief judge is freed of calendar responsibilities, do not provide an aide or aides to the chief judge to assist with administration separate from the administrator's staff.[22] So time becomes a real constraint on chief judges. Even in larger courts where the position is a full-time one, the demands on a chief judge's time are heavy because the number of constituencies is so large.

Second, most administrators' staffs are barely sufficient to handle specifically assigned tasks.[23] In most courts only a minimum number of staff members are provided for the basic institutional support functions, which normally means they are more than fully occupied with their assigned responsibilities. These employees and managers have no additional time to back up either the chief judge or the administrator on their internal matters while these two are networking externally. So, in most courts, the chief judge and administrator fit external relations into their schedules as best they can, often dividing the responsibility. They then normally have to compensate for their external relations time with overtime, evening, and in many cases, weekend time to catch up with and respond to what has been happening internally. Virtually every chief judge and administrator would acknowledge the importance of external relations, but they normally are unable to devote the amount of time to them that they warrant.

7.2.2 Internal Tasks and Skills

When one looks internally, tasks and skills can be identified generically, as Drucker and numerous other business writers have done, or specifically within the context of courts, which the National Association for Court Management and others have done. This section will examine both approaches.

7.2.2.1 Skills, Responsibilities, and Tasks of All Managers

Drucker says of management:[24]

> Management ... is a generic function which faces the same basic tasks in every country and, essentially, in every society. Management has to give direction to the institution it manages. It has to think through

the institution's mission, has to set its objectives, and has to organize resources for the results the institution has to contribute. Management is ... responsible for directing vision and resources toward greatest results and contributions.

Management's job "is to make productive the resources in its trust."[25] The job description of very few, if any, court administrators would include the responsibilities set forth by Drucker, who also makes clear that management is not a one-person task. It is the responsibility of a team of top managers[26] that in a court context would be the chief judge and the court administrator supported by the judges and senior management staff.

Drucker identifies four generic functions of management: give direction, think through the organization's mission, set objectives, and organize resources.[27] To accomplish these functions, a manager must:[28]

- Set objectives
- Organize
- Motivate and communicate
- Measure performance
- Develop people

Of these five, court administrators do the first three fairly regularly, although when Drucker speaks of setting objectives he means organization-wide objectives; many court administrators more likely would set only project-specific objectives. Even chief judge-administrator teams seldom are asked to set objectives beyond specific projects. Courtwide objectives are being included in strategic and long-range plans when courts develop them, but the courts developing such plans remain a fraction of all trial courts. Further, the plans normally are tweaked and endorsed by all judges rather than being delegated solely to the court's leaders.

Measuring performance is the weakest area for virtually all courts, even though organizations such as the National Association for Court Management (NACM), the Conference of Chief Justices, and the Conference of State Court Administrators have been urging use of measurable performance goals for several years.[29] There are a number of reasons for this, which will be explored further in section 12.6.1 in chapter 12.

Because of the potential loss of administrators, managers, and staff as the baby boomers reach retirement age, the development of potential managers is receiving more attention in courts. Until recently, however, it has not been a priority. During times of budget freezes or cuts, training is one of the first items cut or eliminated. Other ways to develop people that do not involve budgeted funds do not receive much attention in most courts. On this point, Jack and Suzy Welch have said: "When you become a leader, success is all about growing others. It's about making the people who work for you smarter, bigger, and bolder. Nothing you do anymore as an individual matters except how you nurture and support your team and help its members increase their self-confidence."[30] Being a good leader means being a servant. It is the manager/leader's job to assure that staff members have the training and tools needed to complete their assigned responsibilities. Further, a manager/leader must assure that the assigned responsibilities fit a person's strengths: "no two people have the same configuration of strengths and weaknesses. And no one has only strengths; … It is the manager's job to optimize resources. And placement is the way to optimize the most expensive resource of them all: the human being."[31]

Harris Collingwood talks about placement in these terms: "Leaders must help their followers discover what they are good at. Leaders enable self-knowledge."[32]

Some court administrators and chief judges understand the concept of being a servant, although the allocation of court funds, which reflects a court's priorities, does not always reflect implementation of the servant role. Whether it is union work rules, lack of attention, or personality issues, optimizing human resources through careful placement is not practiced as much as it should be in courts. When people are moved to a job they prefer or to one that is thought to match their skills, it usually is a reward rather than an effort to maximize a person's strengths or to minimize exposure of the person's weaknesses. Sometimes a manager is most effective when he or she moves a marginal performer to better use the skills and strengths that person possesses.[33]

One of the difficulties in identifying the skills and knowledge a manager needs is that the qualities of good managers and of good leaders overlap. In Drucker's writings, which had their greatest impact in the pre-"leadership" era of management literature, qualities and skills he attributed to management would be called leadership qualities and skills today.[34] Perhaps, the most direct way to identify the skills, knowledge, and qualities of managers is to review more specifically what managers do.

Warren Bennis often is quoted as saying, "Managers do things right. Leaders do the right thing." While clever, it does not help to create a job description. Two professors at the McLaren School of Business, University of San Francisco, succinctly talk about what managers do in contrast to what leaders do: "A manager controls, a leader builds commitment; a manager sanctions; a leader inspires; a manager administers, a leader creates; a manager focuses on the routine, a leader focuses on vision."[35] The difficulty with this statement is that it sounds pejorative when describing managers. Even though these authors might acknowledge that the manager's functions are necessary in organizations, the manager's role suffers by comparison to a leader's (see section 7.3 for a further discussion of leaders).

Abraham Zaleznik, then a professor at Harvard Business School, offered in the *Harvard Business Review* one of the clearest and most complete descriptions of managers in 1977.[36]

A manager is a problem solver. The manager asks: "What problems have to be solved and what are the best ways to achieve results so that people can contribute to this organization?" ... to be a manager, [requires] persistence, tough-mindedness, hard work, intelligence, analytical ability, and perhaps most important, tolerance and good will....

Managers tend to view work as an enabling process involving some combination of people and ideas interacting to establish strategies and make decisions. They help the process along by calculating the interests in opposition, planning when controversial issues should surface, and reducing tensions. In this enabling process, managers' tactics appear flexible....

[What a manager does includes] reconciling differences, seeking compromises, and establishing a balance of power....

Managers relate to people according to the role they play in a sequence of events or in a decision-making process, while leaders, who are concerned with ideas, relate in more intuitive and empathetic ways. The distinction is simply between a manager's attention to *how* things get done and a leader to *what* the events and decisions mean to participants....

Managers see themselves as conservators and regulators of an existing order of affairs with which they personally identify and from which they gain rewards. A manager's sense of self-worth is enhanced by perpetuating and strengthening existing institutions. He or she is performing a role that is in harmony with the ideals of duty and responsibility. (emphasis in original)

Ronald Stupak, an astute observer of institutions and leadership, wrote a short piece for the periodic membership newsletter of NACM that contrasts leaders and managers. His leadership list will be discussed in section 7.3; the manager's list is set forth here.[37] It reflects many of the same elements as Zaleznik's list.

Maintains the present	Is crisis driven
Monitors progress	Uses negative power
Does things right	Communicates rules
Plans from memory	Is activity anchored
Manages things	Is a stability protector
Is tactically driven	Is an "SOP" regulator
Is technically anchored	Protects hierarchies
Is a boundary protector	

A key difference between Drucker's list and Zaleznik's and Stupak's lists, is that many court administrators can relate immediately to the latter descriptions as being close to what they do. Drucker's list is consistent with his definition of management and also more descriptive of actual tasks than Zaleznik's and Stupak's, but very few administrators or even chief judge-administrator teams see the core of their job description as embracing Drucker's list. More importantly, as a prelude to the discussion of leadership needs in courts, Zaleznik's and Stupak's descriptions are consistent with the traditional view of how courts operate and what courts have expected of their administrators.

The skills and qualities that are most useful for fulfilling a manager's role are:

- Technical knowledge
- Communication (a skill leaders also must have)
- Setting performance goals
- Managing toward performance goals
- Contingency planning
- Strategic planning
- Making decisions under uncertain conditions
- Problem solving
- At home with complex and abstract ideas
- Synthesizing and reconciling differences
- Guidance
- Maintenance

Most of these terms are self-explanatory. Two sets might benefit from brief expansion. Drucker and many others endorse setting measurable performance goals ("metrics" is the current nom du jour). It is one thing to set measurable performance goals and another to use them to guide and then determine management decisions. A manager should gauge every decision by whether it is consistent with and will bring the organization closer to achieving its goals. If it is not, the decision should be reevaluated. Only by being rigorous about managing toward established and measurable goals can a manager be effective. Drucker colorfully states the need:[38] "Being able to set objectives does not make a man a manager, any more than the ability to tie a small knot in a confined space makes a man a surgeon. But without the ability to set objectives a man cannot be an adequate manager, just as a man cannot do good surgery without tying small knots." Setting measurable objectives and managing toward them is a weak area in court leadership (see also, section 12.3, chapter 12).

The difference between contingency planning and strategic planning may not be obvious. *Strategic* planning is a standard approach in management that involves defining a future one would like to achieve in the relatively near term (three to five years) and identifying the strategies, personnel, and resources one will employ to achieve those goals. *Contingency* planning is part of organizational maintenance. It involves thinking about things that might go wrong and how the organization should prepare so they do not occur or so the organization can respond appropriately if there is no way to prevent them, such as a natural disaster.

> Many management experts are now saying that pessimists make great managers. Why? Because they're always thinking of what could go wrong and are, therefore, coming up with solutions to problems—just in case the worst happens. So if you're an optimist, force yourself to write down everything that could go wrong with new projects, ideas, employees, etc. Once you do this, you'll naturally be prepared with solutions if disaster strikes.[39]

Contingency planning is very hard to do in government generally and in courts specifically, particularly if any funds must be expended to prevent or minimize possible future problems. The ongoing difficulties at all levels of government of implementing contingency planning after the 9/11 attack and before and after the hurricane devastation along the Gulf Coast and in Florida in 2004 and 2005 are dramatic examples of this difficulty, but they hardly are unique. It is said by some of those in the military—not as a compliment—that they do not have time to do it right but always have time to do it over. The same could be said of those in government about contingency planning. This issue is most dramatic for courts in the context of security and for postdisaster planning for continuity of operations. These issues will be discussed further in chapter 10. For now, it is sufficient to note that it is hard to implement contingency planning when money is needed. Government budget makers seem to have trouble allotting money to possible but not assured needs. Even if no or very little funding is needed, however, contingency planning requires conscious and determined effort, even as a court administrator is busy "swatting away the alligators in the swamp."[40]

7.2.2.2 Skills, Responsibilities, and Tasks of Court Administrators

This section will examine the technical expertise needed by court administrators. It also will review some qualities that are helpful for an administrator that do not appear in NACM's Core Competencies or in the business literature.

Starting in the early 1990s, NACM surveyed its members about the knowledge, skills, and abilities needed by court leaders, including the chief judge. After several iterations and intensive review of drafts by practicing administrators, judicial officers, and others knowledgeable in the field, NACM approved its "Core Competency Curriculum Guidelines: What Court Leaders Need to Know and Be Able to Do" ("Core Competencies"). Technically, the Core Competencies only define a course of training and education that a court leader might follow to expand his or her understanding and competence. "The Core Competency

Curriculum Guidelines are ... not intended ... to test or to grade either practicing or aspiring court managers or their judicial superiors. Rather, their purpose is **self-assessment and self-improvement**... NACM does not assume that any single court leader has or could master every Core Competency ... nor... do they need to"[41] (emphasis in original). Nonetheless, the Core Competencies, in fact, are an excellent listing of the scope of items about which a court administrator should have at least passing knowledge and with which he or she will deal on an almost daily basis. Accordingly, when one assesses what court administrators do and what knowledge, skills, and qualities they need to bring to the position, there is no better place to start than NACM's Core Competencies.

There are ten core competencies:

- Purposes and responsibilities of courts
- Caseflow management
- Leadership
- Visioning and strategic planning
- Essential components [akin to an "all others" category]
- Court community communication
- Resources, budget, and finance
- Human resource management
- Education, training, and development
- Information technology management

Graphically, "purposes and responsibilities of courts" are at the center of a circle, with the other nine competencies arrayed around the circle. Within each competency discussion, there is an introduction explaining the nature of the competency and why it is important, followed by a statement of the "knowledge, skill, and abilities" associated with each competency. For the novice or aspiring court leader, the discussions not only suggest possible courses of study, but also are an excellent introduction to each topic. Every court should have at least one copy in each leader's office.[42] Some of these competencies will be referred to again in subsequent chapters. For now, it is sufficient to note that any court with a strong manager or desiring to hire one must consider the Core Competencies as it evaluates whether applicants have sufficient technical knowledge.

The Core Competencies define knowledge, skills, and abilities administrators should have or seek to obtain. Burrowing down from this level leads to job descriptions. Job descriptions address what a court administrator does from a very different perspective. They mostly are at the level of tasks rather than knowledge, skills, and abilities. The National Center for State Courts (NCSC) posts actual job descriptions for many positions on its website, including for court administrator.[43] Several dozen descriptions were provided in early 2006. Friesen, Gallas, and Gallas provided a generic listing of job responsibilities in the early 1970s.[44]

1. Administrative control of all nonjudicial activities of the court, subject to the general supervision of the presiding judge.
2. Assigning, supervising, and directing the work of the officers and employees of the court except commissioners, hearing officers, and referees with respect to their quasi-judicial responsibilities.
3. Formulating and administering a system of personnel administration subject to guidelines established by the court and subject to limitations that may be imposed by law or higher state judicial authority.
4. Preparing and administering the budget of the court, including coordination of the court budget with guidelines and controls laid down by legislative bodies and constitutional restraints.
5. Maintaining a modern accounting and auditing system for the court with respect to government funds and trust accounts.[45]
6. Establishing and maintaining property control records and conducting periodic inventories to assure that such records and physical inventories are reconciled.
7. Undertaking definition of the space management program, including space design, control, and requirement projections, and representing the court in its relationships with architects and builders.
8. Representing the court in its dealing with other government agencies and the State Court Administrator's Office with respect to the establishment, maintenance, and use of courtrooms, chambers, and offices.
9. Initiating organization, systems, and procedure studies relating to the business of the court and its administration and preparation of appropriate recommendations and reports to the presiding judge, the court, and the state judicial conference [or state supreme court].
10. Defining management information requirements and collecting, compiling, and analyzing statistical data with a view to the preparation and presentation of reports based on such data as may be directed by the presiding judge, the court, and the state court administrator.
11. Representing the courts as its liaison on all management matters to other state courts, the state legislature, the state judicial conference [or supreme court], the local financing authority, the sheriff, the court clerk, the chief probation officer, bar associations, civic groups, news media, and other private and public groups having a reasonable interest in the administration of the court.
12. Arranging and attending committee meetings of the judges of the court and of the entire court, including preparation of the agenda and serving as secretary to the court in all plenary meetings.
13. Establishing procedures for the calling of trial jurors and grand jurors and controlling their utilization and payment.
14. Preparing an annual report to the court and to the public for the preceding

calendar year, including recommendations for more expeditious disposition of the business of the court.

As long as this list is, there are additional items that many job descriptions would have today. The first probably would be in every job description: to oversee the selection, installation, maintenance, updating and upgrading, as needed, of the court's computer hardware and other electronic technologies and its case management and all other software programs, including access to and use of the Internet. Data processing and other technologies were in their infancy in courts when Friesen, Gallas, and Gallas were writing their book. The personal computer had found its way into only a few government offices and even fewer courts, and many of today's other technologies—and the Internet—were unknown. Responsibility for this aspect of a court's operations is a significant part of a court administrator's job today.

Second, Friesen, Gallas, and Gallas's list includes making recommendations regarding caseflow management and the court's calendar processes. In many courts, the court administrator is assigned explicit responsibility for overseeing or directing the court's calendar and caseflow management processes, either on his or her own or under the supervision of the court. In other courts, the judges retain sole authority over calendar organization and caseflow management and also are not interested in the court administrator's recommendations about it.

A third item included in many job descriptions today is the need to oversee the periodic development of and implementation of a strategic plan for the court under the direction of the chief judge and the court. Recognition of the need for and value of strategic planning has come slowly to courts, but it is becoming more accepted and desired now and will gain broader acceptance and use in the future.

The fourth item is most relevant when the administrator also is clerk of court. The administrator also would be responsible for the creation, maintenance, and storage of the court's records and for providing appropriate access to those records to the public and appropriate government agencies, subject to state and federal law and local and state rules of court.

Court administrators will do their jobs better if they have qualities that have not yet been mentioned, either as qualities of any manager or specifically in a court context. Some will surface again in the context of "leadership," but they also are important for strong court managers. These are:

- A sense of self
- Patience
- Perspective
- Flexibility
- Tolerance of different viewpoints

- Curiosity
- People skills

Some court administrators' title is "court executive officer," or CEO. The court administrator is not the CEO in the corporate sense in any court. The chief judge is the equivalent of a corporate CEO. The administrator can be and should be the Chief Operating Officer, if the corporate analogy is continued. Courts belong to judges; the staff supports them so they can do what they are charged to do by the constitution and statutes. As suggested in chapter 6, judges also should belong to courts, but that view is not as broadly shared among judges; the tension in that dual relationship is one of the reasons that administrators need a strong sense of self as they balance the conflicts the dual role of judges can produce.

A sense of self also helps with daily circumstances. There will be times when an administrator believes something must be resolved now but it will be deferred by the judges. There will be times when an administrator believes strongly in the need for a specific program or rule or procedure that will be rejected by the judges or the judges will approve an alternative that only partially addresses the need. There will be times when an administrator has made and announced a decision that will have to be modified or withdrawn because judges insist on it. There will be times when an administrator will point out a potential issue or problem and recommend action but the judges do not see the situation as the administrator does so nothing will be done. And then the issue or problem will materialize and the court or administrative leaders will be blamed or challenged for not preventing it, and the administrator will have to stand silent. There will be times when the administrator or the court desires something from the clerk, the sheriff, or others involved with the court and it will be rejected or ignored. There also will be times when an administrator will make a mistake of judgment or in actions and have to accept both the fact of making a mistake and the adverse consequences, and then seek to address the damage. In all these examples of circumstances that one or more administrators face daily across the country, an administrator must have a sense of self that is strong enough to maintain the course while sustaining faith in one's integrity, basic strengths, and abilities.

The phrase, "close enough for government work" often is used in a sarcastic or belittling way to reference work that is not complete or is done poorly, but that is accepted by government workers because they do not care enough to do work properly or are not required to do a complete, accurate job. That phrase could be paraphrased to, "soon enough for government work." Those in government seem to have their own sense of time. Tasks that most people think should and could be done in a week (or less) and that the private sector routinely completes in that time, may require three weeks or more in government. And the responsible officials believe they are timely. It is, of that is a decision can be thought to be timely that requires several people to meet, a month to set up the meeting, get and review background material, if any, and make a decision. A court that took two years to design a form thought it was moving deliberately but appropriately (see chapter 6). Another court started to design a form in 1995. At the end of 2005, it still had not been finalized and new reasons for delaying final approval surfaced in the Fall of 2005.

"Government time" is not found only in courts. It permeates government, local, state, and federal. It is most obvious within the executive branch because that branch is responsible for implementing most government actions. One need only think about the slow response of several federal and state agencies following Hurricane Katrina in September 2005 or the things that still have not been done by federal, state, and local agencies to avert another 9/11 attack (or recover from one) to appreciate both the pervasiveness of government time and its potential for harm. Although these are highly visible and contentious examples, the combined and cumulative effect of daily examples at all levels of government might make the Katrina and 9/11 examples pale in comparison.

Government bureaucracies grind down time sensitivity in two ways. When decisions are made quickly or actions are taken quickly, normally the decision maker or the actor has to proceed with less than full information. When one does that, mistakes are likely. More often than not, mistakes get bureaucrats in trouble with their bosses or citizens and elected officials. If one takes one's time, the problem may go away (or move to another office), the problem may change so the original decision would have been wrong, or more information comes in and a mistake becomes less likely. Except for humongous crises like Hurricane Katrina, taking time hurts bureaucrats (and elected officials) less often than moving quickly.[46] Self-preservation defense mechanisms are an important element in understanding government time.

Second, some of the delays or apparent indifference to the passage of time are a consequence of low staffing levels. There is too much work for the normal 40-hour work week and overtime is discouraged or denied. Under labor laws and union contracts, morning and afternoon breaks are mandated, as are full lunch hours. In this environment, one can quickly devolve to an attitude that you will do what you can and go home, because not only is that all that is expected, but it is all that is allowed. The budget becomes the client rather than the citizen. Once that mindset takes hold, it is hard to accelerate the pace of work, either for a one-time need or in general. Limited staffing is not a sufficient or complete explanation, however, as there are too many adequately staffed offices that also operate on government time.

Court administrators are not immune from operating on government time. In my experience, however, court administrators normally have a greater sense of urgency about the need for decisions and action than some court staff and many in other units of government. Many court tasks have statutory, rule, or internal administrative procedural deadlines. For example, many courts have internal rules about courtroom minutes being completed and entered into the case management information system within 24 or 48 hours. Papers releasing people from jail must be completed as soon as possible after a judge makes that decision. Calendars for tomorrow's work need to be prepared, normally, by 3:00 or 4:00 p.m. so files can be pulled and given to the judges to examine in advance. Warrants for arrest and bail bond information should be prepared the same day, if not within two hours. When judges need something fixed in their courtrooms or chambers or something else related to their jobs, they normally have a low tolerance for delay. If the administrator can deal with an issue only through court staff, an immediate need normally can be handled immediately, particularly if a judge is affected. Court staff members understand the hierarchy and the deadlines; they try hard to provide judges with whatever they need, be it information, a case file, or fixing a chair. When the administrator has to reach outside direct-line staff, however, government time often seems to kick in. When the occasion for prompt attention are matters that have a longer time horizon, such as a new program or changing an existing program or calendar, however, all stakeholders, including judges and staff, seem to operate on government time with distressing frequency.

Thus, there is the need for patience. Some administrators' personalities allow them to take delays in stride and not to worry about the actions (or nonactions) of those they cannot control. For most court administrators, patience must be learned or they will be in a constant state of stress.

An administrator's need for perspective is related to having a strong sense of self, but also is different. An administrator must be able to see the court from a distance in order to assess whether it is doing its job and to envision how to improve its operations and delivery of service. An administrator who gets too tied up with the daily details of operating a court will be doing only part of his or her job.

The rules are simple:

1. It is not top management work if someone else can do it....
2. People who move into top management work should ... give up the functional or operating work they did earlier.[47]

An administrator also has to understand the context in which courts operate, as reviewed in part I of this book. There simply are a lot of things and critical personnel courts and their administrators do not control and sometimes cannot control. It helps to recognize courts' place in government and in society and the limits of one's power and authority. The absence of control does not mean giving up and not trying for improvement, but it does mean one has to keep the long view in mind while working on what may be only very small incremental steps toward achieving the long-term goal. Most administrators know better than they do, not for want of trying but for all the institutional, political, and personality reasons discussed to this point and because of budget and staffing limitations. Administrators require perspective on both the court as an institution and on themselves to assure the proper functioning of daily operations and to work for long-term improvement.

Flexibility is an important quality for administrators. It can be called into play at two levels. "Trial courts can be dynamic and a bit wild. A courthouse in the full throes of a busy court day can be a scene of frenetic activity and hourly emergencies…. A major breakdown in court operations or case scheduling can be embarrassing and frustrating, so each day presents a new administrative challenge to keep things moving along without fiascoes."[48] During my time as a court administrator, there were many days when I came to court expecting—sometimes needing—to do certain tasks and ended the day not finishing one of them because of unanticipated events that arose during the day. Flexibility at this level probably is not all that different from the daily demands on many executives in both the public and private sectors, however. The greater need for flexibility is in fixing problems and designing new or modified programs or procedures. Refer back to Zaleznik's description of a manager to note his use of the words enabling, reconciling, and seeking compromise. These words could define the concept of flexibility for a court administrator.

I emphasize two ideas when conducting training programs for court administrators and senior managers: (1) "baby steps" and (2) a "bottom drawer" approach to management. "Baby steps" refers to the popular 1991 movie, *What About Bob?* Its story line is set up by a book written by one of the two main characters that says people should seek to overcome neuroses and phobias, making one small incremental change at a time until, in the end, the person has made tremendous changes. The term *baby steps* is simply a cute way of referring to the continual improvement approach of many Japanese and then American companies that adopted Total Quality Management in the 1970s through the mid-1990s.[49] Baby steps also sometimes is all that a court administrator can accomplish at a particular moment of time as he or she seeks to move the court closer to larger, longer-term goals. Court administrators must not be content to accomplish only baby steps for every new idea or program—large, bold, dramatic steps are needed to accomplish major changes—but sometimes one must take what one can get and then use the new position as the launch pad for more improvement later.

A court administrator should never be content with the status quo; some improvements always are possible and desirable. Thus, every administrator's wish list should be longer than his or her current project list. The wish list might include ideas that already have been presented and rejected or ignored, as well as new ideas that have not yet been propounded or tried. The wish list is figuratively kept in the "bottom drawer" of an administrator's desk, near at hand when the right moment arrives. Courts are like all other units of government and the private sector: crises and embarrassment make people much more willing to consider a new idea than they might be while deluding themselves that everything is fine.[50] When one of these moments of opportunity arises, an administrator should check his or her bottom drawer to see if there is something on the wish list that can address or ameliorate the crisis of the moment. If so, it should be brought out and proposed, even if it is an idea that previously had not won favor but is one the administrator believes strongly has merit and should be tried.[51] Flexibility, both in organizing one's priorities day to day and in pursuing longer-term goals, is a necessary quality for court administrators.

"You should no more expect others to agree with your every opinion than you should agree with theirs."[52] Building an environment in which people feel free to challenge and test ideas, either to strengthen those that are accepted or avoid those that do not have merit, is hard. We all would like to be right all the time and to have people always agree with us. Neither desire can be realized; if the latter is true, an administrator probably is more a tyrant than a manager, he or she is certainly not a leader, and the organization will suffer.

In a wonderful management primer, *Leadership Secrets of Attila the Hun*, author Wess Roberts, using Attila's voice, reminds his readers:[53]

■ Do not consider all opponents to be enemies. You may have productive, friendly confrontations, with others inside and outside your tribe.
■ Do not try to conform everyone's behavior unless doing so is critical to tribal discipline or purpose.

Michael Livingston reviewed University of Chicago Law School professor Cass Sunstein's book, *Why Societies Need Dissent*, indicating Sunstein "makes a distinction between interpersonal conflict … and substantive conflict…. 'Diversity of information is the most important variable' in group process, and 'conflicts about substance are most likely to be helpful…. If people are fighting because of personal animus, they are less likely to accomplish their tasks.' If this distinction invites a 'no, duh,' it bears emphasis that personal animus is not inherent in dissent."[54] It can be a fine line at times between an employee or manager who is simply throwing up road blocks, through personal animus or otherwise, and one who is aggressive about suggesting alternative scenarios or views in hopes of strengthening rather than hindering the decision making. To help to identify which is which, the administrator or another senior manager may need to have personal discussions with the person who seems always to be objecting in order to mentor about presenting alternate points in a constructive way, or to surface possible animus. If behavior does not change, it becomes a personnel matter.

The need for dissenting views is not lessened by the fact that some people do not want to be positive contributors, or do not know how to be. Manfred Kets de Vries, an internationally recognized expert on leadership, views the classic role of "a King's fool" to be critical to a leader. "The fool … is a foil for the leader—and every leader needs one…. The fool shows the leader his reflection and reminds him of the transience of power…. To be effective, organizations need people with a healthy disrespect for the boss—people who feel free to express emotions and opinions openly, who can engage in active give-and-take."[55] One need not think in terms of disrespect or naysayers, or difficult people. Diversity of opinion is the goal. John Scully, former CEO of Apple Computer, says: "One of the biggest mistakes a person can make is to put together a team that reflects only him. I find it's better to put teams together of people who have different skills and then make all those disparate skills function together. The real role of the leader is to figure out how you make diverse people and elements work together."[56]

Much of the literature on leadership makes the point about needing dissenters to improve decision making: "All great leaders … cultivate a culture of candor."[57] Martin Winterkorn, the CEO of Audi, the German automaker, says, "Audi's culture … endorses internal debate and argument. As a manager you have to be able to fight with colleagues on an intellectual plane without feeling attacked personally. This is especially important when it comes to discussing mistakes that are made. Everyone makes mistakes, even me."[58] The need is as important in courts as in other organizations. Indeed, the environment of courts may make it even more important. It is a harder role to play in courts, however, because judges are not used to their opinions being challenged openly and vigorously and a number of administrators are not tolerant of dissent. It is because of this environment that strong managers should not only tolerate, but also seek out diverse views and dissenters to help shape and strengthen decisions.

Curiosity is not commonly put on lists of leadership qualities and managers are said to eschew it. Warren Bennis, a leading commentator on leadership, cites it, however. "Leaders wonder about everything, want to learn as much as they can, are willing to take risks, experiment, try new things."[59] Curiosity is important in courts for two reasons, whether one believes administrators should be leaders or managers. First, court administration still is growing as a profession and there remains much to be learned. Administrators should constantly be looking around for training and literature on public administration, the nonprofit sector, and the corporate sector for ideas and guidance about how to improve. Second, change happens in courts largely one court at a time (see also, section 12.2, chapter 12). Even with the Knowledge and Information Service of the National Center for State Courts, whose purpose is to facilitate the exchange of information and ideas among courts, new ideas and programs often move slowly through the court community. An administrator, therefore, must keep his or her eyes and ears wide open to identify and find out about new programs of merit that might work in his or her court. Without curiosity and a sense of discovery about the job, it is easy for an administrator to turn inward and forget to look around at what other courts are doing, both around the state and around the country. An administrator can always decide a new idea or program is not appropriate for his or her court, but unless the basic curiosity exists, the administrator is not in a position to make that judgment.

One of the most important qualities exhibited by leaders is strong people skills. In the literature of leadership, the term *emotional intelligence* is applied most often. The terms used to describe people skills vary, but the need for people skills is almost universally identified as important for leaders. We will return to this point in section 7.3. It is important here because so many court administrators appear to possess and are asked to use the qualities and skills identified for "managers" rather than those identified for "leaders." The label does not matter. If one looks again at Zaleznik's description of a manager, above, a manager needs to understand opposition, reconcile positions, and find compromises. Managers like to interact with people rather than isolate themselves to contemplate new futures, a mental habit that is found most often in leaders. Managers need people skills.

Court administration involves almost constant interacting with important but independent stakeholders, with largely independent minded judges, with state and local government and private agencies, and with the public on the court's behalf. Without some sensitivity to people, without some skill at presenting ideas without being threatening, demeaning, or indifferent to others' views, and without some capacity to recognize and accommodate important interests of others, a court administrator cannot be effective.

7.3 The Need for Leaders in Court Administration

One of the critical competencies for court leaders included in NACM's Core Competencies is "leadership." [60] In explaining why leadership is important, NACM states, "Leadership is the energy behind every court system and court accomplishment…. Absent leadership excellence, courts and court systems cannot take or maintain effective action." [61] Like virtually all writers about leadership, NACM explains leadership, in part, by contrasting it to management. [62]

> Management deals with complexity. Leadership deals with change and growth. Managers oversee and use control mechanisms to maintain predictability and to ensure coordination, follow-through, and accountability. They know how to get things done. Leaders think about, create, and inspire others to act upon dreams, missions, strategic intent and purpose. Courts have an obvious need for both management and leadership.

Courts also have an obvious need for managers with some leadership skills and qualities (see section 7.2.2.2, above). But how do they go about finding them? Can courts train people to be leaders? Can administrators be leaders or can only judges be leaders in courts?

There are three components of the leadership issue: the qualities and skills possessed by leaders; whether leadership can be taught (or learned); and what the consequences of having a leader or leaders would be, how would things be different?

7.3.1 Leaders' Qualities and Skills

The quotes from business writings in section 7.2.2.1 plus the NACM quote immediately above, imply the qualities and skills of leaders, but do not specifically identify them. As just one example, NACM says leaders "*deal with* change and growth" (emphasis added). They do, but how? What enables them to deal with change and growth? The literature goes off in many directions. The Core Competencies' discussion of the "knowledge, skills, and abilities" of leaders is a good summary of the key points in much of the literature.[63] NACM offers 50 bulleted items identifying the knowledge, skills, or abilities leaders should possess, allocated among five major qualities. Those five qualities are:

- Be credible in action
- Create focus through vision and purpose
- Manage interdependencies: work beyond the boundaries
- Create a high-performance work environment
- Do skillful and continual diagnosis.

NACM's list would not be a bad list of the characteristics a strong court administrator should possess, too. "Vision and purpose" are the only items on this list not normally stipulated for a court administrator. Even so, a court seeking a strong manager might desire one who has a vision of what courts should be and who would be purposeful in achieving it, if the judges were comfortable with the administrator's vision. It is just that not many courts give any indication that a new vision of courts is one of the things desired in an administrator.

Ronald Stupak was quoted earlier identifying the qualities of a manager or the results a manager can achieve. He offers a corresponding list for leaders:[64] A leader, he says:

Creates futures	Is opportunity driven
Sets directions	Uses positive power
Does the right thing	Communicates meaning
Is strategically driven	Is performance anchored
Motivates people	Is a change-maker
Is value anchored	Is an option generator
Is a boundary crosser	Cultivates networks
Positions from imagination	

The Army War College offers an interesting perspective on leadership. It surveyed subordinates of highly regarded major generals in Iraq on "what makes a good leader?" The responses, in order of importance, were:[65]

■ Keeps cool under pressure
■ Clearly explains missions, standards, and priorities
■ Sees the big picture; provides context and perspective
■ Makes tough, sound decisions on time.

Another list suggests "the best managerial tools" are "judgment, warmth, communication skills, and intuition."[66] Regarding the need for warmth, Manfred Kets de Vries refers to the "teddy bear factor: Do people feel comfortable with you? Do they want to be close to you?"[67] A corporate board sought a new leader who would demonstrate "technical competence,… people skills, conceptual skills (meaning imagination and creativity), judgment and taste, and character."[68]

There are a lot of lists that could be included here. Some lists merely refer to the same things with a different label. Some lists contain a new thought or two. Rather than provide more lists, I would like to focus on two concepts that seem to be seminal for leaders: emotional intelligence and the ability to match leaders' and followers' values and needs in such a way that followers adopt the leaders' values and thus work with the leader for change. The latter is not the same as empathy, but empathy overlaps to a substantial extent a leader's ability to identify and then reinforce another's values and needs so he or she becomes a follower.

Daniel Goleman, cochair of the Consortium for Research in Emotional Intelligence in Organizations, Rutgers University Graduate School of Applied and Professional Psychology, was one of the first two to identify and explain emotional intelligence and why it is important for leaders. The concept is not unknown in court administration, but it is not well known, either.[69] There are five components of emotional intelligence: self-awareness, self-regulation, motivation, empathy, and social skill.[70] Self-aware people display candor with others and an ability to assess themselves realistically.[71] "Healthy leaders are very talented in self-observation and self-analysis…."[72] Self-regulation is an ability to say no to impulsive urges to act, but also is a propensity for reflection, thoughtfulness, a comfort with ambiguity and change, and integrity.[73] Motivation is the drive within a leader to achieve beyond expectations, including his or her own, and a desire to achieve for achievement's sake.[74] "Socially skilled people tend to have a wide circle of acquaintances, and they have a knack for finding common ground with people of all kinds—a knack for building rapport."[75]

Manfred Kets de Vries sums up emotional intelligence in one phrase: self-reflection.[76] John D. Mayer, a professor of psychology at the University of New Hampshire, who is credited along with Goleman with defining emotional intelligence in the early 1990s, talks of emotional intelligence in the following terms:[77] "... Emotional intelligence is the ability to accurately perceive your own and others' emotions; to understand the signals that emotions send about relationships; and to manage your own and others' emotions. It doesn't necessarily include the qualities (like optimism, initiative, and self-confidence) that some popular definitions ascribe to it." Emotional intelligence remains a hot buzzword in business academic circles, but corporate executives also have internalized it. William George, former chairman and CEO of Medtronic, Inc, a medical device manufacturer, talks about self-awareness as follows:[78]

> Authentic leadership begins with self-awareness, a knowing yourself deeply. Self-awareness is not a trait you are born with, but a capacity you develop throughout your lifetime. It's your understanding of your strengths and weaknesses, your purpose in life, your values and motivations, and how and why you respond to situations in a particular way. It requires a great deal of introspection and the ability to internalize feedback from others.

Why is it important to understand emotional intelligence? Goleman explains:[79]

> When I analyzed all this data [from the efforts of 188 companies to identify leaders and the ingredients that make good leaders,] I found dramatic results. To be sure, intellect was a driver of outstanding performance. Cognitive skills such as big-picture thinking and long-term vision were particularly important. But when I calculated the ratio of technical skills, IQ, and emotional intelligence as ingredients of excellent performance, emotional intelligence proved to be twice as important as the others for jobs at all levels.

Emotional intelligence is highly personal and highly internal. The lists above and the items discussed elsewhere in this book describe the results of being a leader, not the traits that enable one to achieve those results. Emotional intelligence provides insight into the factors and traits that lead one to leadership. It may have become a buzzword in the literature, but it still provides insight into the kind of person who becomes an effective leader. It also is largely overlooked when courts talk about desiring leaders. Typical job interviews for court administrator positions involve asking about accomplishments in one's current position. They ask about how an applicant overcame a difficult situation or dealt with a difficult employee. They may pose a hypothetical situation and ask how the applicant would deal with the facts presented. They almost never seek to learn about an applicant's emotional intelligence (see section 7.4).

James MacGregor Burns authored a seminal book on leadership in 1978.

The book contains many insights, but one of the most important relates to the relationship between leaders and followers. Many people, even today, think of leaders as people who can make others do what the leader wants them to do. Burns defines leadership "as leaders inducing followers to act for certain goals that represent the values and the motivation—the wants and needs, the aspirations and expectations—*of both leaders and followers*. And the genius of leadership lies in the manner in which leaders see and act on their own and their followers' values and motivations"[80] (emphasis in original). Burns identifies three types of leadership.[81]

> The relations of most leaders and followers are *transactional*—leaders approach followers with an eye to exchanging one thing for another: jobs for votes, or subsidies for campaign contributions. [Note that this balancing and compromising is a feature attributed by some to managers today.] … *Transforming* leadership, while more complex, is more potent. The transforming leader recognizes and exploits an existing need or demand of a potential follower. But, beyond that, the transforming leader looks for potential motives in followers, seeks to satisfy higher needs, and engages the full person of the follower. The result of transforming leadership is a relationship of mutual stimulation and elevation that converts followers into leaders and may convert leaders into moral agents.
>
> The last concept, *moral leadership*, concerns me the most. By this term I mean, first, that leaders and led have a relationship not only of power but of mutual needs, aspirations, and values; second, that in responding to leaders, followers have adequate knowledge of alternative leaders and programs and the capacity to choose among those alternatives, and, third, that leaders take responsibility for their commitments.… Moral leadership emerges from, and always returns to, the fundamental wants and needs, aspirations, and values of the followers.

To effect change in courts, leadership must be at least transforming. To effect lasting and transformational changes, leadership must be moral. As discussed at length in chapter 6, there is little or no power one can exercise in courts because all judges are politically equal. Only persuasion is effective to get a critical mass of judges, and, following that, all judges, on board with a major change.[82] Once judges are on board, only persuasion—backed occasionally by judicial power that can be exercised in court—will bring along all the stakeholders who are *in* courts but not *of* them. Courts are wonderful institutions in which to exercise both transformational leadership and moral leadership because the values of law and courts—due process, fairness, the appearance of doing justice, access, even-handedness, preserving order while protecting individuals from arbitrary government power—already are ingrained in virtually all the key stakeholders and in the general citizenry. Courts do not have to seek or create shared values to which both leaders and followers can ascribe, they already exist and are accepted. People may prefer one approach to another or believe a proposed solution will not achieve the stated goals, but that is where leadership takes hold. Leadership seeks needs, motivations, and aspirations that lie below the shared values and affect how people see proposals, either as threatening or as compatible and desirable. Leaders listen—another skill ascribed by almost all observers to leaders *and* good managers—and address these underlying factors so that others see the congruence between what they want and what the leader wants. At that point, change is possible and often is transforming.

An observer of court administration speaks of this convergence, although in somewhat different terms. Bob Tobin speaks of the early pioneers in the court administration revolution of the second half of the 20th century as having "the ability to state a vision in simple and compelling terms. Their greatness did not lie in dreaming up visions, but in their ability to apprehend and mobilize support for ideas whose time had come."[83] It is important as court leaders speak of needing leadership that they remember Burns's concepts of leadership, remember that in an institution of peers, only transforming and moral leadership can be effective. Those who have the emotional intelligence and moral leadership to reach their peers are the leaders of the current and future generations who will move courts forward into leadership courts.

7.3.2 What Difference Do Leaders Make?

Leaders are change agents. Leaders change an institution's direction. They see the present context for an organization, reject it, and create a new context. Then they persuade others to adopt their new context and seek to make it happen. They often reinvent organizations, just as IBM left the mainframe computer business and today is largely a consulting and information integration company and just as Western Union used to deliver telegrams and now is a retail personal finance company.[84] Drucker talks about leadership in these terms: "The foundation of innovative strategy is planned and systematic sloughing off of the old, the dying, the obsolete. Innovating organizations spend neither time nor resources on defending yesterday."[85] And again:[86]

> Innovative strategy ... aims at creating a new business rather than a new product within an already established line. It aims at creating new performance capacity rather than improvement. It aims at creating new concepts of what is value rather than satisfying existing value

expectations a little better. The aim of innovating efforts is to make a significant difference.

Warren Bennis cites three reasons why leaders are important. [87]

First, they are responsible for the effectiveness of organizations....

Second, ... [w]e need anchors in our lives, something like a trim-tab factor, a guiding purpose. Leaders fill that need.

Third, there is a pervasive national concern about the integrity of our institutions.

Bennis's call for integrity was more urgent from his perspective in 2003, shortly after some of the more serious corporate fraud cases had surfaced in the late 1990s and early 2000s. Even so, many writers cite integrity as a necessary quality in a leader. It has value in its own right and also is critical to enable leaders to establish trust, a key consequence of leaders exercising leadership.

Courts need effective organizations. Courts need anchors integrity and to improve the service they now provide. Courts also need new concepts of value. On the other hand, courts do not need to create new businesses because in important ways they cannot. They do not need to slough off the old or cease to defend the old. As just one example of this duality, but one that may prove to be very important in the 21st century, consider problem-solving courts. They are a new way of doing business, but not a new business. They have broken the context of courts and created a new context for thinking about what courts do and how they do it. Courts cannot slough off the adversarial process, even if, as I believe will be the case, the problem-solving approach continues to expand in its application within courts. Some cases still require the safety valve of an adversarial hearing. Centuries of practice, procedures, and provisions of constitutional law compel courts to retain the capacity to resolve disputes using the adversarial process. Courts cannot get out of the dispute resolution, honest government, lawful government, and security-providing business. Courts can use different techniques as they fill these roles, however, which means courts must continue to invent and change while they continue to preserve their function and roles.

The other thing about courts is that it is very hard for administrators to be leaders. Or, perhaps more accurately, it is very hard for administrators to be the visible leaders of significant change. This issue also was addressed in chapter 6. Judges need to be seen by most important stakeholders as involved and committed before the stakeholders will take the idea of a significant change seriously. Before other judges come on board regarding a proposal, judicial leaders in a court often need to be seen to be committed and involved. Normally, it is judges who must articulate the values and the moral positions that will make fellow judges willing followers. Administrators can be leaders in the sense of having vision, of understanding and articulating effectively the values that will move early adopting judges to sign on, and to have the character and integrity needed to bring staff along to a shared vision. These are important qualities; when a court has them in an administrator, it is blessed. But a court whose only leader is the administrator will not achieve whatever vision the administrator may have. As a result, the administrator will feel discouraged and may become isolated, as he or she will be too far out in front of the judiciary to be effective at the day-to-day management level as well as at the long-range change level.[88] There is no doubt that there are courts across the nation with judges who have strong leadership skills and visions of an improved and maybe a changed judiciary. Many of these courts already are recognized as leadership courts in their states and, sometimes, nationally. These courts are in the minority. They will not move to a majority status because we wish for more leadership. Like so much in court administration, courts change one court at a time. And some courts will be very slow to change.

As NACM's Leadership Competency discussion states, courts need both leaders and managers, but they need good strong managers more than leaders. NACM's Core Competencies embrace both judicial and staff leaders, so NACM's call for leadership is not entirely misplaced. To the extent that it suggests that courts need administrators who can and will fill the leadership role, it probably suggests too much.

7.3.3 Teaching Leadership

The difference between leaders and managers is hidden within NACM's and Stupak's lists and those of the other authors cited above. It lies in how they view the world, including their work world, in how they interact with ideas and people, and in who they are. NACM and a number of others say that leadership is, "to a significant extent, learnable."[89] It is learnable only to the extent that one learns from living; the lessons gained from life are not learnable from a book or by following a prescribed curriculum in a classroom or through distance learning. Leaders do not emerge from training, they have innate qualities that grow and strengthen over time as they have a variety of experiences in and out of their work environments, as they take risks, make mistakes and maybe even fail,[90] and as they listen to and learn from others. Gloria Anderson, a newspaper executive and editor, says, "You can't make being a leader your principle goal, any more than you can make being happy your goal. In both cases, it has to be the result, not the cause."[91]

Warren Bennis makes the point repeatedly:

I am surer now than ever that the process of becoming a leader is the same process that makes a person a healthy, fully-integrated human being. And it is the same process that allows one to age successfully.[92]

◊ ◊ ◊ ◊

[The leaders interviewed by Bennis about leadership agree on two basic points:] First, they all agree that leaders are made, not born, and made more by themselves than by any external means. Second, they agree that no leader sets out to be a leader per se, but rather to express him- or herself freely and fully. That is, leaders have no interest in proving themselves, but an abiding interest in expressing themselves. The difference is crucial, for it's the difference between being driven, as too many people are today, and leading, as too few people do.[93]

◊ ◊ ◊ ◊

No leader sets out to be a leader. People set out to live their lives, expressing themselves fully. When that expression is of value, they become leaders. So the point is not to become a leader. The point is to become yourself completely—all your skills, gifts, and energies—in order to make your vision manifest.[94]

As Bennis further notes specifically about training people to be leaders, "I would argue that more leaders have been made by accident, circumstance, sheer grit, or will than have been made by all the leadership courses put together.... Leadership courses can only teach skills. They can't teach character or vision—and indeed they don't even try. Developing character and vision is the way leaders invent themselves."[95] Regarding the central role of character in leadership, Bennis is echoing Drucker. (Recall, Drucker speaks of managers as many today speak of leaders.) "What a manager does can be analyzed systematically. What a manager has to do can be learned.... But one quality cannot be learned, one qualification that the manager cannot acquire but must bring with him. It is not genius, it is character."[96]

Daniel Goleman rejects as ineffective the trained psychologists employed by a number of large companies today who develop what are known as "competency models" to aid them in identifying, training, and promoting likely stars in the leadership firmament.[97] One of the coauthors of the report on the Army War College's study of highly regarded major generals said, "One thing we found is that it's still easier to teach technical skills than to teach people how to gain trust and build teams."[98] Richard Ferry, cofounder of Korn/Ferry International, an executive search firm, has observed the same thing. "You can't really create leaders. How do you teach people to make decisions, for example? All you can do is develop the talents people have."[99]

There is another tension between a desire for leaders and a need for managers. Zaleznik points out that the process of ensuring people are able to assume practical responsibility—tasks associated with managers—may inhibit the development of leaders. The presence of great leaders also can undermine the development of managers. Leaders, by definition, are not maintaining the organization but changing it. Some managers may have trouble dealing with the disorder created by a leader.[100]

One cannot teach intellect, although one certainly can improve knowledge. One cannot teach how to fashion a long-term vision, although techniques may help big-picture thinking. Most of all, one cannot teach emotional intelligence insofar as it is based on the factors identified by Goleman and discussed in the previous section.

Leaders are discovered, not trained. Abraham Zaleznik indicates that managers are fashioned by socialization efforts across the course of one's life. Many of these socialization skills can be taught. But leaders "emerge" from the process of "personal mastery, which impels an individual to struggle for psychological and social change."[101]

Without doubt, technical skills and knowledge can be imparted through training. That is the guiding vision of NACM's Core Competencies. The qualities and experiences that result in the emergence of leaders, however, cannot be captured and presented in tests to identify likely leaders or in workshops to teach people how to be leaders. Leadership is a personal quality gained over time by people who possess qualities that make them open to life's lessons and who relate in a particular way to others, neither of which can be captured in a lesson plan.

NACM is right in the discussion of the leadership competency that courts need leaders. It is not right, however, when it says leadership can be learned, implying classroom or on-the-job training. We need to know how and why leaders are different in order to understand how to recognize leadership qualities. We need to nurture and train those with leadership capacity in technical skills and in a broad range of work and life experiences so their leadership qualities can grow and meld with technical skills. We cannot take people without leadership qualities and train them to be leaders.[102] Nor should we take good, even outstanding managers and expect them to be leaders.

7.4   The Hiring Process for Court Administrators

Too often, judges do a poor job of selecting court administrators. It is not the selected administrators who are poor, but the process used to select them.

Almost all courts select managers through review of an application form and possibly written answers to supplemental questions and then a personal interview. Sometimes there is a panel of interviewers who screen down to the final two or three, followed by a final round of interviews by appropriate senior managers or, most often, judges. The interviews almost always are highly structured, with preset questions asked of all applicants and almost no deviation from those questions. Thus do courts—and almost all public entities—believe they are being both effective and "fair" to applicants. Limit discretion, limit different treatment for different people, and, the lawyers assert, no one can criticize the final selection or the process. Wrong!

In terms of predicting performance, personal interviews are accurate 7 percent of the time.[103] *Seven percent!* With courts' highly structured and inflexible approach, the percent might be even lower. It seems it is mostly dumb luck when courts hire good administrators using this common technique.

The *Handbook of Industrial and Organizational Psychology* indicates the following about the success of other techniques in predicting on-the-job performance.[104]

Selection Technique	Accuracy In Predicting
Résumé analysis (quasi-scientific résumé "sifting")	37%
Work sample test (written skills test)	44%
Assessment Center (lengthy, off-site skills and personality workup)	44%
Situational interview (role-playing mock scenarios)	54%

Situational interviews involve people acting as customers or colleagues bringing characteristic problems or issues to the applicant who has no preparation for the encounter. For example, a problem finding files, a staff member's tardiness problem, or a proposal to overlook an ethical issue.[105] A book by Justin Menkes, *Executive Intelligence*, claims that rather than emotional intelligence and other indicia of leadership, it is "executive intelligence" that best identifies successful executives.[106] Menkes defines executive intelligence as superior reasoning and problem-solving skills. The best way to find such executives is to "measure the ability to accomplish tasks, work with and through others, and evaluate oneself and adapt accordingly."[107] He argues that the best way to test an applicant's abilities in this area is "an oral exam comprising hypothetical business problems";[108] or, in other words, a situational interview.[109] In addition to probing for the qualities of a good manager in which a court is particularly interested, it should explore *how* one addresses a problem or issue. That is one of the advantages of the situational interview.

I know of one court that hired a senior manager whose interview went poorly. The selection committee figured—correctly as his many subsequent years of on-the-job success demonstrated—that someone with the success achieved in his current position should be given credit for those over a "bad day or bad interview." Dion DeLoof, cofounder of a technical staffing firm, says, "Some of our best hires have been people who have little or no experience, but come with a history of overcoming adversity and learning new skills…. 'Past success and performance is a predictor of future success and performance.'"[110] Performance and references should get at least as much weight as a pleasing demeanor and the "right answers" to the preset questions during a one-hour encounter.

Courts also tend to hire for skills or knowledge they believe they need today, too-often ignoring the virtual certainty that tomorrow's problems will be different, because change is the only constant. Asking one to describe experiences and responses to date is like looking in a car's passenger-side mirror; performance-based selection is looking through the windshield.

Many things could be done differently in hiring administrators. First and foremost, a court should plan on most of a day or even two to three interviews for each semifinalist rather than a single 45 or 60 minute interview.[111] Ask for a memo written while in their current position that analyzes and proposes a solution to a problem. Ask for an analysis and proposal regarding a current problem or issue that your court currently has (after providing relevant data and background), either written on site or presented orally, and ask follow-up questions. To heighten the experience and stress, the court could even set up a situational test during what appears to be a traditional interview and ask the applicant to handle it to demonstrate what he or she would do if appointed to the desired position. Have an applicant visit a division or courthouse to assess a problem and see how he or she interacts with staff, as well as how he or she goes about identifying possible solutions. Ask for a one- or two-page memo written after the interview addressing the job opportunity, the applicant's approach to the issues your court is facing, and laying out a high-level plan for making the court successful.[112] Look for an applicant's capacity to examine problems strategically, not tactically. Find ways to observe how people perform rather than have them explain how and what they have done. Seek opinions from the current employer or colleagues in other courts with whom the applicant has worked regarding collegiality, problem-solving skills, and responses to stress. Seek references from two or three past employers, as the qualities identified above do not change much over time. Many employers, particularly government employers, are reluctant today to respond about a former employee with anything beyond title and the dates of employment, but it does not hurt to ask. That also is why it might be useful to find peers who have worked with the applicant on committees or in volunteer organizations. These individuals would not be as constrained in responding as would a former employer. And consider a lunch or dinner at the court's expense. Not everyone feels comfortable being interviewed during a meal, but it need not be a formal interview. It could be simply a sociable break in a long day. Even with people not asking about job experiences or situations, one can learn a lot about a person during an informal discussion over a meal. This also is an excellent way to involve and get input from more staff, judges, and managers.

Related to this point, business school professors Imparato and Harari cite an accountant at Hewlett-Packard who described his interview process to them. "I learned later that once they reviewed my resume, they assumed I knew accounting. What they really wanted to know was how I worked on teams, how fast would I take on responsibilities without being told, how cooperative was I, how did I feel about risk, and how easy was I to work with."[113] Many court interviews fail on the first point made by this accountant: assuming the person has the needed technical skills (other than secretarial or data entry applicants, who may have been given a typing test to determine speed). Note, too, that this person was being hired as an accountant, not the CEO or a senior manager. Yet, it was important to Hewlett-Packard that he be a good team member, that he was willing to assume responsibility, that he was cooperative, and had given some thought to dealing with risk. Based on numerous court job interviews on both sides of the desk, I believe courts do not explore for these qualities much for their administrators, far less for employees further down the hierarchy.

Finally, Drucker inserts a useful reminder about looking for leaders and supermanagers.[114]

> Service institutions can no more than business depend on supermen or lion tamers to staff their managerial and executive position.... It is absurd to expect that the manager of every hospital in the world be a genius or even a great man [or woman]. If service institutions cannot be run and managed by men [and women] of fairly normal and fairly low endowment, if, in other words, we cannot organize the task so that it will be done adequately by men [and women] who only try hard, it cannot be done at all.

If courts start trying to fill their administrator positions with leaders who will be transformational, there are not enough to go around. Courts as a group, nationally, would advance materially if they simply sought strong managers. Even if more courts "only" seek good managers, however, they need to spend time examining the job the administrator is asked to do to see if it is manageable. The new administrator also has to examine the scope and nature of the position to see that it is defined by what Drucker calls "top management" tasks and not operational responsibilities that could be done by others. Too often, the job of administrator seems to grow like Topsy, with everything accepted and nothing moved to others. Staffing levels have a lot to do with this problem, but the absence of attention to what the job is also contributes. "The focus has to be on the job. The job has to make achievement possible. The job is not everything, but it comes first."[115] There is a fine balance to be struck by a court and its administrator regarding the skills and qualities sought and the tasks assumed. If courts want strong managers, as I believe they should, they need to start at the hiring process, carry through to the job definition stage, and then provide the administrator with the support staff needed to do the job defined. This agenda asks a lot of the judges who will be doing a lot of the up-front work, but in the end the investment of time up front will pay substantial dividends throughout the administrator's tenure.

Notes

1. Hays, Steven W., and Cole Blease Graham, Jr, eds., *Handbook of Court Administration and Management*. New York: Marcel Dekker, 1993, p. iv.
2. Saari,, David J., Michael D. Planet, and Marcus W. Reinkensmeyer, "The Modern Court Managers: Who They Are and What They Do in the United States," in Hays, Steven W., and Cole Blease Graham, Jr, eds., *Handbook of Court Administration*, p. 238.
3. See also, Friesen, Ernest C., Jr., Edward C. Gallas, and Nesta Gallas, *Managing the Courts*. Indianapolis, IN: Bobbs-Merrill, 1971, p. 119; Judicial System Leadership Forum, *Final Report*, Dec. 16–17, 2004. Washington, D.C.: Bureau of Justice Assistance and American University, 2005, p. 6.
4. Friesen, Ernest C., Jr., Edward C. Gallas, and Nesta Gallas, *Managing the Courts*, pp. 239–240.
5. Tobin, Robert W., *Creating the Judicial Branch: The Unfinished Reform*. Williamsburg, VA: National Center for State Courts, 1999, p. 179. Tobin is right about a "guarantee," but this may be too pessimistic a view, nonetheless. A number of administrators in smaller courts have moved up to larger courts during their careers. It is hard to move from a medium-sized court to a large urban court, but not impossible for one who has an excellent record of achievement. When Tobin is correct about the difficulty of upward mobility, it often is because the judges in the large courts are asking about experience supervising at least X number of people or budget of Y dollars or more, rather than an applicant's character, judgment, and people skills.
6. Ibid., pp. 179–180.
7. For a few courts, "technicians" should be extended to include human resources specialists. Some judges tend to believe that if this one issue is addressed satisfactorily, that is all the administrator need do.
8. Friesen, Ernest C., Jr., Edward C. Gallas, and Nesta Gallas, *Managing the Courts*, p. 22.
9. Saari, David J., Michael D. Planet, and Marcus W. Reinkensmeyer, "Modern Court Managers," pp. 238–240.
10. Friesen, Ernest C., Jr., Edward C. Gallas, and Nesta Gallas, *Managing the Courts*, p. 150, citing D. Yoder, *Personnel Management and Industrial Relations*. 5th ed. Englewood Cliffs, NJ: Prentice-Hall, 1962, pp. 418–419.
11. Byrne, John A., "The Man Who Invented Management: Why Peter Drucker's Ideas Still Matter," *Business Week*, Nov. 28, 2005, p. 98.

12. Ibid., p. 102.

13. There often were only high school diplomas. A 2005 to 2006 survey of almost half of the members of the National Association for Court Management (NACM)—including judge-members and many who are not the court administrator—indicates that over 30 percent do not have a BA or higher degree (55% have BAs or master's degrees; most of the remainder have law degrees). National Association for Court Management, Membership Profile Survey, as of Apr. 3, 2006, provided to the author by the NACM. Between the mid-1970s into the 1990s, three academic institutions, the University of Southern California, American University, and the University of Denver, awarded a master's degree in judicial administration, in USC's case through the School of Public Administration. Many of the graduates of those programs became senior court managers and court administrators. Their numbers were limited, however, and the programs no longer exist. (Denver's program was converted to one for law firm and court administrators; students pursuing law firm administration now dominate.) The graduates of these programs were unable to change broadly held perceptions about the absence of academic ratification of the field.

14. Chief Justice Warren Burger's vision when he sponsored establishment of the Institute for Court Management was that senior managers from government and the private sector plus retired military officers would receive training about courts from ICM and then become strong court managers. Many early graduates of ICM's Court Executive Development Program fit this model. (see note 15). Soon, however, recruiting such individuals became harder so the model was adjusted to train those already in courts on how to be strong court managers.

15. The CEDP involves a four-part program: (a) certain workshop requirements (ranging in length from three days to a week) as a prerequisite to admission; (b) a one-month residency program devoted to an academic review of management concepts and literature; (c) a research study and resulting paper documenting the study and results; and (d) a one-week closing workshop reviewing each person's research paper, some final management discussions, and graduation.

16. Michigan State University has created a Judicial Administration Program that offers academic credit for seminars attended during conferences of the NACM (and, now, other organizations) "that offers academically-based certificate programs and a master's degree." See Maureen E. Conner and Lawrence G. Myers, "NACM and MSU Collaborate to Add Academic Cre-dentials to NACM Education Programs," *The Court Manager,* vol. 19, no. 4, 2004, p. 24. This program is brand new, however, and thus has not yet progressed far enough to garner recognition among judicial officers.

17. Drucker, Peter F., quoted in John A. Byrne, "Man Who Invented Management," p. 100.

18. Friesen, Ernest C., Jr., Edward C. Gallas, and Nesta Gallas, *Managing the Courts,* p. 111.

19. Judges work in an environment in which litigants determine, almost on a random basis and certainly without warning, courts' inventory of cases while the legislature determines the laws that they apply and interpret and the budget under which courts operate. In a world seemingly controlled by others' actions, it often is hard to get judges to see value in strategic or long-term planning.

20. In fairness, I have known some administrators, now largely retired, who not only were strong personalities and administrators, but also could be very blunt and curt, bordering on rude, when responding to judges' requests or questions. It would have been a natural human response for a judge to denigrate these administrators' performance or decision making and label them unprofessional.

21. Judicial training programs can aid in this effort by designing programs on management that will both inform and appeal to judges.

22. The chief justice of California has a special assistant who primarily deals with administrative and scheduling matters in addition to the staff of the state court administrator. These positions are rare even in very large states.

23. Court staffs generally are a little short of or just sufficient, so administrators seeking new staff normally would seek more courtroom and case processing support staff ahead of "overhead" staff to support the administrator's assigned functions. Also, despite the common complaint that government agencies are "bloated," and "top heavy," most governments hate to fund what are perceived to be "excess" staff to cover time lost to training, illness, and unexpected demands with short time lines. The complaint about bloated government bureaucracies very seldom has validity for a state trial or appellate court.

24. Drucker, Peter F., *Management: Tasks, Responsibilities, Practices*. New York: Harper & Row, 1973, p. 17.

25. Ibid., p. 301.

26. Ibid., pp. 616, 618.

27. Ibid., p. 17.

28. Ibid., p. 400.

29. The most notable example of this is the *Trial Court Performance Standards*, published in 1990. The standards have been widely touted and discussed since, but seldom used with the measures. In an effort to increase usage, the National Center for State Courts developed CourTools, a condensed set of performance standards. CourTools were released in 2005.

30. Welch, Jack, and Suzy Welch, "The Leadership Mindset," *Business Week*, Jan. 30, 2006, p. 120.

31. Drucker, Peter F., *Management*, p. 310.

32. Collingwood, Harris, "Leadership's First Commandment: Know Thyself," *Harvard Business Review*, Dec. 2001, p. 8.

33. This is easier said than done for some staff. A few people—fortunately, very few in most courts—are such difficult individuals that moving them would improve the morale in the section they left, but ruin it in the section to which they are assigned. If the person will not leave, cannot leave because he or she cannot find a new job, or has narrow skills that do not transfer well to other sections, the challenge of dealing with this person is substantial.

34. Drucker used the term *innovative strategy*. Drucker, Peter F., *Management*, p. 792.

35. Imparato, Nicholas, and Oren Harari, *Jumping the Curve: Innovation and Strategic Choice in an Age of Transition*. San Francisco: Josey-Bass Publishers, 1994, p. 73.

36. Zaleznik, Abraham, "Managers and Leaders, Are They Different?" *Harvard Business Review*, 1977, reprinted in *Harvard Business Review*, Jan. 2004, pp. 75–79 (emphasis in original).

37. Stupak, Ronald J., "A Turning Point: From Managers to Leaders," *Court Communiqué*, vol. 1, no. 2, March 1999, p. 1.

38. Drucker, Peter F., *Management*, p. 401.

39. *Briefly*, the newsletter of the Seventh Judicial District, New York, vol. 26, July 22, 2005, p. 3, adapting material from "Optimism Isn't Always the Key to Success," from *Together* in *The Manager's Intelligence Report*.

40. This is a play on the management phrase, "When you are up to your waist in alligators, it is hard to remember that you need to drain the swamp."

41. National Association for Court Management, *Core Competency Curriculum Guidelines: What Court Leaders Need to Know and Be Able to Do*. Williamsburg, VA: National Association for Court Management, 2005, p. 4.

42. Copies of what NACM refers to as a "mini guide" that is devoted to the core competencies are available for a small fee from NACM, through the NCSC (see note 43).

43. http://www.ncsconline.org/D_KIS/jobdeda/main.htm.

44. Friesen, Ernest C., Jr., Edward C. Gallas, and Nesta Gallas, *Managing the Courts*, pp. 122–123.

45. In some courts today, the administrator also would be given responsibility for receipt, handling, and deposit of funds and for banking accounts and activities of the court. Sometimes this responsibility is solely the clerk of courts', sometimes it is shared by the clerk and the administrator, so local circumstances control whether and how this responsibility is phrased. In most courts that are locally funded, clerk or court staff members receive and account for cash and other payments pursuant to rules and procedures established by the responsible local government official. Banking normally is a county or city responsibility rather than a court responsibility.

46. See, Tobin, Robert W., *Creating the Judicial Branch*, p. 162.

47. Drucker, Peter F., *Management*, p. 615. In small courts, the person with the title of court administrator may be expected and to a degree required to do line work. Staff is not large enough in many courts to free the administrator from all line responsibility, even if it is only covering telephones or handling the counter during breaks or when someone is ill.

48. Tobin, Robert W., *Creating the Judicial Branch*, p. 183.

49. On the application of Total Quality Management to courts, see Aikman, Alexander B., *Total Quality Management in the Courts: A Handbook for Judicial Policy Makers and Administrators*. Williamsburg, VA: National Center for State Courts, 1994.

50. For courts, embarrassing newspaper or television stories often make judges much more open to change than they were prior to the story. Budget crises also can create conditions in which people will listen to possible reforms that were unacceptable when funds were sufficient.

51. Whirlpool Corp. started an innovation initiative in 2000. In the years since, thousands of ideas have surfaced, often from line staff. Even when an idea is rejected, it is not killed, it is given an "inactive" status. In 2006, there were 717 inactive ideas waiting for Whirlpool or another company to reexamine them. Arndt, Michael, "Creativity Overflowing," *Business Week*, May 8, 2006, p. 53.

52. From *Daily Inspirations* "quote of the day" calendar.

53. New York: Warner Books, Inc., 1990, p. 57.

54. Livingston, Mike, "A Dose of Healthy Disagreement" *Legal Times*, Nov. 3, 2003, quoting and reviewing Cass Sunstein, *Why Societies Need Dissent*, retrieved at http//www.uchicago.edu/news/news_sunstein.html.

55. Contu, Diane L., "Putting Leaders on the Couch: A Conversation with Manfred F.R. Kets de Vries," *Harvard Business Review*, Jan. 2004, p. 70.

56. Quoted in Bennis, Warren, *On Becoming a Leader*. New York: Basic Books, 2003, p. 98.

57. Ibid., p. xvii.

58. "On a Roll at Audi" retrieved Sept. 23, 2005, from http://www.businessweek.com/innovate/content/sep2005/id20050916_242086.htm.

59. Bennis, Warren, *On Becoming a Leader*, p. 33.

60. National Association for Court Management, *Core Competency Guidelines*, pp. 17–20. The primary authors are Geoff Gallas and Dan Straub (p. 62).

61. Ibid., p. 17

62. Ibid.

63. Ibid., pp. 19–20.

64. Stupak, Ronald J., "From Managers to Leaders."

65. "What Makes a Good Leader?," in "IntelligenceReport," *Parade*, July 10, 2005, p. 10.

66. Ryan, Liz, "Don't Be an Every Minute Manager," retrieved Sept. 22, 2005, from http://www.businessweek.com/ careers/content/sep2005/ca20050915_0127_ca017.htm.

67. Contu, Diane L., "Manfred F.R. Kets de Vries," p. 16.

68. Bennis, Warren, *On Becoming a Leader*, p. 24.
69. NACM's Leadership discussion does not use the term, for example, but does discuss some of its elements. National Association for Court Management, *Core Competency Guidelines*, pp. 17–21.
70. Staff of the *Harvard Business Review*, "Introduction," to Goleman, Daniel, "What Makes a Leader?" *Harvard Business Review*, originally published in 1998; reprinted in *Harvard Business Review*, Jan. 2004, p. 82.
71. Goleman, Daniel, "What Makes a Leader?" p.85.
72. Contu, Diane L., "Manfred F.R. Kets de Vries," p. 71.
73. Goleman, Daniel, "What Makes a Leader?" p. 87.
74. Ibid., p. 90.
75. Ibid.
76. Contu, Diane L., "Manfred F.R. Kets de Vries," p. 66.
77. Ibid., p. 28.
78. "Leading by Feel," *Harvard Business Review*, Jan. 2004, p. 35. This article contains statements by 18 business leaders and scholars about emotional intelligence.
79. Goleman, Daniel, "What Makes a Leader?" p. 84.
80. Burns, James MacGregor, *Leadership*. New York: Harper & Row, Inc., 1978, p. 19. See also, Prentice, W.C.H., "Understanding Leadership," *Harvard Business Review*, 1991, reprinted in *Harvard Business Review*, Jan. 2004, p. 104.
81. Burns, James MacGregor, *Leadership*, p. 4 (emphasis in original).
82. See Judicial System Leadership Forum, *Final Report*, p. 7.
83. Tobin, Robert W., *Creating the Judicial Branch*, p. 259.
84. Western Union delivered its last telegram on February 2, 2006. "STOP—Telegram Era Over, Western Union Says," The Associated Press, Feb. 2, 2006, retrieved Feb. 12, 2006, from http://www.msnbc.msn.com/id/11147506/.
85. Drucker, Peter F., *Management*, p. 791.
86. Ibid., p. 792.
87. Bennis, Warren, *On Becoming a Leader*, p. 4.
88. Tobin, Robert W., *Creating the Judicial Branch*, p. 162.
89. National Association for Court Management, *Core Competency Guidelines*, p. 17.
90. John Wooden, the legendary basketball coach, is reported to have said, "failure is not the crime. Low aim is." Quoted in Bennis, Warren, *On Becoming a Leader*, p. 188.
91. Ibid., p. 122.
92. Ibid., p. xxiv.
93. Ibid., p. xxix.
94. Ibid., p. 104.
95. Ibid., p. 34.
96. Drucker, Peter F., *Management*, p. 402
97. Goleman, Daniel, "What Makes A Leader?," p. 84.
98. "What Makes a Good Leader?," in "IntelligenceReport," *Parade*, July 10, 2005, p. 10.
99. Bennis, Warren, *On Becoming a Leader*, p. 136.
100. Zaleznik, Abraham, "Managers and Leaders," p. 75.
101. Ibid., p. 79.
102. Kasparek, F. Dale, "Leading the Unfinished Reform: The Future of Third Branch Administration," a project report submitted for the Institute for Court Management's Court Executive Development Program, Phase III, 2005, p. 129.
103. Merritt, Jennifer, "Improv at the Interview," *Business Week*, Feb. 3, 2003, p. 63.
104. Dunnette, M.D., and Hough, L.M., eds., *Handbook of Industrial and Organizational*

Psychology. Palo Alto, CA: Consulting Psychologists Press, 1990, cited in Merritt, Jennifer, "Improv at the Interview," *Business Week*, Feb. 3, 2003, p.63.

105. A friend who used to work at the California Administrative Office of the Courts advised the author of a favorite situational question that he used to screen finalists: "You are walking down the hall when you overhear two people talking. One is complaining loudly and bitterly about one of your coworkers. What do you do?" My correspondent thought the answers revealed a lot about how people deal with conflict in the workplace, whether they can think on their feet, and whether they are honest or giving an answer they think you want to hear. E-mail communication from Richard Schauffler to the author, Nov. 1, 2004.

106. Menkes, Justin, *Executive Intelligence: What All Great Leaders Have.* New York: HarperCollins, 2005.

107. Foust, Doug "How to Pick a Business Brain," *Business Week*, Feb. 20, 2006, p. 104.

108. Ibid.

109. While a face-to-face interview probably is best, one also could use a written submission. This not only would test one's reasoning, analytic, and problem-solving approaches, but also test writing skills. See Ryan, Liz, "How a Memo Can Beat an Interview," *BusinessWeek Online*, retrieved Oct. 8, 2004, from http://www.businessweek.com/ careers/content/oct2004/ ca2004104_7927_ca009.htm.

110. DeLoof, Dion,"Getting the Most from Your People." *BusinessWeek Online*, Sept. 22, 2004, retrieved Sept. 25, 2004, from http://www.businessweek.com/ smallbiz/content/sep2004/ sb20040922_9037.htm.

111. I recall that many years ago a friend who worked for a bank told me on a Saturday night that he had spent all of that day screening entry-level management candidates and was going to continue the process with these same candidates on Sunday. The most courts will do is conduct a screening interviews for multiple applicants one day and ask two or three finalists to hold over for a second round of interviews with the final decision makers the next day. The *process* both days is the same, however: interviews talking about general attitudes and how applicants dealt with various situations in their current or past positions.

112. See Ryan, Liz, "Memo Can Beat an Interview."

113. Imparato, Nicholas, and Oren Harari, *Jumping the Curve*, p. 216.

114. Drucker, Peter F., *Management*, p. 139.

115. Ibid., p. 266. Drucker says this in the context of defining jobs for staff, but it applies equally to defining the job of the court administrator.

Chapter 8

Introduction to the Hierarchy of Court Administration

Court administration often is defined in terms of tasks and functions: jury management, bond forfeitures, completing minutes of what happened in court, data entry, records management, security, strategic planning, calendar management, and on and on. The job description for a court administrator discussed in chapter 7, section 7.2.2.2 highlights the range of tasks and functions for which administrators are responsible. On top of these general responsibilities, trial courts across the nation through much of the last third of the 20th century had to deal with reorganizations of trial courts, changed funding sources for many, and significant efforts to improve calendar management and reduce delay in many courts. Problem-solving courts burgeoned, jury management had two waves of reform, one largely procedural and one more related to courtroom activities, and the use of data processing and other technologies exploded. Expectations in the other branches of government and among the public regarding accountability increased, as did courts' ability to respond. Since the mid-1970s, government income was down—whether local or state—during four periods of significant decline in economic activity.[1]

Layered on top of the normal ebb and flow of government revenue was a growing sense among the general public that government was inefficient, wasteful, ineffective, and generally inferior to the private sector. Taxpayer revolts or just general distaste resulted in capped spending, capped or cut revenue, and rejected bond issues and tax increases that might have kept up with the cost of government. During good economic times, many states enacted significant tax cuts. In an era when government funding was under great general pressure, courts needed more funding to respond to all the new demands of the court and judicial administration revolution and had to compete for those additional funds with all other government units that also faced important and growing demands. Meanwhile,

194 ■ *The Art and Practice of Court Administration*

legislatures across the country and the U.S. Congress were mandating the funding of certain programs and earmarking appropriations so that the programs and units of government funded through the general fund, such as the courts, were competing for fewer dollars. In the face of all these circumstances and pressures, courts did relatively well during the 1980s and 1990s compared to other units of government.[2] Even so, trial courts historically have struggled for adequate staffing in trial courts and in clerk of court offices. For several reasons, but often because of budget constraints, the technology and software used in courts lag behind the private sector by at least a generation and often by two generations. Even in average and good years, courts cannot expect significant budget increases, so most trial courts have to decide which one or two new or enhanced programs they will try to fund in a particular fiscal year out of the dozen or more they feel are needed.[3] When a recession hits, courts normally scramble not to have their budgets cut, since so much of their budgets[4] is required for personnel and for constitutionally mandated items such as indigent defense, transcript costs, and mental competency examinations over which courts have no control or discretion.

8.1   Constitutional and Statutory Mandates

It is said that the recession that hit government between 2002 and 2004 was the worst since World War II.[5] During this and other recessions, a common response from both courts and legislatures—after courts take the obvious steps of freezing positions and salaries, cutting travel, training, the use of consultants, and maybe deferring capital projects—is to identify activities that are "mandated" by a state's constitution and statutes.[6] The theory of the other branches seems to be that courts are doing a lot of things they are not mandated to do, so if courts only do what is mandated, they can absorb cuts sought by the two other branches. On the other hand, attorneys and others in those branches who are sensitive to courts' needs recognize courts' unique role in government and do not want to cut to the point where the courts cannot perform as required. Therefore, they seek to preserve funds for "mandated" items. Courts do likewise, seeing identification of mandated tasks as an opportunity to reduce the size of cuts because they believe that the two other branches have no idea how much is mandated. If courts identify all the mandated tasks, they can demonstrate that they cannot absorb as big a funding cut as is being proposed. In addition, if something is mandated, it cannot be left unfunded, so courts should not be made to absorb as large a cut as other units of government. Whatever the incentive, an identification of mandates often is undertaken when courts face actual cuts (as opposed to increases less than increases in costs).

This approach has inherent difficulties. The framers of the constitution, state legislators, and even supreme court rules are addressing specific concerns or are setting up a general structure that is specific to a topic. They are not seeking to address all the functions and tasks courts must perform to function in their adjudicative role and, even more, they are not seeking to establish any kind of priority among all the requisite functions and tasks. Therefore, examining mandates must overlook important institutional needs that simply are not addressed by legislation or rules. When lists of mandates are compiled, the assumption is that all mandates are equal. There is no reason to believe that. The legislature does not address relative priorities among the many statutes it adopts that affect court operations. The legislature may have said courts must do something, but they did not make that judgment in the context of a fiscal crisis or in the context of all the other tasks it has said must be done by courts Particularly in state-funded systems, the legislature can choose not to fund something, and when doing so it is de facto suspending or repealing a previous mandate. In the face of a fiscal crisis, the legislature might well decide its mandate *can* be suspended. Executive-branch officials almost daily make judgments as to whether or not to comply with a given statute. Law enforcement and prosecutors are the most obvious example of officials who determine that even if something is a crime on the books, they will not enforce it or they will enforce it only in some circumstances. The same thing happens in the welfare department, the highway or public works department, and in virtually every other government agency, just not as visibly as when a police department or a prosecutor announces changed priorities regarding certain crimes because of a lack of resources. Some in courts believe that as the branch of government whose responsibility it is to enforce the law, courts should comply with all mandates, regardless of fiscal constraints or the possibility that all mandates are not created equal. In an ideal world, it would be lovely if courts could do that. But legislatures seem to have an easier time passing mandates than funding staff positions or judgeships or even needed technology and facilities. If judgeships do not keep up with filings or staff positions must be left vacant to accommodate cuts in budgets, a court giving a low (or no) priority to a particular mandate is no different from the executive branch declining to buy something for which the legislature has appropriated funds or a prosecutor not filing on certain crimes because the office lacks sufficient attorneys.

At an operational level, for various reasons courts do not comply with some mandates even in good fiscal times. Some staff members in some courts do not learn of new legislation, so they do not comply. Some laws and rules simply are not enforced, not because of a conscious effort to ignore them but simply because of inattention, lack of training, lack of monitoring of performance by supervisors, or any number of other reasons.[7] If a statute says something must be sent by a court to law enforcement or a prison within 48 hours, courts may be late because of poor management or limited staff resources. They may comply eventually, but technically they are not complying. In times of fiscal crisis, courts often say that they do not have the staff or do not have the funds to reprogram their software, so they will suspend complying with a law until the funds are available or staff levels are enhanced. This response certainly is not something that should happen routinely, but it is a more appropriate response during times of fiscal crisis than saying courts have to do everything that is mandated. Mandates are relevant and courts should try to comply with as many as possible, but mandates do not define the scope or extent of the search for what to do when funding is an issue. What courts need to do during times of fiscal constraint is identify the functions and tasks, mandated and nonmandated, that are essential to their maintenance and proper operation. Preferably, identification of these functions and tasks would occur when there is no fiscal crisis. Courts then are better positioned to protect those items already identified when a fiscal crisis eventually surfaces.

The Conference of State Court Administrators (COSCA) and others recognize that identifying mandates is not the end of the discussion and probably should not be the starting point. Rather, they suggest that the discussion now should be in terms of "core responsibilities"[8] or "core functions"[9] or "core elements."[10] These are broader than mandates. For example, in 2001, COSCA included the following in core functions:

- Assignment and calendaring of cases
- Management of court personnel (including hiring, firing, and deployment)
- Management of court and administrative records
- Judicial branch education.[11]

The assignment of cases, deployment of personnel, management of administrative records, and judicial branch education all are important institutional needs but not necessarily adjudicative needs. Except possibly for administrative records or annual education requirements for judges, which often now is mandated by court rule, none is mandated in legislation or court rule.

Two years later, COSCA added planning, policy development, program evaluation, and data collection to the above list.[12] Other than data collection, which may be the subject of legislation or court rule, these, too, are institutional needs that are not mandated and are not case-related. In Arizona, where the chief justice ordered a study to "identify all constitutional and statutory mandates," Maricopa County (Phoenix) included in its review local administrative orders and applicable national standards such as the American Bar Association's Standards Relating to Trial Courts and Standards Relating to Court Organization.[13] Without saying so explicitly, the courts of Maricopa County were broadening the concept of "mandates" to include institutional needs that went beyond the definition of mandates used by the chief justice.

It is time for the judiciary to define, and, if necessary, debate with the other branches its tasks and functions. Which are mission-critical, desirable but not mission-critical, and which advance the judiciary and make it a more effective institution but are not as central as the first two categories. COSCA has said: "We support a national effort … to more precisely identify the core responsibilities for which courts can and should be held accountable…."[14] That is one purpose behind the Hierarchy of Court Administration.

8.2   The Hierarchy of Court Administration Explained

The Hierarchy of Court Administration makes a court a living institution. In chapter 1, court administration was defined as providing and maintaining the infrastructure for the judicial branch so judges can perform their constitutionally assigned duties. The Hierarchy of Court Administration identifies the bones, blood vessels, muscles, and skin that give shape, color, and function to that infrastructure. The Hierarchy of Court Administration, just as Maslow's Hierarchy of Needs does for people, defines the essentials that must exist for a court to function as it should, then identifies higher levels of need to which courts can and should progress as resources and a court's capacity to do more expand. Maslow says humans move up and down his Hierarchy of Needs as the needs at one level are satisfied or as the capacity to satisfy needs at a higher level is lost. That is the case, too, in the Hierarchy of Court Administration. Courts that can perform the mission-critical tasks and functions then can move on to the next level, to address their security and business continuity needs. When those are secured, they can more effectively address external relationships. When these foundational needs are met, a court can start to be proactive (level 4) and, for a few courts, eventually move to being a leadership organization (level 5). The lines between the levels are not barriers and are not limiting. There is some overlap that occurs in seeking and allocating resources. For example, some external relationships must be achieved even if all security or business continuity needs are not satisfied. A court can and should pursue simultaneously some elements of the first three levels. Courts can and should start to be proactive before they have met all their needs in the first three levels. When budgets are cut, courts can try to preserve as much of what they have gained as possible, but if cuts are deeper, then they should withdraw from levels four, three, and two, but not level one. Level one, the mission-critical needs, is the floor below which a court cannot go. When it is unable to perform the functions and tasks identified in this level, it no longer can effectively deliver individual justice in individual cases while according due process and fair and equal access, which are the bedrock purposes of courts.

The Hierarchy of Court Administration is set forth in Figure 8.1. The tasks and functions that are found in each of the five levels are identified in Table 8.1.

Each of the remaining chapters discusses the elements of each level in detail. Note again (see chapter 1) that some of the tasks and functions that are mission critical also can be found in level four, the proactive management level. At the

Figure 8.1   Court Administration Hierarchy of Needs.

mission-critical level, the tasks and functions are performed at the level needed to sustain the organization. At the proactive level, they are more expansive, more technologically and Internet based, more sophisticated, and more effective (see also, chapter 12). Some may quarrel with the allocation of some tasks to level one or to level four, believing something identified here as in level four now is mission critical for them. Or, a state may have a statute or rule requiring courts to do something assigned to level four. If an innovation using technology is assigned in this book to level four but can be shown to be a cost-saver over the previous process or program, it should be protected from cuts regardless of the level to which it is assigned. The use of technology does not define whether a function is level one or level four, the function is the key. If technology already has been applied to improve productivity or access, it needs to be preserved. Level four speaks in terms of applying new technologies for two reasons. First, there are many important functions that still are completed manually; in such courts, applying technology to these functions puts the courts into a proactive mode, which is level four. Second, even if a court uses technology to perform a function now, technology changes rapidly. There always seems to be new hardware or

Table 8.1   Elements of the Hierarchy of Court Administration

Level 1: Mission-critical operations	• Accounting and fiscal needs (cash management; deposits; receiving, recording, and properly allocating fine, fee, and surcharge payments; special delinquent funds collection efforts; daily reconciliations; bond forfeitures; bond postings; accounts payable; budget management and reporting) • Assuring timely and accurate capture and updating of file/case information (creating files; updating files/records; courtroom minutes) • Creating and sending or posting timely notices • Maintenance and protection of confidential case-related information • Counter and telephone inquiries and responses • Capturing data and generating basic statistical reports of case and court activity • Providing timely case-based information to legally-mandated individuals and organizations • Caseflow management to achieve timely disposition of cases • Jury management • Reporting of courtroom proceedings in criminal cases and other legally mandated proceedings • Provision of counsel, transcripts, and expert assistance to indigent criminal defendants • Providing language interpreters where legally required • Securing and scheduling mental health professionals for competency determinations • Human resources (recruiting, selection, evaluation, promotion. retention) and benefits management • Purchasing supplies, equipment, and services • Inventory and maintenance of equipment and technology • Training and cross-training staff in operational tasks and functions and in new and changed laws • Continuing education for judicial officers • Evidence receipt and safe and secure storage • Use of an accessible facility appropriate for court proceedings • Facility daily maintenance, repairs, and reconditioning
Level 2: Security & business continuity	• Physical security of people, building(s), paper records, computer records, and telephone systems • Protection of private/confidential information in otherwise public records • Records management • Business continuity planning and implementation
Level 3: External relationships	• Political and policy units of the two other branches of government. state and local • State Administrative Office of the Courts • Criminal justice agencies, local and state • Government agencies interacting with the court on civil and family cases • Government and private entities providing support services • Bar associations • Social service. mental health, and other community service agencies • Addiction agencies and organizations • Service clubs and community organizations

Continued

Table 8.1   Continued

	• Media relations • Educational institutions and programs, both K-12 and higher education • Credit reporting and other investigative groups • Victim and advocacy groups • Court watchdog groups • Academic and other researchers
Level 4: Proactive management	• Planning (strategic and long-range) • Environmental scanning • Focus is on outputs, not inputs • Assuring data quality and using objective statistical information to set priorities and to manage • Program evaluation • Problem-solving courts • Refining caseflow management • Improving the jury experience • Assuring access (physical, language, including use of Plain English, self-representation assistance) • Supporting and assisting coordinate agencies and organizations • Community input/feedback • Community outreach • Meeting client expectations • Using new technologies • Change management • Adopting best practices from other courts • Nurturing and developing staff skills and capacities • Improved working conditions and opportunities for staff • Maintaining and adapting facilities
Level 5: Leadership organization	• Humanistic or Quality management (continual, incremental change, empowering staff, customer focus, use of data to guide management decisions and gauge performance) • develop best practices • focus attention on stakeholders who are not judges or attorneys • Program evaluation • broad understanding among judges and staff/managers of sphere of influence and scope of authority of each • Institutionalize successful new programs • Scan public, nonprofit, and private sectors for best practices • Develop new technologies and adapt public and private-sector state-of-the-art technologies to a court context • employer of choice • Recognition in the community as a bellwether organization • Community recognition as a place where justice is sought and provided • State-of-the-art courthouse and interior design

software that will improve productivity further. For courts in this second category, installing the newer technology is a level four activity even if technology is used today. The line of demarcation is to preserve whatever means and staff the court now has to complete the required function as it should be completed. Preserving what now exists for a given function is a level one need. Advancing beyond that point is level four. The allocation suggested in this book is an effort to guard the mission-critical functions that allow courts to satisfy the specific requirements of the federal and state constitutions: individual justice in individual cases, plus the institutional infrastructure needed to assure that those constitutional requirements are met.

Without question, some tasks defined being in the proactive level are desirable and make it easier for courts to operate. New technologies adopted at the proactive management level may well move to level one in the future. In allocating some functions to level one and some to level four, the choice that was made for this book is that making life easier is not as critical as survival. The essence of the mission-critical tasks and functions is survival, just as Maslow's first level is reserved for basic human survival by focusing on air, food, water, and other biological survival essentials. All courts must protect the resources needed to function at level one. The essence of level four is to advance beyond where a court is today through new technologies, new management approaches, and new programs. All courts should strive to operate at level four as much as possible, while meeting needs in levels two and three, as well. When choices must be made in tough times, the Hierarchy of Court Administration is a guide to the order in which cuts might be made, not a mandate, except insofar as it defines the mission-critical needs.

Before proceeding to the specifics of the Hierarchy, we should consider a note of caution expressed by COSCA about courts being too specific about tasks and functions. In its 2003 policy statement on judicial branch budgets in times of fiscal crisis, COSCA advised:[15]

> State judiciaries are increasingly finding themselves in debates over what are and are not core functions of the courts. By their very nature, these debates tend to create an adversarial environment, in which the judicial branch is inevitably on the defensive. Court leaders can quickly find themselves bogged down in defensive item-by-item negotiations with the other branches concerning which programs or staff support [are]constitutionally mandated functions. In this context, it can become difficult to justify new or continued expenditures for "innovations" like problem-solving and specialty courts. Yet the state court community has increasingly come to view these reforms as essential, as they stand to improve the quality of justice and provide dramatic savings for government and society.... When resisting reductions, it may be preferable to present a broader description of the functions of the courts—protecting cherished liberties, no discretion to turn people away, serving as society's emergency room, etc.—rather than debating core and non-core functions.

COSCA's caution should be noted, but it should not end the effort to define and establish the Hierarchy of Court Administration. COSCA's statement anticipates a fiscal crisis and an effort in that context to define what is a core function and what is not. The Hierarchy of Court Administration could be adopted during a fiscal crisis, but it would be best for at least two reasons to adopt it in times of relative fiscal tranquility. It offers a new framework for examining not only court functions and tasks, but also how courts go about fulfilling their mission and improving service to their stakeholders. As such, it is best to adopt it, discuss it with the two other branches, and use it before there is a crisis. If it proves to be a useful tool when funds are adequate, its use will not be a surprise and less a topic of debate during tight fiscal times.

One of the most important aspects of the Hierarchy in thinking about COSCA's caution is that it is not task-specific. It defines functions that courts must perform; specific tasks are not laid out. The difference between a task and a function is similar to the difference between a requirements analysis for new software and detail design. The requirements analysis might indicate that cash must be received and accounted for. The detail design document (or a procedures manual for staff) would address the specific tasks, such as counting the cash upon receipt, placing it into the cash drawer, the screen or form on which the cash would be noted, what needs to be entered on the screen or form, reconciling the cash drawer at the end of the day, and so forth. Technology can greatly impact the individual tasks to be completed and how much time one takes to complete tasks, but it does not change the function.

A functional approach leaves to each court's discretion how each function is to be staffed. The technology used, the skills and experience of staff, and volume levels all will vary by court. If cuts cannot be avoided, each court can determine how to allocate staff among the functions. If it is unable to staff a function at the level needed, it can reexamine its allocations or return to the funding source. The Hierarchy does not determine this level of detail, each court does. But the Hierarchy does say that at level one the court cannot cut any more because then it will not be able to perform this function at all or within appropriate time frames and this function is mission-critical. The court will look for cuts at levels five or four first, then at level three, then at level two, but not in level one.

The Hierarchy also provides a conceptual framework the public can understand, just as people have a gut recognition of the value and appropriateness of Maslow's Hierarchy of Needs. Courts can tell citizens: "This is the minimum we need to fulfill our constitutional and statutory duties, but these are the other things we're doing and trying to achieve to provide you with better service to make the experience of using the courts easier for you, and to make more effective use of your tax dollars." The public will understand the gradations and the distinctions between the mission-critical tasks and functions and improved service.

It may be hard to protect some services or programs that are desirable when they are listed as desirable from the outset, that is, in level four rather than level one. But it is most important to save the mission-critical functions. Courts will define these mission-critical functions along the lines already done by COSCA and the courts of Maricopa County. That is, they will move beyond individual, specific mandates to include institutional maintenance functions. If courts are thorough, fair, and principled in the way they allocate functions among the first four levels, their position in budget discussions is strengthened, not weakened. This is particularly true if the definition process is done before the next fiscal crisis occurs and there is dialogue about it with the other branches during the tranquil fiscal times. In 2006, most states are starting to see revenues increase, some significantly.[16] National economic forecasts are positive. The time is propitious for adopting the Hierarchy of Court Administration.

Further, COSCA and the Conference of Chief Justices, among others, advocate other reforms to the budget process that will end the debates about individual functions or tasks. Among those reforms are lump-sum allocations to the judicial branch with individual allocations within the branch left to the judiciary. They also recommend that if courts cannot get lump-sum appropriations, they obtain much greater freedom to move funds among budget line items to meet needs as they arise and change. If either of these reforms is achieved in conjunction with having a Hierarchy of Court Administration, it will be the branch that will oversee where funds are allocated to keep trial courts as high in the hierarchy as possible given the total available resources. The Hierarchy becomes a guide within the branch rather than a weapon that can be used by the legislature or governor to cut court funds further.

The difficulties COSCA cites about debating individual tasks and functions derive from looking at what courts *must* do to adjudicate cases and to respond to legislative and constitutional mandates. The Hierarchy of Court Administration puts these into the broader discussion of what the judiciary needs to achieve these ends *in the context of being a viable branch of government.* The judiciary is saying through the Hierarchy that being a judicial branch is more than just hearing cases one at a time as people (or government) choose to file them. It is saying that an entire institutional framework is needed to enable courts to hear and to fairly resolve these cases. Once the Hierarchy is articulated, there are no guarantees that legislators and people in the governor's office will not try to nit-pick the choices. In a world of limited resources and politics, no such guarantees are possible. But at least the context will be broader and the discussion will be starting with what the courts say is needed and appropriate, not what the legislature has chosen to put into legislation or the statewide rule-making body has chosen to put into rules. A U.S. Senator who was the CEO of a major corporation before going into politics told a law student many years ago that you should always prepare the first draft of a contract because then the other side is arguing about what you want and your language, not what they want. The Hierarchy of Court Administration follows that advice.

Finally, COSCA is right about grounding all budget arguments in terms of broad purposes. It is those purposes that undergird the Hierarchy. The purposes come first. The Hierarchy of Court Administration grows out of the purposes. The purposes that are used to help define the Hierarchy are set forth below.

COSCA's point about the risk to innovations such as problem-solving courts is important, but can be addressed. In the Hierarchy of Court Administration, problem-solving courts are in level four, not level one, so the implication is that they can be abandoned or cut back during recessions. Problem-solving courts are readily sold on the basis of total government and societal savings, even if they are not constitutionally mandated (as I believe they are not). Problem-solving courts may be the vehicle for redefining—or expanding—the role of courts in American society, but they are not what state constitutions say courts are to do. Since they were created and advanced by the judiciary alone, almost none is sanctioned in or required by a statute. To date, problem-solving courts have been sold and sustained on their merits, supported by positive evaluation results for both courts and the rest of government. The savings they generate are documented and substantial. If the case for problem-solving courts is made and if their numerous stakeholders support their value, they can be sustained even in periods of fiscal crisis, but on their merits and general benefits, not because they are part of the judiciary's historical and constitutional role.[17] The same can occur if other positive programs develop as a result of courts operating at levels four or five. Part of being in level four or five involves setting measurable goals, evaluating results, and adjusting programs as needed in light of the evaluation findings. If a program is worthwhile, if it advances the justice goals of courts, is efficient in its use of resources, and saves money for others in government, the needed support will exist and the program can continue to be funded even in tight budget times. There is nothing in the Hierarchy of Court Administration that requires that effective, money-saving programs developed at levels four and five must be cut when budgets are tight. The Hierarchy is a guide. If cuts are needed, the Hierarchy suggests where to look first. It also says where to draw the line and say, "no mas." It is not a straitjacket.

8.3 Adjudicative and Administrative Imperatives

Certain imperatives, related to both adjudication and administration, underlie the ability of the judiciary to be a viable branch of government that can perform its assigned duties. One cannot look only at what happens in the courtroom and with case records. One needs to examine the administrative structure that enables judicial officers and their immediate support staff to perform. The imperatives identified here are the "broader descriptions" mentioned by COSCA in the quote above. They are the policy underpinnings upon which operations are built. If we do not know why we are doing something, it is hard to generate enthusiasm for it or to fight for it during times of fiscal need. If we know why, it often is easier to understand and defend what we do.

8.3.1 Adjudicative Imperatives

Adjudicative imperatives are the purposes of courts plus the tasks and functions courts must carry out if they are to fulfill their constitutional mission. Ernie Friesen identified the purposes of courts in the 1970s. He did so by asking judges and attorneys in workshops he was teaching what they believed the purposes of courts to be. He then distilled them into the eight listed below.[18] This statement has stood the test of time; it should be part of the orientation for all staff and new judges in every courthouse.

1.   To do individual justice in individual cases;
2.   To appear to do justice in individual cases;
3.   To provide a forum for the resolution of legal disputes;
4.   To protect citizens against the arbitrary use of government power;
5.   To make a formal record of legal status;[19]
6.   To deter criminal behavior;[20]
7.   To help rehabilitate persons convicted of crimes;
8.   To separate persons convicted of serious offenses from society.

Some have said this list overlooks other purposes, such as helping to make law, promoting civil obedience, assisting in providing a sense of security among citizens, and helping to sustain democracy. Whether or not Friesen's list can be expanded or refined, no one questions the appropriateness of those eight purposes.

The Trial Court Performance Standards[21] do not speak in terms of purposes, but ask and answer a question that in 1990 was new: If courts worked the way they should, what would the results be? This question was critical in accomplishing two things. First, it shifted the focus from "inputs"—number of judges, number and type of staff, jurisdictional and operational structure—to outputs, the results citizens should expect from courts. Second, it focused attention on court users and away from judges and staff.[22] The Trial Court Performance Standards identify five key areas in which to measure performance, with 22 performance standards distributed among these five areas:

1. Access to justice
   1.1. The court conducts its proceeding and other public business openly.
   1.2. Court facilities are safe, accessible, and convenient to use.
   1.3. All who appear before the court are given the opportunity to participate effectively without undue hardship or inconvenience.
   1.4. Judges and other trial court personnel are courteous and responsive to the public and accord respect to all with whom they come into contact.
   1.5. The costs of access to the trial court's proceedings and records—whether measured in terms of money, time, or the procedures that must be followed—are reasonable, fair, and affordable.
2. Expedition and timeliness
   2.1. The trial court establishes and complies with recognized guidelines for timely case processing while, at the same time, keeping current with its incoming caseload.
   2.2. The trial court disburses funds promptly, provides reports and information and other services on an established schedule that assures their effective use.
   2.3. The trial court promptly implements changes in law and procedure.
3. Equality, fairness, and integrity
   3.1. Trial court procedures faithfully adhere to relevant laws, procedural rules, and established policies.
   3.2. Jury lists are representative of the jurisdiction from which they are drawn.
   3.3. Trial courts give individual attention to cases, deciding them without undue disparity among like cases and upon legally relevant factors.
   3.4. Decisions of the trial court unambiguously address the issues presented to it and make clear how compliance can be achieved.
   3.5. The trial court takes appropriate responsibility for the enforcement of its orders.
   3.6. Records of all relevant court decisions and actions are accurate and properly preserved.
4. Independence and accountability
   4.1. A trial court maintains its institutional integrity and observes the principle of comity in its governmental relations.
   4.2. The trial court responsibly seeks, uses, and accounts for its public resources.
   4.3. The trial court uses fair employment practices.
   4.4. The trial court informs the community of its programs.
   4.5. The trial court anticipates new conditions or emergent events and adjusts its operations as necessary.

5. Public trust and confidence
    5.1. The trial court and the justice it delivers are perceived by the public as accessible.
    5.2. The public has trust and confidence that the basic trial court functions are conducted expeditiously and fairly and that its decisions have integrity.
    5.3. The trial court is perceived to be independent, not unduly influenced by other components of government, and accountable.

The Trial Court Performance Standards offer any court a full agenda. The Standards are aspirational, yet they are grounded in important expectations and realities of trial court operations. Each should be reflected in at least one of the Hierarchy of Court Administration's levels.

Friesen's list of court purposes and the Trial Court Performance Standards together provide most of the adjudicative imperatives of trial courts. There are a few others, however, that the judiciary also needs or the availability of which courts must assure:

■ The ability to provide due process to all parties;
■ Neutrality between and among litigants;
■ Assurance that information and arguments provided by litigants is available to and considered by a judge;
■ A safe facility in which to hold hearings and receive and store safely evidence and records.

Some of these items on these three lists relate solely to judicial officers, while others also affect or involve staff and staffing. For example, both judges and staff must assure the neutrality and the appearance of neutrality of the institution. Staff can and should assist judges to assure the timely adjudication of cases. Sufficient staffing, computerized information systems, and management procedures are needed to assure that information provided by litigants (or otherwise needed by judges) is taken in and processed properly; is provided to judicial officers in a timely way; and is properly and safely stored for timely retrieval as needed. Trial Court Performance Standard 1.3 embraces the ability to communicate to and with the court. This involves the growing need for interpreters to assist litigants who cannot speak or understand English or for whom English is a second language, one in which they would be handicapped during a judicial proceeding. It also relates to illiterates and those with dyslexia. Further, it cannot be overlooked that for most citizens, the language of law is a foreign language with which they need help. With the growing number of self-represented litigants in civil and family lawsuits and even in some criminal cases, the need for language and procedural access is coming to include the self-represented, whatever their English language skills. Litigants and their representatives need access to judicial officers in a facility that is physically safe and accessible (Standard 1.2), but it is staff members who receive and store information, documents, and evidence.

8.3.2 Administrative Imperatives

As just indicated, some administrative imperatives are part of or derive directly from adjudication imperatives. Beyond those, there is a separate list of administrative imperatives Most of these imperatives are addressed by the Trial Court Performance Standards, but some supplemental or clarifying imperatives are worthy of note. The list applies to courts as adjudicators, as well as to courts as complex organizations that require management.

- Accommodate and assist all who seek information about cases, about the judicial process and how it works, or about the court as a government institution.[23]
- Assure judicial officers have the essential equipment, furniture, and staff support to be able to meet the adjudicative imperatives.
- Properly create and store and timely retrieve administrative information such as personnel records, procedural manuals, policies, and rules.
- Create budgets and monitor budget compliance.
- Establish and implement personnel systems and operating policies and procedures for staff.[24]
- Establish and implement purchasing policies and procedures that meet open and fair government standards and that assure the availability of needed goods and services as needed.[25]
- Timely and accurately paying for goods and services provided to the court.
- Ethical behavior on the part of all nonjudicial employees.
- Assure that the assignment of duties and responsibilities to staff is clear, that tasks are appropriately defined, that staff members are properly assigned and allocated, that staff members know how to perform their assigned responsibilities, and that they have at least the minimum resources needed to perform the tasks and responsibilities assigned.

The imperatives just listed, plus those covered in and implied by the Trial Court Performance Standards, are the foundation for court administration and the judicial process. By their nature, most are mission-critical functions that belong in level one. Some are more appropriate for level four of the hierarchy, but even though in level four, they are important and should be deferred or abandoned only reluctantly.

The remaining chapters examine each level of the Hierarchy, how it relates to Maslow's Hierarchy of Needs, and its component elements.

Notes

1. The National Bureau of Economic Research identifies significant declines in economic activity from January 1980 until July 1980, July 1981 until November 1982, July 1990 until March 1991, and March 2001 until November 2001. National Bureau of Economic Research, *Business Cycle Expansions and Contractions,* retrieved Mar. 11, 2006, from http://www.nber. org/cycles.html.

   Government recessions usually lag behind the impact of recession in the general economy by 12 to 24 months because of the delayed impact on tax revenues that are not consumption based. Recoveries lag correspondingly. Thus, even though some measures show that the last national recession began and ended in 2001, state government tax revenue started falling in the last quarter of 2001 and continued to fall for eight straight quarters. Hall, Daniel J., Robert W. Tobin, and Kenneth G. Pankey, Jr., "Balancing Judicial Independence and Fiscal Accountability in Times of Economic Crisis," *Judges Journal,* Summer 2004, p. 5.

2. Cf., Hudzik, John K., and Alan Carlson, "State Funding of Trial Courts: What We Know Now," *Judges Journal,* Summer 2004, p. 13; Tobin, Robert W., *Lessons Learned from Recession Experience.* Denver: National Center for State Courts, undated, p. 1.

3. When I became a court administrator in 1996, the two case management software packages being used were 10 and 12 years old respectively, and neither was Y2K compatible. Eighty percent of the hardware in the court involved mainframe applications and dumb terminals. Even with the year 2000 rapidly approaching, we needed three fiscal years to get the funding for new cabling and for the personal computers required to install the new Y2K-compatible software.

4. In courts of both limited and of general jurisdiction, personnel and legally mandated costs might constitute 75 percent or more of the total budget. See, for example, Conference of State Court Administrators, "State Judicial Branch Budgets in Times of Fiscal Crisis," *The Court Manager,* vol. 19, no. 1, 2004, p. 31. When budgets are frozen, cut, or increased less than the increases in already-negotiated pay increases for staff or nonnegotiable fringe benefit costs, there is little room left for adjustments in other expense categories

5. Hall, Daniel J., Robert W. Tobin, and Kenneth G. Pankey, Jr., "Balancing Independence and Fiscal Accountability," p. 5; Nadeau, Joseph P., "Ensuring Adequate Long-Term Funding for Courts: Recommendations from the ABA Commission on State Court Funding," *Judges Journal,* Summer 2004, p. 15.

6. For example, Reinkensmeyer, Marcus W., "Court Budget Strategies: Stewardship, Accountability, and Partnership in Maricopa County," *Judges Journal,* Summer 2004, pp. 38–40.

7. As a consultant to hundreds of courts across the nation, it seems that a substantial number of my clients would not have needed my advice if they had simply followed their own rules and codified procedures. There normally are several reasons why they are not doing so, but the fact remains that the existing rules and procedures often would go a long way, if not all the way, toward addressing the problem I had been hired to address. Thus, it is not surprising that legislation and state rules of court also may not be fully enforced in every court all the time.

8. Conference of State Court Administrators, "Policy Statement on Effective Judicial Governance and Accountability, adopted Nov. 30, 2001," retrieved from ttp://.cosca.ncsc.dni. us/Resolutions/judgovpolstate.pdf Conference of State Court Administrators, "Effective Judicial Governance and Accountability, A Position Paper Adopted December 2001," *The Court Manager*, vol. 19, no. 1, p. 34.

9. Conference of State Court Administrators, "State Judicial Branch Budgets in Times of Fiscal Crisis," *The Court Manager*, vol. 19, no. 1, 2004, p. 28; John K. Hudzik, "Judicial Independence, Funding the Courts, and Interbranch Relations, " *Judges Journal*, Summer 2004, p. 1.

10. Conference of State Court Administrators, Resolution in Support of Principles of Effective Judicial Governance and Accountability, adopted Dec. 12, 2003, retrieved Feb. 17, 2006 from http://cosca.ncsc.dni.us/Resolutions/resolutionJudicialGovernance.html.

11. Conference of State Court Administrators, "Position Paper," p. 35.

12. Conference of State Court Administrators, "Judicial Branch Budgets," p. 33.

13. Reinkensmeyer, Marcus W. "Court Budget Strategies," p. 38.

14. Conference of State Court Administrators, "Policy Statement."

15. Conference of State Court Administrators, "Judicial Branch Budgets," p. 32.

16. See Tanner, Robert, "Flush with Cash, States Make Pricey Plans," an Associated Press article retrieved Feb. 20, 2006, from http://my.earthlink.net/channel/news/print?guid=20060220/ 43f94cd0_3421_1334.

17. The conscientious use of performance goals, performance measures, and evaluations of the consequences of problem-solving courts—even though required by the executive branch funding agencies that supported problem-solving courts in their early years and not embraced initially by courts—is a model for how courts can and should approach all new programs (see section 12.4, chapter 12).

18. Friesen memorialized these purposes in a video produced by the Institute for Court Management. *Caseflow Management Principles and Practices: How to Succeed in Justice*, VHS (Williamsburg, VA: ICM, 1991). See also, National Association for Court Management, *Core Competency Curriculum Guidelines: What Court Leaders Need to Know and Be Able to Do*. Williamsburg, VA: National Association for Court Management, 2005, p. 9.

19. This relates to functions such as dissolution of marriage, probate of wills, and the resolution of disputes over wills, termination of parental rights, adoptions, and name changes. It also covers the recordation of settlements in other types of cases.

20. This purpose and the two that follow obviously relate to criminal case sanctions.

21. Commission on Trial Court Performance Standards, Williamsburg, VA: Bureau of Justice Assistance and National Center for State Courts, 1990.

22. Ibid., p. 1.

23. I do not know of any studies of how many people enter courthouses or contact courts just for information compared to those involved in litigation, but it would not surprise me if those seeking information outnumber those who are litigants (and their representatives and family members).

24. For many locally funded courts, the county or city develops, controls, and administers the personnel policies applied to court staff. Even so, there are interstices that the court needs to fill to address its special needs. An ethics policy and rules about access to and use of confidential court records are just two examples.

25. As with personnel systems, locally funded courts often are required to follow the policies and procedures of the county or city. Timely ordering and inventory procedures are court responsibilities even for these courts, however.

Chapter 9

Hierarchy of Court Administration: Mission-Critical Functions

Mission-critical needs are those that are essential for the proper operation of the court, both to fulfill its adjudicative role and to be a viable branch of government. The funding source does not matter; the functions are essential whether funds are provided locally or at the state level. They also are essential whether or not there are statutes or rules specifically addressing them. Some of these functions will be described or required by statutes or rules, which helps to define them as mission critical, but their essential character is not determined by those sources. If a court is unable to perform these functions, it cannot operate effectively as a court. Budget cuts—even more, continuing but low budget levels—that preclude a court from effectively performing these functions cannot be accepted.

9.1 Maslow's Hierarchy and the Hierarchy of Court Administration

The Hierarchy of Court Administration parallels Abraham Maslow's Hierarchy of Needs for humans. Table 9.1 shows the parallel between what Maslow described as the physiological needs of humans, the basic survival needs, and the mission-critical needs of courts. Just as humans must and do seek to satisfy their basic physiological needs before they seek to fulfill other needs, so courts must seek to be able to perform the mission-critical functions before they address other needs. It is appropriate to liken courts' mission-critical functions to the air, food, water, and other items that Maslow lists as physiological needs for humans. Without the

Table 9.1 Maslow's Physiological Needs and Courts' Mission-Critical Needs

Human physiological needs	Court mission-critical needs
• Oxygen • Water • Protein • Salt • Sugar • Calcium • Other minerals & vitamins • Maintain pH balance • Temperature • Activity • Rest • Sleep • Waste disposal • Avoidance of pain • Sex	• Caseflow management to achieve timely disposition of cases • Records management • Assuring timely and accurate capture and updating of file/case information (creating files; updating files/records; courtroom minutes) • Creating and sending or posting timely notices • Providing timely case-based information to legally mandated individuals and organizations • Maintenance and protection of confidential case-related information • Counter and telephone inquiries and responses • Capturing data and generating basic statistical reports of case and court activity • Jury management • Reporting of courtroom proceedings in criminal cases and other legally mandated proceedings • Provision of counsel, transcripts, and expert assistance to indigent criminal defendants • Providing language interpreters where legally required • Securing and scheduling mental health professionals for competency determinations • Evidence receipt and safe and secure storage • Use of an accessible facility appropriate for court proceedings • Accounting and fiscal needs (cash management; deposits; receiving, recording, and properly allocating fine, fee, and surcharge payments; special delinquent funds collection efforts; daily reconcilitations; bond forfeitures; bond postings; accounts payable; budget management and reporting) • Human resources (recruiting, selection, evaluation, promotion. retention) and benefits management • Training and cross-training staff in operational tasks and functions and in new and changed laws • Continuing education for judicial officers • Purchasing supplies, equipment, and services • Inventory and maintenance of equipment and technology • Facility daily maintenance, repairs, and reconditioning

ability to perform mission-critical functions, courts also cannot exist or perform as they were designed to do.

9.2 Mission-Critical Functions Explained

The functions identified as mission critical are self-explanatory in some senses, at least for those who work in courts daily. They embrace both adjudicative and administrative needs. The adjudicative functions are those involved in and supporting the resolution of cases. The administrative functions are more tied to viability of courts as government agencies. Some functions straddle both areas, such as responding to public inquiries and some of the fiscal and accounting functions. Although those working in courts understand most of these functions, some deserve explanation or discussion so that their scope or the issues associated with them are clear. In the discussion that follows, adjudicative functions are discussed first and then administrative functions. Because of the overlaps, however, some adjudicative-related functions are discussed within functions that are more broadly administrative.

9.2.1 Caseflow Management

Caseflow management "encompasses all the functions directly associated with moving cases from the point of filing to the point of hearing, trial, or other disposition.... Caseflow management is *strictly* a management process, encompassing all the functions that affect movement of the case toward disposition, regardless of the type of disposition. It embodies planning, organizing, directing, and controlling these functions"[1] (emphasis in original). In the late 1970s and 1980s, caseflow management focused on getting cases resolved on their merits or otherwise disposed; postdisposition activity was acknowledged but not often addressed. As noted in the National Association of Court Management's (NACM) Core Competency discussion of caseflow management, "increasingly, events that follow disposition to ensure the integrity of court orders and timely completion of post-disposition case activity"[2] are an important component of caseflow management.

Caseflow management is at the heart of what courts do. It is the most mission-specific of all the adjudicative-related functions. It is the means by which courts achieve the results delineated in Standard 2.1 of the Trial Court Performance Standards (see section 8.3.1, chapter 8). The primary responsibility for caseflow management falls to judges, but staff members have an essential supporting role. Also necessary in today's electronic world are the software and hardware needed to capture information and to generate the data and reports needed by judges and staff to properly manage caseflow. There should be no compromises in preserving the resources needed to assure the court's ability properly to manage caseflow.

Caseflow management can be done well or poorly. It can assist parties to resolve cases as expeditiously as possible for the circumstances of each case and for the benefit of all cases.[3] It also can operate mostly as a scheduling process for whatever litigants want to bring to a judicial officer whenever they wish it to be heard. The court's role in the latter circumstance is largely to manage the number of cases on each calendar to assure that the calendar does not contain more cases than the judges feel they can reasonably address in any single calendar session.

Most courts today seem to operate between these two models, with some attention paid to the pace of litigation and modest interest in not rubber-stamping all requests for continuances, but with a general lack of interest in a strong caseflow management program. There appears to be some slippage across the nation toward a more passive role regarding caseflow management.[4]

However judges feel generally about assuring the absence of unnecessary delay, almost all states have some kind of speedy trial provision for criminal cases. The exact meaning of "speedy trial" varies from state to state. Sometimes a statute will specify the number of days or months within which a trial must at least start, with the time typically being longer if a defendant is free on bond than if he or she is in jail. In other states the provision is less specific about the meaning of "speedy." In any event, in every state and in the federal court system, there comes a point at which a criminal defendant is entitled to have charges dismissed because the state has taken too long to conclude the matter. No matter how judges approach the issue of court control of the pace of litigation generally, they will track cases that are at risk of a speedy trial dismissal and seek to assure that the court is ready and able to try these cases within the time constraint in their state. Occasionally a case is dismissed for failure to comply with the speedy trial rule, but it is rare and always done with great reluctance.[5]

Every court must devote resources to the caseflow management process. Every court must put cases on calendars for a wide range of reasons. Every court schedules cases for settlement conferences and for trials. Some matters go on calendar so a judge can be advised of and accept a settlement in a civil matter or a plea in a criminal case. Motions increasingly ask for rulings on matters that arise after a case presumptively has been resolved, particularly in family law cases and to a lesser degree in criminal cases. Minutes of what happened in court must be taken and entered into the computerized (or manual) case management information system by staff. Calendars that show what is to happen in each courtroom each day must be prepared, distributed to judicial officers, staff, and, normally, the prosecutor, public defender, and jail, and posted for the public in the courthouse. Notices may need to be prepared and distributed by either regular or electronic mail. And, in most courts, parties in cases scheduled for trials and extended hearings need to be contacted to assure they will be ready to proceed as scheduled and, if not, why and when they might be ready.

Caseflow management consumes a significant portion of a court's resources. Necessary hardware and software, including needed upgrades, direct support staff of judges, central case management staff, file clerks who retrieve and move files around the courthouse, and those responsible for generating statistical reports to advise judges about the status of their caseloads, should be deemed mission critical to the caseflow management function.

9.2.2 Records Management

Records are the lifeblood of courts. Most records in most courts today—and virtually all records in some courts[6]—are electronically created and stored, but paper remains the mode for creating, using, and storing many records in virtually every court. There is a clear trend toward enabling electronic filing of documents by parties, particularly lawyers; toward courts communicating with parties electronically, especially in cases involving many parties; and toward working internally only with electronic records. A number of individual courts and some states over the years have talked about developing paperless courts, but no one has yet achieved that goal. Electronic records materially improve the productivity of staff, enable multiple users of the same record at the same time, and require far less space for storage. They carry other issues, though, such as security from external contamination or tampering, a need for sensitivity to the environmental conditions for storage that courts can overlook, and the long-term deterioration of data stored electronically (see chapter 10). For courts that work mostly or primarily with electronic records, maintaining the capacity to do so is mission critical. Returning to a paper-based records system would slow down processing for both staff and judges and often would increase the number of staff needed. Both at the level of being a critical function and from the standpoint of budget impact, electronic records are mission critical in every court that has them and should be sought by those that do not. The conversion costs from a paper-based system, including training, can be high, but normally are below the continuing cost of staff needed to maintain a paper-based system.

Also mission critical is the need to upgrade the software and hardware that enables the use of electronic records. Statutory changes affecting records must be added into the software annually in most states, biannually in a few states. Programming errors or better ways to achieve the same result should be corrected or changed as they appear. Hardware becomes obsolete every three-to-five years because of improvements and the increasing demands of new software. At a certain point, it is necessary and important for the entire case management information system to be upgraded to enable it to be used with new and better operating systems or to reflect advancements in programming. Maintenance and upgrade of both hardware and software can be expensive, but unless it is done regularly, the court's capacity to complete its mission critical records-based functions deteriorates in both quality and timeliness. Sometimes deferring this upgrading and maintenance for a year can be tolerated, but if this is postponed for two or more years, service quality and functionality can be lost. The political or fiscal wisdom of skipping regular maintenance may have to be determined in each court, but it is not recommended, because without timely and accurate information (see

Standard 3.6, Trial Court Performance Standards),[7] judicial officers and the court as an institution cannot do their jobs.

Records management has several components:

- Receiving records both electronically and in paper form
- Creating and updating case-related and administrative records[8]
- Electronic inquiries, both case-related and for general information
- The court reporters' recordings of courtroom proceedings
- Reporters' transcripts
- Creating and sending notices of upcoming proceedings, of the court's decisions, of parties' failure to appear and failure to pay, and of convictions of crimes and traffic offenses
- Creating and distributing warrants for arrest and the withdrawal of warrants
- The storage and retrieval of records, short term, midterm, and long term.

In all its components, the function of records management is critical for a court. Many of its elements are mandated by statute and statewide court rules or by local rules or administrative directives that reflect local conditions or circumstances. Standards 1.2 and 3.6 of the Trial Court Performance Standards directly address records management needs. Judges cannot adjudicate cases without records. Parties may be denied due process if they cannot access and obtain records, including, in criminal cases, transcripts of proceedings. Without access to records, the public cannot obtain information about cases, rules of procedure, how to use the court, and the forms needed for various court proceedings. The public also needs access to hold the court accountable as a public institution. Statutory law normally contains a number of requirements regarding court records, including:

- What is and what is not a public record[9]
- What must be treated as confidential and who may access confidential records[10]
- Individual items of information within specified case records (usually case type specific)
- The types of records a court must create or store
- The medium for and length of time that court records are to be retained[11]
- Administrative records associated with the court being an employer that must be created, maintained, and retained.

Record retention requirements significantly impact the square footage and environmental conditions needed to store records, both paper and electronic, as well as the medium for storing records long term.

Some refinements and explanations are appropriate regarding some elements of records management. Issues not addressed here include an appropriate definition of "court record," what should be or should not be confidential, how to treat restricted information in otherwise public records, and fees for obtaining access to records. COSCA produced a concept paper that addressed some of these issues in August 2000: "Concept Paper on Access to Court Records."[12] Then, with funding from the State Justice and institutional support from the National Center for State Courts (NCSC) and the Justice Management Institute, COSCA and the Conference of Chief Justices produced guidelines for public access to court records.[13] Readers interested in these specific topics and other issues associated with access to court records should consult these publications.

The primary function of creating, updating, retrieving, and storing records is mission critical, but within the subfunctions there are exceptions. For example, prior to computerized records, sending notices of upcoming case events to parties and interested others (e.g., social service agencies in problem-solving courts) was not done at all in most courts or was assigned to a party. In criminal and a few other case types, the clerk or the bailiff may complete a form with the date, time, and place of the next appearance and hand it to the defendant at the end of the hearing so there is no question of whether the defendant received it. With this history, it is hard to argue that mailing reminder notices of upcoming case events is a mission critical function. On the other hand, better-designed computerized case management systems are designed to generate notices automatically. If the notices also can be delivered electronically, for example to a prosecutor, public defender, and private attorneys appearing in either criminal or civil cases, there are clear case management advantages for the court and there is no impediment to the court providing the notices.

The notices that are not mission critical are reminder notices of upcoming court events. Statutes mandate many notices provided by courts to other government agencies, such as notices of convictions in traffic and criminal cases and notices of outcomes in some family-related matters and in juvenile proceedings. The reason these notices to other government agencies are required is that they often are needed for these agencies to complete important work of their own. With respect to criminal and traffic cases, these notices enable other agencies to take appropriate administrative action within their sphere of control, such as suspending a driver's license or possibly revoking a professional license. Other agencies, such as the state's attorney general, share the information with agencies involved with public safety, such as adding the information to a database used by police and sheriff departments. Jails, prisons, and probation offices need to know the terms of a criminal sentence to do their jobs. The court is the hub of a very complex information system, particularly for information related to traffic and criminal convictions and sentences. Most of the time, the court is the only agency that can initiate and complete the noticing function. Courts must be staffed or have a fully functioning computerized information system that will allow them to fulfill these information sharing functions.

Courts also send notices of the court's judgment to parties in civil and family disputes when a judge takes a matter under advisement. Some courts provide notice of judges' rulings on filed motions either on a telephone recording or through the court's website. Statutes or rules in most states may not mandate these notices, but they are needed to complete the court's purposes of doing justice in individual cases and being seen to do justice. Parties need notice that the court has reached a decision, what that decision is, and of any terms or conditions in the judgment. Only if the parties have notice of the court's decision can the court be seen to be doing justice, can the court treat all parties even-handedly, and can the parties assist the court to assure that its orders are enforced. Thus, even if not mandated by law, these notices are mission critical because they are a necessary part of achieving a court's mission.

All of these noticing functions require some staff time. Even if a court's computerized case management information system generates these notices automatically, staff must input the necessary information into the computer. If the noticing is performed manually, even more staff time is needed. The staff members needed to complete these functions are mission critical.

9.2.3 Making a Record of What Happens in the Courtroom

Making a record refers to the role of the court reporter in taking down verbatim what is said by whom during a court proceeding. Constitutionally, a record is required for all phases of criminal court proceedings. Because there is, as yet, no constitutional right to appeal a civil judgment, a verbatim record need not be made of all civil proceedings. For many years, therefore, until well into the 20th century, if a reporter was used in any civil proceeding, whether a hearing on a motion or a trial, the reporter was hired and paid for by one or both parties, not by the court. If there were no reporter, each party and the judge made handwritten notes of what was said. In some courts today, that still is the case, at least for pretrial hearings but even occasionally for trials. In most courts today, however, court reporters are full-time court employees or independent contractors who report all proceedings in all case types.

Court reporters use stenography to capture the words spoken,[14] using a small machine that enables them quickly to record a type of shorthand.[15] Most new reporters today use a machine that converts their key strokes into electronic signals that are recorded on a digital storage device that is later inserted into a computer for translation of the notes into English text (called computer assisted transcription (CAT). Some new reporters today and a number of longer-term reporters use a machine that looks very similar to the CAT machine but that captures the keystrokes on a paper tape. If these reporters later are asked to prepare a transcript, they have three options: (1) reading the paper tape and dictating the transcript into a voice recorder and having another person type out the transcript while listening to the recording; (2) sitting at a computer and doing the translation personally; or (3) using a transcriber who reads their shorthand off of the paper tape without any further intervention by the reporter.

In addition to reporters' use of technology to capture the record, technology has replaced or supplemented court reporters in a number of courts, particularly courts of limited jurisdiction. It also is used in some general jurisdiction courts for case types that normally result in only a limited number of transcripts. The dominant technology is audio recording. Today, it often is digital recording that facilitates finding witnesses or even specific testimony and produces a cleaner audio sound during any subsequent transcription. A growing number of courts also use, or use instead, digital video recording. Someone should monitor both of these technologies to assure that the machine is properly capturing the sound (and video) and to make notes about who is speaking about what at particular points on the tape. If the proceeding is one from which transcripts rarely are needed and audio recorders are used, many courts skip the monitor. The tape recorder is turned on at the beginning of the calendar and turned off at the end. If there is a subsequent need to review what happened, someone later has to find that hearing (or trial) and transcribe what happened. Whether or not an in-courtroom monitor is used, a transcriber—sometimes a court employee but more often an independent contractor—is employed by the court to create a transcript from the audio recording or the audio portion of the videotape, if one is needed.

As a constitutional requirement in criminal cases, the making of the record and the creation of transcripts are mission critical. The requirement of a record has been extended to a few other types of cases and proceedings (e.g. mental competency), so making a record is mission critical in those areas, as well. When there is a significant budget crisis, the issue for budget purposes seldom is whether making a record is required, even for civil cases, but whether it is necessary to use court reporters or if one of the two alternate technologies would be sufficient. Because of their high skill level and their relative scarcity, court reporters are very expensive employees (and contractors). Salaried monitors of electronic equipment normally cost much less than court reporters and the electronic equipment involves only a one-time expenditure that is feasible because of the salary savings.

A one-to-one relationship between a judge and a court reporter is not necessary from a management standpoint. Many judges believe the quality of the record improves when they work with one reporter all the time, but that advantage cannot be and has not been documented. Nonetheless, the one-to-one relationship is a very strong tradition in most courts and is hard to break. A relatively small number of courts have been able to develop a central pool of reporters who are assigned to courtrooms and hearings as and when needed, which reduces the total number of reporters needed. Pooling reporters definitely is not the norm and would be rejected by judges and reporters alike in most courts. So the discussion about saving money in the court reporting function usually is about technology versus live reporters. Sometimes it focuses on technology for some proceedings or case types and sometimes it is about replacing all reporters with technology.

The use of court reporters can help a judge to control the presentation of evidence and arguments, because everyone has to accommodate the fact that the reporter normally can hear and keep up with only one person at a time. Therefore, court reporters are not effectively replaced by audio recordings when courtroom proceedings involve multiple parties who are prone to interrupt each other frequently, or a single attorney who is difficult to control. Some also argue that when the parties desire an overnight transcript or an hourly transcript because of the nature of a trial, a court reporter is essential. Several side-by-side experiments have shown otherwise, but they have not shaken the general belief that a reporter is needed for overnight or hourly transcripts.

The debate about live reporters with or without CAT, versus audio recordings, versus video recording is too complex to be reviewed in detail here. The key points about the mission critical elements of the function are: (1) the reporting function is mission critical in all proceedings and for all case types for which there is a constitutional, statutory, or statewide court rule requirement; (2) the technology used to capture the record is an item for discussion, but if the fiscal crisis arises suddenly and a court is facing what to do in the next 12 months, there probably is not enough time effectively to change the current technology, so the current technology (including court reporters) probably is mission critical; but (3) even if the existing technology must be retained, it is appropriate to reexamine whether all proceedings for all case types currently reported must continue to be reported by court reporters. However these three points are resolved, the bottom line is that the function of reporting the record is mission critical and some level of both staff and equipment is needed for a court to meet its obligations in this area.

9.2.4   Public Inquiries and Access to the Courthouse

The King County (Seattle, WA) District Court, the county's limited jurisdiction court, which handles about 225,000 cases per year, has a call center to which all telephone calls that do not go directly to a judge or a staff member are directed. In 2003, the call center received an estimated 560,000 calls, the number being projected from an evaluation of the center's operation over a three-month period.[16] That number of calls averages to over 2,200 calls per court day or about five calls every minute of every court day during the year.[17] Every court in the nation must deal with a heavy volume of telephone calls. Sometimes the number is greater than in the King County District Court and sometimes it is less. A small court or branch of a court might receive only a dozen calls an hour, a larger urban court might receive 50 percent more than the King County District Court. In addition, small and large courthouses alike host hundreds or thousands of people a day: lawyers, litigants, media representatives, citizens seeking various information about using the court or about their case(s), military and law enforcement officers, credit reporting companies, probation and parole officers, and an occasional student or historian. They all seek information from staff assigned to public counters. In a growing number of courts, staff and volunteers in information booths and self-help centers also help these individuals.[18]

The commentary to Standard 2.2 of the Trial Court Performance Standards states that, "as a public institution, trial courts have a responsibility to provide information and services to those they serve. Standard 2.2 requires that this be done in a timely and expeditious manner."[19] One feature of being a public institution is that almost all of the records in a court's possession are public records, to which citizens have a legal right of access.[20] The right is not limitless, as a court can impose reasonable restrictions on time, place, and number of records accessed at one time (or, with computerized records, time on the public access computer).[21] But otherwise, the right exists and thus is mission critical.[22]

This mission critical need always has been in jeopardy in difficult fiscal times. To reduce demands on staff, some courts have closed for an hour around lunchtime (when many citizens might otherwise come to court), or close at 4:00 p.m. even though staff works until 5:00 p.m.[23] Between March 1 and June 30, 2003, to address severe budget cuts, all the trial courts in Oregon were closed all day on Friday.[24] In California, such a patchwork of open and closed hours developed during the last recession that the Judicial Council, the policy making body for the judiciary, adopted a guideline for budget management that "recommended" operating hours for the clerk's office from 8:30 a.m. to 4:00 p.m., with hours of 8:00 a.m. to 5:00 p.m. "encouraged."[25] It required trial courts to keep at least one office open 6½ hours per day unless granted specific permission otherwise by the council. Trial courts have to use drop boxes for filings during "periods of shortened hours." Office closures impose impediments on access to public records, but the judgment is made that the right to information seldom is time critical, so restrictions can be imposed. Reduced public hours enable courts that have to eliminate staff positions or leave positions vacant to remain reasonably current with mandated paperwork. (This is another area where courts have made judgments about priorities when staffing levels get too low (see the discussion about complying with mandates in section 8.1, chapter 8).

The judgment to restrict in-person access to public records and to limit responses to public inquiries is understandable when courts experience staff reductions, but it is preferable to make the right of access a mission critical function to be fully funded in the budget.[26] COSCA also suggests that fees may be appropriate for responding to some requests for records.[27]

Treating public access as mission critical poses some risks for court leadership beyond the obvious budget impact. If there is a function desired by some or all judges that is not mission critical that must be cut in order to preserve 40 hours a week for in-person access to records, most judges would favor a cut in public access ahead of whatever function or program they want. Choosing public access because it is mission critical could put a court administrator in a difficult position. Conceptually, public access and preserving service to the public are consistent with the new emphasis in courts on access and public outreach (see chapter 13), but while courts still are in transition in achieving that reorientation, it may not be possible to protect the staff needed to assure that access.

When in-person public access must be limited, courts need to look for alternative service delivery models. The most effective alternative is for a court to use its website to provide full or almost full access to case records and information about use of the court.[28] A website is available 24/7, and it can—and many courts' websites do—provide read-only access to court records and substantial information about how to use the court, as well as forms that are needed for various types of cases. Some websites even provide 3-D video tours of courtrooms with accompanying explanations of the various people found in the courtroom and what they do and what is expected of someone in a courtroom. The website can perform many of the functions of a self-help center and ease any burden on the public from the court having to close its public counter or telephone service for part of the day.

There are two difficulties in replacing in-person inquiries with a website. The first is one with which all of government is struggling: the lack of computer access or limited access of the poor in the community. Many public libraries are trying to fill this need with public-access computer terminals, but libraries also face budget restrictions that have limited their service hours; even if they are open 40 hours a week, a library's service hours outside normal working hours are limited. This is a problem courts need to think about and try to address, but they need the help of the community to do so.[29] The second difficulty is that this solution may be hard to implement fully on short notice. Webmasters can do a lot in relatively little time, but some time still is needed, as are dollars, to produce or upgrade a website appropriately. If a budget cut is unexpected or a recession lasts for three years,[30] finding the dollars to provide full access through the website might not be possible.

The King County District Court, cited at the beginning of this section, found another way. When it faced a cut in its budget of over 20 percent, it had to eliminate or leave vacant dozens of staff positions. These positions came from across the court's operations, other than direct judicial support, so staff members providing public service were reduced. Because of the volume of telephone calls received daily, the remaining staff found it very difficult to answer telephone calls, assist people at the public counter, and complete all the necessary case-support data entry. That was when the call center was started. Positions from throughout the court were reassigned to the call center and all calls to any court location came to the call center first. If calls had to be redirected to a branch, they were, but the call volume at the branches was a fraction of the original number. The call center was a very imaginative way to try to preserve this mission critical function in the face of severe and unavoidable staff cuts.

There also is the issue of physical access. The Americans with Disabilities Act (ADA)[31] became law in 1990. Many of those covered by the act, including government organizations, have been slow to conform to its provisions, particularly regarding physical access. The reason for slow compliance is understandable, as the cost of retrofitting countless government buildings, including courthouses, would be (and still is) enormous. Judges who have ruled in lawsuits that have been filed have been clear—and advocates for the disabled have been clearer—that expense, by itself, is insufficient to defer compliance beyond a reasonable period, although government can seek to accommodate the disabled without major renovations if the alternatives provided reasonably meet the need. Today, more than fifteen years after the act became law, the explanation that more time is needed is beginning to wear thin. In 2004, the United States Supreme Court ruled in *Tennessee* v. *Lane*[32] that citizens' "reasonable right of access to the courts" imposes special obligations on courts to assure physical access to courthouses. The court also upheld the awarding of monetary damages to the 25 named plaintiffs who could not access courthouses in Tennessee.

Access involves more than being able to get a wheelchair up courthouse stairs or through a courtroom door. It also embraces signs that are readable and understandable, clear directions on how to find rooms in the courthouse, and assuring the hearing-impaired can hear what is said in the courtroom. It also should include advice on a court's website how the vision-impaired can increase the font size to make it easier for them to read the material or access an oral version of the text. Asking disabled citizens from the community to visit the courthouse to identify impediments and suggest adjustments could be a fruitful outreach. For additional ideas and approaches taken by courts, readers should consult the National Center for State Courts' ADA Resource Center.[33]

Government generally and courts in particular do not need to spend millions to comply with the requirements of the ADA. Now, however, the Supreme Court has added the right of access to the courts to the statutory weight of the ADA in its particular application to courts. Full, reasonable accommodations to both employees and citizens who are disabled should be mission critical.

9.2.5 Jury Management

Jury management encompasses all the functions required to get an appropriate number of randomly selected citizens to a courtroom when and as needed to start the jury selection process for a specific case and assuring these citizens' payment for services in accordance with law. The functions include identifying citizens eligible for jury service, qualifying them as meeting statutory requirements, considering and acting upon requests for permanent and temporary excuse and for postponement, assuring that the proper number of citizens come to the courthouse when and as needed, caring for and protecting citizens who appear for jury service, allocating them to randomly drawn panels, and getting a sufficient number of potential jurors to courtrooms for the start of a jury trial. Jury management, like caseflow management, embodies planning, organizing, directing, and controlling these functions.

The right to trial by jury in criminal cases is in the federal constitution and in all state constitutions. There is no comparable right to a jury trial in civil cases in the federal constitution or in most states. The right normally is statutory for civil cases. Because there is no constitutional right to a jury trial for civil cases, when budgets get very tight, one of the responses in a number of courts across the nation has been to suspend jury trials in civil cases, sometimes for several months. Civil litigants often pay the fees of the jurors who actually serve on the jury hearing their cases, but the court absorbs the cost of all jurors who appear at the courthouse for possible selection but who do not serve. Normally, there are many more who appear and are not selected than who ultimately make up the trial jury. So even if civil litigants pay the daily fee of their trial jurors, suspending civil jury trials saves courts money.[34]

One way a growing number of states are addressing the cost issue, plus trying to make jury service more attractive generally, is to move to a one trial/one day term of jury service.[35] With this system, citizens' jury obligation is for one trial, however long it may be, or for the time it takes to select a jury, normally one day or less.[36] For those not selected, their jury obligation ends at the end of the selection process for the next 12 or 24 months, depending on the state. Those who serve for one day normally are not paid a per diem fee and may or may not get reimbursed for their mileage, but those who sit on a trial jury are paid much more than formerly—perhaps $40 or $50 a day—from the second day to the end.[37] This system saves the court the first-day costs for civil (and criminal) jurors and reduces the financial burden of serving for those who are selected.[38]

Like many reforms in court administration, however, changing the term of service and the daily compensation for jurors normally involves statutory change, which frequently cannot be achieved in the middle of a fiscal crisis. In many states, these reforms, particularly those involving increases in jurors' daily compensation, have taken several years to achieve. The odds of localities in locally funded systems, or the legislative budget makers in state funded systems, agreeing to increase juror compensation during a recession are slim to laughable. Most effective court reforms need to be pursued as budget conditions start improving or are deemed to be comfortable, rather than when income suddenly drops and cuts must be absorbed relatively quickly.

Another reason for suspending jury trials for civil cases is that fewer staff then are needed in this function, as there are fewer trials, fewer citizens summoned and screened for qualification, fewer jurors who appear at the courthouse, and fewer people to be paid. In my experience, criminal jury trials in smaller courts often represent 80 percent of all jury trials in a year, so in those courts, the savings are relatively small. In larger, urban and suburban courts the number of civil trials as a percent of all trials increases. National totals collected by the National Center for State Court suggest that in recent years, civil jury trials are about one-third of all jury trials.[39] In state-funded systems, the savings from suspending civil trials could begin to add up even if the savings in any one court are limited. In any event, when court budgets are cut, with only limited options for finding items to cut, civil jury trials often are on the list.[40]

No one, least of all those who suspend civil jury trials, favors the idea. Jury trials in civil cases may not be constitutionally mandated in most states, but the public perceives them as an integral part of citizens' rights. Some parties may choose to have their case tried before a judge just to get the matter resolved, rather than waiting until funds are restored. When they choose bench trials, the matter gets resolved, but at the same time, the parties may feel cheated by the process. There also is nothing on the civil side comparable to the speedy trial rule for criminal cases. By suspending civil jury trials, courts may be imposing delay on civil litigants that affects their opportunity to a fair and just trial—eyewitness recollections and memories fade as time goes by. Courts would not be skirting any laws by imposing a delay on those who insist on their right to a jury trial in a civil case, but they may be imposing the appearance of an unjust system rather than a just one.

Because of the history involving civil jury trials, it may be hard to argue that they must be deemed mission critical, but it is easy to say that suspension of these jury trials should be among the last options adopted. On the criminal side, however, jury trials and the staff, hardware, and software needed to manage the process must be protected as mission critical.

9.2.6 Services and Resources Needed By Indigent Criminal Defendants

The U.S. Constitution, applicable to the states through the 14th Amendment, requires government to pay for counsel and other services needed by indigents for a full and proper defense.[41] Today, in most urban areas and many other jurisdictions across the land, at least 80 percent, and often more, of those charged with felonies are deemed to be indigent.[42] The comparable percentage for misdemeanor defendants is much lower,[43] but even here, the costs can be significant because of the volume of misdemeanors involved.[44] The most significant cost is for counsel to represent indigents.

Most often, defense attorneys are provided through a public defender's office, with funds appropriated locally and going to an administratively independent office. In some states and trial courts, however, the funds are funneled through the court's budget, often because the court appoints the chief public defender. In the jurisdictions without public defender offices, private, local attorneys are appointed by the court as needed and at court expense. Even with a separately operated and funded public defender's office, a court's budget will contain funds for indigent defense. In cases involving two or more people charged with responsibility for the same crime, each defendant is entitled to his or her own counsel and as a matter of law the second and other attorneys cannot work for the public defender's office. Some larger jurisdictions have established "conflict attorney" offices, but normally the second and any other attorneys are private attorneys paid directly by the court. So even when a jurisdiction has a public defender's office funded outside the court's budget, the court will pay some counsel and for other services to which indigent defendants are entitled, including the cost of written transcripts. If there is a question of an indigent defendant's mental competency to stand trial and assist in his or her defense, the funds for the psychiatric experts who assist the court to make that determination also normally are in the court's budget.

The U.S. Supreme Court declared the constitutional right to counsel for indigent counsel in the mid-1960s. Even so, many people, including many politicians, accept the public funding of attorneys for criminal defendants only begrudgingly.[45] A number of these individuals find it even harder to accept providing transcripts and experts and psychiatric evaluations at government expense to assist with indigents' defense. In too many quarters, when someone is arrested, they are presumed guilty or citizens believe they have the responsibility to prove their innocence.[46] Those who have this perspective have trouble understanding why guilty defendants need attorneys to get them off through "technicalities," "putting victims on trial," and distorting what people say and mean. Criminal defense attorneys and the tools they need to put on an effective defense are anathema to many. Accordingly, the total public cost of providing indigent defense often is scrutinized, whether the funds are in the separate budget of a public defender's office or in a court's budget. And, it seems, there is scrutiny whether government revenues are high or low. Courts always should be willing to explore and to support efforts to save public funds. They should not accept budget savings that will diminish the quality of service to the point that indigents cannot obtain a constitutionally adequate defense, however. Trial courts are charged to do individual justice in individual cases according to the legal rules established by both the legislature and the appellate courts. That includes assuring that indigent defendants have the same access to counsel, to documents, and to experts as those who can afford to provide their own defense. Courts have the obligation to assure this relatively equal playing field, which makes this function mission critical.

9.2.7   *Interpreters in Criminal Cases and For Jurors*

It does not matter if courts provide justice and are seen to provide it by some people if all people do not have access to the institution. Providing access has many components, some of which already have been discussed. One of the most important is that people with business before the court understand what is happening. Courts conduct their business in English. In an increasingly diverse country, increasing numbers of litigants do not speak English at all or do not speak it well enough to comprehend what is being said in court. Indeed, many Americans with English as their native language have trouble with the language of law. A study of the Miranda warning showed it was phrased at a level understandable to a sophomore in college.[47] So it is not surprising that there are many people who are fluent in a second language who do not know legal terms in that language. On top of that, courtroom translators are to provide verbatim translations both ways, not summarize what has been said or paraphrase it. How does one translate "habeas corpus," "vicinage," or even "subpoena" into Farsi or Korean? Friends and family members who may accompany someone to court do not know about the need for verbatim translation, so when they offer to translate, they most often summarize or paraphrase. Because of the precise nature of some legal phrases and requirements, a summary or paraphrase often is insufficient. Both are insufficient, also, when a non-English-speaking witness is testifying. Being a translator in a courtroom is different from being able to have a social conversation in a living room or even a classroom. "Without qualified interpretation of courtroom proceedings, the trial is a 'babble of voices,' the defendant is unable to understand the nature of the testimony against him or her, and counsel is unable to conduct effective examination."[48]

Just as the pool of people who can be successful court reporters is limited, so, too, is the pool of people who can be successful translators. In both instances, training and understanding of the legal process are needed. Since the early 1990s, courts have been seeking to establish certification procedures for those who serve as translators.

As with court reporting and services for indigents, translators in criminal cases are constitutionally mandated[49]and therefore are mission critical. The right to a translator in a civil case has not yet been declared a constitutional requirement, but if access to courts has any meaning, it will be in time. In 2000, the California legislature established a pilot effort to provide translators in certain child custody and domestic violence cases in seven counties.[50] In its report to the legislature about the pilot program, the Judicial Council said: "The study found strong consensus among judicial officers in the pilot counties that interpreting of family and domestic violence proceedings was a fundamental factor contributing to the quality of justice in their courts. As one judicial officer put it, 'Having interpreters equates to having a bailiff or a record of the proceedings, it is just that basic. The service needs to be provided.'"[51] Even though the right to an interpreter normally is not yet established for civil cases, because access is a key component of courts' mission, the provision of translators in as many languages as needed should be deemed mission critical. It is possible, as some courts do with court-paid counsel, to charge those with sufficient resources the cost of providing a translator, but the availability of a translator in all court proceedings, preferably one certified to be a court translator, should be deemed mission critical.[52]

In order to serve as a juror, a person must understand English sufficiently to understand the evidence and arguments being presented in court. Thus, every state excuses persons who do not speak English from jury service. A growing number of states are mandating by statute that a citizen who is hearing- or visually impaired be allowed to sit on juries, however. If a hearing-impaired person is called and otherwise qualified to serve, and if that person is selected to sit on a jury, he or she needs a translator so he or she can understand what is being said. The translator is specially sworn and then sits with the hearing-impaired juror during the trial and joins the jurors during deliberation.

Some translators are employees of the court. Because Spanish is the predominant language for which courts need translators, employed translators most often speak Spanish. In areas where a second or third language may be prevalent, a court may employ translators who speak those other languages, also. More often, translators for both Spanish and other languages are contractors paid a daily or half-day fee.[53] The fee may be set statewide by statute or by court rule, or it may be negotiated individually with an interpreter.[54] In almost all courts, the need for and cost of translators are increasing significantly. Thus, this cost has become a more obvious expense when a close budget review is needed. As with counsel for indigent criminal defendants, ways to lower the expense can be discussed, but the need for the expense should be nonnegotiable. The need for translators is mission critical for criminal cases. It should be mission critical for all case types. Whenever possible, a court's need to assure access for litigants and witnesses in all case types should be sufficient to support the need for translators regardless of the case type.

9.2.8 Family and Summary Civil Cases

The discussion to this point has been about *functions* that are mission critical, not case types. Some functions are mandated because they are integral to criminal cases but not civil cases. Civil cases clearly are not functions, thus seldom are discussed as being mission critical. If courts are to fulfill their purposes, however, as well as comply with a raft of legislation governing summary civil cases and many cases involving children, thinking of these types of cases as mission critical is appropriate.

Summary civil cases are primarily small claims and landlord–tenant disputes. The dollar value of a dispute below which a case becomes a small claims case varies across the nation, ranging from \$1,000 to \$15,000. In a little over half the states, the cap in 2003 was set between \$3,000 and \$5,000.[55] Landlord–tenant disputes normally result from tenants not paying rent for several months and landlords seeking to evict the tenant or obtain the rent money.

Part of what courts do is help to preserve public order. They also are to do justice and appear to do justice in individual cases. Small disputes over repair of a car, an item of clothing ruined by a cleaner, and small monetary damages resulting from an automobile intersection or parking lot collision, can generate a lot of emotion. Lawsuits seeking payment of unpaid bills ("collection cases") represent a significant percentage of cases on many small claims dockets. These cases may affect the fiscal health of small businesses. Many of the collection cases as well as a significant percentage of the other small claims cases, are resolved with a default judgment, where the defendant does not appear to contest the claim so the plaintiff wins by default. Even if there are no constitutional mandates that these types of cases must be resolved, there is substantial public benefit in doing so. The timely resolution of these cases benefits small businesses and individuals who have suffered an economic loss that may be small in dollar terms but large relative to their assets. Statutes, normally, or court rules recognize the value of resolving these cases quickly by creating summary procedures and mandating short timeframes within which courts should resolve them. If courts are not provided the resources needed to resolve these cases within the time constraints set by statute, they are not fulfilling their assigned role.

Children are the most vulnerable and least able to protect themselves in our society (along with the mentally ill). The reference to "family" in this section covers more than the divorce/dissolution, paternity, child support, and adoption cases that normally are assigned to family divisions. It also covers abuse and neglect of children ("dependency" cases in many courts) and the mental health calendars that normally are placed in a court's probate division, plus the juvenile status offenses[56] that normally are in the juvenile division. (Juvenile delinquency cases involve the commission of crimes by juveniles so are covered by existing constitutional imperatives along with strict time constraints imposed by statute.) There are no constitutional mandates to adjudicate children's cases or those involving the mentally ill ahead of others, or to do so within statutorily defined time standards. This absence is not the end of the review in terms of these cases being mission critical, however.

First, dependency cases are subject to strict time limits in the initial determination of dependency that results in the court assuming control over the care and placement of a child. Then, there are mandated reviews of the child's welfare every six months. The steps to be taken and the time limits now are mandated in federal legislation.[57] In our republic, a federal mandate would make the proper and timely handling of these cases mission critical.

The family division cases of divorce/dissolution of marriage, paternity, and child support, together with adoption cases,[58] touch people very personally and deeply. If a court is unable to devote sufficient resources to resolving these cases in a timely way—not eventually, but timely—many lives are disrupted, but especially those of the affected children. The emotional levels and the impact on society of these cases are even higher than in summary civil cases. Children are affected by all divorces, but divorces that take extended amounts of time because a court lacks the needed resources fester that much longer and can affect children that much more deeply. Children whose financial support is not assured also suffer. Judicial resources may be most critical in handling these cases, but staff support also is essential. In many ways, the last half of the 1990s and the early years of the 21st century have been the "years of the children" in terms of society's concerns and priorities.

Courts should do all they can to assure that the adjudication of cases involving and affecting children are seen as mission critical, so that both the judicial and staff resources needed to adjudicate these cases are preserved. With respect to dependency cases, this also may involve the resources needed by executive branch agencies such as child protective services, as well as funds to assure the availability of attorneys for all parties required to have them.

9.2.9 Technology

Technology has many forms in courts today. Almost all courts now put all their case information into case management software run on networked personal computers, on a mainframe, or, in a slowly growing number of courts, in a remote data warehouse. The private software vendor who sold the case management software to the court or the state's administrative office of the courts normally administers the data warehouse. Internet use and websites for courts are becoming more widely used, meaning court personnel or contractors (including local government IT personnel) are needed to maintain and upgrade the website and to handle any technical problems associated with use of the Internet. Two of the biggest issues involved in Internet use are viruses and hackers. Both threats are addressed through software that is increasingly sophisticated and expensive. The funds to sustain these activities and software packages are mission critical.

Courts increasingly are scanning paper records as they come into the court or shortly after disposition, so that all records come to the court initially as electronic files or are converted to electronic files at some point. The scanning process requires staff up front to separate stapled or clipped papers and otherwise to prepare the documents for feeding into the scanner and then to check to be sure the scanned image is clear. The up-front costs are justified for documents scanned as they are filed by the saving of staff time thereafter, the ease of use, and the fact that multiple users have access to the image at the same time. Using a scanned image also eliminates the risk of damage or loss to the original paper record, if that is kept. The time and costs associated with scanning paper files after a case is concluded are justified by the relative ease of storage and being able to store thousands of records in a few inches versus several yards of shelf (and floor) space.

Once a court has scanning equipment, and staff to scan active files, the staff and the equipment become mission critical. When a court introduces scanning of active records, all of the court's workflow is (or should be) redesigned to reflect the use of scanned and other electronically created files, and further, staff are reallocated. Unless scanning is introduced and used without any change in the existing workflow and staff allocations, switching back to a paper-based system during tight budget periods would be disruptive and probably would require more staff, which is not a good solution in a budget crisis. For all electronic records, safe off-site backup storage also is essential in case something happens to the computers or files in a courthouse (see chapter 10).

Many courts have switched from a staff member initially answering all telephone calls to automated answering systems, normally using a phone tree-type of recording. ("For court hours and location(s), press one, for traffic, press two, for criminal, press three," etc.) Some systems only direct callers to the right department, some provide information in an effort to eliminate a person having to do so (like court hours and locations), and some are highly sophisticated (and expensive)[59] purveyors of substantive information. The rationale is to free staff time that might otherwise be spent answering telephones so staff can serve people at the counter or complete time-sensitive paperwork (see section 9.2.5, above). Whether one likes automated answering systems, tolerates them, or would like them all to go away, many court administrators believe they relieve some staff time to deal with necessary record processing. (The amount of saved time depends on the type of system that is installed.)

Judges need records to accomplish their assigned mission. Courts need records to fulfill their responsibilities to provide access to public records and to respond to citizen and governmental inquiries. If courts' records are in electronic format, as they increasingly are across the country, the ability to create, update, protect, provide access, and preserve those records is mission critical. This function requires staff plus hardware and software, as well as safe and secure off-site storage. Courts should not compromise in this mission critical area.

9.2.10 Evidence Storage

During trials and occasionally in support of what are called evidentiary motions, parties introduce physical evidence. The physical evidence that might be introduced can be extraordinarily diverse and sometimes is quite unusual. Evidence can run the gamut from the normal documents and photographs, to illegal drugs, to guns and other weapons, to clothing (often soiled or containing bodily fluid), to poster-sized charts, to large scrolls showing time lines and events, to doors, parts of automobiles, carpeting, and almost anything else one might imagine that could help a judge or jurors to understand what happened. Once evidence is introduced into a case, it becomes the court's responsibility to store and protect it. At a minimum, a court's responsibility extends for the length of the trial or hearing. Normally, it continues through the time the parties have to appeal an adverse judgment.

By rule or statute, the time to file an appeal normally is 30 or 60 days, but with posttrial motions that might be made and time for sentencing in criminal cases, this time often extends to 90 or 120 days after a trial is over. If an appeal is filed, normally the court remains responsible to protect and store the evidence in case the appellate court believes that seeing the evidence is necessary or in case a new trial is ordered. The trial court retains custody of the evidence so that neither of the parties in the case, nor anyone else, has an opportunity to change, corrupt, or "misplace" the evidence. When the appeal process is over or if no appeal is taken, courts used to just keep the evidence until at some point the evidence storage area was full, at which point they would ask the parties if they wanted it or simply order its destruction. Today, more often than not, courts will order the parties to take the evidence back in civil cases. In criminal cases, the prosecutor or law enforcement will be asked to store drugs and weapons even during the appeal process.[60] By and large, courts are being more vigilant about retention periods today and not keeping evidence indefinitely.

Courts take seriously their responsibility to store and protect evidence, but often do not execute their long-term responsibility very well. "Long term" means different things in different contexts. For a capital murder case, many states require all evidence as well as all records to be preserved indefinitely. In other major felonies, the evidence may have to be preserved for the length of the sentence (decades in some cases). Evidence in misdemeanor cases and in most civil cases may need to be held for only be a few months, but certainly longer than the time allowed to file an appeal. Even with the trend toward giving evidence back to the parties, evidence lockers, closets, and rooms often are jammed full and in only modest order.

Paper and photographic evidence requires the same care for long-term storage that court records do. So do electronic records (audio tapes, video tapes, CDs, and DVDs). Physical items such as clothing and pieces of wood are put at risk for water damage, high humidity or dampness, mold, and other environmental conditions. Yet, many courts use locked closets or small rooms with little or no environmental protection, the same shelving as used for long-term paper storage, and limited indexing and records of what is being kept. Items that fit easily into a storage box are put into one and labeled, but oversized items normally are put wherever they fit. Most administrators recognize the importance of this storage function and the weaknesses in their courts' evidence handling, but often feel that their courts have higher priority needs or have few options.

As with long-term records storage, space often is at a premium in courthouses and budget analysts in the other branches seldom place a high priority on this function. The safe and secure storage of evidence should be deemed to be mission critical, nonetheless. Both staff to monitor and manage the storage area and an adequate and appropriate storage space are part of the mission critical need. Normally, there is a legal requirement for the storage, at least for a period of time. As suggested, there are security issues associated with some evidence that must be recognized and addressed. If a court has not devoted many resources to this function or the evidence is starting to exceed the capacity of the storage area, it may be hard to obtain the needed funds during tight fiscal times. Once again, this need is best addressed when funds are relatively available. In the meantime, whatever a court has at the moment should be preserved as a mission critical function when budgets are at risk.

9.2.11 *Probation*

The probation function is an integral part of judges' sentencing responsibilities. Probation officers in 2003, the most recent year for which data are available, were responsible nationally for about 4 million convicted persons compared to about 2,900,000 people combined in all the jails and prisons and under parole supervision.[61]

The administrative responsibility for probation varies across the country. Sometimes probation is an independent office with the chief probation officer appointed by the executive or legislative branch and with funding going directly to that office. Sometimes probation is seen as solely a judicial function so that the office and its funding are under the court's authority. Some courts are responsible administratively for juvenile probation but not for adult probation. The administrative location of the probation function does not affect the centrality of the function to courts' purposes, but it can affect court budgets and how aggressively a court fights for the probation budget.

Probation, like defense services for indigents, normally is not favored by funding authorities, even though it is far less expensive than jails and prisons. Wherever the function is located administratively, courts often have to fight to keep the budget from being cut, not only in times of fiscal distress, but even in relatively good financial times. As a result, courts and probation offices have created several ways to allocate resources to try to stay on top of those offenders who pose the greatest risk of reoffending, while tracking but not really supervising those who pose a limited risk to the general community.

As is true of several of the mission critical functions identified here, courts often have been unable to forestall cuts in probation's budget during tight economic times. That does not lessen the importance of the function or the need for it to be effective in achieving its assigned tasks. Trial Court Performance Standard 3.5 states that, "the trial court takes appropriate responsibility for the enforcement of its orders."[62] All orders are important, but important components of courts' purposes relate to the sentencing of criminal defendants (see section 8.3.1, chapter 8). If the probation function is diminished too much, the much-more-expensive options of jail and prison will have to be used by judges to provide sufficient public safety. Probation is a mission-critical function. To the extent that it can, a court should do everything in its power to preserve probation funding when budgets are being cut.

9.2.12 Collecting Data and Generating Management Reports

Collecting and using timely and accurate data to assist with management of the adjudicative process, and of the institution, is mission critical. Having and using data is critical because: (1) one cannot manage what one cannot measure; (2) data are needed to make effective budgetary arguments;[63] (3) as public institutions, courts need to account to the public for their use of funds and their performance; and (4) data help staff and judges to manage themselves.[64]

Peter Drucker makes the following point about "service institutions." (He includes government as a service institution.) The need of service institutions, he says,[65] ". . . is not better people. They need people who do the management job systematically and who focus themselves and their institution purposefully on performance and results. They do need efficiency, that is, control of costs, but above all they need effectiveness, that is, emphasis on the right results."

Throughout the modern era of court administration, courts have had an uneasy relationship with assuring timely and accurate data and with using data for management purposes. There are several reasons. One, state administrative offices of the court started to mandate that trial courts send them certain summary "inventory" data, the most common being filings in broad case categories, dispositions in those same categories, jury and sometimes bench trials, and, sometimes, pending case totals for the broad case categories. Either these data were collected and tabulated manually, or early case management information systems generated the mandated data but little else. These data are good for annual reports and gross trend lines, but they have very little value for trial court management. Once the early computerized systems were programmed, it was hard (and often expensive) to expand the management reports to produce more useful reports.

Two, putting the summary reports together at the trial level almost always was an add-on task for someone, which meant probable delay before someone pulled all the disparate reports together to send to the state. Since these data were for an annual report and of only marginal local value, delay month to month was not seen locally as critical; everyone knew the data would not really be used until sometime after the fiscal or calendar year ended. As summary reports often were compiled manually, accuracy was compromised from the outset. When trial courts obtained better computerized case management systems, the computers compiled the data, so the timeliness issue was addressed, but accuracy still was an issue, at least for dispositions and pending totals. If data entry staff members are hard pressed for time, filing data are entered first because judges need information about new cases when the parties appear in court. Data input for dispositions might be deferred because, after all, the case is over so the time pressure disappears. This returned the timeliness issue, only in a different form. The current generation of software generates management reports from operational data, so the totals accurately reflect what was entered and reports that are useful for local management can be generated. Weaknesses persist, however, because many computerized systems still lack automated accuracy checks. Incorrect dates can be entered and incorrect disposition codes used without their being flagged or discovered until someone else looks at the record. It is startling how many courts with computerized information systems still assert that they do not trust their data because, largely, of lack of faith in data entry accuracy or timeliness.

Three, now many of the computerized information systems can generate management reports that are (or could be) useful, but the list of potential reports is very long and the list of reports regularly generated and used is very short. The failure to use the power of computers to provide good management reports stems from two weaknesses. First, many administrators and senior managers—and the chief judge—have not been trained how to use these reports. They might be in the system, but if the leadership does not understand what the reports are telling them, they are useless.[66] The second weakness also is the fourth reason why the use of data has not found favor in most courts.

Many judges see management reports not as useful tools for self-analysis and institutional advancement, but as weapons that might be used against them in the next election; or, that might be used to put them in a relative bad light vis-à-vis their peers on the bench and result in an assignment to hear cases they wish to avoid. The institutional positives that flow from having timely and accurate data about the court's operations can be trumped by the professional and personal concerns of judges (see chapter 7).

There is an interesting duality of perspective among judges about statistical reports, however. Judges' concerns about data being used against them may lead to squelching a report completely or to redesign of a report to the point that it is so general that it is not useful for management. When reports are designed to show results by individual judge and then distributed to each judge, however, many become competitive and want to look good on the reports. If they are performing relatively well compared to their peers, they work hard to stay in that relative position. If they are not doing relatively well, they work harder to do better.[67] Judges do not get too upset if they are somewhere in the middle of such a list, but they love to be at the top and hate to be at the bottom. The State of Kansas applied this phenomenon to courts when it started to publish in the early 1980s how each trial court was doing relative to the new time standards for dispositions. The state court administrator used to note that no court ever was on the bottom of the list (meaning it had the most cases missing the disposition time standard) two months in a row.

A lot of useful management data do not lend themselves to setting up a competition among the judges. When those opportunities arise, they should be used sparingly and with forethought. The fear factor among judges regarding misuse of data by a potential opponent should not be overlooked as a serious impediment to effective use of data in courts to improve management.

A fifth reason that there has not been a strong demand for accurate data that can drive management decisions in courts is that for many years courts have been able to use smoke and mirrors about filings, dispositions, and maybe pending cases, make generalized claims about how these numbers demonstrate the claimed need, and get what they wanted in the budget.[68] Accurate data were not demanded by the other branches and not used. The nexus between the numbers used and the stated need was not demonstrated but also not required. When the value and skill of a court's leadership is largely based on whether or not the budget is increased[69] and results are achieved without rigorous use of accurate and timely data, accurate and timely data have no value.

The Trial Court Performance Standards challenged this thinking and these experiences. Not only did they challenge the factors courts' leaders thought were important, but then they said that whether or not a court was achieving the desired performance should be determined by "the application of data, not on guesswork."[70] COSCA, the Conference of Chief Justices, NACM, and virtually all other significant national organizations have embraced the Trial Court Performance Standards. Several courts try to use them to gauge their performance and to identify how to do better. Virtually every conference of NACM contains several speakers or panelists who say courts have to use the Standards and "metrics" to manage. At an intellectual level, the Trial Court Performance Standards changed the debate and changed the perception about the value of data. Regrettably, they did not change operations in more than a few courts.

One of the issues cited by trial court administrators for why the operational impact has been so limited is the large number of measurements proposed originally to gauge whether a court was meeting the standards. Plus, it was hard for most courts to collect the needed data. Therefore, the National Center for State Courts in 2005 published "CourTools," a restatement of the "10 core measures" a court should use to gauge attainment of the Standards.[71] The hope and expectation is that CourTools will seem less overwhelming to trial courts and that they will lead courts to use and rely on data to a greater extent.

With or without CourTools, courts that wish to be successful in the 21st century have to use data to manage. The collection, entry, and use of timely and accurate data is essential for the ability of courts to keep up with and, one hopes, get ahead of the increasing pace of change they will face in this century. There are several ways administrators can introduce and institutionalize the use of data that might make it less threatening to judges and to staff who might feel that "big brother" now will review all they do. They include:

- Abandon "performance" measures in favor of "service delivery" measures, that is, change the focus from "me" or "us" to "our clients."
- Do not think or talk about "failing to meet" or "falling short of" a goal, but of a need for and opportunities for continuing improvement.
- In judge-related areas, start with court measures rather than individual measures. (Individual results are the long-term goal, but perhaps not a prudent way to introduce the use of data to help manage. The use and sharing of individual judge data should be a joint decision of the leadership team.)
- Sample the staff time spent on specific tasks as a step in determining workloads to justify budget requests for new positions. Make sample time measurements routine. When funds are obtained, so as to document the value of the budget increase measurement is changed from the baseline,. Staff will see how using data can be positive.
- Make data quality a priority. Devote whatever resources are needed, including new case management software, if necessary, and training time to assure data quality. Make this a specific mission critical goal.
- Develop measurable output goals for supervisors and managers that are tied to court goals. Work with the human resources people to devise positive incentives for those meeting and those exceeding their goals (gift certificates, attendance at conferences or training programs, time off, cash bonuses, if possible, etc.).
- Insist that all proposals for changes in procedures or new programs contain statistical analyses of the problem(s) warranting the change and outcome expectations that are measurable statistically.
- The administrator should model proper behavior by obtaining and using data to support his or her own proposals, including goals that use data.

■ Provide training for supervisors and managers in statistical analysis and how to set quantifiable goals.

Data and their use as an aid to management is one of those functions that can be seen to have two levels, that which is mission critical and that which is more extensive and sophisticated and thus fits better into level four in the Hierarchy of Court Administration. In level one, the definition offered in 1971 by Friesen, Gallas, and Gallas is a good articulation of mission critical needs: "Management information … is the data about the work of the court which must *routinely* be considered in making the decisions related to orderly and smooth operations"[72] (emphasis in original). The staff and the software that will enable courts to meet their need for accurate, timely, and complete management information are mission critical.

9.2.13 Accounting and Fiscal Responsibilities

Courts, particularly courts of limited jurisdiction, take in millions of dollars each year in cash, checks, and, increasingly, credit card payments. Consequently, they handle a large number of payment transactions daily, resulting in significant funds that must be recorded, assigned to the proper case, accounted for in the case management and fiscal systems, spread across the proper accounts,[73] and then deposited. (I have heard of a few small courts in which deposits were not made daily. Daily deposits should be standard procedure even if the collected sums are small.) Each year, several courts across the country face either accounting or theft scandals. The problems might arise from lax supervision or controls or simply poor handling and accounting of their funds, but whatever the cause, problems with cash seem to appear in national news reports in several courts a year. If the cause is inadequate supervision, the court either has a training issue or a staffing-level problem. In either case, the funds needed to assure each court and the other branches that this problem will not arise should be deemed to be mission critical.

The form of payment for fines and fees has been a subject of discussion since at least the early 1980s. For many years, only cash was acceptable. Then checks became acceptable, with bounced checks carrying a heavy fee. They also carry a heavy accounting burden. In the 1980s, whether or not to accept credit cards was broadly debated. The issue in those years turned on the fee banks charge. Most state laws require full payment of fines and fees. If someone pays with a credit card and a bank holds back 1 or 2 percent as a fee, the court is not receiving full payment. The first-adopter courts often got a fee waiver from banks to avoid this problem, but as the number of people wanting to pay by credit card and the number of courts wanting to accept them increased, fee waivers became less attractive to the issuing banks and soon disappeared. Some states adopted laws to permit credit card payments and payment of a fee by the payer that covered the banks' fees, but even today some courts do not accept credit cards. In order to sell the idea of accepting credit (and debit) cards, courts need to know how many fines are not paid, how many checks bounce and their staff costs for handling those checks, and how many unpaid fines and fees are uncollected. Based on these numbers, a 1 or 2 percent fee paid to a bank may cost a court much less than not accepting credit cards. Today, debit cards are the issue. The fee issue remains, but the transfer of cash to the court's account occurs faster, which should make debit cards even more attractive. As with credit cards, some courts accept debit cards and some do not.

Further, across the nation, fines, fees, and penalties are increasing significantly, making it harder for most people to pay the full amount in a single payment by cash or by check. The result is that an increasing percentage of defendants are seeking and obtaining installment or time payments. In a few courts, automatic electronic funds transfers are available for installment payments and for regular payments of child support through the court. This option is not available in most courts, but is widely available in the private sector for a wide range of repetitive payments.

Wherever a court is today in terms of the various payment options, that is the mission critical level of staff and technology that should be maintained. The long-term goal for courts should be to accept whatever payment methods are common in the private retail economy. Achieving progress toward that goal would be a level four or five goal in the Hierarchy of Court Administration. To achieve that goal, government requirements for full payment may need adjusting and the equipment that interfaces with bank records may be required, but the goal should not change. Payment should be as convenient as possible for all parties dealing with a court. Defaults would be reduced if there were a variety of payment methods available. And if the risk of nonpayment can be transferred to the private sector through credit cards or eliminated by same-day withdrawal of funds from banking accounts with debit payments, these are desirable outcomes.

Bond forfeitures can be a quicksand area for courts. If someone forfeits bail by not appearing in court as required, the bondsman is supposed to pay the court the full bond amount. These funds, in effect, are "found" money in government; they are funds that do not come from tax or fee income, so they have special value to budget people. Bondsmen have multiple clients and can have substantial accounts with courts. They normally can be counted on to pay. Therefore, there is some tendency in short-staffed courts to defer the processing of forfeitures because they do not carry the time deadlines of some other tasks. In one urban court, the unprocessed forfeitures had reached more than a million dollars at the time of an audit. Consequently, the supervisor of that unit was disciplined. This degree of lack of attention to bond forfeitures is not common, but this court's experience is a caution for others to manage the bond forfeiture area with care. The risks and needs also require that this function be mission critical need.

Courts operate with public funds and are accountable for their use of those funds. Most courts do very well managing their budgets, but two factors lead to overruns. The first is inherent in the constitutional requirements imposed on courts regarding indigent criminal defendants. The second derives from lack of attention by court administrators as to how expenses are tracking to the budgeted sums.

A significant portion of a court's budget is devoted to payments for services needed by indigent criminal defendants. Even with a history of expenses covering several years, budgeting for these expenses involves guesses. No one can be sure how many criminal cases will be filed and, of those, how many will involve indigents, although that percentage tends to stabilize over time. No one can be sure how much time it will take counsel to defend each case. Private attorneys are paid by the hour. If one hundred cases are filed this year and one hundred were filed last year, this year's cost could be 10 percent higher simply because of the time spent per case. No one can be sure how many transcripts will be needed or how many pages will be in the transcripts. (In most states, transcript costs are set at a per-page rate.) A court may estimate a small increase or a small decrease compared to the previous year's budget, but in the end it will have to pay whatever the total amount of the bills. One cannot manage these expenses, one can only monitor them. At all levels of government the budget staffs in the other branches understand the mandatory and largely unpredictable nature of these expenses. In state-funded systems, an underestimate for one court might be offset by an overestimate in another court, but even in state-funded systems, total statewide expenses may not match the number in the budget. In locally funded courts, missing the budgeted sum is an annual event.

Many locally funded courts have had their submitted budgets reduced by the budget staff in the legislature or the executive branch reducing the total budgeted for these mandated expenses, sometimes well below any recent year's expenditures. They may do so with a wink. The budget staffs in the other branches understand that if extra funds are needed late in the fiscal year to cover these expenses, they will be provided through a supplemental appropriation. In the meantime, the budget adopted at the beginning of the year is balanced through the artifice of cutting these mandated expenses. Courts normally do not object because they share the budget meisters' understanding. Occasionally, toward the end of a fiscal year, when these supplemental appropriations are needed, the other branches threaten not to fund them and complain about mismanagement, but in the end the needed funds normally are provided because they must be (assuming an internal movement of funds is not possible).

Mandated costs are not the only at-risk budget item in a court's budget. After the mandated costs for indigents, many of a court's expenses are fixed, since so many are tied to staff salaries and benefits or are ongoing, largely administrative expenses. Cuts seem at times to be arbitrary, even admittedly so sometimes, to achieve a budget that has a paper balance. Or, cuts are made in the face of obvious and documented need, but they are made and approved and the court is asked to do its best. Often, a court is told one of two things. It may be told that there is no time fully to analyze its need so it can come back in X months for a supplemental appropriation. Or, the funding authority has to see how much revenue comes in during the year; if revenues are high enough, the cut funds will be restored late in the fiscal year.

Both approaches work well for budget managers in the other branches, but not for courts. Death and taxes may be certain, but the approval of supplemental budget requests almost never is. Therefore, an administrator has to manage to the smaller sum while keeping in regular contact with the budget people in the other branches to gauge the real likelihood of getting the additional money. If overruns start developing, particularly those driven by staff costs, the administrator may have to make calculated guesses starting in December or January about whether they will be covered in April or May or if more severe cuts must be made now to finish the year within budget. The budget makers in the other branches cannot generate funds for all the worthy late-year demands, however sympathetic they may be to a court's needs. So, if funds fall short, the supplemental appropriation on which the court was counting may not come. Occasionally the budget staff will recommend the supplemental but the appropriating body will not grant it.[74] It is a difficult balancing act, but one that the administrator has to perform, often knowing that his or her original request, if funded as requested, would have obviated the problem.

The need for constant attention to income and expenses versus the approved budget makes the second cause of budget overruns difficult to understand: inattention to income and expenses versus the budgeted sums until late in the fiscal year. Almost all courts, states, and localities have some reporting mechanism that allows the monitoring of expenses and income against budget projections. These reports should be provided to the court administrator, even if the court has an accounting or budget staff with primary responsibility for monitoring these numbers. Court administrators should not assume their budget or accounting people will keep them fully informed and alert them to possible problems. The court's leaders should know via a required report at least monthly where the court should be vis-à-vis the budget and where it actually is. If expenses are too high in specific categories, or income is not coming in as expected, the administrator should seek to determine why and whether there is a possible problem or a temporary glitch that will correct itself. There may be very logical and acceptable explanations—for example, the mandated expenses for indigents that were cut, several juries that went overtime, or a specific problem earlier in the year that produced a lot of staff overtime—but the leadership should know of and start to address the issue as soon as possible. The court then should advise relevant budget personnel in the other branches. This does not seem like a revolutionary idea, but enough courts get into trouble near the end of the fiscal year with actual or probable overruns that it seems this kind of monitoring is not standard practice. Sometimes, the court simply is caught in a crisis made by the budget makers in the other branches because the prospect of a supplemental bailout evaporates. Sometimes, however, the attitude seems to be that such a high percentage of courts' costs are fixed or mandated that they have very limited ability to control costs. So, an overrun is beyond the court's control and the other branches have to fix it.

It may not be easy to control costs, but it is possible. As the Trial Court Performance Standards state, a trial court must seek sufficient resources, but following that, "use those resources prudently (even if they are inadequate)."[75] When it is apparent that a supplemental appropriation is necessary, the court should be able to show its original request and justification, what has happened to that budget item or category in the months since, the steps it has taken to eliminate the overrun, and why the steps were not sufficient. "We're the court and you have to take care of us" is not sufficient.

Income is the other side of the budget/fiscal picture. Commentary to Standard 3.5 of the Trial Court Performance Standards states: "Courts ought not direct that certain things be done or certain actions taken and then allow those bound by their orders to honor them more in the breach than in the observance.... For example, patterns of systematic failures to pay child support and to fulfill interim criminal sentences are contrary to the purpose of the courts, undermine the rule of law, and diminish the public's trust and confidence in the courts."[76]

Beyond the need to enforce its orders, courts are being put under increasing pressure by the two other branches of government to collect a higher percentage of the fines and fees imposed so that the net cost of courts to the general fund is reduced. Courts are vulnerable to this pressure because a number of audits, mostly by local government auditors, have indicated that courts often have millions of dollars of uncollected fines (and fees and penalties) on the books.[77] Courts often feel these audits are unfair because so many of the fines, fees, and penalties are imposed upon people who are indigent or have limited discretionary resources—recall that about 80 percent of felony defendants are indigent—making the sums mostly uncollectible from the outset. As fines and fees increase, more become effectively uncollectible.[78] They may be on the books as accounts receivable, but telling courts to collect a higher percent of these sums will not change the economic circumstances of those who owe them. Perhaps, courts should review with their legislatures whether lower fees and penalties might increase total dollars paid, but in the meantime, the Trial Court Performance Standards' admonition is uncontestable. Courts should do all they reasonably can to enforce as high a percent of their judgments as possible.

Installment payments are the most obvious and often successful approach. These impose a significant burden on staff to receive and account for relatively small payments over many months. Nonetheless, this is an effective collection approach. In turn, however, the staff needed to manage this process should be deemed to be mission critical. Courts have different definitions of when payments are considered delinquent, but at some point that happens. A collection rate of between 50 percent and 60 percent prior to default normally is achievable because so much of what is due is for traffic offenses committed by middle-class citizens who eventually will pay. But that means that 40 to 50 percent of fines and fees due are unpaid. Some courts run their own collection operation for these delinquent sums, some use the city's or county's collection staff, and some use private collection companies. A few courts use their own staff initially but pass the hardest cases to private collection companies. Some courts are confident that using their own staff saves on transaction costs and is as effective as using another government unit or a private company. Some courts feel that the expertise and specialization brought to the process by a private company will increase the net revenue even though transaction costs can be high. In the court for which I was the administrator, the court shifted from the county's collection staff to a private company prior to my arrival and increased collections by about $1,500,000 the first year. Collections started to fall off during my tenure, so the court switched companies and increased collections again by about 40 percent.

In addition to traditional collection efforts, however administered, a number of states have two other effective ways to enforce ordered payments. The first is legislation that authorizes the state's motor vehicle department to deny renewal of either car registration or a driver's license if the department has on file a failure to pay notice from a court. The department then will not issue the renewal document until proof of payment is provided. Multiyear driver licensing in some states separates the imposition of a fine from the final collection point, but the need to pay again is made immediate by the inability to obtain a license. Car registrations are renewed annually, so they suffer less from the time separation between the imposition of a fine and its payment. The second, more recent device is to intercept state income tax refunds. Both devices are proving effective in ensuring that court orders are not ignored indefinitely. COSCA in 2003 and then both COSCA and the Conference of Chief Justices in 2005 have endorsed the interception of federal income tax refunds for "legally enforceable [state court] orders that are willfully ignored."[79] They have not achieved authorization from Congress as of 2006, but such a law probably would increase collections further.

Each state and court needs to assess the pros and cons of the various options for itself, but in the end, it is important that courts devote more attention and resources to complying with Standard 3.5 of the Trial Court Performance Standards, and to treat the collection of fines, fees, and penalties as mission critical.

Purchasing and the handling of accounts payable also impose demands on court staff, regardless of the support provided by local departments or the state (depending on the funding source). Someone needs to identify when supplies and equipment need to be purchased, someone needs to collate these needs into a single order, to place the order, to track its receipt, and assure proper distribution of the items when they are delivered. When the bill arrives, someone needs to confirm that the items were received and that the billed amount is correct. Depending on the size of the court, this is a relatively small function or a fairly large one. Whichever, it is a function for which a court should have sufficient staff.

Some of this discussion has referenced the responsibilities of a court's leadership. They will not be accountants (normally) and will not have time to address all the items covered in this section. It is essential to the institutional integrity of the court that the functions covered in this section be adequately staffed.

9.2.14 Administrative Records

In 2001 when COSCA was defining core responsibilities of the judiciary, it included the creation and maintenance of administrative records.[80] Employers, including courts who operate any portion of their personnel system independent of the city, county, or state that funds them, must adhere to many labor and worker safety laws, both state and federal. Many of these laws carry requirements that employers create and retain written or electronic records of their actions. Even without a legal requirement, there are important institutional needs that are met by having a personnel file for each employee and keeping some of its contents for a long time, if not indefinitely.

In addition, policy statements, procedures manuals, desk manuals, training materials, strategic plans, purchasing invoices, payables vouchers, and warranties and contracts for equipment and software all are important for the institution, whether or not a specific law or court rule requires their retention.

These records are mission critical, as are the staff members who are needed to create, retrieve, and store them.

9.2.15 Human Resources Management and Training

As just mentioned, courts as employers have a number of legal responsibilities for and toward their employees. Normally, in locally funded systems, basic personnel functions are handled by the city or county providing the funding, such as, recruiting, testing, and screening applicants, benefits administration, workers compensation claims management, often discipline appeals and advice regarding discipline. Local executive branch employees also may negotiate contracts with an employee union on the court's behalf. In larger courts, court employees may undertake some of these functions even if the court is locally funded. Court administrators often feel particularly strongly about the need for court staff (often including themselves) to negotiate new contracts and amendments to existing contracts with unions.

Friction often exists between localities' human resources staff and courts when it comes to recruiting and screening applicants. The position of "clerk" in the auditor's office or the welfare department is different from a clerk in a court. The level of independence, the public contact, the intelligence, and entry-level skill needed by a court clerk normally are higher than for someone with that title in another government department or agency. Courts often feel that the HR department in local government sees "clerk" and does not differentiate between a clerk for the welfare department and a clerk for the clerk of court. Similar issues arise when hiring a judge's secretary versus a secretary for a manager in a county or city department. Problem-solving courts require new kinds of employees. They need people who can coordinate and work with a wide variety of people. They need people who are organized and can organize others. Some social service training or experience often is helpful. These individuals may have the same job title as others in the court (e.g., Court Clerk IV), but their skills and experience should be different. Court staff will understand that, but local (and even some state) HR people may not. Therefore, some courts have negotiated or simply insisted on screening and testing their own applicants, regardless of any other human resource services provided by the locality's government.

In state-funded systems, the role of the administrative office of the courts in personnel administration usually turns on whether the state merely reimburses localities for their services, so court employees remain local employees, or whether everyone working for trial courts becomes a state employee. In the latter case, the judicial branch usually administers a full human resources department with regional or local HR staff responsible to the AOC.

Training is the one element of human resources management for which courts remain responsible regardless of any other accommodations provided by local government. Even in state-funded systems, trial courts may have some obligations to assure staff training that is independent of or that supplement any training provided through the administrative office of the courts.

Judicial training also is very important in today's world. Some state supreme courts (or policy-making bodies) have begun to impose continuing education requirements on judges. Some require only specific topics, but normally the requirement is broader. Most states offer at least an annual judicial conference at which various substantive workshops are offered, possibly along with information about administrative and procedural changes. A few states have elaborate and excellent continuing education programs that provide dozens of courses a year on various subjects. The National Judicial College in Reno, Nevada, has provided excellent courses since the 1960s; some states rely heavily on the Judicial College to supplement local training programs. There are ample reasons for judicial education: the law changes quickly and trial judges often have trouble keeping up with all the new statutes and court opinions; generalist judges who are assigned new calendars need to get up to speed on the law of the case type;

statewide administrative rules or responsibilities often change over the course of a year; and there is a general need for judges to network with each other. Whether or not judicial training is mandated, it has become very critical.

When budgets get tight, training often is near the top of the list of items to be curtailed or eliminated.[81] We diminish training too readily, not only in courts but also generally in government. Training is an easy target for government budget cutters. Normally, for both judges and for staff, some travel is involved. When budgets are tight, travel outside the state but even within the state is made to appear like a luxury. There certainly have been occasions when travel has involved 90 percent play and 10 percent ostensible work. Some "education" providers even brag about an hour or two of workshops early in the morning so attendees will have the rest of the day to play golf, go fishing, go to a beach, shop, or whatever. Legislators, executive branch officials, attorneys, and some judges all have taken out-of-state "training" courses that fit this mold.[82] When many in the public hear of out-of-state training programs, it is the image of these boondoggle trips that comes to mind. Some judges and administrators will not attend workshops in New Orleans, Miami, San Francisco, and Las Vegas because of the image these cities project.[83] Even with in-state travel, judges and court administrators are very sensitive to the subliminal message they may be sending to staff if they travel to another city for training. When they are in another city, they are reimbursed for staying in a nice hotel and eating in nice restaurants. If, at the same time, budget constraints have led to staff being denied raises, staff positions being left vacant, and other items needed by the court being deferred, staff may question the court's priorities. Most administrators and judges recognize the value of training, even when budgets are tight, but also believe that deferring training for a year or so is preferable to appearing to be insensitive to the sacrifices being made elsewhere to meet budget cuts.

This attitude is commendable at several levels, but it depreciates too much the value of training. Training is as much a needed tool as an upgraded software program that facilitates staff's work or the pens and paper used throughout the court. This attitude also overlooks that most recessions last for two or three years, not one. Once you defer training for a year, it cannot be restored in the second and third year of constricted budgets. The better approach has two elements. First, training must be provided for everyone and its value continually emphasized, so staff recognize that they are not being excluded and that they will gain something, too. Second, less costly training programs, even those involving travel, can be devised to preserve what is important while minimizing the less desirable image issues.

Tom Peters, the author of several best selling management books, urges: "Don't cut the training budget when crises come; increase it!"[84] He also notes, "Our investment in training is a national disgrace.... Despite lip service about people-as-our-most-important-asset, we value hardware assets over people, and have done so for the last century."[85] Even during the most recent recession, many companies reduced but did not eliminate their training budgets for their technology staff: "With good reason, according to Laurie Koetting, director of the Center for the Application of Information Technology at Washington University. 'If you think training is expensive, try recruiting,' Koetting said."[86]

Courts should take the approach of the private sector, at least insofar as their technology staff is involved: curtail if you must, but do not eliminate. Because of the salaries paid for skilled technology workers by most governments, compared to the private sector, government generally and courts in particular have a hard time competing for these workers. Plus, court technologies often are a generation or two behind the private sector. One of the few things courts can offer new technically strong staff—besides making a contribution to an important social and political institution, a not insignificant draw for some—is to promise to bring them up to speed on some new software, programming language, or hardware, or to keep them up to speed through training.[87] Most people understand the need to train technology staff. Courts have to extend the rationale (and be strong in its defense if attacked) to all staff positions.

Training should be mission critical. It is essential for both judges and staff. If a court introduces a new program, judges and staff must be trained. If courts are to adapt to the new world of constant change—yes, constant change even in traditionally slow-moving courts—staff needs training. If courts want to distinguish themselves in the local employment market and keep good employees, if they want to reward high performance staff, training needs to be provided. When staff believes the organization cares about them, that the organization wants to enrich them professionally, and enhance their capacity to perform better now and to advance later, they will be happier, morale will be higher, and they will stay even if compensation cannot keep up with the private sector.[88] Even if some should leave after being trained, however, the court will come to be known as a place that cares about its employees and helps them succeed. With that reputation, other good employees will replace departing employees.

As has been the case for several functions denominated here as mission critical, courts' history does not reflect this level of commitment. Training normally is sacrificed because of the good reasons cited above plus it traditionally has been an easy target when there is budget pressure. In addition, budget personnel in the other branches do not see training as critical, so they are quick to point to training as an area to be cut if the court does not volunteer it. As is the case for several functions, therefore, it is best to establish the policy that training is a mission critical function during "normal" or good budget years and then to preserve as much as possible during lean years. If training is pursued aggressively when budgets are reasonably good, staff will be better prepared to cope during difficult budget times and they may not be as quick to see out-of-town travel as a luxury that can be abandoned without cost.

Cross-training is something done out of necessity and naturally in small courts, but once staffs begin to exceed 25 or 30, cross-training seems to become a burden. It is not and should not be seen as such. It may be the best hope for courts of any size during tight budget periods if positions need to be left vacant or cut and should therr be a major disaster. Desk manuals, initial orientation programs for all new staff, and supervisor training all can be and should be developed when budgets begin to get restored. Then the court will be better prepared for the next downturn in revenue and the next round of cuts.

Also, whatever the status of the budget in any given year, there are less expensive ways now to provide training—and to preserve training in difficult times—such as distance learning, e-learning,[89] in-house workshops, or "brown bag" sessions conducted by knowledgeable staff, and even videos on relevant subjects. As many dollars as possible should be preserved even in tight budgets while also exploring how to preserve training at a reduced cost until budgets can be restored. It has to start, however, with both a policy commitment to training as mission critical and then an operational priority accorded to this function. More broadly, the staff and costs associated with human resource management, however much or little is actually performed by a trial court's staff, should be seen as mission critical.

9.2.16 Equipment, Furnishings, and Facilities Maintenance and Inventory Control

These functions have been addressed as part of some of the functions already discussed. Reference has been made several times to maintaining and upgrading critically important computer hardware and telephone systems. Larger items of equipment—air conditioners, heating units, and alarm and security systems—often require maintenance, too. (It may be worth noting in this context that "temperature" is one of Maslow's physiological needs that parallels court's mission critical needs.) Facility items such as cracked sidewalks, damaged roofing, broken windows, and damaged locks arise with some regularity. Even in hard budget times, maintenance funding seldom disappears, but it often may be cut to a marginal level, at which only the most critical, potentially life-threatening, health-threatening, or security-threatening items can be addressed. Courts often share facilities with other government agencies or departments, so the local government controls what is repaired and when. Even if a courthouse is dedicated to a court, the judicial branch owns or is responsible for court facilities in only a few states; in the balance, local government owns the courthouse(s) and is legally responsible for maintenance. All courts can do is plead their case and get in line.

Throughout government, significant facility repairs are seen as capital expenses and a courthouse is just one facility of many for which the local government is responsible. For facility repairs and repair of major equipment items such as heating and air conditioning, courts compete for priority with all other government buildings. The idea that a small repair now might forestall a larger, more expensive repair later is rejected or minimized too often in government. Public budget makers focus too often only on getting through this fiscal year and not enough on longer-term infrastructure needs. This is not true of all government officials, but one need only look more generally at governments' problems over the last 20 years in maintaining their infrastructure to understand the difficulty courts have in pressing for maintenance and repair of larger items of equipment and of courthouses.

Fixing a broken chair or the leg of a desk or a broken desk drawer is not as significant a problem and is not met with the same level of resistance in the other branches. It is not always easy to achieve, however. I have been in courthouses where one or two juror seats in the jury box were broken and had been broken for some time, so that a folding or some other chair had to be carried into the box and used during trials. And this chair or chairs had been broken for several months and would remain broken because funds to fix them or buy new ones were not available. I have seen desk chairs of staff set aside because funds to repair or replace them did not exist. Files have been put into boxes and left on the floor or on top of file cabinets because funds were unavailable to buy new shelving or file cabinets.

A broken chair in a jury box sends a loud message to the citizens who come to court as potential jurors. The message is not that the court (or the funding agency) is being frugal so that taxes do not have to be raised. The message is that the court does not care enough about jurors to get them a decent chair to sit in for six hours a day. The message to staff is that the court's leaders do not care about their needs or safety. When a judge's chair is broken, it is fixed or replaced immediately. When a staff member's chair is broken, she is asked to make do for a while until funds can be freed up in the budget. Piles of boxes of files on the floor may make passage difficult, create a risk of people tripping, and, in extreme cases, a risk of fire. Boxes of files on top of cabinets create risks of back problems or muscle strain or, should a stool be available to help, of slipping off the stool while lifting down the box. Staff is not asking for much when they see these conditions go unattended, they are just asking for the respect and support they deserve.

In a court's overall budget, these items are not significant. It might be only several thousand dollars a year, unless some major equipment or facility repair is needed. If no one has been hurt, if buckets can catch the water from the leaking roof and they are not in a courtroom, administrators (or the funding agency) have accorded these needs a low priority. Certainly, it cannot be said that these types of maintenance are mandated by the legislature or court rule—unless they create a fire danger and thus violate local fire regulations. As a viable and independent branch of government, however, courts should be able to have sufficient funds to provide ordinary and necessary maintenance on equipment, furniture, and facilities. This function should be deemed mission critical.

Inventory control seems obvious enough and simple enough that: (1) it should be done regularly; and (2) it should not be affected by the ups and downs of budgets. Appearances can be deceiving. Inventory control almost always is an add-on task and thus can be overlooked among all the other things that a court's staff is asked to do. Larger courts may have staff charged with equipment and furniture maintenance or someone in the accounting or fiscal department to whom this function can be assigned. In smaller courts, however, it often falls to the administrator's secretary (if she or he has one), to a first-level manager, or to an accountant who is pressed daily to keep up with receipts, accounts payable, and accounts receivable. The staff time needed to conduct and then update an inventory would not appear in a budget. As an add-on task, it also is something that might be overlooked if positions are left vacant or staff actually is cut. Inventory control is not time-critical unless there is a fire or other major disaster (flood, tornado, earthquake, bomb) that damages or ruins furniture and equipment. Since the timing of a fire or other disaster is random and unpredictable, a failure to have an inventory and to keep it current might turn out to be a significant difficulty. Therefore, the need for this function must be recognized and the staffing impact of inventory control should be accounted for when courts argue for maintenance of mission critical positions.

The functions discussed in this chapter embrace most of what courts do, both for the processing of cases and for institutional maintenance. They also in some instances are functions that have been deferred or minimized by courts when budgets have become tight. In applying the concept of mission critical functions, therefore, some degree of wisdom is needed. If a process or the use of technology has become part of the normal processing of a court, they may now be mission critical for that court, even though some other court does not have that technology or process. If, however, a court can separate some component of a process or use of some technology can be abandoned without having to add more staff to compensate, then that step should be taken. When in doubt, courts should look to what is mandated. What they should not do is stop with that examination. Nor should they assume that because a statute exists on a subject, that all statutes are created equal. Courts also need to assure that their institutional-integrity needs are met and recognized as equal to their adjudicative needs. Two things the mission critical list will not contain are brand new programs and new technology that has not been used before and thus cannot legitimately be deemed to be a necessary upgrade. As to the essentials, Friesen, Gallas, and Gallas spoke eloquently of the need in 1971:[90] "If the court lacks the resources to perform its functions, loses control over its procedures, or contributes to the inadequacy of presentation, the individual before the courts will not receive justice. The rationale that justice will prevail in the majority of cases even if some money is saved here or there, some books are left out of the law library, some space is reduced, or some staff displaced is indefensible."

Notes

1. Solomon, Maureen, *Caseflow Management in the Trial Court, Support Studies—2*, for the American Bar Association Commission on Standards of Judicial Administration. Chicago: American Bar Association, 1973, p. 4.

2. National Association for Court Management, *Core Competency Curriculum Guidelines: What Court Leaders Need to Know and Be Able to Do*. Williamsburg, VA: National Association for Court Management, 2005, p. 12.

3. There are many excellent sources for learning the principles and techniques of good caseflow management. The seminal book of the modern court administration era is Church, Jr., Thomas, et al., *Justice Delayed: The Pace of Litigation in Urban Trial Courts*. Williamsburg, VA: National Center for State Courts, 1978. The most recent comprehensive treatment is Steelman, David C., with John A. Goerdt, and James E. McMillan, *Caseflow Management; The Heart of Court Management in the New Millennium*, 3rd edition with revisions. Williamsburg, VA: National Center for State Courts, 2004. Many additional sources can be found through the website of the National Center for State Courts, http://www.courtinfo. org.

   Also, the Institute for Court Management of the National Center for State Courts offers two workshops per year on caseflow management. Information on these also can be obtained through the National Center's website.

4. Beyond anecdotal stories and court administrator opinions coming to the author, one sign of the lower level of interest generally in caseflow management is that in early 2006, it was not one of the top 14 areas of interest on the opening page of the National Center for State Courts' website.

5. Just before Mardi Gras 2006 in New Orleans, a judge of the district court said he might have to order the release of about 4,000 jailed defendants because there were insufficient funds for the public defender's office. That office had reduced its lawyer staff from 42 to six because of budget cuts associated with the aftermath of Hurricane Katrina. Clearly, this was exceptional. Although the issue was phrased in terms of a right to speedy trial, the real issue in this instance was lack of funds for defense counsel. Associated Press, "New Orleans Could Be Forced to Free Suspects," Feb. 23, 2006. retrieved Mar. 1, 2006, from http://msnbc.msn. com/id/11532547.

6. A federal bankruptcy court clerk advised the author in several e-mail communications that in 2005, about 90 percent of all new filings are electronic with no paper backup. Overall, about 20 percent of the cases have or generate paper. The paper is retained for 60 days after scanning and then, if the quality of the scan is not questioned, destroyed. E-mail communications in 2005 from Norman Meyer, Clerk, Bankruptcy Clerk for the U.S. District Court of New Mexico to the author.

7. Commission on Trial Court Performance Standards, *Trial Court Performance Standards, with Commentary*. Williamsburg, VA: Bureau of Justice Assistance and National Center for State Courts, 1990.

8. The type of file folders used, case numbering systems, and control of access to files all are subcomponents of this component.

9. See Conference of State Court Administrators, "Concept Paper on Access to Court Records," Aug. 2000, retrieved from http://cosca.ncsc.dni.us/PositionPapers/courtrecordaccess.pdf.

10. Ibid.

11. This aspect of records management is starting to move from the legislature to the judicial branch, so records retention policies and procedures increasingly are being determined through court rules, but the authority for these rules remains statutory in virtually all states.

12. See note 9.

13. Steketee, Martha Wade, and Alan Carlson, *Developing CCJ/COSCA Guidelines for Public Access to Court Records: A National Project to Assist State Courts.* Williamsburg, VA and Denver, CO: National Center for State Courts and Justice Management Institute, 2002. See also, Carlson, Alan, and Martha Wade Steketee, *Public Access to Court Records: Implementing the CCJ/COSCA Guidelines, Final Project Report.* Williamsburg, VA and Denver, CO: National Center for State Courts and Justice Management Institute, 2005.

14. The one exception is called "voice writing." Voice writing is like simultaneous translation from one language to another. The reporter wears or holds a mask over his or her mouth and speaks what is said into an audio recording machine. Most voice writers are trained in and work for the military, although there also are some employed by the U.S. Congress and a few in state courts.

15. A very few "pen writers" remain. Pen writers, as the name implies, use a pen and pad to take shorthand notes. Pen writers were moderately common into the 1950s, but their numbers declined as machine shorthand became more common and pen writers retired.

16. Moriarty, Casey, "King County District Court Automatic Call Distributor Evaluation," August 2003, a study provided to the author by the court.

17. If comparable figures for the direct calls to staff and judges' chambers were available, the average might well reach or even exceed five per minute.

18. These individuals would not include all those visiting the court who are filing documents and paying fines or child support payments (when such payments are made through the court).

19. Commission on Trial Court Performance Standards, *Trial Court Performance Standards*, p. 11.

20. See Sections 2.0, 3.2, and 4.10 in Steketee, Martha Wade, and Alan Carson, *CCJ/COSCA Guidelines for Public Access*, pp. 10, 17, 23.

21. For example, ibid., at pp. 4, 9.

22. See also, Conference of State Court Administrators, "Access to Court Records," p. 2.

23. See, for example, "Courts' Public Service Hours by Location," p. 4, a table showing the public service hours of all of Oregon's courts, retrieved Feb. 26, 2006, from http://www.ojd.state.or.us/documents/CourtHoursChart.pdf.

24. Order Directing State Courts' Day of Closure and Service Limitations to Address Budget Cuts," Chief Justice Order No. 03-028, retrieved Feb. 26, 2006, from http://www.ojd.state.or.us/sca/WebMediaRel.nsf/Files/CJO03-028.pdf/$File/CJO03-028.pdf.

25. Judicial Council of California, "Operating Guidelines and Directives for Budget Management in the Judicial Branch," section II, adopted Aug. 2003, and revised Dec. 2004, retrieved Feb. 28, 2006, from http://www.courtinfo.ca.gov/jc/documents/reports/1204item20.pdf.

26. See Conference of State Court Administrators, "Access to Court Records," pp. 8, 9–10.

27. Ibid., pp. 8–9.

28. See also, ibid., pp. 7, 9.

29. For example, if there are community centers in relevant areas of the city that are open for at least part of the evening or on weekends, a court might place a public access terminal in those locations to help address this problem.

30. See Tobin, Robert W., *Lessons Learned from Recession Experience.* Denver, CO: National Center for State Courts, undated, p. 2.

31. Public Law 101-336, 104 Stat. 327, 42 U.S.C. 12101 et seq.

32. 541 U.S. 509 (2004).

33. http://www.ncsconline.org/D_KIS/ADAResources.htm

34. Civil jury trials normally last several days, with an average in most courts between three and five days. So the total dollars paid by civil litigants for jurors by the end of the trial may equal

or exceed the court's cost for the first day, but that offers no comfort to those responsible for the court's budget.

35. The more common name is "one day/one trial." I reverse the two phrases because occasionally jury selection requires more than one day. Putting "one day" first may mislead some people.

36. If they do not get to a courtroom for the selection process but spend the entire day in a jury assembly room—something that seldom happens in a very well run system or that happens a lot in a less tightly managed system—that day in the assembly room counts as their day of service.

37. There are some variations on this theme, with some states paying more per day, some paying less, and some paying one amount up to a certain number of days and then even more for extra days.

38. Someone working at the federal minimum wage in 2006 would be paid a little less than $50 for an eight-hour day. Someone earning $20 an hour would get only a little over 30 percent of their salary if paid $50 a day, but even that is much better than the $5 and $10 a day paid by many states through the 1990s.

39. In 2002, the last year for which the National Center for State Courts has verified data (from 23 general jurisdiction courts), there were 35,664 criminal jury trials and 17,617 civil jury trials. See the NCSC's Trial Trends Report, retrieved Mar. 3, 2006, from http://www. ncsconline.org/d_research/csp/TrialTrends/CSPtrialtrends.html.

    Both felony and civil jury trials have been decreasing in number since 1976, but civil jury trials have decreased faster. Thus, in 1976, the first year for which data from these 23 courts are available, there were only 1.6 criminal trials for each civil jury trial.

40. The political impact of suspending civil trials cannot be overlooked. One rule of budget politics is for departments and agencies to cut popular programs so there will be an outpouring of support saying the program(s) cannot be cut, so the budget authorities have to restore the funds. Sometimes this works and sometimes it does not, but it is a well-understood tactic when budgets start getting cut. Courts are not oblivious to this phenomenon. In one of the fastest growing counties in California, jury trials were suspended for two years because the criminal filings and the workload associated with those cases overwhelmed the judges' capacity to deal with all cases. The population had increased by 150 percent over 25 years; the increase in judgeships did not keep up. George, Chief Justice Ronald, State of the Judiciary Address to the California Legislature, Feb. 28, 2006, p. 12, retrieved Mar. 1, 2006, from http://www.courtinfo.ca.gov/reference/documents/soj022806.pdf. The degree to which resources fell behind need in this county is not common, but it occurs in fast growing areas and is another reason that civil jury trials may be suspended.

41. The seminal case for this principle is *Gideon v. Wainwright*, 372 U.S. 335 (1963).

42. National Center for State Courts, Knowledge and Information Service, "Indigent Defense FAQs," Dec. 30, 2005, p. 3, retrieved Feb. 23, 2006, from http://www.ncsconline.org/WC/ FAQs/IndDefFAQ.htm.

    In November 2000, the Bureau of Justice Statistics announced that, "66% of federal felony defendants in 1998 as well as 82% of felony defendants in the 75 most populous counties in 1996" were indigent. Bureau of Justice Statistics, "Two of Three Felony Defendants Represented by Publicly-Financed Counsel," Press Release, Nov. 29, 2000, retrieved Feb. 23, 2006, from http://www.ojp.usdoj.gov/bjs/pub/press/iddcpr.htm.

    At the time the Supreme Court decided *Gideon*, indigents represented about 60 percent of state criminal defendants. See Anthony Lewis, *Gideon's Trumpet*. New York: Random House, 1964, p. 197.

43. The U.S. Supreme Court in *Scott v. Illinois*, 440 U.S. 367 (1979) clarified its 1972 ruling in *Argersinger v. Hamlin*, 407 U.S. 25 (1972) that defendants cannot be incarcerated unless

they are represented by counsel. A 1965 study indicated that at that time, between 25 and 50 percent of misdemeanor defendants could not afford to pay for their counsel. Silverstein, Lee, *Defense of the Poor in Criminal Cases.* New York: American Bar Foundation, 1965, pp. 8–9

44. In 2003, about 17.6 million misdemeanor charges were filed nationally versus about 3 million felonies. National Center for State Courts, *Examining the Work of State Courts, 2004.* Williamsburg, VA: National Center for State Courts, 2005, p. 14.

45. The idea of the public paying for counsel for indigents who have civil claims is even harder for many people. Funding of these programs barely addresses the needs. In a 2005 report, the Legal Services Corporation, the federal agency charged with distributing federal funding for civil legal services provided to low-income individuals, estimates that 80 percent of low-income persons' civil legal needs are unmet. Press Release, Legal Services Corporation, Oct. 17, 2005, retrieved on Mar. 2, 2006 from http://www.lsc.gov/press/pr10170501.php

    A Washington State judicial branch commission concluded in 2004 that, "the additional funding necessary to meet the need for legal services of poor and vulnerable people is $28.1 million annually," which would have meant more than doubling the funds being spent at the time. Board for Judicial Administration Court Funding Task Force, *Justice in Jeopardy: The Court Funding Crisis in Washington State,* p. 50, retrieved Mar. 2, 2006, from http://www.courts.wa.gov/programs_org/pos_bja/wgFinal/wgFinal.pdf.

46. For example, Yankelovich, Skelly, & White, Inc., "Highlights of a National Survey of the General Public, Judges, Lawyers, and Community Leaders," in Fetter, Theodore J., ed., *State Courts: A Blueprint for the Future: Proceedings of the Second National Conference on the Judiciary held in Williamsburg, Virginia, March 19–22, 1978.* Williamsburg, VA: National Center for State Courts, 1978, p. 6.

47. Davis, William E., "Language and the Justice System: Problems and Issues," *Justice System Journal,* vol. 10, no. 3, Winter 1985, p. 358.

48. California Judicial Council Advisory Committee on Racial and Ethnic Bias in the Courts, *Final Report.* San Francisco: Judicial Council of California, 1997, pp. 99–100.

49. *United States v. Carrion,* 488 F.2d 23 (1st Cir., 1973).

50. See Judicial Council of California, "Family Law Interpreter Pilot Program: Report to the Legislature." (2001), p. 1, retrieved from http://www.courtinfo.ca.gov/programs/cfcc//pdf-files/FLIPP.pdf

51. Ibid., p. 2.

52. The whole issue of certifying translators' proficiency and knowledge of legal terms and the languages for which certification is available, is a difficult one for courts. As of the early 2000s, the number of languages with which litigants and witnesses need help far outstrips the capacity of courts to find people who are able and willing to act as translators, not to mention the judiciary's capacity to certify them through a rigorous testing process. In California, for example, the 1990 Census indicated that 244 languages were spoken in citizens' homes. Commission on the Future of the California Courts, *Justice in the Balance, 2020.* San Francisco: Judicial Council of California, 1993, p. 20. The California Department of Education in 2000 tracked 56 languages spoken by students in K–12 who are English learners. Tafoya, Sonya M., "The Linguistic Landscape of California Schools," *California Counts, Population Trends and Profiles,* vol. 3, no. 4, Feb. 2002, pp. 2–3, retrieved from http://www.ppic.org/content//pubs/cacounts/CC_202STCC.pdf.

    A national consortium of 34 states certifies translators in 14 languages. See http://www.ncsconline.org/D_Research/CourtInterp.html. Most states that are not part of the consortium, if they certify translators at all, certify only in Spanish and one or two other languages, at best. Qualified American Sign Language translators are among the hardest to find outside of large urban areas. The court for which I was the court administrator had to call an agency that was 100 miles away to try to find an American Sign Language translator. Consequently, when courts need a translator for a hearing-impaired person, some try to find a real-time court reporter who is skilled enough to take the verbatim record and have the transcription appear almost immediately on a computer screen (a laptop in a courtroom). In that way, the person can read what is being said almost as it is being said, similar to the streaming text one can get on television when "mute" is pushed.

53. Mileage fees also may be involved, but these are small compared to the per diem or half-day fees. When the supply is very limited and the demand great, some translators also charge an "appearance fee" in addition to their per diem fee.

54. In the absence of a fee set statewide, some courts will publish a schedule of fees they will pay, often adopted by the judges as a court policy. In practice, however, the schedule is more of a guide than a hard-and-fast rule when dealing with languages for which it is hard to find interpreters. When an interpreter insisted on a fee well beyond my court's schedule, my interpreter coordinator or I talked to the judge presiding over the case for which the translator was needed. Sometimes we then agreed to the requested fee and sometimes we kept looking.

55. National Center for State Courts, 2003 State Court Structure Charts. Williamsburg, VA: National Center for State Courts, 2004. Retrieved from http://www.ncsconline.org/D_Research/csp/2004_Files/2004_SCCS.html.

56. Cases like truancy, being out after curfew, and beyond parental control that only can apply to juveniles but that are not denominated as crimes.

57. Family Preservation and Support Act (Omnibus Budget Reconciliation Act of 1993, P.L. 103-66). See also, Publication Development Committee, Victims of Child Abuse Project, *Resource Guidelines: Improving Court Practice in Child Abuse and Neglect Cases*. Reno, NV: National Council of Juvenile and Family Court Judges, 1995; Edwards, Leonard P., "Improving Juvenile Dependency Courts: Twenty-three Steps," *Juvenile and Family Court Journal*, Nov. 1997, pp. 1–23.

58. These may be in the family division or probate division, depending on how a court allocates its caseload.

59. The Maricopa County (Phoenix, AZ) Superior Court spent $190,000 on its telephone tree system in the mid-1990s when it established the first self-help center in the country for self-representing litigants. The system provided substantive information useful to self-representing litigants in addition to directions to the center and other basic operating information. Based on an e-mail to the author from the Maricopa County Superior Court, March 2006, plus information gained by the author during a training workshop presented by the Court.

60. Courts have found that storing large quantities of marijuana, cocaine, or other illicit drugs may affect the health of the employees who enter or work in the evidence storage area. Having this type of evidence also raises the security risks.

61. Pastore, Ann L., and Kathleen Maguire, eds. *Sourcebook of Criminal Justice Statistics—2003*, Washington, D.C: U.S. Dept. of Justice, Bureau of Justice Statistics, 2005, p. 478.

62. Commission on Trial Court Performance Standards, *Trial Court Performance Standards*, p. 16.

63. Many trial court administrators and state court administrators believe politics and personal relationships rather than rational arguments with supporting data determine most budget decisions. There certainly is evidence to support that view. In state funded systems, however, courts' share of the state budget has grown from 1 percent or less to several percentage points and the dollar values have become significant. The state-funded California judiciary's budget for FY2004–2005, for example, was $2.85 billion. Judicial Council of California,

Cornerstones of Democracy: California Courts Enter a New Era of Judicial Branch Independence. San Francisco: Judicial Council of California, 2005, p. 30, retrieved from http://www. courtinfo.ca.gov/reference/2_annual.htm.
At the local level, administrators are more sophisticated and more demanding of documentation of need. Therefore, politics and personal relationships do not hold sway as much today as they may have previously. Important needs that are well supported with data still may get rejected, but important needs without supporting data and a strong rationale will be rejected more readily and faster today than they might have been in the past.

64. See Drucker, Peter F., *Management: Tasks, Responsibilities, Practices.* New York: Harper & Row, 1973, p. 401.

65. Ibid., p. 166.

66. During a statewide effort to reduce delay in civil cases in California in the late 1980s and early 1990s, I directed a team of consultants who worked with the administrative office of the courts to design several management reports that would help judges and senior managers know what was happening and where trouble spots might be developing. After about six months of sending these reports to the pilot courts, many judges asked that the next quarterly meeting of the pilot courts address what these reports were and how to use them. We thought the reports were self-explanatory. Clearly, we were wrong.

67. There are many anecdotes testifying to this phenomenon, particularly to judges and courts not wanting to be last on a list. I also have personal experience where a judge who had been at the top of the list for several months moved to second place one month. She called the senior manager responsible for compiling the list to ask how her clerk had messed up the data or whether the manager's staff had made a mistake that resulted in her moving down a slot.

68. I was consulting in one state whose annual report showed a disturbing increase in pending cases for the last two years in the court of limited jurisdiction. I asked the person in the state court administrator's office who had overall responsibility for the data and for these courts what had been happening to cause so many pending cases. He responded that I should ignore those data, that they wanted new judgeships for the court of limited jurisdiction; the numbers in the annual report were there to support the application for new judgeships that had been filed that year. I never learned if there also was an important caseflow management issue.

69. Tobin, Robert W., *Creating the Judicial Branch: The Unfinished Reform.* Williamsburg, VA: National Center for State Courts, 1999, p. 182.

70. Commission on Trial Court Performance Standards, *Trial Court Performance Standards*, p. 6.

71. CourTools is available through the National Center for State Court's website, http://www. courtinfo.org, or in hard copy ordered directly from the National Center. The ten core measures involve access and fairness, clearance rates, time to disposition, age of active pending caseload, trial date certainty, reliability and integrity of court files, collection of monetary penalties, effective use of jurors, court employee satisfaction, and cost per case.

72. Friesen, Ernest C., Jr., Edward C. Gallas, and Nesta Gallas, *Managing the Courts.* Indianapolis, IN: Bobbs-Merrill, 1971, p. 193.

73. Funds collected by courts seldom can be assigned to only one account or budget fund. By local ordinance or state statute, various amounts or percentages are allocated to specific fee accounts, to the local and state general funds, and, often, to the localities whose law enforcement agency made the arrest in a criminal or traffic case. In the court for which I was the administrator, most fine and fee payments were potentially spread across 14 accounts. Although California spreads funds across a large number of small accounts, it is not alone

and the number of accounts is relatively typical.

74. See the discussion in section 4.1.2, chapter 4, about legislators punishing courts through the budget process for case decisions the legislators do not like.

75. Commission on Trial Court Performance Standards, *Trial Court Performance Standards*, p. 19.

76. Ibid., p. 16.

77. This problem is not limited to state courts. Federal courts and federal administrative agencies that impose fines have the same problem. See Mendoza, Martha, and Christopher Sullivan, "Corporations Stiffing Government on Fines," an Associated Press article retrieved on March 19, 2006 from http://enews.earthlink.net/article/bus?guid=20060319/441ce550_3421_13 34520060319.211.316383.

78. Ibid.

79. "Tax Refund Offset Proposal to Further Compliance with Court Orders," Resolution 1, Conference of State Court Administrators, adopted July 27–31, 2003 and "In Support of Tax Refund Offset Legislation in the United States Congress," Resolution 15, Conference of Chief Justices and Conference of State Court Administrators, adopted August 5, 2005, both retrieved Feb. 23, 2006 from http://cosca.ncsc.dni.us/Resolutions/courtadminresols.html.

80. Conference of State Court Administrators, "Effective Judicial Governance and Accountability, A Position Paper Adopted December 2001," *The Court Manager*, vol. 19, no. 1, p. 35.

81. See Tobin, Robert W., "Lessons Learned from Recession."

82. I have not known of any conferences or workshops for court administrators sponsored by court organizations that fit this pattern, although some workshops sponsored by groups other than court groups might. I have known of a few individuals, both judges and administrators, who attended national court training programs in name only, taking the occasion of a court-paid trip to visit a fun area and avoiding the inconvenience of having to spend some time in a workshop. I cannot speak for other training programs, but in these circumstances, the Institute for Court Management (ICM) will not award a certificate of completion.

83. I know of a senior manager of a court who paid her own travel expenses to an ICM workshop in New Orleans in order to avoid the appearance issue for her court.

84. Peters, Tom, *Thriving on Chaos: Handbook for a Management Revolution*. New York: Alfred A. Knopf, 1987, p. 328.

85. Ibid., p. 324.

86. Offer, Annemarie, "Spending On Training Can Lower Recruitment Expenses," *St. Louis Business Journal*, July 30, 2001, retrieved March 4, 2006, from http:// bizjournals.com/stlouis/stories/2001/0730/focus14.html.
    The average cost per hire for all positions in the private sector in 2004 was $3,270. See "UpFront," *Business Week*, Oct. 24, 2005, p. 16, citing data in PriceWaterhouseCoopersSaratoga,2005/2006 Human Capital Index Report.

87. One court with which I am familiar is located in an urban area with a lot of high-powered technology companies and with several large hospitals that use the same programming language as the court. The court followed the advice offered here and gave its staff good training, but found the tech companies and the hospitals then recruited court staff with bigger salaries and benefits. The court, therefore, was having trouble keeping enough staff to operate its hardware and software. Although this seems to be a Catch-22 for the court, had it not provided the training, it would have been even harder to maintain and improve its operations. It had to endure high turnover, but at least it was able to benefit from these individuals for 12 to 18 months.

88. See Peters, Tom, *Thriving on Chaos*, pp. 325–326.

89. Using online learning an dother innovations, IBM's training budget fell by $10 million between 2003 and 2004 (1.4% of IBM's training budget) while the number of classroom and e-leaning hours rose by 29 percent. Mandel, Michael "Why the Economy is a Lot Stronger Than You Think," *Business Week*, Feb. 13, 2006, p. 66.

90. Friesen, Ernest C., Jr., Edward C. Gallas, and Nesta Gallas, *Managing the Courts*, p. 19.

Chapter 10

Hierarchy of Court Administration: Security and Continuity of Operations

As a public institution, court security needs to extend not only to judges and employees but also to all those who enter a courthouse with an expectation of safety. To that extent, a court's security needs differ from those of an individual. An individual can choose to take a risk with his or her own security, but an institution has to consider others' security. For some, therefore, security is a mission critical function. It is not mission critical in the Hierarchy of Court Administration for two reasons. First, Maslow made it the first level of need above a person's physiological needs, so maintaining the parallelism is appropriate. Second, courts themselves have not defined it as mission critical, although there has been some shift in that attitude since 9/11. Many courts still lack effective perimeter security. Many offer token security in courtrooms. Some believe security concerns have been met once magnetometers, hand-held wands, and X-ray machines are in place at the front doors. Few courts have security plans for each facility and the people in it. Even when such plans exist, they may not be kept current.

There are courthouses across the country, mostly in urban areas, where daily security risks are great and security is a very high priority. There are individual cases in many more courts that carry security risks; most courts respond appropriately, at least at and in the courtroom. These are not the common circumstances, however. Most courts still make security a lower priority than adjudicative and institutional needs. A failure to provide adequate security can have a number of adverse consequences for any court, but security for the institution and the people in each courthouse is not part of a court's mission. Therefore, it is appropriate to consider it as a level two need rather than as mission critical.

259

Security and continuity of operations are related and overlap to this extent: a court's computerized records need several security protections, as do its paper files. A court that has a major disruption will have to rely on these security steps to restore continuity of operations. In some circumstances, the absence of security may lead to a need to implement a business continuity plan. Thus, one stated goal of continuity planning is to avoid risks, which returns us in large measure to security.

This chapter examines both physical security and business continuity.

10.1 Maslow's Hierarchy and the Hierarchy of Court Administration

The Hierarchy of Court Administration parallels Abraham Maslow's Hierarchy of Needs for humans. Table 10.1 shows the parallel between what Maslow described as the safety and security needs of humans and the security and continuity of operations needs of courts.

A person whose security is breached and who is badly injured might have trouble providing for his or her own physiological needs, but until that person has sufficient air, water, food, and the other needs identified by Maslow, security is a lesser priority; and so most mission or vision statement of a court, but a sense of fear and a lack of security can make it difficult for judges and staff to focus on their mission. A breakdown in security not only threatens individuals' safety, but the safety of a court's records and its capacity to deliver justice. These realities are subordinated by a number of courts, however, when there is no imminent or obvious threat. Similarly, when a court's operations suffer a major stoppage or disruption, it must restore the continuity of its operations in order to fulfill its mission. This must take place before the court can think about again reaching out to the community or being proactive in addressing problems and improving operations. A court located along the Gulf Coast will be very attuned to the

Table 10.1 Maslow's Safety and Security Needs and Courts' Security and Continuity of Operations Needs

Human safety and security needs	*Court security and COOP needs*
• Safe circumstances • Stability • Protection • Avoiding fears and anxieties	• Physical security of people, building(s), paper records, computer records, and phone systems • Protection of private/confidential information in otherwise public records • Long-term records storage • Business continuity planning and implementation

risks of disruptions to business continuity after 2004 and 2005 and is likely to have taken steps to assure continuity. If it has been many years since a court in another part of the county has suffered a natural disaster or fire that disrupted operations, however, or a court has never had that ill-fortune, it may not have a sense of urgency to deal with continuity issues.

10.2 Security

In section 7.2.2.1, chapter 7, one of the qualities identified as desirable in a court administrator was "contingency planning." Security is one of those areas that require contingency planning. If security is done well, a court may not know the number or nature of serious risks it avoids, but the absence of visible security breaches does not mean security is unnecessary.

Fortunately for everyone, almost all courts only rarely suffer security break-downs or even security threats. They are far too common in some urban courts, but for most courts, they surface only occasionally and are relatively random.[1] (There are occasional individual cases in which a security risk of physical danger is apparent and for which specific plans are made. These normally can be identified in advance and with sufficient time to allow for planning.)

Security risks involve more than weapons inside (and immediately outside) the courthouse. Fire, chemical and biological weapons, fights, and even abductions in family law disputes also are risks with which court security must deal. Significant health incidents within the courthouse often are put within security personnel's purview, at least for the initial response. Security personnel will be the first called if there is an incident near the courthouse that requires evacuation or lockdown of the courthouse.

It has been said that humans react inversely to risk and the likelihood of serious harm. That is, if something is relatively likely to happen but the risk of injury or harm is small, no precaution or only modest precaution will be taken. If the possible injury or serious harm is great, such as death or a very serious injury or disease, people will take much greater precautions even if the likelihood of that injury or risk is very small. So it is with court security. A rational analysis of the likelihood of harm for most courthouses might show a fairly small risk of any threat greater than a fistfight in or outside a family law courtroom or an attempt to smuggle drugs to a criminal defendant. The consequences of a very rare but very serious incident could be so great, however, that a court's leadership must plan to preclude that catastrophic event despite the low odds.

There are two broad categories of risks against which courts must protect themselves: physical harm to people and buildings, and corruption, theft, and destruction of computer and paper-based records. Both topics only will be outlined here, as there are excellent sources elsewhere devoted specifically to these needs. The National Center for State Courts (NCSC) has a lot of information about both topics, especially following the tragic killings in Chicago and Atlanta (see section 5.2.3, chapter 5) and the devastation to scores of courthouses by hurricanes Katrina and Rita in 2005, as well as the hurricanes that slammed Florida in 2004.[2] The National Association for Court Management has produced two excellent miniguides on the subjects of this chapter: *Court Security Guide* (2005)[3] and *Business Continuity Management Guide* (2006).[4] The latter contains information from courthouses in Alabama, Louisiana, and Mississippi about their prehurricane planning and posthurricane responses to Hurricane Katrina. Two other post-9/11 documents also could be helpful: National Center for State Courts, *Emergency Management for Courts*[5] (containing seven simple steps plus a few resources for each step based on 9/11 and the natural disasters in Florida) and a State Justice Institute-funded publication developed by American University's Justice Programs Office, *Planning for Emergencies: Immediate Events and Their Aftermath: A Guideline for Local Courts.*[6] The National Sheriff's Association, the U.S. Marshal's Service, and the U.S. Department of Homeland Security and state equivalents also are excellent sources for information about both subjects of this chapter, but particularly about security. The U.S. Marshal's Service and the National Sheriffs Association also have conducted security audits that are very helpful to state courts.

10.2.1 Physical Harm to People and Buildings

The physical security that courts should have in place parallels humans' needs identified by Maslow for safe circumstances, protection, and avoidance of fears and anxieties. Even if they are not as critical as physiological needs for humans or mission critical needs of courts, they are not far behind those foundational needs.

Security is not just magnetometers, hand wands, and maybe X-ray machines at courthouse entrances or bailiffs in a courtroom. Security includes these plus: appropriate locking devices on doors; circulation patterns for criminal defendants that separate them from the public, witnesses, jurors, judges, and staff as they move around the courthouse; video cameras where there is a possible risk but people cannot monitor the area; fire and door alarms and possibly sprinklers, at least in parts of the courthouse; plans for what to do in the event of a security incident; drills for staff and judges, a recognition and acceptance by staff and judges that there are risks against which the court must be protected and they are part of the security apparatus; and most of all, a knowing and watchful eye by staff, judges, attorneys, and the general public while in and around the courthouse. Also, family members, well-known local attorneys, and former staff cannot be treated as if they were staff, with unfettered access, keys to doors, or knowledge of security codes. Domestic violence is a problem across the nation and across all social and economic classes. There are far too many incidents of domestic violence coming into workplaces, including courts. (Men can be victims of domestic violence, as well, but women overwhelmingly—85 percent in 2001[7]—are the victims. In my experience, most court employees are women.) No administrator should or would suggest that staff treat their spouses as potential threats to the court, but all staff can recognize that the problem might arise for some staff member at some point in the future. Thus, they should cooperate in following all the rules about restricted access to the building and to interior sections of the building.[8] Such caution is easier to sell post-9/11 than it might previously have been. So far as attorneys are concerned, in one court with which I am familiar, staff would provide favored attorneys with new security codes to the back door of a courthouse before some staff members and judges obtained them. In many courts, attorneys access staff work areas and file shelves as easily as staff and so frequently that staff members hardly pay attention. One need only read any state's news releases about attorneys who have been disbarred or disciplined to recognize that even well-known and well-liked attorneys can have problems unknown to most outsiders that might lead to security concerns for both people and files. Within the legal "family," such accommodations for attorneys can be understood, particularly in smaller communities, but ultimately it is foolhardy to assume that there is no risk when people who do not work for the court can readily by-pass security measures.

Another element of security is to recognize its breadth. There are five zones to consider. The first is outside the courthouse,[9] in the parking lots, in underground garages,[10] on the sidewalks across which people can drive vehicles, and in bushes and planted areas beside the courthouse in which people can hide themselves or dangerous devices or weapons. In urban areas and when there are a lot of trees near a courthouse, roofs of nearby buildings and the trees nearby become potential locations for a sniper who might call in a false fire or bomb threat to cause people or a particular person to exit the courthouse.[11] For judges, it extends to driving to and from home and to growing instances of providing security systems in judges' homes. Posting security personnel in all parking lots and outside the courthouse all day may not be feasible for all courthouses, but some courts already post personnel at parking lot entrances and high-intensity lights and/or video cameras are being added around parking lots. A security person outside the main entrance(s) during heavy arrival and departure times might be feasible and video surveillance might be more broadly used outside courthouses so there is at least some security presence.

Security zone two is the first line of defense within the courthouse: the entrances protected by security personnel and equipment, locked doors, windows, and the areas of public access within the courthouse (other than courtrooms). Most people now are familiar and have experience with airport security and similar security in some public buildings, particularly post-9/11. Therefore, these devices no longer surprise people who enter courthouses and may even give them some sense of relief that within these walls there are no weapons other than on authorized security personnel. Weapons are not the only threat in this zone, however. Chemical and biological weapons might slip by a weapons check; security has to be alert for body language and other signs that might suggest a person is particularly nervous or trying to hide something. Packages or backpacks may be left in a hallway. Disgruntled litigants or their distraught family members can start fires in trashcans or in bathrooms. The raw emotions often associated with family law cases sometimes spill out into the halls and results in shouting matches or fights. Friends or family members of criminal defendants may intimidate witnesses in corridors. In one California court, a gang member killed a juror while he was using a public restroom during a break in a criminal trial.[12] (How he got a knife or knifelike device into the courthouse is unknown.) The public access areas of courthouses once one gets past the entrances are not risk free merely because weapons may be stopped at the door. Yet, very few courthouses provide for surveillance, either personnel or cameras, in these areas.

The third zone is the staff work areas. Increasingly, some kind of locking device (a keyed lock, a numeric pad, or a card-reading lock) protects these areas. Before too long, biometric devices will be used in high-risk courthouses. The biggest risk in these areas is inattention. Staff may go through a locked door and then let someone who is not authorized to be in that area to "piggyback" through the door with them. Similarly, when staff members exit the building, someone might be allowed to enter. Staff may see someone in the work area that they do not recognize, but assume that if he or she is in the staff area, he or she belongs there so nothing is said, particularly if the person is well dressed or dressed in maintenance clothing. If a court uses identification badges for staff and for visitors and the unknown visitor does not display his or her badge, something might be said, but if badges are not required, often the unknown visitor is accepted.

The other aspect of security in this third zone is assuring that staff members know what to do when a security incident arises. Who gets called and advised if they observe a problem? If they witness something, what do they need to observe so they can fully advise law enforcement or security? Where do they go when they exit the building, if necessary, and by what route? What should they do if they see a suspicious package? What are they to do with personal valuables, their computers, and any file folders on their desks when they leave? When there is an authorized guest in the area, who is responsible for helping that person exit the building or respond appropriately? All these issues can be addressed by "crib sheet" reminders at each desk,[13] security manuals designed for staff (in contrast to such manuals for security personnel), and drills to help cement the knowledge. It also is recommended that volunteers test staff's awareness on a random basis by testing elements of security (e.g., piggy-backing or trying to get through a secure door without obvious authorization) to see how staff respond.

The fourth security zone is the courtrooms themselves and their associated areas (judges' chambers, attorney–client conference rooms, holding cells, and jury rooms). Judges need the same information as just discussed for staff, except judges also might be prime targets in hostage situations so they may need special instructions. Staff and judges need to know what to do with and for all those who are in a courtroom during a security incident, including jurors and parties in the case. Jurors need a gathering area outside the courthouse that is separate from others, in order to preserve their integrity. Criminal defendants may need yet another place, particularly if the building, including prisoner holding areas, must be evacuated. Procedures need to be identified for handling files and evidence in the courtroom if evacuation is needed. The proper location of the bailiff in the room has to be addressed, so he or she has a full view of both the public seating area and the people in front of the bar.

The fifth and final zone is the staff, judges, and security personnel and assuring they are adequately prepared, educated, and sensitized to the need for security. Some of this was suggested in the discussion of zone three. There also is a need for an overall security plan that is reviewed periodically and amended as needed. Security personnel need more training than staff; the court should assure that they are receiving the training needed even if these personnel are the responsibility of another agency. Medical emergencies can arise in zones two, three, or four. A plan, developed with local emergency responders, has to be in place about how to handle each possibility, particularly if an in-custody criminal defendant is involved who might or might not be faking.

The enormous physical and emotional impact of 9/11 and the hurricanes of 2004 and 2005 have tended to push back in our memories things like mail bombs and the anthrax mail scare. The mail rooms of the county or city and then of the court should be considered a sixth zone of security need because these threats resurface from time to time. There are clear guidelines about how to handle mail and what clues to look for to identify possibly dangerous mail and packages.[14] These should be available to the responsible personnel, training should be provided, and procedures put in place in case suspicious mail enters the courthouse.

It is important to plan on and to follow through with periodic audits (preferably annual) of the security plan to see if changes or additions are needed and to test responses to specific threats. One need not wait until the annual audit, however, to remind people of the need to remain alert. Taking a page or a section of the plan and testing that one aspect of the plan on a random basis also keeps people focused on the fact that assuring security requires constant vigilance.

The physical security of the courthouse and the people in it is not easily achieved. Some of what is needed requires funds, but not everything. Attitude changes, attentiveness, and acceptance of personal responsibility by staff and judges all can be achieved without any funds—or very limited funds for training—and can do a lot to increase a courthouse's security. At some point, the necessary equipment also is needed, but it is not sufficient. A court's leadership can help create an environment in which people are more sensitive to security risks and knowledgeable about what to do even without magnetometers, X-ray machines, and video cameras. Sometimes after such equipment is in place, people relax, believing the equipment now will assure security. Attitude, attentiveness, and acceptance are necessary supplements.[15]

A court's leaders should not try to be or become experts in security. They are surrounded by competent law enforcement, fire fighting, first responder, and medical personnel who have the expertise needed. The court's leadership brings two things to security, one of which these experts cannot bring and the other of which they may not bring. The first is a focus on the court as an institution and the special responsibility that the leadership has for the institution, the people who live in it daily, and the hundreds or thousands of visitors who come to it every day. Experts should not cow the leadership team when that team believes strongly that something is a concern or is needed. If something goes wrong, law enforcement or others might be embarrassed, but the court will be blamed. The experts may, in fact, have let the court down, but the public will look only to the court.

The second thing that the court's leadership can bring to both planning and the execution of the plan is "what if" thinking. This returns us to the "contingency planning" role of an administrator (chapter 7). The court's leaders can listen and ask, "But what if X happens or Y does not happen?" They can walk around the courthouse and think about how things could go wrong and where weaknesses seem to exist today. They can encourage staff and the judges to do the same. If the answers of the experts do not seem to be sufficient, they can keep asking questions and explain why they do not understand how the answer addresses the issue they just highlighted. If the experts cannot satisfy the court's leaders that they have thought about the issue being raised and their solution is sufficient, it probably is not sufficient. ("Trust me" seldom is an adequate response or a basis for trust.) Here is where a lawyer's (and judge's) training can be especially helpful. They know how to push scenarios to extremes to test concepts and plans. That is exactly the skill needed on the court's side. The court's leaders should not back down about their need to understand that the experts are ready to respond to all the contingencies. This process also should be continuous within the court. No one person or group is wise enough to identify every possible contingency in advance. When another court has an incident, the court's leaders should check to see if their security plan addresses the circumstances that arose in the other court. If not, amend the plan and conduct new training.

This issue of working with the security experts highlights one difficult element of security for courts: courts seldom have formal legal responsibility for security. Formal, legal responsibility almost always is assigned to law enforcement personnel, normally the sheriff or, for city courts, the police.[16] Some courts hire private security companies for some or all of their security needs and some employ their own security personnel, known as marshals. The clearly predominant model, however, is for a sheriff or police chief to provide whatever security the court has. Law enforcement may or may not accord weight to the desires and preferences of court representatives.

No law enforcement agency wants something bad to happen to a judge or someone else in a courthouse because of an omission or a mistake by one of its officers. At the same time, even if a court's budget reimburses the law enforcement agency for its costs, thereby eliminating cost as a direct concern of the agency, the personnel come from the agency. If a law enforcement agency has to make a choice between seeking more officers to be on the street or to add to a court detail, all the institutional incentives of law enforcement are for adding more officers to the street. These agencies' leaders do not favor special hires or special job classifications, by and large, because the agency does not gain any flexibility in assigning personnel. Also, deputy sheriffs and police officers, even older officers whose careers are winding down, see themselves as crime fighters, not monitors of electronic equipment and largely passive peacekeepers in courtrooms. It is necessary to note however, that some bailiffs of all ages and with varied years of service do an outstanding job representing the court and their agency to the public at the point of perimeter security and in the courtrooms. Many become valued—even invaluable—assistants in the courtroom, helping both the clerk of court and the judge with duties found nowhere in their job descriptions. It is just that their basic orientation is crime fighting, not guarding a building and the people in it from a threat that may not materialize. Therefore, a court seeking more security or new forms of security may have to argue first with the responsible law enforcement agency before it even gets into budget discussions.

One effective way to address this challenge is to follow the advice of all the experts and set up a security oversight or advisory committee. The court should convene and chair this committee, as it is the entity whose security is involved. These committees contain representatives of the court and the responsible law enforcement agency, of course, but also citizens, attorneys, preferably an elected official from the budget-making body, a representative of the county administrator or the city manager, and representatives of other occupants of the building(s) in which courtrooms are located. In a tightly packed urban area, there might even be a representative or two from adjacent buildings, as they might be affected should there be a serious security incident in the courthouse. Such a committee can be an important leavening agent for both law enforcement and the court. It can support the court if its position is sound and support law enforcement if the court is pushing beyond what reasonably seems necessary. It can help the court consider and set priorities if the court's needs exceed the capacity of the city, county, or state to fund those needs. It then also provides a broader support group when the matter comes to the budget approval process. Finally, this group can take information back to their constituents so they are aware of the court's security plan and what others need to do in the event of a security incident in the court (for example, a hostage situation calling for evacuation).

Budgetary authorities in the other branches also heavily influence a court's capacity to provide security at the level courts believe to be needed. If there have been no obvious or recent risks, budgetary authorities may feel there is no need or no urgency to provide what the court desires. Even if they acknowledge a need, the preferred approach of budget personnel in the two other branches is to move incrementally toward meeting a need. That is, if a change or new program carries a relatively high cost (as equipment or several new personnel would), budget staff will try to spread the cost over two or three years to reduce the financial impact of the change or program on any single year. An incremental approach makes sense on the budget side because of the many demands for additional funds coming from across government. It may not make sense from a security standpoint. If nothing adverse from a security standpoint has happened recently or happens during the incremental phase-in, incrementalism works. If something goes wrong in year one or year two of a three-year plan, the funds for the balance of the effort (and maybe more) will be found almost immediately, but by then they are too late.[17] Courts should seek all the funds in one year if there is any feasible way to do it.

The idea of setting priorities makes sense, but sometimes is not sufficient. No one, including budget analysts, can predict when a security breach might occur. As with so many aspects of court administration, a court's leaders should not be unreasonable regarding the level of funding for court security, but they also should not accept that a delay poses little or no risks. The *risk* is high every day. A court in which there is no incident today has only beaten the odds for today. The cover of NACM's 1995 security guide displays a banner that reads: "Warning: Premises may be protected by a false sense of security."[18] A court's risk of someone being injured or worse does not lessen because there has been no injury this week, this year, or for the last five years. The absence of any fires in a courthouse does not mean none will occur. That message is a hard sell, but it is a point courts should make whenever possible. The message should not be given only to budget people in the other branches of government. A court's staff and even its judges need to be reminded, too. It is the vigilant who remain secure.

No one wants to deal with the consequences of a serious breakdown in security similar to what happened in Atlanta in 2005. They especially do not want to deal with them after the fact. Before the fact, however, what rules the day is a lack of belief that a problem will arise or else budget limitations. Yet, court leaders need to recognize that when there is a serious breakdown that results in injury or death, it is not necessarily a lack of funds that led to the breakdown. Often, the rules for security or the security plan, if there is one, would have precluded the problem *if only they had been followed*. Thus, a national summit on court security convened in 2005 following the Chicago and Atlanta killings listed as its first element for effective courtroom safety and security, "Standard Operating Procedures are not being following [sic] and for full safety, there needs to be 100 percent compliance."[19] Complacency in the absence of problems is at least as big a threat as potential security risks themselves.[20] Atlanta could happen anywhere. The surprise is that there are not more Atlantas, given the lack of security in some courthouses and the relaxed attitudes that develop in many others.[21] Courts are not serving their constituents, judges, and staff well if they forget that or allow officials in the other branches to deny that.

10.2.2 Electronic and Paper Record Security

This aspect of security has two elements: active records and long-term record retention and protection.

10.2.2.1 Active Records

Electronic and paper records in active cases share certain risk factors (fire, water damage, temperature and humidity, mold). Electronic records are subject to the unique threats of viruses and hackers. Paper records can be removed from the courthouse or simply misplaced and so become effectively unavailable.[22] Older but still active paper records also may be subject to damage from moisture, mold, or vermin if the storage facility is not adequate. Electronic records also pose the unique challenge that once they are made available for viewing, public download-ing, or copying via the Internet, control is lost, so changes and corrections in the court's records are not made on the record picked up on the Internet prior to the change or correction. Also, later efforts to legally expunge the record(s) or make records confidential are for naught. E-mails that raced around the globe discuss-ing what was in court records were threat enough, but now with the explosion of blogs, a record made available for viewing on the Internet can be given a life totally independent of the court.[23] This latter issue is not necessarily a security issue, per se, but it is an aspect of electronic records that can be affected by a court's efforts to secure its electronic records.

Key reasons that a number of courts were slow to create websites and some still are uneasy about electronic filing of documents and public access to active records through the Internet, are the virus (and worm) and hacker threats. More than just having virus protection software, courts must have stand-alone servers that enable "read-only" access to current records and that serve as buffers against incoming electronic documents that might contain viruses or worms. The issue can be addressed, but both administrators and judges who may not be technically fluent may be concerned, nonetheless.

Hackers can harm court records in two ways. There is the obvious one, and there is the one that probably has received greater attention: an unauthorized person from outside the court gaining access to the court's files and changing information in a file, either to the advantage or disadvantage of a party. The less obvious but potentially more embarrassing risk for a court is the hacker who gains access to a court's files and steals the personal information of staff, litigants, or attorneys contained in those files. Whatever a hacker's purpose, probably all hackers would use the same portal to gain access. While each individual court must protect itself against hackers, the risk of hacking probably is greater for courts whose records are kept in a data warehouse. If one court's records are hacked, this is a problem, possibly a big problem. If all or many of a state's records are hacked, especially if the goal is personal information in the courts' records in a data warehouse the personal information and credit records of millions of citizens could be put at risk. Given the number of incidents noted in the media in the early 2000s of theft of personal information from commercial databases and those of educational institutions, it would be unwise for courts to assume their databases will not be subject to attempts to gain this type of information.

The focus through the 20th century was on protecting entire case records for case types denominated by law as confidential (e.g., juvenile records, termination of parental rights). Now, there also is concern about protecting parts of files and individual records within otherwise public records.[24] As of 2006, this is a relatively new area of concern for courts. The presumption until recently has been that private information in a public record becomes public. With the growing theft of personal identities around the world, however, courts and legislatures are becoming sensitized to the issue and the many records, particularly of government institutions, that contain information that puts people's identity and very personal information at risk (bank accounts, medical records). There are questions of what the law requires and how courts should approach the handling of records in which people have a legitimate privacy interest but that may not be protected from disclosure by law. Computer experts say that markers or codes can be added to electronic records to hide or deny access to private information that is prohibited by law or by a local rule from disclosure. We must hope that these protective devices are effective. Another approach is to identify certain categories of information about people that should be confidential and then require that they be separated from the public record in advance by the filing party.[25] It will take time to determine the most effective approaches for protecting sensitive information in a public record, perhaps another five to ten years. Meanwhile, whatever the final answer may be, there may be millions of electronic records already in courts' computerized records that contain these items of information and that are not coded or masked. It is critical for courts to seek to protect themselves and those who have filed information from hackers. Courts also need to regularly upgrade their capacity in this area. If a hacker should break through, courts also must be confident that their masking devices protect information that is to be confidential within case records. This is a money issue for many courts. New or modified hardware or programming may well be needed to deal with information filed from this point forward. Money and significant staff time will be needed to try to address records already entered into the electronic system.[26] With growing concern about privacy rights and thefts of identity across society and in many legislative bodies, funding authorities may be sympathetic.[27]

The need to back up electronic files and to protect the backup records off site is well understood today. Here is where security and business continuity concerns overlap. If there is a major catastrophe, a fire, flood, or a major collapse of a roof, a tornado or earthquake, or a chemical or biological incident,[28] a court may have to relocate and will need to be able to access or re-create its records to continue its operations. A court's leadership should seek to understand precisely the steps taken off site to preserve and to protect backed up records, including environmental protections such as heat and humidity. If the storage location is in the same flood plain or along the same earthquake fault line as the courthouse(s), for example, an alternative site may have to be considered.

A quasi-security issue relates to the incidence of spam (unsolicited commercial e-mail) on the Internet and its impact on a court's computers and workplace. "The volume of pornographic spam is so great it could contribute to a hostile workplace, a national survey says.... Many legal analysts said there is a growing belief employers will be subjected to a wave of lawsuits if they don't implement systems to stop spam."[29] Obviously, this is an issue that does not directly affect a court's records. Spam is just another, albeit an unwanted, record. If too much spam gets through a court's filtering software, it might slow down the network's response time, but it will not harm the information already on the hard drive the way a virus might, or alter or steal a record the way a hacker might. Spam may contain code that will open a window to the court's system, however, which then becomes a security risk. Spam is another security issue akin to viruses that deserves a court's attention.

The biggest security issue that involves paper and is independent of the physical threats to the building itself is the lost or misplaced files. Some courts have controlled-access file rooms and staff assigned specifically to retrieve and reshelve files as needed. When files are removed from these rooms, they are signed out (or scanned out using bar code readers) and their return is noted. This approach reduces the incidence of misplaced files, but it still does not protect against person A taking the file from the file room and then passing it to person B without telling the file room, and then forgetting that person B has it when someone else needs it. The problem of "unable to locate" files is reduced materially, but not eliminated.

The more common situation, by far, is open file shelves accessible to everyone on staff with either no effort made to note who has the files or a sporadically-used, and therefore ineffective, out-card system. Most of the time the file shelves are behind some kind of barrier and within the staff's work area or behind a door that only staff and judges can access, but as noted, attorneys known to staff may be given unfettered or reasonably easy access to files. The theory behind this easy access is that it facilitates the handling of cases in the courtroom and attorneys are officers of the court and thus have an ethical responsibility to protect and return the files, but it is only a theory. In years past I visited small courts and learned that attorney A or attorney B may have a missing court file in his or her office down the street. I have not been told that in recent years, but I continue to see attorneys with ready access to file areas. This is unacceptable in a world much more conscious of security than it was in the past.

Many courts have to live with cramped and inadequate file storage areas. With electronic records starting to dominate, the issue of active file space will diminish in the future. In the meantime, the inadequacy of space ties to security in two ways. First, many courts deal with the lack of space by putting older file folders into boxes which then are filed in a more remote area of the courthouse, off site, or stacked on the floor, on top of cabinets, and anywhere else space can be found. Beyond the threat of injury to staff, often the somewhat cavalier approach to piling boxes wherever they seem to fit enhances the risks of fire and hinders exit routes should staff have to evacuate in a hurry. This problem is difficult to resolve in many of the courts facing it because there simply are too few alternative storage sites that can protect the files and also are readily accessible for file retrieval. The second relationship to security is the fact that some courts solve their in-courthouse space limitations by finding nearby storage space outside the courthouse. In Orange County, California, *800,000 active files* are stored in three off-site storage areas.[30] Staff members then need to move files back and forth to the alternate location as well as around the courthouse. Sometimes, the alternate storage area is more secure than courthouse storage areas, sometimes not. Strange things can happen whiles files are moving back and forth. Ordinarily, the use of another site increases security issues only marginally, but there is a slight increase, even so.

Some courts seek to provide citizens with access to case files but also some control over the file folders by setting up reading rooms. A small counter is staffed by a court employee, who takes requests, provides the files, keeping some record of who has what, and then generally monitors those in the room to see that they do not misuse or harm the documents in the files and do not leave the room with them. This is a good idea, except very few rooms have enough staff to protect both the files and the door. As public access computer terminals increasingly provide computerized access to electronic records, this problem, too, will dissipate.

A mechanism to help reduce misplaced files is color-coding the case numbers and using terminal-digit filing. Without going into a lot of detail, both mechanisms help someone to see quickly if a file is misfiled when returned to a shelf. If the file is not returned, color-coding the file numbers does not matter. Some courts also color-code the file folders themselves by case type,[31] so if one is looking for a family law case, one need only look for the files with the color assigned to family law cases. None of these approaches provides security for paper files, per se, but they reduce the incidence of unable-to-locate files.

Technology soon should materially improve the security associated with paper-based file folders. Radio frequency identification (RFID) tags in file folders offer a substantial likelihood of reducing file searches from hours to minutes and for creating electronic fences to keep files within areas or, at least, alert staff when files are being removed, much as electronic tags on clothing do in retail stores.

RFIDs are dot-sized computer chips that can store hundreds of characters of data (vs. 12–15 for a bar code)[32] that contain a tiny antenna for communicating with a receiver. If a tag were embedded in a file folder, a handheld receiver could identify in seconds the presence and location of a file in a room. RFID tags still are relatively expensive compared to plain manila folders without bar codes or RFIDs (around 1–2¢ cents each) and compared to bar coding files (1–10¢ each). Also, external radio interference issues have not yet been fully resolved; the effect of interference on a court looking for files or trying to keep files from walking off is unknown. The cost of RFID tags has come down considerably in the last three years because several large retailers, the Department of Defense, and a growing list of manufacturers are requiring that RFID tags be placed on items (or pallets of items) they buy. They may not yet be cost-effective for most courts, even given the cost of staff time to find unable-to-locate files, but they soon should be. The technology, and especially its cost, should be tracked for eventual widespread adoption, assuming this technology is not replaced within the next five years with another innovation (see the next section).[33]

Paper records and the technology represented by RFID tags will compete with electronic records for dominance in courts over the next several decades. Electronic records do not need RFIDs. Thus, if courts really were to become paperless, the RFID technology would be obsolete, except for two features in courts that need to be recognized. The first is that there are literally millions of existing and old file folders with paper records; the old files go back scores of years (over 100 years in many courts) in long-term storage. Courts will not replace all the old file folders with new tagged folders, but RFID tags might be helpful if added to pallets or to boxes of folders to gain better inventory control. The second reality of courts is that each tends to change on its own timeline (see section 12.2, chapter 12). The early adopter courts may be entirely or largely paperless within a decade. Thousands of courts will continue to receive and use paper records for several more decades. During this transition period, RFID tags might be very useful in those courts. (Again, however, note the discussion in the following section).

10.2.2.2 Long-Term Records Storage[34]

The creation and use of electronic records is not yet universal in courts, at least insofar as filed documents are concerned. A majority of courts still receive their documents in paper form. Virtually every court then uses computers to create an electronic record for the case, but the documents themselves remain in paper form and are used in paper form. This is changing, however. Increasing numbers of courts will receive all or virtually all of the pleadings in a case and other filed documents in electronic rather than in paper form. Law enforcement slowly will move to electronically generated citations that will be filed electronically with the court. The paperless court, although not yet here, is coming. The current widespread use of electronic records and the inevitable expansion of their use pose several challenges that courts have not yet fully addressed. Every state has either statutes or statewide court rules, and sometimes both, defining how long various court records must be retained and which must be retained forever. Every state now allows courts to accept electronically generated and filed documents and either to retain records electronically or convert paper records into electronic form and to retain the electronic form in lieu of the original paper-based document.

Electronic records are very important for courts that are working to improve the productivity of staff and judges to increase the accuracy of records and of data about case processing, and to help courts deal with short-term space demands. Electronic records are not going away, nor should they. The use of computers to create, update, retrieve, and store case records is mission critical today in all but the smallest courts. Even in these very small, often part-time courts, computer-based record keeping may facilitate more rational and economic staffing patterns than paper-based records.

Electronic records also challenge courts in new ways. The challenges associated with hackers, viruses, and backing up records have been addressed above. They also pose challenges regarding midterm and long-term storage requirements, which is fraught with potential problems. Those who are fully committed to computers often argue there is no issue or challenge regarding long-term storage,[35] but the evidence does not support their confidence.

In its Core Competency statement regarding information technology management, NACM says:[36] "The line between vision and hallucination is a fine one. Effective court leaders are realistic about what technology can do, what it will cost, how long it will take to implement, and what is involved in its maintenance and upgrade." Unstated but implied in this statement and equally important is the caution that leaders must understand what technology *cannot* do. The Core Competency also cautions that court leaders, "not allow technology to compromise the judicial process or bedrock political and legal principles."[37]

Thomas Norris makes a similar point in a paper written for the New York State Archives entitled, "The Seven Attributes of an Effective Records Management Program."[38]

> [Because of the wide variety of technology tools available,] … it becomes critical that we choose the right ones for the right occasions and

not be swayed in selection decisions either by fear of new technologies
or by the desire to have the newest and brightest technology "toys."

Technology must be appropriate to the need it fills. As administrators decide on
the proper technology, important responsibilities of court administrators should
not be overlooked. It is easy to become enamored of computers and their promise
to the point that one overlooks or excuses away their limitations or difficulties. A
particular technological solution must contribute to a court achieving its purposes.
A tool good for one purpose may be unhelpful to a court for another purpose
because of courts' unique legal or institutional constraints. Beyond the natural
allure of easy solutions and marvelous results, there are real-world limitations that
affect courts' obligations for long-term records storage.

The long-term storage obligations of courts are not easily met. Records retention
laws or rules mandate that about 20 percent of all records received be retained for
50 or more years, some indefinitely.[39] Many more civil records must be kept up to
20 years to enable enforcement of civil money judgments. As a result, almost all
courts struggle with long-term records storage. Substantial storage space for the
old paper records is needed. To do it right, there are many elements of the process
that require attention. Files must be purged before they go into long-term storage,
which is a labor-intensive process. There are a number of requirements for proper
storage, but courts seldom have or lease the space that meets those requirements.
If microfilm is used to replace the paper and thereby reduce the space demands,
both a capital investment and staff investment is needed or expensive microfilming contractors must be obtained. And then even microfilm requires attention
from time to time (see below). Many courts have trouble obtaining the funds for
either option. Thus, it is easy to understand the allure of using electronic records
for long-term storage in the form of CD and DVD disks that can store thousands
and maybe tens of thousands of records in a few feet of space. Plus, if electronic
records already are backed up, the immediate time and cost of putting the records
on CDs and DVDs is minimal. Familiarity with the benefits and ease of use of
computers should not dull one's sense of caution about record integrity.

The use of computers and digital records for long-term storage carries at least
two risks. First, many technology companies, even those with respected products, go out of business, occasionally in only a few years. Also, some technology
companies survive but are sold to a company uninterested in supporting the
old/former equipment or software. Initial planning needs to consider a fallback
or "fail safe" position, particularly for solutions that are to be used to meet a
long-term need. If equipment cannot be serviced any more, it cannot be useful
for long-term storage.

Second, when the second or third generation of a technology is developed, the
vendor's support for the original machine or software often is withdrawn, either
forcing a court to make an unwanted or too-expensive upgrade or leaving the

court "bare" in its use of the original technology. This withdrawal of support has been seen for software packages, for operating systems, and for hardware. The probability of future upgrades needs to be part of the initial decision-making process in terms of how it will affect the cost as well as the feasibility of long-term records storage in digital form.

These difficulties and considerations require that court administrators adopt and adapt technology, understanding the realities of the marketplace along with any limitations in the technology itself. The technology environment and the cautions suggested here have a direct bearing on how courts should approach their long-term records management responsibilities.

Records management is pretty low on court administrators' list of favorite topics. The common responses to this topic are: "talk to the techies," "boring," "too expensive," "no staff time to deal with it," and "a nuisance." Sometimes these statements are preceded by, "I know it's important, but...." Administrators seem increasingly to see long-term records storage as an "old" problem because of the universality of computerized records. In tech-heavy courts, most documents now come to the court in electronic form, are created or summarized on courts' computers by court staff, and are scanned into a computerized format after being received in paper form. Even if most working records in a court remain in paper form, many administrators believe that if the paper is scanned and stored once a case is concluded, hard-drive storage or storage on a CD or a DVD will eliminate the storage space and access problems of paper records. These views are wrong. Those who believe they are correct need to undertake much closer examination of their premises and the strength of the justifications. Courts have a legal obligation as well as some societal responsibility[40] to preserve many records. The low priority accorded long-term records management in most courts, combined with a growing reliance on digital record storage and preservation, may lead courts to fail to meet either their legal or their societal responsibilities.

A "Technical Report" from the Association for Information and Image Management states that some DVD storage can maintain record integrity for up to 100 years.[41] The strong consensus among records experts, however, is that *digital storage can be relied on only for records whose retention period is 10 years or less.*[42] The key impediment to long-term storage is not the DVD, but the obsolescence of the hardware and software needed to read old disks and tapes. Manufacturers of hardware and developers of software upgrade frequently. IBM released the first personal computer in 1979. Eight years later it introduced and installed on its PCs the PS/2 operating system, hoping to create a standard for operating systems to rival Microsoft's. It sold over 2 million computers in less than two years after the PS/2 system was introduced.[43] Seventeen years later, it is doubtful that IBM, or any company, supports any of the PS/2 technology, assuming anyone is still using it. Indeed, today IBM is encouraging use of Linux, a totally different approach to operating systems and software development. In 2005 it sold its personal computer business. In 2003, Hewlett-Packard introduced 158 new products; in 2002 it introduced 50 new printer models for its consumer line *plus* additional printers for businesses.[44] How many of those printers and other products does HP still support? How many will it be supporting in 2002?

To support development of new hardware, vendors push purchasers to abandon their old equipment through pricing incentives, or improved quality, or by abandoning support for the older machines or software. Soon, often within 10 years, expertise to maintain the old software or hardware has vanished. This makes sense from the manufacturer's or developer's standpoint because it builds sales of the current products. From the user's perspective, all the documents, files, videos, and other electronic records must be converted, abandoned, or reentered to be usable with the current technology. For most of us, the records are abandoned (e.g., 8-track music tapes) or converted (e.g., DOS-based documents).

"Backward compatibility," the ability of new hardware and software to read old technology records, has not been provided by the industry to date and likely will not be in the future. Even if you can find a working personal computer that reads 5-1/4 inch disks, what are the odds of finding another 20 years from now, or repairing in 2026 the one the court has kept? Is it prudent to expect today's DVDs to be the storage medium in 30 or 50 years? In 2004, Bill Gates of Microsoft predicted that DVDs will be obsolete within ten years.[45] Bar codes were a wonderful advance when introduced 30 years ago. In another 20 years they may be obsolete, as RFID technology becomes dominant. Courts that bar-coded their long-term storage files may not be able to find or identify files in 25 years.[46] Floppy disk readers no longer are being built into new personal computers.[47] The laws defining records retention requirements take no account of the marketing strategies of manufacturers and software developers. They require long-term and permanent retention of certain types of records, whether or not computer manufacturers provide backward compatibility. Computer quality and capabilities advance seemingly on a daily basis, while costs continue to plummet. This almost compels the widespread and expanding adoption and use of technology. But the planned obsolescence of these same computers raises a huge red flag about relying on them for long-term records storage.

Nor is it prudent to rely on "migration" (conversion) of records to whatever format and form future developments might bring as a prudent response to this planned obsolescence. Migration is a process "designed to achieve the periodic transfer of digital materials from one hardware/software configuration to another, or from one generation of computer technology to a subsequent generation... [so as] to preserve the integrity of digital objects and to retain the ability for clients to retrieve, display, and otherwise use them in the face of constantly changing technology."[48] Those who support reliance on digital record storage say that old records can be migrated readily to new formats and software requirements, so reliance on digital records poses no problems. The cost of digital collection and storage of records decreases substantially every year, so digital advocates argue that in 10 years, when prudence suggests old records should be refreshed (migrated), costs will be lower, technology will be improved, and everything will be "hunky-dory."

Migration from today's hardware and software to tomorrow's in 10 years and then, again, in 2026 to the generation after that, then again in 2036, and so on, is too risky to satisfy courts' legal requirements. The risk of hardware and software obsolescence is real and cannot be ignored. Equally critical are the risks of insufficient funds being available in government coffers when it is time to migrate records and of lack of managers' or staff's attention to the target times for migration. The record is generally poor of most government entities, including courts, staying on schedule for reviewing records for destruction and preservation. When paper records are not reviewed on schedule, the medium (paper) remains intact, as does the information on the medium (the record). Not so for electronic records. When one misses the target time for migrating electronic records to the then-current medium and electronic format, the risk of record degradation grows. Record degradation in this context means the potential loss of records that by law should be preserved permanently, or at least for many decades.

The 1960 census data were the first stored in digital form. Twenty-five years after capturing the data digitally, only two computers in the world could read the original census data tapes, one in Japan and one in the Smithsonian Institution. Clearly the Census Bureau had a problem! This experience is an important object lesson about the difficulties associated with the obsolescence of hardware and software. Equally instructive is what happens when data are migrated from old technology to new technology. In the late 1970s, the Census Bureau, recognizing the hardware obsolescence problem, migrated the data from its original storage medium to industry-standard computer tapes. But 10,000 records out of 1.5 million (.7%) were lost during the migration process.[49]

How would those numbers convert if this experience were replicated in a court? A large urban court can accumulate two million records and a small court can obtain 100,000 records very quickly.[50] Records retention policies would require about 20 percent of the records to be preserved for 50 or more years.[51] In a court with two million records, about 400,000 records and in our hypothetical small court, about 20,000 records would need to be migrated five or more times during their preservation period. There are two unknowns about these long-term records. First, has today's migration process reduced the potential rate of loss? Would the risk today still be 0.7 percent or less? Second, would a 0.7 percent loss, or even 0.3 percent, of a series of court records every ten years be functionally or historically critical? The answers are unknown, but the odds of critical records being lost with each migration probably remains. In the two hypothetical courts, if the rate of loss were, say, 0.5 percent, almost 2,000 and 100 records, respectively, would be put at risk every ten years. The loss of record integrity during the second, third, etc. migration might be the same as, higher than, or lower than the original migration. If it is the same as the original migration, however, over a 50-year span, potentially 10,000 and 500 records, respectively, might be corrupted or lost. The potential loss of records then is 2.5 percent, not less than 1 percent. When permanent retention is legally required, the law says *all* records of certain kinds are to be preserved, not 99 or 96 percent. In light of legal requirements for records retention, that is a high potential price to pay for an as-yet unfulfilled promise of archival quality digital storage.

Digital storage may, in time, provide archival quality storage with a full capacity to retrieve the information[52] and full backward compatibility of equipment, but for now, digital storage cannot be relied on for permanent or even long-term records retention. *Only microfilm remains a certified medium for permanent and long-term storage.* Moreover, as microfilm supporters point out, to read microfilm, one needs only a light source and a magnifier; multiple generations of software and hardware are not needed. If only the information in a record is needed, it is hard to match, far less beat, the low-tech reliability of microfilm.

Certain conditions must be met with microfilm for it to retain its archival quality. Just as some administrators place unwarranted faith in digital imaging, some are too simplistic regarding microfilm. It certainly is not self-executing. The proper film for long-term storage and retrieval must be used. The images obtained during the filming process must be checked to be sure they are clear and complete; a percentage of images will need to be refilmed or the effort will be for naught. And the conditions under which the film is stored must meet archival standards. A good image can be damaged or lost if storage conditions are not appropriate and if the stored film is not checked from time to time. Environmental conditions, particularly temperature and moisture, affect both digital and microfilm records, but the risks are greater with microfilm. If care is taken at all stages of using microfilm, however (see below), microfilm will retain its archival quality for up to 500 years.[53] A gap still remains between 500 years—or, if one wants to be conservative, 250 years—and "permanent" retention, meaning forever. Most retention schedules require permanent retention for some records. The burdens and issues associated with having to regenerate images every 250 years are materially different from the burdens and issues associated with digital images having to be migrated every 10 or 20 years, however.

Cost is another factor when considering either technology. On the surface, it might appear that digital storage would be significantly less costly, because you just create a disk in a couple of minutes, put it in a box for storage, and forget it. That is not what the research by records experts shows. The relative cost of digital versus microfilm storage is not crystal clear; the conclusion often turns on assumptions about future costs associated with both methods.

There are four steps to which costs must be applied when comparing the two media: preparation, image capture, storage, and retrieval. Preparation costs are similar for the two media if the image is captured from a paper original. If the original record is digital, the cost advantage clearly lies with digital in the preparation stage. Microfilming has a clear cost advantage at the capture stage. The microfilm cost advantage is less when storing text-only records, which most court records are, but microfilm remains cheaper based on current costs. Digital either gets closer, catches up, or becomes cheaper than microfilm for retrieval, depending on future cost assumptions. Retrieval of a microfilm record is more labor-intensive than retrieval of a digital record, so over time increasing labor costs undercut microfilm's initial cost advantage. The driving factors for digital's costs are the initial capture costs and then storage and migration costs, all of which are helped over time by decreasing technology costs. If only limited retrieval of records is needed during the retention period, as is the experience in libraries and normally in courts, microfilm retains its life-cycle cost advantage for at least 10 years and possibly longer.

In 1992, Don Willis produced an influential report for the Commission on Preservation and Access entitled "Hybrid Systems Approach to Preservation of Printed Materials."[54] The paper focused on preserving printed materials similar to court records, except that Willis worked with bound library books rather than stapled or clipped, typed documents maintained in courts' file folders. Willis compared the technological features of both microfilm and digital technologies, but also examined comparative costs. His cost comparisons were complex and multitiered, but at that time, comparing archival optical disk storage and archival microfilm, optical disk technology was 20 times more expensive than microfilm.[55] Willis postulated that increasing labor costs over time (important on the microfilming side) and decreasing technology costs (critical on the optical disk side) might at some point produce equal filming and optical imaging costs, but that certainly was not the case in 1992.[56]

An even more detailed review of both technologies and costs of digital capture and storage versus microfilm was undertaken from 1994 to 1996 by the Colgate University Library's Department of Preservation and Conservation.[57] The final report echoed Willis' recommendation of five years earlier that a combination of digital storage to meet short-term access needs and computer-output micrographics (COM) for long-term archival storage is best. Comparing cost estimates from five different studies, the cost of archiving a single book in a digital form ranged from one-sixth to ten times the cost of archiving that same book on COM. The extreme range in cost estimates turned, as did Willis's postulate about eventual equal costs, on how positive the study author was regarding assumptions about the decreasing cost of digital storage over time. Even with a cost advantage, however, the potential loss of records during migration should guide a prudent court administrator to the use of microfilm rather than digital storage.

COM is today's most cost-effective, operationally effective merger of the operational advantages of digital records and the long-term storage needs served by microfilm. With COM, records start in electronic form, whether as filed or transformed from paper to an electronic record by scanning. The electronic record then is transferred to microfilm for permanent storage. COM is needed until the archival quality and long-term retrievability of digital records is assured.

Microfilm clearly is low tech, but low tech does not mean bad tech. A very popular book in the 1970s was titled, *Small is Beautiful*.[58] The author's premise was that high tech had become so complicated and so expensive that developing countries and even the United States could not afford it, ordinary citizens could not use it, and workers could not maintain it. Therefore, the author argued, we should look for simpler, less expensive, low tech answers to support both industrial and farming development. Microfilm certainly is not new and it is a relatively low tech answer to a continuing need. Being low tech is insufficient reason to warrant turning our backs on it, however. Indeed, it is microfilm's simplicity that keeps it both viable and desirable in these high tech times, much like the tortoise in the Tortoise and the Hare fable. Digital records are great for improving productivity, enabling simultaneous use of records, distributing use of records among many users, providing public access to records in the short term, and lessening short-term storage space needs. They are not yet great for meeting courts' archival responsibilities.

Most courts store their paper and electronic records in the courthouse or in a nearby storage area also used by the rest of their local government's agencies (even if the court is state funded). Some use commercial records storage companies, either exclusively or to supplement other government storage. As mentioned, most administrators generally assign a low priority to records management. Long-term records storage seems to get even lower priority. When an administrator accepts the responsibility and tries to meet the court's long-term storage obligations, the local government or the state funding apparatus often stymies him or her. Budget personnel in the other branches normally assign a very low priority to this need and seldom will endorse funding for proper long-term storage.

As part of several records management studies, I have had to look for old files. As a young attorney I spent three months looking through long-term storage areas of scores of local governments as part of the discovery process in an antitrust suit. Out of perhaps 60 long-term records storage areas I personally have seen, I can count on one hand the number of storage areas that would meet even modest standards for the long-term storage of records and none that meets all the standards promulgated by records management experts.[59] Labeling, indexing, storage cartons, shelving, ease of access within the storage area, fire and water damage protection, temperature controls, and protection against insects and vermin all are deficient in most court records storage areas.[60] Even if courts feel they can meet their long-term retention responsibilities with only electronic records, the effort will be for naught if these electronic records are stored with the same carelessness as most courts display regarding their paper records. Courts should do much better than they do for long-term records storage.

Long-term retention of many records is a mandate for courts, but this clearly is one of the areas where courts ascribe a lower priority to a mandated function (see chapter 8). Records management, especially records for cases that still are active (or, in family matters and many juvenile-related matters, that might be reactivated with some regularity for up to 20 years) should be mission critical. Long-term records storage also should be mission critical. In most courts today, however, it has been given such a low priority historically that courts may be precluded in a near-term time of fiscal distress from arguing that proper long-term storage conditions must be achieved and maintained and, thus, the funds needed must be added to the budget. But at least administrators should insist that funding not be cut. When budget conditions are more favorable, however, long-term records storage should receive more attention so that over time it can achieve the status of being a mission critical function.

10.3   Continuity of Business Operations

The idea of planning for and assuring business continuity is relatively new in modern court administration. For centuries, courts that have experienced fires, floods, and other natural disasters have had to deal with the issue. Even asbestos removal from a courthouse that closed the building down for months required continuity planning and execution. These events were called recovering from a disaster. The topic of "continuity of business operations" (COOP) has not received a lot of attention until recently in court administration literature or at conferences. Perhaps it has not claimed a lot of attention because normally disaster recovery surfaces as a need one court at a time. Unless that court is your court, it is fairly easy for a court administrator in another state or even another county who is waist-high in daily problems of his or her own to overlook the operational impacts on the other court. Hurricanes Katrina and Rita changed that, because they devastated scores of courts at one time. Chunks of the judiciary of Mississippi and southern Louisiana just washed or collapsed away, along with the employees in some of the worst hit areas. Florida had a similar experience, although not quite so widespread, in both 2004 and 2005. Courts around the country were asked if they could donate chairs, desks, filing cabinets, out-of-date or at least unneeded computers, and basic office equipment to the damaged courts. The magnitude of what happened along the Gulf Coast alerted many throughout the nation in ways that a fire in a single courthouse or news of flooding in an area had not. If any court's leadership was inclined to overlook continuity planning prior to 9/11 or to the hurricane season of 2005, it will be hard to do so hereafter.

Continuity of business operations is related and tied to security issues, for breakdowns in security may lead to a need to implement a continuity of operations plan, but it clearly is a separate topic. Because of its close ties to security, it is a level two need of courts rather than a level one. But, like security, it is easy to overlook until one is staring it in the face.[61] Also like security, planning for continuity of operations is a classic test of and draws almost entirely on an administrator's capacity to do contingency planning. It is a classic "what if" exercise.

The difference between the more traditional concept of "disaster recovery" and "business continuity" is that "the business continuity planning process provides a broader focus of prevention by using techniques to identify risks and establishing processes to ensure the continuing of critical court functions."[62] Disaster recovery emphasizes restoration and picking up the pieces; business continuity emphasizes continuity and resiliency while trying to avoid disruptions and maintaining and resuming mission critical functions.[63] Business continuity includes such recovery aspects as freezing and restoring water-damaged paper and cleaning and restoring damaged buildings, but also covers communications with staff and the public following an interruption of business and having an emergency cache of supplies and equipment on standby to facilitate continuity. The objectives of COOP, as articulated in Federal Preparedness Circular (FPC) 65 issued by the Federal Emergency Management Agency (FEMA) in June 2004, are to:[64]

- Ensure the continuous performance of an agency's essential functions or operations during an emergency
- Reduce the loss of life, minimizing damage and losses
- Execute as required successful succession to office and delegation of authority
- Reduce or mitigate disruptions to operations
- Ensure that agencies have alternative facilities from which to perform their essential functions during a COOP event
- Protect essential facilities, equipment, vital records, and other assets
- Achieve a timely and orderly recovery from an emergency and resumption of full service to customers
- Ensure and validate COOP readiness through testing, training, and exercise programs to support the implementation of COOP plans.

There are many details involved in developing a COOP plan and in executing such a plan, if needed. All those details will not be identified here. The sources cited at the beginning of this chapter contain them. Rather, some key elements needed to support the planning effort are offered, as well as a few thoughts about the plan itself.

A court may need funds before it is fully prepared to implement a continuity plan. Because of the national response, those funds may be available from the federal Homeland Security Department or from state equivalents. Courts, at least as of early 2006, have not done a very good job tapping into those funds. Generally, any special needs of courts have not been considered when their localities have sought and obtained such funds. This is similar to what happened in the early years of the federal Law Enforcement Assistance Administration (LEAA) and its state progeny in the 1970s. Once courts woke up to their inclusion in the list of possible grantees, and after some clarifying language was inserted into the federal legislation funding LEAA, courts obtained important funding from this agency and the state counterparts. The same can happen with the homeland defense funds. In the large picture of funding for homeland defense, courts' needs are modest. Courts simply have to make the case for the importance of the continuation of a court system during local and regional disasters that fit the criteria for homeland defense funding.

The good news is that, like security, much can be done with little or no funding, particularly the part about developing a plan. As is true of so many initiatives in courts, the leadership has to support the initiative and be visible in the beginning, if not all the way through the planning process. The chief judge should be the one announcing the initiative. He or she should be the one asking people to join the planning committee. The chief judge or the chief judge's designee should chair the committee. The court administrator can play an important behind-the-scenes role and either the administrator or a senior manager designated by the administrator should sit on the committee, but visible judicial leadership is needed. Judicial leadership is essential, first, because it emphasizes the importance of the initiative so far as the court is concerned to staff and to others outside the courts whose help is needed. Second, it confirms the institution's commitment to carry through. As discussed in both chapters 6 and 7, significant new efforts undertaken by courts without visible judicial support usually falter. Should a court thereafter experience a major disruption that would have benefited from having a COOP plan, it would be disappointing (at least) for the court and very disruptive for the community if the court turned out to be unprepared. There simply are too many details that can take too much time to resolve if a court starts at zero the day after operations must be discontinued. Every area of the country has some natural disasters that might disrupt a court's operations for more than a few hours. Fires occur everywhere without warning. Toxic spills and fires at chemical plants that can close sections of a town or city occur without warning. Developing a full COOP plan takes an effort, but not nearly as much effort as trying to establish continuity after the fact.

Because of the availability of homeland defense funding, many localities have undertaken some COOP planning. If a locality still is working on its plan, a court immediately should ask to join that group. If a locality has completed its planning, the court can piggyback on that effort. Necessary communication equipment and alternative means of communicating among government officials and staff may be in place already. Evacuation plans from public buildings may be in place, along with plans for evacuation of entire areas of the town or city. Detailed plans may exist for continuation of the executive or legislative branch. The court can draw on and build on all of this as it develops its COOP plan. That should make the effort for the court somewhat less overwhelming and time-consuming than it might be otherwise.

The local planners may even think they have considered the court in their planning. The problem, however, is that normally the court is not at the table when all this planning is taking place. Planners from the executive branch and law enforcement, who usually create these plans, do not know or understand the legal requirements affecting courts and seldom know the operational details needed for a court to continue to operate. They also are in a very poor position to determine for the court, if they even attempt to do so, the essential functions that must be restored immediately and those that can be brought up in a phased way over time. Nor would they be able effectively to determine a court's facility needs. Further, they cannot develop communication protocols within the court family or determine where and which judges would convene to continue operations or how to advise jurors, attorneys, and litigants where to find the replacement court.

The other branches normally overlook the court's needs when they plan, so the court has to take an independent look at the situation. The court then can either write a court supplement to an existing plan or develop its own independent plan that still would draw on the best aspects of an existing plan. Some of the other branches' plan could be incorporated into the court's plan with little or no change. The public information function is the most obvious, along with interagency and intracourt communication needs. It is likely in a small community that the court would want to use the city's or county's information officer as the main spokesperson for all of local government and feed that person the information the court has to get out. Even for larger courts, which already have a public information officer (or a person who fills that role), at a minimum the court's public information officer should coordinate with the local government's spokesperson. The court would want the same alternative communication means that are to be used by the rest of local government to facilitate important communications with law enforcement and agencies supporting infrastructure. In all the major disasters of the last three years and during the 9/11 disaster, communication breakdowns have been one of the common elements. There was a lot of publicity after 9/11 and after Hurricane Katrina about how various emergency responders could not communicate with each other. Beyond the issue of radios that can be tuned to the same frequency, in major disasters some of the normal means of communication simply are not available, be they telephone land lines or even satellite telephone communication. Thus, two or three ways need to be considered to connect with staff and with the public. Presumably, if the other branches have completed their planning, this issue will have been addressed and the court can simply adopt the plan.

To facilitate both the court's planning and the necessary coordination with the rest of government, key people involved in the other branches' planning efforts should be asked to join the court's planning committee. The court will need to include its own staff, one or more judges, representatives of the Bar, and social service agencies, both governmental and private, who might not have been involved with the effort of the other branches. Indeed, the local bar association(s) may want a committee of its own to develop its own contingency plans for assuring the availability of counsel and their files in the first week or two following a significant disaster that might affect law offices as well as the court.[65] A full list of those in the community who might participate in the court's planning committee can be found in the sources suggested at the beginning of this chapter.

There are three tasks that only the court can complete: (1) deciding upon the key functions and case types for which continuity is most critical; (2) defining an order of succession within the court hierarchy; and (3) reviewing state laws and any standing orders (or preparations for these) of the supreme court regarding filing documents, suspending statutes of limitations and speedy trial deadlines, and other time-critical events that are disrupted in a disaster, as well as developing templates for appropriate local orders. Regarding the succession issue, if the chief judge is unable to act, who will be the backup and who will back up the first backup? The same issues must be considered for the court administrator. Who will declare a court emergency, the local government because it owns the building or the court because it is court functions that are disrupted? Or will there be two declarations? Increasingly, state supreme courts and administrative offices of the courts also are looking at continuity of operations and beginning to develop protocols of actions and orders they will initiate upon the occurrence of a natural disaster or other disruptive event. Local courts need to know what these are, how to obtain them when needed, and then, in turn, advise the state supreme court and the administrative office of their plans so everyone can work together when and as the need arises. There may even be value in regional planning by trial courts regarding a sharing of facilities or emergency orders.

Natural disasters and fires can happen at any time of the day or night. Many plans focus on what to do when a disaster strikes during normal work hours. That is important because staff and maybe hundreds of citizens and attorneys plus files and evidence have to be cared for. Most discussions about developing plans omit references to what one does if the disaster strikes at, say, one o'clock in the morning. Does it make a difference in the plan if court personnel are present in the courthouse and have to respond quickly versus when no one is present and access after the fact may be difficult or impossible? For some disasters (e.g., a forest fire, which normally takes time to arrive), it might make a difference. For others, it may not. This question at least needs to be asked during the planning process.

Periodic drills are important to assure the viability of COOP plans. They also help staff to know what to do when an emergency occurs. Without drills, it is hard to remember, far less execute, what one was told to do a year or two ago. There is a natural tendency if a major incident or disaster has not occurred in several years to dismiss the drills as a waste of time. It is one of the responsibilities of leadership to counter that attitude and to sensitize staff to the need to be prepared.[66]

There are two planning considerations that may require funds. One is assuring an alternative facility and the other is a cache of equipment, supplies, furniture, and telephones (or other communication equipment) to be used if the courthouse must be abandoned. The former might be obtained with only a contingency contract, with no funds changing hands (other than a limited "good faith" fee) unless and until the alternative facility is needed. Trailers for temporary courtrooms and office space can be rented after the fact so long as a supply is identified. Most equipment and furniture can be rented, if needed, and the telephone company may be able to supply temporary equipment, as well as installing new telephone lines. Even so, advance purchase of some items, including laptops, maybe one computer sufficient to serve as a network hub, and basic supplies stored in a transportable storage bin away from the courthouse might be desirable. Even if many items can be rented and facility contracts signed after the fact, some contingency authorization of funds from the funding authority may be appropriate in case the funding authority's operations also are disrupted.

The extraordinary regional breadth of the destruction caused by Hurricanes Katrina and Rita in 2005 and the several hurricanes that hit Florida in 2004 probably was beyond the thinking of many prior to their occurrence. It is hard to plan for half or more of a city's population leaving at one time and hundreds of square miles of area physically devastated for, perhaps, several years. Now that it has happened, however, COOP plans at least have to consider everything from one courthouse being affected for a few weeks to a major regional disaster and all the possibilities in between. The breadth of the challenge may caution setting some priorities for the planning process, starting, for example, with the courthouse remaining intact but needing evacuation for a while, then a courthouse being destroyed with all or most of its contents but the rest of the community intact, then an area of town affected, and so on. The key is not to think about a specific type of disaster, such as a fire, but to think in terms of the myriad responses needed when the courthouse is closed for whatever reason. If a court will do that, then whatever specific event triggers implementing the plan, the court will be ready. Most of all, each court needs to develop a COOP plan as soon as possible, run regular drills for staff so they will remember what to do when the time comes, and be as prepared for the unexpected and undesirable as the court can be.

Notes

1. In the eight-judge semirural county in which I was the court administrator, the court over the five years I was there had two or three bomb or other unspecified telephone threats a year, none of which, fortunately, was valid. When we finally installed magnetometers and

X-ray equipment, we uncovered a lot of knives and a few guns that previously had perhaps been brought into the courthouse (and we saw some people walking away when they saw the equipment and then coming back). The most serious risks of physical danger before and after security was upgraded were a few fights associated with family law matters. I suspect our experience was typical of many smaller and midsize courts. See also, National Association for Court Management, *Court Security Guide*. Williamsburg, VA: National Association for Court Management, June 2005, p. 3, where only a little over a third of courts responding to a survey in 2004 indicated that an "incident relating to security " had occurred in the last five years

2. These resources can be found through its website at http://ncsconline.org.

3. See National Association for Court Management, *Court Security Guide (2005)*. See also NACM's largely but not fully superseded earlier guide: National Association for Court Management, *Court Security Guide*. Williamsburg, VA: National Association for Court Management, June 1995.

4. Williamsburg, VA: National Association for Court Management, 2006.

5. Williamsburg, VA: National Center for State Courts, 2003.

6. Siegel, Lawrence, Caroline S. Cooper, and Allison L. Hastings, *Planning for Emergencies*. Washington, D.C.: Justice Programs Office, School of Public Affairs, American University, 2005, retrievable from http://www.spa.american.edu/justice/resources/SJI.pdf.

7. Rennison, Callie Marie, *Intimate Partner Violence*, 1993–2001. Washington, D.C.: U.S. Dept. of Justice, Bureau of Justice Statistics, 2003, retrievable from http://www.ojp.usdoj.gov/bjs/pub/pdf/ipv01.pdf.

8. When staff slips, some form of discipline should be considered. At a minimum, a discussion is needed. If rules supporting security exist but they are not enforced, the message to staff is clear that they are not important.

9. A bomb placed next to a wall in a planted area hit one suburban California court in the dark early morning hours. Security personnel ordinarily would not have been present to stop the placing and detonating of this bomb, but maybe exterior lighting and external cameras would have been some deterrence. There also was the widely reported incident in 2004 of a client who felt abused by an attorney, chasing the attorney around a small tree on the lawn of the courthouse and shooting at him. In another incident, a husband shot his wife's attorney in a divorce case in the parking lot as she and the wife were going to court.

10. I was consulting in a court whose administrator picked me up at my hotel and drove me to the courthouse. This courthouse had underground parking for judges and the administrator with a security person at a gate at the entrance. After the security guard waved us through, I was struck by the administrator's off-hand but very insightful comment that the guard had no idea who I was or whether I had a gun in my lap and was forcing my way into the courthouse. Admittedly, the odds of that happening are small, but it is exactly these small possibilities that end up being deeply regretted after the fact.

11. The building in which I had my office when I was a court administrator was at the bottom of a natural bowl, with a lot of foliage around and several spots along the driveway on the hill where a sniper could hide. I recall during one building evacuation for a fire drill, several staff members and I were standing in our assigned evacuation spot and noting how easily a sniper up the hill could pick us off. So far as I know, however, no one, including me, talked to the sheriff about how to deal with the problem.

12. George, Chief Justice Ronald, State of the Judiciary Address to the California Legislature, Feb. 28, 2006, p. 21, retrieved Mar. 1, 2006 from http://www.courtinfo.ca.gov/reference/documents/soj022806.pdf.

13. Some courts also provide small laminated cards to all staff that contain key telephone numbers and vital steps.

14. For example, National Association for Court Management, *Court Security Guide (2005)*, pp. 30–31.

15. In Atlanta, the corridor in which the prisoner allegedly assaulted the escorting deputy sheriff and reportedly took her gun was subject to video surveillance. Seemingly, no one was watching when this incident took place, or, if they were, they did not react in time to save a judge and a court reporter from being killed (and, maybe, a deputy sheriff from being subsequently killed outside the courthouse).

16. In a limited survey that produced responses from ten urban courts in 2002, the Justice Management Institute announced that all ten courts indicated that a "law enforcement authority" provided security, although three of the ten said security was provided by a combination of court employees and contractors. Justice Management Institute, "2002 Security Survey Results."

17. For example, Fulton County (Atlanta), Georgia, was able to fund 40 additional deputy sheriff positions shortly after three people were killed in and immediately outside the courthouse, but did not fund those positions prior to the shootings. *American Justice*, Episode no. 247, first broadcast Apr. 27, 2005, by A&E Network. Produced by Judy Cole.

18. National Association for Court Management, *Court Security Guide (1995)*, cover.

19. Element 1, "Essential Ten Elements for Effective Courtroom Safety and Security Planning," retrieved Nov. 21, 2005, from http://www.ncsconline.org/What'sNew/TenPointPlan/htm.

20. See note 15.

21. I have been in an urban courthouse where a deputy sheriff turned his back to the audience and leaned against the rail that divides the public area from the adjudication area, his gun handle ending up on the public side of the rail. Neither he nor anyone else inside the rail was paying attention to the audience. His gun was strapped down in its holster, but someone determined to get his gun could have done so. Many courts still exempt attorneys from security screening. Observing that accommodation during several visits to an urban courthouse, a victim's father hollowed out a law book enough to fit a gun into it, dressed in a business suit, put the law book in a briefcase, and was waved past the magnetometer by the deputy sheriffs, who assumed he was an attorney. When he got to the courtroom, he shot the defendant. The Chief Justice of California told the legislature in early 2006 of a judge who had stacks of law books in front of his bench. The judge was in a rural court in which there had been an attempted hostage taking. The books were not there for scholarship, but because he could not get local funds for a steel plate to be installed in the bench for protection. George, Chief Justice Ronald, State of the Judiciary Address to the California Legislature, Feb. 28, 2006, p. 20, retrieved Mar. 1, 2006 from http://www.courtinfo.ca.gov/reference/documents/soj022806.pdf.

22. Traditionally, these misplaced files have been referred to as "lost." A newer, less pejorative term is *unable to locate*.

23. A related but severable issue is blogs created and maintained by court employees. Some corporations have established policies about what employees can discuss on their personal blogs or contribute to discussions on others' blogs. See Jesdanum, Anick, "Blog-Related Firings Focus on Policy," Mar. 6, 2005, retrieved Mar. 7, 2005 from http://enews.earthlink.net/channel/news/print?guid=20050306/422a8e50_3ca6_15 ....

    Court employees may inadvertently (or consciously) share information about a case or cases that should not be public from an administrative standpoint or that the law says is confidential. Courts need to consider the policies they wish to adopt, if any, regarding both employees' personal blogs and contributions to others' blogs. Among other concerns, courts have to consider the First Amendment rights of their employees, which private corporations do not. See Henry, Ray, "Federal Court Drops Proposed Gag Rule," (Associated Press), Dec.

12, 2005, retrieved from http://start.earthlink.net/article/nat?guid=20051212/439d03d0_3ca6_155262005.... See also, *Garcetti v. Cebalos*, 461 U.S. 138 (2006).

24. See Steketee, Martha Wade, and Alan Carson, *Developing CCJ/COSCA Guidelines for Public Access to Court Records: A National Project to Assist State Courts*. Williamsburg, VA and Denver, CO: National Center for State Courts and Justice Management Institute, 2002, pp. 45–57.

25. For example, Conference of State Court Administrators, "Concept Paper on Access to Court Records," Aug. 2000, pp. 6–7, retrieved from http://cosca.ncsc.dni.us/PositionPapers/courtrecordaccess.pdf. General Rule 31(e), Access to Court Records, State of Washington Rules of Court, 2004.

26. Courts will have to decide whether to seek to protect all records in their system at one time or only add markers and codes to files as they return to court for some purpose. Either way, considerable staff time may be required, but if files are protected only as cases return to court, the time and therefore the expense can be spread out a bit.

27. For example, Tanner, Robert, "States Steadily Restrict Public Info," (Associated Press), Mar. 11, 2006, retrieved Mar. 11, 2006, from http://enews.earthlink.net/article/nat?quid=2006 0311/44125950_3ca6_1552620060311-1295840942.

28. It could be a spill from a passing truck or train; it need not be an attack on the courthouse.

29. United Press International, "Spam Seen as Workplace Problem," Oct. 16, 2003, retrieved Oct. 16, 2003, from http://start.earthlink.net/newsarticle?cat=4&aid=Lifestyles02003101 61240.

30. Judicial Council of California, *Cornerstones of Democracy: California Courts Enter a New Era of Judicial Branch Independence*, San Francisco: Judicial Council of California, 2005, p. 25, retrieved from http://www.courtinfo.ca.gov/reference/2_annual.htm.

31. This makes the cost per file significantly higher than the cost of traditional manila file folders because colored folders start out more expensive and often the volume of folders needed for each case type is not sufficient to get significant price breaks from bulk orders. I do not know of any cost-benefit analysis that factors in any staff time saved looking for misplaced files, but such an analysis should be done.

32. This version of bar code is the now recognizable strip of vertical lines. A more recent version is a square of lines that can be read up, down, and side to side, thus storing far more information. An invention in 2006 adds color to the square, thereby creating a capacity of 600 kilobytes. "The Bar Code Learns Some Snazzy New Tricks," *Business Week*, Apr. 3, 2006, p. 113. Whether this bar code design is better for courts than an RFID will have to await further development of both technologies.

33. See also, Phillips, Dale, "Strategic Applications of Technology: Radio-Frequency Identification (RFID) Technology and the DeKalb County, Georgia, Juvenile Court," *The Court Manager*, vol. 20, no. 2, Spring 2005, p. 24.

34. This discussion is adopted from an original article by the author appearing in Greisler, David S., and Ronald J. Stupak, eds., *Handbook of Technology Management in Public Administration*. New York and Boca Raton, FL: Taylor & Francis Books, 2006. Used by permission.

35. See Winters, Roger, "Time for Electronic Court Records," in National Center for State Courts' Trends in 2004, retrieved from http://www.ncsconline.org/D_KIS/Trends/Doc-ManTrends2004.html.

36. National Association for Court Management, *Core Competency Curriculum Guidelines: What Court Leaders Need to Know and Be Able to Do*. Williamsburg, VA: National Association for Court Management, 2005, p. 57.

37. Ibid., p. 56.

38. Albany, NY: Government Records Services, New York State Archives, the State Education Department, The University of the State of New York, 2002, page 5, retrieved from http://www.archives.nysed.gov.

39. Dibble, Thomas G., *A Guide to Court Records Management.* Williamsburg, VA: National Center for State Courts, 1986, p. 56.

40. In one court with which I am familiar, the court had a number of old records and even pictures that the court administrator felt strongly had historic value for the county, but the county historical society turned down her offer to provide them to the society. Because of her belief in their ultimate value, she was keeping them in the court's records in case the historical society changed its mind, for once she destroyed the records they would be lost. Some argue that the broader society, not courts, should assume whatever "societal" responsibility there may be to preserve old records. That is, if courts no longer need records for court purposes but the records still may have some historical value, museums or local historical societies should assume responsibility for their preservation. The fact that courts were the original depositories is insufficient to impose a long-term, even permanent obligation on them for retention. Many court record retention schedules call for very old records to be offered to local or state history repositories, but do not require these entities to accept and preserve them. If the historical society turns them down, as in the example just given, these old records fall into a sort of limbo of neglect, indifference, or lack of funding.

41. Association for Information and Image Management, International, *The Use of Optical Disks for Public Records, ANSI/AIIM TR25-1995.* Silver Springs, MD: Association for Information and Image Management, International, 1995.

42. According to an IBM "information storage expert," popular CD-R and CD-RW disks available in all office supply stores can be expected to maintain record integrity for only two to five years, barely enough for traffic tickets in most court retention schedules. See "Life is Short," *AARP Bulletin,* vol. 47, no. 3, Mar. 2006, p. 32.

43. White, Stephen, "A Brief History of Computing—Products Notable for Their Technical Achievement or Popularity" (2002), retrieved from http://www.ox.compsoc.net.

44. Spooner, John G., "HP Offers 'Simple' Message to Consumers," Aug. 11, 2003, retrieved Nov. 1, 2003 from http://news.com.com/2102-1041_3-5062002.thml?tag=st_util_print and Edwards, Cliff, "The New HP: How's It Doing?," *BusinessWeek Online,* Dec. 23, 2002, retrieved Oct. 31, 2003 from http://www.businessweek.com/print/magazine/content/02_51/b3813086.htm?tc.

45. "Floppy Disk Becoming Relic of the Past," Sept. 7, 2004 (Associated Press), retrieved Sept. 7, 2004, from http://start.earthlink.net/newsarticle?cat=2&aid=D84UQEN80_story.

46. Green, Heather, "The End of the Road for Bar Codes," *Business Week,* July 8, 2002, p. 76B.

47. "Floppy Disk Becoming Relic."

48. Task Force on Archiving of Digital Information, *Preserving Digital Information.* The Commission on Preservation and Access, Washington, D.C.: 1996, p. iii.

49. Ibid., pp. 2–3.

50. For example, the seventh largest trial court in California, the Santa Clara County (San Jose) Superior Court, had 141,438 nontraffic case filings in FY2002–2003 and another 145,952 nontraffic case filings in FY2003–2004. If each file averaged only ten documents (not pages, but documents)—a modest number for some case types but a fair number for others—the court would have received in just two years over 2,873,900 documents subject to records retention schedules. In the California court with the seventh smallest number of nontraffic filings, the Lassen County Superior Court, with only 2.3 judgeships, there were 3,664 nontraffic case filings in FY2002–2003 and another 4,080 in FY2003–2004. Using

the same formula, it would have received in two years almost 77,500 documents needing to be preserved for anywhere from five years to permanently.

51. See Dibble, Thomas G., *Court Records Management*, p. 56.

52. See the thoughtful proposals in Task Force on Archiving of Digital Information, *Preserving Digital Information,*. So far as this author is aware, however, these ideas remain only ideas, with no current implementation efforts underway.

53. This contrasts to the 100 to 150 years for ideal recording and storage conditions for CDs, ignoring the issues of hardware and software obsolescence.

54. Retrieved July 30, 2003 from http://www.clir.org/pubs/reports/willis/intro.html.

55. Ibid., at p. 2.

56. This study and other similar studies did not compare costs when the original record already is in digital form, which would be the case in most courts for at least some records and in some courts, such as the New Mexico Bankruptcy court, for virtually all records. This may not be determinative, however, as the big cost for digital is the migration cost.

57. Kenney, Anne R., *Digital to Microfilm Conversion: A Demonstration Project.* Ithaca, NY: Cornell University Library Department of Preservation and Conservation, 1997.

58. Schumacher, E.F., *Small is Beautiful.* London: Blond & Briggs, 1973. Harper & Row published both a hardcover and paperback version in the United States. See also, Hof, Robert D., "Do We Have to Have a Digital Revolution?," *Business Week*, Feb. 2, 2004, p. 37; Nussbaum, Bruce, "Technology: Just Make it Simpler," *Business Week*, Sept. 8, 2003, p. 38.

59. See, for example, Dibble, Thomas G., *Court Records Management*, chap. 4. See also, Kline, Laura S., *Developing an Inactive Records Storage Facility.* Local Government Records Technical Information Series, No. 48. Albany, NY: Local Government Records Services, State Archives and Records Administration, the State University of New York, the State Education Department, 1995.

60. In the oldest courthouse of five used by the court for which I was the court administrator, we also had flaking asbestos from insulation on overhead pipes falling into file folders. A major effort was needed to clean the file folders and address the asbestos issue in that storage area.

61. A survey by NACM for its COOP miniguide that produced 238 responses showed that smaller and more rural courts are most likely *not* to have continuity of operations plans. National Association for Court Management, *Business Continuity Management Guide.* Williamsburg, VA: National Association for Court Management, 2006, p. 3.

62. Ibid., p. 4.

63. Ibid., p. 5.

64. Federal Emergency Management Agency, "Federal Preparedness Circular 65" (2004), retrievable from http://www.fema.gov/txt/library/fpc65_0604.txt.

65. One California attorney suggests that the failure of attorneys to plan for continuity of representation following a natural disaster is an ethical violation. See Langford, Carol M., "When Disaster Strikes … The Ethical Duties of Disaster Preparation," *California Bar Journal,* Feb. 2006, p. 1. See also, Williams, Mark, "When Disaster Strikes … Protecting Electronic Data and Paper Files," *California Bar Journal,* Feb. 2006, p. 1.

66. The American University guide to emergency planning cites one court where a judge simply refused to vacate his courtroom during a declared emergency, not just a drill. The chief judge later issued an order that when an emergency is declared, everyone shall be removed from the courthouse. If a judge chooses to stay, s/he may do so in an empty courtroom. See Siegel, Lawrence, Caroline S. Cooper, and Allison L. Hastings, *Planning for Emergencies*, p. 8.

Chapter 11

Hierarchy of Court Administration: External Relationships

The external relationships of courts are diverse, multifaceted, and difficult to manage. They also are very important and are undergoing some changes. Some relationships are imposed by law, some by virtue of the structure of government, and some by the nature of the litigation process, particularly the relatively new problem-solving courts. Some external relationships exist by virtue of courts being governmental and political institutions, and some as a by-product of the judicial branch becoming both more coherent and more accountable. The opportunities and challenges they pose for courts are the subject of this chapter.

11.1 Maslow's Hierarchy and the Hierarchy of Court Administration

The Hierarchy of Court Administration parallels Abraham Maslow's Hierarchy of Human Needs. Table 11.1 shows the parallel between what Maslow described as the belonging and love needs of humans and the external relationship needs of courts.

An institution will not have sweethearts or children, but it needs friends and it certainly needs and has organizational affiliations. The latter is an area to which we will return in levels four and five. In level three, the focus is on relationships that exist—or, in a few cases, should exist—for basic operations or in the ordinary course of a court's existence. Refinements and advancements beyond the relationships discussed here come in the next two levels.

Table 11.1 Maslow's Belonging and Security Needs and Courts' External Relationship Needs

Maslow's belonging and security needs	Courts' external relationship needs
• Friends • Sweetheart • Children • Affectionate relationships • Organizational affiliations	• Political and policy units of the two other branches of government, state and local • State Administrative Office of the Courts • Criminal justice agencies, local and state • Government agencies interacting with the court on civil and family cases • Government and private entities providing support services • Bar associations • Social service, mental health, and other community service agencies • Addiction agencies and organizations • Service clubs and community organizations • Media relations • Educational institutions and programs, both K-12 and higher education • Credit reporting and other investigative groups • Victim and advocacy groups • Court watchdog groups • Academic and other researchers • General public

11.2   Relationships Based on Law

State statutes mandate a number of relationships for courts. They are not called "relationships," as most involve courts being mandated to share information generated as a result of court cases with various government agencies or with individuals. The list is long and has grown over time as legislatures have seen gaps or responded to a particular crisis or political issue that might have been averted or lessened ("if only ___ had had the information"). Information alone seldom is sufficient—one must do something with the information—but it often is a starting point. Courts are mandated to send information to a number of government agencies, normally at the state level, plus, increasingly, to the federal government.

The list of agencies to which trial courts must send information generally includes:

■ The state administrative office of the courts;[1]
■ Local and state law enforcement agencies;
■ Federal agencies, some law-enforcement and some administrative;
■ Local and state prosecutors and state databases regarding those convicted generally and also those convicted of specific crimes, particularly those involving children;

- State administrative agencies, particularly the motor vehicle department and state agencies charged with the care and/or welfare of children and the elderly;
- Local and state financial authorities;
- Local school officials regarding children involved in court cases;
- Local and state corrections institutions and probation offices.

Legislative mandates about the information trial courts should send to administrative offices of the courts normally involve caseload statistics. If the legislature does not mandate some minimum information to be shared, the state supreme court (or other policy-making body) will establish the requirement by rule, which has the force of law. The state supreme court also may supplement legislation with a rule or rules that require more statistical information than the legislature wants. As noted in chapter 9, these data usually give only the very broadest of perspectives on courts' operations; they are summary data meant to identify common caseload elements and sometimes workload-related information (e.g., jury trials, sometimes by broad case categories such as "civil" and "felonies"). They have limited or no value for daily case management, but because they are mandated, they are captured in all trial court case management information systems.

The far larger obligation (and burden in most courts) relates to sending case-based conviction and sentencing information to state and local law enforcement, to correctional institutions, to probation offices, and to licensing agencies. Law enforcement agencies know and share information about arrests through the Federal Bureau of Investigation (FBI) and state agencies (normally within the Attorney General's Office), but the burden of closing the loop and advising those who compile arrest information of the disposition of a case falls largely to the courts.[2] The FBI and state "rap sheets" are lists of arrests. They also are supposed to contain disposition information, but too often in the past and still sometimes today, the result of an arrest is not added to the rap sheets. In the absence of disposition information, people whose charges were dismissed or who were found not guilty are treated by law enforcement (and, normally, the media) as if they were guilty of the previous offense if they are rearrested.[3]

If someone is sentenced to a jail term or to time in prison, the local sheriff or the state department of corrections must know the exact terms of the judge's sentence. If there is probation at the end of a jail term or instead of jail, the probation department needs comparable information, plus the conditions of probation so the probation officer can enforce those conditions. The court is the best agency to advise the driver licensing department of traffic convictions. It also is the best source of information for professional licensing agencies such as the state bar association or supreme court for convicted attorneys and medical and dental licensing boards for doctors and dentists. The court is at the end of a linear progression from crime to arrest through sentencing, but it is the hub of information for the array of agencies broadly comprising the criminal justice system. Accordingly, the sharing of information by the court with these other agencies is highly important. This is part of the noticing function discussed in section 9.2.2, chapter 9, and why this function is mission critical for courts.

The mandatory information sharing function of courts has expanded in recent years and may continue to expand. Now, the federal government requires information about domestic violence cases and some drug offenses. Parties in lawsuits must be informed if certain things happen, or people who are deemed interested, such as crime victims or state agencies overseeing the temporary care of children or the elderly, need notices.

It stretches the concept of "relationships" a little to speak of these mandates as creating a relationship, except to this extent: The agencies getting the court's information usually prescribe the information to be provided and a form on which that information is to be provided. Therefore, training on completing the form is needed, communication is needed between the agencies and the court if there are any questions or problems, and courts can advise the agencies if there are problems completing the forms. Relationships develop at the operational level that are important to enabling the court to comply with its mandates.

11.3 Relationships Based on Structure and Funding Sources

Relationships based on structure have at least two components: (1) separation of powers and the role the legislative and executive branches play in how courts operate and do their business; and (2) institutional support and affiliations. The relationships that fall into this category are:

- The funding authority, local or state (or both)
- The state administrative office of the courts, particularly in state-funded systems
- Local and state legislatures
- State and federal agencies and occasionally private foundations that distribute grant funds
- Local government agencies and officials that provide direct support services (clerical staff, computer support, building maintenance, billing or accounts payable services, banking support, collection services, and possibly probation services).

11.3.1 Funding Relationships

The differing approaches when a trial court is funded locally versus being funded by the state were discussed in section 4.3 in chapter 4. The key for this level of the

Hierarchy of Court Administration is that a trial court's relationships vis-à-vis its funding source determine in large measure what it can do and how successfully it can fulfill its mission. The relationship is determined by law: if a court is locally funded, it must relate to local officials to obtain funds. If it is state funded, it relates to the budget staff in the administrative office of the courts, and very little or not at all to the budget staffs in the two other branches. When the state is the source of funds, the AOC tries to make itself the sole voice regarding the budget with the two other branches. Ordinarily, this is the only way the judiciary will be successful. When there is a cacophony of trial court voices in addition to the AOC's, it is too easy for the other branches to say, "No. Get your house in order and then we'll talk." On occasion, however, the AOC may ask for help regarding specific budget requests from key or all trial courts.

The degree and character of the relationship with the funding authority is not mandated, but operationally it is mission critical. If a court does not know and understand the requirements of the funding entity, if it does not know the personalities of the key staff people, if it does not understand the priorities that drive budget decisions, it will not obtain the level of funding needed to function properly. Without such knowledge, particularly at the local level, a trial court also will not know when to press hard and when to back off completely or to a fall-back position. As noted in chapter 4, it also may not understand how successfully to phrase or support a request for a new or increased budget item.

State funding does not remove trial courts from the local funding process, however. Even if there is state funding, the local government unit usually provides needed institutional support services such as daily maintenance, building and heavy equipment maintenance, and possibly some billing or banking support. The clerk of court normally remains locally funded. Obviously, this office's budget and staffing levels are critical to a court's operations. If this office is not being funded at an appropriate level, it is in the court's direct interest to support the clerk's budget request regardless of the court's own source of funds. The prosecutor remains locally funded. The importance of the prosecutor to the court's operations is discussed in chapter 5. Beyond the policy choices of the prosecutor discussed in that chapter, there are resource issues that impact the court. If the prosecutor's budget does not keep up with a rising incidence of arrests or if salaries are not sufficient to attract good attorneys, the court is negatively affected. The work of the prosecutor's office can be affected as much by the presence or absence of clerical staff and investigators as by the number and pay of attorneys. If the prosecutor's office is causing delays in court because it cannot complete needed paperwork, the court may choose to support a request for additional clerical or investigative staff. Similar situations occur with the public defender's office and the probation office, if they are separately funded. There are other attorneys and social service agencies in local government involved with child support enforcement, dependent and neglected children, and guardianship cases that are funded by local government and that all end up in court. These other agencies are affected by the priorities and funding decisions of local government, as well. A court that is state funded will be more removed from the tug-and-pull of local politics and funding priorities than when it is locally funded, but it cannot turn its back on these issues, either. There may be occasions when it will be necessary for the court to add whatever moral and political suasion it has in support of the budget request of one of these entities that impact the court so directly. Such support is most likely to be given for increased funding of the public defender's office and the probation office, but only because of their historically low funding priority in local government; court support also may be extended to any of the other agencies.

Grant funding from state and federal agencies (and, rarely, from a foundation interested in some aspect of what courts do, often associated with children) has been important to courts since the 1970s. Recently, few courts would have been able to start their drug courts without grant funding assistance, normally from the federal government. Federal grant funding also has boosted some of the other problem-solving courts, such as domestic violence courts. In chapter 2, I noted the importance of this funding in the early and middle years of the revolution of modern court administration. I argued that because the dollars provided through the normal budget process for courts often are so close to or slightly below what is needed to do all of courts' assigned tasks, a few extra grant funds have a significant marginal impact. For the most part today, both administrative offices of the courts and at least larger trial courts try to follow federal grant programs and seek these funds when they can. The current federal priorities within the Department of Justice and the recent skimpy funding of the State Justice Institute have diminished the opportunities for courts to take advantage of such funding. The marginal impact of these funds can continue to be great, however. It is beneficial if the court administrator or someone on staff regularly checks for the availability of grants and determines if the court might use a particular grant.

Before a court starts seeking and accepting grant funds, it needs to ask itself four questions. If any is answered in the negative, it should not seek the funding. The first question is whether the court has a need for the program or equipment (or whatever) is involved. If there is no need other than the fact that there is a possible grant out there, a proposal should not be written. Second, if the grant supports new staff positions, is the court confident that it can fold the new positions into the ongoing budget or will it be willing to see the positions and the program disappear when the grant ends? The 1970s, in particular, saw a number of programs and staff positions created that were having a positive effect, only to see them end when the grant funding finally ended. Saying no because of concern about being able to build a new position or positions into the budget is hard, because the program might be a good one. There are no guarantees in the budget process, but if the program is needed and there is a strong evaluation component that can document the program's value, it might be worth the gamble. If the court's leaders are uncertain whether they can or will want to preserve a new position when the grant ends, they should not bother seeking it to begin with. Third, are the staff resources available to put together a good proposal? Unless someone has the time to commit to doing a thorough and well-documented proposal within the deadline set for submissions, it is best not to waste both the court's time and the time of the grant-making body. A bad proposal could be and often is as bad as no proposal at all, but the court also has wasted the time to write a bad proposal. Finally, does the court have the staff to monitor compliance with grant conditions, to prepare progress reports, and to prepare financial accounting reports? The time demands for each of these elements of grant administration can be substantial. If the court is uncertain whether its staff has the time and the capacity to administer the grant once it is received, it is best not to pursue it.[4]

11.3.2   *The Administrative Office of the Courts*

Most of the discussion to this point about the state administrative office of the courts has been tied to the budget process, with some limited discussion of lobbying on state legislative bills affecting the courts. The relationship is much deeper and more complex.

The administrative office of the courts is the staff arm of the state supreme court (or designated policy-making body) regarding the administration of all courts in the state. Thus, it helps with rule making covering the adjudicative process and with administrative rules. It works on and lobbies for the budgets of the appellate courts regardless of how the trial courts are funded. It normally develops and promulgates new forms that are to be used statewide. It runs annual (and, in some states, more frequent) conferences for judges and for administrative management and staff of both trial and appellate courts. It usually supports statewide training programs—the number and character of which vary by state—for judges and staff. It normally will staff statewide advisory committees studying various topics for the supreme court or other policy-making body. Often, it also undertakes research projects and makes suggestions for changes and evaluates new programs being tried by either appellate or trial courts. In a state-funded system, it may have a great deal to say about trial court operating policies and procedures and human resource management.

The range of activities and the effective power of AOCs vary greatly state to state. An AOC's power and influence are much lower when trial courts are mostly funded locally. The model for the AOC then tends to be advisory and research oriented, although at times it may create and operate a statewide case management information system because of the recognizable economies of scale involved and because of the value of a common statewide database. Unless the AOC serves as no more than a pass-through agency, its power can be considerable when the power of the purse is located at the state level.

Robert Tobin succinctly states the tensions between AOCs and trial courts:[5]

> State AOCs tend to think of their trial court outreach as a service. This is not always the perception of trial court administrators, who may regard the service as a form of control or interference. There is, therefore, a certain tension between state court administrators and trial court administrators.…
>
> [This can extend to staff, as well, in that] trial court administrators often regard the state court administrative office as a nuisance operation staffed by persons ignorant of the real world of trial courts. For their part, state court administrators tend to see trial court administrators as parochial, idiosyncratic, and narrowly focused on minor local concerns.

In many respects, both perspectives are correct and to be expected. The relationship often is akin to tension between headquarters and a branch operation. Headquarters does not understand the special needs and circumstances of the branch and the branch does not understand the need for and value of adhering to headquarters' policies and procedures. This type of tension will not go away.

All organizations that operate in multiple locations struggle with finding the right balance between common policies and procedures developed by management and staff in the headquarters and local flexibility and responsiveness. The judiciary is no different. It has two overlays that do not exist in the private sector or in the rest of government, however. The first is that large trial courts develop a political—and hence operational—life of their own, whether the judiciary is state funded or locally funded. Most states have one or two metropolitan areas that dominate in population and economic power within the state. If the judiciary is locally funded, the trial court or courts in those areas can and usually do operate as independent entities that will cooperate with the AOC but not be controlled by it. The political and economic power of the metropolitan area transfers to the trial courts in terms of daily operation. If the judiciary is state funded, the AOC has more effective power, but it still treads lightly when dealing with the largest court or two. Just as the legislature may adopt legislation with differing impact on jurisdictions with different population totals, court rules can create similar strata based on the number of judgeships or filings. Or, there will be a statewide policy, but it will mirror in large part what is done in or preferred by the largest court or two; the smaller courts simply have to adjust to what makes sense for the largest or larger courts. Budget decisions by the AOC staff or the state court administrator are not made blindly and may reflect the relative judicial-branch power of the largest court or larger courts. State court administrators who are too aggressive in trying to impose a state perspective on the largest court or larger courts normally have a short tenure.

The second overlay on the headquarters–branch tension for the judicial branch is that judges across the state view administrative decisions made at the state level much as they do administrative decisions made locally: judges are professionals who know best what works and does not work for them and in their courtrooms and thus are free to accept, modify, or reject AOC administrative decisions. Judges follow substantive and procedural rules for the adjudication process, but may not feel the same level of commitment to use statewide forms and to follow decisions and directives that relate to the administrative structure and operation of the institution. The trial court administrator can reflect this perspective, as well, in some cases. Some states, therefore, have sought to break the one-to-one tie between a trial court's judges and their administrator by having the state court administrator appoint the trial court administrator[6] or having regional administrators. This latter solution does not address the issue with the large urban courts, as they normally become a region of one court, but it can help in smaller, more rural areas.

The pressure for more uniformity and common practices across the state does not arise solely from the AOC having a headquarters perspective. Just as happens at the local level (see chapter 4), many budget staff in both branches of state government and some legislators and governors view the judiciary as similar to an executive branch agency that should do everything the same way across the state and thus, in their minds, save money. Therefore, they continually press the supreme court and AOC to achieve that result. Factors about trial courts that judges and administrators alike take for granted are lost on or deemed to be irrelevant by officials in the other branches. The factors include the:

■ Historic development and operation of locally based trial courts
■ Unique perspective and needs of professionals (the judges)
■ Election (in most states) of judges, leaving few of the disciplinary options available that could be used with appointed managers and staff
■ Mandate that judges have and require discretion to seek justice in individual cases; that mission-based aspect of their work may require some flexibility regarding procedures
■ very uneven decisions by local governments prior to state funding about: staff levels and staff compensation and the impact of the latter on recruiting; the level and type of technology available to facilitate operations; and whether there will be branch courts and where they would be located, which affects staff economies of scale and staffing patterns
■ Locally determined allocation of staff and workflow.

Even if a state has had state funding for some time, and thus, conceptually, there has been time for the AOC and supreme court to impose more uniformity, state-level budget officials often overlook their own contribution to the continuing variety: they seldom are sympathetic to the funding requests needed to bring all courts up to a certain commonality of staffing, compensation, and technology that would then provide the foundation on which to build uniformity. There are echoes of a Catch-22 in the process, with AOC and supreme court leaders wondering how they became the bad guys in the drama when they have only been trying to advance the entire branch despite the institutional and historic constraints. When the state judicial leadership makes these points during the budget process, budget officials in the other branches are as likely to see the statements as whining and avoidance as they are to hear them as legitimate constraints.

As headquarters–branch tensions are not new issues, for either institutions generally or courts in particular, are there any useful models to minimize the tension? Even in a small state, the AOC cannot manage the trial courts directly. The complexity of daily processes is too great. Giving the AOC authority to hire and fire trial court administrators probably would facilitate achieving more uniformity and might upgrade the management skill level brought to the position in smaller courts, but it would not address the other institutional impediments and would not eliminate some of inevitable us–them tensions. The best chance to achieve a workable balance seems to be a three-step process: (1) the state-level authorities set specific and measurable policy goals applicable to all trial courts; (2) allow the trial courts to achieve those goals in whatever manner best fits their personnel and other assets, and provide needed resources if they are lacking; and (3) then tie rewards and the lack of rewards (budgetary and otherwise) to meeting the goals. The structure also should encourage and give meaningful scope to trial court innovations. If a state-funded system becomes too directive and controlling, innovation can be stifled.[7]

Each element of this prescription challenges the AOC and state-level policy leaders in the other branches. Despite all the talk about performance standards within the judiciary since at least 1990, measurable goals and measuring to see if goals are met remain an aspiration in most states. It is hard to quantify some goals and harder to collect the data and then let the data determine one's judgment about whether a goal has been reached.[8] Too many computerized case management information systems still lack the programming flexibility to draw out ad hoc data to determine if new goals have been met. Efforts to overcome computer programming limitations by collecting real time or daily data that require completion of forms have been only marginally successful. Again, the difficulty goes back to two consistent themes in courts: (1) virtually everyone in courts works against daily deadlines, and staffing levels are merely adequate or less than adequate, so there is little or no flex time to complete new data collection forms; and (2) most judges have a strong aversion to completing any data collection form, but especially one that might take their attention on the bench away from the cases with which they must deal. The most successful data collection efforts that have required special forms have been those in which courtroom staff completed the forms, not the judges.[9] If such forms were routinely devised and required, however, some accommodation for the staff time consumed would have to be built into staffing levels, which might be hard to achieve through the budget process. So, the first step in the process is a challenge in both its parts: data-based goals and collecting needed data.

The second step is easy in its first part (let the trial courts do what they want to reach the goal), but hard in the second part (give them the resources they may lack to achieve the goal). Many individuals and some institutions are remarkably inventive in achieving goals with limited or no resources, but it is unrealistic to ask every trial court to achieve the same goal if the resources available to achieve that goal are unevenly distributed and, for some, insufficient. New resources may be needed, which could be a hard sell in the budget process.

As hard as it is to set measurable goals, to obtain needed data, and to provide resources, the hardest part of the process at the state level would be to withhold rewards based on performance. Even when such actions have been threatened, it has been very hard for the policy-making body or the administrative office of the courts to follow through. It has been hard on at least two levels. The first is simply professional courtesy and identification. State-level policy makers recognize how difficult it can be to "herd the cats" that are the judges and to reorganize staff workflow, if that is required, to achieve new goals. If one big but manageable thing kept a trial court from reaching the goal, perhaps that would be easier to identify and assess whether the withholding of a reward is warranted. If it were several little things that kept a court from achieving the goal, as is more likely, it is harder to determine if there was a lack of effort or a real effort made that simply fell short. And if there was a conscientious effort to reach the goal, should the AOC ignore the effort by withholding resources? Evaluations of new programs sometimes will identify that a court's lack of commitment to a goal was a major contributor to a failure to achieve that goal.[10] The reasons for failure and their relative importance normally are harder to assess and thus, it is harder to withhold rewards. The second reason why it is hard to withhold a reward is that if a reward (e.g., an increase in staff, new technology) is withheld, it is as likely to be the innocents who will be punished, the staff and judges who tried hard to meet the goal and the customers (the litigants). Policy makers at the state level do not want to compound a problem.

A greater uniformity among trial courts is desirable. Attorneys and citizens who move from county A to county B should not need to learn a whole new way to operate and have to use a new set of forms merely for crossing a county line. If we can accept the validity of the goal—and, if such is the case, ignore that the pressure comes from the budget officials in the other branches—the approach most likely to move all the trial courts in that direction is the one suggested here. Because of the difficulties, it is not an approach that will be fully implemented overnight, in a year, or maybe even in five years, but it is the only hope for getting the two sides to move in the same direction and with some congeniality.

The quotation from Tobin above referenced the unflattering views of trial court administrators about AOC staff. That view contains a large element of truth in many states' AOCs. Many AOCs recruit and hire some staff and managers with substantial trial court experience who are both knowledgeable and sensitive to trial court perspectives. Over time, however, these individuals gain a "headquarters" perspective and their sensitivity to the need for local flexibility and variance diminishes. More critically, bright, eager people who have had no exposure to trial courts except through books, memoranda, reports, and committee meetings seem to predominate on many AOC staffs. That would be acceptable if their roles were merely advisory or to conduct studies. Often, however, they shape or even decide policy and, worse, operating procedures, without the hands-on experience that might leaven their decisions and make those decisions more workable in trial courts. They certainly do not set out to devise policies or procedures that are difficult to implement at the trial level, but they often do so.

The reasons why AOCs do not attract a lot of trial court people probably are more complex than can be suggested here. A few possibilities can be offered, however. One factor is that administrative offices of the court almost always are located in the state capital. Trial courts are scattered throughout the state. The pool of experienced people who are willing and able to leave their current town or city to move to the state capital is limited.[11] The trial court or courts in and immediately around the state capital can supply staff for the AOC, but even then, the pool is limited and the experience of those trial courts may not correspond to how trial courts in other parts of the state operate. As suggested above, trial court size, the degree and design of computerization, how cases are managed by the judges, how staff workflow is organized, and the preferences of local judges all affect what trial court staff learn and how broadly their experience can be applied. Thus, something that worked for AOC employee A when he or she was in trial court A may not make sense in trial court B, or at least may cause problems in trial court B that did not have to be faced in trial court A. Unless employee A has had a chance to work in several trial courts before joining the AOC, or is sensitive enough to listen closely to trial courts if their opinions are solicited,[12] his or her perspective may simply be too narrow to develop sound policies and procedures for all trial courts.

The roles of staff in an AOC and in a trial court differ. The type of work being done at the AOC simply may not be appealing to many trial court staff. AOCs tend to attract those interested in policy, in devising new solutions to shared problems, and in studying patterns rather than addressing one case at a time. Trial court personnel tend to be somewhat more energized by working with the public, tend to feel comfortable with assembly-line processing, tend to be able to tolerate detail work, and tend to like the hustle and bustle of a trial court compared to the relative calm and staidness of an AOC. The two entities may simply attract people whose personality tendencies differ.

Clearly, these characterizations are drawn broadly, but together they start to suggest why relatively few trial court people end up working for AOCs and why both sides' staffs feel the other side just does not understand.

To the extent that AOC staff members do not have broad trial court experience, how can that weakness be addressed? The solution imposes additional time demands on trial court judges, staff, and management as well as some financial and time demands on AOC staff, but there are few options. If the expertise needed is not in-house, it must be obtained from the trial courts themselves. The effort to gain it requires not just trial court input, but a shared search for the best response. Everyone should work together to be sure the problem is correctly identified and that the solution is the best fit for all or virtually all courts. Some rules or administrative directives must be specific. Not all administrative matters addressed by the supreme court or AOC can be resolved with a broad policy goal. When a new rule or directive must be specific and directive, more time for broad input should be allowed. And AOC staff members have to at least remain open to the possibility that an in-house solution may need to be scrapped or significantly changed.

Most AOCs and supreme courts use advisory committees on significant issues and many use them for any rule change or administrative change of consequence. The weakness in their use is twofold. First, even with experienced representatives on the advisory committees, it is very hard to have all germane views and levels of expertise represented on the committee. Second, once an advisory committee has worked hard to come up an appropriate program, rule, or procedure, there is a tendency to think that additional extensive trial court input will add very little. This tendency exists particularly if surveys were done to aid the advisory committee. Asking for written comments within the next two weeks and then making minor changes, if any, tells trial courts that they are not being given a meaningful opportunity to provide input. The management mantra is that if one asks for advice, one had better listen and be prepared to adopt at least some of the suggestions. A positive response at the state level does not mean that every comment or suggestion for change is accepted, but that suggestions are considered and there is feedback to those commenting, which indicates that their idea was reviewed and this is why the committee chose to go another way. If staff cannot give that type of explanation, something is wrong with the decision-making process. This kind of response certainly adds time and effort to the jobs of AOC staff, but it opens a dialogue between the AOC and all the trial courts that can only benefit both in the long run. It also gives trial court judges, staff, and managers who respond the sense that their time was not wasted. As is true in courtrooms, sometimes trial court representatives do not have to see their ideas accepted if they see that their input was considered on its merits. The commentator may or may not be convinced that the final decision is best, but he or she knows the idea was treated substantively.

Some AOCs try to do what was just suggested. Some others would like to, but the calendar time available for this process is not available, often because of the legislative calendar or a deadline for a meeting of the supreme court. The absence of time may be genuine or a ploy to minimize trial court "interference" with AOC decisions. If there never is enough time, trial court representatives may come to believe their input is not desired or valued. If most of the time a meaningful exchange takes place, but sometimes does not take place, the dialogue will remain open. The AOC also will get more enthusiastic support from the trial courts if the AOC has to go to the legislature for assistance to implement the proposal.

Consideration should be given to the staffing impact for both the AOC and the trial courts if AOCs pursue this approach. Few trial court judges, staff, or managers are looking around for work. (Yes, some people in each category have extra time, but by and large, those with extra time who wonder how to fill their day stand out as exceptions, not the norm.) Most trial court personnel are straining to do their assigned duties plus the extras that always seem to crop up. Reviewing proposals from the AOC normally is expected to be in addition to whatever else someone is being asked to do. Similarly, if AOC staff have to allow more calendar time to finalize proposals and then respond personally to everyone who might comment, this extra time demand should be recognized in the staffing patterns of the AOC. If the legislature and the AOC see value in more uniformity among trial courts, the AOCs and supreme courts have to press for an add-on staffing factor to cover the time required to obtain meaningful input that will lead to greater acceptance of uniformity.

Following this suggested approach still does not assure greater uniformity. There was a second part to the Tobin quotation above: the view of state court administrators that trial court administrators are parochial, idiosyncratic, and narrowly focused on minor local concerns. There is a lot of validity to this perspective, also. Again, the headquarters–branch tension has to be acknowledged as a factor in the trial court administrators' response. Beyond that, the factors that lead to differences among trial courts influence these qualities. Trial court administrators are hired locally to work for—and to a degree, to protect—local judges. The institution and the people drawn to work for the institution are not structured to embrace rapid and significant change. The problem lies in not embracing relatively minor change, either. The first question from local staff and judges when a new procedure or rule is proposed is whether the trial court has to change anything it does now. If it does, the second question is "How much?" If the answer is or sounds like "a lot," resistance kicks in. Questions such as "why?" and "how will this help address a statewide problem?" are not raised or are given little weight. Trial courts certainly are not the only institutions where change is resisted; changes, even small changes, are hard for all institutions and many people. The institutional biases of trial courts, however, seem to make them a little more resistive and testy than components of other institutions.

Trial court administrators at this point in the maturation of the field should be able to see and help the judiciary of a statewide branch move forward with more coherence, but there are three impediments. First, in most states, they continue to be hired and fired locally and get no points locally for advancing greater uniformity in the statewide branch of government. Indeed, in some trial courts, trying to do so will get an administrator in trouble. Second, the idea of a coherent, statewide branch remains an emerging concept.[13] Many states still have significant progress to make toward a coherent statewide branch of state government. So long as trial courts continue to be largely independent of state-level control, trial court administrators will appear to be and in many instances will remain parochial, idiosyncratic, and narrowly focused. Finally, many trial court administrators do not have a meaningful opportunity to participate in each state-level decision about changes. Nor is it realistic to have such participation, even in small states. Given the difficulties of getting everyone's input, it should not be entirely surprising that there is some initial resistance from some trial courts. Some of it simply comes with the territory. But that is why it is so important to try to open up the input process and to add calendar time to allow for that. In the meantime, some understanding and accommodation is needed on both sides.

11.4 Attorneys, Bar Associations, and Others Who Participate in Litigation

Three categories of attorneys are critical to court operations: government-funded and employed criminal attorneys (prosecutors and defenders); government-funded and employed civil attorneys who appear on behalf of government social service agencies and their clients (children owed support payments, neglected and abused children, and those unable to care for themselves); and attorneys in private practice. Because they are critical to the proper administration and disposition of cases, positive relationships between the court and attorneys are essential. The court can interact with and obtain input from private attorneys through their bar associations, both general and specialty. The public attorneys usually interact through the managers of their offices and interbranch comittees.

Traditionally, many attorneys, supported by some judges, have thought that court administration's job was to facilitate and support the attorneys in their interactions with the court. The priorities for court administration were thought to be the judges' needs and desires, attorneys' needs and desires, staff's needs and desires that did not conflict with either of the first two priorities, and then individual litigants and the general citizenry. Attorneys' grip on second place on the priority ladder may be slipping (see chapter 13), but the need for strong relationships and open exchanges with bar associations and the various public litigators remains great.

In litigation, judges tend to study the law and facts in a case and then announce their decision. The litigants state their positions, but the litigation process is not a collaborative process. (Settlement conferences and mediations run by judges tend to be collaborative, but these still are not seen as the norm.) Judges have tended to, and often prefer to, approach administrative decisions the same way they handle cases: the administrator and senior managers gather the facts, propose one or more decisions, and the judges decide. The need for collaboration with others outside the court is not necessarily the first instinct.

This approach certainly is changing in many courts, but in many others it still is not intuitive. Yet, practicing attorneys often are very bright and they have perspectives on problems that judges and court staff do not have, so they can help fashion solutions to problems that will facilitate success. And, even in the era of "Rambo" litigators who lean toward beating the other side into submission, attorneys see themselves as part of the judicial system and feel an obligation to help make it better. Plus, if attorneys are involved in planning, the involved attorneys can sell the solutions more readily to the attorneys who could not sit on the planning or advisory committee. Finally, it is in the court's interest to consult with and involve attorneys in overseeing operations and planning changes because if they are not involved, attorneys can scuttle, or at least undermine, what otherwise looks like an excellent plan.

Just as courts traditionally have changed slowly, attorneys are not big fans of change, either. Private attorneys particularly do not like changes they believe may affect their pocketbooks. Public attorneys do not like changes that they believe will disrupt their established workflow and workload. When attorneys are able to help define the issues and fashion solutions, they gain understanding of the hows and whys of the change and gain assurance that their world will not radically change. (In some instances, such as when there are significant delays in disposing of cases, attorneys' world *should* radically change, but those situations are rare and in those instances the court simply may have to insist.)

Attorneys also can be strong political allies of a court with the two other branches of government and with the public to help explain problems, respond to criticism, and help sell budgetary or legislative changes desired by the court.

A strong working relationship with the bar through the associations and the public offices is very much in a court's self interest. The working relationship is not just going to bar association meetings and dinners (or luncheons) and telling them about the court's needs or what new program or rules the court is putting in place. It means a partnership in which the bar has an important advisory role on how to move the court closer to achieving its mission. The bar's role ultimately must be advisory, however, because the court remains an independent entity with goals and objectives separate from those of both the organized bar and individual litigators. Attorneys normally will seek to advance the self-interest of attorneys. The court must advance the interests of justice and the public it serves. If the bar were given a veto, important objectives of the court might be defeated.

Beyond attorneys, there is a growing list of other organizations and government units that are involved in the litigation process. These organizations sometimes participate as a matter of law, but more often they are interacting with courts because of conditions of probation or the growing use of problem-solving courts (see section 4.2, chapter 4). These organizations include:

- Government child protection agencies and public and private foster care agencies
- Government agencies that address addiction, mental health issues, and job training
- Local school districts and adult education programs
- Community service providers dealing with physical and mental health and addiction issues, education, direct services to children, psychological counseling, job assistance, and welfare assistance
- CASA organizations (Court Appointed Special Advocates), community volunteers trained to assist the court in child abuse and neglect cases to assure that the interests of the child are properly represented to the court.

There are three elements involved in the relationship with the above agencies. First, the court needs to know what they do, how they go about what they do, the level of success they have, and the quality of their staffs. Too often, at least when these agencies only worked with probationers, judges had a short written description of the program or a probation officer told the judge he or she had heard it is a good program, so the judge started to use it and continued to do so unless and until a problem arose. Now, both for probationers and for problem-solving courts, judges understand that they need more information, which may require visits to these organizations' offices and discussions with their personnel. It also may require reviewing any evaluations of their work that exist.[14] Especially for problem-solving courts but even for probationers, it is important for judges to understand the strengths of various programs, the differences among them, and their personnel so they can better match people with programs.

The second element is that these organizations need to know what the court expects from them. These agencies all are in the helping business. Probation officers also see themselves more in the helping business than the police officer business. But for probationers and even more for those in problem-solving court programs, judges need to know in detail of a person's progress and, as critical, of any slips or failures. and the judge needs that information quickly. Those who see their roles as helpers often do not want to "rat" on someone, but the court cannot do its job unless they do. The judges and the programs, but especially the programs' personnel, need to understand the court's needs and the consequences of the court not receiving needed information. Many judges have found this may take several meetings and that some people just cannot adjust to assist the court as it needs to be assisted. In these latter instances, a judge may have to stop using a particular agency.

Schools normally would fall into a separate category, because the role of a school and a school's administrators vis-à-vis students who may be involved in a court matter is different from the role of a counselor or someone assisting an adult to find a job or obtain job skills. Truancy, late arrivals, performance in the classroom, already are tracked by schools and are as important to school officials as they are to the court. Even so, it helps if a judge extends him- or herself to meet with school officials to explain what the court is doing and the importance of the school's assistance. Thereafter, regular contact can be maintained by the assigned probation officer or court-based liaison.

The third element of intersection is general support for the organizations. All of these organizations other than CASA, which normally has an affiliation with the court and receives some of its funding through the court's budget, are independent of the court. In important respects, however, they are adjuncts to the court, and very important to the success of its programs. As these organizations seek public or private funding or need support in the community, or if they desire their role in the court's program(s) to be explained to a board or constituents, they often ask judges for help. There are ethical constraints on judges regarding fund raising, but judges normally try to help as they can.

11.5 Broader Societal Relationships

The above relationships either are mandated or follow naturally from institutional conditions. Relationships with the groups identified below are important to a court because it is a public institution, or so it can gain support for and understanding of what it is doing.

- General public and citizens using the court who are not involved in litigation
- Local colleges and universities regarding volunteers and intern programs
- Local victims rights and advocacy groups
- Court watchdog groups
- Local school officials and teachers regarding student education programs, including peer courts and court tour programs
- Community service organizations

- Volunteer coordinating programs, both public and private
- Credit reporting and other investigative groups
- Academic and other researchers
- Local media outlets.

When courts consider external relationships, the focus often is on organizations and entities, either in their own right or as surrogates for the public. In today's electronic world, courts can reach out directly to citizens, most commonly today through websites but possibly in the future through blogs, instant messages about what is happening in courts, or other communication means not yet developed. These direct communications are important now, as reflected in the explosion of court websites across the country since the early 2000s, but may be even more important in the future. The wired (and wireless) world already is changing the way people gain information, work, and communicate and some say it will change the way people learn and how ideas and innovations will develop.[15] For the moment, it is clear that websites, at least, are critical direct links between courts and citizens, whether or not they are litigants. Many courts now are using their websites to provide general information about the court, its judges, and its personnel. They post news releases, job announcements, and requests for proposals from vendors. They offer special sections with information about jury service and for summoned and serving jurors. Some courts have developed online information sheets about various types of cases and how they are processed, and supplemented these with streaming video tours of the courthouse and courtrooms. Online self-help centers also are being provided for those who represent themselves rather than using an attorney. Courts also are posting their annual reports, statistical and financial information online, sometimes with expanded hyperlinks to provide information not available in the printed version of a report. Clearly, courts are beginning to think in terms of directly communicating with citizens about all aspects of who they are, what they do, and how best to use the services available. Courts will continue to seek new ways to communicate directly with the public through computers, telephones, iPods, and other electronic devices that may come along in the future. The opportunity provided by technology to communicate directly with litigants and the general public is one of the exciting opportunities of the twenty-first century (see also, section 12.10, chapter 12).

Some of the organizations listed above assist the court with supplemental personnel to assist citizens using the courts or to help complete required work (colleges and universities, community volunteer coordinating programs). Researchers also can help by conducting evaluations of court programs, either directly for the court or as part of a broader research effort, or simply to provide the court with insight into how it is doing in the area being researched. Academic researchers often appreciate being asked to undertake evaluation efforts because they can be helpful to the education process for students, as well.

Several types of court users only want information from court files: credit reporting companies, the military, and, sometimes, corporate recruiters. The court gains no direct benefit from these users other than meeting its obligation to provide access to public records. In fulfilling that obligation, courts also advance societal interests in advancing credit to those who should have it, assuring a properly constituted military, and facilitating people otherwise qualified to get jobs. Courts are almost entirely passive in this relationship, but relationships develop, nonetheless.

Advocacy groups and court watcher groups may or may not start out supportive of the court, but their interests are legitimate and it is important for the court not to appear to be hiding information or to be afraid of being accountable for its work. Court watcher groups scare many judges because they often are seen as having a predetermined agenda and judges fear that they will use selectively collected information to attack, either immediately or during an election cycle. One particular advocacy group, a diverse committee addressing the needs of victims of domestic violence, often is sponsored by the prosecutor's office. The court normally is invited to participate on these committees to facilitate coordination of these cases and to iron out any procedural issues or problems that might affect the disposition of cases or the execution of restraining orders. Judges sometimes sit on these committees, but it is a delicate situation that judges probably should avoid. Because they are advocacy entities for one side of court cases, in addition to being coordinating bodies, judges' participation on these committees can raise questions about the neutrality of the court. Assuring that the court is seen to be doing justice is an important purpose of courts about which judges are very sensitive. Because there are legitimate coordination issues surrounding this case type, however, administrative staff or managers can and should participate as committee members. It probably is unwise for judges to do so, however.

Community service organizations are included on this list for several reasons. They can provide a forum for court representatives (judges or senior management) to explain what is happening in the court, discuss current issues or changes, and respond to citizens' questions and concerns. They also can be a source for volunteers. Those attending meetings can serve as a sounding board of public opinion about how the court is doing in the public's eyes or what it should select as its future priorities. Judges often appreciate the opportunity to appear before these groups because members of these groups vote.

The entity on the above list that causes judges and courts the most angst is the media, print, radio, and television. Some courts and many judges have a love-hate relationship with the media. Many judges believe courts and judges cannot get a balanced or positive story from one or more of their local media outlets. Judges have told me that the editor of their local newspaper sends reporters to the courthouse to find or create negative stories about a judge or the court. And that reporters routinely misquote them or quote them out of context. Many judges will not talk to reporters, in part because of ethical constraints but more, because they just do not like the coverage provided to court cases.

Anyone who watches the cable news networks understands how they can whip viewers across the country into a frenzy about any case if the story line is good or can be made to look good. Because judges can make mistakes, because the adversary process itself is not perfect, and because real life as played out in courtrooms involves emotional and difficult issues,[16] the media looking for "good" stories have opportunities. If a news network or a popular anchor on those networks believes a judge has made a mistake, he or she can vilify that judge. They can and have called for judges to be impeached or to resign, sometimes with only superficial efforts to gain all the facts. Any judge seeing those stories has to feel concerned about how complex and difficult situations can be simplified and distorted by the media.

Further, judges across the nation are more wary of televised trials in notorious cases since the O.J. Simpson trial in the mid-1990s. The presiding judge in that trial, Judge Lance Ito, has become both a symbol and a noun about how notorious televised trials can significantly impact both the judge and the justice system. Some judges are not strongly adverse to the media, but still believe that court cases are too complex to be properly explained by the electronic media and that even newspapers (particularly headline writers) are mostly looking for the angle that will sell newspapers and not to inform the public.

The debate about courts and the media has raged since at least the Scopes trial in the 1920s and the Lindbergh baby kidnapping case in the 1930s. In the years since, an accommodation between bench and the press has been reached about the mechanics of having cameras in the courtroom, but *whether* there should be cameras continues to generate debate. Courts try to control parties' conduct outside the courtroom, but with no more than modest success. The reporters and commentators outside the courtroom remain largely beyond control. Media representatives and some others see that lack of control as highly desirable and mandated by the Constitution. Others, including many judges, see it as regrettable and a threat to fair trials, not only for those subject to the publicity but to all defendants, even those charged with relatively routine, low-level crimes that get no publicity. This debate is beyond the scope of court administration; it is a judicial administration issue (see chapter 1). All court administrators can do is be prepared to respond to whatever decisions judges make in particular cases and, in notorious cases, to handle the crush of humanity, questions, and equipment that will follow (see below). They also need to know the general rules about media access to courthouses, courtrooms, and case information for routine cases as well as high-publicity cases.[17]

The focus on courts and the media as they report about and involve themselves (mostly) in criminal cases[18] has influenced and somewhat distorted the discussion about use of the media in and for court administration. In many important ways, courts need the media, particularly on the court administration side. The media is a critical surrogate for the public. Courts need the media to inform citizens about new programs, a new or improved website, expanded ways to pay fines, improvements in the courthouse building or furnishings, or whatever else a court is doing to improve itself. The media can run "feel good" stories about the problem-solving courts' successes, which then can build support overall for the court. They can help the court find volunteers. The media can share the news about staff members who have been recognized for good work and for long-term service. They can spread the word about improvements in jury service.[19] The media also assist courts to be accountable to citizens as a public institution. The need for accountability is embraced by the Trial Court Performance Standards (Standard 4.2) and most leaders in the judiciary.

One of the purposes of courts is to provide general deterrence, that is, to deter the general public from crime by the example of people being convicted of and sentenced for specific crimes. Without the publicity provided by the media, that purpose of courts cannot be achieved effectively in the modern world. Although many judges doubt the value and accuracy of the education about courts provided by the media—and the public opinion polls cited in chapter 4, among others, support their skepticism—the media could be an effective ally in combating the misleading images created by some television dramas and movies and help explain how courts really work.

The California public's impressions of their courts in the early 1990s were similar to those in other states and in the national polls, not very good: less than half felt that the overall performance of the courts was good, very good, or excellent.[20] The judiciary of California has undergone tremendous changes since the early 1990s, and many of them have been designed to improve operations and productivity and to make courts more fair, accessible, and accountable. Each trial court has had to develop community-focused strategic plans. The process has compelled invitations by courts to the community for its opinions and input about improvements. State leaders have flooded the media with press releases, held public forums across the state, and worked hard to spread the word about positive evaluations of new programs. The supreme court and intermediate appellate courts regularly hold one or two sessions a year in high schools around the state (as a number of other states are doing now, also). In the latest public opinion poll, completed in 2005, there was a 20-point improvement in the public's general opinion about courts compared to 1992.[21] If California's judiciary had done exactly what it did, but had not reached out to the public to tell them what it was doing and how it was changing the courts, I doubt that there would have been that level of improvement in perceptions.

The court for which I was the court administrator regularly issued press releases to the county's and area's newspapers (and to area television stations for particularly newsworthy items, such as our night court for small claims); they all were printed by the two main local newspapers, almost always without changes. The local reporters assigned to the court routinely checked with me if a story touched on administration (as opposed to a case, about which they would contact the involved judge). I returned reporters' telephone messages as quickly as I could to help them meet their deadline and answered their questions as fully and honestly as I could. I met with each newly assigned newspaper reporter and oriented him or her to how we worked and to our key personnel. I even suggested some stories they might develop on their own about how the court worked. When we had a rough patch involving an administrative matter and some staff went to the county's main newspaper to put pressure on the court's management, its court reporter wrote as sympathetic a story as one could hope for because of the positive relationship we had built. Our court was in a small (roughly 150,000 people) but growing suburban–rural county without substantial competition among the local news outlets. Those factors doubtless helped the court to get publicity and to build positive personal relationships. The judges to whom I have spoken who are most negative about the media are almost all from larger urban areas where judges are more anonymous and media competition is intense, so a juicy negative story about the court or a judge might be seen as giving the news outlet an edge. Even so, positive experiences in urban communities can be found, as well.

Many courts have positive stories of improvement and achievement involving court administration that they can and should share more aggressively with the media. The media may have trouble understanding hundreds of years of evidence law that leads to evidence being excluded at a trial, or the complexities associated with sentencing a multiple offender when the judge is not given or cannot consider circumstances reporters consider to be important, or even separation of powers issues. The media does not have trouble understanding the installation of wireless computer access in the jury assembly room, however, or higher pay for jury service, or allowing credit or debit card payments of fines, or documented money savings or recovered lives from a new court program. The list could be extended and it exists in most courts across the country. If all a court does is share the list with other courts or put a line or short paragraph on its website, the community served by the court will not learn of these improvements. The media is the best way to share the news. Whatever merit exists in judges' concerns about the weaknesses of media coverage of cases and their outcomes, these do not extend to the advantages of media coverage of the court administration side of the institution. Courts can and should do better in that regard.

Notorious cases are one of the areas of intersect between judicial administration and court administration. Like fire, pestilence, and floods, these cases can surface at any time and anywhere. A court in a small community in Iowa, for example, should not assume it never will have to deal with this type of case because it is not in California, New York, or Florida and because of the type of community it is. Bad people doing extraordinarily bad things to appealing victims are everywhere. Celebrities can travel to or through any community and get involved in strange doings. Just ask the small skiing community of Eagle, Colorado, where basketball star Kobe Bryant was accused of rape. A case that becomes notorious can arise anywhere.[22] The need for contingency planning again comes into play. The judge presiding over the case will determine what happens inside the courtroom and will seek to control parties' communication with the media, but it is the administrator, court staff, and courthouse security who will have to generate order out of chaos.

It is difficult to identify a notorious case at the outset.[23] A case that generates a lot of local or area interest may have no national appeal and thus not become "notorious." A case that seems to be routine when filed may spark remarkable interest and suddenly become notorious. One court administrator who experienced a notorious case has suggested it is like Justice Potter Stewart's definition of pornography: you know it when you see it. More specifically, when an administrator sees television network satellite trucks arriving and nationally known reporters or news anchors, the court probably has a notorious case.

Some common factors in making a case notorious stand out.[24]

- One or more child victims
- Celebrity status of the alleged perpetrator or victim
- Multiple victims, particularly if the person accused is alleged to be a serial killer
- Female victim, especially one who is relatively young
- Homicide involving intimate and family relationships.

A relatively recent notorious case was the Scott Peterson murder case in California's San Joaquin Valley, the richest agricultural area in the nation. Stanislaus County had a population estimated at a little under 500,000 in 2002, when on Christmas eve that year, Laci Peterson, due to deliver a son within a few weeks, was reported missing by her husband, Scott. Within days, Laci's disappearance captured the nation's attention. By the time the bodies of Laci and her son Connor washed up on the shores of San Francisco Bay in early April 2003, every cable news channel, most network news and magazine shows, local and regional television stations, local and national newspapers and magazines, and even national tabloids were reporting daily on the search for Laci. On Monday, April 22, the day charges of double murder were filed against Scott Peterson, a notorious case started.

Until the point of Scott Peterson's arrest on April 18, no one in the court knew who, if anyone, would be charged or, more critically, when. The notoriety surrounding the disappearance and search was clear. Even so, the local sheriff's department, which ran the jail and court security, the local police department, the investigating and arresting agency, and the court were unprepared for the deluge of media representatives and all their equipment that started April 18, escalated on April 22, and did not diminish for the next nine months, at which point the case was transferred to another county for trial. Within that first court week, the court, police department, and sheriff's department cooperatively established the framework for organizing the frenzy. They set up a special website for the media, excluded cameras from the courthouse, and organized the media representatives' use of the street and the area outside the courthouse.[25] Creation and use of the website were essential elements in gaining control of a difficult situation. The approach adopted in this case has set a new standard for how courts should respond if they happen to get a notorious case. The key lessons learned and the elements of the model that courts should follow are set forth below.

Serendipitously, in 1999 and again in 2001, Modesto, the county seat of Stanislaus County, became a center for media activity in two unrelated crimes that garnered national attention. Neither of the crimes had occurred in the county, but in one case Modesto was the closest city of any size and in the other case the victim and the married U.S. Congressman representing Stanislaus County, who was having an affair with the victim, were from Modesto. The experience of dealing with the media during those two previous situations taught both the sheriff's department and police department some essential principles that then were applied during the Peterson case. When dealing with the media in all cases, but most especially in high-profile cases, the following principles should guide one's actions.

- The court executive officer (the title used in California) created the acronym FAT to describe the provision of information:
  - *Fair*
  - *Accurate*
  - *Timely*
- The messenger must build and sustain credibility with all the media.

These rules are critical because if a court adheres to them, the media will play by the rules established. If a court does not adhere to them, the media *will* get their story and get it any way they can, accurate or not. If a free-for-all for information develops, physical chaos in and around the courthouse may be the least objectionable consequence. Moreover, if a court adheres to these rules, the media will adhere to them and self-police their enforcement, so long as the rules are clear, understood, and followed strictly by the information source.

What does it mean to be "fair"? It means all media get the same access to information at the same time. Thus, the local newspaper is not favored with a quote or a document or other information over anyone else. A news outlet that gives a "spin" to the court's information that the judge or administrator may not like continues to get the same information at the same time with the same courtesy as all other media. Their spin is not the court's responsibility. Tabloid newspapers are treated the same as the national TV networks and nationally respected newspapers. During the Peterson investigation, when individual Modesto police officers began to leak information, the Chief ordered that only his department's public information officer (PIO) and he could talk to any media representative; anyone caught violating that order would be disciplined. There may be times when the hometown media will exert whatever pressure they can to get an advantage they believe they "deserve." If the PIO (or court administrator) succumbs to this pressure, it is an immediate and possibly irretrievable message to all other media that it's "Katie bar the door" for information gathering.

The value of fairness became clear to the court executive officer in the Peterson case when a senior executive of a national network sat in his office and kept asking if he could trust that every document filed would be posted on the web and posted as quickly as possible. The network executive said if the executive officer would give him that assurance, he would take his satellite truck away from the courthouse. The court executive officer gave him that assurance; the executive removed his satellite truck.

"Accurate" is fairly self-explanatory. The one element of "accurate" that should be highlighted is that it embraces "complete." When the Peterson court shared filed documents, the entire document, as filed, was provided. If there were later misinterpretations or misquotes, it was the news outlet's responsibility; it was not because the court had provided only a portion of a document.[26]

Information is "timely" when it is provided to all as soon as reasonably possible. The media have to believe the court will provide timely information and that it will be provided to all of them at the same time. In Stanislaus County, one element of this was the case's administrative rule (issued by the judge) that all filings that came in after 4:00 p.m. in the afternoon would be provided first thing the next morning, unless they related to a hearing to be held the next day, in which case they were provided shortly after being filed. Many in courts and law enforcement believe the media will not—some say cannot—police themselves, that the economic and ratings pressure to be "first" will lead all to seek an advantage any way they can. Stanislaus County proved these cynics wrong.

There also are many people in the justice system who believe that if the media are not given any information, they will go away and the "media circus" will be avoided. This approach might work for a small drug bust or a standard domestic or assault case—or even a local high-profile case—but those in Stanislaus County closest to its handling of the media advise that such thinking is wrong for notorious cases. They go back to their experience that if information is not FAT, the media will get what they want any way they can. Rather than avoiding a "circus" in a notorious case, withholding information creates the "feeding frenzy" one is trying to avoid. Being open and applying the FAT principles creates an orderly flow of information to everyone, thereby avoiding the circus.

The other rule for the court administrator is to be jealous of his or her time when called by the media. For the Peterson case, the executive officer's secretary screened his calls. If a call came in from a media representative about a document that had been posted on the website, she referred the caller to the website and declined to put the caller through. It took about two weeks, but once the media learned about the site and came to trust what was posted, the calls dwindled quickly to a trickle.[27]

The court executive officer in the Peterson case summarizes his experience with the following suggested rules:

1. Do not be afraid to field questions from the media. Yes, they are smart, but you know a whole lot more about court operations than they do.
2. Never give an opinion. You can and should share facts (events, dates, what happened and what events will happen), but your opinion is irrelevant and probably will cause problems far more than withholding it.
3. You cannot be bullied, you won't be bullied. That attitude will come out in your voice and will be sufficient; they will recognize it.
4. "I don't know" is an acceptable answer. It may frustrate them, but it is a good and honorable answer.
5. "That question is premature" also is an acceptable answer. It is appropriate, especially, when talking about what is to happen. (They'll want to know what "might" happen.)
6. Do not worry about trick questions. You can spot them and dodge them.
7. Always respond like an administrator, not a lawyer; it is easier to be understood if you do not try to talk "lawyerese."
8. Explaining legal terms to the smaller media outlets—who lack attorneys on staff or on call—is okay, so long as it is off the record.
9. Keep the quotes short. If you make a mistake, you can back up and start over.
10. Keep a copy of your local criminal laws and procedural rules handy and refer to them as necessary.
11. This case is not your "Andy Warhol" 15 minutes of fame or your "hour on the stage." You are part of the chorus for this one. (The temptations are great; it takes a lot of discipline to remain an unidentified member of the chorus.)
12. All in all, this is a wonderful learning opportunity and should be approached with that attitude.

Other than a few courts in the nation, those in New York City and Los Angeles being the prime examples, no court knows whether it will have to deal with a notorious case. They are like lightning: they hit suddenly and without warning.

Yet, if a court becomes the locus for a notorious case and it has not made any contingency plans—similar to the COOP plans discussed in the last chapter—the time it requires to gear up may materially weaken the court's chances to control the situation. Based on the experience of the Stanislaus County Superior Court, there are six things all courts can do "just in case." The preparation may never be needed, but if it is and is not available, the administrator and the court will have serious regrets.

1. *Develop a plan.* There are two ways to approach this, one much less likely to result in plans being prepared than the other. The one with the lowest likelihood of being implemented broadly is to expect each trial court to establish its own plan. Some large urban courts and, perhaps, courts in locales frequented by many celebrities may develop such plans, but virtually all small courts and courts that incorrectly believe "it can never happen here; we're too inconspicuous and quiet for a notorious case to develop" will wait until lightning strikes. Then, like Eagle, Colorado, and Mariposa County, California (where Yosemite National Park is located), they will scramble to respond and lose valuable time.

The second way is for the state administrative office to take the lead, to form a committee to design the outline of a plan that all of the state's courts can use, with appropriate blanks to be filled in by each court. This approach maximizes the use of existing skills and experience, avoids reinvention across the state, allows for a good portion of the needed work to be done in advance, and is the most effective use of resources for an event that even in very large states usually happens only once every several years.

Two elements of the plan are essential: (1) what to do "in the meantime," that is, until the website is ready and the media personnel and trucks are organized; and (2) the shell of a website. Some thought also might be given in each location to where the media tents and the satellite and microwave trucks might go. The City of Modesto had the good luck to have a fenced vacant lot across the street from the courthouse for the trucks. Most courts will have to search more broadly and be more creative than Modesto had to be. It certainly does not hurt to start looking, however, as that will make the final decision easier when the time comes.

One of the obvious lessons from the Peterson case is that even when a website is started almost immediately, it takes some time for the site to be fully operational. Along the way, it also is necessary for the media to learn to trust the site and the credibility of the court and law enforcement PIOs. In Stanislaus' case, it took about two weeks. If a court—or a state committee—has not thought through what a website would contain, it will take longer. Fortunately, Stanislaus County now has created a template. Imitation is the sincerest form of flattery. It also is a reflection of the quality of the imitated product. The courts in San Mateo and Santa Barbara, California, and Eagle, Colorado, already have used Stanislaus' template—including a good part of the exact language used in Stanislaus—to cut their development time. Even so, one must plan on needing development time and, therefore, also must plan on a more manual, people-intensive approach at the beginning.

2. *Finding a public information officer.* One position that exists in only a few larger courts is a public information officer. Where would most courts, then, find a public information officer when that rare event of a notorious case comes along? The three representatives of the court, the sheriff's office, and the police in the Peterson case all recommend against going out and hiring someone after the case arises. Such a person may not know the community, the agencies involved, or the media well enough to be effective. Therefore, the person would have to gain knowledge and establish a rapport with everyone before he or she could be effective. During that time, valuable liaison and control time would be lost.

The Stanislaus County court executive officer believes that most court administrators can be their own PIO during a notorious case. No one will know the court better or be better able to access needed information. Most court administrators also develop some facility in talking to the public and, to a lesser degree, the local media during their tenure. They also, more than anyone else, will have the trust of the judge.

The police department and sheriff's office PIOs offer another option: look around today to find PIOs in other government agencies who seem to be most effective with and respected by the media. Talk to that person or to several people and line them up on a contingency basis: "If we should get a notorious case at some point, would you be willing to help out the court and serve as our spokesperson?" Because they previously had experienced the value of cooperation among agencies and also knew of the need for "back up," these two Stanislaus County PIOs also recommend regular meetings and training sessions for the PIOs in various agencies in the community. That way, they will get to know each other, develop some knowledge of the issues and concerns of different agencies, and get training they can call on when needed. In Stanislaus County, because of events since 1999, the PIOs of government agencies meet regularly and always try to build some training into their meetings. The court executive officer and the judge who presided over the Peterson case in Stanislaus County also endorse the local criminal justice agencies meeting regularly so they can build both knowledge and trust before a crisis arises.

3. *Review existing rules and statutes.* California adopted a special rule, Rule 2073, to deal with notorious cases as a result of the Peterson and Michael Jackson cases, which arose within less than a year of each other. A new rule was needed because different people interpreted existing rules differently insofar as they allowed or did not allow certain case information to be placed on the website. Each state's administrative office of the courts or a committee of trial court administrators should review all existing rules and statutes with an eye to how they would affect

the management of a notorious case. If there is some ambiguity or a prohibition that would inhibit a website or what could be posted on such a site, amended or new rules should be put in place as soon as possible.

4. *Build a photo gallery.* When the website eventually used for the Peterson case was built on that first weekend following Peterson's arrest, the sheriff's PIO already had file copies of photographs of the jail, which was the focus of attention that first weekend. Courts should develop a similar set of generic pictures of the courthouse, courtrooms, possibly public hallways and perimeter security locations, the local jail(s), and, perhaps, the facades of other criminal justice agencies' buildings. These could be built into the shell website so they will be ready when and if needed later. Or, they could be kept handy in digital or hard copy form to be added as appropriate if a notorious case ever comes along. Specific additional photos, such as a defendant's mug shot and a photo of the assigned judge, could be added quickly as the final version of the web site is put together.

5. *Write biographies for all judges.* Judicial biographies can be developed today and then used if needed. These should be more than just a statement of the judge's current assignment and when he or she went on the bench for the first time. In Stanislaus, the biographies of the two judges that were posted provided details about their legal and full judicial careers plus civic organizations to which they belonged. Each bench may have different views about how much detail to provide, but once there is a consensus, it is easy to develop the template and fill it in for each judge. It then will be ready should it be needed.

6. *Consider how to handle the provision of services and fees.* Service fees were not a significant issue in Stanislaus County, but could be. Stanislaus County did not charge for access to the website, but there were clear accounting costs—although very limited out-of-pocket costs—associated with developing and maintaining the website. (The volunteer citizen who helped build and maintain the website donated all his time.) It would not hurt to address the issue of fees in advance, so there is one less item to address when a notorious case actually appears in the court.

Can the court legally charge anything for setting up and maintaining a website? If so, can it charge only its actual costs or can it recover more than its documented costs? Are accounting, billing, and collection time part of the jurisdiction's costs? Does the court desire to recapture actual costs or also a premium? Can the court charge a premium under the law?

Likewise, with the parking and tent spaces for the TV stations and networks. Stanislaus County did not charge the media for the hearing days, other than during the ten-day preliminary hearing. Yet, the City of Modesto incurred police costs on those other, one-day occasions. Prior to actually having a notorious case, one cannot estimate costs. What a court could do, however, is determine whether to charge, for which events to charge, and the components of the charge (law enforcement officers only, accounting staff time, and a "service fee" for the community's inconvenience in being unable to use the street for vehicular traffic). Is there any basis for distinguishing the media from a local neighborhood party or a street fair that results in a closed street? Does the court or community want to get into the business of ordering and collecting the fee for port-a-potties and electric generators or would it rather leave ordering and paying for these items to the media? If the media is allowed to obtain port-a-potties and other rented items for single-day hearings, would they have to remove them in between hearing days or be allowed to rent them for X days at a time and put them in a place where they could remain?

A notorious case generates its own energy, but it also creates unique issues and challenges. The court's leadership has to focus on the issues and challenges more than on the energy. It is easier to do so if there is an outline of how to respond developed in advance. Few courts will need to implement their plan, but few courts also see their courthouses burn down or flooded or evacuated because of a toxic spill. A notorious case is one of those contingencies about which courts' leaders must think and for which they should prepare. If they act as contingency planners, their lives will be much easier should it ever turn out that they need the plan.

External relationships cover the gamut from incidental and occasional to frequent, very important, and necessary. None can be ignored, although the latter clearly require more attention and concern than the former. The handling of external relationships is one of those areas about which the chief judge and the court administrator should talk and allocate responsibility (see section 6.5, chapter 6). As suggested in the brief discussion of websites, the method of communication, at least with the general public and maybe with many of those identified in this chapter, may well change over the next 20 years, but there will be three constants. Some communications will continue to be and need to be face-to-face. Second, if critical relationships are ignored or allowed to sour because of a lack of communication, the court will suffer adverse consequences. Third, the need to establish and build these relationships will not change.

Notes

1. The state administrative office of the courts often is mandated, in turn, to advise the legislature about the courts' work or about the results of pilot projects established with legislative authorization.
2. If a prosecutor chooses not to charge a crime, that information remains in the prosecutor's office; the court would have no way of knowing. The court is the official repository only of outcomes for cases filed.
3. In the state courts of the 75 largest counties in 2000, of all those charged with felonies, 27 percent were not convicted, with almost all of those having their charges dismissed. Pastore, Ann L,. and Kathleen Maguire, eds. *Sourcebook of Criminal Justice Statistics—2003*, Washington, D.C: U.S. Dept. of Justice, Bureau of Justice Statistics, 2005, p. 457. In the federal

district courts in 2001, 11.2 percent of all defendants (felony and misdemeanor charges) were not convicted. Ibid., Table 5.17, p. 418,

4. The court could seek to enhance its staff's capacity, but seldom can it do so within the time required to prepare a specific grant. Staff enhancement would have to be step one in a longer-term effort to obtain more grant funding.

5. Tobin, Robert W., *Creating the Judicial Branch: The Unfinished Reform.* Williamsburg, VA: National Center for State Courts, 1999, p. 171.

6. In Idaho, for example, a state-funded judiciary with regional administrators, the supreme court by rule has authority to appoint the administrators, but that same rule delegates the selection of the administrator jointly to the state court administrator and the administrative judge of the district. *Idaho Court Administrative Rules*, Rule 43 (1988).

7. Tobin, Robert W., *Creating the Judicial Branch,* p. 261.

8. Interviews rather than numbers might best gauge some measures. That should be acceptable if key measures are quantified.

9. A few studies, most notably the 1980s study of trial time; see Sipes, Dale Ann, *On Trial: The Length of Civil and Criminal Trials.* Williamsburg, VA: National Center for State Courts, 1988 and some of the self-representation studies, have been successful in getting judges to complete information questionnaires. These required a lot of follow-up effort by the research staff, however, so they are not necessarily encouraging models of what would be possible on a regular basis.

10. For example, Mahoney, Barry, *The Ventura Day Fine Pilot Project: A Report on the Planning Process and the Decision to Terminate the Project, With Recommendations Concerning Future Development of Fines Policy.* Denver, CO: The Justice Management Institute, May 1995 (draft report provided to the author).

11. The private sector also is finding it harder today than previously to find people willing to move to new cities or countries to advance their careers.

12. Unfortunately, even if there is an advisory committee of trial court personnel and judges working on an issue, normally it is not possible to solicit and obtain input from all trial courts. Coming up with a solution and then asking trial courts to advise if there are any problems is not the best way to obtain real input. Beyond any appearance that the decision already has been made, many trial court staff and managers do not have time to give AOC proposals close examination within the timeframe requested.

13. Tobin, Robert W., *Creating the Judicial Branch.*

14. One aspect of this need that is not recognized by the public or most legislators is the time required for judges to perform this task well. Since judges have calendars all day and the programs are working with clients during normal business hours, judges often have to devote late afternoons and evenings to these meetings and inspections. They are happy to do so because they believe in the programs with which they are involved, but it is time that cannot be identified or measured by looking into a courtroom to see if a judge is on the bench, as some court watchers, journalists, and local legislators are fond of doing.

15. Frank Moss, Media Laboratory of the Massachusetts Institute of Technology, quoted by Perman, Stacy, in "How the Masses Will Innovate," *BusinessWeek Online,* Mar. 13, 2006, retrieved Mar. 13, 2006 from http://www.businessweek.com/technology/content/mar2006/tc20060308_265863.htm?campaign_innovate_mar14&link_position=link16.

16. Deciding cases is not easy, even though everyone thinks they can do it. See also, Pound, Roscoe, "The Causes of Popular Dissatisfaction with the Administration of Justice," speech delivered Aug. 29, 1906, reprinted in A. Leo Levin and Russell R. Wheeler, eds., *The Pound Conference: Perspectives on Justice in the Future.* St. Paul, MN: West Publishing, 1979, p. 341.

17. Because of the relative frequency of and impact of notorious cases in California, there now is a special rule about administrative responses allowed and encouraged for notorious cases. Calif. Rules of Court, Rule 2073 (2005).

18. The specter of reporters appropriating for themselves the role of law enforcement or the prosecutor to solve cases, to assure the filing of an accusation against a specific person, or to obtain a guilty judgment is very hard to watch in some cases, but it sells newspapers and is "good television," so it probably will not diminish.

19. One of the judges of the court for which I was the administrator was called for jury service and was allowed to sit on a jury. After his service he wrote an "opinion" piece for the main county newspaper about how much he enjoyed and learned from the experience. It was not written as a press release about how people should serve on juries, but it generated several supporting letters to the editor and had a very positive impact.

20. Rottman, David B., "What Californians Think About Their Courts: Highlights from a New Survey of the Public and Attorneys," *California Courts Review*, Fall 2005, p. 7

21. Ibid.

22. The court in Dallas, Texas, did not know about the Andrea Yates case until she called the police to tell them her five children were dead. There was no warning or hint of the Bryant case until the event and arrest shortly thereafter. Even in the Elizabeth Smart case in Salt Lake City, the abduction was "notorious," but the arrest of her alleged abductors—and therefore the arrival of a notorious case for the court—was totally unexpected.

23. This discussion of notorious cases and the Peterson case is adopted from a portion of an original article by the author, "From Chaotic to Copesetic: Lessons in Media Relations for Courts from *People* vs. *Scott Peterson*," *The Court Manager*, vol. 19, no. 4, Winter 2004–2005, pp. 6–21. It is used with permission. Michael Tozzi is the court executive officer in Stanislaus County. The sheriff's department's PIO at the time was Kelly Huston. The police department PIO was Doug Ridenour.

24. The core of this list derives from a summary of an article by Derek J. Paulsen that appeared in the November/December 2003 National Criminal Justice Reference Service Catalog, p. 12. The original article was, "Murder in Black and White: The Newspaper Coverage of Homicide in Houston," *Homicide Studies*, vol. 7, no. 3, pp. 289–317 (August 2003).

25. For additional information about handling notorious cases, see Murphy, Timothy R. et al., *Managing Notorious Trials*. Williamsburg, VA: National Center for State Courts, 1998.

26. The California Rule of Court adopted after the Peterson case, note 17, above, now restricts some information from being made public. (See text below.)

27. Tozzi's approach is not unlike dropping a manual work process once it has been computerized and the software has been tested. If the court maintains the manual process "just in case," the manual process will remain in use forever. Likewise, if calls about items posted on the web are allowed through, the calls will not stop. The reporters will talk to the administrator "just in case" they can get something that others will not get.

Chapter 12

Hierarchy of Court Administration: Proactive Management

All courts should be proactive in their management. If courts do not change and improve, either others will change them or they will stagnate and become increasingly irrelevant. Being proactive in the context of courts means looking for opportunities to move beyond the status quo—whatever that is for any single court—to improve operations, improve productivity, increase effectiveness, introduce new programs that will move the court closer to achieving its mission, and improve the court's outreach to the public, both to improve access and services and to improve two-way communication. Most courts are proactive, the main issue being only the extent to which they are. Once courts assure their mission critical needs and fulfill the needs and obligations in the second and third levels of the Hierarchy of Court Administration (chapters 10 and 11), they should look to be and do all they can to be proactive.

12.1 Maslow's Hierarchy and the Hierarchy of Court Administration

The Hierarchy of Court Administration parallels Abraham Maslow's Hierarchy of Needs for human beings. Table 12.1 shows the parallel between what Maslow described as the esteem needs of humans and the proactive management needs of courts.

In Maslow's Hierarchy, esteem has two elements: self-esteem and the esteem of others. Proactive management by courts brings both types of esteem to courts:

Table 12.1   Maslow's Esteem Needs and Court Proactive Management Needs

Maslow's esteem needs	Court proactive management needs
Respect of others:	• Planning (strategic and long-range)
	• Environmental scanning
• Status	• Focus is on outputs, not inputs
• Fame	• Assuring data quality and using objective statistical
• Glory	information to set priorities and to manage
• Recognition	• Program evaluation
• Attention	• Problem-solving courts
• Reputation	• Improving the jury experience
• Achievement	• Assuring access (physical, language, including use of plain
Self-esteem:	English, self-representation assistance)
	• Supporting and assisting coordinate agencies and
• Confidence	organizations
• Appreciation	• Community input/feedback
• Dignity	• Community outreach
• Dominance	• Meeting client expectations
• Mastery	• Using new technologies
• Independence	• Change management
• Freedom	• Adopting best practices from other courts
	• Nurturing and developing staff skills and capacities
	• Improved working conditions and opportunities for staff
	• Maintaining and adapting facilities

a sense of accomplishment and pride from improving court operations and delivering better service and access, which also improves the lives of the judges and staff, and citizens' appreciation of the improvements the court is making. If a court is effective in conveying to the public what it is doing to improve and how that helps those who use the court, the court gains the public's respect. Just as humans seek and gain status, recognition, attention, reputation, and achievement when respected by others, so too will courts, except that courts also will be stronger politically and will gain budgetary support to continue to advance. A court that is not proactive will only be marking time and will be compared adversely by the public and the other branches of government to other courts and organizations. A court that is not proactive either will be forced to change by the other branches or will find itself unable to meet its basic obligations without a massive infusion of money, which may be denied because of a lack of demonstrated ability to use funds effectively. Self-esteem in the context of a court will be manifested in several ways: increased confidence among staff; the ability of the institution to take on new challenges; recognition by management of staff's efforts and staff's own sense of being with a positive organization; mastery of new skills; and a sense of dignity that derives from knowing they are doing well and doing good.

12.2   One Trial Court at a Time

Court reform is difficult and ponderous. As Arthur Vanderbilt stated many decades ago, court reform is "no sport for the short-winded."[1] Nor is proactive management. There are several very important reasons why some of the things discussed in this chapter are commonplace in some courts and revolutionary in others.

A lot of individual trial courts have survived for decades by changing very slowly, explaining that because the common law changes in small incremental steps and because courts are to resist majoritarian sentiments, it is appropriate for administrative changes to be similarly slow and deliberate. The parallels are specious. Courts can introduce new or changed programs or administrative functions or tasks as quickly as they can plan, implement, and evaluate them; the pace of change in the law and the judiciary's role in society are irrelevant.[2] Judges' and staff's capacity and willingness to absorb change are very relevant, however.

Too often court leaders have converted legitimate concern for and recognition of the equal status of all judges and the importance of protecting judges' professional and decisional needs into paralysis regarding administrative changes when individual judges oppose a change. Larger courts and some smaller courts may come to reject or ignore one or two judges' opposition, but frequently limited opposition is sufficient to slow things down and, sometimes, to kill an idea for several years. Anecdotes and finely spun "what ifs" by people trained in "what if" thinking often rule the day, even in the face of contrary hard data and alternative anecdotes. (The data are dismissed as wrong or measuring the wrong thing and the counter-anecdotes are seen as not being as compelling as theirs.) A significant change that was tried and failed often is dead for at least a decade, even if lessons were learned as a result of the failure that could preclude failure for a modified plan. If an idea is delayed long enough, by the time a court is able to consider it again, circumstances and technology may have changed enough to require a new planning cycle. Continuing and effective advancement is very hard in that environment. Finally, judges often gauge whether something is good or bad by whether it hurts or helps them in their courtrooms. If it does not help, the old saw, "If it ain't broke, don't fix it" gets called out. It may not be "broke" in one judge's courtroom, but it may be broken courtwide. Nonetheless, the more parochial view can carry the day because few people actively seek change and confrontations with fellow judges are avoided in almost all instances, so they accede to the "let's not rush this" argument.

Leaders need to take into account that most courts operate very much like small groups. James MacGregor Burns defined a small group as, "a collection of persons with shared purposes and values; with face-to-face or otherwise physically close relations to one another; with extensive social contacts among themselves as a result of shared interests and influence on one another; and with some sta-bilization of roles."[3] Individual judges can divert proposals for change because, "the group is assumed to be a collection of persons in a state of equilibrium. In this state, efforts to change the group to a new level or type of activity will bring pressures to return the group to its former equilibrium."[4] Plus, when there are conflicts within the group, it often is tied to members having subsidiary affili-ations with one or more other groups, in this context, most often with the bar. Group members, "must respond to other group needs and demands as the price of maintaining membership in those groups. Such overlapping group member-ship is a seedbed of potential conflict that becomes overt when group members responding to competing group claims, challenge those of the central group."[5] Conformity within a group (such as judges) is based on shared goals and norms. When there is a conflict, "a kind of appeal may take place—an appeal to tradition, 'group unity,' the written or unwritten procedures, constitution, or declaration of purposes of the group, or to some 'higher' moral code."[6]

The small-group dynamics explain why a few judges can halt or materially change a new program even if a majority favors the change. They also suggest that if a new program is seen to further higher values tied to a court's purpose and so is broadly accepted among the judges, the new equilibrium also will be strong. Therefore, significant proposals for change should start with and continue throughout to emphasize the purposes of courts and their relationship to the proposed change. Constitutional and statutory provisions also can be cited. The public's long-standing frustration with courts—justified or not— also can be an ally (see also, section 12.12).

These difficulties in selling changes contribute to the extremely uneven pattern of change in trial courts across a state and, even more, across the nation.[7] Unless in a particular state the supreme court is able and willing to mandate by rule or administrative directive that all courts must make a specific change, each court gets to evaluate it for itself.[8] Some courts embrace the change and some do not, while a third group may modify the change and then adopt it. Patchwork quilts, not smooth, one-color coverlets, are the norm in court administration, whether viewed from within a state or nationally. If one can get a court to buy an idea, another court's solution may be adopted, but like the traveling salesman of old, selling the idea is a new experience with each new customer (court).

There also are important structural impediments outside the judiciary that cannot be overlooked. Courts have suffered in the budget wars from being rela-tively weak in political terms. When funds are needed to introduce a change, courts seldom deal from a position of political strength.[9] Further, courts have had trouble articulating convincing reasons why a strong court system is as important or more important to the community as hungry or poorly schooled children, health and safety issues, and the crisis *du jour* that demands attention and dollars. The philosophical arguments in favor of strong courts normally cannot stand up against a hearing room full of voters angry or fearful about some other issue. Often, a court's request for funds is quite modest compared both to its own budget and to requests made by others and the total funds available. This seldom is sufficient to obtain the funds, however, for two reasons. First, court representatives do not have all the facts about other requests or the funds available, so they cannot make an effective argument about limited cost. In a world where budget decision makers feel validated when they cut a thousand dollars here and three thousand there in a budget of several million (or scores of millions), the argument about only a relatively few dollars being needed often is ignored. The broad lack of understanding among most citizens of basic civics and political science[10] compounds courts' efforts to argue the importance of a strong and improving judiciary. Three arguments can carry the day, although sometimes only after a fight: (1) "the constitution requires it"; (2) we will save you more money than you give us, either in the court's budget or in some other budget you fund; and (3) we will generate enough income to offset the expense, so there is no net cost (and possibly a savings) because of this change.[11]

In locally funded courts, these arguments must be made again and again from community to community. If they are effective in one community, they may be rejected in three others, so even if there are, for example, four courts that want to do the same thing at the same time, local fiscal conditions and the persuasiveness of individual courts determines whether and which courts can change. Even in state-funded systems, the judiciary's desire to implement a change may be stymied by getting no funds or only a fraction of the funds requested. In that situation, either each court gets less and makes its own compromises to stay within the funds available or only some courts can implement the change. In either case, the state ends up with a patchwork reform.

During the two centuries when trial courts were almost all local institutions locally administered and locally oriented, all changes became local issues. If court A developed and implemented something new, even if court A was in the next county or a separate court in the same county, court B was free to adopt it or not. Court B could tweak and improve court A's change and court A could ignore what court B did. A state might have as many ways of handling a specific task or function as there are trial courts. In any given state, both trial court administrators and the state court administrator still struggle with how to introduce and implement reforms to be adopted by all trial courts. Reforms that were adopted by one or more courts across the country in the early 1980s still have to be sold court by court today. Changes that have improved operations in dozens and sometimes hundreds of courts across the country still can be hailed by a "court B" as a major new innovation when court B finally adopts it.[12]

A variance on the difficulty of serial innovation involves the court in which a program or procedure was instituted at one point but it did not become institutionalized and thus disappeared when the champion left the bench or simply faded away over time. The current generation of judicial officers, who were not on the bench when the earlier program was put in place, may be unaware that it existed. At a minimum, the new generation is not steeped in the original rationale, in the planning, and in the results formerly achieved. Caseflow management efforts to reduce delay and jury management efforts to improve juror response to summons or juror care and use in the courthouse are the most prominent examples of these forgotten reforms. Years later, our hypothetical court may again face delay and wish to reduce it or again feel it needs to improve citizen response to jury summons, but effectively starts over because it failed to institutionalize the changes the first time.

These realities need to be addressed at the national level and at the state level. In the last chapter it was proposed that the state leadership set policy goals for all trial courts but let them meet the goals however works best for them. This risks perpetuating solutions devised "one court at a time," but at least all courts would be working toward a common goal at the same time. If a specific program has to be implemented exactly the same way in every trial court, the challenge is immense. Only a few programs and the use of statewide forms require this degree of conformity. Using the "carrot" of new funding to support change can be effective, but the other branches of government might not provide the funds to enable an AOC to make this offer. Federal funding for each implementing trial court plus for a major national training program through the State Justice Institute or another agency has proven effective in the past. Even with federal support, however, the new program will be widely adopted only if the state's leadership sees the reform as something that should be implemented statewide and therefore reinforces the efforts of the federal funding agency. The models used in the 1970s and 1980s to spread new programs broadly across the nation should be reviewed and maybe revived.

At the trial court level, this range of incomplete and unfinished reforms and improvements adds three layers of complexity to a court administrator's job. The first layer is the need to identify and respond to the many possibilities for improvement already implemented by other courts. Every year thousands of courts are introducing maybe dozens of good new ideas and improving perhaps scores of existing programs. Each trial court's leadership has to go through a six-step checklist:

1. Learn of the ideas and changes.
2. Decide if the idea(s) has merit for their court.
3. Set priorities about which new ideas are most important.
4. Determine if the time, staff, and resources exist to implement it/them.
5. Sell the change to the bench, staff, and stakeholders.
6. Implement it/them successfully.

An administrator has a significant number of different improvements and new programs from which to choose. He or she also has to assure that the daily operations are not compromised or overlooked, that key policy makers concur with his or her assessment of need, and that he or she stays within the budget provided.

The second layer of complexity is associated with recurring problems. If a court faces a recurring problem that had been addressed once, in addition to reeducating judges and staff, the leadership team may have to overcome the attitude that the court tried that once and it did not work. In fact, it may have worked but fell into disuse, or it may have worked somewhat and the lessons learned will improve the chances for success this time. People may only remember prior use and the lack of current use and be uninterested in the reasons why. Returning to something that did not work well, or worked but was not institutionalized for whatever reason, sometimes is harder than gaining acceptance of a totally new idea.

The third layer of complexity occurs when a court creates a new approach that is very effective and from which other courts would benefit. How does an administrator get the word out to other courts? After one court alerts others to a better way, how does it find time to respond to the inquiries and maybe on-site visits that will follow from other courts eager to improve?[13]

There are several X factors in the improvement process related to the time needed to put change into place and the additional staff, equipment, or other resources not covered by normal operating budgets. The judges may not see the advantages the administrator sees or may prefer a different change to the one the administrator believes would be most helpful (see chapter 6). Sufficient funding may lag by a year or two. Managing the "meanwhile" between an idea and when it can be fully implemented can be a significant challenge.

The complexities of being proactive should not discourage courts from being so. Further, every improvement, each effort to improve productivity, and each new application of technology need not involve major surgery on a court's operations. Many improvements are incremental and made with relative ease. No court in the nation has done everything that can be done to optimize its capacity to deliver justice and serve the public, so opportunities exist for improvements no matter how many other courts' ideas have been adopted. Plus, staff and judges probably have ideas for further enhancements that no one has tried yet. Whether improvements happen in many courts at one time or court by court over time, there is ample need for and sufficient opportunities to introduce improvements. That is why in section 7.2.2.2, chapter 7, it was suggested that good administrators always should have several ideas "in the bottom drawer" that can be pulled out when the moment is right.

12.3   Outputs, Not Inputs

The publication of the Trial Court Performance Standards in 1990 changed the nature of the discussion about court and judicial administration.[14] The results and consequences of what courts do became the measuring stick for effective and successful courts rather than the number of judges, the number of staff, or how the court organizes itself or its calendars. Although the discussion has changed, management's actions and budget allocations lag far behind.

The need for, value of, and impediments in courts to using data were discussed in section 9.2.11, in chapter 9. Proactive management goes beyond "the data about the work of the court which must *routinely* be considered in making the decisions related to orderly and smooth operations"[15] (emphasis in original), to judging whether or not the desired performance is being achieved by "the application of data, not [based on] on guesswork."[16] It means using at least the performance measures and measuring techniques suggested in CourTools,[17] the ten "core measures" derived from the 75 originally developed in 1990.[18] Courts from time to time also should examine the measures in the 1990 publication of the Trial Court Performance Standards[19] and use those as supplementary measures.[20] There is broad consensus within the judiciary on the appropriateness of the performance goals. It is hard for any court to argue that it should not be seeking to meet those goals. Organizing resources, allocating funding, and measuring whether a court has met those goals are the hard parts. If a court accepts the challenge, however, it will grow both its self-esteem and the esteem of others.

One caveat may be in order. A court cannot focus on only one output measure or goal to determine if a program or the court is meeting its goals.[21] That mistake has been made from time to time when assessing the success or failure of a delay reduction project, particularly in midterm assessments. Because of the complexity of the court system, the numerous actors beyond the court's control, and the inability always to guess in advance how a program will play out, some outcomes are likely to be positive and some less than desired or negative. If only one outcome goal is examined, the program may be considered a success or a failure, whereas a comprehensive examination of the results might suggest the opposite. In real life, no court today is likely to be meeting or exceeding all ten of the core measures identified in CourTools. Nor is a new program likely to succeed in meeting all the goals set for it. If progress or success-but-with-room-to-do-better is the result, that is a good outcome and should point the way to doing better.

Focusing on outcomes will produce better results for the court than orienting budget discussions and staff allocations around whether a department needs one or two new staff members to keep up with its work. The need should be driven by whether one, two, ten, or zero staff will help the court to get closer to meeting its outcome goals. If a new staff position would help the court complete work in a more timely way, but the work is not central to what the court should be doing to achieve desired outcomes, creating that staff position is not good. The questions we ask determine the answers we get. If the questions are formed around the outcomes we seek, the answers will follow naturally and, normally, point in the right direction.

A court does not need to reinvent its entire operation or undertake a zero-based budget exercise to focus on outcomes. It can start with the next budget cycle and with proposals for new projects or programs. Management should require that proposals for new programs contain three elements in addition to a description of the program: (1) an explanation of how the new program will advance one or more of the goals and objectives or the vision of the court (see section 12.6.2); (2) the specific, measurable goals of the program;[22] and (3) the evaluation methodology to be used to determine whether the goals have been achieved. If specific goals are set, the new program may meet them, fall short, or exceed them. If the program falls short, having defined goals allows a more focused discussion of whether the shortfall is critical and means the program is not working or disappointing but not enough to decide the program is not worthwhile. The shortfall and, perhaps, subjective explanations that explain the data may also point to how the program can be improved to enable it to meet the original goals.

12.4   Evaluating Programs and Projects

Proactive management evaluates what it does and whether new and ongoing programs and functions are meeting goals. A focus on outcomes means more than the outcomes one desires from a court. It also assumes one knows the outcomes of new projects or programs so one can evaluate whether they meet their goals and whether they will help the court to move closer to meeting its mission and objectives. The way to do that is to evaluate new programs and projects. Over time, existing programs and functions should be evaluated, as well, to assure they continue to contribute to the court's desired outcomes. "No success ... is 'forever.' Yet it is far more difficult to abandon yesterday's success than it is to reappraise failure.... A success that has outlived its usefulness may, in the end, be more damaging than failure."[23]

Evaluations offer courts a number of positives.

- ■   They test whether goals are being achieved.
- ■   They show everyone involved and those to whom the court is accountable that the effort expended in starting and sustaining the program was/is worthwhile.
- ■   Opportunities are identified to improve or expand programs that are working.

- ■ Changes in staff allocations are supported.
- ■ Justifications for budgetary changes and increases are provided to sustain current budget levels, increase budgets, gain new staff, and justify staff salary increases.
- ■ Justification is provided for changing or terminating a program.
- ■ The focus is kept on overall results rather than anecdotes.
- ■ Public support is gained and retained for both a new program and for the court generally.

There also are risks associated with and impediments to evaluations in a court setting. These often contribute to, if not determine, the common absence of evaluations for new programs.

- ■ Fear that an evaluation may not show positive results leads to stopping the evaluation before it starts.
- ■ Fear that less than stellar or negative results may be used against a judge or all judges in the next election can kill an evaluation being started.
- ■ Concern that if the evaluation uses random assignment to the new process and the current process, and if the new process has a significantly positive or negative impact, parties and judges alike will want to use the new process only or shun it completely before all the data are collected and longer-term results are known; therefore, before–after evaluations are more common but also less powerful in their conclusions. Because courts are to provide justice in individual cases, terminating a failing idea is an acceptable response, but sometimes termination comes too early to be confident that it is the correct response.
- ■ When there are negative unintended consequences or failure of a program to meet its goals, the evaluator may be blamed, not the program design or weaknesses in implementation.
- ■ When a strong judicial champion favors a program even in the face of a less than positive evaluation, the evaluator and data are pitted against the advocate with the court's leaders often put in the middle.
- ■ Similarly, a positive evaluation does not assure continuation of a program if it has not gained political support inside or outside the court, or both.[24]

Too often, judges, in particular, or senior managers may have an idea or hear that a program in another court works wonderfully and convince the court's leadership to try it. Clear goals are not set, data are not kept, and a formal evaluation is not undertaken, particularly if there was an evaluation in the other court. After a period of time, the judge, possibly supported by other participants, declares it a success and it continues, or says it was not a good program and it is abandoned.[25]

One of the more famous examples of the phenomenon of declaring victory is the "Scared Straight" program started by a judge in New Jersey. Juveniles, originally those under the jurisdiction of the juvenile court but later teenagers in high school with no juvenile court record, met with prison inmates who advised the juveniles of all the terrible things that had happened to the inmates as a result of their criminal activity and being convicted. These meetings were supposed to scare the juveniles so much that they would not commit crimes. The logic of the program is appealing. Early reports were very positive. The judge gave speeches to other judges around the country and newspaper and magazine articles praised the program and encouraged its extension. It was adopted by a number of courts, schools, and correctional institutions across the country. It was not rigorously evaluated for several years, however. When an academic evaluation finally was completed, the conclusion was that the program had no discernable long-term impact on the juveniles' criminal activities.[26] To that point, anecdotes plus the enthusiasm and persuasiveness of the original judge carried the day. The program may have helped the self-esteem of the inmates, but it did not meet its goals. Juveniles were not "scared straight," they just were entertained. Some studies indicated some juveniles were harmed.[27] Too many court programs have developed and been spread from court to court in similar fashion. Some of them may have been wonderful programs that achieved their goals, but some surely were not.

A positive example of the value of evaluations involves drug courts. The creation of hundreds of drug courts followed a number of positive evaluations of their efficacy and the fiscal savings they produced. There even have been annual evaluations of the evaluations, done in an effort both to share the results more broadly and to add some rigor to the process.[28] A few evaluations were relatively superficial and many asked different questions or studied different elements of similar programs, so cross-comparisons were difficult. There was enough commonality, however, and the results were sufficiently consistent, that people felt comfortable trying drug courts and other problem-solving courts themselves.

The reason drug courts and some of the other early problem-solving courts were evaluated with such regularity is that most were started with grant funding and an evaluation was a condition of the grant. Grants for new programs normally will carry evaluation requirements. Courts fall down when they start a new program on their own without grant funding and when the grant funding ends.[29] It is here that proactive courts lead the way: they set goals for all new projects and programs and then evaluate them to determine if they meet the goals. Periodically, they return to existing programs to determine if they remain effective.

Although listed above, one positive of doing evaluations should be emphasized: it can show staff and judicial officers that their efforts are worthwhile. Too often staff and judicial officers are asked to work extra hard to put a new program in place and collect data on how the program works, but the data are not shared with them. All of the staff and all of the judges who work on a new program are curious about how it is going. If they do not get the feedback, they may lose commitment and energy. If the data show the desired results have not been obtained, everyone can examine them and possibly identify ways to modify the program to improve it. It becomes a courtwide effort that not only will help it succeed, but also help to institutionalize good programs.

It often is easier to say an evaluation should occur than it is to find someone who can and will do it and do it at a price the court can afford. The good news is that not every evaluation needs to meet the standards of a doctoral thesis. Every evaluation requires some investment of time and money, but if most of the data can be gleaned from operational data already in the court's computerized information system and ad hoc reports can be obtained from the system, the investment of time becomes more manageable. Some evaluations done with limited funding lack refinements that might be nice to have, but this is an instance where some timely information can be much better than no information or information that comes two years after a pilot effort ends.[30]

The Detroit Recorder's Court, now merged with the Circuit Court of Wayne County, used to have a professor at a local college on an annual retainer. When the court's leadership had a special study or evaluation to be done, they would call the professor, he would assign some students to help, and within a relatively short time they had a quick but effective answer to an ad hoc question about case processing or an evaluation of an ongoing program. Courts that have institutions of higher learning nearby can use this resource. Sometimes students can undertake a small evaluation for course credit, so the cost to the court is nothing or very limited. If courts can make arrangements with local institutions of higher learning for interns, or even with high schools for honors program students, interns can design and conduct evaluations. From a cost and effectiveness standpoint, it would be best if a court could hire college or advanced-degree graduates who are interested in courts, law, statistics, or political or social science and use them to do special studies while they also learn how courts work. Some large urban courts have a researcher employee or even a small research unit. These courts often have relatively more resources than smaller courts and also some economies of scale in their staff operations that enable them to free up funds for this type of position. Smaller courts have to be more creative, but the absence of funds for a PhD researcher should not end the search for evaluators.

The goal is first to instill the mentality that new projects and programs should be evaluated. (Eventually, existing programs should be reviewed as well, but it is easiest to start with new programs.) Once that idea takes hold, then many bright minds within the court can be put to work to decide how best to undertake any single evaluation or to build an internal capacity to do evaluations in house.

12.5 Assuring Data Quality and Using Data to Determine Management Decisions

Focusing on outcomes and undertaking evaluations of current and new operations both require accurate data. Proactive management assures that data entry is done in a timely way and is accurate. It also assures that the software that generates reports using those data does so properly so reports can be trusted. This is achieved by internal programming edits to catch obvious entry errors such as date or number transposition or a date for step five in the processing of a case that is earlier than the date for step one. It tracks data entry by person and reviews reports on the number and type of mistakes made for each data entry operator. Errors are reviewed not for punishment but to determine if the errors are the result of a programming or tabulation error or a lack of or deficiency in training. If the latter, is it a training need for everyone or just for one or two? Whichever it is, the needed training is provided. If there are programming errors, they are corrected. There should be no excuse for operations-based data not to be accurate. It is management's responsibility to see that it is. (If summary and ad hoc reports are not being generated from operations-based data, that would be the first change to be made; the current case management information software has to be abandoned in favor of a system that pulls needed data from operational entries and allows for ad hoc reports to be generated based on queries.)

Peter Drucker argues forcefully for the value of data to management, but also cautions that data be used to help individuals to do better, not to punish or manipulate the staff. Needless to say, a court's leaders should not seek to use data to manipulate or punish judges.[31]

> We … know that people can control and correct performance if given the information [about their own performance], even if neither they nor the supplier of information truly understands what has to be done and how….
>
> The information the worker needs must satisfy the requirements of effective information…. It must be timely. It must be relevant. It must be operational. It must focus on his job. Above all, it must be *his* tool. Its purpose must be self-control, rather than control of others, let alone manipulation. (emphasis in original)

An anecdote from my experience confirms what Drucker is saying. A small mid-western state with a centralized information system generated a by-trial-judge list monthly showing each case older than two years. Then, for each case, the judge had to indicate the next action date, and what was scheduled to happen on that action date, and return it to the administrative office. (If there were no action date, the judge had to explain why.) Reports of cases that were really old—based on AOC staff's judgment—were shown to the chief justice, who often called the trial judge to encourage disposition of that case and to reinforce the need for timely disposition of all cases. When the report was first used, many judges had multiple pages of cases. After a few years, most judges had only one or two cases. I asked if there were any follow-up by AOC staff comparing consecutive reports to see if the next action date had been met and what had happened. I was told, "No, judges do not want to have to keep explaining what is happening in old cases and, especially, to get a call from the chief justice. They get rid of the cases on their own. We just file the reports."

Data are important to help structure management issues and identify possible solutions. Many people in courts, staff and judges alike, know why a program or task is not working as it should. Sometimes they share their opinions with management and sometimes they do not, but they seldom doubt their conclusion(s). As complex organizations and as entities in which the professionals (the judges) seldom meet and share experiences informally, courts are similar to the elephant in the story of the blind men and the elephant. Each person has a different opinion about what it is he or she is touching because each is "seeing" a different part of the elephant. So it is with judges and staff. Case processing staff may have a broader view because they may see cases from several or even all judges, whereas the judges and their immediate support staff see only their own work. Because of their myopia, data that look at the entire elephant are especially important. Sometimes, the anecdotal views turn out correctly to identify the problem and the way to address it. At least as often—in my view, more often—the anecdotes are wrong or only partially validated. The data show something different.

When the data are shared and some anecdotes are not supported, the validity of the data normally is questioned, particularly if a sampling technique was used.[32] Once the group accepts the validity of the data, having data does three things. First, it changes the focus of the discussion to the data and away from personalities or institutional jealousies or conflicts. Second, the data highlight any differences in processing by various judges or staff that are not as clear when the discussion is based on anecdotes. (The differences should be acknowledged without casting blame or aspersions.) Third, they facilitate a discussion about the real causes of the problem and often point the way to solutions, or at least to one or two possibilities around which test solutions can be built and tried.

This is just one way that data can facilitate management. Summary reports also can serve as diagnostics, warning of a problem that merits further attention and review. If bonuses or performance-based rewards can be provided to staff, data will help identify the court's best performing staff, as opposed to those who are most liked or who are closest to a particular judge. Data can guide management to areas that need more resources and that are overresourced. "Achievement is never possible except against specific, limited, already defined targets, in business as well as in a service institution. Only if targets are defined can resources be allocated to their attainment, priorities and deadlines set, and somebody be held accountable for results."[33]

Reports are needed at two levels: the macro level that provides an overview of how the entire court is doing and the micro level, reports for each judge about his or her own cases and calendars. Macro reports should go to the court's leadership; some may be provided to all judges and staff supervisors. Micro reports go only to each judge so he or she can use those reports to guide his or her performance. If there are problems, the court's leadership can examine an individual judge's reports, but ordinarily it is not necessary or helpful to do so.

One mistake often made is to overwhelm people, particularly judges, with data. Most judges are not statisticians and do not want to be. Almost all judges when given data look first for their own numbers. Then they look at where they stand vis-à-vis their colleagues. Courts that have the most effective management also discuss the reports and what they show at each judges' meeting. The key is to keep the first level of reports at a high, summary level. Whenever possible, charts and graphs should be used instead of or in addition to tables. Someone who wants and needs only a quick overview of what the data show can get it faster and possibly better by looking at graphs and charts rather than at tables.

Both in the public and private sectors, the term *dashboard* reports has become popular. Like the dials on the dashboard of a car, the first-level reports should focus on only a few key items and should be as easily read as a street stop light, as being good (green): "we may have an issue (yellow)," or "we have a problem (red)."[34] The statistical systems that produce these dashboard reports allow users to "drill down" to lower levels and greater detail to gain greater understanding. Most judges need their own micro reports and the key dashboard reports. The leadership needs the dashboard reports. All the judges and senior managers should have access to the more detailed data, but ordinarily only the chief judge, administrator, and a few key senior managers would use it. The other and final thing to remember about any predesigned reports, in contrast to ad hoc reports, is that they can only be diagnostic. If they reveal or suggest a problem, more study and evaluation will be needed, which may involve more detailed reports, some ad hoc reports, or special studies of files.

For all the institutional reasons cited throughout this book, it is difficult for a court administrator to inculcate an ethos of seeking data and then using it to guide management decisions. It is necessary, however, and thus should be a goal of proactive management.

12.6 Planning, Mission and Vision Statements, and Environmental Scanning

Proactive management thinks long-term, engages in strategic planning to bring the court closer to the long-term vision, and scans the environment as an aid to planning. It agrees on a mission and vision statement that not only can unite those within the court, but also advise citizens in a few sentences how the court sees its role in the community.

12.6.1 Long-Term and Strategic Planning

Yogi Berra, Baseball Hall of Fame catcher and manager famous for his malapropisms, once said: "You've got to be careful if you don't know where you're going 'cause you might not get there."[35] Berra's observation is why courts need to plan for the future. If they do not plan, they may not get to where they want to be. Another sports figure, hockey great Wayne Gretsky, said he was successful because he did not skate to where the puck was, but to where the puck was going to be. Gretsky's observation is why courts need strategic planning. If you know where you want to be, you can develop strategies to take you there and avoid obstacles and pitfalls. Yes, things may change and require an adjustment to the strategies. If a court does not plan and set out a strategy for how to achieve its plan, however, it will bob and bounce along like a fallen leaf on a river's rapids. It will be subject to all the external political and social forces and personalities that will sweep up and change courts in ways that may be very undesirable. Having a plan does not assure that a court will achieve the hoped-for end, but without a plan, it surely will fail.

By and large, judges, and therefore courts, have not seen much advantage in planning, believing that courts are subject to the whims of people who file cases, of the legislature, and of budget makers in the two other branches. Many judges have felt and many still may feel that little is gained and a lot of time can be wasted trying to plan for an unknown future over which courts have little or no control. "Courts engage in planning if they are forced to do so by some external pressure that makes planning inevitable [such as a new courthouse, a major change in technology, or court unification].... Judges prefer to react rather than initiate."[36] In response, consider this question, posed by two business professors in their book about managing significant changes: "Is it reasonable for us to decide that while our societies and businesses are being completely reshaped, we have the luxury of maintaining traditional habits, behaviors, strategies, and priorities as we attempt to guide our organizations through the unfamiliar turbulence going on around us?"[37] I submit that the answer must be "no."

Despite this resistance, there were two waves of planning in the 20th century: in the 1970s in response to funding initiatives by the U.S. Department of Justice's Law Enforcement Assistance Administration for "criminal justice planning;" and in the 1980s looking ahead to and beyond the new millennium. Both of these efforts involved long-range planning rather than strategic planning, which has a shorter horizon, usually three to five years. Both of these efforts produced some interesting and challenging documents in a number of states, but little or no action directed to achieving the changes outlined in the plans.[38] The other characteristic many of these plans shared was that although the plans in the 1980s were to address 20 or more years down the road, they focused largely on the issues and problems current when they were written. It was hard for those in the judicial branch (in contrast to citizens who participated) to scan the environment and think about entirely new challenges and issues—and significant new ways to address them—that might arise 20 years hence but were not yet beginning to materialize.

The effort to introduce strategic planning has been more successful. There may be two reasons. First, the timeframe is shorter and thus more manageable than trying to envision a court system 20, 50, or more years from now. For the most part, a court is looking at issues recognizable today and setting strategies to avoid a near-term problem or achieve a near-term goal. Second, judges and senior managers seem to take more readily to the development of relatively short-term strategies than to envisioning a world that may not exist.

The fact that many judges may not embrace planning as a discipline does not absolve court leadership of the responsibility. One of the core competencies for courts' leaders developed by the National Association for Court Management (NACM) is "Visioning and Strategic Planning." As stated in the introduction to that competency discussion, "Visioning and strategic planning help courts and court leaders avoid isolation, create and maintain momentum for change, and improve day-to-day court management."[39] The discussion continues to identify six reasons why court leaders invest in visioning and strategic planning. Three are particularly compelling:[40]

1. A strategic plan develops priorities and goals that are clear and accepted throughout the court and justice system.
2. A vision of the future, the long-range strategic plan, and its implementation help ensure continuity when the leadership of the court changes.
3. Strategic planning supports a positive response to public demand for increased court accountability.

The third point should be part of a two-way dialogue with the community. As the Core Competency discussion notes, the planning process and the promulgation of a plan enhances court-community communication, particularly if the court seeks community input into problems and issues it sees and the future citizens envision for the court. A well-conceived and shared plan increases public understanding of and satisfaction with the court and the justice system.[41]

One of the most important traits of leaders (see section 7.2.2.1, chapter 7) is the ability to form a new vision of an organization, work with others so it becomes their vision too, and then oversee attainment of that vision. In broad terms, these are the components of a strategic plan. In developing a strategic plan, a court's leadership does not do it alone and, indeed, should not do it alone. It is a collaborative effort involving not only the court family but also key stakeholders.

Society at large is changing very rapidly. The pace of change is not likely to slow any time soon. Constitutional and statutory law assures that courts will not be eliminated no matter how society changes, but some in courts have assumed that courts can resist change and survive intact. Where the use of courts is not legally mandated, this assumption is not well founded. Arthur Vanderbilt, while he was President of the American Bar Association, noted the removal of many adjudicative matters from courts to administrative agencies.[42] Administrative agencies' jurisdiction has grown over the years since and the discussion continues in 2006. Today there are proposals for "health courts," which are not courts but administrative tribunals to deal with medical malpractice cases because some in Congress and society at large do not like the size of the awards that plaintiffs can obtain in courts.[43] In the 1980s and 1990s, expansion in the use of private judges and alternative dispute resolution organizations to resolve a wide range of civil and some family law matters also should have been a reminder that courts need to adapt or others will marginalize them. The way to adapt is to strategically plan a desired future and work toward it. If proactive management does not do this, external rather than internal forces could shape the nature of courts.

12.6.2 Mission and Vision Statements

Mission statements define a court's purpose, its fundamental values, qualities such as providing all litigants with due process, equal treatment and access, and independence and impartiality. The core values remain and sustain organizations regardless of their current vision of the future or today's challenges. "People in the organization must share a 'center' of core values and priorities around which diversity circles like planets around a fixed star.... In whatever way the center is fashioned, it must engender a sense of ownership, agreement, and commitment throughout the organization—and generate a deep mindfulness of the organization's purpose."[44] The centrality of a mission statement also is emphasized by Ronald Stupak, who reminds leaders to "preserve core values, accentuate the power of positive purpose.... [Leaders] never, ever allow mission to become subordinate to operations, fund raising, or egocentric hubris."[45]

Most trial courts and state court systems have adopted mission statements, some of which are excellent. No effort will be made here to reproduce samples. One reminder might be offered to any court that has not yet adopted a mission statement or is considering amending its statement, however. Most mission statements talk in terms of resolving disputes and criminal charges consistent with the key qualities mentioned above and doing so in a timely way. Some are very tightly written while others are longer paragraphs. Whatever their style, they share two qualities. First, it is hard to put them on a letterhead or business card. Second, judges often are the authors; the writing style is consistent with the style of those legally trained. Most people are not legally trained. Therefore, the mission statements do not speak readily to the general public.

At one level, any difficulty an average citizen may have following and understanding a mission statement is not critical, since mission statements articulate values that drive the organization and around which people within the organization can rally. Law and legal principles drive the purposes of courts, so a mission statement cannot ignore or avoid them. At another level, however, courts need to think more of marketing themselves to the public. It might help to ask a teacher or newspaper writer or editor to review the language used to improve readability for the average citizen. Also, some thought might be given to including broad goals or purposes of courts that transcend resolving individual cases. For example, courts:

- Help to protect and sustain democracy
- Protect, value, and improve people's lives
- Protect society and individual citizens from wrongs committed by people and by government
- Protect and preserve American values as expressed in our U.S. and state constitutions and laws
- Protect citizens against arbitrary and unlawful government actions, criminal activities, and wrongs committed contrary to civil laws.

Some mission statements seek to convey these ideas; others might consider the inclusion of these concepts. Some trial courts post their mission and vision statements on the walls of public corridors, entry areas, and staff work areas. Many more do not. A mission statement not only should bind and inspire within the court family, but also be a statement of purpose for the public. A court that takes the time to develop a mission statement—and done well, it will take some time—should share it with the public, first in a press release, then on public-area walls, and, if possible, on the court's letterhead.

NACM's Core Competencies' discussion of Visioning and Strategic Planning provides a good summary of visioning and a vision statement:[46]

> Visioning is a creative, collaborative process that asks court leaders and their justice partners to articulate a preferred future: what the court will look like and be doing when performing at its very best. A vision statement, which is the outcome of a visioning process, describes that future. Research suggests that vision statements are most effective when they "tell a story" of a new reality—a lucid and detailed preferred

future. Effective vision statements elevate and compel action because they are both bold and inspirational and believable and achievable.

Most people do not spend a lot of time thinking about the role of courts in government or society, including people who work in the courts. The latter are too involved in the day-to-day details to step back and think about the policy and social implications of the institution of which they are a part. Yet, there is a sense among almost all court staff that what they do is important, relative to both the manufacturing plant in town and the deli on the corner, and relative to the other components of government. Courts have a strong message to impart and can create an exciting vision of how they will fill their roles in the future. They are poised for another wave of innovation in the delivery of service. Developing and promulgating a vision statement allows courts, together with their stakeholders, to define their aspirations.

As with mission statements, vision statements should be shared broadly, within the court family (on laminated cards, if brief enough), within the justice community, with leaders of the other branches of government, and with the public. They also should be posted in a public area of the courthouse and in appropriate staff locations.[47]

Vision statements inspire, but they also should be management tools. A vision "tells people what's expected of them. And that makes it a lot easier to tell them when they're not meeting expectations. You can discuss their conduct and their performance in terms of the vision."[48] This point ties back to the discussion in section 12.3, where it was suggested that the court administrator ask those who propose new programs or projects how they advance the court's goals and vision. An administrator who wishes to reinforce the importance of reaching the court's vision should make bringing the court closer to its vision one of the elements in job performance evaluations of senior management. The chief judge should hold the administrator to the same standard, as well. Choices among several ideas for budget requests should be settled by measuring each request against the court's vision and deciding which is most likely to help the court achieve its vision. Articulating a vision should not be an exercise to pacify the court administrator or the state supreme court, but to establish a road map for the court's administration for the next several years. It makes little sense and becomes a waste of time to struggle to articulate a vision of the future, post it on the wall (or put it in the annual report), and then ignore it when setting budget priorities and evaluating job performance. For that reason, it is important that all judges understand what a vision statement is, why it is important for them to be involved and take the exercise seriously, and how it will be used.

If a vision statement is to be used for job performance evaluation and budget decisions, it cannot be too vague; it also should focus on outcomes, not inputs. One example of the difference may be sufficient. Black and Decker, a company that makes power tools, is reported to have said, "Our customers want quarter inch holes, not quarter inch drills." Courts' customers want a full and fair hearing, an opportunity to present their evidence and position, prompt resolution of their cases, a neutral arbiter, and courteous treatment, among other outcome-oriented elements of having to be in court. These ideas take us back to performance standards and the use of data. They all are related and they all will improve courts' service to all stakeholders and the perception of courts among those stakeholders.

12.6.3 Scanning the Environment

Traditionally, "environmental scanning" has meant surveying broad social, economic, political, and demographic trends to determine their nature, to consider how they might affect an organization, and then to plan how to prepare for the time when their impact is more imminent. That type of scanning is helpful occasionally, but is more useful for the long-range planning attempted by courts in the 1980s that was only marginally successful. As used here, environmental scanning is more limited and immediate. It requires that a court's leadership constantly survey the government, private, and nonprofit sectors to explore what they are doing that might apply in a court setting. Plus, what near-term social, economic, political, and demographic trends (three to five years) will or might affect courts and what can be done to use them to the court's advantage or to avoid their impact? A current example is the challenges and the opportunities offered by the aging of the Baby Boomer generation. If one thinks of the innovation curve, where there are innovators, early adopters, early majority, late majority, and laggards,[49] very few judges and court administrators are innovators and only a few more are early adopters. Courts usually pick up on ideas late in the early majority or in the late majority timeframe, although some clearly are laggards. For reasons that are discussed in section 12.11.1, that characteristic of courts and their leaders may not be all bad. In the context of planning, however, court leaders should seek to identify ideas and trends earlier in the innovation cycle. It does not mean that they have to become early adopters. It only means that they try to become aware of trends earlier so there is time to consider their meaning and potential impact on or application in courts and to devise possible responses. It also gives them the chance to be early adopters if that will benefit the court. Further, it means they try to be more alert to current economic conditions, management ideas, and human resource issues and responses in order to broaden the pool of ideas from which they can draw when they evaluate how to respond to issues facing the court. "If we are responsible leaders, we're constantly scanning the environment for changes and for hints of how it will change in the future."[50] One of the qualities specifically identified for court administrators in chapter 7 (cited for leaders of the corporate world, as well[51]), is curiosity. Curiosity should be the impetus for constant scanning of the environment for proactive management. "Discovery consists of seeing what everybody has seen and thinking what nobody [yet] has thought."[52]

12.7 Identifying and Adopting Best Practices from Other Courts

While scanning the environment, proactive management looks for best practices adopted by other courts and seeks to implement as many as appeal and can be accommodated by the court's staff and budget. A number of state judiciaries have been pressing the idea of "best practices" within courts. The National Center for State Courts established a Best Practices Institute in 2000 to identify and further what are regarded as best practices across the country. Best practices are new or materially improved programs, processes, procedures, or approaches that increase productivity, save significant sums of money, or bring a court materially closer to achieving its mission. According to the National Center's Best Practices Institute, best practices also have been documented and evaluated. A best practice may be a new form or a new way to handle fine payments, but to be widely adopted by other courts, it is more likely that it is something that has a relatively significant impact on the initiating court and early adopters. "The Institute assumes that there may be several best practices to reach a desired end and does not adhere to a 'one-size-fits-all' approach."[53] Best practices also will change over time, as more is learned, as new programs are developed, and as older programs are refined and changed.

The idea of seeking and implementing particularly successful practices of others grew out of the quality management movement in the 1980s and 1990s. It makes sense to learn how others do things better and seek to implement those ideas in your organization without reinventing the wheel each time (see section 12.2). Proactive management seeks and is happy to adopt good ideas from other courts.

12.8 Problem-Solving Courts

According to one source, in 2005 there were more than 2,000 problem-solving courts across the nation;[54] there were none in 1988. The first of what now are called problem-solving courts started in Miami, Florida, in 1989.

The basic approach of problem-solving courts is described in section 4.2, chapter 4. There are five basic elements: "(1) immediate intervention; (2) nonadversarial adjudication; (3) hands-on judicial involvement; (4) treatment programs with clear rules and structured goals; and (5) a team approach that brings together the judge, prosecutor, defense counsel, treatment provider, and correctional staff."[55] Problem-solving courts also ask the judge to assume a new role. No longer does a judge declare a sentence and then pass the case off to corrections for incarceration, to court staff to collect a fine, or to a probation officer. In problem-solving courts, the judge is heavily involved once someone submits to the court's jurisdiction. The judge uses the power of the court to encourage as well as compel compliance with the conditions to which those subject to the process have agreed. The judge praises and supports but also demonstrates there are consequences for failing to do what is required if someone slips. The judge also actively works with public and private agencies that deliver the needed social services. Some see problem-solving courts as a desirable turning away from the adversarial process to embrace an outcome perspective that looks beyond a case to the defendant (or family members) and seeks the best long-term outcome for each person. This approach has been shown to be successful for those who complete the process,[56] for government through savings across several components of the justice system, and for society at large. That is why the Conference of Chief Justices (CCJ) and the Conference of State Court Administrators (COSCA) twice have endorsed the principles and methods of problem-solving courts.[57] They have called upon courts to "take steps ... to expand and better integrate the principles and methods of well-functioning drug courts into ongoing court operations" and encouraged "the broad integration over the next decade of the principles and methods employed in the problem-solving courts into the administration of justice...."[58] Yet, others see problem-solving courts as placing courts in roles with which they are unfamiliar and for which they are not equipped.[59] "[M]ore of the resources of the judiciary are going to be committed to supervising and providing such services, a fact which has large implications for our ability to handle our more traditional work in the old relaxed manner."[60] The extensive adoption of problem-solving courts across the nation and the numerous social issues to which the techniques have been applied, together with the CCJ and COSCA endorsements, suggest that problem-solving courts will continue their growth for some time.

Problem-solving courts are another area of intersection between judicial administration and court administration. Court administrators cannot set up problem-solving courts and cannot keep them from being set up. Whether or not a court establishes a problem-solving court is a uniquely judicial decision made in conjunction with prosecutors, the defense bar, sometimes the family law bar (when family courts are involved), and the social service (and sometimes educational) institutions with which the judges will work.

Court administration has several supporting roles to play, however. First, court administration can advise those who are making the decision what the operational impacts will be, including how such a court will affect workflow, possibly the court's information system, and staffing allocations or the need for new staff.[61]

Second, once the decision is made, court administration has to assure that the institutional support is provided. Third, if a new staff position is created, court administration has to handle the human resources side (job description, pay level, advertising, and selection) and assure that needed funds for compensation, furniture, and equipment are available. Fourth, court administration needs to review calendars and either itself make the needed adjustments or assist the judge(s) in reviewing existing calendars so that cases can be reallocated as needed. Fifth, court administration also should work with the planning group to assist in the formulation of goals for the program. Sixth, court administration should seek to assure that there is an evaluation, assist in finding a qualified evaluator, and then assist with design of the evaluation plan. The evaluation should parallel other evaluations in other courts as much as possible, both to add to the community's knowledge base and to enable some comparison between these other programs and the court's. Seventh, court administration should at least attend the post-implementation oversight committee's meetings (preferably as a member of the committee) to inform the committee of any operational concerns that might arise. Finally, court administration needs to assure that staff and the responsible judicial officer(s) have the training they need to undertake this new project.

Two elements of court administration's responsibilities deserve further discussion, because to date the literature on problem-solving courts has not recognized these matters to any degree. The first is the components of the program that are evaluated. An excellent book that endorses problem-solving courts succinctly reminds courts, "to ask hard questions about the impact of case processing on victims, offenders, and communities. This includes documenting the safety of victims, the number of offenders who are rearrested, and local perceptions of neighborhood quality of life."[62] Other common evaluation issues relate to jail and prison days (and dollars) saved, number and types of relapses, work history, impact on the family of the offender, and, for women drug addicts, number of babies born drug free and the cost savings for society these births represent. In juvenile drug courts, school days missed, disciplinary matters, and grades also are examined. Evaluations almost always are preprogram and postprogram. All of the areas of evaluation just mentioned are legitimate; the largely positive results across all these elements have been the major reason that problem-solving courts have been adopted so widely. The savings in correctional costs, in law enforcement costs, and in improved health for offenders and new babies, together with many graduates working and keeping jobs they could not have held previously, virtually guarantee a positive cost-benefit analysis (see note 56).

Court administration has let itself down by not insisting that evaluations also examine the impact of these programs on the court itself. There are a number of questions affecting court operations that either are simply not asked by the academic or law enforcement-oriented evaluations or by court administration itself.

- What is the judge's workload in a problem-solving court and how does it compare to the workload of a judge handling similar cases but not in a problem-solving fashion?
- The same question should be asked for courtroom and operations support staff.
- How, if at all, does workload change over time in courtrooms and for operations support staff that continue to use traditional processes?
- How much time do problem-solving judges spend outside normal court hours on community liaison and education?
- What percent of the total workload of the court is contributed by each phase in problem-solving cases?
- How much time, if any, is saved by directly involved staff as a consequence of familiarity with cases and parties in problem-solving courts?
- How much added time is spent on out-of-court "team" and "progress" meetings?
- How critical are the out-of-court team and progress meetings to success?
- What skills, if any, do staff in problem-solving courts need that are not needed by other court staff?
- Can those skills be purchased at the same cost as comparably classified court staff or do they cost more?
- What happens to the program when the original judge and the second judge are replaced?
- Did community groups and other government agencies support these programs because they could afford to in the flush economy of the late 1990s, or because they recognize and value the benefits for clients and their organizations even in a tight economy?

The above questions are important for at least four reasons. The first is the obvious one of documenting added workload for problem-solving court personnel. Second, courts should know the extent of offsetting workload savings, or their absence, in other courtrooms. Third, if the evaluations remain generally positive regarding clients and society, is there a net cost to courts that needs to be recognized and addressed, a net cost saving, or no courtwide workload and cost impact? If there are net costs for courts, these should be identified and addressed. The last two questions above address whether a court and the broader community institutionalize the problem-solving court, a critical issue if, as seems to be the case, problem-solving courts are a new paradigm and the court faces budget pressures.

The second element of concern for courts regarding problem-solving courts is hinted at by the two evaluation questions regarding the type and cost of staff needed for problem-solving courts. Because these questions have not been raised systematically, one can only speculate, but there is some likelihood that at least those who serve as coordinators with the outside agencies should have different backgrounds from the usual court employee. It is likely that a social work or psychology or even an education background would be helpful. Strong people and coordination skills and an ability to handle a lot of details will be necessary. These positions may evolve into a professional or quasi-professional status that may create a need for higher pay, and, thus, create a need for a budget increase. At the moment, court administrators and their human resource staff need to monitor the situation. The local labor market may affect the answer in different areas. Based on conversations with some court administrators whose courts have problem-solving courts, it seems that problem-solving courts may require a position upgrade for staff directly supporting the judge.

Problem-solving courts may be regarded as mission critical by some judges and courts. There is no doubt they are effective for certain types of cases and seem to be having a positive impact on their communities. Their value does not yet make them mission critical, however. Problem-solving courts challenge the traditional approach of adjudicating cases by focusing more on the entire person and circumstances rather than the initiating case. They challenge the concept of how courts achieve justice and, indeed, the current concept of justice itself. And they challenge the idea of doing individual justice in *individual cases*. A strong argument can be made that courts always have used the therapeutic approach used in problem-solving courts, just not for the case types to which it is applied now and not with the judicial involvement in the postadjudication processing that one finds in problem-solving courts. Problem-solving courts, either as they exist in 2006 or on an even broader scale, say of ten or 20 years hence, may result in either a redefinition of, or amendment to the purposes of courts. At this point, however, they remain one tool among many being used by only a fraction of all trial judges on a fraction of the caseload. (If there are 2,000 problem-solving courts, there probably are no more than 3,000 judges presiding over those courts. There were over 37,000 trial court judges as of 2003.) Therefore, if a court has to absorb significant cuts in its budget, problem-solving courts should not yet be deemed to be mission critical. That does not mean they must be abandoned, however. The funding authorities might well look at the broader picture and provide the extra funds the court needs to keep operating its problem-solving courts in order to achieve the governmentwide savings that problem-solving courts provide. ("The leadership role open to the courts is justifiable solely on financial grounds."[63]) If that argument is made and accepted by the funding authority, that is a good result. Absent this type of trade-off by the funding authorities, however, courts responsible for absorbing cuts within the confines of their own budgets cannot yet deem problem-solving courts to be mission critical.

12.9   Refining Caseflow Management

Proactive management makes excellent caseflow management a core value of the court. Again, the specifics of exemplary caseflow management can be obtained in the sources identified in note 3, chapter 9. In making caseflow management a core operating priority, proactive management assures the following:[64]

- Institutionalization of the concept of court control of the pace of litigation for all case types.
- Constant attention to achieving the same or better levels of justice sooner.[65]
- An understanding of and commitment by all judges that individual justice in individual cases guides caseflow management decisions in specific cases, not time standards or a perceived need for disposition totals.
- Differentiation in the handling of different types of cases within the broad case categories of felonies, misdemeanors, general civil, summary civil, family, probate, juvenile, and traffic, with the calendar type (master, individual, or hybrid), the expected steps leading to disposition, and early mandatory discovery tailored to the case type.
- Overall case processing time standards supplemented by intermediate time goals selected to assure meeting the overall time goals.[66]
- Separate case processing time goals for whatever problem-solving courts the court operates.
- Time standards for postdisposition matters, with the standards and processing differentiated by case type and type of matter.
- Several means of resolving civil and family disputes and some criminal charges are used (traditional adversary process, arbitration, mediation, minitrials), with cases sent to the process most appropriate for each case, together with the capacity to move cases among processes and a formal trial before a judge or jury as the final choice.
- Firm commitment to the credibility of assigned dates for both hearings and trials (there is no such thing as a "first" date).
- Management of trial time, balancing parties' right to present their cases fully with a need to assure they focus their cases to narrow issues and to avoid unnecessary and duplicative evidence, thereby not wasting the time and funds of all involved in the trial process.
- Macro and micro statistical reports providing a full picture of the pending, active caseload and the cases that have been disposed, with individual "early warning" reports for each trial judge identifying cases assigned to the judge that are close to missing a preset checkpoint in case processing.

- ■ Discussion at each judges' meeting of the court's case management performance using the macro statistical reports.
- ■ Key macro statistics are shared regularly with all staff.
- ■ A bench-bar-citizens committee (or one for each major case type) that oversees caseflow management and offers suggestions for refinements and any needed new rules or rule amendments.
- ■ Orientation materials for new judges about why the court places a high value on strong caseflow management and the basic approaches all judges are to take.
- ■ Orientation materials for new staff covering the same topics as the judges' orientation materials but directed to staff's needs.
- ■ Continuing education for all judges and staff regarding caseflow management.
- ■ Support training for attorneys on how to manage cases effectively within their offices.
- ■ Sharing of both its goals and its performance with the public and the other branches of government.

It is easy for courts to continue to do whatever they are doing regarding caseflow management. It is harder to decide to assert (or reassert) the court's control of the pace of litigation and to reduce whatever delay exists in the processing of each major case type. It is hardest to keep that focus and to sustain the commitment to exercise judicial control and assure that cases do not require more calendar time for disposition than needed to assure justice in individual cases.

All the pressure on judges is to accept delay. Requests for delay happen daily and in many cases. Often the reason for a request sounds plausible. It is hard to determine which requests further justice in the individual case, which flow from a lack of attention and preparation, and which are needed because of game playing designed either to induce delay or to drive up costs. Judges who are elected periodically do not want to antagonize the bar by being unduly strict about continuances.[67] The court has to counter this daily pressure by reinforcing judges' (and staff's) resolve both institutionally and individually, showing them with data and their colleagues' advice and support that employing strong and effective caseflow management helps both litigants and the court. Proactive management does all it can to provide that assurance and to sustain the court's shared commitment.

The bar at large will give up its power over case progress only with great reluctance and a sustained fight.[68] This resistance of many in the bar can lead some judges—particularly those fearful of the next election cycle—to challenge either starting a delay reduction program or sustaining it in the face of the constant pressure to back-slide noted above. Leaders who recognize these dynamics and address them daily sustain strong caseflow management programs over time.

As suggested in the list above, proactive management also is concerned that those who use the court do so as efficiently and effectively as they can.[69] Many attorneys seek and need continuances because they lack strong case and client management within their offices. If they were to improve their office management, the court would benefit materially. Therefore, it is appropriate for a court to encourage and support the local bar association's sponsorship of such training, even to the extent of helping to write a grant proposal if that would facilitate the process. Such support tells attorneys that the court is not indifferent or oblivious to the changes litigators may have to make to adjust to court control of the calendar and the pressure to be prepared when the court schedules a hearing or conference. It also gives attorneys an improved capacity to earn a living. They may or may not be able to bill the same number of hours for any given case, but they will be able to handle more clients over time and bill more frequently because they will manage their time and cases better.

12.10 Improving the Jury Experience

Jury management's first wave of change was in the 1970s and 1980s and involved mostly court administration. The focus was on improving source lists, responses to summons, utilization of jurors once they got to the courthouse, improving random selection practices, and juror orientation and information. Both in this early period and continually to the present, court administration has sought improved jury management software that assists with the items just mentioned plus facilitates one trial/one jury (discussed in section 9.2.5, chapter 9) and the postponing and excusing of jurors.

A second wave started in the 1990s. This wave primarily involved judicial administration and focused on the juror experience in the courtroom. The changes, still to be made in many trial courts, provide for juror questions of witnesses, juror note taking, pre-final argument reading of instructions (and sometimes pre-opening argument and interim readings), and a second, more effective wave of plain-English jury instructions. While the judicial administration changes were occurring in this second wave of reforms, court administration directed energy toward improved assembly rooms, in appearance, comfort, and thoughtfulness. Beyond nicer chairs, quiet areas were added, as were smoking areas where smoking in a building still is allowed, television viewing areas, and work and computer access areas. There also was a successful movement to reduce the automatic, legislatively mandated excuses from jury service for various work and other categories of citizens (sick, elderly, disabled). A growing number, but still only a limited number, of courtrooms also have been equipped for electronic presentation and viewing of evidence to facilitate jurors following the presentation of evidence.

These systems not only use large screens for viewing by everyone in the courtroom, but also provide monitors for each juror or every two jurors. This latter improvement deserves broader adoption in courthouses around the country, but the cost per courtroom is significant (as of the early 2000s), so in many jurisdictions, availability of this electronic presentation capacity may have to await a significant drop in cost or new courthouses (see also, section 12.11.2).

Proactive management seeks continual incremental improvements in jury management and for jury service. Specifically, proactive management:

- Tracks juror usage during voir dire[70] and uses juror exit questionnaires, tabulates results, reviews comments, and adjusts service as appropriate.
- Reviews the provisions of the "Jury Patriotism Act,"[71] a model law that seeks to codify the changes mentioned above, and seeks, along with other courts, adoption in their state of desired provisions of the law;
- In courts that have not yet adopted one trial/one day terms of service, proactive management seeks to convince the legislature, if terms of service are set by state law, or, if not, the judges of the court, to adopt a one trial/one day term of service and then institutes procedures to make it work.[72]
- Supports statewide efforts to change and upgrade juror compensation.
- Endorses the development of plain-English instructions;[73]
- Supports the management of trial time in order to minimize the burden of jury service on citizens.
- Actively solicits citizens' opinions about their service and advertises the positive experiences; in place of or to supplement a paper questionnaire, proactive management sets up a jurors' blog page within the courts' website on which citizens, both those who served on juries and those who came to the courthouse but did not serve, can comment on their experience, their views of the attorneys, and their views of the judge and staff.
- Uses press releases, appearances on local television and radio, and speaking engagements to civic groups by judges and senior management to encourage jury service.

The number of jury trials in both civil and criminal cases has been declining since the mid-1980s, as has the percent of all dispositions achieved by jury trials.[74] Even so, a court with a strong jury management program that tries about 100 jury trials a year (roughly two jury trials a week) might bring to the courthouse between 3,000 and 4,000 citizens a year as potential jurors. A court that has a low juror utilization rate probably brings between 5,000 and 6,000 citizens to the courthouse. These numbers can be doubled or tripled to arrive at the number of citizens summoned to serve. Proactive management thinks of each juror as Scandinavian Airlines in the 1960s thought of each customer contact by an employee: a moment of truth.[75] Jurors who have positive experiences will become ambassadors of the court to the community, not only for jury service but also for the court generally.

The issue of juror privacy and juror protection was recognized in high-profile and high-security criminal cases a number of years ago. More recently, the need to protect juror identity has surfaced, so that in some courts for most or all trials, jurors are assigned numbers; court records, judges and staff, and parties in the cases refer to them by number rather than by name.[76] Starting in 2005, identity thieves started to contact citizens saying they were calling from the court because of their pending jury service and seeking personal information to confirm that they were talking to the right person. Courts began to hear from citizens and immediately distributed press releases, put notices on their web pages, and advised citizens during orientation that these calls were fraudulent and that a court would not do that. It is unknown if this quick response, plus many courts getting out ahead of these thieves by advising citizens in advance, will end this particular ruse. All of these instances suggest, however, a need for heightened sensitivity to the need to protect important personal information of jurors that is in court files. This issue should be addressed as part of broader records management issues (see section 10.2.2.1, chapter 10), but jury staff may need specific training in how to address the issue if prospective jurors raise it.

There is a looming issue that is not a court administration responsibility, but one that may mandate some rethinking of the trial process and how evidence is presented. In the process, court administration may be called on in some fashion as yet unknown. Many adults who grew up on Sesame Street, but especially those who are 25 and younger, seem to suffer from attention deficit deriving from almost continually multitasking and being bombarded by sights and sounds from multiple sources. In 2005, a Kaiser Family Foundation survey revealed that, "Fifteen-to-eighteen-year-olds average nearly 6½ hours a day watching TV, playing video games, and surfing the Net.... A quarter of that time, they're multitasking."[77] The Pew Internet and American Life Project indicates that among the 24 million American teens 12 to 17 years old, 65 percent instant message, 29 percent keep several instant message conversations going at once, and 25 percent instant message people in the same room.[78] In a cover story on what is now being called the "@ generation," *Business Week* magazine profiled two college dorm mates:[79]

> [One of the dorm mates, a 20-year-old junior, at 7:00 p.m. on a Saturday night] has just sweated her way through an online quiz for her advertising management class.... She checks a friend's blog ... to find out where a party will be that night. Then she starts an Instant Messenger (IM) conversation about the evening's plans with a few pals.
>
> At the same time, her boyfriend IMs her a retail store link to see

a new PC he just bought, and she starts chatting with him. She's also postering for the next Buzz-Oven concert by tacking their flier on various friends' MySpace profiles, and she's updating her own blog.... The TV is set to TBS ... but she keeps the volume turned down so she can listen to iTunes over her computer speakers. Simultaneously, she's chatting with dorm mate ... who's doing pretty much the same thing from a laptop on her bed.

Ellen Goodman, a nationally syndicated columnist, discussed the issue this way in 2005:[80]

Linda Stone, a former Microsoft techie, characterizes ours as an era of "continuous partial attention." At the extreme end are teenagers.... But adults too live with all systems go, interrupted and distracted, scanning everything, multi-technological-tasking everywhere.

We suffer from the illusion, says Stone, that we can expand our personal bandwidth, connecting to more and more. Instead, we end up overstimulated, overwhelmed and, she adds, unfulfilled. Continuous partial attention inevitably feels like a lack of full attention.[81]

Courts expect these individuals to sit for four to five hours a day for three to five days listening as jurors to the traditional presentation of witnesses and documentary evidence in a typical criminal or civil trial. Kind and supportive treatment of prospective jurors by court staff will not overcome the sense of ennui and, perhaps, the inability of people living in a world of electronic stimulation to concentrate on what is being presented meticulously and sometimes in excruciating detail during a trial. This comment has nothing to do with the merits of presenting evidence in detail and in tiny bits that can be tested by (or withstand) cross-examination. It has everything to do with the people who, as jurors, will be trying to pay attention to and sort out all that evidence. It also is not fair to blame only computer technology. Sesame Street is a national treasure, but it also has raised a generation of people who learned in six-second bits of stimulation. A clash of cultures is on the horizon that will need to be addressed if jury trials are to remain viable options for those who need them.

Courts will not change these behavior tendencies in the general public, so judges and attorneys, possibly with the help of sociologists and psychologists, must seek to address the challenges to the conduct of trials presented by this hyperstimulated society. Court administrators have a simpler issue to address that already is beginning to appear: ubiquitous cell phones, a growing number of which have picture-taking and streaming video capacity in addition to instant messaging. Courts are beginning to ban cell phones from courtrooms and denying jurors the use their phones for instant messaging and taking pictures or otherwise communicating with anyone about the trial while they serve on a jury.

This cell phone issue has been recognized and dealing with it will become a standard order to jurors soon, if it is not already. The challenge for court administrators in this context is to keep current with all the latest technological gadgets and how people are using them so they do not taint the jury process. Cell phones may give way to wrist phones or wired clothing, eyeglasses that are communication devices (they already can be used for close-circuit TV and eyeglass phones are available), and who knows what else might come along during this century. Judges, with the bar, will determine how best to respond to these challenges, but court administration, including staff, may be able to identify the risks and offer solutions if they keep their eyes and ears open and their imaginations fertile.

The jury process is a fundamental element of America's justice system. Court administration plays a vital role in assuring that the right to a jury of one's peers is available to all those who desire it. Proactive management constantly looks for ways to enrich the experience for jurors and those who might be jurors while adhering to all legal requirements.

12.11   Embracing Technology and Finding New Ways to Benefit from It

Proactive management uses technology in various ways to improve productivity and to reach out more efficiently and effectively to litigants and citizens. Proactive management constantly is scanning developments in software and hardware for new ways to extend service and to improve the effectiveness of judges and staff. Proactive management recognizes and embraces the value of technology while not being seduced by its appeal to the point of using it in ways that might undermine the basic purposes of courts.

12.11.1   *The Need For and Limitations of Technology*

Technology is an essential tool in aiding courts to live within funding limits while continuing to upgrade service and the productivity of staff. The structural and funding changes that have occurred since the mid-1950s required changes in law. Beyond these changes in law, a significant percentage of the improvement achieved in court administration over those years is traceable to the use of technology.

The impact of technology on people's daily lives is huge and will only expand. People today use the Internet and its associated technologies in ways that were unimagined in the 1970s. Telephone and similar devices now are shirt- or pants-pocket minicomputers and sophisticated cameras and television monitors. People not only instant message others but also get instant stock and news reports, participate instantly in sporting and entertainment shows on radio and television, order virtually anything from ham and cheese on rye for lunch to custom-designed automobiles and fine jewelry online with shipping within 24 hours. Home mortgages and consumer credit can be approved or denied in minutes. Business has been transformed by online links between suppliers and manufacturers, virtually eliminating manufacturers' inventories greater than a few days' needs. If someone ships something, he or she can track its every step on the Internet. Television reporters sit outside a courthouse and share testimony with viewers almost instantaneously because of instant messages from someone inside the courtroom.

Part of America's character is a restless spirit impatient to get on to the next great thing. The Internet specifically and technology generally have reinforced the sense of impatience. In this world, unless courts embrace technology with enthusiasm and find ways to conduct most business digitally and even to adjudicate disputes more rapidly, the public will come to see courts as archaic and unworthy of support.

Yet, there is an inherent tension in this vision of digital courts. Courts cannot become just like the corner deli, an automobile company, a mortgage lender, or a mail order catalog company. As a unit of government, courts face constraints not present for most businesses. Those constraints mean courts probably never will be able to provide the instantaneous access and responses that technology might afford in the private sector. Courts must assure:

- Access
- Equal treatment of all litigants
- Due process of law (i.e., adequate and full opportunity to prepare and present one's case, which often takes more time than customizing a car or deciding one's opinion on a news show's "e-mail question of the day")
- The appearance of justice, which would not support instant, seemingly nondeliberative decisions
- Compliance with legal restraints on information that can be made public
- Long-term preservation of records (see section 10.2.2.2, chapter 10).

Access and equal treatment dictate caution by courts about making access to and use of courts' services entirely digital. Courts must serve the poor who cannot afford computers and may not know how to use public-access computers in, for example, public libraries or even courthouses. Beyond this clientele, there simply is a significant segment of society that does not have and does not want Internet access. The use and ownership of computers and the use of the Internet is not as broadly entrenched in society as some may believe. Until their penetration into virtually all households has occurred, courts have to plan for alternate access and use modalities for those without the resources or the interest to buy computers, computerlike telephones and other communication devices, and Internet access. A survey completed in early 2006 indicates that Internet connectivity has plateaued at around 64 percent of all households, with growth of only 1 percent a year expected through 2009. Some say their access to the Internet at work is sufficient (a different issue, to be addressed by employers), but six million households say they will not subscribe to an Internet service provider at any price. Nearly 60 percent of people 65 or older do not use the Internet and 33 percent of people 45 or older are not connected.[82]

Unquestionably, courts have a lot of room between where most are today in terms of technological adaptation and use and developments that might jeopardize the values and requirements listed above. They also can make enormous strides in developing information networks with stakeholders that facilitate and speed the exchange of information. Thus, proactive management has ample room to expand the use of technology for the benefit of both courts and the public they serve. At the same time, the rush toward greater use of technology must not blind courts' leaders to its limitations or to the need to manage its installation and use very carefully.

Information technology (IT) "can make justice more accessible, improve timely processing, promote fairness, and make more effective use of resources allocated to courts. Or it can bog down the court in costly mismanagement, bad press, and lower credibility with funding authorities."[83] The management side of adopting technology is critical to success. Courts are not alone in having to overcome the pitfalls. "A 1995 report from the Standish Group, a leading software design consultancy, revealed that more than 70 percent of efforts to build new computer systems fail."[84] The Standish Group also reports that half of all technology projects cost twice their original budget.[85] If these data remain valid today for the world at large, they pose special challenges for courts. Trial courts seldom develop new software or introduce significant technologies using their own staff. Normally, they use technology personnel of local government, consultants or private vendors, or software developed by the IT staff of the state administrative office of the courts. Whoever has the lead role, however, trial courts still must manage the process with their own personnel: development of requirements, detailed design, testing, modification, training, and installation. Some courts have been able to train their personnel to manage technology projects and to make the project their sole responsibility. Normally, however, management of these efforts is an add-on to the daily assignments of a court's technology staff or senior managers. Even the technology staff, which at least has some understanding of the technical side of the project, if pulled in different directions will have a hard time staying on top of the project and avoiding the pitfalls that lead to high failure rates and a high percentage of budget overruns. Courts are improving their capacity to manage these projects, but there are many examples of failed, unsatisfactory, overrun, and very late implementation efforts, particularly of new case management information systems. One of the key challenges of proactive management regarding technology is to assure the proper management capacity and the time for the court's project manager to see that the effort proceeds as planned, as scheduled, and within budget. These projects drain a lot of time and energy from a court; it is critical that they be managed properly.

There is another factor when considering the many advantages of technology: if it does not work as advertised or as effectively as in other environments, its use may undermine a court's ability to fulfill its mission. This could be due to the technology's inherent limitations, because the technology ends up limiting access or due process, or because its cost and the management energy it requires diverts resources from other court needs. Thus, courts normally should not seek to be early adopters of each new technology breakthrough. There are three reasons for caution by courts. First, that major breakthrough may turn out to be a major bust, which could result in significant wasted resources and possibly jeopardize record integrity. Implementing the "next great thing" too early also might lead a court to miss another opportunity or delay a court from recognizing the value of another approach because of the effort needed to get the new "thing" in place and working properly. Second, an application that works well for a department store, a manufacturer, or a hospital may not transfer effectively to a court environment. There probably are many applications used by department stores, manufacturers, and hospitals that can be and should be adapted for use in courts (see chapter 13). It also is true, however, that the fact that they work in those environments does not assure they will work in courts or satisfy all the constraints with which courts must live. Courts need time to assess both the technology on its own merits and then to assess the application of the technology in courts. If courts rush into adoption of new technologies too quickly, either one or both levels of review may be short-changed, to the long-term detriment of the courts. The third reason is that courts are part of government and government leaders normally are risk averse because the public seems to be risk averse when it comes to expenditures of public resources. Both the public and government leaders are of two minds when it comes to innovation. The public, elected officials, and, of course, the administrators who implemented the innovation love it when a government unit is a leader and has a wonderful new idea that works. All three groups run away quickly from a new idea that fails and either pretend they were not involved or that the failure was X's fault. Government officials also have a long memory regarding those failures, particularly if a lot of money was involved.[86] If a court examines a new technology closely and considers both the upside of adopting it and the downside, there is nothing inherently wrong with being an early adopter. The

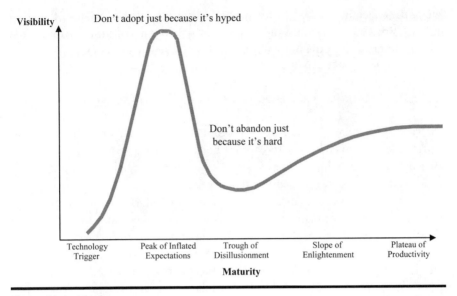

Figure 12.1 The hype curve.

judiciary needs some courts to be early adopters for an innovation to be tested, proven, and spread. It is just that caution is needed, fueled by skepticism that the product is as good as the hype.

Another way to envision this process is to consider the " technology hype curve"[87] (see Figure 12.1). If "visibility" is on the vertical scale and "maturity" is the horizontal scale, there are five stages of maturity. The first is technology trigger, where there is almost no visibility. As the innovation moves to the peak of inflated expectations it gains its greatest visibility and hype. The high visibility and hype almost invariably are followed by the trough of disillusionment, when visibility falls significantly, as do general opinions about the value of the innovation. Then, as the technology passes through the "slope of enlightenment," and finally gets to the "plateau of productivity," visibility improves and the curve tends to flatten out. It takes different innovations different amounts of time to pass through each of the five stages that lead to a productivity enhancement. Therefore, there is no formula one can provide as to when a court would be best positioned to adopt the innovation, other than to suggest that the peak of visibility and inflated expectations may not be the best time. Courts with strong technology staffs and a sound base of technology use might serve as early court adopters at the peak of the visibility and inflated expectations cycle, but the average court might be served best by waiting for the experiences of the early adopter courts.[88]

There is a fine line between rushing too quickly into use of new technologies and waiting too long to take full advantage of them. There also is a need to assure sound project management and execution. If a court must err on one side of the line or the other, it may be best for the typical court to err on the side of waiting and assessing rather than rushing to be an early adopter. In most instances, it is best for others to find the bugs and limitations in new technology.

12.11.2 Technological Responses to Consider In the Near Term

The variety of software and hardware products in use that might be useful in courts is far too great to try to capture here. There are some approaches and concepts, however, which if not already in place in a court should be considered for its strategic plan in the next five to ten years.

Facilitate electronic filing and exchange of information. Manufacturers and large retailers have built sophisticated networks with suppliers using the Internet to allow "just in time" inventorying, outsourcing of parts manufacturing, and even far-flung design teams that include people who are not only from different offices but also from different companies. The concepts that lie behind these private-sector electronic communities have been talked about for years in courts, but courts have been much slower to implement them. Integrated criminal justice information systems, electronic filing, remote access to file information through the Internet, and electronic communication of information and notices to other agencies all are similar to these private sector initiatives, and a number of courts have implemented them. They remain remote concepts in many other courts, however. These other courts should do all they can to obtain the needed funding, the cooperation of other agencies, and the expertise to design and implement these systems over the next five years.[89]

When this effort has been completed, consider how the following two developments, one in another country and one in a local government executive branch agency, could be applied in a U.S. court. The South Korean government is delivering progress reports on legal proceedings and notices of fines for traffic and environmental violations through text messages to people's cell phones. The government hopes to save half the cost of noticing parties by using this technology.[90] New York City's Comptroller is using the Internet to help settle cases more efficiently. Both sides submit blind offers up to three times until a match is made. If there is no match in three iterations, the parties meet face-to-face. The Comptroller's office estimates saving $17 million in less than two years.[91]

Use technology to facilitate access. As with the filing and exchange of information, the applicable concepts for using technology to facilitate public access have existed for many years and have been implemented, at least to some extent, in many courts. Most courts have websites now. If a court does not, that addition to its technical arsenal should be added as soon as possible. Websites, at least until the next breakthrough occurs, are a key portal to court information, files, and forms. A well-designed site can save courts a great deal of staff time that otherwise would be spent answering questions and improves the uniformity and quality of information being provided to citizens. It also can enable the completion and filing of forms.[92] The more courts can put on their websites about what the court does, how it operates, the information and forms citizens need to use, accessing case file information, and virtual tours of the courthouse, the more likely citizens with Internet access will use the site. The result will be an improvement in both staff productivity and citizen education. One should be realistic about what a website can achieve, however. "It's a Website myth that 'if you build it, they will come.' The truth is that a percentage of your audience will visit your Website on a regular basis, but the vast majority of your constituents will only do so if you actively remind them."[93]

Language translation software now is available for websites and documents on websites.[94] One company's product in 2003 could translate English-based documents on web pages into ten other languages: Dutch, French, German, Hebrew, Italian, Japanese, Portuguese, Spanish, and two Chinese languages. In 1999, the *New York Times* started using this translation service for its international website readers. This might be a very cost-effective way to expand access to a court's website. Note, however, that at least one person who has used this type of software for a language in which he is conversant says it is good for a first-draft translation, but a human translator familiar with legal terms still is needed to refine and complete the translation.[95]

One of the Internet search services as of 2006 offers an Internet-based translation service for over 100 languages for either specific words or an entire page on a website. Someone using this service would have to toggle back and forth between a court's website page and the translation service,[96] but if no other option existed, this may be acceptable to a user. The court would have to provide a link and explain how to proceed. The lesson is an old one: technology changes rapidly, so courts have to be alert for new aids that can expand the reach of their website in a cost-effective and substantively effective way.

Because of the significance of a website, courts should examine how much information they contain and how easy it is to navigate around the site. For several years, Justice Served, a consulting firm to justice agencies,[97] has rated websites of both AOCs and trial courts and selected the Top 10 each year. The list of these ten sites is provided on Justice Served's website and the website of the National Center for State Courts.[98] A review of these highly rated sites plus the sites of other trial courts that a court's leadership knows to be well managed might provide clues to what to include and how to present the information. It also might help a court to have a few citizens who do not use the court regularly and a few who do, use the website and evaluate both readability and ease of use. In that context, the University of Wisconsin at Stout has a Website Usability Testing Center that seeks to "discover problems in the use of a website, preferably before that product is released for use by the customer."[99] Other colleges or universities may offer a similar service. Jonathan Palmer published an article on website usability in *Computer*, the magazine of the IEEE Computer Society.[100] An Internet and library search should identify other sources, as well. The point is that courts need to consider usability when they design (or have others design) their websites. "[B]usinesses whose homepages address usability and incorporate other essential design criteria report higher traffic, more repeat visitors, and greater customer satisfaction."[101]

A widely used technology application is video arraignments, through which prisoners to be arraigned (and sometimes for other appearances) are left in jail but appear in a courtroom through a video hookup between the jail and the courthouse. This application has proved to be so useful that it is being used in some jurisdictions even though the jail is next to the courthouse and connected to it by a secure passageway.

Many courts now are using video conferencing equipment for internal meetings and for long-distance training. Existing applications are not widely extended to other possibilities, however. For example, video appearances could be extended to emergency domestic violence cases, to civil matters such as small claims cases, to traffic infraction cases, and landlord–tenant disputes.[102] Parties could appear in special "video appearance rooms" in selected public buildings around the county or in branch courts when they have to appear in a branch that is some distance from their homes.[103] Law enforcement officers could appear in traffic cases from their assigned precinct's or office's video appearance room to save time and facilitate appearances in more than one branch of a court on a given day, if that could be done to facilitate an officer's schedule. Attorneys could appear via video for hearings such as scheduling or status conferences and, in some courts, to argue short-cause motions. (This courtesy should be extended to self-represented litigants, as well.) When a party or witness in a civil matter (and occasionally in a criminal matter) is very ill, a video deposition is authorized, with the video then being used in the courtroom. Live video appearances also might be feasible if the person is coherent enough to testify, but not well enough to travel to the courthouse to testify.[104]

A growing number of courts now offer in-person assistance to self-represented litigants, either through a forms and book library or through a staff person who assists with completion of forms and information about the evidence they need to bring to court. In each of those courts, the reach of this service can be extended through video conferencing or an Internet connection.[105]

A number of courts now are using telephones to extend their capacity to provide language interpreters. There are commercial services that provide interpreters for a wide range of languages via the telephone, but only for short periods of time (normally 15 minutes or less). Some states share certified interpreters by "lending" an interpreter in one city to a court in another city via telephone. Videoconferencing is another way to address this need. In 2005, a judicial district in upstate New York used videoconference interpreters between two courthouses in the district and, again, between a court in the district and a New York City court (for Vietnamese speakers).[106] The use of video technology may be a better answer than telephones to the great and growing demand for interpreter services.

Some courts allow arguments to be made for and against motions in civil cases through a dialogue occurring through a bulletin board or Internet court site. Arguments are posted, the other side responds, the judge can ask questions, and this can go on any time day or night and for several days. When the parties indicate they are through, the judge considers the matter, rules, and the motion is resolved without anyone appearing in court.[107]

Electronic courtrooms. Reference was made in the jury management section to electronic presentation equipment. All courtrooms should have an enhanced capacity for parties to present and use electronic evidence and exhibits, including exhibits that facilitate attorneys' arguments.[108] Electronic discovery is more and more important in both civil and criminal cases. DNA evidence and other science-based evidence may be presented more readily through a computer presentation. Today, in a significant number of courtrooms in the nation, if this type of evidence is needed, parties bring their own equipment unless a court has a courtroom in which this equipment is installed and the trial is being held there.[109] In an increasingly digital world, it is likely that digital evidence will be used increasingly. An excellent resource for what is needed and how to set it up is the high-tech demonstration courtroom in the William and Mary Law School, next to the headquarters building of the National Center for State Courts in Williamsburg, Virginia, referred to commonly as "Courtroom 21."[110] The courtroom is administered jointly by the law school and the NCSC. The National Judicial College in Reno, Nevada, also has set up a high-tech demonstration courtroom in its facilities.

Built-in television viewing and television broadcasting equipment also is needed. Virtually any courtroom can be equipped with stand-alone television viewing equipment, often placed on a rolling stand so it can be moved aside when not needed. For remote television access and the video conferencing discussed above, high-speed wiring has to be added, but compared to adding the capacity to broadcast television, adding cabling for video conferencing is a relatively simple operation.

Televising trials and hearings immediately generates debate in most jurisdictions. Yet, Florida courts can and do televise trials daily across the state and have done so for about three decades. Kentucky introduced video as the medium for taking the verbatim record in the early 1980s. A by-product of selecting that technology for reporting cases is that local cable channels can pick up court cases for broadcast. Other states also either routinely or from time to time allow televised proceedings. If televising proceedings is only an occasional event, normally a television station would provide a pool camera with an operator set up in the back of the courtroom, with a feed to other stations' equipment set up in another room or in trucks outside the courthouse. It is preferable for the conduct of court proceedings if a courtroom is prewired for television transmission, with cameras discretely placed in predetermined locations. Most courts would require a new courthouse or a major new wing to a courthouse to equip courtrooms with a built-in capacity to both receive and broadcast television signals. If that opportunity arises, these capacities should be built in. In the meantime, all courts should seek to equip one or two courtrooms (depending on the size and configuration of the courthouse) to serve as an electronic courtroom.

Some courts now use electronic white boards for internal meetings. These boards electronically produce hard copies of what was written on the board. A percentage of these courts also use them in the courtroom. Now, there are electronic white boards that are large touch screens that can project what is written or drawn on the board onto wall monitors or into computers.[111] Electronic white boards would be useful additions to electronic courtrooms.

Courtrooms today normally have a small white board, a roll-in chalkboard, portable flip charts and stands, and a pull-down screen for viewing overhead slides or a computer-based slide presentation. They are offered to facilitate the presentation of evidence and, in some cases, arguments on motions. These items are grounded in an analog world. It is time for the capacity needed for a digital world to be added to courtrooms.[112]

Impact of the Web. The Internet is transforming business, government, social interactions, and virtually every aspect of life. It is starting to transform courts, as well.[113] The Internet permits telecommuting by workers, which is not a widely used practice in courts to date, but may become so, particularly for data entry and customer service positions (see section 12.13). The use and potential of websites have been discussed in several places in this book. There are some potential impacts that may or may not be positive, however.

The expanding use of blogs is one such uncertain development. Should the court administrator or jury clerk/manager have a blog to comment on administrative matters affecting or involving the court? Should the court be monitoring blogs to see what people are saying and respond to criticism or false information?[114] Should judges use blogs to respond to citizens' general questions about courts—a number of courts have done this from time to time in public forums—or to explain their side of a controversial decision?

Companies now are using the Internet to enable customers to help with design and marketing decisions and even product development ideas. A number of courts put comment cards on counters to get feedback on problems and to learn about excellent service by staff. These capacities easily could be added to a court's website or made available through a court blog.

Judges now usually respond to requests for warrants during noncourt hours via telephone, with supporting documentation faxed to their homes, if needed.

Internet communication could be more efficient once the judge is alerted that he or she is needed. Often judges have to respond in the middle of the night. Unless their computers have an alarm device that would wake them up during those hours, a telephone call or some other means of alerting the judge still would be needed. There also needs to be a way to get information to a judge who is out of the house when he or she is needed. In time, cell phones may fill all these needs, but not yet.

Finally, on Court TV and some cable news shows, citizens call in to ask show hosts or guest attorneys questions about what is happening during televised trials or notorious trials that have daily coverage or to offer opinions. It is a small step from these calls to the existence of notorious case blogs, with the nation serving as a mock jury for the trial attorneys. How, if at all, that might affect what happens in the courtroom is uncertain, but some impact is likely, either on the trial itself or people's view of the trial and courts generally.

Modern case management information systems. It took 40 years for almost all courts to have computerized case management information systems. Many courts have upgraded their systems once or twice since the original installation—particularly if they had a Y2K issue prior to 2000—so many systems are reasonably integrated, complete, modularized, and flexible, with the capacity to generate predesigned and ad hoc reports. Courts that do not yet have these capacities should seek to obtain them as quickly as possible. When they do, they should assure that the system also provides or accommodates networking with other agencies, either with hard wiring or through the Internet. Even more than other agencies, the software and hardware should enable remote work by staff. This is a human resource issue more than a technological one, but with the changing workforce and increasing numbers of businesses operating with at least some remote staff, courts should not be precluded from doing so by their technology.

To date, courts have relied on in-house development of their case management information systems or commercially developed software that can be customized to the needs of each court. The market for commercial development of case management information software is quite small compared to the volume sales desired by most software development companies. Because of the pervasive variations among courts, there also is a lot of customization needed, which discourages larger software developers from trying to enter the market. The record of successful software development efforts for courts, either in-house or commercial products, has been very spotty.[115] County and city staffs who develop the software do not know courts, so try to force standard and easy programming choices on courts that do not work or are incomplete. Plus, regrettably, they seldom are skilled at using current generations of programming language, so the court is denied the chance to have a current generation system. Commercial vendors are more flexible, but customization is so expensive that it is hard for these generally smaller companies to make enough profit to stay in business for many years, which, in turn, creates upgrade and support issues.

Courts are a small, somewhat sui generis market difficult to serve. The Department of Defense (DOD) is a very large market, but it also presents challenges because of its special requirements. Both courts and the DOD, therefore, have mostly developed, or had developed, customized software. In recent years, however, the DOD has been using more off-the-shelf software to meet its needs.[116]

> The synergy produces real savings. "About 15 years ago, we would have to build systems from the ground up," says Frank C. Lanza, CEO of [a DOD supplier]. "But now,… we can buy their graphic processors modify them to suit the needs of an F-16 [simulator], and spend our time with the operational scenarios to train pilots."

The DOD can use a wider range of off-the-shelf products than courts because the scope of its needs is much greater. Nonetheless, it may be possible for courts to modularize their software without jeopardizing the need for case information to be readily transferable among case types and various users so that commercial products could benefit courts the way they are benefiting the DOD.[117] Courts, at a minimum, need to be open to this possibility and to have their computer staffs follow developments in the field with this idea in mind.

Radio Frequency Identification (RFID). This technology was discussed in section 10.2.2.1, chapter 10. The technology already is two decades old and can be traced back to World War II.[118] It is only recently, however, that chip technology and high-volume mandated use by suppliers to the Department of Defense, major retailers, and some major manufacturers have begun to bring the cost down to a level that it makes sense for courts to use RFID chips to track paper files and evidence. As mentioned in chapter 10, some interference issues remain.[119] This is one of those technologies, therefore, where it might be prudent for courts to be among the early- or late-majority adopters. That would allow sufficient time for all the bugs to be worked out and the cost to come down enough to warrant the expense that the RFID chips would add to the cost of ordinary file folders.

Voice-recognition telephone answering systems. As voice recognition software improves, more and more companies in the private sector are using it in their telephone trees, so that now orders for merchandise, credit card inquiries and payments, and travel reservations can be made without talking to a human being. For some, this is not progress. For court administrators, use of this technology at least has to be explored as a complement to the court's website for information about the court and to enable telephone payments of fines and fees.

Internet-based telephony. New Internet-based software for telephones, voice-over-Internet-protocol (VoIP), may aide the blind and deaf to communicate better and more productively (in addition to reducing the cost of traditional voice and data communication). It integrates the phone, voice mail, audio conferencing, e-mail, instant messaging, and Web applications on a secure network. The deaf can read voice mails from their e-mail program while the blind can hear a caller ID or a missed-call log, or line status.[120] An employer can make reasonable accommodations for disabled employees. The technology also may help courts expand access for the disabled, as an increasing number of telephones sold to companies currently use VoIP technology, and its use in residences also is growing.

Verbatim court technology. There are many real-time court reporters in courts today, but even though their ranks are growing, they still are a minority of reporters in almost all courts. Real-time court reporting is harder than using computer-assisted technology or the older machine stenography. It takes longer to learn to write well enough for the translation to be seen by others immediately. Plus, the equipment and software are more expensive than CAT. It offers a court significant benefits, however. Many judges now have a computer on the bench. The real-time system can be hooked to the judge's computer so he or she can see the transcript as it is being produced and make marginal notes for later review. The technology also aids the hearing impaired to follow proceedings in real time without a separate interpreter. To the extent that the reporter market allows a court to do so, it should seek real-time reporters as its first choice.

The other technology gaining in use is digital audio and video recording. This technology can be placed courtroom by courtroom or the entire courthouse can be wired, with the equipment operated from a central control area from which each courtroom's equipment is monitored to be sure it is operating properly. Digital recording equipment has become much more sophisticated. There is ample discussion whether the quality of a record captured via audio or video equipment is comparable, of lower quality, or of a higher quality to reporters using stenography. Studies comparing stenographic reporters with audio dating back to the early 1970s documented the two technologies were comparable, but the court reporting profession has claimed error in every study done. Many judges also seem to feel more comfortable having a stenographic reporter sitting in the courtroom who can do read backs and help to control the dialogue, so the debate continues. (These two functions also can be provided by an in-court recording monitor, but the trust level does not seem to be the same for some judges.)

Today's world is dominated by computers and video entertainment. Video reporting is used in some courts, but the extra cost compared to audio recording has limited its widespread adoption. It is reasonable to assume that the use of video to capture the record will grow as new courthouses are built.

The debate about which technology is best may well continue for most of this century. Court reporting for the last century steadily and consistently moved to increasing reliance on technology. That trend is not likely to change; the only questions are the pace of change and the skills and role of the in-court monitor. It is probable that both audio and video reporting technologies will be used increasingly, both for technical and for economic reasons, but it could take decades before technical solutions dominate over technologically-assisted stenographers.

Secure pay systems. Most courts are simply happy to have fines paid, without much concern whether the payment is from a defendant, a family member of the defendant, or a friend. With telephone and Internet payments, so long as the credit or debit card is cleared, courts have not worried much about whether the defendant was using his or her own card. With the rising tide of identify theft, however, all payees have to be more careful. There also may be conditions placed on a probationer that make it important for the judge to know that the defendant himself or herself is making a payment. Therefore, as more courts make it possible for defendants to pay fines via the Internet, some system of assuring the identity of the payer will become important. There now are systems available that use fingerprint identification at the payer's end.[121] Other bioidentity systems may come along in the next several years. Courts should remain alert for these possibilities and then weigh their cost against the need to identify exactly who is paying a fine.

12.11.3 Future Possibilities

I know of no survey, but I would not be surprised if over 90 percent of all court PCs use Microsoft operating systems and office software. Linux is an alternative, open source operating system that is gaining ground in the private sector and with some foreign governments. Other alternatives may come along, Microsoft Corporation is fighting hard to keep its market share and is particularly targeting government. The fact that Microsoft will fight hard does not mean it will win the fight to remain the dominant operating system and top producer of the associated software, however.[122] Courts will need to keep their eyes and ears open to see how the fight progresses. Should it happen that Linux gains substantial market share and a significant number of courts convert, the conversion process would touch all aspects of a court's operations. Switching to Linux or another operating system would introduce a long list of issues and could involve significant up-front out-of-pocket costs. Very careful cost-benefit analyses will be needed. That is one of the arguments Microsoft uses when trying to keep customers. Should Microsoft begin to lose its current dominance, whether to stay with Microsoft will be a major consideration for courts. The technology of security is bound to get more sophisticated and complex as the century progresses. Courts will have to decide which new technologies are useful, which are necessary, and which can be by-passed.

If Bill Gates is right that DVDs (and, presumably, CDs) will become obsolete storage media within ten years[123]—or if he is wrong and it takes 30 years—courts will have to adjust, but then the conversion and storage issues discussed in chapter 10 move to the forefront again. The issue will have to be addressed, not only for current records but also for older paper and electronic records.

As mentioned above, voice recognition software is getting more sophisticated and competent annually. The wide range of speech patterns of those who appear in court plus the technical language—not just legal, but medical, forensic, law enforcement, psychiatric, and some business—used in court probably means it will be decades before it will be sophisticated enough to be considered as an alternative to current court reporting technologies. Voice recognition technology and its possible application to court reporting needs to be watched, however, and considered as the century progresses.

Artificial intelligence used to be largely a pipe dream of computer nerds and philosophers. Today, it, too, is growing in sophistication, in quality, and in productive applications. Possible court applications would be in responding to telephone or Internet inquiries for information, and in handling requests for information about fines and calculating fines due. Although the prospect will concern many judges, artificial intelligence also may be a useful aid to decision making in the courtroom and to settling civil cases. Artificial intelligence will be very slow to find its way into courtrooms and courthouses, but it is something court administrators should watch, just in case.[124]

There probably will be a dozen new technological applications (hardware and software) by 2020 that are unknown in 2006 that might be useful in courts. Part of court administration's responsibility as it undertakes the environmental scanning discussed in section 12.6.3, is to keep a sharp eye out for technologies that may have a significant impact on how courts work. Once those technologies are identified, a court can assess whether and how they might be used. But first, they must be found and understood.[125]

12.12 Inducing and Managing Change

By definition, proactive management induces change. Some changes will be minor, some significant, and a few major, but change is necessary to maintain a viable institution. In today's world, a strong case could be made that change should join death and taxes as the only certainties in life. Courts cannot halt change: The legislature, administrative regulations, technology, societal expectations, and even international treaties will impose change, even if courts do nothing. Being proactive allows courts to make choices, to set priorities, and to determine the parameters of their organizations and operations for themselves. If courts try to minimize or delay the impact of change, external forces that eventually will compel change may not be as sensitive to the institution's substantive, cultural, and timing needs as the court itself would be. There is no evidence to support the proposition that waiting until a change is imposed will turn out better for a court than facing it and shaping the process to the court's advantage. A court cannot anticipate and organize its way around every change, but being proactive puts it in a better position to respond even to changes it cannot anticipate.

The goal is not to halt change but to manage it and make it a part of a court's culture. One of the most appealing elements of the Total Quality Management movement of the 1970s and 1980s was the concept of incremental change. No process and no organization is so good or so complete that it cannot continue to improve. An organization that is open to change encourages everyone to participate in identifying areas of need and suggesting improvements. It remains management's role to make final decisions, but everyone has a responsibility—and should be recognized when they exercise it—to remain alert for doing things faster, better, and smarter.[126] In section 7.2.2.2, chapter 7, the idea of "baby steps" was introduced. Giant steps are necessary and desirable at times, but every organization also benefits from baby or incremental steps in between the giant steps.

Three stories about major changes may be instructive about the benefits to be gained from giant steps. The first story is about the Spanish explorer Hernando Cortez. When he landed in Mexico near Veracruz in 1519 and established a base camp, he burned the ships to prevent any thought of retreat in his men. His troops in time gained control of Mexico and established Spain's first colony in that country.[127] Seldom can a court's leaders do the equivalent of burning the ships. One cannot overlook the power of seeming to have no option but victory, however, when the need for change is critical and there is reason to believe that a significant portion of the troops do not see the same level of need as the leadership does.

The second story is less dramatic but also possibly more helpful. When I was in graduate school, I worked with a sociologist who often had perspectives on a situation that the lawyers surrounding him did not. When I joined the staff of the National Center for State Courts, I wrote to tell him that my first assignment was to study whether staffs of two trial courts in a county could be consolidated functionally without a formal, legal unification. He wrote back about how Illinois had recently consolidated its trial courts into a single court and consequently had made some improvements, but he foresaw that the courts soon would slip back into old habits. His advice was that courts that are consolidated should be split apart and courts that are separate should be consolidated and they should go back and forth every five years of so. As he saw it, it was the change process itself that induced improvements, but after a while people adjust and start to get settled and predictable. If, at that point, another major change is induced, problems and issues will surface, improvements will be made while shifting to the new arrangement, and then the organization can move on until the next change.

The third story is an anecdote that supports that view. A former National Center for State Courts colleague was a trial court administrator in two courts successively before joining the National Center's staff. In the first court, the judges used a master calendar to manage cases. He convinced them to change to an individual calendar, with significant improvement in the time to disposition. In his next court, they already had an individual calendar so he convinced them to change to a master calendar. The second court experienced improvements in the time to disposition similar to the first court. Just as my sociologist friend had indicated, it was the process of changing that resulted in the improvement, not the particular change.

Few courts will tolerate the introduction of significant change every five or so years, particularly if it is thought that the change is being introduced "merely" to induce improvement. If one looks at the nation's judiciary broadly since the mid-1950s, in contrast to what any single court may have done, there have been tremendous changes in many states, as a result of which most courts have improved operations. Many individual courts also have changed and improved dramatically. In individual courts, leaders have to monitor how the court is performing using the performance standards and data discussed earlier in this chapter. When the data indicate slippage, a court's leaders need to look for ways to convince the organization that change is needed and then find an appropriate response.

Many changes can and should be of the baby steps variety. Some changes will be broader and involve judges and staff in reexamining the overall processing of a case type, or the organization of staff's workflow, or even introducing a significant new technology. When significant change is required, a leader's empathy and integrity are most needed and in play.

> Essentially, the leader's task is consciousness-raising on a wide plain.... The leader's fundamental act is to induce people to be aware or conscious of what they feel—to feel their true needs so strongly, to define their values so meaningfully, that they can be moved to purposeful action.[128]
>
> The leader takes the initiative in making the leader-led connection; it is the leader who creates the links that allow communication and exchange to take place.... The leader is more skillful in evaluating followers' motives, anticipating their responses to an initiative, and estimating their power bases, than the reverse. Leaders continue to take the major part ... and will have the major role in ultimately carrying out the combined purpose of leaders and followers. Finally, and most important by far, leaders address themselves to followers' wants, needs, and other motivations, as well as their own and thus they serve as an *independent force in changing the makeup of the followers' motive base through gratifying their motives.*[129] (emphasis in original)

Courts should embrace change *unless* there are too many changes to absorb at one time. Sometimes, the impediment to more change is simply physical. The staff and judges simply do not have the time and expertise to do their normally assigned tasks plus handle additional changes. Sometimes, the impediment is psychological, when there have been several significant changes occurring at one time or one or two major changes and people simply need time to absorb them and learn what to do now. A leader has to be sensitive to the signs of stress and resistance and to understand the difference between "normal" resistance to change and a stressed response that says, "Whoa." As Attila the Hun might advise: "Retreat is noble when continuance with the battle or the issue at hand would result in further losses or total annihilation of your resources. In order to return on another day, you must salvage all the warriors and materiels [sic] possible."[130] Calling a short "time out" in these circumstances is not a rejection of change, merely part of the management of change and being sensitive to the workforce. Change mandated from the outside by the legislature or a major catastrophe in the community cannot be postponed, although priorities can be set for the steps needed to effect the change. Change induced internally can be regulated to avoid burnout and stretching people beyond their physical limits.

There are many fine books and articles about managing change. No effort will be made here to duplicate them. A few reminders are offered, however.

- "If they don't know why, the price is too high."[131] A leader needs to communicate early and often the identified need or impetus for change, why *this* response, and how the change will affect individuals
- Thus, be prepared to respond to the question, "What's in it for me?"
- "To get the bad customs of a country changed and new ones, though better, introduced, it is necessary first to remove the prejudices of the people, enlighten their ignorance, and convince them that their interests will be promoted by the proposed changes; *and this is not the work of a day*" (Benjamin Franklin[132]; emphasis added).
- People who believe they should be consulted or advised in advance of a change but who are left out of the loop can and will work against a project.
- *Who* delivers a message about a need for or a plan for change may be as important as the message itself; select messengers carefully.
- Many factors influence people's opposition to change, including fears of incompetence following the change, loss of contact with coworkers, uncertainty about what the change means, and no longer being the one in control of a process.
- Acceptance of change is not necessarily driven by the merits; otherwise, it would not have taken the British Navy 194 years after proof that lemon juice prevents scurvy to approve its use on Navy ships and the chairman of Sony would not have had to step in at the last minute to save its Walkman.
- Change leaders need to be ready with a two-minute speech that will hit the high points of where things should be and where they are, positive

results to date, remaining issues and concerns, and what the leader(s) is doing.

- If a court's leadership gets too far ahead of where most judges (or the most influential judges) feel comfortable, the court administrator is at risk of being terminated (as well as the change).
- Feedback, feedback, feedback.

12.13   Attracting and Retaining Staff

There are many elements of human resource management; this section will focus on attracting and retaining staff. Proactive management values staff, but also shows staff that they are valued. Proactive management adopts policies and compensation packages that will draw people to want to work in courts. Proactive management provides a wide range of training and prepares staff for advancement, both within the court, and, if they choose to leave, outside the court. Proactive management provides appealing working conditions and opportunities for growth. Proactive management seeks and values staff input, and recognizes staff input into how to improve operations and service to stakeholders. Proactive management develops staff's strengths. Once again, Peter Drucker has a compelling way to highlight this last point:[133]

> People are weak; and most of us are pitifully weak. People cause problems, require procedures, create chores. And people are a cost and a potential "threat." But these are not the reasons why people are employed. The reason is their strength and their capacity to perform. And ... the purpose of an organization is to make the strengths of people productive and their weaknesses irrelevant.

Drucker certainly is not alone in urging the value of building up people's strengths. Marcus Buckingham in the *Harvard Business Review* has said: "Good managers know how to ferret out the strengths and weaknesses of their employees—then figure out how to build those strengths and minimize those weaknesses. This is a big job and the reason managers are such an important aspect of successful businesses."[134] When a young basketball coach's team at the U.S. Military Academy got off to be poor start (5-7), she called her brother, who was the basketball coach of the University of Pittsburgh. One of the key pieces of advice he provided was not to berate the players, but always find something positive to say and build them up. At the end of the season, Army's women's basketball team made the NCAA basketball tournament for the first time ever.[135] Proactive management understands this aspect of personnel management and practices it.

Courts normally have to provide whatever the funding authority provides in the way of fringe benefits. Even when courts have their own personnel system independent of the executive branch, most courts seek to provide the same as or very close to the executive branch's benefits for two reasons: (1) they want to facilitate the movement of employees in other government agencies to the courts and from courts to the other branches; and (2) they do not want to get into a budget argument with the two other branches that they are being too generous. Nonetheless, in the tight labor market that can reasonably be anticipated over the next ten to 15 years, courts can and should examine some improvements that would make court employment attractive to more workers. Courts also have to recognize that they do not draw evenly from men and women in the workforce; women predominate in the workforce of trial courts. That reality may affect the choices made regarding benefits.

Low-Wage America: How Employers Are Reshaping Opportunity in the Workplace,[136] discusses the evaporation of the American dream of upward mobility of workers, even across generations. Without citing a lot of numbers here, suffice to say that compared to the 1970s, there is less movement among income brackets, more downward movement in income by sons compared to their fathers, and more of the sons in the top income bracket started there than worked their way into it.

> [America's] economy is slowly stratifying along class lines. Today, upward mobility is determined increasingly by a college degree that's attainable mostly by those whose parents already have money or education.[137]
>
> Although college enrollment has soared ... more children from poor families can only afford to go to community colleges.... The number of poor students who get a [four year] degree—fewer than 5% in 2001—has barely budged in 30 years ....[138]

There is a clear trend to requiring a college degree for most court jobs. This shift may not be serving courts well. Americans have long shown that intellect, integrity, competence, imagination, and sound work habits are not the province only of those with college degrees.[139] Courts may be able to take advantage of the continuing American dream of upward mobility by seeking bright, hard-working, ambitious people who lack a college degree. Courts can use "premium pay" or "bonuses" for advanced education if desired, but they should allow job entry without it. An education benefit, if one does not already exist, should be added to the court's benefits package that provides reimbursement for tuition and book expenses for degree-required courses upon their satisfactory completion. Plus, such a package should provide leave time for college-level courses given only during the workday or to allow on-time arrival for an evening course. A few states are enacting imaginative ways to expand higher education opportunities to more citizens, but at the moment, the share of the nation's wealth devoted to enabling a higher education is shrinking. Courts can improve their recruiting and retention opportunities by recognizing this need and responding to it.

Another area of opportunity is being acknowledged and catered to by the private sector, but only to a lesser degree by government: the X and Y Generation and mothers of young children who want to work, but only part time or from their homes without set hours. Also, baby boomers who do not want to fully retire are potential candidates. Of this generation it is said, "seasoned workers are less likely to job-hop, get torn apart by issues of work-life balance, engage in egocentric battles with colleagues, or suffer from burnout. What they do want … is meaningful work, recognition of experience, and a flexibility that will allow them to reduce or alter responsibilities at the sunset of their careers."[140]

Part-time employment and job sharing arrangements are provided in courts, but normally as an exception rather than as a policy option. One of the reasons part-time jobs and job sharing are not favored is that in many courts, if someone works half or more time, full benefits must be provided. This is deemed too high a price for flexibility by many in government—particularly in an era of skyrocketing medical benefit costs. Starbucks pays full health benefits to part-time employees. Its board of directors questioned the wisdom of doing so, as government budget analysts and taxpayer groups do, until the CEO documented for the board that doing so saved money because turnover was dramatically reduced.[141] Perhaps the judiciary can serve as a local or state-level pilot program for two or three years to determine if similar benefits accrue in government, along with attracting quality employees and improving staff morale and productivity.

Telecommuting staff have not been favored in courts because many, if not most, jobs require customer contact or working with the hard-copy files, neither of which can be done from one's home. For over a decade, the private sector has been shipping technical support, catalog orders, and other telephone-based services abroad. Today, an increasing quantity of these services are staying home, being provided in American kitchens, extra bedrooms, and portions of living rooms by the very people who desire part time or flexible work hours. Compared to regular call centers, which have a 100 percent turnover rate, home-based call services have a 20-to-30 percent turnover rate.[142]

Flexible hours are another accommodation to the modern worker that is used a lot in some courts but not at all in many others. As more retail and other service organizations extend the hours that they remain open for service, pressure will grow on government agencies to do the same. Courts across the country have felt pressure for years from the legislative branch to extend their hours, particularly to establish night courts for traffic and small claims and other summary civil cases in order to accommodate working litigants. Some courts have night courts but most do not. Normally, if courts extend hours, it is to accept filings after hours in a drop box or via the Internet, not with staff at the courthouse.[143] Flexible hours will enable courts to extend their hours. There are management issues for courts using flexible hours if staff comes to work without a supervisor being present, but if a court extends its hours and uses flex time to fill that need, supervisors also would need to be accorded the flex time option. There also are other ways to check on presence and staff being productive. Plus, some effort may be needed to select the right people to work with less supervision. Germane to this thought is a comment by Peter Drucker: "A manager who starts out with the assumption that people are weak, irresponsible, and lazy will get weakness, irresponsibility, and laziness. He corrupts. A manager who assumes strength, responsibility, and desire to contribute may experience a few disappointments. But the manager's first task is to make effective the strengths of people, and this he can do only if he starts out with the assumption that people ... want to achieve."[144]

This thought is echoed by others. Lionel Tiger, Charles Darwin Professor of Anthropology at Rutgers University, says, "Leaders often forget that people arrive predisposed to do a good job.... One of the things good leaders do is to allow people to do what is built into them to do anyway, which is to contribute."[145] Two professors at the McLaren School of Business, University of San Francisco, in discussing the value of guarantees of service or products, say the following about customers. The word *employee* could effectively be substituted for *customer*.[146]

> [I]t is necessary to adopt a twofold premise: one, customers are trust-worthy; two, the overwhelming number of customers will not only *not* take advantage of you, but they will help make your business a success... the overwhelming majority of customers are quite honest and decent. The ones who aren't trustworthy can be isolated and weeded out, but as one successful manager told a colleague of ours: "If 2 percent of our customers are jerks, why would I want to create a system that tells the 98 good people 'we don't trust because we think you're jerks, too?'" Customers are remarkably tolerant and forgiving when they believe that the organization—even when it messes up—sincerely cares about doing right by them.

All of the employment options discussed above can be found in some courts, but not broadly across the country. All pose some management challenges, but those can be addressed. At least one study indicates they can be beneficial. In a study of 103 married and employed women who used at least one family-friendly benefit, "eighty percent ... said the work/life policies they utilized did make a difference in their marriages." The policies did not necessarily save them from gender-based work at home, but it gave them the time to do it without feeling resentment or extra stress.[147] In another study of 941 telecommuters from 20 countries, 46 percent of the women and 52 percent of the men said they feel more productive working at home.[148] Boeing Company's director of the workplace of the future, Jeffrey Hobbs, says flexible hours are necessary to attract younger workers.[149]

Health improvement is a low-cost way for courts to benefit their staffs. Some courts allow or provide nutrition and exercise training for staff. A court can furnish a small inside exercise/wellness room where staff can use low-impact exercise equipment either during a short break to get their juices going again or during lunch. Some businesses now are providing resting rooms for staff. (Midday rest breaks are becoming recognized as desirable for both employees and employers.) Lake Havasu City, Arizona, in 2004 paid 37 employees to attend Weight Watchers.[150] Courts also could create and expand wellness programs beyond substance abuse and psychological counseling. Studies show that people who come to work while sick often infect others, so courts might review their sick leave policies and be stricter about people staying home when they are ill. The court administrator could set an example by staying home when he or she is ill.

Finally, courts can seek to address lifestyle challenges that impact their staffs. For example, courts can survey staff about their needs, especially as they relate to the "sandwich" generation's problems,[151] and develop programs that respond. Courts can work with others, in either the public or private sector, to establish subsidized adult and child day care facilities for staff.

Another way to improve staff morale and cut turnover is to improve the training of first-line supervisors. "[T]he data are very clear that ... the direct supervisor is most influential [in the decision about whether] the employee will stay or leave.... Does the individual's leader or supervisor talk to that employee to understand his aspirations, educate him to help him meet those aspirations, and encourage him to do so? The more successful companies are finding ways to keep talented people engaged."[152] Supervisors should understand that their primary responsibility is staff support. IBM does not use the term *supervisor*. Rather, the job description is "assistant." "His [or her] job is to be the 'assistant' to his [or her] workers. His [or her] job is to be sure that they know their work and have the tools. He [or she] is not their boss."[153] Drucker also suggests that during job performance evaluations, the following questions be asked[154] (emphasis in original).

1. What do I do as your manager, and what does your company [court] do that helps you the most in *your* job?
2. What do I do as your manager, and what does the company [court] do, that hinders you the most in *your* job?
3. What can you do that will help me, as *your* manager, do the best job for the company [court]?

Frederick Smith, former Chairman and CEO of FedEx, advises that managers also should be prepared to answer five questions that new employees have:[155]

1. What do you expect from me?
2. What's in it for me?
3. Where do I go if I have a problem?
4. How am I doing?
5. Is what I'm doing important?

One effective way to keep talented people engaged is to emphasize internal promotions, review internal candidates before advertising openings, and give "point" credit for previous court employment, similar to veteran preferences. Good people also can be attracted to join the court is it gives a hiring preference to employees of other courts who have moved into the area, including noncompetitive hiring when one's performance in the previous court was good.

Some of these ideas involve additional funds. Seeking increased salaries to compete with the private sector and failing to fill positions with good workers also cost money. The lower-cost alternatives discussed here can, to a degree, offset any salary and benefits weaknesses the court has relative to the private sector. Almost anything courts do to improve salaries or the benefits of employees will offend some taxpayers. Some people seem to believe that government should operate on the cheap because "it's our money." Good workers make government better. Most citizens want their money spent wisely, which means attracting good staff to courts initially and keeping as many as possible. Government does not have to match the employers in the community whose compensation is highest, but it also should not apologize for trying to be competitive for good employees. Either courts can do nothing to improve benefits beyond whatever the executive branch is willing to do or they can rethink what will allow the judiciary to get the skilled people it needs. Proactive management seeks to attract good staff and to keep the good staff it has.

12.14 Assuring Access

Access has many components: physical access to the courthouse; the ability to get to a courthouse; electronic access; language access, including the use of plain-English for forms; finding one's way around the courthouse (signage); and self-representation assistance. Proactive management is sensitive to assuring access in all these components and to assuring that any new means of access that arise are broadly available. Physical access and language access were discussed in sections 9.2.4 and 9.2.7, chapter 9. Here, brief reference will be made to signage and assistance to the self-represented.

People who work in courts quickly find their way around and become familiar and comfortable with where to go to see specific people and do specific things. It is easy to forget the feeling one has the first time one steps into a courthouse and has to find the clerk's office or a courtroom. Finding the right room is harder if different case types are handled on different floors with corresponding clerk's operations on each floor and when one does not know the courtroom but only a party's name or a judge's name. Almost every court posts each courtroom's calendar outside that courtroom and many post all calendars near the building's entrance in a public lobby. Some of these also post an alphabetic list of parties to facilitate finding a name and then a courtroom and time. In most courts, a visitor then is on his or her own.

Courts generally are becoming more sensitive to the need for clear, understandable signs to help people navigate the courthouse. Some are adding diagrams of each floor of the courthouse, much as a shopping mall does to help shoppers find specific stores. A growing number have opted for information booths near the main entrance, normally staffed by volunteers, to direct people to the proper place. A limited number of courthouses now have television monitors posted in several locations in the courthouse that scroll the names of cases and their assigned courtrooms, much as airport monitors show arriving and departing flights. Despite all these efforts, there continues to be an unmet need for more attention being given to helping visitors navigate through a courthouse so they can complete their business.

In addition to ordinary signs and electronic monitors, as the population ages, more people are becoming sensitive to the needs of senior citizens. They might benefit most from a human being giving them instructions so the information person can assess whether the instructions are understood. Or, larger type may be needed on the posted calendars or TV monitors (and signs). Hand-out diagrams of each floor may prove to be helpful. Courts also have to be sensitive to the needs of the visually impaired, the hearing impaired, and the mentally impaired who will be visiting the courthouse.

In today's world, courts also need to pay more attention to building evacuation and emergency procedure signs. An advisory committee was suggested in section 10.2.1, chapter 10, to assist with security issues. Either an advisory committee or a group of citizen volunteers representing a variety of backgrounds and needs could be very helpful to a court if periodically its members entered the courthouse to review and test signage and the ease with which a relative stranger can find people and things. Proactive management reviews signage and physical access issues annually.[156]

Until 1995, self-represented litigants (also known as "pro per" or "pro se" litigants) were on their own. The feeling was that if they wanted to represent themselves that was their right, but the court could not help them because that would be favoring one side over the other and be contrary to the appearance of justice. Courts felt they just had to put up with the self-representeds' lack of knowledge of applicable law and what law is not applicable, incomplete and incorrect paperwork, and lack of supporting evidence when they got to trial. The

American Bar Association accredits law schools teaching people to be lawyers. There are no schools teaching citizens how to be a self-representing litigant. In 1995, the Maricopa County (Phoenix) Superior Court set up the first program in the nation to facilitate the use of courts by self-represented individuals. The care put into planning the center and the positive response from the community created a paradigm shift in courts' thinking about the needs of the self-represented and how helping them also helped the court.[157]

Many courts across the country now provide some form of assistance to self-represented litigants. The number of assisting courts not only is growing, but the assistance also is getting more sophisticated, as courts and the local bar gain more experience with these programs. The assistance ranges across a broad spectrum:

- Forms packets, usually organized by case type and sometimes by type of action to be filed, organized to assist the self-representeds to find and complete the correct form;
- A broader library with law books, including some directed solely at helping the self-represented;
- On-site staff to guide self-representeds to the right materials;
- Website assistance with descriptions of the process, forms (sometimes allowing online completion), and occasional virtual tours of courtrooms and the process;
- Group workshops, normally run by an attorney and sometimes available in different locations around a county, to inform people about court processes, forms and information needed, and to guide them through completion of the correct forms;[158]
- Assistance by attorneys at a courthouse location, either volunteers from the bar or employed attorneys, who identify the proper forms for self-represented to use and who can help them complete the forms, but not represent them in a lawyer–client relationship.[159]

Most recently, some courts are developing computer-based programs that assist with the completion of forms. Like tax-preparation software and online travel sites, the software asks the self-represented a series of questions about who, what, where, when, and how, and then selects the proper form and fills the information provided into the proper part of the form(s). At that point, the computer either prints out a hard-copy paper version for subsequent filing or allows electronic filing of the computer-generated forms. Normally, nonattorney court staff are handy to assist with use of the computer and to answer questions about the information being requested, but not to provide legal advice.

Evaluations of these programs have been very positive in terms of customer satisfaction and the improved results judges see in the courtroom.[160] Every court and each program has room for improvement, but generally these programs are a marked improvement in the service provided by courts and they make the court process both more understandable to and more accepted by self-represented litigants. Any court totally lacking assistance to self-represented should develop some level of assistance as soon as possible. For most courts, the challenge is to expand the services offered using limited additional funds. The focus in many courts, therefore, has been to enhance the information and assistance available through the court's website and to refine information available at the courthouse. In very diverse communities, there also has been an effort to provide information and form completion directions in the major languages used in the community in order to expand access. For some from countries whose courts are not seen as independent of the government or whose cultures frown on the use of law and courts to settle disputes, there also are information packets and occasional on-site workshops to explain the American legal system and how it can help. The relatively new computerized "paralegal" programs for completing court complaints/petitions and other documents also will be a growing area of assistance.

In proactive management courts, enhancing access for all citizens is a very high priority. Proactive management continually looks for opportunities to assure and then to expand access opportunities and services to citizens, whatever their particular need or limitation.

12.15 Interaction with the Community

The interaction between a court and its community should be a two-way interaction. Citizens should have opportunities to provide input to courts and courts should reach out to the community, first with messages about itself, and then as a contributing partner to community life. Proactive management addresses both aspects of this interaction.

12.15.1 Reaching Out to the Community[161]

Most of the elements of this task have been mentioned previously:

- Appearances by judges and senior managers before community service clubs and other civic organizations
- Press releases about court administration achievements and changes and news of the court plus parallel information on the court's website, including personal and professional achievements of judges such as running a triathlon or marathon, participating in a long-distance bicycle ride or race, charitable work in another community following a disaster, serving as faculty to train other judges or court administrators, and similar noteworthy activities

- An "ask a judge" column in the local newspaper(s) of screened questions a judge can answer, possibly supplemented by comments by an attorney
- Possible blog sites for comments about and for the court by attorneys, litigants, the public, judges, and senior managers
- Annual reports on court activity and accomplishments;[162]
- Allowing community groups to use court facilities for meetings
- School group tours
- Judges or judge-attorney teams appearing in local schools to teach one, two, or a series of segments on legal issues or the role of courts in society[163]
- Television broadcasts of all trials or trials of local significance
- Judges and court staff taking a more visible role in community functions and charitable events (e.g., walks, marathons, local fairs, fund raising for a community charity or following a community disaster, and even parades).

12.15.2 Obtaining Community Input and Feedback

There also are several ways courts have obtained and could obtain community input and suggestions for changes:

- Comment cards on public counters
- A section of a court's website for both comments about the website and comments about one's experience(s) with the court
- A jury section on the website that includes a space for the juror exit questionnaire and comments about jury duty
- Establish advisory committees for significant changes in court operations or major study topics and include members of the general public on the committees along with attorneys and representatives of the criminal justice community
- Add members of the pubic to the committee(s) developing a court's strategic plan
- Solicit community comments on administrative rules and budget priorities prior to adopting final versions
- If a new courthouse is to be built or a major renovation is to be undertaken, set up a citizens' advisory committee comprised of former jurors, self-represented litigants, the bar, local elected officials, and the general public.

The only caution in soliciting community input is that a court should not ask if it is not prepared to listen. Some comments will be hard to hear, some out of bounds, and some off the subject, but these are not sufficient to foreclose the idea. When customers indicate an expectation regarding the level or quality of service received from the court, the court should seek to respond. Drawing on a tenet of quality management, courts should seek to meet and exceed customer expectations. They can do so by listening to feedback from customers and from staff who have regular contact with customers.

The private sector is using the Internet increasingly to solicit product ideas, reactions to new designs and design changes, and marketing ideas. There is no reason courts could not do likewise.

12.16 Working with and Supporting Stakeholder Organizations

The numerous interdependencies in which courts are involved have been mentioned throughout this book. In most cases, if courts' institutional stakeholders do not function well, the courts will have a harder time functioning well. Therefore, proactive management supports stakeholders' efforts to increase resources and to introduce programs that will make the entire justice system work better.[164] One court administrator used to help other agencies to write grant proposals and provided letters of support for other proposals. His court also urged that the prosecutor obtain additional secretarial support because that extra position would enable the prosecutor to get papers filed in court in a more timely fashion.

Similarly, when a stakeholder indicates that a court procedure is having an adverse impact on its operations, the court, at a minimum, should be willing to listen to and understand the nature of the problem and consider whether there are adjustments that can be made. If making an adjustment to or change in the court's procedures would not have a negative impact on other court users, the adjustment or change should be made. If it would negatively affect others, the court should convene a meeting of affected stakeholders plus its own staff to try to find a response that would benefit all.

12.17 Maintaining and Adapting Facilities

In both locally and state-funded courts, maintenance of the courthouse(s), including janitorial services, normally is the responsibility of the local government.[165] The intergovernmental logistical and funding issues associated with the maintenance of courthouses were discussed in section 4.1.2, chapter 4, and in section 9.2.15, chapter 9. This section will focus on adapting facilities.

Proactive management considers the impact of changing programs and technologies on the courthouse facility itself and works with the responsible agency or agencies, normally in local government, to assure that the adjustments in facilities needed to support new programs or technology are provided in a timely way.

The facility changes may be little more than running a few new cables to a courtroom or section of the courthouse. It may be a child care facility that needs to be carved out of a space currently used for something else. Perhaps a courtroom should be converted into two smaller hearing rooms. If most of a court's records now are digital, perhaps the stored paper files can be moved to a long-term storage facility and the now-vacant records space converted into staff work areas or offices, conference or hearing rooms, or space for new technology equipment. Many new programs and changed programs do not occasion any need for adjustments to the courthouse itself. When an adjustment is needed, however, court administration should work with the responsible authority as closely as it does with those planning the new program so that the program is not delayed unduly because of facility restraints. (Sometimes the only option is new, rented space; when that is the case, the court's budget may need to be increased, unless the program is supported by a grant and the grant carries rent money with it.)

Proactive management often juggles several projects and changes at one time. From time to time it will appear to some to be doing too much at once. A court's leadership should never be at a loss for ideas of things that can be improved or newly introduced. Nor should it ever assume that all the changes needed to improve the institution have been identified and put in place. Being proactive means never being satisfied about what has been accomplished or timid about what remains to be done. Many courts across the nation have done exceptionally well in conceiving and implementing their own improvements and borrowing generously from the good work of other courts. Because of the phenomenon of "one court at a time," however, many courts still have much that might be accomplished. That is not a criticism, just an acknowledgment of the vast number of ideas for improvement that exist and might yet be formulated in this complex institution. Being proactive is what makes court administration a challenge. It also is a set of challenges that, when met, invigorate and produce much satisfaction for all involved.

Notes

1. Vanderbilt, Arthur T., "Foreword," *Reports of the Section of Judicial Administration*. Chicago: American Bar Association, 1938, reprinted in American Bar Association, *Improvement of the Administration of Justice*, 5th ed. Chicago: American Bar Association, 1971, p. xix.
2. See also, McConnell, Edward B., "Court Administration," in *The Improvement of the Administration of Justice*. 5th ed. Chicago: Section of Judicial Administration, American Bar Association, 1971, p. 28.
3. Burns, James MacGregor, *Leadership*. New York: Harper & Row, 1978, p. 290.
4. Ibid.

5. Ibid., p. 293.

6. Ibid., p. 291.

7. Green, Milton D., "The Business of the Trial Courts," in *The American Assembly, The Courts, The Public, and the Law Explosion.* Jones, Harry W., ed. Englewood Cliffs, NJ: Prentice-Hall, 1965, p. 7.

8. Even an administrative directive is insufficient sometimes, at least immediately. In the 1970s, the then-Chief Justice of Ohio ordered all trial courts to switch from master calendars to individual calendars for handling cases. He did so without consultation or warning. There was a significant revolt in some courts.

9. The judiciary nationally and in some states has shown it has remarkable political strength when it feels strongly about an issue and uses the powers of persuasion of its leaders. In many states it has achieved significant reforms needed to create a statewide judicial branch. It has convinced Congress to include courts in various funding programs. CCJ and COSCA also have convinced Congress several times not to adopt a law that would have a significant adverse impact on state courts. This strength seldom seems to extend to discussions about budgeted money, however.

10. See chapter 4.

11. The difficulty with the second and third arguments is that questionable assumptions or unduly optimistic conclusions often support them. Then, in years two or three, there are further arguments because the savings are not realized or the income falls short. The budget process, like the making of sausage, is not pretty to watch.

12. See, for example, "Help Desk Offers Advice to Civil Litigants," an Associated Press article retrieved Jan. 7, 2006 from http://abcnews.go.com/US/wireStory?id=1481106. The article describes how a federal district court announced the start of a program in which an attorney employed by the court would be assisting self-represented litigants with their civil case filings. The news report says that, "experts say it is believed to be the first of its kind in the nation." It may or may not be the first such program in a federal district court, or there may be some slight variation that the article does not report, but the "experts" being cited did not even hint that this service was started in the State of Washington a dozen years earlier and has been replicated in many state trial courts since. The federal court is providing a valuable service to both itself and to self-represented litigants, but it is hundreds of courts shy of being "the first of its kind in the nation." Similar announcements about improvements in jury management are made across the nation each year, including changes that first were proposed and implemented in some courts in the 1970s or 1980s. It almost seems to be against human nature (or government nature) to say, "We're way behind in doing this, but it's a great idea and we're delighted to be joining dozens (or hundreds) of other courts in providing this service to our customers."

13. The district court in Minneapolis, Minnesota undertook in 2002 to prepare to apply for a Baldridge National Quality Award, a national award of the Department of Commerce's National Institute of Standards and Technology to business, health care, and education entities. (Government units were added to the list of eligible organizations in 2004, but quality criteria for these organizations had not been established as of early 2006.) Applicants for the award must meet very strict criteria for a quality organization. Putting an application together is very time consuming. One of the statutory requirements of the Baldridge program is that award recipients must be willing to share what they have done and learned with anyone interested. Were the court to become an award winner, the subsequent time commitment might dwarf the time devoted to preparing for and completing the application.

14. Commission on Trial Court Performance Standards, *Trial Court Performance Standards.* Williamsburg, VA: Bureau of Justice Assistance and National Center for State Courts, 1990.

15. Friesen, Ernest C., Jr., Edward C. Gallas, and Nesta Gallas, *Managing the Courts*. Indianapolis, IN: Bobbs-Merrill, 1971, p. 193.

16. Commission on Trial Court Performance Standards, *Trial Court Performance Standards*, p. 6.

17. Williamsburg, VA: National Center for State Courts, 2005, with updates at http://www.ncsconline.org/d_research.

18. See also Conference of Chief Justices and Conference of State Court Administrators, Resolution 14 In Support of Measuring Court Performance, adopted August 3, 2005, retrieved Dec. 23, 2005, from http://ccj.ncsc.dni.us/CourtAdminResoultions/resol14Measuring-CourtPerformance.html.

19. Commission on Trial Court Performance Standards, *Trial Court Performance Standards*, pp. 23–41.

20. These earlier measures of performance are not deficient, just more than most courts could handle in terms of the time and cost to undertake them all. Using them selectively as a supplement to the ten core measures in CourTools is a desirable goal.

21. See also, Tobin, Robert W., *Creating the Judicial Branch: The Unfinished Reform*. Williamsburg, VA: National Center for State Courts, 1999, p. 231.

22. Determining if a program is successful does not mean every goal must use case-based data. Opinions can be obtained through interviews or questionnaires/surveys that can be valid supplements to case-based data. But even with opinion assessments, one can be more or less rigorous in stating expectations. Thus, one way to phrase a goal would be: "judges believe the new program has reduced problem X [that the program is seeking to address]." A more refined goal would be: "two-thirds or more of the judges will believe the new program has reduced problem X." A similar goal could be set for the opinions of users of the new program or their attorneys; for example, "the percentage of users who believe they understood the forms and how to complete them will increase by at least 20 percentage points." Or, "The mistakes made by self-represented litigants who complete ABC form are reduced by 50 percent [or, from an average of X per form to no more than Y per form]."

23. Drucker, Peter F., *Management: Tasks, Responsibilities, Practices*. New York: Harper & Row, 1973, p. 159.

24. Prosecutors and law enforcement can kill a court program if they believe it puts their agencies in a bad light or imposes too much effort on them compared to what they see to be advantages to them.

25. This is not an issue only for courts. In the book *Hard Facts, Dangerous Half-Truths & Total Nonsense: Profiting from Evidence-Based Management*, "the authors (Jeffrey Pfeffer and Robert I. Sutto) fret that managers' fondness for casual bench-marking ('GE does it? We should too!'), past practices, and pet ideologies may hold serious harm for their organizations." McGregor, Jena, "Forget Going with Your Gut," *Business Week*, Mar. 20, 2006, p. 112.

26. Petrosino, Anthony, Carolyn Turpin-Petrosino and John Buehler, "Scared Straight and Other Juvenile Awareness Programs for Preventing Juvenile Delinquency," (updated, 2003), retrieved at http://www.campbellcollaboration.org/fcontend2.asp?ID=4.

27. Ibid.

28. For example, Belenko, Steven, "Research on Drug Courts: A Critical Review, 2001 Update." New York: The National Center on Addiction and Substance Abuse, Columbia Univ., 2001.

29. A study of drug courts by U.S.Congress, General Accounting Office in 2002 found that most of the drug courts in existence at that time had stopped tracking recidivism because the funding agency stopped asking local courts in 2000 to collect recidivism information. McMurray, Jeffrey, "Study: DOJ Has Lost Track of Drug Courts," *ABAJournal.com*, Apr. 24, 2002, retrieved May 6, 2002 from http://www.abanet.org/journal/redesign/apdrug.html.

30. See also, the description of the effort to do evaluations in less time with less cost reported in Maryland Administrative Office of the Courts, *An Executive Program Assessment for State Court Projects to Assist Self-Represented Litigants*. Annapolis, MD: Maryland Administrative Office of the Courts, 2005.

31. Drucker, Peter F., *Management*, pp. 268–269. See also, Imparato, Nicholas, and Oren Harari, *Jumping the Curve: Innovation and Strategic Choice in an Age of Transition*. San Francisco: Jossey-Bass, 1994, p. 147: At Mrs. Fields Cookies, "Information is not used to control but rather to elevate awareness and understanding."

32. This argument is easier to make and has more force when there are doubts about the validity of the data drawn from the case management information system. That is why the accuracy of the data is so important.

33. Drucker, Peter F., *Management*, p. 140.

34. See Ante, Spencer E., "Giving the Boss the Big Picture," *Business Week*, Feb. 13, 2006, p. 48.

35. Berra, Yogi, *The Yogi Book: I Really Didn't Say Everything I Said*. New York: Workman Publishing, 1999, p. 102.

36. Tobin, Robert W., *Creating the Judicial Branch*, p. 111.

37. Imparato, Nicholas, and Oren Harari, *Jumping the Curve*, p. 53.

38. The largest effort at criminal justice planning undertaken nationally to date was the in early 1970s effort funded and overseen by the Law Enforcement Assistance Administration, the National Advisory Commission on Criminal Justice Standards and Goals. The Commission produced an overall report, *A National Strategy to Reduce Crime*. Washington, D.C.: U.S. Gov't Printing Office, 1973, while each of its 12 task forces, including one on courts, also produced an independent report with analysis and recommendations that fed into the overall report. This effort was significant in several respects, but the two relevant here are that: (a) all 13 reports are excellent and thoughtful with many ideas worthy of serious consideration; and (b) many of the recommendations could be made as readily and as appropriately today as they were in 1973.

39. National Association for Court Management, *Core Competency Curriculum Guidelines: What Court Leaders Need to Know and Be Able to Do*. Williamsburg, VA: National Association for Court Management, 2005, p. 21.

40. Ibid., p. 22.

41. Ibid.

42. Vanderbilt, Arthur T., "Foreword," *Reports of the Section of Judicial Administration*. Chicago: American Bar Association, 1938, reprinted in American Bar Association, *Improvement of the Administration of Justice*, 5th ed. Chicago: American Bar Association, 1971, p. 144.

43. See, for example, "'Health Courts' Offer Cure," *USA Today*, July 4, 2005, retrieved from http://usatoday.com/news/opinion/editorials/2005-07-74-our-view_x.htm. See also, Howard, Philip K., and Stephanie Mencimer, "The Doctor's Court," *Legal Affairs* Debate Club, Mar. 14, 2005, retrieved March 29, 2006, from http://www.legalaffairs.org/webexclusive/debateclub_medmal0305.msp.

44. Imparato, Nicholas, and Oren Harari, *Jumping the Curve*, p. 192.

45. Stupak, Ronald J., "The Advocacy Arena: Who Shall Lead Us?," *The Journal of Volunteer Administration*, vol. 23, no. 2, April/May 2005, p. 40.

46. National Association for Court Management, *Core Competency Guidelines*, p. 21.

47. During a hospital visit a number of years ago, I discovered the hospital's excellent mission statement posted on the wall by the coffee refill station in the public cafeteria.

48. Hesselbein, Francis, "All in a Day's Work," *Harvard Business Review.*, Dec. 2001, p. 64. (Ms. Hesselbein is a former CEO of the Girl Scouts and Chair of the Peter F. Drucker Foundation.)

49. See "Marketing—Target Market, Innovators, Early Adopters, Influencers," retrieved July 19, 2005 from http://www.determan.net/Michele/mtarget.htm.

50. Hesselbein, Francis, "All in a Day's Work," p.58.

51. For example, Bennis, Warren, *On Becoming a Leader.* New York: Basic Books, 2003, p. 33.

52. Chemist Albert von Szent-Gyorgy, quoted in Good, Irving John, *The Scientist Speculates.* New York: Heinemann & Basic Books, 1962.

53. Statement of the Best Practices Institute retrieved April 2006 from http://www.ncsconline. org/Projects_Initiatives/BP/index.htm.

54. Berman, Greg, and John Feinblatt, *Good Courts: The Case for Problem-Solving Justice.* New York: The New Press, 2005, p. 9.

55. Rottman, David, and Pamela Casey, "Therapeutic Jurisprudence and the Emergence of Problem-Solving Courts," *National Institute of Justice Journal*, July 1999, p. 15.

56. In one recent study, only 9 percent of the drug court participants who completed the four evaluated programs were rearrested within a year, while 41 percent of those who were terminated were rearrested. Abstract of "Evaluation of Program Completion and Rearrest Rates across Four Drug Court Programs," *Drug Court Review*, vol. 5, no. 1, 2005, retrieved from http://www.ncjrs.gov/AbstractDB/Details.asp?fromWAL=1&perpage=1&index=10&ncjn um=234584&docIndex=928chkBoxBitFlag=0000....

57. Conference of Chief Justices and the Conference of State Court Administrators, Resolution 12, In Support of Problem-Solving Court Principles and Methods, reaffirming their Aug. 3, 2000, resolution on July 29, 2004, retrieved from http://ccj.ncsc.din.us/CourtAdminResolu- tions/ProblemSolvingCourtPrinciplesAndMethods.pdf.

58. Ibid.

59. Tobin, Robert W., *Creating the Judicial Branch*, p. 224.

60. Then-Chief Justice Michael D. Zimmerman, Utah Supreme Court, in a speech to the Utah Bar Foundation, quoted in ibid., p. 227.

61. Many problem-solving courts have been set up with no additional staff; the judge and his or her existing support staff just take on the extra work because of belief in the program. Most models of successful courts, however, include a coordinator position to work with and monitor the outside agencies and sometimes a scheduling and coordinating position for in-court coordination. Sometimes, these are new positions, sometimes just a reallocation of existing staff.

62. Berman, Greg and John Feinblatt, *Good Courts*, p. 7.

63. Friesen, Ernest C., Jr., Edward C. Gallas, and Nesta Gallas, *Managing the Courts*, p. 211.

64. For analogous suggestions focusing on criminal cases, see American Bar Association, *Standards for Criminal Justice: Speedy Trial and Timely Resolution of Criminal Cases* (2004), retrieved from http://www.abanet.org/crimjust/standards/speedytrial_toc.html.

65. Caseflow management and court control of the pace of litigation are about controlling the calendar time that cases remain in the court. Preparation time for attorneys (and self-representeds) must be preserved to assure due process of law. Delay comes from confusing the two, from thinking that if parties have more calendar time, they will spend more time preparing this case. That might be true for self-represented litigants, who have only one case at a time, but attorneys are more likely to use extra calendar time to handle other cases before returning to the instant case shortly before it is due back in court or just before some discovery event. If judges ignore the reality that attorneys handle more than one case at a time they might unfairly impinge on preparation time, but judges also have to recognize that attorneys have no legal or moral right to take more cases than they can handle in a reasonable amount of time.

66. Mostly, this refers to stating expectations that each step in the processing of each type of case will be achieved within a certain time, with the sum for all steps equaling the overall time goal. When a court considers the differentiation of cases, there is a second set of subgoals it should keep in mind. As a broad, general rule, two-thirds of the cases in a broad case category should be disposed within half the time set in the time standard (e.g., 65–67 percent of cases with a one-year standard disposed within six months) and about 85 percent of all cases disposed within three-quarters of the time provided in the time standard (within nine months in this example). If a court manages to that type of subgoal, judges will have the time needed to manage the cases most requiring their attention.

67. During one caseflow management workshop, a judge was asked to identify his goals for the workshop. He said his goal was to find out whether he could manage cases better without upsetting all his fellow judges and the bar, because he wanted to get reelected the next time he ran. He was from a state with a very partisan political environment.

68. A well-planned program will/must involve bar leaders in the planning effort and in helping to advise the bar of its purposes and how it will work. The visible support of these leaders will lead some attorneys who might otherwise oppose the program to give it a chance to see if the promises pan out. The bar is very diverse and attorneys are strong willed, however, so even with leaders' support, there will be nay-sayers who will oppose the change.

69. One of the most-frequent irritants for self-represented litigants is the delay and repeated continuances tolerated by courts.

70. The number of prospective jurors needed to select a jury for most cases (95% or more) varies in each court in each state, based on local practice, the number of peremptory challenges available and typically used (by case type), the typical number of jurors removed for cause, and, sometimes, the trial judge. Within a given court, a relatively narrow range of jurors needed is discernable through analysis of data kept by the courtroom clerk during voir dire. The goal for jury management staff is to have as few citizens as possible who are "unused" when a jury finally is selected. ("Unused" means never called to the jury box for voir dire.) Therefore, jury staff wants to err on the side of a judge running out of jurors prior to getting a jury once or, at most, twice a year, based on the data. Judges' goal (and that of many attorneys) is to err strongly on the side of never running out. Courts with strong jury management programs work with their judges to agree on a "typical" number of jurors sent to start the voir dire process. In these courts, judges accept the risk that maybe once or twice a year they may run out of jurors before a jury is selected. They do so to further the goal of the organization to save money and not to overburden too many citizens with a needless appearance at the courthouse. Suspension of voir dire is anathema to other judges, so that they insist on starting voir dire with a large "cushion" of jurors. Judges control the trial process and their courtrooms. When a judge insists on a number of prospective jurors to start voir dire that is well above his or her typical needs, jury staff has only one option: keep the data and continue to work with the judge to convince him or her over time that a smaller number initially will not threaten his or her chances of selecting a jury in all but the most unusual case. And in those unusual cases, the judge probably knows in advance that they are unusual, so the judge and jury staff can agree to bring in extra jurors for those cases.

71. Available through the website of the sponsoring agency, American Legislative Exchange Council, http://www.alec.org/meSWFile/pdf/0309.pdf.

72. If the judges do not accept the one trial/one day model, the administrator at least should seek agreement to shorten the term of service.

73. Developing plain-English instructions is easier said than done because of the complexities and subtleties introduced into the instruction process over decades, if not centuries. Therefore,

the effort usually takes several years. If the jury system is to remain a viable part of the fact-finding process in courts, however, it is a necessary commitment of time and resources.

74. See the NCSC's *Trial Trends Report*, retrieved Mar. 3, 2006, from http://www.ncsconline. org/C_Research/csp/TrialTrends/CSPtrialtrends.html.

75. See Carlzon, Jan, *Moments of Truth*. New York: Harper & Row, 1989, esp. p. 6.

76. It was interesting to hear jurors in two high-profile cases in California in 2004 and 2005, during post-trial interviews, indicate that they used made-up nicknames or first names while sitting as jurors so they could talk and refer to each other. It was only after their verdict was delivered in court that they learned the real names of their fellow jurors.

77. Hempel, Jessi, and Paula Lehman, "MySpace.com Generation," *Business Week*, Dec. 12, 2005, p. 89.

78. Ibid., p. 88.

79. Ibid.

80. Goodman, Ellen, "In Paying Attention, the Coin Is Time," Redding (CA) *Record Searchlight*, Aug. 12, 2005, p. A-6.

81. See also, "Zen and the Art of Thinking Straight, *Business Week*, Apr. 3, 2006, p. 116. This article contains a condensed version of an interview of Dr. Edward Hallowell about his book, *CrazyBusy: Overstreched, Overbooked, and About to Snap—Strategies for Coping in a World Gone ADD*. New York: Ballantine Books, 2006.

82. All of these data are reported in Crockett, Roger O., "Why the Web Is Hitting a Wall," *Business Week*, Mar. 20, 2006, pp. 90–91.

83. Crawford, Chris, "Technology Facts," *The Court Manager*, vol. 20, no. 2, p. 31.

84. Wolfe, Gary, and Vince Kasten, "Bringing Courts Into the Future," *The Court Manager*, vol. 20, no. 2, p. 9.

85. Ibid., p. 10.

86. In the county where I was a court administrator, an effort was started several years before I arrived to create an integrated criminal justice information system. The court was skeptical, but agreed to participate until about a year and a half into the project, when the court pulled out and the effort collapsed. Well over a million dollars had been spent up to that point. When I proposed that the court buy a new case management information system more than two years after the collapse, virtually everyone in the court and some in the county's Information Technology Department and the county administrator's office told me about the criminal justice information system debacle and cautioned that neither the court nor the county could withstand another failure.

87. Prepared by Fenn, Jackie, Gartner Fellow, Gartner Group, and used by permission. Gartner Group is a provider of research and analysis about the global information technology industry. Additional information about Gartner Group may be obtained through http://www.gartner. com.

88. The difference between the early adopter courts and the others is the best illustration of the difference between leadership courts and proactive management courts. Proactive management courts seek technological advantages and scan the environment to find them; leadership courts are able and eager to be early adopters.

89. See also, Conference of State Court Administrators, *Position Paper on the Emergence of E-Everything*. Dec. 2005, especially pp. 9–10, retrieved from http://cosca.ncsc.dni.us/White-Papers/E-EverythingPositionPaper/ApprovedDec05.pdf.

Because of the multitude of different computers and computerized information systems in trial courts across a state and the nation, this goal is yet another example of one court at a time. See the project description of the electronic filing project in California, retrievable from http://www.courtinfo.ca.gov/programs/efiling. Because of this limitation, it may not be possible for the remaining courts to have their systems operational within the next five years, but the effort can be started.

90. "Text Message Nation," *Business Week*, Jan. 28, 2006, p. 14.

91. "Pacesetters Streamlining," *Business Week*, Nov. 21, 2005, p. 94.

92. A number of courts have posted forms on their website for downloading, but do not yet provide for completing the forms, either online or offline with subsequent electronic filing after the form has been filled in. This capacity should be added.

93. Brehe, Todd A., 'E-Publications—A Means to Improve Communications Processes for U.S. Courts," *The Court Manager*, vol. 20, no. 2, Spring 2005, p. 28.

94. "Instant Translations," *PC Magazine*, Dec. 14, 1999, p.11.

95. Richard Schauffler in e-mails to the author in 2003.

96. If a user translates one page, say the opening page, and then wants to link to another page on the website, the second page will appear in English again. Then the user would have to paste that web address into the search company's translation and start over. It is a bit awkward, but it works. A court also would have to be clear that all documents filed with the court must be in English.

97. http://justiceserved.com.

98. http://www.ncsconline.org.

99. http://www.uwstout.edu/webusabilitycenter/.

100. Vol. 35, no. 7, July 2002, pp. 102–103. (IEEE stands for the Institute of Electrical and Electronics Engineers.)

101. Palmer, Jonathan, Abstract of "Designing for Web Site Usability," retrieved from http://csdl2.computer.org/persagen/DLAbsToc.jsp?resourcePath=/dl/mags/co/&toc=comp/mags/co/2002/07/r7toc.xml&DOI=101109/MC2002.1016906.

102. In King County (Seattle), Washington, jail officials proposed to the court a few years ago that the video arraignment equipment be extended to civil courts so inmates involved in civil matters could appear via video. Memo provided to the author during a consulting assignment in King County.

103. The U.S. Department of Health and Human Services now is using televised appearances as the primary mode of handling Medicare coverage appeals. Some trial court judges have expressed concern that they cannot properly evaluate body language and subtle movements by those testifying if they see a party or witness through a television screen. As credibility always is an issue and these clues help to determine credibility, the objection needs to be taken into account. With the improvement in camera lenses and transmission capabilities, however, objections that carried weight in the 1990s may not be as significant today. To be certain that the technology has overcome this issue, pilot efforts would seem to be in order. The other consideration would be staffing in the video appearance room, as it would not be prudent to assume that the equipment could and would be operated properly without someone trained in its use being present.

104. A 2005 Australian study compared the impact on juries of live testimony, prerecorded video, and closed circuit television appearances in adult sexual assault cases. The mode of presentation of evidence "did not have a significant impact on jury decisionmaking." Abstract statement of Taylor, Natalie, and Jacqueline Joudo, *Impact of Pre-Recorded Video and Closed Circuit Television Testimony by Adult Sexual Assault Complainants on Jury decision-Making: An Experimental Study*. Retrieved Apr. 3, 2006 from http://www.ncjrs.gov/AbstractDB/Details.asp?fromWAL=1&perpage=1&index=11&ncjnum=234815&docindex=53&chkBoxBitFlags=0000…

105. See "Ontario County Family Court Pro Se Remote Assistance Project," *Briefly* (the newsletter of the Seventh Judicial District, in Rochester, NY), Feb. 10, 2006, p. 1.

106. "Videoconferencing to the Rescue," *Briefly*, June 10, 2005, p. 1.

107. There is an issue of court proceedings traditionally occurring in a public forum. This can be addressed by the arguments and questions being made a part of the case file to which the public would have access.

108. Conference of State Court Administrators, *Emergence of E-Everything*, pp. 16–17.

109. Representatives of Courtroom 21 told the author that a 2003 survey of federal district courts indicated that about one-quarter of all district court courtrooms were high-tech at that time, with a growing number installing equipment as time goes by; likewise in state courts, although no data are available. A growing number of state courthouses are creating multiple electronic courtrooms, with a significant but as-yet uncounted number of courthouses having at least one courtroom that is enhanced technologically. Because of the continuing decline in the cost of this equipment, it is expected that more and more courtrooms will be outfitted with electronic presentation equipment over the next ten years.

110. Formally, the entire high-tech courtroom operation, a joint project of the law school and the National Center for State Courts is the Center for Legal and Court Technology and the Courtroom 21 Project.

111. "Polyvision's Thunder," *BusinessWeek Online*, retrieved Feb. 15, 2006, from http://images. businessweek.com/ss/06/02/demo_show/source/5.htm.

112. Conference of State Court Administrators, *Emergence of E-Everything*, p.17.

113. Thus, the name of COSCA's position paper cited in note 89, "The Emergence of E-Everything," seems particularly apt.

114. For example, "The Simpson Jurors," *Jur-E Bulletin*, Apr. 7, 2006, p. 1, available from the NCSC at http.www.ncsconline.org/Juries/bulletin.htm.

115. Courts are not alone in this regard. See Kerstetter, Jim, "Business Software: Comes the Revolution," *Business Week*, June 23, 2003, pp. 82–83.

116. Coy, Peter, "Beating Plowshares into Swords," *Business Week*, Apr. 7, 2003, p. 41.

117. "[S]tandardized programming technologies like the Extensible Markup Language, which makes it easier for different kinds of software to work together …" would help. Kerstetter, Jim, "Business Software," p. 82.

118. "Technology Primer: Radio Frequency Identification," *TechBeat*, Summer 2005, p. 6.

119. In the 1980s, suppliers were arguing for the use of radio-transmitter wireless microphones in courts so attorneys could walk around rather than standing at a podium to be heard through a microphone. In one courthouse I visited that used these microphones, from time to time radio broadcasts and passing truckers on CBs could be heard over those same microphones during a trial. If external radio interference would interfere with finding files when needed, that could be a problem for a court.

120. Robitaille, Suzanne, "How VoIP Can Connect the Disabled," *BusinessWeek Online*, April 28, 2004, retrieved Apr. 30, 2004, from http://www.businessweek.com/technology/content/apr2004/tc20040428_43 ….

121. "Pay by Touch Online," *BusinessWeek Online*, Feb. 15, 2006, retrieved Feb. 15, 2006, from http://images.businessweek.com/ss/06/02/demo_show/source/7.htm.

122. For example,Wildstrom, Stephen H., "The View Beyond Vista," *Business Week*, May 8, 2006, p. 20.

123. Associated Press, "Floppy Disk Becoming Relic of the Past," Sept. 7, 2004, retrieved Sept. 7, 2004, from http://start.earthlink.net/newsarticle?cat=2&aid=D84UQEN80_story.

124. For a description of an interesting application of AI in a far-flung retail organization, see Imparato, Nicholas, and Oren Harari, *Jumping the Curve*, pp.158–160.

125. A fall 2004 article in *TechBeat*, a newsmagazine of the National Law Enforcement and Corrections Technology Center of the National Institute of Justice, discussed how corrections

officials have identified numerous uses for an environmentally friendly portable toilet. The first idea was to use the toilet, which does not use water, to help catch contraband drugs that had been swallowed. From there, brainstorming sessions identified many other possible uses. The manufacturer never had considered the corrections market. The person who first thought of the connection just happened to be attending a small business innovation research conference. Others know technology, but court people know courts. If they ask, "How could this help in my court?," many technologies not used now might surface.

126. See Drucker, Peter F., *Management*, p. 258.
127. Retrieved from http://library.thinkquest.org/J002678F/cortez.htm.
128. Burns, James MacGregor, *Leadership*, pp. 43–44.
129. Ibid., p. 20.
130. Roberts, Wess, *Leadership Secrets of Attila the Hun*. New York: Warner Books, 1990, p. 88.
131. R. Dale Lefever, frequent trainer and lecturer to judicial branch personnel on managing change.
132. Franklin, Benjamin, *The Works of Benjamin Franklin*, John Bigelow, ed. New York: GP Putnam's Sons, 1904, vol. 11, p. 361.
133. Drucker, Peter F., *Management*, p. 307.
134. Buckingham, Marcus, "What Great Managers Do," retrieved from http://www.marcusbuckingham.com/press/newPress/articles/HarvardBusiness/greatmanagers.php. See also, "What Not To Do," *Business Week*, Oct. 10, 2005, p.74.
135. For example, Berkow, Ira, "West Point Stands at Attention for Army's New Women's Coach," *New York Times*, March 15, 2006, retrieved Apr. 15, 2006, from http://patriotleague.cstv.com/genrel/031606aaa.html.
136. Bernhardt, Annette, Richard J. Murnane, and Eileen Appelbaum, eds. New York: Russell Sage Foundation, 2003.
137. Bernstein, Aaron, "Waking Up From the American Dream," *Business Week*, Dec. 1, 2003, p. 56.
138. Ibid.
139. A 2005–2006 survey of almost half of the members of the NACM—including judge-members and many who are not the court administrator—indicates that over 30 percent do not have a bachelor's or higher degree. (Fifty-five percent have a bachelor's or master's degree; most of the remaining 69 percent have law degrees.) National Association for Court Management, Membership Profile Survey, as of Apr. 3, 2006, provided to the author by the NACM.
140. Brady, Diane, "Take This Job and Customize It," *Business Week*, April 24, 2006, p. 108, a book review of Ken Dychtwald, Tamara J. Erickson, and Robert Morison, *Workforce Crisis: How to Beat the Coming Shortage of Skills and Talent*. Cambridge, MA: Harvard Business School, 2006.
141. Gallo, Carmine, "Saying It with Passion," *BusinessWeek Online*, Apr. 6, 2005, p. 2, retrieved Apr. 8, 2005 from http://www.businessweek.com/smallbiz/content/apr2005/sb2005046_2194_sb....
142. Conlin, Michelle, "Call Centers in the Rec Room," *Business Week*, Jan. 23, 2006, pp. 76–77.
143. Some urban and large suburban courts have a second shift of data entry staff or even 24-hour data entry, but these employees do not serve customers at the public counter.
144. Drucker, Peter F., *Management*, p. 441.
145. "All in a Day's Work," *Harvard Business Review.*, Dec. 2001, p. 62.
146. Imparato, Nicholas, and Oren Harari, *Jumping the Curve*, pp. 264–265.
147. Kleiman, Carol, "Studies Reveal Surprises About Work/life Programs and Gender Roles," Associated Press, Dec. 3, 2003, retrieved Dec. 3, 2003, from http://start.earthlink.net/newsarticle?cat=4&aid=Lifestyles8200312030900.

148. "Slippers and Stubble," *Business Week*, Apr. 3, 2006, p. 13.

149. Conlin, Michelle, "The Easiest Commute of All," *Business Week*, Dec. 12, 2005, p. 80.

150. "Arizona City Paying for Weight Watchers," *Today's News-Herald*, a story from Associated Press, Apr. 27, 2004, retrieved Apr. 27, 2004, from http://start.earthlink.net/newsarticle?c at=4&aid=D8278FQ01_story.

　　See also, "Mich. Companies Tout Dieting Incentives," Associated Press, Dec. 27, 2005, retrieved on Dec. 27, 2005, from http://enews.earthlink.net/challen/news/guid=20051227/ 43b)ca_3ca6_.... "Dieting for Dollars: Corporate Trimming," *Business Week*, Nov. 3, 2003, p. 10.

151. This is the generation of people who care for both a parent and their own children. See, for example, "Care-Giving Women Shortchange Personal Needs," Sept. 22, 2004, an Associated Press article, retrieved Sept. 22, 2004 from http://start.earthlink.net/newsarticle?cat=4&aid =Lifestyles2200409220927.

152. "The Right Bait for Keeping Staff," Patricia O'Connell, ed., *BusinessWeek Online*, Feb. 2, 2005, a edited interview of Christopher Mulligan, chief operating officer of TalentKeepers, a global employee-retention research organization, retrieved Feb. 4, 2005, from http://www. businessweek.com/careers/content/feb2005/ca2005022_ca...

153. Drucker, Peter F., *Management*, p. 261.

154. Ibid., p. 309.

155. "All In a Day's Work," *Harvard Business Review,* Dec. 2001, p. 63.

156. Related to this issue but somewhat apart from it is testing the audibility of proceedings in each courtroom. Court sessions are public proceedings that are supposed to be audible to anyone sitting behind the bar. In a significant number of courtrooms around the country, it is very hard to hear what is happening in front of the bar, even if the judge has a microphone on the bench. See Standard 1.1, *Trial Court Performance Standards.* Williamsburg, VA: National Center for State Courts, 1990. The citizen volunteers could test this aspect of access, as well, while visiting the courthouse.

157. The court also did something unique in court annals: it conducted workshops in the new center for court representatives from around the country to explain what it had done, why it had done it, and what the impact had been. These workshops helped spread the word faster than might otherwise have occurred.

158. Legal aid offices that provide attorney assistance for individual civil cases to the indigent and near-indigent in most communities often offer group workshops for family law cases (and, sometimes, consumer-oriented cases), as well, so they can maximize the reach of their limited resources.

159. In some programs, volunteer attorneys may only provide advice and assistance but not enter into an attorney–client relationship. In others, the attorneys can enter into an attorney–client relationship if the client desires. Attorneys employed by the court are precluded from entering into an attorney–client relationship.

160. For example, Hannaford-Agor, Paula, "Access to Justice: Meeting the Needs of Self-Represented Litigants," *Civil Action*, vol. 1, no. 3, Fall 2002, retrieved from http://www.ncsconline. org. Maryland Administrative Office of the Courts, *An Executive Program Assessment for State Court Projects to Assist Self-Represented Litigants*. Annapolis, MD: Maryland Administrative Office of the Courts, 2005; Judicial Council of California, *Model Self-Help Pilot Program: A Report to the Legislature*. San Francisco: Judicial Council of California, 2005. See also, Zorza, Richard, *The Self-Help Friendly Court: Designed from the Ground Up to Work for People Without Lawyers*. Williamsburg, VA: National Center for State Courts, 2002.

161. This aspect of interacting with the community is identified as a core competence in NACM's Core Competencies, National Association for Court Management, *Core Competency Guidelines*, pp. 32–36.

162. The circuit court in Lake County, Illinois, puts its annual report on a CD, which includes a streaming-video message from the chief judge.
163. If one looks for them, there are a remarkable number of materials/modules for various grade levels that have been developed over the years by bar associations, educators, and judges themselves that could be used as models for new material or simply modified and used in a court's local schools. A state's administrative office of the courts, the state bar association and, in large cities, local bar associations, the American Bar Association, the local law library, and the state's education department would be good starting points to find materials.
164. See also, Imparato, Nicholas, and Oren Harari, *Jumping the Curve*, pp. 243–244.
165. In New York, localities retain ownership of courthouse buildings, but a state statute provides that if localities do not maintain courthouses in a "suitable and sufficient" manner, the state court administrator can notify the state Comptroller of the value of providing the needed services, which the Comptroller then will withhold from "any monies" the state pays the locality. New York Judiciary Law, NY State Session Laws, Chap. 825 of the Laws of 1987, section 39(3)(a). This is a remarkable hammer that no other state has given to the judiciary.

Chapter 13

Hierarchy of Court Administration: Leadership Organization

A leadership organization does all the things that a proactive management court does but "kicks it up a notch," to borrow a phrase from a well-known television chef. A leadership organization not only is a leader among courts, but also among all organizations in the community. A leadership organization is known in the community to provide outstanding service, to welcome citizens and cater to those who are not familiar with court processes, to do all it can to decide cases properly and promptly, and to be an excellent employer.

13.1 Maslow's Hierarchy and the Hierarchy of Court Administration

The Hierarchy of Court Administration parallels Abraham Maslow's Hierarchy of Needs for human beings. Table 13.1 shows the parallel between what Maslow described as the self-actualization needs of humans and the leadership organization needs of courts.

Self-actualization means individuals are operating at their highest, most fulfilled level: "Musicians must make music, artists must paint, poets must write, if they are to be ultimately at peace with themselves. What humans *can* be, they *must* be. They must be true to their own nature. This need we may call self-actualization."[1] As it is with humankind, so it is with courts. The two elements of humans' self-actualization needs that resonate with courts' needs are growth and the desire to fulfill one's potential. Growth for courts means having both staff numbers and judgeships keep pace with workload as much as possible, as well as with any new

Table 13.1 Maslow's Self-Actualization Needs and Courts Leadership Organization Needs

Maslow's self-actualization needs	Court leadership organization needs
• Growth • Motivation • Desire to fulfill one's potential	• Humanistic or quality management (continual, incremental change, empowering staff, customer focus, use of data to guide management decisions and gauge performance) • Develop best practices • Focus attention on stakeholders who are not judges or attorneys • Program evaluation • Broad understanding among judges and staff/managers of sphere of influence and scope of authority of each • Institutionalize successful new programs • Scan public, nonprofit, and private sectors for best practices • Develop new technologies and adapt public and private-sector state-of-the-art technologies to a court context • Employer of choice • Recognition in the community as a bellwether organization • Community recognition as a place where justice is sought and provided • State-of-the-art courthouse and interior design

workload associated with being proactive and a leadership organization. Courts also seek to grow their capacity to achieve their mission and goals. Courts also would like to be and strive to be the best they can be, both in the adjudication process and in serving all their stakeholders. The closer they can come to fulfilling all elements of their mission and vision statements, the closer they are to being self-actualized.

Most states have one or more trial courts that are recognized as that state's leaders. They are the ones who always are striving to improve, to be the best court they can be. They are the ones that always are willing to participate in pilot programs. They are the ones that usually are first to introduce and operationalize new technologies. These courts' leaders and senior managers are among the leaders in the state and sometimes in national organizations, too. There is an aura of excellence that surrounds these courts that draws others to observe what they are doing and try to emulate it. These courts often are in one of a state's leading cities, so they are larger than most courts in the state, thus benefiting from some economies of scale not available to all courts and, normally, from salary and benefit levels that attract excellent staff. Some suburban and rural courts are leadership organizations within the judiciary, but larger urban courts predominate.[2]

Leadership organizations do not tolerate change, they embrace it. They understand the need to institutionalize significant changes and use proven techniques to achieve institutionalization. They value training and do all they can to keep all judges and staff—but particularly the judges and the technology staff—up to date with the latest developments. These courts have formal orientation programs for all new judges and staff independent of whatever the state judiciary may provide. Their orientation includes an emphasis on the court's ethos, mission, and vision and how and why cases are managed the way they are. Training starts the first day on the job and continues throughout one's time with the court. Some peer-to-peer training may be provided, but most training is classroom oriented and formal. Because of the "one court at a time" syndrome (see section 12.2, chapter 12), there are good ideas these courts have yet to adopt. Everyone, however, from the chief judge and administrator through the file and data entry clerks knows and appreciates that the court is a leader and wants to help it remain so.

Being a leadership organization is about attitudes more than specific programs, rules, or technology. Just as individuals who become leaders grow into the job rather than being trained or anointed into it (see section 7.3, chapter 7), so, too, leadership courts grow over time from being proactive to being leaders. Having individual chief judges and administrators who are leaders (see section 7.3) is very helpful, if not essential, in making the initial transition from proactive management to leadership. Once the momentum is generated, however, it can be sustained over time because leadership organizations institutionalize their attitudes and approaches.

Leadership courts arise from proactive management, so this chapter will not review all the elements of being a proactive management court discussed in chapter 12. It will cover only those things that leadership organizations do that distinguish them from proactive management courts.

13.2   Qualities of Leadership Organizations

Leadership organizations value staff involvement, as well as that of all judges, in generating ideas and solving problems. The responsibility to make decisions remains with the court's leaders, but staff and judges not in a leadership position are given a stake in identifying problems and finding solutions. "Participation … is not in decision-making. It is in 'decision-thinking.' … It is … participation in responsibility."[3]

13.2.1   Staff Involvement in Decision Thinking

In leadership organizations, everyone knows they have the right and the opportunity to suggest improved ways to do business. Management's response to new ideas is "tell me more," not "I can see some problems," or "yes, but," or "we tried that three years ago and it didn't work." Leadership organizations have enough confidence in their people to try ideas that may not work.

> In the innovative organization, the first and most important job of management ... is to convert impractical, half-baked, and wild ideas into concrete innovative reality. In the innovative organization, top management sees it as its job to listen to ideas and to take them seriously....
>
> Top management in the innovative organization ... not only "encourages" ideas, ... [i]t asks continuously, "What would this idea have to be like to be practical, realistic, effective?" It organizes itself to think through rapidly even the wildest and apparently silliest idea for something new to the point where its feasibility can be appraised.[4]

Imparato and Harari urge leaders to think of the modern organization as interconnected networks of information and knowledge, not as a series of linear steps or processes that produce products or services. "The emphasis in the new work environment is on information and knowledge.... Successful organizations will see themselves as 'brains' or reservoirs of the accumulated intelligence of their employees and business partners—focused toward best serving their customers."[5] Leaders' role is to draw on this knowledge and experience and to provide coherence to the diverse range of ideas.

Possibly silly ideas are not the same as silly proposals. Offering ideas should be easy. Assessing and developing ideas into concrete plans should be structured. There can be a two-step process for receiving and assessing ideas. For the first step, someone with an idea, whether a judge, a manager, or a staff member, should be able to provide the answers to three questions: (1) What is the problem? (2) What is your proposed solution? and (3) How will your proposal be better than what we are doing now? Some process for reviewing ideas is needed that is relatively quick, that answers Peter Drucker's question, above, and that includes written feedback to the proposer. Once an idea is deemed worthy of further development, in step two the proposer or whoever is assigned to follow through should be able to identify the following:

- What is the problem being addressed?
- What is the idea being proposed and how will it address the problem?
- How does this change bring the court closer to achieving its mission and its vision statements?
- What are the known costs and benefits? If dollar values are unknown, what are the direct and indirect elements of cost and benefit that need to be calculated and how do we obtain needed dollar values?
- What needs to be done to implement the proposal?
- About what is the proposer uncertain regarding the idea or its implementation that requires further study or refinement?

- Who will benefit from the change being proposed, both inside the court and among the court's external stakeholders?
- Who might oppose the idea and why?
- Who needs to be involved in planning for implementation and in implementing the proposal?
- Who needs to be aware of the proposed change, why, and at what point does each person or agency need to be advised or involved?
- What results are expected?
- How long before the results will be realized?
- How will the court know if the results have been achieved?
- Are the data needed to evaluate the results available in the court's case management information system? If not, how will the court collect the data needed to determine whether or not the change achieves its goal(s)?

The process just outlined has the potential to become bureaucratic and to slow things down. Therefore, the court's leaders have to assure that at least step one does not fall prey to bureaucratic cautions.

When groups brainstorm, they are told that there are no bad or silly ideas and all ideas should go up on the board without criticism or comment for subsequent discussion and consideration. The first step in soliciting and receiving ideas for changes has to be treated as an endless brainstorming session. There might even be a "fast track" exception for smaller or no-cost ideas where someone can tell a supervisor or manager the essence of a new idea, try it out, and see what happens without a formal proposal that conforms to all the points identified above. The person should be required to track some data to show that the idea worked or did not, but preimplementation review could be very limited.

Leadership organizations find ways to recognize those who propose improvements, even improvements that do not work out. This can range from a formal thank you in person with a copy in the person's personnel file and then in a court's internal newsletter (if there is one), to token gifts, to larger monetary rewards or gift certificates. An annual recognition dinner hosted by the judges and senior managers might be in order if the generation of good ideas really catches on and the court's staff is large enough to warrant a courtwide event.

Peter Drucker reports that when 3M Corporation was growing fastest, employees were given wide latitude to try ideas and were not penalized if the idea did not work out. Yet, each person was held accountable for taking responsibility, for organizing the task of implementing or testing the idea, for working on it, and for appraising progress realistically, in addition to keeping management informed of progress.[6] The approach can be applied as well in courts.

13.2.2   An Institutional Perspective

Leadership organizations have an institutional perspective. Judges remain professionals and get full support for their decisional independence and needs. More than in most courts, however, there also is a recognition of and identification with the court as an institution. Judges recognize and support that the institution has legitimate needs independent of and different from their individual needs and concerns. Judges see the value of institutional integrity and coherence that is severable from their decisional independence. There is general agreement among the judges and between the judges and senior management about the proper sphere of influence of each group and a willingness to support each other within their respective spheres.

Leadership organizations understand the need for and have developed standard approaches to institutionalizing changes. They build strong teams in the planning stage; learn about and address stakeholders' issues as much as possible before implementation; possibly start with pilot projects to be sure an idea works; evaluate results and adjust the program as needed; train all involved judges and staff (and, if appropriate, outside stakeholders); develop manuals and standard operating procedures and keep them current; and constantly review and adjust the program as needed to keep it viable. Also, deviations from the common approach are identified, the reasons for the deviation are discussed, and either the entire program is adjusted to reflect a better idea or the deviation is adjusted back to the norm.

13.2.3   Shift in Courts' Priorities Among Stakeholders

One of the consequences of the significant changes in courts since the mid-1950s is a shift in emphasis for court administration. Initially, judges and attorneys were the focus, sometimes the only focus.[7] The delay reduction efforts across the nation of the 1980s and the release of Trial Court Performance Standards in 1990 started a transition in thinking and emphasis to court stakeholders other than judges and attorneys, particularly to the litigants and the general public. The rise of problem-solving courts and their need to reach out to and work with many agencies in different ways reinforced this transition. The two jury management reform efforts (1970s and early 1980s and in the 1990s and 2000s) also reflect a shift. The first wave had an internal focus on getting more people and a more diverse group of people to the courthouse and using the ones who appear more effectively. The second wave has focused on the juror:[8] increasing understanding, improving comfort, and changing the perception of jury service from something citizens should avoid to something that is a worthy undertaking. Even the effort by the two other branches to induce courts to increase the collection of imposed fines and fees and courts' acceptance of the value of enforcing their judgments is focused on the institution's needs and meeting courts' external obligations, not on what is best for attorneys and judges. Providing and improving access to courts for litigants in particular and citizens in general is part of virtually all judiciary's values and orientation in the early 21st century but was largely absent from the debate in the 1960s. From the 1970s into the 1990s (and still today, to an extent) courts spoke of community outreach in terms of community education, having citizens better understand courts so they would like and support both the institution and judges. Today, there is more discussion about how courts can get feedback from citizens about their needs and how to meet those needs. The impact of the growing demographic diversity in the country is being addressed by courts, not to make it easier for courts to be understood by the new waves of citizens and residents, but to make the courts more accessible to those who need effective courts. Some leaders are even discussing how citizens appropriately can have input into administrative decisions by courts[9] (see section 13.2.6). Leadership organizations understand the shift in perspective, embrace it, and organize both the delivery of service and management priorities to reflect this new emphasis.

In terms of the history of courts and even of the modern court administration revolution, this shift in perspective is new and still being defined. Consequently, the transition in thinking across a critical mass of courts and then all courts will take time. Some will resist it. The tension that will be felt from time to time between those who want to retain the former focus on judges' and attorneys' needs and those who look to shift the focus outward is not a new issue. In the 1930s, Arthur Vanderbilt, while president of the American Bar Association, looked back to the legal reforms of the early 1800s in England and noted, "the bar for the most part was blind to the problems of judicial administration in the interest of litigants and of the public. It was laymen ... aided by a few far seeing judges and barristers, who forced obviously needed improvements on a reluctant profession that was imbued with the curious notion that the courts were created for the benefit of judges and lawyers."[10] An issue that has not resolved in almost two hundred years will not be resolved in the next five years.

Dr. Jonas Salk, the physician responsible for the first effective vaccine for polio, spoke from a doctor's perspective of the tension inherent in change, as retold by Imparato and Harari:[11]

> Salk contended that attitudes and values appropriate for one epoch are inappropriate for the next. He noted that epochal transitions are marked by a deep conflict between the opposing tendencies... "These conflicts and uncertainties can be seen as part of an orderly if somewhat difficult process of nature. Looked at this way, the disturbances of the present time may be seen not as a symptom of a disease ... [but as] the uncertain beginnings of new patterns appropriate to the emerging

conditions." ... Successful organizations continually search for new
root ideas that will serve as the bases for new growth curves.

These authors offer a metaphor for moving from the old focus to solidifying
the new. It may be most useful for the judges who must lead the transition, but
it also may help those who are affected by the change.[12]

> We are out at sea, having pushed away from one shore yet still a dis-
> tance from the other side. Like sailors who can't see their destination
> but can still see the shore they have just left, we are pulled by memories
> of the security and familiarity we once experienced. In the face of this
> reluctance, success rests in going forward.

These authors offer one other observation that may not yet seem apt to court
administration, but that carries weight as one looks at the deep changes throughout
society and the economy that started in the 1990s: "Our organizations need to
change because our civilization is changing, and nothing short of radical trans-
formation in management will suffice."[13]

The shift in focus for courts is not as radical as the economic and social shifts
that seem to be occurring in the United States, but some may see them as such.
In courts, the interests of litigants, the general public, and stakeholder organizations, and the idea of institutional accountability, all existed and have had value
since 1950. As the focus has started to shift to externals, however, judges' and attorneys' interests are no longer preeminent by a significant margin. They certainly
are not being ignored or undervalued, nor should they be in the future. Judges,
in particular, need not be concerned, because the institution still is judge-centric
and court administration must meet judges' professional needs if courts are to
fulfill their mission. The new focus simply requires that the interests of judges
and lawyers not trump these external interests to the degree that they used to.
Further, on occasion their interests may have to yield to others' interests.

> It is obvious that the relationship of judges to lawyers is being tested.
> The institutional culture of the judiciary is fixated on the transcenden-
> tal importance of attorneys, but lawyers, as important as they are to
> the functioning of the courts, are only one group of court users and
> a partially endangered species. Judges have obligations to the public
> and litigating parties that transcend traditional bonding. It may be
> an exaggeration to say that judges have to choose between the people
> and the legal profession, but this is not far from the truth.[14]

The choice for judges posited here by Bob Tobin may not be as stark as this
quotation suggests, but there are some on the bench who have not always acted

as if their "obligations to the public and litigating parties" transcended their obligations to the bar. Were it otherwise, delay reduction would not be so hard to institute and sustain in so many courts.[15] A strain between judges and the bar will be hard for many judges. It is similar to the tension between judges being part employer and part employee (see section 6.3, chapter 6). It also reflects back to the emphasis by small groups on maintaining equilibrium, satisfying demands of subsidiary affiliations (i.e. the bar), and fighting forces that upset equilibrium and undermine the subsidiary affiliations (see section 12.2, chapter 12). Despite this, it is the right thing for courts to do. Attorneys are adjuncts of the courts and very important contributors, but they are not "the court." Judges are "the court" in fundamental ways, but "the court" still transcends each judge and all judges. Progress has been made since the mid-1990s in giving greater weight than previously to external forces and interests. This is a change that testifies to recognition by many within the judiciary that it is the right thing to do. Leadership organizations are closer to making a full transition in their perspective than other courts.

13.2.4 Scanning the Environment

Part of the broadening of perspective in leadership organizations is to look beyond courts for ideas. Proactive management scans what other courts are doing to identify best practices and adopt the most appropriate for their environment and circumstances. There is a tendency among courts to see themselves as unique, as unable to learn from a private business or even another government agency. There even is a tendency among large courts to overlook or dismiss new developments and ideas from smaller courts because the latter do not have to deal with issues of size. In short, there is a tendency to insularity in courts' thinking. Leadership organizations eschew insular thinking. Leadership organizations scan developments in other public agencies, in education, in the nonprofit sector, and in the private sector to find the best and adapt them to the courts. They do not limit their scope to what other courts have done. For example, the second largest long-haul truck manufacturer in the nation routinely looks to Wal-Mart, Dell, Wells Fargo, and Microsoft to find ways to improve its processes so it can produce trucks faster and for less money and handle the funds associated with its huge financing operation.[16] The one place it does not look is to other truck manufacturers. Leadership organizations do not think of what they do solely in terms of "decide cases." They examine their operations more discretely so they can identify others who might be good models from which to borrow. Courts answer telephones, provide customer service at the counter, store and retrieve information via computers and hard-copy files. Courts schedule lots of small, discrete events which often do not occur and frequently are rescheduled for another day, host a lot of people with different interests and needs in the courthouse, and run or oversee a large collection operation. Courts accommodate the needs of professionals while sustaining institutional imperatives, and on and on. Organizations other than courts also must deal with discrete tasks or functions that are similar to those of courts. Nonprofit organizations such as the Red Cross and the Boy Scouts and Girl Scouts must deal daily with a number of scattered, independent, and independent-minded subunits that must be led to share the same values, adopt similar practices, and implement changes along with all the other units. In light of the issue of "one court at a time," courts may be able to learn from these or similar organizations how to counter the "one court at a time" dilemma. How do universities schedule and reschedule thousands of students to attend several hundred classes taught by scores of professors? And now they are doing it on line. Maybe colleges and universities know something that would improve juror scheduling or case scheduling. A number of corporations can be models for motivating workers with incentives other than higher wages, bonuses, or stock ownership.[17] Leadership organizations understand that important lessons for courts exist outside the judiciary and they seek them out. Some promising ideas from other sectors may work in courts and some may not, but leadership organizations constantly and broadly scan the environment for any and all good ideas that are adaptable.

Leadership organizations establish best practices within the judiciary, rather than just adopt the best practices of other courts. As suggested above, no court can be the lead innovator in every area every time, but leadership organizations are looked to by other courts as the ones who usually find new ideas and try them before others in the state and occasionally before others in the nation. Over time they have developed sufficient staff numbers to allow some staff to scan the environment, assess ideas, determine how they will work in courts, and implement them. Their technology staff members attend workshops and national conferences and have access to magazines and organizations that feature innovations so they have an early warning system in place. Leadership organizations are defined mostly by their attitudes and approaches to new ideas and to customer service, but also by their ability to take ideas that seem promising and test them and then refine them to work in a court environment. Some court within the judiciary has to be an early adopter, at least in terms of court adoption. Normally, it is a leadership organization.

13.2.5 Managing Court Reporting

Leadership organizations seek to rationalize and gain control over the court reporting function. Court reporting poses dilemmas for courts with respect to taking the record in court and producing transcripts. The dilemmas exist at three levels: technological, human resources management, and political.

The different technologies available for court reporting were discussed in chapter 12, section 12.11.2 (see also, section 9.2.3, chapter 9). The dilemma associated with technology was suggested in section 6.8, chapter 6: If technology is used increasingly to capture the record, court reporters will be needed less, which shrinks the demand, which can lead to fewer people going into the field, which could produce a shortage of reporters for courts who wish to continue to use reporters. This cycle already is appearing. Given a trend that already is surfacing, should courts embrace technological solutions to reduce personnel costs and avoid the shortage, limit the types of proceedings in which technology will be used in order to assure a market for reporters, or, as in California, effectively ban the use of technology for some cases so courts have to use reporters?[18]

In part it is a question of whether technology can be as effective as a live court reporter in capturing the record, and that record then being a basis for producing the transcript. There has been a debate since the early 1970s about whether technology is as good as, worse than, or better than are human reporters. All the studies other than those commissioned by court reporter associations have shown that technology is at least as good as court reporters. A cost saving normally is documented, as well.[19] The debate continues, however. Many judges are willing to accept court reporters' claims of superiority without reviewing the data. They do so because of their personal attachments to the people who work in their courtrooms daily:[20] concern about the time required for read-backs using machines versus a reporter; how to deal with the situation of "overspeaks;" and dealing with something on a tape being unintelligible. The basic fallacy in the attacks on technological methods of capturing the record lies in reporters skillfully highlighting errors or omissions in the record captured electronically without acknowledging their own errors.

The key phrase in the debate should be "comparable," not error free. Every independent test has shown comparability. In fact, court reporters make mistakes all the time in capturing the record, which is why audio and video are comparable.[21] Anyone who has watched a real-time transcript projected live on a television screen knows that real time reporters, who usually are the best of the shorthand reporters, are not perfect. It is less widely known, and normally overlooked, that the testing boards certify reporters with scores of 97 or 98 percent accuracy, depending on the type of matter being tested (Q&A, narrative, technical). These scores are attained under ideal physical conditions but with a lot of pressure on the person being tested. In a courtroom, there is much less pressure but also less than ideal conditions. There also is the fatigue factor that must enter into a courtroom setting that is not a factor in the certification test. A test situation usually lasts five to ten minutes. A short courtroom trial session would be one hour. Finally, certification tests are conducted with an "average" rate of talking, about 200 words per minute (higher levels of certification test at faster rates of speech, but the basic test usually is at 180 or 200 words per minute). In a courtroom, pauses, "ums," and "ahs" often slow the rate of speech to under 200 words per minute, but there also are times when a witness or an attorney will speak at well over 200 words per minute. Whatever the actual rate during any specific hearing or trial, one can estimate the number of errors during the process of capturing the record by a human reporter.

If the overall average rate of speech is 180 words per minute and a proceeding lasts for one hour, the reporter must record 10,800 words. If the error rate is only 1 percent—bearing in mind that a 2 or 3 percent error rate is acceptable to become certified in most states—the reporter makes 108 errors. If testimony during a trial were to last four hours a day, which is about average in many general jurisdiction trials, the reporter makes over 400 mistakes. These can range from punctuation, to incorrect spelling or capitalization, to an omitted word, to a word that was not understood. As the transcript is being produced, the reporter catches virtually all of these, so the transcript looks clean. It is a fallacy to argue that if electronic recording equipment misses a word, phrase, or even a sentence, it is missing something that a reporter usually would pick up. In fact, in one of the more rigorous tests side by side, the transcripts created from audio recordings missed some things the reporters' transcripts picked up, but reporters also missed some things that the machine transcripts captured. Overall, transcripts from audio recordings were more accurate than the reporters' transcripts.[22] Yet, many judges, I suspect a significant majority of judges, defend the skill of the reporters who work in their courtrooms and doubt the accuracy of electronic reporting. On one level, the judges are right. The reporters are highly skilled and most transcripts end up with no substantively meaningful errors. That does not mean, however, that the obverse is true, that electronic reporting and its resulting transcripts are substantively inferior. A growing number of courts are using electronic reporting and producing acceptable transcripts, and this in itself supports at least "comparability."

Court administration has to balance the objective data about comparability, the cost advantages of electronic reporting, the potential shortage of reporters occurring over the next two or three decades, and the normally strong support of court reporters from judicial officers.

The human resources dilemma involves administrators in two ways: (1) court reporters are very independent personalities often protected by judges; and (2) they are independent contractors when it comes to producing transcripts, which materially complicates any effort to manage the production of transcripts. The first dilemma was reviewed in section 6.8 in chapter 6. Beyond the tie between reporters and judges, because of the technical nature of what court reporters do, many reporters argue that only another court reporter can manage them effectively. This is not a problem in large courts with enough reporters to warrant a first-line supervisor, as the number of reporters justifies a dedicated supervisor and a reporter normally can be recruited to be the supervisor. Smaller courts seldom have the luxury of dedicating someone just to supervise the court reporters, far less one of their reporters, so a nonreporter supervisor given the assignment often struggles to exert any supervisory control. De facto, a judge becomes the supervisor of each reporter, which effectively means they have no supervision.[23] Most reporters use free time during the court day to work on producing transcripts, but that reflects their self-control and professionalism, not that someone is monitoring their performance or the use of their time.

Which leads to the second human management dilemma, how to manage the production of transcripts? The only effective management in most states comes from the appellate courts. If a reporter is to produce a transcript for an appeal, attorneys cannot start writing their briefs until they have reviewed the transcript for citations to the parts of the record that support their position that error occurred or did not occur. State rules vary, but at some point the reporter who is late in completing a transcript needs to obtain an extension of time from the appellate court. If a reporter is very late on one transcript, or late on several, the appellate court may contact the trial court seeking removal of the reporter from daily reporting duties until the transcript(s) is produced. Short of such an order or request from the appellate court, most trial courts do not monitor and are unaware of a reporter's transcript production. There are courts that are not so in the dark, however.[24] Pursuant to court rule, they track transcript orders and when transcripts are produced. Some courts also track the reporters' progress on transcript production. This is a monitoring function, however, not a management responsibility, because as an independent contractor, the reporter owns the transcript, controls its production, and gets the income.

This reality in most states is one element in courts' decisions to shift to electronic reporting. The court owns the electronic recording, so it can determine who produces the transcript and therefore can exercise some control over that process. As the owner, it can give the transcript away or sell it for the statutory or rule-based fee. If it sells the transcript, the revenue belongs to the court, not to a reporter.

Monitoring transcript production normally involves simply noting the case, the estimated transcript length, and the reporter's estimated date by which the transcript should be produced. Whatever the reporter tells the monitor, the monitor writes it down and tracks dates. It need not be such a passive exercise. There is a fairly simple formula one can apply to determine how many calendar days are needed to produce a transcript of X pages.[25] A court needs only four numbers:

1. The hours of courtroom time that were reported (or, as a surrogate, the number of trial days if it was a trial);[26]
2. The number of hours needed by a court reporter or a reporter's transcriptionist or scopist[27] to produce a finished transcript for each hour of courtroom testimony;[28]

3. The number of pages of transcript resulting from a standard hour of a trial or a hearing and of argument before a judge; and

4. The total number of transcript pages currently on order.

Different reporters and different technologies require different amounts of time to produce a finished transcript for each hour of courtroom testimony. On average, a reporter requires between two and three hours for each courtroom hour. So a 12-hour trial (roughly three days) would require between 24 and 36 hours of reporter time for a final transcript.[29] (A transcriber's time or scopist's time would be extra, but that time is not constrained by having to be in court and some of it can parallel the reporter's courtroom time.) If a reporter had only eight hours a week to work on transcripts—perhaps four hours on the weekend and an hour a night for four nights a week or an hour a day during four court days—it could take up to four and a half calendar weeks to produce the transcript. Many reporters could produce it in less time.[30] Then the court has to factor in the number of total pages already on order. The total number of transcription hours needed can be determined from the number of pages. The standard is that an hour of trial testimony produces between 40 and 50 pages of transcript.[31] If a reporter has a total of 1,000 pages of transcript still to be transcribed, that represents between 20 and 25 courtroom hours, which then can be used in the formula above to determine how many calendar days are needed to complete those 1,000 pages. These calculations can help a court to assess how busy a reporter is, whether or not the reporter is likely to miss appellate court deadlines, and, therefore, whether it is necessary to relieve the reporter of some courtroom reporting time to assure that transcripts are completed on time.

The third dilemma faced by court administrators regarding court reporters is political. In virtually every state and nationally, court reporters and their associations are very powerful politically. Although this varies from state to state, mostly it is done the old fashioned way, with political contributions and hiring well known and influential lobbyists. Plus, if they want an increase in transcript fees, for example, they obtain the support of individual judges. The consequences are severe for courts. When a court or the state-level judiciary goes against court reporters in the legislature, the judiciary almost always loses. One of the most dramatic illustrations of this occurred at the national level, although comparable stories can be found in almost every state. In the late 1990s, two regional offices of the U.S. Department of Labor determined that court reporters' transcript work derived directly and solely from their court employment and not from an independent contractor status. Therefore, under applicable federal labor laws they had to account for their time spent producing transcripts and be paid overtime for those hours by the court. This greatly upset court reporters across the nation because it opened the door for courts to claim ownership of transcripts.[32] In less than a year, Congress changed the federal labor code to exempt court reporters from the overtime provisions.[33]

If reporters want an increase in transcript fees and those fees are set by the legislature, as they are in many states, reporters generally will get them. The best the judiciary can hope for, if it is state funded, is a corresponding increase in the budget to cover the added costs for the transcripts it buys. If reporters want a statute that limits or excludes the use of technology to replace court reporters in courts of general jurisdiction, where the big-money transcripts are, they often have the political muscle to get such a law even if the judiciary opposes it. Combined with their intracourt support from individual judges, this political power greatly constrains normal management responses to court reporter issues.

This is an issue for leadership organizations rather than proactive management courts because it is so challenging. An individual court can seek and probably obtain some control over the scheduling for completion of ordered transcripts. An individual court may be able to audit transcript bills to try to bring billing practices closer in line with legal requirements. Individual courts may be able to move reporters into a common pool arrangement, ending the one-to-one relationship that exists between judges and reporters in most trial courts. (This has proven to be very hard to do, however.) Individual courts cannot successfully undertake a frontal attack in the legislature; even a combined effort by all courts often fails. Leadership organizations can keep data, however. They can keep records of time spent in court, time spent on producing transcripts during the court day, and the calendar time required to produce transcripts. The data may push the burden of engaging in a discussion back onto the reporters. The management of the court reporting function is as great a challenge in most states' judiciaries as obtaining state funding, consolidating trial courts, and putting the clerk of court under court control. They all require a firm third-branch commitment, strong leadership at the state level with significant trial court leaders supporting the state effort, time, and maybe some good luck. Some states have met each of the other challenges, so there is some reason to hope that in time factors will shift to allow changes in court reporting management, as well.

13.2.6 Public Input into Administrative Decisions

The movement to state funding and to more central control of both money and functions at the state level means courts' accountability for both funds and how they use those funds has gained in importance. Accountability is an important component of the Trial Court Performance Standards.[34] One of the five major areas of performance is "independence and accountability." Within that category, two standards address accountability directly (Standards 4.2 and 4.4). Only recently have courts begun to struggle with what accountability means and how to provide it. For the most part, they still are looking inward, that is, they are looking at how they can tell the public what they are doing and what results they are achieving. As mentioned in section 12.15.1, chapter 12, they do this in a number of different ways and are increasing their effectiveness. Courts have been less effective in seeking, obtaining, and incorporating input *from* the public.

Many courts across the country now put comment cards on their public counters. This is a good but passive effort. Likewise with similar efforts through the court's website. If courts set up advisory or study committees for specific topics or issues that include attorneys and representatives of stakeholder agencies, it is likely today that they will at least consider adding one or two "public" members to the committee, as well. In California's effort to develop community-focused strategic plans, trial courts found several ways to obtain stakeholder input. Some held public forums, some set up focus groups, some met with community and civic groups who served as surrogates for the general population. A few asked jurors for input and some set up advisory groups, also as surrogates for the general public. The effort was very successful, but to date has not had any impact on other administrative processes. Strategic plans are reviewed every few years, but there is no mechanism for ongoing input. The state judiciary provided small stipends to each court to help in the initial development of the strategic plans. Many courts used these funds to hire outside consultants to obtain public input. Without an annual infusion of funds, few courts have either the staff time or expertise to continue the process regularly.

Leadership organizations search for ways to obtain feedback from users and the general public on a regular basis. They may use one or more of the techniques indicated in the paragraph above or find other ways to conduct surveys of users and the general public.[35] More than just obtaining this input, however, leadership organizations then use the input to identify weaknesses in the delivery of service and to guide needed improvements. The feedback is cycled back into the court's decision-making process and budget development process to influence future directions and changes. The public input, however obtained, is treated as part of the ongoing brainstorming process referenced above. (Praise of staff performance also is noted and shared with everyone in the court.)

Courts want public input so they can improve customer service. Customer service is a hallmark of leadership organizations. It involves several items already touched upon, mostly in chapter 12, but more than that, it involves converting the atmosphere in the courthouse into a welcoming one. Staff receives customer service training so that they greet and interact with customers positively. The courthouse has a welcoming ambience in the public areas. The jury assembly room has comfortable seating and different areas for different types of activities. The clerk's office is staffed at a level and procedures are set up to aid the customer rather than facilitate the office. Waits in lines during busy times do not exceed ten minutes.[36]

The next frontier for courts is to explore how to obtain citizen input prior to making administrative decisions. One way would be only a slight extension of the current practice of advising the general bar of proposed changes to court rules: post the proposed rules on the website and solicit public response. A few courts and administrative offices of the courts are doing that now. A more controversial idea is to include citizens on a new governing body that sets policy for the court.

The judicial council concept of court administration developed in the 1930s. The idea was that the various interested parties, judges, lawyers, legislators, and maybe a representative of the executive branch, would be given authority to study courts, propose needed changes, and generally oversee court administration and some elements of judicial administration. California adopted the first judicial council in the country; several other states, mostly in the West, also have adopted judicial councils. Over time, these bodies have moved from study-and-recommendation bodies to policy-setting and control bodies. Some also expanded their membership to include members of the public.[37]

As Bob Tobin points out in *Creating the Judicial Branch*, courts in the 21st century "have to distinguish between the privacy surrounding adjudication and the necessity for more administrative openness."[38] Peter Drucker analyzed the role of a board of directors and found two roles: one of advising the chief executive on sensitive internal matters and the other of advising on matters touching on the public face of a corporation. Courts' leaders have the same two needs. Drucker posited the possibility of two boards of directors.[39]

> One is the executive board which gives top management somebody to talk to, a review organ, a conscience, a counselor, an advisor—but also an informed and prepared "stand-by" in case there is a "power failure," that is, failure of a company's top management or need to find successors to today's top management.
>
> The other organ is the public and community relations board which gives a company ... access to its various publics.
>
> There is no reason why these two could not legally be one body. But they have to operate differently. With its public and community relations board, top management needs to discuss what the various publics want, need to know, and need to understand. With its executive board top management needs to discuss what top management itself needs to discuss, what top management itself needs to think through, needs to decide, needs to understand.

Drucker points to a way to think about opening court administration to formal and continuing public input. It would not substitute for the other efforts suggested above, but it could be a centerpiece for making courts both more accountable and more open. A second "board" of citizens and court stakeholders can be created to address "what the various publics want, need to know, and need to understand." This board would have its own agenda and its decisions could be either advisory or final unless the judges withdraw them.[40] Or, public and stakeholder representatives can sit with the judges[41] during the "public and community relations" portion of the agenda and be excused for internal management discussions and decisions.

Adding formal public input to decision making about court administration would aid in resolution of another current issue: the continuing difficulty defining what is proper policy making and guidance to management by judges versus improper efforts to substitute for or overrule daily management decisions. A court that creates a public and community relations board or advisory committee has to think through and define the kind of matters that would be addressed by such a board/committee, but also discuss and decide about the matters properly and solely to be brought to the judges. If citizens sit with and get to vote equally with judges on matters on the public and community relations portion of the agenda, for which matters do they withdraw and have no involvement? Even if a court decides in the end not to formalize citizen input, the discussion leading up to that decision might be very helpful for the court's leaders, as it might help clarify the scope of judges' involvement in court administration. Courts should at least discuss whether the judges can live with the model suggested by Jack and Suzy Welch, Jack Welch being the former CEO of General Electric: "Boards have only one job more important than developing internal candidates [for the next CEO]: coaching and supporting the current CEO. Boards can't do the work of management. They can only make sure the right management is in place, now and in the future."[42]

The court for which I was the court administrator established a citizens' advisory committee to do three things: to alert the court to developments in the private sector, especially in technology, that might benefit the court, to serve as a sounding board for ideas the court had for new programs; and to be an advisor on general management issues that the court shared with the private sector, such as human resources. The court felt this charge to the advisory committee was specific enough to get started, although there was no special problem or issue facing the court at the outset. Each of the court's six judges was asked to nominate at least three business or community leaders, from which it was hoped between 12 and 15 would agree to serve. Almost everyone agreed to serve, however, so the committee ended up with 19 members. The thought was that the group would meet every six months. The first meeting was a general orientation to what the court does and some of the administrative and political issues it faced. I was delighted to have these extra eyes and ears and the years of experience represented by the committee members (they all were business or community leaders). The committee started with great enthusiasm, so much so that it requested quarterly meetings. After a year, however, attendance was falling off and discussion topics were limited. Without a specific focus—an issue, a problem, a new project—the committee felt uncertain of its role and whether it was making or could make a meaningful contribution. The committee was in place when the state judiciary required each trial court to develop its first community oriented strategic plan. It provided valuable input into the plan and the priorities the court should set with the plan. Once the plan was completed, however, the committee disbanded by mutual agreement.

The experience suggests three lessons. First, busy executives and civic leaders prefer a specific focus around which they can wrap their ideas and experience. Asking for their help with a specific issue would have been a better way to start than saying we needed a general sounding board. Second, the committee met too often because there was no specific assignment—until the need for a strategic plan came along—on which to focus their attention. Third, the nomination process was a mistake; judges tended to nominate friends who, in turn, did not want to let their friend the judge down by saying no, so they said yes even though they were not especially interested in the committee's charge or did not really have the time.

My court's experience supports Drucker's approach in two ways. First, the public members could be invited to join a functioning body, the regular judges' meeting, that always has an agenda and that deals with concrete issues during each meeting. (If it is set up as a stand-alone advisory committee, it still would have specific areas of responsibility and an agenda.) Second, the focus of issues on which citizens would have an equal voice would be defined more precisely at the outset because clear areas of responsibility would be needed to obtain judicial approval. Using a limited number of citizens in this way also would address two of the issues that arose for my court with its advisory committee: the people selected would be limited in number (probably under ten if an advisory group and only two or three if added directly to the judges' board) and screened more intensively, and both the scope and hours of their commitment could be defined better at the outset.

Virtually all trial court meetings in every court with which I am familiar, during which administrative matters are discussed, are held in private. And neither the agenda nor minutes of these meetings are published beyond the judges and possibly senior managers. The privacy occurs not because it is necessary, but because, as Tobin suggests, judges are used to making case decisions in private so judges' meetings just followed along. The possibility that the judges might be doing the public's business when they set budget priorities, adopt a new strategic plan, or decide on a vendor for a new case management information or telephone system does not arise. The discussion about what is public and what should be decided in private should be aided by thinking about different needs and different kinds of input. It also tests the perspective that all administrative decisions by judges must be made in private.

If an administrative agenda were open to public attendance, the number of people attending in most cases would be very limited. Depending on the items on the agenda, a union representative might appear, in locally funded courts someone from the city manager's or county administrator's office might attend, a court staff member or two might attend, or vendor representatives if the purchase of a major item were on the agenda. Most states have public meeting laws that require most government entities to conduct their business openly. If these laws do not cover trial courts, the judiciary, as an independent branch, has a chance to create a new model. It could borrow the best aspects of the open meeting laws and modify the more restrictive elements to truly open up the process of administration without adding the burdens of current legislation.

It would be an important step in refocusing the priority accorded to different court stakeholders to add public input to the judges' discussion of administrative matters and then to open its meetings to public attendance. Leadership organizations will lead the way in finding a balance between an appropriate need for private discussions and conducting the business aspects of courts in public.

13.2.7 Facilities Design

Leadership organizations reexamine all aspects of a court's operation, including their courthouse(s). Buildings, particularly courthouses, convey symbolism. They speak in metaphors. There has been a fairly standard model for courthouses for decades, if not centuries. Limited finances have led some courts to build or take over buildings that are quite modest and do not fit the standard model.

One used to be able to drive into almost any suburban or rural town and find the courthouse with no directions. It was near the middle of town and reflected its importance in the community. It is much harder to do so today, both because a courthouse may no longer be in or just off the center of town and because the building is hard to distinguish from all other government or office buildings in the immediate vicinity. Unless one finds a sign saying "XYZ Courthouse," a stranger often has to ask which of several similar-looking buildings is the courthouse. Courthouses built since the mid-1980s sometimes preserve some of the "feel" of older courthouses in the public areas, but it is equally likely that it will be hard to distinguish the vestibule, corridors, and the clerk's office from the welfare department or the county auditor's office. Courtrooms today seem to be the last bastion fore reflecting the majesty and importance of the law and its role in society. They look largely as courtrooms looked 100 or 200 years ago.[43]

Much of the homogenization of the appearance of courthouses in states is attributable to finances.[44] States and localities often require a trade-off between the special construction needs (and costs) of courthouses[45] and "surface" items such as enhanced exteriors, special wood treatments on walls, and comfortable public seating areas in and outside the courtrooms.[46] The symbolism of a courthouse's design is losing out to the realities of most jurisdictions' finances. Plus, in a post-9/11 world, security concerns may lead to a look more akin to a fortress than to an inviting place that dispenses justice.

One response of state judiciaries to efforts to save money on courthouses has been the development of "facilities standards."[47] The standards address courtroom size and accoutrements, sight angles and necessary furnishings within a courtroom, workspace per employee, file storage areas, public corridors, security equipment and physical needs, and many other details that go into creating a complete courthouse. These standards then become ammunition for individual courts to fight efforts to make a courthouse too much like a standard office building.

Existing facilities standards are good, but mostly updates of long-standing concepts. They define the square footage needed for various rooms and functions and they recognize the impact of computerization and other technology, but they contain no or very limited options for adapting to unknown futures. Facilities standards mostly address individual rooms or areas rather than a court*house*. The thought doubtless is that if all of the parts are the proper size and configuration, when put together the court*house* will be sufficient. In contrast to the specificity of these standards, work*flow*, people *flow* (other than for security), relationships among work areas, and potential new technologies are addressed in only the most general terms. The standards may mention the need to reflect courthouses' purposes, but they are silent on exterior materials, wall coverings, how one can reflect courts' purposes architecturally, or money-saving, emerging energy technologies or interior and exterior design concepts. Individual courthouses must address these matters, but each is a reinvention, not a reflection of accumulated inspiration and skill.

We know two things about the future: (1) courthouses are used for decades and some for 100 years; and (2) changes in society, technology, how work is processed, concepts of employment, the handling of disputes, population shifts, and other unpredictable developments will significantly impact courts' space needs. Facility standards are valuable and a significant advance over the "let's all figure it out for ourselves" approach of the 1950s. Both proactive management courts and leadership organization courts will use the standards if they get a chance to build a new courthouse. The standards are not enough, however. There are important institutional needs that limit how imaginative or "leading edge" the design of a courthouse can be. There even are germane political and budgetary reasons why courthouses should not appear to be too avant-garde. All these understandable constraints are insufficient to explain the glacial changes in courthouse design.

Imaginative design need not be expensive. Flexible design need not be expensive. Changes that recognize the evolving role of courts, changes in litigation, and opportunities opened by new technologies need not turn a new courthouse into a politically risky, glitzy embarrassment. Some new construction technologies and materials reduce life-cycle costs and, sometimes, construction costs. If courthouses cannot look like courthouses of the 19th century—assuming that is how a courthouse "should" look—then perhaps new models of 21st century courthouses are needed.

One issue not addressed by facilities standards, other than by indirection, is the total size of a courthouse. Courthouse designers should not assume ever-upward growth. Many jurisdictions over the next 30 to 50 years may face increasing population and all courts may have to handle more, and more complex cases, and add both staff and judgeships. Even so, technology, changes in how cases are resolved, and changing work styles could reduce the space needs of courthouses within a generation. At a minimum, they will change how courthouse space is used. If so, what is to be done with space no longer needed? How do courts respond to new needs that will develop over time?

In the early 2000s, architects at the leading edge are designing office and some government buildings that have more glass and less steel. The buildings offer an almost transparent look. Would such a look not be appropriate for the evolving role of courts in our society?[48] Commercial buildings increasingly are designed to be "green," in the sense of using natural light to improve interior lighting and technologies to reduce heating and cooling costs and even to reduce water consumption, so that life-cycle costs are lower than traditional technologies. Even interior design is being refined and offering many more options for both comfort and practicality in staff and in public areas than has been available in the past.[49]

Three changes in courts or society that can be discerned today will affect how courthouses are used within 10 years. The first is how cases are resolved. We know two things today that should be affecting courthouse design: (1) the number of jury trials and the percent that they represent of total dispositions has been declining since the mid-1980s; and (2) alternative dispute resolution techniques are being broadly used in civil, family, and criminal cases, leading to a need for more conference or small hearing rooms and fewer full-size, full-service courtrooms. These two known developments suggest that every courtroom does not have to be designed to accommodate jury trials. More conference and small hearing rooms are needed and the traditional tie between a judge's chambers and his or her courtroom is not essential. This latter point is a sensitive one for many judges. A number of newer federal courthouses have separated judges' chambers from courtrooms, but a number of judges in state courts still may resist the separation. Both judges and administrators may resist efforts to build courtrooms that cannot accommodate jury trials on the theory that if every courtroom has that capacity, the court has the greatest scheduling flexibility. An analysis of the number of days of trial per court day, per week, and per judge should be done, but most courts will have difficulty arguing that the data justify the significant cost increases associated with every courtroom being jury-compatible.

The second change in both courts and in society is the impact of technology.

impacts courthouse design in two ways. First, it enables substantially greater remote use of the court's services such as obtaining information, paying fines, and filing documents, thus in time reducing foot traffic at the courthouse. A courthouse and parking lot/garage that will accommodate 1,000 people per day and peak usage of 400 vehicles will be larger than a courthouse and parking that needs to serve only 600 visitors per day and 250 cars at peak usage.[50] The second impact of technology was discussed in chapters 9 and 10: the growing use of electronic documents and either the diminution or elimination of paper records. This changes the dynamics of staff work areas and will lead in time to much smaller filing areas for hard-copy records. In some courts, this change will simply enable the court to fit its paper files into the storage areas that were built in the 1950s and outgrown in the 1980s. In most courts, it will free up previously needed space either for new services and staff work areas or to reduce the size of a courthouse. Today's facilities standards do not yet reflect these shifting use patterns.

The third impact on design is the changing pattern of work in the general society. As discussed in section 12.13, chapter 12, flexible hours and working from remote locations (distributed workers) change the amount of physical space needed by the work force. Some major companies already are finding significant facility cost savings because of increased off-site work by staff. For the reasons mentioned in section 12.13, courts do not have the same flexibility as many corporations to allow a substantial percentage of their staff to work off-site, but it is probable that changing work patterns in society at large will impact work patterns in courts, as well. This, in turn, may affect the amount of square footage needed in courthouses.

The other societal change that feeds into the amount of workspace needed for staff and the number of courtrooms needed is the emerging 24/7 lifestyle. The Internet is a 24/7 operation, but retail businesses, as well, increasingly are extending hours of operation with both more hours per day and more days per week. Courts have been under pressure since the 1970s and before—largely resisted to date—to add evening calendars to accommodate people who must be in court but do not have the freedom to come and go from work as they please. If more hours per day are scheduled or Saturday hearings are added, it will have an impact on future building use and building design. The number of people coming to the courthouse and working in the courthouse between 8:00 a.m. and 5:00 p.m., Monday through Friday, will be reduced, but evening security may have to be increased. If the building is designed for 20 judges, a court with extended hours might need only 15 or 16 courtrooms because some courtrooms can do "double duty" at night. Or, courtrooms might be smaller because fewer people would be scheduled per calendar. (Remote television appearances also can affect the people coming to a courthouse.) Staff may share work space. Courts will not transition to longer or additional court days and more public counter hours all at once or within the next few years, but these changes are likely at some point in the next

50 years. Courthouses built today will be used for at least 50 years, so they have to be able to accommodate these changes or end up with space that is unused or no longer appropriate for current needs.

Leadership organizations understand these trends and are open to reconsidering the design of courthouses. Some will build courthouses that test new approaches to what courthouses should look like and how they should function, thus again demonstrating their leadership qualities. Leadership organizations will think about and try to respond to the following considerations within the limits of the budgets they have.

- The courthouse should be currently functional and require no major structural changes for at least 50 years, but if the courthouse footprint will allow, there will be the capacity to add a new wing or even small, separate buildings for different functions that reflect changes in the court's processes over time.[51]
- Courtrooms, hearing rooms, and conference rooms should meet a variety of litigation and conferencing needs rather than every trial courtroom designed as a "full service" jury-ready courtroom.
- A limited number of "hard wired" courtrooms should be available for high-security, notorious, or complex cases.
- Spaces, particularly courtroom areas, that meet current needs should be modifiable and capable of being reconfigured fairly easily into several smaller rooms or expanded to absorb adjacent areas.
- A focus on "consumer" needs, including the self-represented and visitors, should be built in.
- The building should accommodate maximum use of current technology, including television signal transmission and receipt, and be readily adaptable to new technologies.
- Equal priority should be accorded to designs that reflect access and openness as to those reflecting the law's "majesty" or "grandeur."
- Consideration should be given to providing multi-purpose rooms, including community meeting areas to build a bond with the many community agencies with which courts are beginning to partner.[52]
- Public areas that facilitate small-group communication should be provided.
- Public areas should assure ready access to courthouse information.
- Special spaces for children accompanying parents to the courthouse and for child witnesses should be available.

Courts are changing in some subtle but also in some dramatic ways. So is society. Courthouses need to reflect those changes and be able to accommodate the changes to come. Leadership organizations are open to trying some "zero-based design" to surface new ways to reflect both the majesty and the functional needs of courts today and of courts in 75 years.

Leadership organizations focus on customers' needs; seek and respond to customer and public feedback; expand access; look beyond courts for new ideas; use new technologies to improve productivity and access; reach out to the community to enhance understanding of what the court does and how it fits into our tripartite system of government; and use design principles to enhance service. When they do so, the community will see the court as a place that tries to assure justice and in which justice is served. A court that also is an employer that provides a competitive compensation package, offers opportunities to advance one's education, provides significant training opportunities, seeks and values staff input into decision making, and provides an appealing physical environment in which to work, will be an employer of choice in the community. If, in addition, staff and judges are seen as contributors to community life, the community will recognize the court as a forward-looking organization worthy of both respect and support. Support from the community for new court initiatives can be marshaled. Funding authorities often rewarded courts in the 1980s and early 1990s with additional budget funds after they reduced delay and showed other management improvements. Leadership organizations are in an even stronger position to garner funding support along with community recognition for their efforts.

Becoming a leadership organization takes time. Staff must be built up, both in numbers and in quality. The use of technology must be improved and expanded. Management must demonstrate skill, foster the talents of staff, and show positive results using data and customer responses. Judges must become more comfortable with limiting the scope of their activities to resolving cases and setting policy and leaving daily administration to the administrators. It takes time to demonstrate competence and to garner trust, both internally and externally. Courts that can do so become leadership organizations.

Notes

1. Maslow, Abraham, *Motivation and Personality*. New York: Harper & Row, 1980, p. 22.
2. Many smaller courts have been responsible for new ideas that spread across a state and the nation and for showing other smaller courts how to adapt ideas from larger courts to the small-court environment. Nothing in the concept of leadership organizations is meant to detract in any way from these important contributions. The difference is that the attitudes and qualities that separate leadership organizations from proactive management courts are pervasive in the former and more sporadic in the latter.
3. Drucker, Peter F., *Management: Tasks, Responsibilities, Practices*. New York: Harper & Row, 1973, p. 258.
4. Ibid., pp. 797–798.
5. Imparato, Nicholas, and Oren Harari, *Jumping the Curve: Innovation and Strategic Choice in an Age of Transition*. San Francisco: Jossey-Bass, 1994, p. 75.

6. Drucker, Peter F., *Management*, p. 798.

7. Tobin, Robert W., *Creating the Judicial Branch: The Unfinished Reform*. Williamsburg, VA: National Center for State Courts, 1999, p. x.

8. For example, "Colorado Publishes Annual Report," *Jur-E Bulletin*, Apr. 14, 2006, available from the National Center for State Courts at http.www.ncsconline.org/WC/Publications/KIS_JurInnJurE04-14-06.pdf.

9. More than just discussing the matter, in California, trial courts now are required to make their draft and final budgets available for inspection by the public and by employee unions. 2006 California Rules of Court, Rule 6.620d, retrieved from http://www.courtinfo.ca.gov/rules/titlesix/title6-83.htm.

10. Vanderbilt, Arthur T., "Foreword," *Reports of the Section of Judicial Administration*. Chicago: American Bar Association, 1938, reprinted in American Bar Association, *Improvement of the Administration of Justice*, 5th ed. Chicago: American Bar Association, 1971, p. 145.

11. Imparato, Nicholas, and Oren Harari, *Jumping the Curve*, pp. 100–101, citing Salk, Jonas, and Jonathan Salk, *World Population and Human Value: A New Reality*. New York: Harper & Collins, 1981, p. 116.

12. Imparato, Nicholas, and Oren Harari, *Jumping the Curve*, p. xx.

13. Ibid., p. xiv.

14. Tobin, Robert W., *Creating the Judicial Branch*, p. 202.

15. One example may highlight both the accommodation judges have accorded—and still accord—to attorneys and the challenge that this accommodation puts to courts' purposes. The issue arises most obviously in criminal cases involving privately retained counsel, but also can influence requests for continuances in family cases. If a privately retained counsel comes to court but has not been paid yet by his or her client, most courts have a catch phrase that alerts a judge that the attorney has not been paid. Common phrases include, "Witness Green is not here today, your Honor," or "I'm awaiting the arrival of Mr. Green," or some other locally recognized phrase that may not be quite so direct. When this alert is given, judges continue the case with no further questions, in recognition of the attorney's need to be paid before the case is resolved because the chances that the attorney will be paid after the case is resolved are slim. The court becomes part of the collection effort for the bar. It is true, of course, that if too many private lawyers do not get paid, the criminal bar will shrink and many cases may be slowed because there are not enough attorneys to represent criminal defendants. Other interests—those of alleged victims and their families, of the defendant's family, of the general public, and of law enforcement, who also may be present—are given no place in the conversation. Indeed, it would be considered bad form by many judges and defense counsel if the prosecutor injected these other interests. This is one of the examples of accommodations between the bench and bar, but it is not isolated. Part of the shifting in emphasis is to heighten the visibility of a broader range of interests than those of litigating attorneys.

16. Arndt, Michael, "Thinking Outside the Truck," *BusinessWeek Online*, Jan. 9, 2006, retrieved Feb. 2, 2006 from http://www.businessweek.com/innovate/content/jan2006/id20060106_876067.htm.

17. For example, "Making the Job Meaningful All the Way Down the Line," *Business Week*, May 1, 2006, p. 60.

18. California Penal Code §869 and California SB 2140.

19. For example, Greenwood, J. Michael, et al., *A Comparative Evaluation of Stenographic and Audiotape Methods for United States District Court Reporting*. Washington, D.C.: Federal Judicial Center, 1983, p. 81.

20. It was noted many years ago by a researcher that one reason judges favor reporters over audio

recorders is that a judge cannot talk to an audio recorder while driving to a branch court in a geographically large judicial district. Judges also cannot talk to an audio recorder during trial breaks and down times during a regular court day.

21. Indirect evidence of reporters' own recognition of their inability to capture everything said is the use by a fair number of reporters of personal or the court's recording equipment that they consult in their offices while finalizing the transcript. If they captured everything as it was being said, which is the implication on their side of the debate, they would not need the recording machine.

22. Greenwood, J. Michael, et al., *Comparative Evaluation*, pp. 36–50.

23. Hewitt, William E., with Jill Berman Levy, *Computer-Aided Transcription: Current Technology and Court Applications*. Williamsburg, VA: National Center for State Courts, 1994, p. 97.

24. See ibid., pp. 97–100.

25. Just as when considering caseflow management, there is a need to distinguish processing time from calendar time. Court rules always speak in terms of calendar days within which a transcript should be produced. The number of work hours needed to produce a transcript within those calendar days is entirely different.

26. Courts seldom track how many courtroom hours are spent on a particular matter, so for trials, the trial days may be a necessary surrogate. Then, the court has to use an average number of hours of courtroom time per trial day to estimate reporting hours. For motions and extended hearings, the clerk's minutes could be consulted.

27. A scopist is someone who takes the electronic record and does a first edit of it on the computer for the reporter. This can be done while a reporter is taking the record in court. It also saves the reporter considerable time. See note 26.

28. This number can be based on the most recent research or on a number agreed upon with the court's reporters.

29. Computer-assisted transcription requires less time per courtroom hour than transcription processes that do not have the computer produce the first draft. The one exception would be a CAT reporter who does all the editing work herself versus a regular machine reporter who uses a note reader, someone who can read the reporter's shorthand without the reporter spending time translating it. See National Center for State Courts, *Computer-Aided Transcription in the Courts*. Williamsburg, VA: National Center for State Courts, 1981, pp. 34–35.

30. If a reporter could spend ten hours a week on transcripts rather than eight, and nothing else changed, the calendar time would fall to under a month even if three hours were needed for each courtroom hour of testimony or argument.

31. This figure can be calculated in two ways. The first way is to assume an average rate of speaking for an hour. If it is 180 words per minute, in a hour there would be 10,800 words. If a court or state has transcript format standards (which it should), the number of expected words per page can be determined. Most states' standards anticipate 250 or 300 words per page. In point of fact, in the half-dozen or so studies I have done over the years involving hand counts of words per page, the actual number of words per page often is between 150 and 200. Only rarely is it as high as 250 words per page for an entire transcript. It is this discrepancy and the fact that in most states reporters bill on a per-page basis, that is the basis for my saying in note 46, chapter 6, that I normally find overbilling by a significant number of reporters. If an average page has 200 words per page, an hour of testimony would produce 54 pages. If average transcripts should have 250 words per page, there would be 43.2 pages of transcript derived from an hour of testimony. The other way to calculate this is to count the words in a sampling of completed transcripts where the start and end times are noted and determine an average number of words per hour and then calculate the average number of pages of transcript that are produced.

32. It is uncertain if their projected total income also would have been reduced, but for some it clearly would. Transcript income varies considerably from court to court and reporter to reporter, often depending within a court on the calendar(s) to which a reporter's judge is assigned. Very broadly, transcript income a year can range from under $10,000 to over $100,000 for busy reporters in urban courts.

33. Court Reporter Fair Labor Amendments Act of 1995, S. 190 and HR 1225. See "Fair Labor Standards Act," at http://www.ncraonline.org/infonews/key/fairlabor.shtml.

34. Commission on Trial Court Performance Standards, Williamsburg, VA: Bureau of Justice Assistance and National Center for State Courts, 1990.

35. They could use short questionnaires handed to litigants following a court appearance or use volunteers administering surveys in the corridors or even telephone surveys of a sample of court users.

36. The physical restrictions in some clerk's offices may not allow enough staff to serve customers to reduce the wait to ten minutes. If that is the case, courts might take a page from some airlines in busy airports who assign a staff person to greet each customer, find out what they need, and try to facilitate as short a wait as possible. In some banks, when lines get long, an extra person steps forward to help with transactions that do not require a cash drawer. Courts might have public information terminals and pay kiosks in a nearby hallway if the filing area is too small. Existing architecture may limit some elements of good customer service, but it need not preclude all efforts to minimize the inconvenience of visiting the courthouse during busy periods of the day.

37. Public members also are part of some mandatory state bar association boards of directors today, whereas originally, these boards contained only attorneys.

38. Tobin, Robert W., *Creating the Judicial Branch*, p. 114.

39. Drucker, Peter F., *Management*, p. 634.

40. It would be possible to provide that the judges could modify the stakeholder board's decisions. If the members of this second board are to feel they are making a real contribution, it probably would be best to limit the judges' response to either accept the decision or reject it entirely, with an explanation.

41. Most of the smaller courts, those with 15 or fewer judges, have a regularly scheduled meeting of all judges, normally once a month but sometimes more frequently. At these meetings, the judges are asked for advice, asked to make policy decisions and adopt new rules, and are advised of administrative decisions or developments of consequence since the last meeting. Such courts may or may not have an "executive committee" of the chief judge, assistant chief judge, and court administrator that acts for the court between meetings. Larger courts, those with 16 or more judges, often set up a board of judges or an "executive committee" of the administrative judges of each division, plus sometimes, one, two, or three other judges. This smaller group conducts the business of the court on behalf of all judges. The full bench then, normally, would meet once a year or at the call of the executive committee. In this discussion, when reference is made to "judges" making a decision or sitting as a board of directors, it is a shorthand reference to whatever each court uses as its vehicle for making policy decisions and overseeing what management is doing.

42. Welch, Jack, and Suzy Welch, "Paying Big Time for Failure," *Business Week*, April 10, 2006, p. 112.

43. In restored Colonial Williamsburg, Virginia, one of the popular attractions is the courthouse, a reproduction of the building where many of this country's most important founders practiced law or met as members of Virginia's Assembly. The courtroom could be transposed into the modern courthouse less than a mile away with only minor modifications. Similarly, courtroom scenes in movies made in the 1940s and 1950s show courtrooms virtually the

same as courtrooms in almost every courthouse in the nation today, except for the presence of computers today.

44. The federal government by and large has continued to build expensive and impressive court-houses for both trial and appellate courts. Whether that will continue through this century remains to be seen.

45. For example, holding cells, three separated corridors for different traffic flows, greater height to each story to accommodate the courtroom's "feel," security needs, and judges' chambers that are larger in size than are those of other local government managers.

46. The cost per square foot of a courthouse is two to three times the cost per square foot of other government office buildings. Priced another way, a courthouse in the early 2000s cost $1 million or more per courtroom.

47. For example, Hardenbergh, Don et al., *The Courthouse: A Planning and Design Guide for Court Facilities*, 2nd ed. Williamsburg, VA: National Center for State Courts, 1998; *Trial Court Facilities Guidelines*. San Francisco: Judicial Council of California, Administrative Office of the Courts, 2002; *The Michigan Courthouse: A Planning and Design Guide for Trial Court Facilities*. Lansing, MI: Michigan Supreme Court, 2000; New Jersey Supreme Court Committee on Courthouse Facilities, *Courthouse Facility Guidelines, State of New Jersey*. Trenton: The Supreme Court Committee on Courthouse Facilities, 1991.

48. See Hockenberry, John, "Fear Factor: Security in a New Age," *BusinessWeek Online*, May 2, 2005, which discusses, in part, the new (Summer 2006) federal courthouse in Eugene, Oregon. This courthouse was designed to convey openness as well as solemnity, with the security protections largely hidden, retrieved May 4, 2006, from http://www.businessweek.com/innovate/content/may2006/id20060502_628628.htm?campaign_id=innovate_May3&link_positon=link16,

49. Even the use of "cubicles" is being questioned, not only by interior designers but also by the person who invented the first workstation prior to his death in 2000. See Schlosser, Julie. "Cubicles: The Great Mistake," CNNMoney.com, Mar. 9, 2006, retrieved Mar. 9, 2006, from http://money.cnn.com/2006/03/09/magazines/fortune/cubicle_howlwork_fortune/index.htm.

50. These numbers are purely hypothetical, but not outlandish. Courts traditionally have scheduled calendars for all case types to start at the same time in the morning (8:30 or 9:00 a.m.) and in the afternoon (1:00 or 1:30 p.m.), so there is a big rush of people and cars just before those times, followed by a winnowing out of people during the course of the morning or afternoon. One easy response to this phenomenon is to spread out the starting times of calendars in order to reduce the number of peak parking spots needed, at least. This is resisted strongly in some courts, however.

51. Perhaps thought should be given to a "campus" approach in order to reduce the mass of a courthouse needed for larger courts. A campus arrangement could have several smaller buildings clustered around a central filing/self-represented and public information/cafeteria building. The criminal and family buildings would have all the security requirements associated with these cases, but the family building also would have more conference rooms and only one or two courtrooms for jury trials. The civil building could have a complex litigation courtroom plus clustered courtrooms for standard trials. There might even be a trial building that houses all the needed trial courtrooms, and other buildings would house all the nontrial needs of the court. (Some courthouses use "wings" off a central core to achieve these purposes, but not to the extent suggested here.) There are at least four impediments to this approach. One is that the comparative cost is uncertain. Someone would have to be willing to pay for a design to see how a campus approach would compare in cost to a single, more traditional high-rise building. Second, this approach might require some judges to

move among the buildings and either not have any assigned chambers area or have two, one for most of the time and one that is shared with all the other judges that is tied to a trial courtroom. Whichever approach is taken, many judges will resist. Third, the security costs associated with having several buildings to secure will be high, probably much higher than current courthouses that open only one or two doors for public entry. Today, most courts are looking to reduce the number of public entries in order to reduce the need for security personnel, rather than open more public entries. (Maybe there could be only one or two entrances to the campus, following which there would be no need for additional screening at the entrance of each building, but that is a design issue that cannot be resolved here.) Finally, this approach needs a large footprint, so would not be feasible for urban, downtown courthouses. As mentioned, in most states, it is the larger urban courts that serve as leadership organizations.

52. This type of room was built into the courthouse of the federal District Court for the District of Massachusetts. Information obtained during an international conference, "Implementing the Vision: Second International Conference on Courthouse Design," Oct. 11–14, 1995, San Francisco, CA.

Chapter 14

Concluding Thoughts

Court administration has made remarkable strides since the 1940s. As political scientists Hays and Graham have said:[1]

> Courts' accomplishments over the past few decades have been remarkable.... The courts have embraced (with varying degrees of enthusiasm) innovative managerial techniques and technologies. In doing so, an entire new profession has been recruited, trained, and allowed to spread its influence throughout America's courthouses. With no risk of overstatement, the changes that have occurred in just three decades can truly be termed revolutionary.

Two elements have been missing from the revolution: a distinction between what is judicial administration and what is court administration, and a perspective on court administration that enables a court's leadership to set priorities and seek to determine which of several possible projects should be implemented next. This book fills these voids.

The focus here clearly is on court administration. It has been instructive at points to note the overlap between court and judicial administration, however, because the overlap helps to distinguish the areas of particular judicial concern and responsibility versus the concerns and responsibilities of a court's administrative leadership. Judicial administration needs and supports court administration, just as court administration in turn needs and supports judicial administration. In many respects, however, court administrators properly have no say in whether a change affecting judicial administration should occur. Court administration only becomes involved after the basic policy choices have been made and the parameters set. One example of this distinction is the reforms in how jury trials are conducted; so, too, are the policy choices for or against state funding or consolidation of trial courts. Court administrators can inform the debate and should not sit on the sidelines as mere observers. They can explain the differing administrative and fiscal implications of various choices, both pro and con, along with the intangible consequences. In the end, however, it is not their choice to make. These are policy choices that rightfully belong to others, after which court administrators must come to the fore to implement whatever the policy choice may be. The literature of court administration has used the term *judicial administration* to apply to issues and questions of both judicial and court administration. Perhaps the delineation of all the functions and responsibilities inherent in court administration will help readers to draw the line more finely.

The context in which court administration is practiced is critical to understanding its scope, but more, to understanding the challenges posed and why court administration becomes more art than practice. Court administration is complex for the obvious reason that courts are complex organizations that cannot control key factors that influence or determine their success or lack of success. It also is complex because of the context, the social, legal, fiscal, and structural factors that influence and sometimes determine what court administration can and cannot accomplish. The context also is what helps to make court administration so challenging in a positive way. The internal challenges layer on top of the challenges provided by the context. Administrators must understand the context and apply themselves either to neutralizing inhibiting factors or to using these external factors to assist courts to achieve their goals. It also should be clear that all the challenges are not external. The rewards of working with judges can be great. There are wonderful individuals in the judiciary with and for whom it is a pleasure to work and with whom much can be accomplished. In addition, the institution is important to many citizens, so that being a court administrator carries psychic rewards that are not found everywhere. At the same time, cultural, professional, and individual predilections of some judges, and the path and criteria by which they come to the bench, pose challenges not found in any other organization, including other professional institutions. Especially difficult for many administrators is many judges' seeming inability to stay away from personnel administration. Judges solve problems every day in their courtrooms, so when a staff member comes to them with a claimed problem, they "solve" the problem, failing to recognize it is not their problem to solve. Instead, they should follow the example of Alfred P. Sloan, Jr.:[2]

> Sloan ... was the undoubted head of General Motors.... Yet Sloan said again and again, "I think you'd better take this matter up with [one of the three other members of the top-management team].... I would be interested to hear what they decide; perhaps you'll let me know." After the caller had left, ... Sloan would sometimes take the telephone and quietly call up Mr. Brown and ask him to come to the office to discuss the matter. Sloan usually had very definite opinions

and fought for them. But he disciplined himself never to express an opinion outside the top group, unless he himself had direct responsibility in the matter under discussion.

Judges certainly can and should listen to staff members, but they then should direct them back to the manager, as Alfred Sloan did. The tendency to try to solve the problem themselves, often with partial information, hampers the growth of court administration.

The interplay between administrators' desire to be seen as professional managers in their own right, and the need for leadership within the institution and on behalf of the institution, is another layer of complexity seldom found in other institutions, including other government units. Many believe that court administrators need the qualities of a leader, yet court administrators cannot be the visible, public leaders in a court setting. The judges must be. There is the concept of "leading from behind" that administrators with leadership qualities can try,[3] but that hardly is a good substitute for being the leader in front. In courts, the leader in front has to be a judge. Leading from behind also is a very limited option when the judicial leader, the chief judge, changes every year or each two or three years.[4] A few extraordinary politicians in Europe led effectively from behind in centuries past, but that approach has its limits in a court context. It certainly cannot be the model for many courts or many court administrators. The model, as has been suggested for decades, yet implemented even today in only a minority of courts, is a team of the chief judge and the court administrator. Each team member contributes his or her professional expertise and personal perspectives on issues and together they divide the myriad tasks assigned to court leadership to match their interests, skills, and available time.

A critically needed change in many courts is for judges to change their views about the court administrator and senior managers and the scope the administrative team will have to be administrators. The advantages that professional court administration can bring to the judiciary are diminished by the willingness of too many judges either to intercede in various management decisions or, of equal concern, to proceed as if administrative decisions have no relevance within what they see as their "judicial sphere." Their "judicial sphere" simply is too broad for an institutional perspective to develop and for administration to add value. Judges must come to see their administrators and senior managers as professionals whose areas of influence and responsibility are separate from the judges' own decisional responsibilities and sphere of influence. For administrators to be effective, judges need to demonstrate their acceptance of a division of responsibility to both staff and outside stakeholders by keeping out of the administrative side of court operations. Only when and as this transition in thinking occurs will courts fully realize the potential inherent in the proactive management and leadership organization levels of the Hierarchy of Court Administration.

This transition in thinking will take at least a generation to be widely accepted. In the meantime, judges are being short-changed regarding the time required for administrative matters. As noted in chapter 6, administrative time for judges in all but the largest courts is "add-on" time. Judges in most courts carry a full judicial load and then the chief judge and others with administrative responsibilities in divisions or as chairs of committees have to handle administrative matters in addition.[5] Depending on the size of the court and how it organizes dealing with administrative issues, every judge may have to put in some administrative time at judges meeting at least once a month. These meetings often are over lunch or at the end of the day so judges do not lose courtroom time. Today, in almost all courts, there is no way to capture administrative time and judges get no credit for it. The need for new judgeships is based on various case-based data.[6] States that have developed systems for weighting caseload to reflect that case types require varying amount of judicial time normally count "case-related" and "non-case-related" time separately, but the latter is just one big number. Case-related time is broken down among a number of case types, but non-case-related time is an amorphous "other." No effort is made to distinguish reading appellate opinions, court administration time, talking to civic groups, helping schools with peer courts, or the many other non-case-related things judges do. In states with judicial councils as the statewide policy making body, the additional time demands for judicial members are enormous.[7] Judges who chair and are active on statewide committees also must devote significant extra time. State judiciaries have fought hard since the 1970s to create a unified, statewide judicial branch. One consequence of winning that battle—or at least getting closer to winning it—has been judges assuming more responsibility for administering their branch of government. They have not taken the next step, however, of seeking recognition from the two other branches of the additional time demands that accompany that responsibility. With responsibility comes accountability, which courts have accepted as part of their obligations for the 21st century. If they are to have both responsibility and accountability, however, the time demands on judges of the administrative obligations also have to be acknowledged by the other branches of government. The root of "judicial" branch is "judges." Therefore, judges cannot shirk the time demands that are involved. They now have to seek recognition of those demands when judgeship needs are being assessed.

The Hierarchy of Court Administration fills a gap in court administration: the development of a conceptual framework to guide the setting of priorities when funding is restricted and to help courts set priorities when funding improves. Abraham Maslow developed his Hierarchy of Needs to help explain and guide how we examine the development of successful human beings. The parallels between Maslow's Hierarchy and courts' institutional needs are remarkably strong. Hence, the Hierarchy of Court Administration is structured to parallel Maslow's Hierarchy. The Hierarchy of Court Administration parallels Maslow's Hierarchy to explain and guide the development and maturation of successful trial courts as institutions. It provides a framework for answering two important questions. Which tasks and functions are central to courts being viable and which are nice to perform and even possibly important but not critical? Within the many competing needs of courts, which should be addressed first and which can be deferred until funds and staffing size or expertise are in place?

The different levels of need for courts are not walls that cannot be breached in either direction any more than Maslow's Hierarchy defined barriers for humans. Maslow expected and allowed for humans to satisfy some higher needs before all lesser needs were met and accepted that one might slip back to a lower level of need if circumstances changed. So it is with courts. Some needs in higher levels must be met even as mission critical needs are being protected. Some proactive management will and should occur at the same time as efforts to assure, for example, business continuity or to build new external relations. Also, as courts mature, programs that might be in the proactive management level for one court may move to the mission-critical level for another.

The Hierarchy of Court Administration is not a straitjacket, but a way for each court to envision where it is in the process of trying to fulfill its mission and what remains to be done. The one caveat is that a program or a technological enhancement that is not yet essential for the court to fulfill its basic mission should not be deemed to be mission critical if all other courts in the state are providing justice without this program or technology. It might be a wonderful program or an imaginative use of technology. It even might move a court closer to achieving its mission. If the court stands alone (or nearly alone) in its use of the program or technology, however, it is hard to see how the program or technology can be called mission critical. Something does not become mission critical, either, simply because it saves money for others or achieves a worthy end, both of which problem-solving courts do. Programs such as problem-solving courts might readily be justified on both of these grounds, but the justification for continued funding should be based on the global savings and the improvement in outcomes, not on the argument that they (or similar efforts) are mission critical. As mentioned in chapter 12, over time problem-solving courts may compel a reexamination of what courts are supposed to do and how they are to go about it. At that point it would be appropriate to revisit whether the staffing and approaches of problem-solving courts have become mission critical. Until that point, they are a wonderful innovation that is not yet mission critical.

There are no hard and fast rules about when something transitions to the mission critical category from being in the proactive management or the leadership organization level, but two important guidelines can be suggested. The first was just implied: broad implementation in the state. As more courts adopt the innovation and document how it helps courts get closer to fulfilling their mission, the more likely it is to become mission critical. The second is whether it is integrated into a court's workflow to the extent that it reduces staff needs, is documented to improve staff or judicial productivity, or is documented to materially advance access. If *not* retaining the innovation will necessitate increasing staff or other costs, redesigning a critical workflow pattern (again), or foreclose improved access, then continuing the program or technology will save money and improve court operations. Therefore, in tight economic times it is better to continue the new effort than to abandon it. The argument to preserve the innovation should be based on the efficient use of resources that already is responding to the need to conserve funds, however, rather than on the innovation being mission critical.[8] If everything that saves money—or avoids a need to increase funding—were mission critical, the concept would become meaningless.

When establishing priorities for funding, trial courts need to think in terms of mission critical needs[9] that embrace not only adjudication but also institutional integrity needs. It also is essential for the judiciary to be the one defining those needs, since the judiciary is best positioned to know about and to care about institutional integrity issues. There is a limited understanding of the judiciary, among both the general public and many leaders in the two other branches of government. This also dictates that the judiciary must frame the discussion about what it sees as mission critical needs.

Thus, the Hierarchy of Court Administration challenges state judicial leadership to define for the branch the mission critical functions. When courts are locally funded, the resulting list will be an important, possibly essential tool for trial courts to preserve funding. When the judiciary is state funded, it moves the discussion beyond what is "mandated" to what the branch needs to be able to perform its assigned roles. The nature of the discussion is changed and should limit the opportunities to nit-pick individual items. Even if the other branches attempt to nit-pick, however, they will be challenging a coherent, comprehensive list developed by the judiciary with input from stakeholders and thus they are in a weaker position to attack individual items on the list.

Once a statewide list of mission critical functions exists, it, along with the overall Hierarchy of Court Administration, can serve as a guide for both trial courts and the state's judicial leadership in setting priorities for new funding. The mission critical functions need to be protected at all costs. Trial courts should seek to preserve some proactive management initiatives even in difficult times, but not if doing so puts mission critical functions at risk. At the state level, judicial leaders should seek to assure that trial court needs in levels two and three of the Hierarchy are a higher priority than undertaking major new initiatives that legitimately would be thought of as proactive management. Once all trial courts are able to meet their needs in levels one through three of the Hierarchy, a state judiciary, together with the individual trial courts, is will positioned to move forward rapidly with new initiatives at the proactive management level.

Being proactive is not an add-on function, however. Modern court administration shows its mettle at the fourth level of the Hierarchy of Court Administration, the proactive management level. The pace and scope of change in the society generally and in the law specifically dictates that courts be proactive in their management if they are to remain a viable branch of government. It is here that leadership skills and strong management skills elevate in importance. It is through proactive management that courts will begin to connect with and gain positive recognition from citizens in ways that are not possible when fulfilling the needs of the first three levels. Being proactive is essential to survival, but in a qualitatively different way from the mission critical, security, business continuity, and external relationship needs. Even when times are hard economically, a state's leaders should seek to preserve some funding to support proactive management initiatives by trial courts, even if it is only in the form of short-term grants.

The Hierarchy of Court Administration creates a new vocabulary and introduces new ways to look at old concepts. In the 21st century, courts have to end the use of inputs in the dialogue with both the other branches and the general citizenry (e.g., number of staff, number of judges, a particular type of telephone system or case management information system). The focus has to be on performance measures on mission and vision statements. In the world of government budgeting and politics, efficiency cannot be ignored as part of the dialogue, but it has to come behind effectiveness. The Hierarchy of Court Administration is an added tool for the dialogue.

Some currently in court administration think the field is stagnating, that it has lost the visionary leaders of the 1960s through the early 1980s, and the next generation of leaders may not be as capable in advancing the interests of courts and of court administration. That view is too pessimistic. Much remains to be done, both in individual courts and in the field of court administration. If court administration focused only on the matters discussed in chapter 12 regarding proactive management, there is a full agenda. Leadership courts have even more to do. Plus, there doubtless are many ideas that have yet to surface or to win wide recognition that can and will add to the agenda. Yes, the field was blessed by visionary leaders in its early years, but they, in turn, were blessed by the infusion of a lot of federal money that supported trying out new ideas and spreading the word widely about those that were most effective. There not only was an interest in research and development, but opportunities to test the ideas and techniques that surfaced. Today's and tomorrow's leaders deserve the same opportunities. Shaking funds from the federal government for priorities of the states' courts is a hard sell, but it was done successfully once and is worthy of a renewed effort today.

Other sources of funds need to be explored, as well. All states now contribute to the general operating funds of the National Center for State Courts. It continues to need those funds. In addition, however, a shared research fund could be set up to which both the states' judiciaries and individuals could contribute. It would require significant funding from larger states, but pooling funds from many states might create a critical mass that could justify each state's additional contribution. Very few foundations have criminal or civil justice reform as a stated purpose and some of those who do also have a particular "solution" or program they wish to advance. Basic research and pilot programs for new court programs seldom generate enthusiasm in the foundation world. There may be some foundations, however, including some smaller family or individual foundations, interested in children, families, women's or elder-care issues, in conquering drug addictions, or in some other subset of what courts do that could be parlayed into a research fund or as a challenge grant to the states. Some bright individuals have pursued these avenues in the past and will continue to do so. To date, the results are disappointing, not because of lack of effort or ideas but because of an inability to find the right key to foundations' purposes. If the entire field were to devote time and attention to the effort, creative ways to fund research, development, and training might be found. If they can be, visionary leaders of the 21st century will emerge. Combined with judges letting administrators administer and a full agenda of proactive and leadership items to implement, the golden days of court administration may well lie ahead rather than being viewed fondly as a historical artifice.

Notes

1. Hays, Steven W., and Cole Blease Graham, Jr., eds., *Handbook of Court Administration and Management*. New York: Marcel Dekker, 1993, p. iv.
2. Drucker, Peter F., *Management: Tasks, Responsibilities, Practices*. New York: Harper & Row, 1973, p. 622.
3. Tobin, Robert W., *Creating the Judicial Branch: The Unfinished Reform*. Williamsburg, VA: National Center for State Courts, 1999, pp. 260–261.
4. Leaders on a court are not necessarily the judges with the title of chief judge, but if the chief judge is not the or a leader among the judges, that introduces another layer of complexity. A court administrator who is trying to promote change, who regularly ignores or goes around the chief judge to engage with another judge whose leadership capabilities are stronger, will not be the administrator very long.
5. In some midsized courts, the chief judge (but no others) is assigned only 90 or 80 percent of a full load in order to free some time for administration. In my experience, this offset is insufficient for the chief judge who is conscientious about fulfilling his or her responsibilities. In small courts (six and under), which predominate in terms of the number of courts and the total number of judges, this luxury is not available.
6. A variety of methodologies have developed in states across the years, but even today, filings, sometimes dispositions, and sometimes trials or jury trials dominate the discussion about whether new judgeships are needed—putting aside for a moment the critical factors of finances and politics.
7. All members of the policy-making body devoted considerable time to the effort; we are focusing here only on accounting for judges' administrative time. When the state supreme court doubles as the policy-making body for the third branch, the time demands on the chief justice are huge and on the associate justices, large. They get no credit for this time,

either, but as the focus of this book is trial courts, their needs are not explicitly discussed here.

8. In the circumstances just posited, it is incumbent on a court to document the extra costs that would be needed and why these extra costs cannot be avoided if the new program or technology is abandoned or suspended. It is insufficient to simply state to the funding authority that giving up the program or technology will increase costs.

9. COSCA refers to them as core responsibilities or core functions. See, for example, Conference of State Court Administrators, Policy Statement on Effective Judicial Governance and Accountability, adopted Nov. 30, 2001, retrieved from http://cosca.ncsc.dni.us/Resolutions/judgovpolstate.pdf. Conference of State Court Administrators, "Effective Judicial Governance and Accountability, A Position Paper Adopted December 2001," *The Court Manager*, vol. 19, no. 1, p. 34.

Bibliography

Aikman, Alexander B., *Total Quality Management in the Courts: A Handbook for Judicial Policy Makers and Administrators*. Williamsburg, VA: National Center for State Courts, 1994.

Aikman, Alexander B., "From Chaotic to Copesetic: Lessons in Media Relations for Courts from People vs. Scott Peterson," *The Court Manager*, vol. 19, no. 4, Winter 2004–2005.

"All In a Day's Work," *Harvard Business Review*, Dec. 2001 pp. 55 et seq.

"All Too Human," *The University of Chicago Law School Record*, Spring 2004, pp.3–5.

American Bar Association, 1938, *Improvement of the Administration of Justice*, 5th ed. Chicago: American Bar Association, 1971.

American Bar Association Judicial Administration Division, *Standards Relating to Court Organization*. Chicago: ABA Press, 1990.

American Bar Association Judicial Administration Division, *Standards Relating to Trial Courts*. Chicago: ABA Press, 1992.

American Bar Association, "Civics Education," retrieved from http://www.abanet.org.

American Bar Association, *Standards for Criminal Justice: Speedy Trial and Timely Resolution of Criminal Cases* (2004), retrieved from http://www.abanet.org/crimjust/standards/speedytrial_toc.html

American Justice, Episode no. 247, first broadcast Apr. 27, 2005 by A&E Network.

American Legislative Exchange Council, *Jury Patriotism Act*, retrieved from http://www.alec.org/meSWFile/pdf/0309.pdf

Ante, Spencer E., "Giving the Boss the Big Picture," *Business Week,* Feb. 13, 2006.

Argersinger v. *Hamlin,* 407 U.S. 25 (1972).

"Arizona City Paying for Weight Watchers," *Today's News-Herald* (Associated Press), Apr. 27, 2004, retrieved from http://start.earthlink.net/newsarticle?cat=4&aid=D8278FQ01_story

Arndt, Michael, "Creativity Overflowing," *Business Week*, May 8, 2006.

Arndt, Michael, "Thinking Outside the Truck," *BusinessWeek Online*, Jan. 9, 2006, retrieved from http://www.businessweek.com/innovate/content/jan2006/id20060106_876067.htm

Associated Press, "Floppy Disk Becoming Relic of the Past," Sept. 7, 2004, retrieved from http://start.earthlink.net/newsarticle?cat=2&aid=D84UQEN80_story

Associated Press, "Help Desk Offers Advice to Civil Litigants," retrieved June 7, 2006, from http://abcnews.go.com/US/wireStory?id=1481106

Associated Press, "New Orleans Could Be Forced to Free Suspects," Feb. 23, 2006, retrieved from http://msnbc.msn.com/id/11532547

Association for Information and Image Management, International, *The Use of Optical Disks for Public Records*, ANSI/AIIM TR25-1995. Silver Springs, MD: Association for Information and Image Management, International, 1995.

Belenko, Steven, "Research on Drug Courts: A Critical Review, 2001 Update." New York: The National Center on Addiction and Substance Abuse, Columbia Univ., 2001.

Bennack,, Frank A., Jr., "Remarks of Frank A. Bennack, Jr." in *National Center for State Courts, How the Public Views The State Courts: A 1999 National Survey*. Williamsburg, VA: National Center for State Courts.

Bennis, Warren, *On Becoming a Leader*. New York: Basic Books, 2003.

Berkow, Ira, "West Point Stands at Attention for Army's New Women's Coach, *New York Times*, Mar. 15, 2006, retrieved from http://patriotleague.cstv.com/genrel/031606aaa.html

Berman, Greg, and John Feinblatt, *Good Courts: The Case for Problem-Solving Justice*. New York: The New Press, 2005.

Bernhardt, Annette, Richard J. Murnane, and Eileen Appelbaum, eds., *Low-Wage America: How Employers Are Reshaping Opportunity in the Workplace*. New York: Russell Sage Foundation, 2003.

Bernstein, Aaron, "Waking Up From the American Dream," *Business Week*, Dec. 1, 2003.

Berra, Yogi, *The Yogi Book: I Really Didn't Say Everything I Said*. New York: Workman Publishing, 1999.

Best Practices Institute, Statement, retrieved April 2006, from http://www.ncsconline.org/Projects_Initiatives/BP/index.htm

Bickel, Alexander, *The Least Dangerous Branch: The Supreme Court at the Bar of Politics*. New Haven, CT: Yale University Press, 2nd ed., 1986.

Bigelow, John, ed., *The Works of Benjamin Franklin*. New York: G.P. Putnam's Sons, 1904, vol. 11.

Board for Judicial Administration Court Funding Task Force, *Justice in Jeopardy: The Court Funding Crisis in Washington State*, retrieved from http://www.courts.wa.gov/programs_org/pos_bja/wgFinal/wgFinal.pdf

Brady, Diane, "Take This Job and Customize It," *Business Week*, April 24, 2006.

Brehe, Todd A., 'E-Publications—A Means to Improve Communications Processes for U.S. Courts," *The Court Manager*, vol. 20, no. 2, 2005, pp. 28–29.

Buckingham, Marcus, "What Great Managers Do," retrieved from http://www.marcusbuckingham.com/press/newPress/articles/HarvardBusiness/greatmanagers.php

Bureau of Justice Statistics, "Two of Three Felony Defendants Represented by Publicly-Financed Counsel," Press Release, Nov. 29, 2000, retrieved from http://www.ojp.usdoj.gov/bjs/pub/press/iddcpr.htm

Burns, James MacGregor, *Leadership*. New York: Harper & Row, 1978.

Byrne, John A., "The Man Who Invented Management: Why Peter Drucker's Ideas Still Matter," *Business Week*, Nov. 28, 2005.

California Rules of Court, Rule 2073 (2005).

California Judicial Council Advisory Committee on Racial and Ethnic Bias in the Courts, *Final Report*. San Francisco: Judicial Council of California, 1997.

California Penal Code 869.

California Rules of Court, Rule 6.620d, retrieved from
http://www.courtinfo.ca.gov/rules/titlesix/title6-83.htm

"Care-Giving Women Shortchange Personal Needs," Sept. 22, 2004 (Associated Press), retrieved from http://start.earthlink.net/newsarticle?cat=4&aid=Lifestyles2200409220927

Carlson, Alan, and Martha Wade Steketee, *Public Access to Court Records: Implementing the CCJ/COSCA Guidelines, Final Project Report*. Williamsburg, VA and Denver, CO: National Center for State Courts and Justice Management Institute, 2005.

Carp, Robert A., and Ronald Stidham, *Judicial Process in America*. Washington, D.C.: CQ Press, 2001.

Chicago Judges Project, The, A transcript of a video interview, retrieved July 14, 2005, from http://research.uchicago.edu/highlights/documents/judges_transcript.htm

Church, Thomas, Jr., et al., *Justice Delayed: The Pace of Litigation in Urban Trial Courts*. Williamsburg, VA: National Center for State Courts, 1978.

Clarke, John A., "The Role of the Executive Component of the Court, *The Court Manager*, Summer 1990.

Cohen, Thomas H., and Brian A. Reaves, *Felony Defendants in Large Urban Counties, 2002*. Washington, D.C.: Dept. of Justice, 2006.

Collingwood, Harris, "Leadership's First Commandment: Know Thyself," *Harvard Business Review*, Dec. 2001.

"Colorado Publishes Annual Report," *Jur-E Bulletin*, Apr. 14, 2006, retrieved from the National Center for State Courts retrieved http.www.ncsconline.org/WC/Publications/KIS_JurInnJurE04-14-06.pdf

Commission on the Future of the California Courts, *Justice in the Balance, 2020*. San Francisco, Judicial Council of California, 1993.

Commission on Preservation and Access and the Research Libraries Group, Task Force on Archiving of Digital Information, *Preserving Digital Information*. Washington, D.C.: The Commission on Preservation and Access, 1996.

Commission on Trial Court Performance Standards, *Trial Court Performance Standards, with Commentary*. Williamsburg, VA: Bureau of Justice Assistance and National Center for State Courts, 1990.

Conference of Chief Justices and Conference of State Court Administrators, Resolution 22, "In Support of Problem-Solving Court Principles and Methods," adopted July 29, 2004, retrieved from http://ccj.ncsc.dni.us/CourtAdminResolutions/ProblemSolvingCourt-PrinciplesAndMethods.pdf

Conference of Chief Justices and Conference of State Court Administrators, Resolution 14, "In Support of Measuring Court Performance," adopted Aug. 3, 2005, retrieved from http://ccj.ncsc.dni.us/CourtAdminResoultions/resol14MeasuringCourtPerformance.html

Conference of State Court Administrators, "Concept Paper on Access to Court Records," Aug. 2000, retrieved from http://cosca.ncsc.dni.us/PositionPapers/courtrecordaccess.pdf

Conference of State Court Administrators, "Effective Judicial Governance and Accountability," a Position Paper, adopted Dec. 2001, *The Court Manager*, vol. 19, no. 1.

Conference of State Court Administrators, "Policy Statement on Effective Judicial Governance and Accountability," adopted Nov. 30, 2001, retrieved from http://.cosca.ncsc.dni.us/Resolutions/judgovpolstate.pdf

Conference of State Court Administrators, "Resolution in Support of Principles of Effective Judicial Governance and Accountability," adopted Dec. 12, 2003, retrieved from http://cosca.ncsc.dni.us/Resolutions/resolutionJudicialGovernance.html

Conference of State Court Administrators, "State Judicial Branch Budgets in Times of Fiscal Crisis," *The Court Manager*, vol. 19, no. 1, 2004.

Conference of State Court Administrators, "Position Paper on the Emergence of E-Everything," Dec. 2005, retrieved from http://cosca.ncsc.dni.us/WhitePapers/E-EverythingPositionPaper/ApprovedDec05.pdf

Conlin, Michelle, "The Easiest Commute of All," *Business Week*, Dec. 12, 2005.

Conlin, Michelle, "Call Centers in the Rec Room," *Business Week,* Jan. 23, 2006.

Conner, Maureen E., and Lawrence G. Myers, "NACM and MSU Collaborate to Add Academic Credentials to NACM Education Programs," *The Court Manager*, vol. 19, no. 4, 2004.

Contu, Diane L., "Putting Leaders on the Couch: A Conversation with Manfred F.R. Kets de Vries," *Harvard Business Review,* Jan. 2004, pp 65–71.

Court Reporter Fair Labor Amendments Act of 1995, S. 190 and HR 1225, retrieved from http://www.ncsconline.org/What'sNew/TenPointPlan/htm

Coy, Peter, "Beating Plowshares into Swords," *Business Week*, Apr. 7, 2003.

Crawford, Chris, "Technology Facts," *The Court Manager*, vol. 20, no. 2, pp 31–32.

Crockett, Roger O., "Why the Web Is Hitting a Wall," *Business Week*, Mar. 20, 2006.

Daily Inspirations "quote of the day" calendar.

Davis, William E., "Language and the Justice System: Problems and Issues," *Justice System Journal*, vol. 10, no. 3, Winter 1985.

DeLoof, Dion, "Getting the Most from Your People." *BusinessWeek Online*, Sept. 22, 2004, retrieved from http://www.businessweek.com/ smallbiz/content/sep2004/sb20040922_9037.htm

Dibble, Thomas G., *A Guide to Court Records Management*. Williamsburg, VA: National Center for State Courts, 1986.

"Dieting for Dollars: Corporate Trimming," *Business Week*, Nov. 3, 2003.

Donn, Jeff, "Feds assuming expanded role against common crime," Redding (CA) *Record Searchlight*, Dec. 28, 2003, p. A-12.

Drucker, Peter F. Management: *Tasks, Responsibilities, Practices*. New York: Harper & Row, 1973.

Dunnette, M.D., and Hough, L.M., eds., *Handbook of Industrial and Organizational Psychology*. Palo Alto, CA: Consulting Psychologists Press, 1990.

Dychtwald, Ken, Tamara J. Erickson, and Robert Morison, *Workforce Crisis: How to Beat the Coming Shortage of Skills and Talent*. Cambridge, MA: Harvard Business School, 2006.

Edwards, Cliff, "The New HP: How's It Doing? " *BusinessWeek Online*, Dec. 23, 2002, retrieved from http://www.businessweek.com/print/magazine/content/02_51/b3813086.htm?tc

Edwards, Leonard P., "Improving Juvenile Dependency Courts: Twenty-three Steps," *Juvenile and Family Court Journal*, Nov. 1997.

Epstein, Lee, *Contemplating Courts*. Washington, D.C.: CQ Press, 1995.

"Essential Ten Elements for Effective Courtroom Safety and Security Planning," retrieved from http://www.ncsconline.org/

"Evaluation of Program Completion and Rearrest Rates across Four Drug Court Programs," *Drug Court Review* [Abstract], vol. 5, no. 1, 2005, retrieved from http://www.ncjrs.gov/AbstractDB/Details.asp?fromWAL=1&perpage=1&index=10&ncjnum=234584&docIndex=928chkBoxBitFlag=0000....

Family Preservation and Support Act (Omnibus Budget Reconciliation Act of 1993, P.L. 103-66).

Federal Emergency Management Agency, "Federal Preparedness Circular 65" (2004), retrieved from http://www.fema.gov/txt/library/fpc65_0604.txt

Fetter, Theodore J., ed., State Courts: *A Blueprint for the Future*. Williamsburg, VA: National Center for State Courts, 1978.

Flango, Victor E., "Court Unification and Quality of State Courts," *Justice System Journal*, vol. 16, no. 3, 1994.

Foust, Doug "How to Pick a Business Brain," *Business Week*, Feb. 20, 2006.

Freedman, Robert B., "'Promise and Potential for Pro Tems," *California Courts Review*, Spring 2006.

Friesen, Ernest C., Jr., *Caseflow Management Principles and Practices: How to Succeed in Justice*, VHS. Williamsburg, VA: produced by the Institute for Court Management, 1991.

Friesen, Ernest C. Jr., Edward C. Gallas, and Nesta Gallas, *Managing the Courts*. Indianapolis, IN: The Bobbs-Merrill, 1971.

Gallas, Edward, "The Profession of Court Management," *Judicature*, vol. 51, 1968.

Gallas, Geoff, and Gordy Griller, "The Court Management Profession: Questions and Issues," *The Court Manager*, vol. 19, no. 2, 2004, pp. 5–12.

Gallo, Carmine, "Saying It with Passion," *BusinessWeek Online*, Apr. 6, 2005, retrieved from http://www.businessweek.com/smallbiz/content/apr2005/sb2005046_2194_sb

General Rule 31(e), Access to Court Records, State of Washington Rules of Court, 2004.

George, Chief Justice Ronald, State of the Judiciary Address to the California Legislature, Feb. 28, 2006 retrieved from http://www.courtinfo.ca.gov/reference/documents/soj022806.pdf.

Gideon v. Wainwright, 372 U.S. 335 (1963).

Goleman, Daniel, "What Makes a Leader? " *Harvard Business Review*, originally published in 1998; reprinted in *Harvard Business Review*, Jan. 2004, pp. 82–91.

Good, Irving John, *The Scientist Speculates.* New York: Heinemann & Basic Books, 1962.

Goodman, Ellen, "In Paying Attention, the Coin Is Time," Redding (CA) *Record Searchlight*, Aug. 12, 2005.

Gossett, William T., Bernard G. Segal, and Chesterfield Smith, "Foreword," to A. Leo Levin and Russell R. Wheeler, eds., *The Pound Conference: Perspectives on Justice in the Future.* St. Paul, MN: West Publishing, 1979.

Green, Heather, "The End of the Road for Bar Codes," *Business Week*, July 8, 2002.

Green, Milton D., "The Business of the Trial Courts," in Jones, Harry W., ed., *The American Assembly, The Courts, the Public, and the Law Explosion.* Englewood Cliffs, NJ: Prentice-Hall, 1965, pp. 7 et seq.

Greenwood, J. Michael, et al., *A Comparative Evaluation of Stenographic and Audiotape Methods for United States District Court Reporting.* Washington, D.C.: Federal Judicial Center, 1983.

Greisler, David S., and Ronald J. Stupak, eds., *Handbook of Technology Management in Public Administration.* New York and Boca Raton, FL: Taylor & Francis Books, 2006.

Hall, Daniel J., Robert W. Tobin, and Kenneth G. Pankey, Jr., "Balancing Judicial Independence and Fiscal Accountability in Times of Economic Crisis," *Judges Journal*, Summer 2004, pp. 5 et seq.

Hall, Kermit L., "Judicial Independence and the Majoritarian Difficulty," in Hall, Kermit L. and Kevin T. McGuire, eds., *Institutions of American Democracy: The Judicial Branch.* New York: Oxford University Press, 2005.

Hamilton, Alexander, *The Federalist Papers* (1788; Library of Congress), no. 78, retrieved from http://thomas.loc.gov/home/histdox/fed_78.html

Hannaford-Agor, Paula, "Access to Justice: Meeting the Needs of Self-Represented Litigants," *Civil Action*, vol. 1, no. 3, Fall 2002, retrieved from http://www.ncsconline.org

Hardenbergh, Don et al., *The Courthouse: A Planning and Design Guide for Court Facilities*, 2nd ed. Williamsburg, VA: National Center for State Courts, 1998.

Harris Poll, The "The Terri Schiavo Case: Paradoxically Most U.S. Adults Approve of How Both Her Husband and Her Parents Behaved," retrieved from http://www.harrinteractive.com/harris_poll/index.

Hays, Steven W., and Cole Blease Graham, Jr, eds., *Handbook of Court Administration and Management.* New York: Marcel Dekker, 1993.

"'Health Courts' Offer Cure," *USA Today*, July 4, 2005, retrieved from http://usatoday.com/news/opinion/editorials/2005-07-74-our-view_x.htm

Hempel, Jessi, and Paula Lehman, "MySpace.com Generation," *Business Week*, Dec. 12, 2005.

Henry, Ray, "Federal Court Drops Proposed Gag Rule," (Associated Press), Dec. 12, 2005, retrieved from http://start.earthlink.net/article/nat?guid=20051212/439d03d0_3ca6_155262005

Hewitt, William E., with Jill Berman Levy, *Computer-Aided Transcription: Current Technology and Court Applications.* Williamsburg, VA: National Center for State Courts, 1994.

Heylighen, Francis, "A Cognitive Systematic Reconstruction of Maslow's Theory of Self-Actualization," *Behavioral Science*, vol. 37, 1992, pp. 39–58.

Hockenberry, John, "Fear Factor: Security in a New Age," *BusinessWeek Online*, May 2, 2005, retrieved from http://www.businessweek.com/innovate/content/may2006/id20060502_628628.htm?campaign_id=innovate_May3&link_positon=link16

Hof, Robert D., "Do We Have to Have a Digital Revolution?" *Business Week*, Feb. 2, 2004.

Hoffman, Richard B., "The Revolt of the Judges," *The Court Manager*, vol. 19, no.2, 2004.

Hofland, Gina, "Senator Complains to Nominee about Court," (Associated Press) retrieved Aug. 8, 2005, from http://start.earthlink.net/channel/news,

Howard, Philip K., and Stephanie Mencimer, "The Doctor's Court," Legal Affairs Debate Club, Mar. 14, 2005, retrieved from http://www.legalaffairs.org/webexclusive/debateclub_medmal0305.msp

Hudzik, John K., "Judicial Independence, Funding the Courts, and Interbranch Relations, " *Judges Journal*, Summer 2004, pp. 1 et seq.

Hudzik, John K., and Alan Carlson, "State Funding of Trial Courts: What We Know Now," *Judges Journal*, Summer 2004, p. 13.

Huitt, W., "Maslow's Hierarchy of Needs." Educational Psychology Interactive, Valdosta GA: Valdosta Univ., retrieved Sept. 12, 2005, from http://chiron.valdosta.edu/whuitt/col/regsys/maslow.html

Idaho Court Administrative Rules, Rule 43 (1988).

Imparato, Nicholas, and Oren Harari, *Jumping the Curve: Innovation and Strategic Choice in an Age of Transition*. San Francisco: Jossey-Bass, 1994.

Implementing the Vision: Second International Conference on Courthouse Design, Oct. 11–14, 1995, in San Francisco, CA.

"Instant Translations," *PC Magazine*, Dec. 14, 1999.

"IntelligenceReport," *Parade,* July 10, 2005.

Jesdanum, Anick, "Blog-Related Firings Focus on Policy," Mar. 6, 2005, retrieved from http://enews.earthlink.net/channel/news/print?guid=20050306/422a8e50_3ca6_15

Johnson, Anna, "Study: Few Americans Know 1st Amendment," (Associated Press) retrieved Mar. 1, 2006, from http://enews.earthlink.net/channel/news.

Judicial Caseload Profile Report, 2002, retrieved from http://www.iscpirts/gpvcgo-bin/cmsd/2002.

Judicial Council of California, "Family Law Interpreter Pilot Program: Report to the Legislature," 2001, retrieved from http://www.courtinfo.ca.gov/programs/cfcc//pdffiles/FLIPP.pdf

Judicial Council of California, "Operating Guidelines and Directives for Budget Management in the Judicial Branch," section II, adopted Aug. 2003, and revised Dec. 2004, retrieved from http://www.courtinfo.ca.gov/jc/documents/reports/1204item20.pdf

Judicial Council of California, *Cornerstones of Democracy: California Courts Enter a New Era of Judicial Branch Independence*. San Francisco: Judicial Council of California, 2005, p. 25, retrieved from http://www.courtinfo.ca.gov/reference/2_annual.htm

Judicial Council of California, *Model Self-Help Pilot Program: A Report to the Legislature*. San Francisco: Judicial Council of California, 2005.

Judicial System Leadership Forum, *Final Report,* Dec. 16–17, 2004. Washington, D.C.: Bureau of Justice Assistance and American University, 2005, retrieved from http://www.american.edu/justice/resources

Justice at Stake Campaign, Press release of June 27, 2005, retrieved from http://www.justiceatstake.org/files/JASnewsrelease062705.pdf

Kasparek, F. Dale, "Leading the Unfinished Reform: The Future of Third Branch Administration," a project report submitted for the Institute for Court Management's Court Executive Development Program, Phase III, 2005.

Kenney, Anne R., *Digital to Microfilm Conversion: A Demonstration Project*. Ithaca, NY: Cornell University Library Department of Preservation and Conservation, 1997.

Kerstetter, Jim, "Business Software: Comes the Revolution," *Business Week,* June 23, 2003.

Kerwin, Cornelius, Thomas Henderson, and Carl Baar, "Adjudicatory Processes and the Organization of Trial Courts," *Judicature,* vol. 70, no. 2, 1986.

Kleiman, Carol, "Studies Reveal Surprises About Work/life Programs and Gender Roles," Associated Press, Dec. 3, 2003, retrieved from http://start.earthlink.net/newsarticle?cat=4&aid=Lif estyles8200312030900

Klein, Fannie J., ed., *The Improvement of the Administration of Justice,* 6th ed. Chicago: ABA Press, 1981.

Kline, Laura S., *Developing an Inactive Records Storage Facility.* Local Government Records Technical Information Series, No. 48. Albany, NY: Local Government Records Services, State Archives and Records Administration, the State University of New York, the State Education Department, 1995.

Lahey, Mary Anne, Bruce A. Christenson, and Robert J. Rossi, *Analysis of Trial Court Unification in California: Final Report.* Palo Alto, CA: American Institutes for Research, 2000.

Langer, Gary, "Poll: No Role for Government in Schiavo Case," retrieved from http://abcnews.go.com/Politics

Langford, Carol M., "When Disaster Strikes … The Ethical Duties of Disaster Preparation," *California Bar Journal,* Feb. 2006.

Law Enforcement Assistance Administration, the National Advisory Commission on Criminal Justice Standards and Goals, *A National Strategy to Reduce Crime.* Washington, D.C.: 1973.

"Law School Welcomes Three New Faculty Members, The," *The University of Chicago Law School Record,* Fall 2005.

"Leading by Feel," *Harvard Business Review,* Jan. 2004, pp. 27 et seq.

Lefever, R. Dale, "Judge-Court Manager Relationships: The Integration of Two Cultures," *The Court Manager,* Summer 1990.

Lewis, Anthony, *Gideon's Trumpet.* New York: Random House, 1964.

"Life is Short," *AARP Bulletin,* vol. 47, no. 3, Mar. 2006.

Livingston, Mike, "A Dose of Healthy Disagreement," *Legal Times,* Nov. 3, 2003.

Lombard, Patricia, and Carol Krafka, *2003–2004 District Court Case-Weighting Study: Final Report to the Subcommittee on Judicial Statistics of the Committee on Judicial Resources of the Judicial Conference of the United States.* Washington, D.C.: Federal Judicial Center, 2005.

Mahoney, Barry, *The Ventura Day Fine Pilot Project: A Report on the Planning Process and the Decision to Terminate the Project, With Recommendations Concerning Future Development of Fines Policy.* Denver, CO: The Justice Management Institute, May 1995.

"Making the Job Meaningful All the Way Down the Line," *Business Week,* May 1, 2006.

Mandel, Michael, "Why the Economy is a Lot Stronger Than You Think," *Business Week,* Feb. 13, 2006.

"Marketing—Target Market, Innovators, Early Adopters, Influencers," retrieved from http://www.determan.net/Michele/mtarget.htm

Martin, John A., and Nancy C. Maron, "Courts, Delay, and Interorganizational Networks: Managing an Essential Tension," *Justice System Journal,* vol. 14, no. 3 and vol. 15, no. 1, pp. 268–288.

Maryland Administrative Office of the Courts, *An Executive Program Assessment for State Court Projects to Assist Self-Represented Litigants.* Annapolis, MD: Maryland Administrative Office of the Courts, 2005.

Maslow, Abraham H., *Motivation and Personality,* 2nd ed. New York: Harper & Row, 1980.

Maslow, Abraham H., and B. Lowery, ed., *Toward a Psychology of Being,* 3rd ed. New York: Wiley & Sons, 1998.

McConnell, Edward B., "Court Administration," *Improvement of the Administration of Justice,* 5th ed. Chicago: American Bar Association, 1971.

McGregor, Jena, "Forget Going with Your Gut," *Business Week*, Mar. 20, 2006.

McMurray, Jeffrey, "Study: DOJ Has Lost Track of Drug Courts," *ABAJournal.com*, Apr. 24, 2002, retrieved from http://www.abanet.org/journal/redesign/apdrug.html

Mendoza, Martha, and Christopher Sullivan, "Corporations Stiffing Government on Fines," Mar. 19, 2006 and articles retrieved Mar. 19, 2006, from http://enews.earthlink.net/article/bus?guid=20060319/441ce550_3421_1334520060319-211>316383.

Menkes, Justin, *Executive Intelligence: What All Great Leaders Have*. New York: HarperCollins, 2005.

Merritt, Jennifer, "Improv at the Interview," *Business Week*, Feb. 3, 2003.

"Michigan Companies Tout Dieting Incentives," Associated Press, Dec. 27, 2005, retrieved from http://enews.earthlink.net/challen/news/guid=20051227/43b)ca_3ca_

Michigan Supreme Court, *Michigan Courthouse: A Planning and Design Guide for Trial Court Facilities, The*. Lansing, MI: Michigan Supreme Court, 2000

Moriarty, Casey, "King County District Court Automatic Call Distributor Evaluation," Aug. 2003.

Murphy, Timothy R. et al., *Managing Notorious Trials*. Williamsburg, VA: National Center for State Courts, 1998.

Nadeau, Joseph P., "Ensuring Adequate Long-Term Funding for Courts: Recommendations from the ABA Commission on State Court Funding," *Judges Journal*, Summer 2004.

National Association for Court Management, *Core Competency Curriculum Guidelines: What Court Leaders Need to Know and Be Able to Do*. Williamsburg, VA: National Association for Court Management, 2005.

National Association for Court Management, *Court Security Guide*. Williamsburg, VA: National Association for Court Management, June 2005.

National Association for Court Management, *Business Continuity Management Guide*. Williamsburg, VA: National Association for Court Management, 2006.

National Bureau of Economic Research, *Business Cycle Expansions and Contractions*, retrieved from http://www.nber.org/cycles.html

National Center for State Courts, Charter, adopted June 1971.

National Center for State Courts, Annual Report, 1975.

National Center for State Courts, *Computer-Aided Transcription in the Courts*. Williamsburg, VA: National Center for State Courts, 1981.

National Center for State Courts, *CourTools* (2005), retrieved from http://www.courtinfo.org

National Center for State Courts, *2003 State Court Structure Charts*. Williamsburg, VA: National Center for State Courts, 2004, retrieved from http://www.ncsconline.org/D_Research/csp/2004_Files/2004_SCCS.htm

National Center for State Courts, *Caseload Highlights: Examining the Work of State Courts*, vol. 12, no. 1, Oct. 2005.

National Center for State Courts, *Examining the Work of State Courts, 2004*. Williamsburg, VA: National Center for State Courts, 2005.

National Center for State Courts, Knowledge and Information Service, "Indigent Defense FAQs," Dec. 30, 2005, retrieved from http://www.ncsconline.org/WC/FAQs/IndDefFAQ.htm

New Jersey Supreme Court Committee on Courthouse Facilities, *Courthouse Facility Guidelines*, State of New Jersey. Trenton: The Supreme Court Committee on Courthouse Facilities, 1991.

New York Judiciary Law, NY State Session Laws, Chap. 825 of the Laws of 1987, section 39(3)(a).

New York State Archives, Government Records Services, *The Seven Attributes of an Effective Records Management Program*. Albany, NY: Government Records Services, New York State Archives, the State Education Department, the University of the State of New York, 2002, retrieved from http://www.archives.nysed.gov

Nussbaum, Bruce, "Technology: Just Make it Simpler," *Business Week*, Sept. 8, 2003.

O'Connell, Patricia ed., "The Right Bait for Keeping Staff," *BusinessWeek Online*, Feb. 2, 2005, retrieved from http://www.businessweek.com/careers/content/feb2005/ca2005022_ca

Offer, Annemarie, "Spending on Training Can Lower Recruitment Expenses," St. Louis *Business Journal*, July 30, 2001, retrieved from http://bizjournals.com/stlouis/stories/2001/0730/focus14.html

"On a Roll at Audi," retrieved from http://www.businessweek.com/innovate/content/sep2005/id20050916_242086.htm

"Ontario County Family Court Pro Se Remote Assistance Project," *Briefly*, Feb. 10, 2006, p. 1.

Oregon Chief Justice Order No. 03-028, retrieved from http://www.ojd.state.or.us/sca/WebMediaRel.nsf/Files/CJO03-028.pdf/$File/CJO03-028.pdf

Oregon Courts' Public Service Hours by Location, p. 4, retrieved from http://www.ojd.state.or.us/documents/CourtHoursChart.pdf

"Pacesetters Streamlining," *Business Week*, Nov. 21, 2005.

Palmer, Jonathan, Abstract of "Designing for Web Site Usability," retrieved from http://csdl2.computer.org/persagen/DLAbsToc.jsp?resourcePath=/dl/mags/co/&toc=comp/mags/co/2002/07/r7toc.xml&DOI=101109/MC2002.1016906

Parker, John J., "Improving the Administration of Justice," *American Bar Association Journal*, vol. 27, 1941, at p. 71.

Pastore, Ann L,. and Kathleen Maguire, eds. *Sourcebook of Criminal Justice Statistics—2003*. Washington, D.C: U.S. Dept. of Justice, Bureau of Justice Statistics, 2005.

Paulsen, Derek J., "Murder in Black and White: The Newspaper Coverage of Homicide in Houston," *Homicide Studies*, vol. 7, no. 3, August 2003.

"Pay by Touch Online," *BusinessWeek Online*, Feb. 15, 2006, from retrieved from http://images.businessweek.com/ss/06/02/demo_show/source/7.htm

Perman, Stacy, quoted in "How the Masses Will Innovate," *BusinessWeek Online*, Mar. 13, 2006, from retrieved from http://www.businessweek.com/technology/content/mar2006/tc20060308_265863.htm?campaign_innovate_mar14&link_position=link16

Peters, Tom, *Thriving on Chaos: Handbook for a Management Revolution*. New York: Alfred A. Knopf, 1987.

Petrosino, Anthony, Carolyn Turpin-Petrosino, and John Buehler, "Scared Straight and Other Juvenile Awareness Programs for Preventing Juvenile Delinquency," (updated 2003), retrieved from http://www.campbellcollaboration.org/fcontend2.asp?ID=4

Phillips, Dale, "Strategic Applications of Technology: Radio-Frequency Identification (RFID) Technology and the DeKalb County, Georgia, Juvenile Court," *The Court Manager*, vol. 20, no. 2, Spring 2005.

"Polyvision's Thunder," *Business Week Online*, retrieved Feb. 15, 2006, from http://images.businessweek.com/ss/06/02/demo_show/source/5.htm

Pound, Roscoe, "The Causes of Popular Dissatisfaction with the Administration of Justice," reprinted in Levin, A. Leo, and Russell R. Wheeler, eds., *The Pound Conference: Perspectives on Justice in the Future*. St. Paul: West Publishing, 1979.

Prentice, W.C.H., "Understanding Leadership," *Harvard Business Review*, 1991, reprinted in *Harvard Business Review*, Jan. 2004, pp 102–109.

Public Law 101-336, 104 Stat. 327, 42 U.S.C. 12101 et seq.

Publication Development Committee, Victims of Child Abuse Project, *Resource Guidelines: Improving Court Practice in Child Abuse & Neglect Cases*. Reno, NV: National Council of Juvenile and Family Court Judges, 1995.

Reinkensmeyer, Marcus W., "Court Budget Strategies: Stewardship, Accountability, and Partnership in Maricopa County," *Judges Journal*, Summer 2004.

Rennison, Callie Marie, *Intimate Partner Violence*, 1993–2001. Washington, D.C.: U.S. Dept. of Justice, Bureau of Justice Statistics, 2003, retrievable from http://www.ojp.usdoj.gov/bjs/pub/pdf/ipv01.pdf.

Roberts, Wess, *Leadership Secrets of Attila the Hun*. New York: Warner Books, 1990.

Robitaille, Suzanne, "How VoIP Can Connect the Disabled," *BusinessWeek Online*, April 28, 2004, retrieved from http://www.businessweek.com/technology/content/apr2004/tc20040428_43

Rosenberg, Maurice, "Court Congestion Status, Causes, and Proposed Remedies," in Harry W. Jones, ed., *The American Assembly, The Courts, the Public, and the Law Explosion*. Englewood Cliffs, NJ: Prentice-Hall, 1965.

Ross, Thomas W., "Judicial Independence under Attack," retrieved from http://www.meckbar.org/newsevents/news_detail

Rottman, David B., *Trust and Confidence in the California Courts*. Williamsburg, VA: National Center for State Courts, 2005.

Rottman, David B., "What Californians Think about Their Courts: Highlights from a New Survey of the Public and Attorneys," *California Courts Review*, Fall 2005.

Rottman, David, and Pamela Casey, "Therapeutic Jurisprudence and the Emergence of Problem-Solving Courts," *National Institute of Justice Journal*, July 1999.

Rottman, David B., and William E. Hewitt, *Trial Court Structure and Performance: A Contemporary Reappraisal*. Williamsburg, VA: National Center for State Courts, 1996.

Ryan, Liz, "How a Memo Can Beat an Interview," *BusinessWeek Online*, retrieved from http://www.businessweek.com/ careers/content/oct2004/ca2004104_7927_ca009.htm

Ryan, Liz, "Don't Be an Every Minute Manager," retrieved from http://www.businessweek.com/careers/content/sep2005/ca20050915_0127_ca017.htm

Saari, David, "New Ideas for Trial Court Administration—Applying Social Science to Law," *Judicature*, vol. 51, 1967.

Saari,, David J., Michael D. Planet, and Marcus W. Reinkensmeyer, "The Modern Court Managers: Who They Are and What They Do in the United States," in no. 162, chapter 11.

Salk, Jonas, and Jonathan Salk, *World Population and Human Value: A New Reality*. New York: Harper & Collins, 1981.

Schauffler, Richard Y. et al., *State Courts Caseload Statistics, 2004*. Williamsburg, VA: National Center for State Courts, 2005.

Schauffler, Richard Y. et al., *Examining the Work of State Courts, 2004: A National Perspective from the Court Statistics Project*. Williamsburg, VA: National Center for State Courts, 2005.

Schlosser, Julie, "Cubicles: The Great Mistake," *CNNMoney.com*, Mar. 9, 2006, retrieved from http://money.cnn.com/2006/03/09/magazines/fortune/cubicle_howlwork_fortune/index.htm

Schotland, Roy A., "The Crocodile in the Bathtub ... and Other Arguments to Extend Terms for Trial Judges," *California Courts Review*, Fall 2005.

Schumacher, E.F., *Small is Beautiful*. London: Blond & Briggs, 1973.

Scott v. *Illinois*, 440 U.S. 367 (1979).

Siegel, Lawrence, Caroline S. Cooper, and Allison L. Hastings, *Planning for Emergencies: Immediate Events and Their Aftermath: A Guideline for Local Courts*. Washington, D.C.: Justice Programs Office, School of Public Affairs, American University, 2005, retrievable from http://www.spa.american.edu/justice/resources/SJI.pdf

Silverstein, Lee, *Defense of the Poor in Criminal Cases*. New York: American Bar Foundation, 1965.

"Simpson Jurors, The," *Jur-E Bulletin*, Apr. 7, 2006, retrieved from http.www.ncsconline.org/Juries/bulletin.htm

Sipes, Dale Ann, *On Trial: The Length of Civil and Criminal Trials.* Williamsburg, VA: National Center for State Courts, 1988.

"Slippers and Stubble," *Business Week,* Apr. 3, 2006.

Solomon, Maureen, *Caseflow Management in the Trial Court, Support Studies—2,* for the American Bar Association Commission on Standards of Judicial Administration. Chicago: American Bar Association, 1973, p. 4.

Spooner, John G., "HP offers 'simple' message to consumers," Aug. 11, 2003, retrieved from http://news.com.com/2102-1041_3-5062002.thml?tag=st_util_print

Steelman, David C., with John A. Goerdt and James E. McMillan, *Caseflow Management: The Heart of Court Management in the New Millennium,* 3rd printing with revisions. Williamsburg, VA: National Center for State Courts, 2004

Steketee, Martha Wade, and Alan Carlson, *Developing CCJ/COSCA Guidelines for Public Access to Court Records: A National Project to Assist State Courts.* Williamsburg, VA and Denver, CO: National Center for State Courts and Justice Management Institute, 2002.

Stumpf, Felix. F., *Inherent Powers of the Courts: Sword and Shield of the Judiciary.* Reno, NV: The National Judicial College, 1994.

Stumpf, Harry P., and John H. Culver, *The Politics of State Courts.* White Plains, NY: Longman Publishing Group, 1992.

Stupak, Ronald J., "A Turning Point: From Managers to Leaders," *Court Communiqué,* vol. 1, no. 2, March 1999.

Stupak, Ronald J., "The Advocacy Arena: Who Shall Lead Us?," *The Journal of Volunteer Administration,* vol. 23, no. 2, April/May 2005.

Sunstein, Cass, "Why Societies Need Dissent," retrieved from http//www.uchicago.edu/news/news_sunstein.html

Tafoya, Sonya M., "The Linguistic Landscape of California Schools," *California Counts, Population Trends and Profiles,* vol. 3, no. 4, Feb. 2002, pp. 2–3, retrieved from http://www.ppic.org/content//pubs/cacounts/CC_202STCC.pdf

Tanner, Robert, "Flush with Cash, States Make Pricey Plans" (Associated Press), retrieved from http://my.earthlink.net/channel/news/print?guid=20060220/43f94cd0_3421_1334

Tanner, Robert, "States Steadily Restrict Public Info" (Associated Press), Mar. 11, 2006, retrieved from http://enews.earthlink.net/article/nat?quid=20060311/44125950_3ca6_1552620060311-1295840942

Taylor, Natalie, and Jacqueline Joudo, "Impact of Pre-Recorded Video and Closed Circuit Television Testimony by Adult Sexual Assault Complainants on Jury Decision-Making: An Experimental Study," retrieved Apr. 3, 2006, from http://www.ncjrs.gov/AbstractDB/Details.asp?fromWAL=1&perpage=1&index=11&ncjnum=234815&docindex=53&chkBoxBitFlags=0000...

"Technology Primer: Radio Frequency Identification," *TechBeat,* Summer 2005.

"Text Message Nation," *Business Week,* Jan. 28, 2006..

Tobin, Robert W., *Lessons Learned from Recession Experience.* Denver, CO: National Center for State Courts, undated.

Tobin, Robert W., *Creating the Judicial Branch: The Unfinished Reform.* Williamsburg, VA: National Center for State Courts, 1999.

Trial Court Facilities Guidelines, San Francisco: Judicial Council of California, Administrative Office of the Courts, 2002.

Trial Court Realignment and Efficiency Act of 1991, Chap. 90, Statutes of 1991, 1991–1992, California State Legislature, Regular Session (June 30, 1991), 406-409, § 6.

Trial Trends Report, retrieved from http://www.ncsconline.org/C_Research/csp/TrialTrends/CSP-trialtrends.html

United Press International, "Spam Seen as Workplace Problem," Oct. 16, 2003, retrieved from http://start.earthlink.net/newsarticle?cat=4&aid=Lifestyles0200310161240

United States v. *Carrion,* 488 F.2d 23 (1st Cir., 1973).

"UpFront," *Business Week,* Oct. 24, 2005, p. 16.

Vanderbilt, Arthur T., "Foreword," Reports of the Section of Judicial Administration. 1938, reprinted in Section of Judicial Administration, *Improvement of the Administration of Justice,* 5th ed. Chicago: American Bar Association, 1971.

Vanderbilt, Arthur T., ed., *Minimum Standards of Judicial Administration.* New York: The Law Center of New York University, 1949.

"Videoconferencing to the Rescue," *Briefly,* June 10, 2005.

Vogel, Nancy, "Lawmakers Say Nonvote as Significant as Yes, No," reprinted in Redding (CA) *Record Searchlight,* August 29, 2005.

Wahba, M., and L. Bridwell, "Maslow Reconsidered: A Review of Research on the Need Hierarchy Theory," *Organizational Behavior and Human Performance,* vol. 15, pp. 212–240.

Welch, Jack, and Suzy Welch, "Paying Big Time for Failure," *Business Week,* April 10, 2006.

Welch, Jack, and Suzy Welch, "The Leadership Mindset," *Business Week,* January 30, 2006.

"What Makes a Good Leader?" "IntelligenceReport," *Parade,* July 10, 2005.

"What Not to Do," *Business Week,* Oct. 10, 2005.

White, Stephen, "A Brief History of Computing—Products Notable for Their Technical Achievement or Popularity"(2002), retrieved from http://www.ox.compsoc.net

Wildstrom, Stephen H., "The View Beyond Vista," *Business Week,* May 8, 2006.

Will, George F., "The Value of 'Activism'," Washington *Post,* Sept. 1, 2005.

Williams, Mark, "When Disaster Strikes … Protecting Electronic Data and Paper Files," *California Bar Journal,* Feb. 2006.

Winters, Roger, "Time for Electronic Court Records," in *National Center for State Courts Trends in 2004,* retrieved from http://www.ncsconline.org/D_KIS/Trends/DocManTrends2004.html

Wolfe, Gary, and Vince Kasten, "Bringing Courts into the Future," *The Court Manager,* vol. 20, no. 2, pp. 8–11.

Yankelovich, Skelly, & White, Inc., "Highlights of a National Survey of the General Public, Judges, Lawyers, and Community Leaders," in Fetter, Theodore J., ed., *State Courts: A Blueprint for the Future: Proceedings of the Second National Conference on the Judiciary* held in Williamsburg, Virginia, March 19–22, 1978.

Zaffarano, Mark A., "A Profile of Ed McConnell," *The Court Manager,* Summer 1990.

Zaleznik, Abraham, "Managers and Leaders, Are They Different?" *Harvard Business Review,* 1977, reprinted in *Harvard Business Review,* Jan. 2004, pp. 74–81.

"Zen and the Art of Thinking Straight," *Business Week,* Apr. 3, 2006, p. 116.

Zorza, Richard, *The Self-Help Friendly Court: Designed from the Ground Up to Work for People Without Lawyers.* Williamsburg, VA: National Center for State Courts, 2002.

Index

Numbers in italics indicate figures or tables.